W9-BPN-957

Critical acclaim for
EVIL ANGELS

"OUT OF THE COMPLEX STORY OF HIS COUNTRY'S MOST FAMOUS MURDER TRIAL, AUSTRALIAN LAWYER, JOURNALIST AND NOVELIST JOHN BRYSON HAS FASHIONED A REMARKABLE BOOK, ONE THAT RESONATES WITH MORAL AMBIGUITIES AND WRENCHING EMOTIONS . . . BRYSON'S HANDLING OF THE COMPLICATED TESTIMONY ABOUT PHYSICAL EVIDENCE IS A MODEL OF CLARITY AND COHERENCE . . . FAR MORE IMPORTANT, HOWEVER, IS HIS QUIETLY DEVASTATING PORTRAIT OF THE UGLY UNDERCURRENT OF IGNORANCE AND PREJUDICE THAT RAN AGAINST LINDY CHAMBERLAIN ALMOST FROM THE BEGINNING."
—*Newsday*

"ONE OF THE MOST INTERESTING AND DISTURBING BOOKS I'VE EVER READ ABOUT THE SOCIAL AND EMOTIONAL RAMIFICATIONS OF A CRIMINAL TRIAL. . . . [BRYSON] TURNS THE WORST NIGHTMARE OF FALSE JUSTICE INTO AN AFFIRMATION OF HONEST GRIT, WITHOUT LOSING SIGHT OF HOW EASILY LINDY CHAMBERLAIN COULD STILL BE IN JAIL . . . TERRIFIC." —Erika Munk, *Village Voice*

"FIVE HUNDRED AND FIFTY PAGES OF CINEMATIC EXCITEMENT."—Maeve Binchy

"NON-STOP EXCITEMENT . . . BRYSON PILES SHOCK UPON SHOCK AS HE SPIRITS READERS ALL OVER THE MAP: TO COURTROOMS IN DARWIN AND ALICE SPRINGS; TO THE HOMES OF ABORIGINAL TRACKERS; TO FORENSIC LABORATORIES IN AUSTRALIA, ENGLAND AND THE UNITED STATES; EVEN TO AN ADELAIDE ZOO, FOR BIZARRE EXPERIMENTS IN THE LIKELY BEHAVIOR OF DINGOES . . . BOOKS DON'T GET MORE INTERESTING THAN THIS ONE." —*The Virginia-Pilot* and *The Ledger Star*

"AN IMPRESSIVE LITERARY DOCUMENT." —*London Times*

EVIL
ANGELS

JOHN BRYSON

BANTAM BOOKS
TORONTO · NEW YORK · LONDON · SYDNEY · AUCKLAND

EVIL ANGELS

*A Bantam Book / published by arrangement with
Summit Books*

PRINTING HISTORY

Summit Books edition published February 1987
Bantam edition / June 1988

*Bantam Books are published by Bantam Books, a division of
Bantam Doubleday Dell Publishing Group, Inc. Its trademark,
consisting of the words "Bantam Books" and the portrayal of a
rooster, is Registered in U.S. Patent and Trademark Office and
in other countries. Marca Registrada. Bantam Books, 666 Fifth
Avenue, New York, New York 10103.*

PRINTED IN THE UNITED STATES OF AMERICA

O   0 9 8 7 6 5 4 3 2 1

Lesley Weber

CONTENTS

SO VOID WAS NIGHT

EVIL EYE

THE SECRET ASSUMPTIONS OF SCIENCE

NECROMANCY, SO TO TRIAL

SO VOID
WAS NIGHT

PHOENIXVILLE

1

IT WAS AUTUMN. Roadside aspens and hickories were already lean and spiky. Leaves lay in the waggon ruts, and grass in the field was still damp late in the afternoon.

This field was at Phoenixville, on the south bank of the Schuylkill. In 1844, the year this was, the river left the woods here to flow through the rich plains of middle Pennsylvania. The meadow was owned by Josiah Levitt. The Levitt family had invited friends to pass a day there, in prayer, though it was not the Sabbath but a Monday.

Nearly twenty families arrived, most shortly before dusk. They were not late, because a day for these folk was measured from sundown to sundown. Some had come from Vermont, some from New Jersey. The waggons and the sulkies were drawn into a circle. Horses were unharnessed, the warm bits slipped from their mouths and, without halter or hobble, were turned out to graze steaming by the stream.

Some of these folk had not met before. Newcomers were welcomed with the words 'Brother' and 'Sister', and with familiar phrases from the Bible. There was greater warmth than was usual in people who valued solemnity. On this day solemnity was an effort. Adults graced each other with their smiles. Shy children held hands. All were joyful for themselves and for one another. When they looked about they saw only the glad faces of the servants of God.

This was the twenty-second day in October. Everyone was here to watch the second coming of Christ and to be drawn up into the heavenly throng.

* * *

The evening was cold, and many had brought only their Sabbath clothing. Some had dressed in white muslin robes they thought suitable for an Ascension. There was little food, for most believed they would be well provided for. Elder Joshua Himes had said: 'Go not into your houses to take anything out, leave everything upon the Altar of God, and if He wants any part of it He will take care of it.' The sceptics among them brought fruit and water for the journey.

Night passed with hymns and recitations from the Testaments. No one wanted to spend the last mortal night in sleep. Their singing swelled. Sarah Smollett, after consulting with her husband, asked if their voices might not drown out the approach of the Heavenly Choir, but it was generally thought more important to give than to receive, and the verses rolled on.

The darkness was parted, not yet by angelic light, but by the advent of a pale sun rising behind the woods. Children stretched, and crawled out from underneath the carriages. The sun found everybody bright and warm, a condition they all recognized as curious. Nathaniel Brett said this was a sign.

The year had been full of signs. Most were warnings of destruction to a sinful world. The month of March had seen earthquakes close to the southern seaboard. Towns in the Carribean splintered, and American ships were hurled up on the shores of Texas. A comet was bright in the New England skies. Beneath it the northern weather had begun to change. It snowed in Philadelphia on the summer solstice. Boston was covered with frost on 21 July. Cold in Austinburgh had killed an entire season of buckwheat. A God who would confiscate the summer would send his faithful a sign.

So they sang. They arranged to face the east, since that was from where their sign had come.

Mad Mary Chase, wife of Captain Chase, who now refused to be seen with her, sat next to her daughters. Four of these she placed in a line of diminishing size, but held the fifth in her lap because it was twelve weeks old. Old Amos and Martha Gower, childless all their seventy years of marriage, chose to be surrounded by the children of others. Matthew Lockitt, a fruit vendor, sat happily in his empty box-cart. Matthew was a seller of toffeed apples until last August, when he set up his stall in a Washington park near an Advent meeting. By the time the preacher finished, Matthew had given all his apples away to the crowd. His cart had been empty since.

Behind, Adin Shortbridge sat in company, though with a space on his left. He would allow no one to fill it. Adin's brother William had died while awaiting this Advent on a mistaken date. The Boston *Liberator* reported that William climbed a high tree, and 'mantled in his long white ascension robe he made one aspiring effort, but was precipitated to the ground, and instantly died from a broken neck'. The space on Adin's left was for the use of William Shortbridge at the time appointed for the dead to rise.

That time was brought closer by the passing of the sun overhead. It also brought sightseers from Phoenixville township and from the *Inquirer* newspaper in Philadelphia. The townspeople leaned on the fence. A persistent wit loudly counted the dissipation of time. The reporter took a notebook from his pocket. He made across the grass just as the startlingly resolute voice of young Hannah Ballou began Psalm 23. He made, too, an effort to seriously compose his face, to better his chances of an interview with somebody.

The friends in Levitt's green meadow were well accustomed to the presence of those that troubled them. Adventist meetings in the cities were often disrupted by volleys of detonating firecrackers. Howling youths pranced the aisles in white sheets. On windy days, smirking men loosened the pegs on the marquee in which Adventists prayed, so that the poles tottered and the canvas fell in. Their children were jeered in the streets. Cartoonists lampooned their earnest faces in the press, and employers' doors were closed on them because they thought it wrong to work on the Sabbath.

Threat of intrusion by the press retreated now with the sudden appearance, from somewhere behind a cartwheel, of the Ballous' mastiff. With no command from anyone, it set the man from the *Inquirer* over the fence. Hannah finished her verses, then wondered aloud what sort of man could so merrily count down the time to his own destruction, as did the wag on the rails. The severe wisdom of the child, and that of the dog, stiffened their backs and their resolve. The day was growing cold, but no winter was ahead of them.

'And Jesus said: "If thou shalt not watch, I will come on thee as a thief, and thou shalt not know what hour I will come upon thee." Third, Revelations, three.'

'Yes, Brother. Watch for Him. He will come in the clouds of Heaven.'

' "And with them that are raised from the dead." First Corinthians, fifteen fifty-two.'

'And first Thessalonians, four sixteen, sister.'

There was but half an hour to sunset. The portly Moses Clark, who had once been chairman of the land commissioners at Landoff, suggested they should form the waggons in a cross. This was accomplished without the help of their discarded horses. They had the advantage that rows of the seated now faced each of the quarters of the compass, and wondered why they had not thought of it before. Nathaniel Brett took up the count-down that was once the delight of the wag by the fence. Old Amos and Martha Gower held each other's sparse hands. Mad Mary Chase prettied her little ones.

They sang and they sang, and the sun absconded with their dreams.

Darkness fell silent. Adin Shortbridge rested his hand on the empty space beside him. George Florida, a blacksmith whose hot trade had numbed the breath in his throat so he had not been able to sing, fingered his collar. Within a week the Boston *Liberator* will report that he has hung himself with a chain. Mad Mary Chase nursed the youngest three of her daughters all together. Already she had started to cry. The same newspaper will record her finding under the dray, tomorrow morning, the bodies of the other two children dead from cold.

Hiram Edson will recall, in a memoir, the way they passed the long night. They wept until the dawn came up.

2

THE SAME SUNLIGHT falls on New Hampton. There is a small church. The forest walls here are cut back only far enough to allow for a sacrarium tiled with fallen leaves. This gives the pleasing impression that the church is the presbytery within a greater tabernacle. The trees are as straight as organ flutes.

Two wooden dwellings share the ground here. Both belong to a family by the name of Miller. It was for this church that William Miller felled timber, drove pegs, and carved plans into the blaze of a tree. It was also by Miller's calibrations that the time was set for the Second Advent of Christ.

Eleven families are here now. All were joined to the event by Miller's persuasive teaching. They sit on the porches and in the doorways. The most common expressions are of resolution and piety, but this hides a deep spirit of dejection. It is a time they will later call the Great Disappointment.

Continued silence from the church is an increasing distraction for them all. An hour after sundown, William Miller strode inside, alone, and has not yet come out. His brow was heavy. The corn of Adventist farmers stands unshucked in the field because he advised them so. Potatoes lie wet in the ground, their unweaned heifers follow irritable cows, their store-rooms are dark and empty, their windows are boarded over. They are, in the eyes of the world, a people jilted by their Redeemer.

William Miller led them here. He led them into error, but the sound they now await is that of his invigorated step to the church door.

3

IN DECEMBER 1849, five years after the Great Disappointment, mourners at the funeral of William Miller filled the church. There were two days to Christmas, and roads to Low Hampton were sluggish with snow. Latecomers found room to stand and, during the hymns, quietly eased their boots from the floor to prevent them freezing to the boards. The voices of children were as many as the voices of adults, since schools were closed in west New York State by a winter so harsh that school-houses were not habitable.

More than half the congregation were either named Miller or were related to a Miller. William Miller was once the eldest of sixteen siblings. His casket lay by the lectern. Those who had seen him laid out were heartened that his expression in death was his expression in life. It confirmed for them his calm in the sudden presence of his Redeemer, for it was their firm belief that this meeting takes place during the last moments in which the spirit prepares to leave the body.

Joshua Himes gave a eulogy. He spent little time on Miller's scriptural calculations or on the Error. Such was the faith of Adventists that these issues were already well resolved. The year 1844 was not to have been that of Advent, but that of Heavenly preparations for Advent. A time of Advent was itself certain, imminent, and incalculable.

The words Joshua Himes gave were so familiar that most knew them by heart. This passage William Miller used near the end of his sermons, and by his own count he had given 3200 sermons in ten years. 'At this dread moment, look, look! O look and see! What means that ray of light? The clouds have burst asunder, the heavens appear, the great white throne is in sight! Amazement fills the universe with awe! He comes! Behold the Saviour comes! Lift up your heads, ye saints, He comes!—He comes!—He comes!'

They lifted the coffin. The six pall-bearers were short and stocky. All were Millers. They walked, in step, carrying their brother towards the grave they had dug through the snow that morning. Some of those who followed the burial procession will carry their burdens far further. The Sabbath-keepers among them would, in 1863, after bitter argument, inaugurate the Seventh-day Adventist Church according to secular law. The elders Hiram Edson and Joshua Himes will press the need for repentance throughout the northern states until they die. Joseph Bates will be remembered for using the message of Adventism as a force in the anti-slavery movement. The preacher Jones, yet to withdraw from the Baptist clergy, will prove so successful an evangelist that his Christian name will be forgotten and he will be known simply as Increase Jones.

The first woman to fell soil into the pit was Miller's widow. Her pallor was not due to the cold. She had spent the past four years nursing William through illnesses. The path to their house had deepened with the passage of well-wishers. But now she was tired, and will not live long.

The second woman to cast soil was also to cast her presence so powerfully over the church that the work of William Miller would be obscured. This was Ellen Harmon White. With her husband James she will move the centre of Adventism to Michigan. The town they select for a sanitarium there has an auspicious name. It is called Battle Creek. Ellen White will then move for a time to Cooranbong to begin an Adventist colonization of New South Wales.

Her voice was soon to carry the highest doctrinal authority, for Jesus will frequently choose to appear to her in person. She will then be able to detail recent progress in the great clashes between the massed brigades of Satan and the platoons of heavenly angels who, during lulls in the fighting, peer down to see how saints on the world below are faring in similar circumstances.

The crisis of credibility caused by her visions will split the church in 1905, beginning another cycle of public derision. But her stern path was to carry the message of Adventism through, as she described it in 1868, 'the exulting, sneering triumph of evil angels'.

The grave was filled. A stone had not yet been cut, so the head was marked with a cross. Two harrowed Miller daughters drew their mother away. There were no words of leave-taking. They were all to travel from here to Fairhaven where the Congregational church was large enough for a public service. The men went directly to rig the carriages. Ice was shaken from the leathers so not to chafe the horses. Fairhaven lay over the mountains.

Quiet snow continued to fall. By the time the last sulky cleared the gate, William Miller's white grave had already taken on the order of well-settled ground.

DESERT

1

MOST OF US are pilgrims of one kind or another, although what we are truly in homage to might not come clear until our pilgrimages are done. There is a memorial near the Stuart Highway, five hundred kilometres north of Alice Springs, standing to the left of the southbound lane. The roadway is sealed, but the face of the marker is often red with vagrant dust from the plains, for this is the edge of the central Australian desert, and there are not many days in a year on which it rains.

The memorial is to John Flynn. Flynn was a missionary from the south, concerned with the distribution of the gospel by squads of meandering padres. He came to be more famed for his distribution of medicines by aeroplane, and it is this memory which still causes grateful homesteaders to dust off his monument so that tourists can read the inscription without leaving their automobiles.

Another five hundred kilometres further south-west is the Hermannsberg mission. It has been here a hundred years. Most of those who live and work at this settlement are Aranda, a people with the light step of hunters and gatherers. Implacable sunshine, over forty thousand years, has bleached their hair. Missionaries brought them here to raise cattle beside the sandy bed of the Finke River, grow irrigated vegetables, and worship in Lutheran churches. Around the turn of the century, the pastors translated into Aranda the twenty-seven books of the New Testament so that the desert people could recite verses wherever they were. The mission was considered successful until 1975, when legislation gave Aboriginal people the right to choose where to live. Many then chose the desert. Now the Lutheran pastors of Hermannsberg are best known, not so much for their attempt to make farmers of hunters, but as authorities in local languages and for the first English-Aranda dictionary.

Anglicans, Baptists, Catholics, Methodists, and Seventh-day Adventists have all, at one time or another, sent missions to the sparse tribes of the desert. This resulted in an abnormally high incidence of Christian instruction. Mission bulletins recorded astonishment that a people could live here at all.

2

THE MOST COMMON ACTIVITY in this part of the country is transit. Alice Springs has been the waypoint here since the 1870s, when the attractions were water and shade. Now the attractions are gas-stations and motels, and the most expensive drink in town is mixed at the bar of the casino by a costumed girl who takes your money equally quickly when she doubles as a croupier at the roulette tables.

The casino now claims to be the most important part of Alice Springs, a boast that only city folk can take seriously. Those who come here for the gambling don't go far beyond the gaming rooms and the swimming pool, unless the bell-hop has a taxi-cab handy, but the township is not much more than a kilometre away, and the walk is worth taking for more reasons than exercise.

Alice Springs lies in a basin, at the southern edge of the Macdonnell Ranges. From here the vegetation on the rocks is hard to see, and amateur painters generally colour them in shades of red and brown. These ranges have given the basin the Todd River, rainfall enough to have it flow once every year or so, and shelter from the south-easterlies, which are so insistent outside that the climatological tables given to tourists don't record a wind from any other direction. The ranges also make a rim for the horizon to sit on all the way around, and it is this periphery, as much as the trees and the river-bed, which accounts here for the sense of oasis.

The casino lies on one side of the Todd and the rest of the town on the other. The road between carries over a concrete bridge but sometimes, when the Todd floods, the bridge is submerged and guests take a helicopter. The casino is separated from the river and the rest of Alice Springs by well-watered grass verges and fetchingly arranged stands of desert oaks. It is also protected by a wire-mesh fence as high as those used to surround prison compounds in times of war.

The fence diminishes the danger of a hold-up, as gambling officials will say, but there are only two feasible ways out of town so the prospects for a successful getaway can't be great. In any event, everyone in Alice Springs knows the fence has quite a different objective. The river-bed here is green and shady. Although the gravel is dry, the Todd flows happily through the shale about a metre down, and the river eucalypts are wide and strong. Small fish swim the waterholes. People from the Aranda, Pintubi and Pitjantjatjara camp on the Todd, until they are moved on, sleeping in automobiles or under gabled sheets of tin. It's not unprecedented to find a grand iron bedstead, of Edwardian design, steadied against the trunk of a stringybark. These people like to sit around, generally in a circle, singing their own undulating songs, then skipping a millennium or so of musical form by passing on to country and western ballads. This can go on late into the night, while they pass a flagon of sweet wine from hand to hand, very often getting as drunk as the people allowed into the bars of the casino.

The town boundary, just here, is the west bank. All the longest streets of Alice Springs parallel the river, conforming still to the plans of earlier settlers, who thought buildings ought to be close to the sources of water. But the riverside is no longer considered a desirable address. Many of the buildings here now are not well kept. The houses are cut off from the footpath by mesh fences and irritable guard-dogs. The most usual traffic on this side of town is that of delivery vans and cruising police cars. The further you walk to the north-west the richer real-estate values become and then, happening quite suddenly, the street is busy.

The shopping mall is the centre of things in Alice Springs. Although this is the biggest town for a thousand kilometres of road in any direction, the people who permanently live here number less than eighteen thousand. But from March to November, when day-time temperatures are consistently cooler than forty-five degrees in the shade, a hundred and seventy thousand people come in as tourists. Hawaiian shirts and printed frocks are everywhere. Cameras are the common adornment. Postcards are the common mail. The busiest shops are fast-photo centres and souvenir dealers. Pharmacies do brisk trade in sunglasses, skin lotions, and floppy hats. Street corner shopfronts are not often banking corporations, as they are in other cities, but airline terminals and travel agencies.

3

THERE IS A SCENE presented so regularly in the Mall that only tourists take notice of it anymore. The corner here has an awning. By early afternoon the shadow has moved enough that it is a shady place for men from camps nearby to pass an hour or so. The chances are high that they're in no hurry, because the local rate of unemployment among Aborigines runs at ten times the rate for others. Employers firmly believe that blacks have a deep and ineradicable need to wander.

Many of these people wear shorts and coloured shirts like everyone else, but for one, quite elderly man. He is in riding gear. The heels to his boots were once higher, and his shoulders are now depleted, but his wide hat is well brushed, and there is pride enough under his shirt so that tourists know they have happened on the real thing. In the days when cattle were moved across country in dusty mobs, the man was a drover. The window-pane behind him belongs to a travel office. This agency, like others along the Mall, advertises passages to all the seven continents. Its owners are sufficiently confident about white people's ineradicable need to wander to believe that the firm has a bright future. Much of their business is arranging flights and coach tours to destinations not so far away, and the window is hung with posters showing the red bluffs of the Escarpment, Ayers Rock, Mt Olga, Corroboree Rock, and the Standley Chasm. Aborigines have been the custodians of these places, as they believe, since their time began. They call that time the Dreaming, because they have not found an adequate method of calculation to better convey how long ago that was. They were here, still with no thought of moving on, while Romans pushed through into Gaul, Saxons into Germany, and Hellenes into Asia.

Posters of his Dreamtime land make a fine backdrop for the old drover. He must have been photographed more times than he could count, standing right there.

4

IN THIS PART of the country, according to the best guesses of statisticians, the average drinker takes in around forty-nine grams of alcohol, in one agreeable form or another, for every day of the week. This compares courageously with the national standard, which is twenty-eight. It is simply a mean, as everyone understands, and if you charge someone who lives here with the figure, the riposte is likely to be this: someone else must be drinking an astonishing amount. The answer has a familiar ring, but you have only to watch the behaviour of tourists in hotel-bars and restaurants to feel some sympathy with it.

Whoever is doing the drinking, the parking-lot closest to an Alice Springs hotel is the place to stroll through if you want to find out, in quick time, what sort of town this is. Around five on any Friday afternoon, the lot will be full. A tourist bus stands, in front, at the kerbside. The guide, a young woman dressed in the style of an air-hostess, helps each of her passengers step gingerly down to the hot footpath. 'Take care,' she says, since many of them are elderly. They move slowly, as if recently woken from a deep reverie, for they have travelled more than one thousand five hundred kilometres to get here, whether this bus has driven north out of Adelaide or south out of Darwin.

Close to the back of the lot you are likely to see a light van or two of the sort used in the cities to deliver smallgoods. They are now fitted with roof-racks and gas bottles. The positions in which they are parked represent attempts at obscurity, but the panels are painted with scenes of a gaudy surf-beach, or of a garish sunset, and the kids who own them will be dismayed how quickly police suspect that these are being lived in.

A few four-door sedans here belong to local housewives who are now driving shopping trolleys speedily through the supermarkets not far away. Another driver nowhere near the hotel-bar is the owner of an empty road-train which, although it has been truncated by winching the second jinker onto the tray of the first, still occupies eight parking spaces. The driver is asleep in the cabin. It is his first rest in thirty-six hours, although the entries in his log-book will deny it. Tomorrow he will breakfast at an all-night roadhouse, load a hundred and fifty wild-eyed bullocks at Yambah and begin the eighteen-hundred kilometre drive to Adelaide.

The four-wheel drives, most of them Toyotas, fall into two classes: the battered belong to men who are younger than they seem and are looking for any work at any place, and the straight belong to departments concerned with wildlife conservation, municipal services, and law enforcement. Pick-up trucks and utilities, with implausibly large spanners and wrenches in the back, are used by drill workers in town for the weekend. They are from mines with names like Santa Teresa, El Dorado, and Indiana. Old model V-8s, well down on their springs, were parked here by young blacks from the Papunyah Reserve. It would be difficult to say who owns those cars, for people with many relatives and little money don't find sole ownership at all sensible. The mini-mokes, with hoods as gay as beach umbrellas, are parked here by rental companies waiting on another planeload of cut-fare holidaymakers. The rest of the lot should be taken up by estate waggons, and family sedans fitted with camping-racks, all interstate and washed as soon as they hit town, tourists now ready to take in Palm Valley, Mt Olga, and Ayers Rock.

At around this time of day on 15 August 1980, which was also a Friday, there was an unusual number of Chevvies, Broncos, and Renegades. They were painted snappy colours, fitted with bull-bars, and with tow-balls of the sort needed to pull oversized caravans or horse-floats. Anyone here before, at this time of year, knew what it meant. The rodeo was in town.

5

THE CAR IN THE LEAD, as their headlights broke through the Gap, was a Ford pick-up, but it was a close contest. By the time they swung for the driveway, the pick-up had dropped back to fourth. A fanfare of engine noise pealed from the bluffs, and campers in Heavitree Park knew they were coming.

They pulled up at a fireplace. The dust blew past, though the night was still. Any flame had long gone, but the logs were hot. They called for beer-cartons and kicked up a blaze. There were five cars, most with the doors now left open wide. Perhaps this was so not to further disturb anyone still asleep nearby, but that hadn't occurred to the driver of the GT Monaro, who loaded his tape-deck and turned up the music.

There were eight or nine, in jeans and jackets, by the fire. All men, except for a blonde girl who sat in the back of a blowsy Dodge and who, in the lulls between numbers on the tape, sang on. Music rolled, and the fire grew with coals and with blackening beer-cans. On the front of the Monaro, where the bonnet had stayed warm, lay a wiry young man of around twenty-five, whose slim jeans showed patches sewn over the calves. Every time he climbed down from there, he complained what time of night it was but, since he unzipped a fresh can before he said anything else, no one seemed to take him too seriously.

'Got to get some sleep,' he said.

'Sure, Pardy. Better have a drink first.'

'I got a ride in the morning.'

'You never done any good sober. Don't risk it, pal.'

Nights here are cold at this time of year and by two o'clock, when the fire was running low, the number standing around it was down to five. The roughrider Purdy was not yet gone, but had made it as far as the fireside. The soft dew around the bonnet where he'd sat had turned hard and glossy. No one now bothered to reload the music. If there was a time at which the sleepless in caravans and under nylon further along might have thought the party had died, this was it. But, from the cabin of the Ford pick-up, a dog began to bark. The Ford was parked between the Monaro and a toilet-block. The dog, a black-jawed Doberman, made a lot of noise. The man who owned it reached down for a bottle. He picked it up by the neck. There was no suggestion of hospitality in that gesture.

'Darkies,' he said.

It was not a darky, but a pale boy who was walking past the front of the Ford. Most of him was under a blanket he held around his shoulders. The dog quietened. The dog-owner put the bottle down.

'What d'you doing there,' he said.

'Nothing. Been at the toilet.'

'Didn't see you go in.'

'No.' The boy cocked his head. 'The other side.'

'Then don't bother the dog, kid.'

'No. It's just I'm a stranger.'

'My dog don't bark at strangers.'

The boy was around fifteen, at most. He had short sandy hair and freckles. He looked down at his feet, which were pale and cold. He was certainly not trouble, and seemed stuck for a more helpful answer.

'No,' he said, 'I'm on holidays.'

That might put the dilemma at some sort of rest, so the boy moved on. But this was the first camper to appear since the cars pulled up here, and the occasion was not to pass without recognition by Purdy.

'The dog knows more than you do, kid,' he said. The boy kept going.

'Got to get some sleep,' Purdy said.

By morning the pick-up had gone. Daylight found the rough-rider lying full length on the front seat of the Monaro. No one else was in sight. He was still there while tousled campers hung sleeping-bags in the sun and made for the water-tanks with tooth-brushes. Campers are usually gregarious folk, even at breakfast time, but many from tents and vans nearby were choosing to cook somewhere else, although the only memorial to revelry now was a cairn of beer-cans in the ashes.

When Michael Chamberlain woke, the sun was up, but it was difficult to guess how high it was, for light was so diffuse inside the tent that day seemed to have dawned equally all over the sky. The tent was empty. By the time he got outside, he found the boys already into breakfast. His wife Lindy had changed the baby and fed her, and was patting her on the back to unlock some gust or other of digestion.

It was a matter of pleasant and recurring wonder to him how quickly after childbirth her figure became girlish again. After each of the boys was born—six years ago for Aidan and four for Reagan—she was back playing tennis and squash inside a few weeks. She had borne Azaria at the hospital in Mt Isa, the mining town to which he had been assigned, less than ten weeks ago now, yet the only detectable residuum was a certain slowness at the bosom when she moved.

Michael had no doubt that blessings like this were direct and well-considered gifts from Jesus. Michael was a pastor in the Seventh-day Adventist Church. He knew that, although some of God's works are mysterious, many are plainer than pikestaves. It was his wife's duty, and that of his children, to treat their bodies as proper agencies of the Lord, and the result to be expected from this was health and vigour. If Michael had been the priest of a denomination in the older European tradition, he might by now, at thirty-eight, have begun to spread and to allow himself tobacco and alcohol. But his obligation as an example, and as a co-ordinator, of mortal obedience was too clear for confusions of that sort. Without being hardy, he looked trim and efficient.

They finished breakfast quietly. It was a Saturday, and their Sabbath since sundown Friday. They had hoped to spend another two days in the park before driving on to Ayers Rock. If things had run according to plan, the family would have spent today here at the camp, and much of it in devotion. The tent was pitched far from the rowdier arrivals of last night, but still too close for unbroken rest. Beer-cans and cigarettes were appearing now at the breakfast tables of campers not far away. The peaceful temper of Heavitree Park had changed overnight.

Their decision was not long coming. This was no fit place to pass a Sabbath. Their immediate inclination was to make back to Alice Springs. The Cuzins family would take them in. Bert Cuzins was the district pastor. But they had farewelled the Cuzins's yesterday, and retreat seemed an unnecessarily dispiriting start to a holiday. Better, Michael now said, that they spend their Sabbath in the car. Devotion, he thought, can have no less validity in motion than at rest.

So they lowered the tent and loaded the gear. The boys piled in. There was so much equipment inside that they had to sit on parts of it. Lindy held the baby in front, and arranged nappies and washers neatly within reach, for Ayers Rock was four hundred kilometres away by road. Michael was pleased, because everyone was plainly happier for the decision to go on. When he drove them out of the park and turned south to the highway, it seemed to him that his earlier thoughts of refuge were not as manly as he would have liked, even a little absurd.

GOD PUT IT HERE, HIMSELF

1

SO VOID WAS NIGHT in the desert that the Wests were lost. It was near midnight Friday, and the moon was down. They were somewhere to the south-east of Ayers Rock but couldn't find the camping-ground. The only part of the world's surface Bill West could see was where the headlights touched it. There was a frost, and it was as if the spindly desert oaks and wattles that lived out here were too inert to reflect light, except in a moment of brief warmth from the headlamps.

Bill and Judy West, and Catherine, who was then twelve and riding in the back seat, had driven overland twelve hundred kilometres to get here. They lived on a sheep station near Esperance, in Western Australia. That is not a well-populated region either. The city nearest home is Albany, five hundred kilometres overland, and the nearest capital is Perth, at six hundred. Esperance is a town with absolute water frontage to the Southern Ocean and the next landfall in that direction is Antarctica.

So the Wests were quiet and resourceful people, well used to the outback, and to unfamiliar terrain. But it seemed the camping-ground they were looking for was not where the duty ranger, in the office by the gate, had supposed it to be. Bill pulled the car off the road at the next clearing he saw. Another two vehicles, both pulling caravans, drew in alongside. The Wests were travelling in convoy with the Daniell family and the Mayberrys. They all pitched camp here, and turned in.

Next morning they were not awake long before the first sounds of traffic. This was a square four-wheel drive, rolling high on sand-tyres, and driven by an amused park ranger who paused long enough to point further down the road. The Wests could see then, across the scrub, a row of caravans and tent peaks, and a haze from breakfast fires. The turn-off was barely two hundred paces away. They loaded the cars again, grinning. This seemed a comical start to the day. Besides, the place they had thought so secluded by night was becoming unexpectedly busy. The Wests had camped at a bus-stop.

Catherine West ducked out under the tent-fly, leaving her parents inside. The afternoon was almost gone, but she had pulled on a tracksuit and she had warmth in her still from the shower. There was yet enough light out here to write by. The writing Catherine had in mind was her diary. She sat in the deck-chair and nudged it around into the best light, and into the direct gaze of an intrigued dingo.

It stood on the empty campsite at the side of their tent, just two or three paces from her, a big rusty brown dog with a large head and tight frame. Most of its weight was held forward, whether from menace or habit she couldn't tell. This didn't seem to her like a tame animal, yet it wasn't behaving like those she had seen in the wild. Perhaps dingoes which roamed the lanes of camps were different, as were those kids who roamed the streets of cities. She hoped it would go away soon. 'You're not even supposed to be here,' she said. When it turned and padded off, it seemed to carry an air of exaggerated off-handedness. If it could, it might have been whistling. Catherine was a little weary. After setting up camp here this morning, the Wests had explored the caves and the rockfalls around the base of the Rock, and after lunch they climbed it. That took up most of the afternoon, but was worth every minute; from up here you could see all the red plains, gently blurred by the desert oaks, across to Mt Connor and the Olgas, so far away, and peering over, but not too close to the edge, pick out the motels and the rangers' houses down below, neat and tidy, and the fine lines that must be roads, laid out so astonishingly straight they might have been drawn with a ruler. And the sky was blue to the edge of the world. You felt a little impossible, up here, like flying in dreams.

Catherine was about to inform her diary of this when she lurched from a blow on the arm. It was the dingo. It had her about the elbow. She tried to call out but hadn't the breath. The grip was commanding, painful, and she couldn't shake it off. The vapour of arrogance in its eyes was unmistakable and terrifying. She found her breath, the dog tugged at her arm, she screamed for her mother.

When Judy burst from the tent, the dingo's response was merely to watch her. Evidently Judy amounted to a novel, but not unmanageable, complication. She shooed at it, as she would a troublesome farm dog, but it stood fast. Judy West's bearing did not falter for a second. She made at the dingo as if boxing it about the ears was not entirely out of the question. The mounting squalls of her anger turned it then, but its retreat was insolently slow.

Twenty minutes later, Judy West left the tent to walk along the camp row. This part of the camping-ground was closest to Sunrise Hill, the high but scrubby dune from which keen photographers will catch the first warm reflections of dawn on the east bluffs of the Rock. The hill was darkening. Along the near side of the dusty road, the camps stood in a row like a linear village, kept in neat place by a low single-log fence, and a sandy strip occupied intermittently by gas barbecues. Judy was heading for a caravan parked further down. It was the Daniell's. Evidently they had been washing, for a clothes-line now declined from the caravan to the log rail. The clothes were flapping, which was curious because the evening was calm. Judy and a dingo then saw each other at much the same moment, but this time the dingo bolted. What a dingo wanted with underclothes, Judy couldn't guess. She gathered them up. There wasn't a mark on anything.

2

NIGHT HAD FALLEN. Michael Chamberlain turned the yellow Torana off the highway and on the camping-ground road. They rolled past tents and vans, to the end. The baby was asleep, but Aidan and Reagan were cramped and anxious. There seemed to be no allotments large enough. The camp's few lights were far apart, with dark pauses between, and space was not so easy to judge. Twice they drove the length of the row, turning gently so not to raise dust, before they found one. Michael pulled up facing the fence, leaving room on the right for the tent. Here an overhead lamp gave light enough to unpack by. Benches, barbecues, not far beyond the railing. The night was still. It was just fine.

So quietly did they unload the car and rig the tent that the Wests knew nothing of it. The first Judy heard was the cry of a baby. Quite a loud cry, as she remembers it, and very close by, for it was in the space beside the Wests' tent that Michael Chamberlain had chosen to park his car.

3

AT THE INSTANT sunlight touched the dome of the Rock, the most obtrusive sound from the crowd on the dune was the clatter of camera-shutters.

The bluffs filled and richened. It was a moment of redemption. For a minute, two minutes, the dome stood bright and splendid, high above the retreating night.

Then it bleached, and the scene was done. The crowd began to turn away, moving quietly down the hillside as if leaving the event with some reluctance. But the plains were already hard and clear. It was indisputably day.

4

AT BREAKFAST-TIME the barbecues were soon busy. Judy West and the Chamberlains cooked over a common hot-plate. It did not take them long to get acquainted.

The Chamberlains seemed to belong to that fortunate group for whom the paths of life are clear, and alternatives are not worth bothering about. They were both attractive, confident, and sporty. Lindy's tracksuit was well cut, she wore late-model Puma Rockettes on her feet, and reached for handy-packs of chemically impregnated tissues when it was time to wipe the boys' faces. The boys were clean, boisterous, and when they turned around Judy saw each had his name on the back of his T-shirt, like American junior-leaguers.

Michael, judging by the number of tricky accessories in his kit, was a photographer of unusual persistence, and was quite proud of the overintelligent watch he wore on his wrist. That he had chosen a Queensland mining town in which to live was something of a surprise, until this was exposed as a transfer, and one might then have first suspected a teaching post at, say, senior primary-school level, rather than a Christian ministry. After a few moments' quiet observation, all this seemed faintly predictable. So when Lindy had Judy guess in which denomination that ministry was, Judy chose well.

'How did you know?' Lindy asked.

The clue was in their sausages, which were indignantly vegetable.

'Vegelinks, there're called,'' said Michael, 'because they are links between people.'

Lindy was keen to show Judy the baby. 'It's okay, high time she woke up,' she said.

They walked to the fence where a bassinet lay. The baby was tiny, not yet double her birthweight, with a fine, soft nap of brown hair. 'Bubby's name is Azaria.' Lindy sounded the melody in it so that the musical rhyme was with aria. 'Azaria means Blessed of God, you know.'

'I didn't know that,' Judy confessed.

'Don't worry, neither did my mother,' Lindy said. 'When I told her, on the phone, you know, from the hospital, she thought it meant we'd had another boy.'

'Two boys already, so you'd prayed for a girl?'

'Certainly did. Boys are such little monkeys. Fancy three of them.' Lindy sat on the rail and dandled the baby on her knee. 'And Bubby is just the girl we wanted.' There was something in this which spoke of pride in the management of two boys and an infant of swaddling age, on an excursion into a desert.

Judy asked if they were well used to camping out. 'We sure are,' Lindy said. 'We go everywhere.' Her parka was emblazoned with travel badges. 'Michael's got one just the same, and the boys.' She had, snug in a drawer at home, a parka for the baby to grow into.

In her smile was the heady complicity of motherhood. 'Two badges on Bubby's already,' she said.

5

THE EMBLEM of the Conservation Commission shows the wedge-tailed eagle, *Aquila audax,* over a map of the Northern Territory. It illustrates, as much as anything else, the Territorians' respect for things of great magnitude. Their eagles commonly better three metres between wingtips, and the size of their Territory is, for example, twice that of Texas.

Now, a bird and a map might amount to a merely convention-al montage, in design terms, if it were not for a tidy trick of repeated dimension, ad infinitum. The picture is drawn from a position stratospherically high. The eagle hangs, with upswept wings, in the motionless instant before a free-fall that will take it away, sleek and diminishing, to the earth beneath (where, in a concurrent life, we also stand), and where it appears again on this next level of illusion down, on signboards everywhere, as an emblematic eagle with an identical earth far below.

Around Ayers Rock, this prodigious eagle appears on office doors, trucks, pamphlets, and shoulder-tags worn by the eight park rangers. It signifies the pursuit of freedom and the splendour of isolation. But freedom can become burdensome, when the isolation is as splendid as it is out here. In August 1980 the average length of service by rangers was only four years.

The exceptions were much admired. Derek Roff and Ian Cawood each had twelve years, Ian Marshall three. Roff was the most senior. He was born in Yorkshire where he stayed happily until his adolescence had well run out, dreaming of adventures in the wild. The wildest place he could think of was Africa. He joined the police force in Kenya, saw service around the mountains 'up country' and became assistant superintendent of Tsavo wildlife reserve, where his duty was to prevent poachers pilfering, among other things, the skins of leopards, the feet of elephants, and the horns of rhinoceruses. A white policeman from Kenya might not be thought so wise an appointment for Ayers Rock, where the Pitjantjatjara live, but Roff's friendship with these people is deep and respectful. He is entrusted with certain secrets of ritual and of song. He has, as he sees it, a 'simple' grasp of the language and its complex structures of tense and, should he use Pitjantjatjara words in an English conversation they carry the correct melodies of the 'singing-music'. It is his belief that the Pitjantjatjara are the spiritual custodians of the land. When Roff speaks of the Rock he uses, without embarrassment, the local name: Uluru.

Earlier this August, Roff was sitting at his desk in the rangers' office, beginning a memorandum for quick despatch to head office in Darwin.

He was worried. Much of a ranger's time is spent keeping fauna and tourists respectfully apart. Under the conditions he was used to here, the threats to co-existence generally came from the tourists. But the behaviour of dingoes was changing. About forty lived around the Rock, all from lairs in caves and diggings near the base. Twelve or fifteen of these, as near as he could judge, thought of the camping-ground and buildings as within their legitimate influence, and were causing unexpected trouble. Their forays were now frequent and fearless.

'It is most probable,' Roff wrote, 'that conditioning by humans may be a contributing factor. By this I do not just mean feeding, but the inducement to permit patting, to further encourage animals to enter camps, and even houses.'

The houses Roff was referring to were occupied by staff. He knew of houses in which dingoes were fed on the back porch. In another, a dingo slept by the hearth on cold winter nights.

Roff's memo took a didactic tone: 'The dingo is an alert, extremely intelligent predator.' To administrators in Darwin, whose decisions more commonly involve crocodiles and buffalo, mischievous dingoes might not seem a weighty problem.

In fact, Roff's files now held several complaints of menace, and four of attack. One was laid by Ian Kelly, the lessor of the Red Sands. Kelly's child was bitten on the back by a dingo which was then prowling the motel rubbish bins. Late in July, a three-year-old girl was dragged from the seat of a car. That family had arrived at the camp barely a half hour earlier. Ian Cawood had tended the injury. The girl had welts on her skin where the dingo had gripped her around the neck. Cawood noted in the file that he had shot the animal he guessed was responsible. In the same month Paul Cormack, who was nearly four years old, was knocked down by a dingo while he was playing on the road near the barbecues. His mother was preparing dinner. By the time she got to him, the right side of his head was bloodied where the dingo had bitten through the hood of his parka. Four weeks later, in August, the Fisher family was also preparing dinner at the barbecues. The two boys were kicking a soccer ball around. When one of them bent down to pick it up he was savaged from behind by a dingo. The animal could open its jaws sufficiently wide that it took the ball in its mouth and made off.

'It is well able,' Roff wrote, 'to take advantage of any laxity on the part of prey species and, of course, children and babies can be considered possible prey.'

Other rangers had suggested a fence, but Roff forsaw difficulties with gates. The problems should be thought through carefully. Meantime he asked for permission to nail up cautionary notices, and to shoot the most troublesome animals. Roff had dealt with administrations long enough to know that building an enclosure did not begin with a pick and shovel, but with a typewriter and a file-reference.

6

A FOUR-WHEEL DRIVE Toyota pulled up outside the rangers' office. Greg and Sally Lowe had driven over from Alice Springs, Sally nursing the baby. The day was slipping away fast. It was Sunday afternoon, already around 3.40. They had agreed to set aside the rest of the afternoon for climbing the Rock, and tomorrow for climbing the Olgas.

The Lowes found it easy to agree about things. They were each from Tasmanian country families, both once worked as tellers in Hobart banks, they were teenagers when they married and, if they were ever separately questioned about their interests, each would be confident that the other would also list family-life and bush-walking.

Greg opened the driver's door and slid out. He was bearded and lanky. The cabin was dusty, outside and in, a hazard they had come to accept, since the Toyota was borrowed from a relative in Alice Springs. Greg wiped the windscreen with the flat of his palm, slapped it clean on his thigh, and walked into the office.

Inside, he was a little hurried. The duty ranger gave him directions to the camping-ground and a registration form. Greg filled in as much information as he could quickly muster, squandered a moment on a courteous grin, and left.

The ranger was Derek Roff. He filed the Lowes' registration. The space requiring the licence-plate number of their vehicle was blank. It was not, he thought at that moment, worth bothering about.

7

THE BUS-DRIVER, who had asked to be called Peter, made a right turn to the circuit-road for a counter-clockwise loop of Ayers Rock. He had nearly thirty passengers aboard. They had all spent the morning walking the Olgas, and were scheduled for the western slope of the Rock so that those who chose could make the climb. The route would take them past the ritual-keepers whose timeless duties had turned them to stone: the Mala men guarding their initiates, the initiates asleep, the bodies of the dead Kunia. No stops were permitted along this stretch, and the bus passed by the places of totemic legend while Peter, over the address system, described each of them in tones of receding interest.

He drove more slowly past the Pitjantjatjara settlement. The fence was built in order to keep enthusiastic tourists outside it. There were two dwellings. 'Those houses there were built for the families of Aboriginal trackers,' he said, 'and each one cost eighty-five thousand dollars,' The dwellings were made from vertical timber-boards and, to the keen eyes of vacationing speculators from the south, might not have seemed worth half that amount. 'But those blacks won't live inside at all,' he said. 'They say it gives them claustrophobia.'

This earned laughter along almost the length of the bus. Florence Wilkin, whose hearing was not quite so good as it was when she was younger, caught the end of it. She looked out. Indeed, in the shade of the Casuarinas ahead, sat a group of black people. But as they rolled closer it became clearer that these were not adults but children, maybe six to ten year olds. Someone asked Peter what game it was they were playing. 'Who can tell?' he said. 'They have their own games out here.'

While the circle of children watched, the game involved two of them producing, on the third beat of the hand, a pair of splayed fingers, or a palm, or a fist. Whatever the game was called in Pitjantjatjara, it was known to every English-speaking child in the world as Scissors, Paper, Stone.

8

MT OLGA is taller, but Ayers Rock has more the quality of enormity, because it is one piece. Mt Conner is older, but the Rock has more the quality of endurance, because it resists emaciation. Although these three inselbergs, as geologists call them, are within sight of one another, it is the Rock which draws the eye. It runs silver in the rain, shines red in the sunlight, and gold at the beginning and at the end of auspicious days. Glitter is provided by silicate laid down when the sandstone was formed, in Cambrian times. There was a sea here then. The sandstone hardened, was tilted on end, and the new peak became an island. Erosion has been slight and equitable, so the shape it is now is the shape it was always.

The process took five hundred million years. This was also time enough for the completion of three major earthly movements: the first journey of life from the seas, the passage of magnetic north from a point near the equator, the emigration of all the continents from a single landmass.

The present geological period, the quaternary, has so far lasted one million years. For about half that time now, this land has been desert, but a colony of aquatic crustaceans still lives on the dome of the Rock. These, and smears of lichen near the base, are the only living things the Rock allows. The crustaceans are *Triops australiensis,* shrimps. Once, they were swimmers in the sea below. Up here they swarm from the crannies to the puddles when it rains. Triops have become accustomed to living three hundred and fifty metres high because this is now the altitude closest to water.

9

WINMATTI, for whom one of the dwellings at the Pitjantjatjara camp was built, stood in the sun at the very edge of Uluru, on the side the sun goes down. The afternoon was half spent. It was a busy day. The parking-circle was two-thirds filled and, near the foothill which tourists call Chicken Rock, stood four empty buses.

Climbers plodded diligently upward. They made a line from the bottom to the smooth rim of the sky. Another plodded down. So steep is the slope that the descending line is often the slower.

Should those climbers be suddenly rearranged, Winmatti could have re-ordered them, in sequence, with astounding accuracy. If the findings of anthropological psychologists are any guide, his recall is likely to be ten times more accurate than the recall of an alert European adult. But Winmatti cannot count. He could not convey a precise number of climbers, for his language does not have a precise numerate system. The usual Pitjantjatjara word for every number greater than five is 'many'.

Winmatti's years were very many. The hairs on his head and face were white and his eyes as calm as waterholes. Long ago he was christened Nipper, a term by which Australian children describe their young brothers. As closely as he could fix it by the European scale, that name had not been appropriate for Winmatti for somewhere between sixty and seventy years now.

While Winmatti watched, two boys ran up and down the base of Chicken Rock. They were both arrestingly blond, and it was not difficult to pick out, from an ascending group, the man who might be their father. Their mother, a much darker-haired young woman, who kept looking around to see where they were, nursed an infant in her arms. Although Pitjantjatjara women carry tiny babies about, this does not seem so usual among travelling whites. She passed the infant to an older woman, with whom she'd been chatting. The older woman accepted the baby with exaggerated care, as if it were quite fragile.

10

FLORENCE WILKIN and Lindy Chamberlain began chatting about the Rock because their husbands were both somewhere high above. It was a calm, blue, sunny afternoon, no warmer than a pleasant summer's day in the south, and when the conversation drew on the weather, this was not to fill in time but because heat and exertion are major hazards up there. Set into a vertical slope, not far to the east from where Lindy and Mrs Wilkin stood, were plaques dedicated to the memory of climbers who died on the Rock. Falls killed four. Eight died of heart-attacks. A better choice of time is the morning, since after midday the arcose surface gives off enough heat to be felt through the soles of boots.

When the topic turned to children, Lindy Chamberlain looked around. 'Oh, my. Where have they got to now,' she said, and offered the baby to Mrs Wilkin. 'Would you mind? I'd better go looking again.'

The baby was clean, sleepily good-humoured, and prettily dressed in pink. Florence Wilkin took her happily, but with enough care to impress so dauntingly cautious a mother.

11

AIDAN AND REAGAN ran to the base of the climb. Michael was nearing the bottom. He was flushed and smiling.

'Is it great?' Aidan asked.

'It really is,' he said.

'Good,' said Aidan. 'I want to go up. Now.'

First Michael needed to repair his toenails, which were giving him trouble. Then they started up the rock-slope. Since it seemed Aidan was having no difficulty with the steep grade, Reagan scrambled to catch them up. Michael turned to wait, but Aidan thought it important to maintain the impressive lead he had won by default. Michael and Lindy both called for him to stop, but Aidan evidently was having some trouble hearing them. He kept climbing, feet and hands, and slowed only when he tagged the tail of a group higher up.

Lindy turned away to hide her smile. 'Little monkey,' she said.

12

THROUGH THE VIEWFINDER, the tableau they made wasn't at all satisfactory. The boys in the foreground, whose idea it was to have a snap taken in the first place, would not now be still even for a moment, and their father standing behind, who had to climb down here first with Reagan and then go back up to look for Aidan, seemed to have lost all sense of the vertical. Lindy heard the baby cry and lowered the camera. 'Oh. Hold it,' she said.

She had left Azaria with Gwen and Jack Eccles, themselves grandparents from Melbourne, whose intrepid Land Rover was parked at the bottom of Chicken Rock. By the time she got down there, Gwen Eccles had taken the baby to the passenger seat of the cabin, and was rocking her gently.

'Well, thanks anyway,' Lindy said. She gathered up the baby and quieted her. But perhaps she had seemed too hurried, overly ready to intercede. 'Never mind. I wanted a shot of Bubby up there with us all anyhow,' she said, for the kindly and patient Eccles were both a little crestfallen.

13

COME HOLIDAY-TIME on the eastern seaboard, families from the temperate south head for the tropics, and cross paths on the highways with northern families who need to see snow. In an isolated parody of this, for an instant around four-thirty in the afternoon the Lowes, who lived on an island of lakes and streams and now needed to see the desert from atop the Rock, crossed with the Chamberlains, who lived in an overheated mining town and were now heading for cool sanctuary at Maggie Springs.

Greg Lowe was a part-timer in geology, enrolled with the University of Tasmania. For geologists, the processes of destruction are as intriguing as the processes of genesis. Ayers Rock has come through to the present remarkably intact despite the abrasion of waves, at one time, and sand-blasting since. The most notable damage has resulted in parts of the surface splitting away. This is called spalling, and has nothing to do with weathering. It is caused by a phenomenon of far greater drama. After the gritty constituents of the Rock were laid down, it was covered by an overburden of sediment and, on the next layer up, by the sea. The immense weight of those burdens compressed it, until the pressure inside the maturing rock was sufficient to support the weight above. The pressures were built in. Since that time, the Rock has lifted to the surface, the sea has drawn off, wind is blowing the sand away, and the extravagant energies inside are not needed. It is the unloading of those forces which has split off the great slabs that the Lowes saw above them. The Rock is expanding.

Observations of this kind were taking up too much of the waning afternoon, so Greg parked the car, and they carried the baby over to the slope beneath the climb. Sally elected to stay below, alone. She settled the baby snugly in Greg's rucksack for the journey, buckled the flaps to make an acceptable harness, and waved as they climbed away.

On the way towards the pools at Maggie Springs, Michael Chamberlain stopped the yellow hatchback on the gravel verge and reached for his camera. The inexplicable interest that adults take in things of no real consequence was making the boys fidgety, and the ascending strokes of lichen here on the bluff were not worth much more than a passing comment.

Michael crossed the road, and backed off through the scrub trying to fit much of the bluff into the frame. Depending on the shade of belief you chose, those marks were either a mossy growth on the damp side of the slope or smoke stains from the Camp of the Sleepy Lizard. Of course, there was a convincing third: it was all part of the grand and intricate design of Creation.

The boys had put up with enough delays of one kind or another.

'You must have taken a hundred pictures of this old rock by now,' they said. 'What's so great about it?'

'The Lord put it here for us, Himself.'

This mollified them for hardly a second. 'Yeah. But apart from that.'

They shouted to make echoes. Aidan could touch the roof of the cave with upstretched fingers. Reagan had to jump. It was dim and narrow, and faint shapes daubed on the walls in ochre and mud seemed like gloomy messages from lost souls. The boys found a slim opening at the far end and were gone.

Lindy Chamberlain took her time. Michael was, perhaps, now on his way from the car, although small difficulties in the changing of film in his camera caused delays the family knew well.

She held the baby to her shoulder and picked a path between the forms now looming on the sandy floor. The rocks here were ovoid and smooth-skinned. It was as if she could dimple them with a firm hand. Undulations in the walls and the ceiling were damp and anatomical, in contraction where she stood and dilating all the way out to the light. The insistent association was with the foetid passage of human birth, decorated along the side with the fancies of passing hands. The connection was recognized long ago by the people whose sacred place this was. Its name is translated now as the Cave of Fertility.

She found Aidan and Reagan outside, exploring niches in a clutter of boulders a little way up the slope. James McCombe and his family, campers from Geraldton on the far western seaboard, had already thought that an inviting idea. It was the place for a discovery of some kind, but all the nooks were bare, and the McCombes said they hadn't been able to find anything either. Shadows were lengthening. This wasn't easy terrain over which to carry a baby, and just when it seemed everyone was

ready to leave for territories of brighter promise. Lindy saw they
were under surveillance. She pointed up the slope.

'Is that your dog?' she said.

On top of a boulder, not four paces from them, stood a
dingo. McCombe was instantly too busy with serious matters of
photography to suspect Lindy of making a joke. He lifted his
camera and right-flanked the animal, which curiously wasn't
distracted by that manoeuvre at all.

'No,' he said. 'That's a dingo.'

14

SUNSET. There were enough spectators, lined along
the low dune out to the west of the Rock, to make a respectable
crowd for a football match. The parking-lot was jammed with
tour-buses, campervans, and automobiles. The Lowes, who had
expected to enjoy some sort of quiet reverie as the sun went
down, turned their Toyota about and made back for camp. The
Chamberlains were already parked, the boys washed and wearing
pyjamas, Michael fiddling through the camera-bag for filters
with which to entice attractive hues.

'You go ahead,' Lindy said. 'I'll feed Bubby here.' Her suntanned
face, which had held all day the kind of breezy college-girl energy
she was remarkable for, was drawn and tired. Close, maybe, to a
short display of what some friends referred to as 'her fine little
temper'. Aidan had already wandered off, and Reagan was close to
sleep in the back. Michael gently closed the door. 'Okay,' he said.

The sky turned bluer, and the western face of the Rock
moved through ochre into deep rose. But anyone hoping for
walls of polished gold was disappointed. That phenomenon,
although it appears often on postcards, happens only when there
is sufficient cloud above the setting sun to somehow bounce the
light. In a paradox of fortunes, the evening was just too fine.

But Michael was irrepressible. He had taken enough snaps to
be confident some must be vivid and neatly balanced. On the
way back to the car, he found tiny anonymous tracks in the sand
and followed them until they fled into a clump of spinifex. Every
two or three paces he stepped over desert daisies, and discovered
a mauve bloom that attempted to replicate precisely a tropical
orchid but couldn't make a tenth the size. This time of day
Michael customarily composed a small prayer, and the list of
gifts for which he could give thanks seemed immeasurably rich.

EVENSONG

1

THE AXIS of busy activity moved, as soon as it was dark, from the line of tents and vans over to the row of barbecues and benches on the other side of the log rail. Fires were lit. Smoke lay across the air in faint watermarks, giving precise graduations of warmth. In the beams of solitary lamps, exuberant insects blazed through at heroic speeds. Voices in conversation far away sounded near and intimate. Laughter moved between groups like a delighted visitor of whom everybody was fond. A strong belief in some sort of momentum of abundance was abroad and, although the day had closed, no one seemed to have any doubt that the next would turn out every bit as good as the last. The Lowes and the Chamberlains were pleased with each other's company. They had explored some of the same places in the afternoon, perhaps an hour or so apart, but statistical improbabilities did not stand in the way of a welcome feeling that they might have met earlier. The attraction, certainly, had nothing to do with likenesses. Standing beside the pert, chatty Lindy Chamberlain, Sally felt overly tall, and her words sounded lazy. Sally's hair hung to the waist in a muscular plait, and it was easy to imagine her washing and braiding it, barefoot in some gliding Tasmanian stream. While Michael made fussy preparations for cooking, Greg stood back gripping a beer-can with tough and spiky fingers.

Talk turned to matters of family. Reagan was already bedded down, asleep somewhere behind them inside the tent. Aidan, scorning oblique suggestions that a bed was comfortably prepared for him, shuffled about waiting for something more to eat. Lindy Chamberlain held the baby, who was sleepy from the last of a bottle fed to her with some seriousness by Michael, and who was now so snugly wrapped in a cot-rug that only her eyes and nose were abandoned to the night air.

Lindy loosed the folds, the better for Sally to see in. Greg, to whom Lindy had already listed the disproportionate evils to be found inside a can of beer, looked on, but a pace or two further away.

The Lowe child, big for her eighteen months age, rode astride Sally's high hip. Lindy asked her name. 'Chantelle,' said Sally.

'Really?' Lindy asked.

'We like it,' Sally said, a little surprised.

'That's Azaria's second name, Chantel.'

However it was spelled, it seemed that the odds favouring a meeting of two babies named for the same muse, at a campfire in the empty centre of a continent, must belong to a scale unimaginably remote. The Lowes were content to ascribe this to the happy disorder of chance, the Chamberlains to forces a good deal more deliberate.

2

THERE HAPPENED THEN a short serial of events, the exact sequence of which was quickly lost, but it began at the Haby's camp.

When the Habys arrived at the grounds, it was already too dark to pitch the tent. They found a site close to the entrance and pulled in to the log rail. The barbecues, for as far along the line as they could see, were all in use. But this neat and capable Combivan was well used to the demands of its travelling family, and they decided to eat in. The routine came easily, because the Habys had been on the road now for three months. Diana cooked, Kerry and Stephen made salads and set table. It was during that meal, with the side door wide open and the cool desert air drifting in, that Murray Haby looked up to a movement outside. In the fall of light from the doorway stood a dingo. Haby, a schoolteacher from Melbourne with a dark beard and a long reach, moved stealthily for his camera. The animal was interested enough in the fragrances and gestures of mealtime to trot closer and peer inside. Haby attached his flashgun, selected a setting, aimed and fired. He needn't have worried so much. It stayed for a retake.

* * *

Sally Lowe gathered together the debris from the meal-bench, rubbed the boards over with a paper towel, and set off for the rubbish bins. Although it was dark, she knew they were along here somewhere, for she'd seen them earlier, littered around by some scavenging dog or other. Someone had tidied them now. She wiped her fingers against the paper wrapper, jammed the bundle tightly into the bin, and started back.

Something was following her. She looked around. Four or five paces behind her padded a dingo. It was careful to keep the distance between them noiselessly even. What had made her glance behind? The only sound here was of her own footfalls. She walked more quickly. By the time she reached the lights of the fire, the dingo had gone.

Awaiting the coming of eight o'clock, Amy Whittacker and her daughter Rosalie stood over a camp table washing dishes in a steaming bowl. Max Whittacker was tidying things somewhere inside the tent. The hour was important to them because Sunday nights at this time united all those with a radio and a devotion to programmes of hymn-singing, wherever they happened to be.

The table over which Amy and Rosalie worked was lit by a gas lantern they had hung on a stake by the end of the tent. It cast light over a calm circumference and touched the log rail on one side and the roadway on the other. A form moving by the rail caught Rosalie's eye. She paused. 'Oh,' she said, 'it's a dingo.'

It was a very attractive dingo. Light brown, almost orange in this light, she thought, with an inquisitively upcurled tail. Neat and handsome, rather like an Arctic husky if you shaved the fluff away. It rounded part of the lighted circle, scrutinizing them all the while, and turned off again in the direction of the barbecues. But something had not ridden well with its handsomeness. The way, perhaps, it had stepped out so exactly the compatriot boundary of darkness. It was altogether too clever.

They bent again to the washing. The time was seven minutes to eight.

3

AIDAN PLIED THE LIGHT of his torch about under the barbecue bench but couldn't find the mouse. It could not have got far. It seems a mouse knows where you're going to look, and then it's not there. Aidan's concentration was dispirited enough by so unequal a contest to withdraw of its own accord, when his father said, 'Look, here's a dingo.'

The dingo seemed shy of the light. Michael Chamberlain threw down a crust of bread to entice the animal closer. Lindy's reaction was instant. 'That's really silly, Michael,' she said. 'You shouldn't encourage them.' This was as sharp a tone as the Lowes had heard her use to her husband, and caused Greg, who was then lowering Chantelle so she might pat the dingo, to straighten. As the dingo carried the bread off, evidently to assess it in privacy, Aidan turned back to a renewed pursuit of the mouse. The flashlight made a slim beam which tapped along, side to side, like the tip of a blind man's stick, Michael was the first to see something. 'There,' he said. But before Aidan had time to see where it was his father was pointing, the dingo was in there, pouncing and fiercely gone, mouse and all.

4

AZARIA WAS ASLEEP. It had taken Lindy ten or twelve minutes of patiently mesmeric swaying to achieve this, and she stood up from the rail with relief. 'It's time I put Bubby down,' she said.

Sally Lowe watched her walk away, with Aidan following close behind, towards the tent. There was about Lindy Chamberlain, Sally thought, a sense of stoic virtue. It had something to do with judging her own merit, perhaps. Lindy was clearly tired but was, just as clearly, pleased with maintaining a spotlessly swaddled infant, two enthusiastic youngsters and a neat and well-humoured husband. After a third child one might have expected the off-handedness of a well-practised matron. Instead, Lindy carried the consistent glow of the new mother.

Aidan, now heading fast towards one side of the barbecue, and Lindy, to the other, were racing each other back. Aidan won. Lindy was hampered to some extent by the can of beans and the can-opener she held in her hands, but Sally considered the more likely handicap was that of the good-natured parent. They had not been away ten minutes. Lindy upended the beans into a pan to heat them for Aidan. It was then Sally Lowe realized that Lindy had not planned to eat until the rest of the family was contentedly fed. Quite typical, she thought.

5

TO EVADE the descending cold, Judy West pulled her camp chair inside the flap and settled down again to read. The tent was divided. In the outer half, where she now sat, part of the floor was occupied by Catherine in a recumbent sleeping-bag. Billy lay on a mattress on the other side of the fabric wall. The sounds of the night were clear but not intrusive. Judy could hear voices around the nearest fireplace and might have ascribed the dialogue to the appropriate Lowe or the appropriate Chamberlain had she wanted to listen. But Judy was more absorbed by her reading. She was a longstanding member of the Wildflower Society, and the Australian Bird Atlas bore notes of her observations around Esperance, so the days here were as much excursion as holiday. The words she was most interested in, right now, were to be found in the pages of a wildlife book which lay on her lap.

The sound which made her look up was the growl of a dog. A deep sound, guttural with menace, and it recalled something quite familiar. The farm dogs at home growled like that, in prowling circles, while Bill stripped the warm cavity of a suspended sheep, slaughtered for the table, and threw them coils of bloodied offal. They growled to keep the others off.

Judy could see nothing from where she sat. The growl had come from the direction of the Chamberlains' tent. Since the voices she could hear indicated that the family was still at the fire, there seemed no reason not to go back to her book.

6

SALLY LOWE HEARD the baby cry. Not loud, but sharp in the cold air, and somehow unfinished. It was this property of curtailment which moved her to look at Lindy. Lindy was not bothered and, given that a mother's ear for the sounds of her own is naturally more accurate, it seemed best to Sally Lowe that she hitch her Chantelle higher on the hip and say nothing.

Considerations of parental infallibility were lost on Aidan. 'That was Bubby crying,' he said fearlessly. Michael then agreed he'd heard it too, and Lindy turned for the path, through the low bush to the tent, with sceptical strides.

'But she was fast asleep,' she said.

7

FROM THEN ON, it would seem to everyone that things happened in different dimensions of time for each of them.

Lindy Chamberlain's quick legs, as she makes over the scrub, take on the jerky impulses of panic. She falters, but this is associated somehow with taking the last eight or ten paces to the tent at a run. Sally now realizes that Lindy has shouted something to them all, something terrifying and engulfing, but cannot yet arrange the meaning of it in her mind. An earlier thought is not yet displaced: the sports parka Lindy has on looks comical over a floral frock and bare knees. Lindy, who curiously seems to be the only one with the capacity for movement, drops to all fours and scrambles inside the tent. It is her reappearance then, with unrewarded arms, that locates for them what it was she had said.

Sally, sturdily akimbo, thinks she has heard the word 'Michael' before anything else, and makes an effort to look at him. Greg, leaning on the bench, misses the first words but is slowly getting the rest. Michael, holding over the flame his wife's tardy meal, seems to understand least of all. And Judy West, now bolt upright in the chair inside her tent, has heard the cry, 'My God. My God. The dingo's got my baby.'

Greg was the first to escape whatever force it was that held them down. By the time he reached Lindy she was already at the rear of the tent, facing the road. Michael was now abreast them, but not yet abreast the train of events. 'What?' he said. Lindy's response was no answer but an attempt to part the currents of turmoil: 'Will somebody please stop that dog?'

But Greg could see only an empty road and night beyond. 'Where?' he asked. 'That way,' she pointed, across the road and to the right. That way was pitch black, a fact which struck them with the force of a new and unpredictable circumstance. They needed light. Lindy threw back her head. 'Has anybody got a torch?' she shouted.

Sally Lowe made for her car. Aidan scrambled to find the torch he had a minute ago. Judy West, who had found no one at the barbecue, reached them all in time to grasp what was going on and headed back for Bill and Catherine and for a lamp. Greg snatched a flashlight from Sally's advancing hand, as though he were about to run the final leg of a relay race, and sprinted for the brush.

There was an inexplicable moment between the assent of the switch and the sudden expression of light. The tops of bushes shone back, unruffled. The shadows were dark and abrupt. The brush seemed more tangled than it was in daytime, the sand softer. Spinnifex and wattle slapped his thighs. Somewhere to his right, he could hear someone else stumbling through the growth. Greg held the beam higher. It was Michael, threshing the scrub aside with both arms and squinting at the ground. Evidently he hoped the dingo might have discarded his baby in flight. He had no torch. The blind flailing of those arms moved Greg to a declaration of sympathy and of common anguish, but the thought was inexpressible.

'What a hell of a thing to happen,' was the best he could do.

Other lights were beginning to dot the scrub. Word was, somehow, travelling fast. Campers pulled on jackets and stomped into hurried boots as they crossed the road. Already Bill and Catherine West were in there somewhere. Lindy had run off to find torches. Sally Lowe stood by the tent, hugging Aidan on one side and hold Chantelle tightly to the other. She heard Greg shout an instruction so obvious she was appalled that no one had thought of it earlier. 'Get the police here,' he said. Sally had turned in the direction of their Toyota before it occurred to her that she could not drive that vehicle.

Michael came back, defeated by the dark. Sally caught, in the light by the tent, the glint of tears dribbling his cheeks. Judy West arrived with a lantern, but it had a fluorescent tube and cast no beam, so Michael handed it back. He kept patting his pockets. There was, he said, a lamp which plugged into his car, but the door was locked. Now he had lost his keys.

Aidan, who had found his own torch, thrust it forward, but although it had once seemed substantial in his own hand it was now absurdly small as it lay on his father's. The beam was sickly. Aidan had been tearful for some time, but it was clear enough to those consoling him that he was crying then over the paucity of his offering.

* * *

Something was happening in the grounds outside, but Murray Haby did not yet know what it was. When Lindy Chamberlain told him, and asked for a torch so that she could search for her baby, his abundant beard was not nearly sufficient to cover the incredulity on his face. How did she know it was a dingo?

'I saw it come from the tent,' she said, 'and when I got there my baby was gone.'

Haby needed to fix so monstrous an event more firmly in his mind. 'Did you see it carry the baby away?'

'No,' she said, 'it wasn't carrying anything.' This fact seemed as new to her as it was to him. 'Please,' she said, 'I need a torch.'

Haby fetched his flashlight from the Combivan. The batteries were new and the beam strong. 'Which which way did it go, the dingo you saw?' She pointed toward the scrub, and reached for the torch. 'No,' he said, 'it's better I go.' The children, inside the van, had caught a little of this. 'What is it?' Kerry called. 'A dog's taken a kid's teddy-bear.' But to Diana, close by the door, he whispered: 'No, it's a baby that's gone.'

Murray Haby was a practised, if amateur, tracker, a skill he had kept up since childhood. It had occurred to him already that the dingo Lindy Chamberlain saw might not be the one which stole off with her baby, a possibility that made the tracking quite tricky.

Organ music and the congregation of hymnal voices were, to the Whittackers sitting inside their tent, rich and vital enough to have come from an outdoor recital close by, rather than from a radio sitting on the bonnet of their car. This had something to do, perhaps, with the purity of night air. It was then Michael Chamberlain appeared at the tent-flap, and Amy Whittacker's first thought was that someone had come to complain about the volume.

'You are playing Christian music,' he said. 'What does that mean?'

Now, Amy Whittacker was not unaccustomed to defending the strong beliefs she held, in any arena. She had worked, in her time, at three Melbourne hospitals as a double-certificated nurse, had tutored in midwifery, lately had taken out a bachelor's degree in social work, and it was in that profession she now practised. But this man, as she watched him then, was not far from losing control of himself, and it took her a second or two to compose a truthful and peaceable reply.

'It means we are Christian people,' she said quietly.

'Then pray, please pray,' he said. 'A dingo has taken our baby. She is probably dead by now.' He passed a hand over his face. 'She was nine weeks old.'

Rosalie and her father considered some other sort of action more appropriate and grabbed for torches and for jackets. Michael followed them out and waved in the direction of the scrub. More exact intelligence was beyond him.

Amy Whittacker bowed her head. She then heard Michael outside, above the organ and the songs of praise, call to Max and to Rosalie an item of information so removed from the needs of the present that it seemed he might not be capable any longer of logical thought.

'I am a minister of the gospel,' he shouted.

Greg Lowe saw a flash of light behind him and a little to his right. A voice, Murray Haby's as it turned out, called over. 'Seen anything?'

'Nothing yet,' he said, and waded on.

The next sounds he heard were from Michael, who had caught him up this time with a torch, though it cast a pitiful light. They walked together, playing the beams under the bushes and on the paths between. No wind had swept the ground for days, and the sand was as pocked as a beach after a busy day. Greg imagined they had begun to climb. He shone his beam ahead. Up there was the dune, Sunrise Hill.

While Greg searched for intelligible marks on the ground, he had also composed something he wanted to say. The words did not come easily.

'Whatever we find,' he said, 'there's no joy for you.' It was too rough a statement of fact, and caused Michael to halt, but Greg was not at all sure Michael understood what they might stumble upon. The chances were high now that, if they happened on anything it might be some fearfully savaged remnant, a sight not fit for a father's lingering memory.

'I should see to Lindy,' Michael said, and turned away.

Amy Whittacker prayed until the hymns ended. She then closed the tent-flap, unplugged the radio as she passed the car, and set off to see what she might do for the child's mother. She found Michael, who led her to a group of three women sitting on the rail. The small dark-eyed woman in the centre he introduced as his wife. It was a choice Amy could have made without help, so stricken was the face and bewildered the gaze. Taking on adversity face to face was Amy Whittacker's style, and she now enclosed the young mother in her arms and said, 'God is good.'

'Whatever happens is His will,' came the reply, an antiphony. 'And it says, doesn't it, that at the Second Coming "babes will be restored to their mothers' breasts"?'

This was no question, but litany. They both knew the answer.

-8

FRANK MORRIS ARRIVED in the grey police Toyota, swung off the road until the headlamps shone over the plain, and left it there, blue light spinning. Two vehicles halted alongside, one carrying Bill and Catherine West, who had located Morris's house beside the darkened police station, and the other carrying the rangers Cawood and Marshall, whose abbreviated dinner still lay on a table back in the Chalet restaurant.

The sturdy and amiable Morris was in charge of the station here, a command only large enough to give him authority over one subordinate. He was currently dressed as if he were a hastily summoned civilian, which spoke of the fact that seven minutes ago he was in bed.

Morris crouched in the tent, Lindy Chamberlain behind at the flap. Cramped quarters, he thought, for a family of five. His torch-beam peremptorily swept the floor. Here were mattresses, sleeping-bags and, in the far right corner, a bassinet with two tiny rugs and a miniature pillow. Speckles glinted from one of the rugs. He held it up. It was blood, all right.

Not yet disposed to act on the assumptions of a mother disabled by shock, he moved to examine the ground outside. The sand at the entrance was scuffed by many shoes, some corroboration of her statement, at any rate, that she and the pastor had twice checked the tent in case the baby was miraculously mislaid at the source. Morris, in five years of service out here, had been called variously to houses and motels, and to tents like this, after complaints about intruding dingoes. When he found, now under the light of his torch, the clear passage of paws away from the entrance, he felt relief more than surprise.

The prints turned left at the tent corner. He followed, between the tent and the Chamberlains' car, until they faded on the road. Morris backtracked to the clearest imprints. He was not yet satisfied that the paws were those of a dingo rather than a camp dog. A dog's foot, as blacktrackers instructed him, will leave the clear line of the nail. A dingo elevates the claw to protect so useful an implement from wear. Morris held the flashlight low, tilted to best define the ridges. The pads here were crisp and smooth, all of them.

Since a dingo might be expected to head for a lair or for other safe territory before beginning in earnest to eat, it seemed to Morris that the search ought to be planned by someone familiar with the likelihoods. He glanced about. 'Where the hell is Derek Roff?' he said. By the faces around him it was plain no one had yet thought to alert the head ranger.

'This will make you feel better,' said Judy West, who had made hot chocolate. The cups steamed like chimneys. She was as much concerned about warmth as about nourishment, but didn't like to say so. Cold and its effect on Azaria, now an abandoned bundle out there on the plain, God willing, was a topic sure to bring on another bout of shaking and tears in one, or both, of the Chamberlains. The temperature was falling so quickly that it might reach freezing point well before midnight.

But Michael refused his cup, and Lindy handed hers back, saying, 'I'd only throw it up again.' The point had been reached where the most helpful and optimistic subjects for conversation were exhausted, and although Judy West, Sally Lowe and Amy Whittacker knew they must stay, no one knew what to come up with next. It was Michael who did. 'Would it be rude of us to go off by ourselves for a minute?' When they came back, from somewhere in the barbecue area, as far as Judy West could see, Lindy appeared a little more composed. Michael drew them together. 'I'd like us to pray,' he said. He laid both hands upon his wife's head. 'Let us all now remember that this is not the time for anger or for bitterness.' That Michael Chamberlain was again able to assume some sort of pastoral authority seemed to everyone a heartening sign.

The scrub just beyond the road was the area already most thoroughly searched, but it was also the focus of Lindy's most frequent obsession. 'Bubby might be just out there,' she cried, 'nearly dead.' The way things were going, 'nearly' was their best hope. Michael took her arm, drew her up from the rail and, the West's torch in hand, walked into the knee-deep brush.

Sally Lowe was to watch this several times tonight: the Chamberlains, an arm around each other's waist, in slow step one way then back again, her cheek against his shoulder, walking out as they might have done in happier days, this now a promenade of sorrow.

Aidan's obsession lay with the dingo. This was beginning to worry Sally more deeply, since enticing his attention elsewhere was meeting with briefer success. The events of the night were altogether too eloquent. The conversations, to which he listened with an avid horror, spoke endlessly of hope when the faces of every adult around bore the marks of the most unanswerable defeat.

'Don't let the dingo eat our baby,' he wailed.

Sally led him towards the tent. The hyperactive combination of fright and fatigue must be broken. She couldn't use his age as an argument for putting him down, since she still toted Chantelle about on her hip. 'Show me which is your bed, Aidan,' she said.

He climbed on his mattress eagerly enough. Reagan, undisturbed by their entry, lay on the other side of the tent. Sally was about to cajole Aidan further into bed when a mark on the mattress caught her eye. It was a smear of blood, perhaps once a pool. Aidan had seen it too.

'Reagan's dead,' he said.

'No, of course he's not.'

'Reagan's dead. Reagan's dead.'

Sally reached across and shook Reagan by the shoulder, with pressure sufficient to draw an irritable twitch and a mumbled complaint.

'There. See, he's fine.'

But the blood, the empty bassinet, the small pillow, and the disarranged baby-rugs were no longer static; they were now the continuing properties of an event, vivid and irresistible, and Aidan covered his eyes and followed the event all the way to its unbearable conclusion. 'The dingo has our Bubby in its tummy,' he cried.

* * *

Derek Roff's thought, as he put down the phone, was, So it's finally happened. He left home at a run, drove hard to the camp, and was there within five minutes of summons.

He found the Chamberlains by the tent, a few people around them. Someone, in fact the thoughtful Catherine West, had rigged a gas lamp on a staff, so the tent showed up orange and green and, with the primrose car beside, looked not unlike a movie set arranged to make best use of colour. Mrs Chamberlain, wan and watchful, sat erect on the railing with her husband, the pastor, standing behind, his hands on her shoulders. Perhaps it was the formality of this tableau which caused Roff to introduce himself, though everyone seemed to know already who he was. 'I am the chief ranger,' he said. 'What happened here?'

'Our baby girl has been taken by a dingo, and we are fully reconciled to the fact that we will never see our baby alive again,' Michael Chamberlain said. 'The dingo would have killed the child immediately, would it not?'

Roff was unprepared for a display of fatalism, however pious it was, or of composure, however humble it was. He suspected that Michael's emotional balance was now perilously atilt. 'Look,' he said, 'just tell me what happened.'

Lindy answered, to Roff's relief, lucidly and briefly. When she finished, he asked: 'Did you see anything in its mouth?'

'No, nothing.'

'Are you sure the baby is not in the tent somewhere?'

'Of course she's not. How many times do you think I've looked there already.' He followed her to the tent-flap, while she crouched inside beside her sleeping son, lifting the rugs, the clothes, and letting them fall, crying, 'Look. She's not here. She's not here.'

'I can see that,' he said quietly. 'It's all right. I'm sorry.'

VIGIL

1

SEARCHERS ON THE PLAIN were called in for briefing. Joined by fresh volunteers from motels, staff quarters, and camps further away, they made a crowd of heartening size, Derek Roff thought. He waited for silence enough to speak. There must be close to three hundred men and women here, and a few teenagers, serious and eager. Earlier, the owners of dogs had brought their animals with them: a pair of energetic young women with an Alsatian, and a man whose Setter had been given some article of the baby's clothing to sniff but then remained as confused as anyone else. But the dogs were ordered off, in case their tracks led the search astray.

'First, thank you all for coming,' Roff said. 'Sometime before eight-thirty, that is, maybe three-quarters of an hour ago, a small baby was taken from a tent, there. We think it was taken by a dingo. The dingo headed south-east, so from the camp here, over the track and across the flat, in the direction of the hill. We're going to form into a human chain. I don't want anyone more than two paces away from the next.' That ought to cover, as Roff then calculated, about half a mile across. Not at all bad.

'We are not only looking for a dingo or a dog. Tracks, pieces of cloth, anything at all. The baby was a few weeks old. Very tiny. She was wearing...'

'All white,' said Frank Morris, who had this moment returned from the Chamberlains with the information.

'White. Be careful to look under the scrub as much as between it. Now, does everyone have a torch?' There were torches, lanterns, fluorescents, and floods, but evidently more people than lights. 'Okay, then anyone without a light walks between two who do.'

Roff looked up at the stars. They were bright and crisp. 'Now, it's cold already, and it's going to get colder. Anyone without a jacket had better fetch one now. We are arranging a supply of batteries from the store, so when you need one just call out. I think we're ready to get started.'

'No, there's one other thing. Be alert for signs of digging. That is very important, any digging.' In fact, this was the sign Derek Roff hoped for least. The sort of digging he had in mind would end any chance of finding the baby alive.

2

WHILE THE SEARCHERS filed across the road and into the brush, Frank Morris walked back to the Chamberlains. He thought to look again through the tent, and to draw from the parents some, any, item of information useful if something identifiable came of the search. He found them at the rail, Amy Whittacker and Sally Lowe standing by, and asked if Lindy Chamberlain wouldn't mind recounting again what it was she had seen.

He interrupted midway. 'The dingo had nothing in its mouth?'

'Nothing, so far as I could see.'

'I thought earlier you said it did.'

'No,' she said.

Morris was not confident enough of his own recollection, and it seemed an unimportant detail considering the turmoil of things so far. He pursued it no further. 'Tell me what clothes the baby was wearing,' he said.

Lindy Chamberlain counted them off. 'Disposable nappy, with a plastic cover; a singlet; a jump-suit over everything. Yes, and booties underneath. White, everything white.' She had begun to shake, perhaps to the chill passage of memory. 'I told you white already,' she said.

It was not colour in which Frank Morris was currently interested, but temperature. 'You should understand,' he said, 'that if we don't find her quickly, she won't survive the cold.'

Although this was addressed to Lindy Chamberlain, it was her husband who responded. 'The will of God,' he said. 'There is nothing anyone can do about the will of God.'

'Oh, look,' said Sally Lowe.

She pointed over the dark plain, where lamps and torches blinked and swung, in preparation for the first long sweep. Sally saw in this a resurgence of hope, but Michael Chamberlain seemed to be affected by quite a different emotion.

'Our daughter should be brought to us,' he told Morris, 'no matter what condition you find her in.'

The succession of lights reached far into the night, stately and processional. 'We want her back,' he said.

3

THE NURSE, Roberta Downs, was a slim woman with long sandy hair and a liking for oversized, round spectacles, which made her look so young that everyone in the settlement preferred to call her Bobbie. She had been a nurse, by this time, for five years, enjoyed her posting to the Rock, and was engaged to marry a bushpilot who lived here.

When she joined the Chamberlains, and the vigil on the railing by the tent, the time was around nine-thirty. She found Michael Chamberlain quiet and remote, as if formality was the last preserve of strength. His wife was shaky, despite the tracksuit slacks she now wore under her frock and the blankets around her shoulders. Lindy Chamberlain had entered that talkative stage of sorrow which revisits every small memento of a happier past and anoints them all with sanctity.

Bobbie's concern, after a half hour or so of this, was that neither of the Chamberlains was well enough prepared for the debilitating course of grief. When Lindy, from a rare silence, burst out suddenly with the words, 'Nine weeks of joy,' and covered her eyes with a soaking kerchief, Bobbie Downs decided they must stay here no longer.

'Time we moved you away from here, into a motel, okay?' she said. This suggestion met with approval from Sally Lowe, Amy Whittacker, and Judy West, but not from the Chamberlains.

'We can't afford a motel,' was Michael's slow reply.

'I'm sure no one will ask you to pay.'

'The police won't know where we are.'

'I'll tell the police. And the rangers. Right?'

'Thank you,' Michael said, 'but this is where we should wait.'

Across the plain, the chain of lights had begun to hang irregularly in the dark, the higher tinged with pink. So the search had reached the first slopes of the red sand-hill and, presumably, without finding a trace so far. Bobbie Downs wondered how long it would be before the Chamberlains were forced away from here, by either despair or the merciless cold.

But there were traces to be seen on the plain. Rather too many, in fact. It was a surprise, even to the rangers, to discover how much of the ground here was cross-hatched with dingo tracks, for never before had such an exercise been carried out. Only the Aboriginal trackers seemed to find it a commonplace. The Pitjantjatjara group had arrived just as the search got underway. Winmatti was not among them for the night was already too cold for so old a man, but his wife Barbara was there, with her father Nuwe Minyintiri, and Daisy Walkabout, all trackers whom Derek Roff much admired. Roff thought it best to keep them separate from the chain, and available when the search happened on prints. Each time, the tracker determined the size, the age, and the gender of the dingo, whether or not it had recently fed and, on more than one occasion, in which of the lairs nearby it lived.

When Frank Morris came back to the tent again, it was a little after ten. 'Nothing yet, I'm afraid,' he said.

The group around the Chamberlains had dwindled. The Lowes were gone. After Greg had stumbled out of the brush, tired and despairing, Sally decided it was time to take Chantelle somewhere safe, and they made off for a motel. It seemed like the first obvious recognition of defeat and, to take the edge off it, Morris now said: 'We'll keep looking, of course.'

'Keep us informed,' Michael Chamberlain asked.

'No trouble. We'll send you progress reports.' Morris found it hard to keep optimism uppermost in his voice.

'There is another thing, Constable. We are very grateful for all you are doing. My wife and I would like to thank you.'

Frank Morris was used to many of the tasks an outback policeman is called on to perform, but the comforting of bereaved parents was not one of them. 'Sure,' he said and walked away, back to the hopeless plain.

4

'TABLETS to dry up the milk in your breasts,' Bobbie said.

'What's that?'

'Lasix. I've got it at the clinic.'

'To do what?'

'Dry up the milk. I mean, just in case.'

'Oh. Yes.'

5

MURRAY HABY had not joined the main search. This was only partly to do with individualism in his temperament; rather more with his sense of urgency. Haby had two advantages, a prompt start and early information, and he wasn't about to waste either of them.

Searching through the scrub on the plain he made across the direction Lindy Chamberlain had pointed, as much as along it, in somewhat the same pattern as a sailboat tacking upwind. He must suppose, he thought, that the dingo had purpose in its direction. His best course, then, was one which gave the most chance of intersecting the animal's line, and that course was the zig-zag.

The quick beam of his flashlight intersected plenty, and this called for another earnest marshalling of the available arguments. The dingo he wanted was carrying a baby, was in flight, and had headed south-east. He should assume it would not begin to tear the child apart until safe from pursuit. So Haby dismissed those prints which seemed to him aimless or meandering, those which seemed somehow light-footed, and those which did not have enough fleetness in them to kick up the sand. The trouble was that those criteria got him to the foot of the sand-hill without happening on any prints which qualified.

The sand-hill gave him pause. It was a dune, really, though a dune substantial enough to have some structure or other at the top he remembered seeing in daylight. There was also a place for flag-raising ceremonies, on which days it was known as Anzac Hill rather than Sunrise. The slope presented Haby with a fresh set of possibilities altogether. This was a margin, a discrete piece of ground over which the dingo must pass if it was to hold direction. The bushes were sparse. And the incline was such that an animal might have more difficulty holding its load clear of the ground.

Haby had climbed close to the brow, and completed much of his planned first traverse under the ridge, when his torch-beam picked up the sign he was hoping to find. The prints were deep and plain. A larger animal. And, here, dragging something. A furrow, soft, and pitifully compliant.

6

WORD WAS AROUND that fresh batteries had arrived, so Judy West drove Bill across the plain to join in the main search. When she got back, Lindy Chamberlain was well into another bout of overactivity. 'Why are they all searching so far away?' she cried. 'Bubby could be just out here, somewhere.' This was close, Judy thought, to frenzy.

'Do take her again, Michael, so she can see for herself,' said Amy Whittacker, and Judy added, 'I'll be here if the children wake up.'

They were not long gone when one of the children cried. Judy crawled into the tent. It was the first time she had been in there. Light from the grounds, and more from the gas lantern, loomed through the fabric. She found the boy, who was struggling with some unidentifiable fear, in a sleeping-bag close to the tent-flap, and quietly hushed him to sleep.

She could see blood on one of Azaria's small rugs. It seemed to have been caused by a blot and a fine spray, which gave it the appearance of an exclamation mark. But the real drama in here was provided by the empty bassinet. It held Judy still for a moment, while she considered how shocking a mere space can be.

7

THE PRINTS and the furrow led Murray Haby higher, and to a quite different mark in the sand. This dingo was carrying something, all right. Here was a depression where it had laid the burden down.

Haby was taking care, now, to walk well to one side of the track so not to distort it, in case he lost the trail and had to begin again. The prints climbed to the top of the ridge, then over. The sand here was much more densely packed, the prints not so deep. In another thirty paces he lost them.

The night was so dark that without the flashlight he could not see his own feet. He plied the beam about, walking this time in widening circles. Nothing. The strange thing was that the sand here was level, and so firm he was making little mark himself. He shone the light further out, and discovered he was now standing in the centre of an empty car-park.

8

DEREK ROFF HALTS the chain of searchers at a water-tank on the east slope of the ridge, turns them all about, ready to start back again. The older stragglers cough steam and cigarette-smoke. Roff orders a minute's rest.

At the campsite, the Chamberlains come in from the scrub. They are cold and silent. Bobbie Downs drapes rugs over Lindy's shoulders, and decides against reintroducing the subject of a motel just yet. The only cheerful topic Judy West can think of is that one of the boys woke but has gone back to sleep. Amy Whittaker holds Lindy's bleak hand.

9

BECAUSE HE COULD FIND no record of the dingo's departure from the car-park, Murray Haby decided to backtrack. His priority should be, so he thought, to establish the full validity of his find. At the depression in the sand, a little below the ridge, he squatted for as intense an inspection as the yellowing beam would allow: the shape of something soft, oval, and nearly the length of his hand. There was a moist drop alongside, blood perhaps, but not as red as he would have expected. Saliva, maybe. It was the pattern in the imprint he thought most startling. It reminded him of a soft-knitted fabric.

Backtracking downhill to the plain was not difficult. The prints were clear on this surface, and came, more and more clearly now, from the camping-ground. The nearer he drew to the camp, the more often was the trail obliterated by the brief passage of human feet, but these paws were familiar to him now, swift and bold. He decided to short-cut, and made for the roadway. About here the animal first burst into the scrub, the prize held high, the eyes hot.

Haby stepped out on the road. To his right was the yellow car, the gay tent, the parents by the rail with friends, their children asleep, no shadow of danger. Everything as it once was. The impulse rose in him to shout a warning. It was as if he had successfully run against the tide of events, and had somehow arrived in time for the beginning.

10

'MUCH BETTER,' said Roff, plying a flashlight about with some vigour, the first indication to Haby that the main search had found nothing nearly so significant. Nuwe Minyintiri was without a torch. He plucked stalks from the grass and patted his pockets for matches. He twirled the stalks into a wick, lit it, and held the fire-stick low. Roff and Haby followed. They seemed to be following a weightless flame, an autonomous pair of shorts and a shirt, for Minyintiri is so dark-skinned it was difficult to see the rest of him. He moved swiftly up the slope, soft and barefooted, not at all hesitant now where the marks were overprinted by footfalls, relying confidently on a momentum of direction and choosing correctly every time.

They neared the crest of the ridge. 'Not far now,' Haby said. Minyintiri having found the first of the furrow, flashed the light back to be sure he had missed nothing of it earlier. A dozen paces further, he halted and peered at the ground. Here was the depression Haby had found. Haby said, 'There's only the one,' but it wasn't long before the old Aborigine pointed to another, and then a third. 'Mmm,' he said, a syllable which infected the others with disquiet. Perhaps they were now standing at the very point where, after flight, this dingo was considering behaviour of quite a different kind.

The size of the prints much impressed the tracker. 'Big feller,' he said. But Roff was more interested in the imprint of the bundle in the sand. The pattern put him in mind of crepe, or a knitted weave, perhaps. 'But is it the baby?' was what he needed to know.

'Maybe, maybe,' Minyintiri said. He held a palm upward to indicate the weight of the body. 'Something like.' Then touching the unfussed periphery of the mark with a finger, sad and gentle, he indicated something they had seen but not yet recognized.

'Not move anymore,' he said.

11

THEIR COFFEE-MUGS EMPTIED, the searchers were ready to go back to the unwelcome night. A ragged silence began to fall, in pace with the realization here and there that someone was about to address them. It was Michael Chamberlain. They yielded space, curious and quietened.

'Thank you, all of you, for the efforts you are making to find our baby,' he said. 'Although we cannot believe there is hope, any longer, of finding her alive.'

As it seemed to James McCombe, who had seen the Chamberlains during the afternoon at Maggie Springs, the pastor was delivering all this with astonishing, if brittle, composure.

'I am a man of God, a minister of religion. I know that nothing happens in the world unless the Good Lord wills it should be so. I know our baby has passed from us into heaven. My wife and I must not be sad, but jubilant that our little daughter is safe in the arms of Jesus.'

On James McCombe, the effect of Michael Chamberlain's attempt at joy was an appalled sadness. Evidently the feeling was well shared. One of the crowd, a big man in a coarse woollen bush-jacket, took the pastor by the shoulders and hugged him. They stepped apart. Michael Chamberlain was in tears.

As everyone turned away, suddenly intent on other things, McCombe wondered what sort of religion it was which made demands of such magnitude. And Michael Chamberlain might have made it all the way through, if it were not for the candid opposition of human compassion, vehement and unexpected.

12

'GONE,' MINYINTIRI SAID, sweeping the fire-stick over the sand. The prints it showed were of boots and shoes, from a time the main search made over the ridge. Anyway, Murray Haby thought, the tracker got further than I did. Minyintiri led them back the way they had come. He began afresh, hoping evidently that something in the dingo's run, here, might show a preference for direction, there. He lost it again.

'Not now.' Minyintiri shook his head. 'Daylight, maybe. Not now.'

Turning for the descent, and for camp, Roff was already deciding how to reorganize the search from here on. The dingo might have moved along the ridge. It might have returned to the flat. If it crossed the ridge and headed east into the spinnifex country, well, goodbye. Impossible territory at night-time, bad enough during the day. So the drill was, for as long as they had volunteers, separate squads now for the flat and the sand-hill.

Murray Haby fell in alongside him. 'I guess I should join the main group,' Haby said.

'Do that.' The tone was brusque and uncharacteristic, but Roff was thinking through his next problem: What now to say to the parents. We found the trail but lost it? Your baby was dead by the time the animal first laid her down? He inclined his wristwatch to take the light of Haby's torch. Eleven-fifteen. His hands were stiff and clumsy. He rammed them deep into the pockets of the jacket. God, it was cold.

The women watched as Roff approached. Lindy wore a blanket as though it were a cape and she was ready for the keening. There was something of Africa in all of this.

'Nothing?'

'No. We'll search on. But I don't think we will find her, not now.'

'Not anything?'

'Not even her clothing.'

13

BOBBIE HAD JUDGED her time. 'Let me get you into a motel; you can't do anything here.' And Judy West said, 'You can't sleep in that tent. It's unthinkable.'

Michael Chamberlain looked towards the tent. 'That's true,' he said.

Bobbie didn't wait around for any firmer statement of assent.

When Bobbie drove back into camp, it was well after midnight. She brought with her the news that the Uluru Motel would take them. She also brought with her Gordon Noble in the police truck. His usefulness, in Bobbie's scheme, was partly to provide transport and partly to provide a certain official impetus to the move.

They loaded blankets, sleeping-bags, clothing, all into the tray of the truck; an unruly and profligate pile, exaggerated by the way they heaped it in, which provided them with small jokes about the mutable dimensions of the Chamberlains' car. So cold was it that their breathing steamed like the snorting of work-horses. Bobbie was glad to be getting out of there.

She held the torch as Lindy checked the tent. Not much was left inside. Lindy backed out, holding an uncovered ice-cream container. Evidently it held a solution of some kind. She walked four or five paces, poured it on the ground, and sobbed.

Bobbie sat Lindy on the rail. The container, which she took from Lindy's unresisting hand, was filled with the baby's bottle-teats.

The short cabin in the police truck had space for Noble, the two sleepy boys, and Lindy Chamberlain, but no more. Michael, at the door of the yellow hatchback, said to Bobbie, 'You'd better ride with me.'

She settled into the passenger seat, her feet on gear in the well. Michael's bulky camera-bag was under his knees. Bobbie told him there was room for it on her side.

'It's okay,' he said, 'I always keep it here.' Bobbie stretched out, thinking that Michael's driving habits were, keen photographer or not, quite foolhardy.

14

ROFF DESPATCHED CAWOOD and a detail of rangers to check all known lairs between here and the Fertility Cave. He trudged then towards the weakening thread of lights to find Morris. One more sweep, and they can all turn in. The radio-telephone link opens at sunrise: he must then arrange a call, high priority, to Conservation Commission headquarters in Darwin.

Four hours to dawn. With the morning sun, the discomforting first light of publicity. God, what a mess it could make in the newspapers.

IT'S TIME WE ALL WENT HOME

1

THE ADELAIDE *NEWS* got its first tip at 7.30 a.m. The message came through to the managing editor's desk where Greg Reid, a very large man who worked in shirtsleeves whatever the time of day, scanned it. He recognized the source as a trusted informant in Alice Springs. It was too early to decide, just yet, how much space the story might be worth. The *News* was an afternoon daily. The presses downstairs were already set with the first edition, but it might make something for the second. The *Advertiser*, their rival in this city, did not go to the streets until morning, so the timing was fine.

Reid called Geoff DeLuca in from the newsroom and briefed him. DeLuca, senior police roundsman here for the last five years, was in his early thirties. He was the sort of reporter who ate and drank enough to give him a weight problem but stayed nervously wiry. 'They're still searching this morning,' Reid said. 'What do you want to do?'

Known on the newsfloor as a quick mover, DeLuca was not ready to move yet. 'Try for an interview with the parents by phone, and see what develops from that,' he said.

Reid, whose management style relied heavily on volume, said, 'There's a flight north at ten-thirty, and you're on it.'

'Sure, but put through a call to the Rock first. We'll take it right here.'

You have to feel lucky to be lucky, so DeLuca believed. A telephone interview, in time for the second edition, would claim the story for the *News*, whatever tips the *Advertiser* got later.

2

THE OUTSTANDING QUALITY of the Uluru Motel was impermanence, like those lone suburban buildings standing on land long rezoned for some other use. The Uluru was rezoned for demolition. Aggressive grasses over-ran the paths. The garden belong to other climatic zones. The tropical hibiscus and temperate rhododendrons were comfortable enough until an hour or so after daybreak, when the morning sun gave an indication of the temperatures to come. The swimming-pool, which might be considered a disappointing gesture by coastal standards, was an astonishing extravagance here, and it was the early morning duty of the groundsman to sieve from the water the slippery bodies of those small lizards and desert rodents which had thought it astonishing overnight.

The eaveless units were as narrow as box-cars. They carried flimsy and identical appointments: curtained robe, en suite toilet, and resonantly dripping shower. Over the doorways—and from the one numbered 34 the Chamberlain couple now step, closing the door on the two irritable boys—paint faintly dimmed the name of an earlier owner, Apex Hire.

The path was warming, although it was barely eight o'clock, and flies hummed around a corner of the bar-room where damp plumbing from the urinals came through the wall. A unit close to the bar accommodated the office. Here the manager, Alan Barber, booked calls on the radio-telephone. In a thin voice Lindy Chamberlain asked for a south-coast number, at Nowra where her mother lived, and Michael asked for two, one north to his church headquarters in Townsville, the other to Wellington, New Zealand, the home of his parents. They waited for the connections.

Michael was taking the call to his mother when Frank Morris walked in. Morris nodded to Barber and pointed to the phone, indicating that he wanted to be considered in the queue somewhere.

Evidently the New Zealand line was poor. Morris and Barber, wordlessly in concert, left the room for the path outside; absentia in form only, since Michael's voice was as plain outdoors as in.

'They are doing everything possible, Mother,' Michael said, 'but we don't ever expect to find the body. Don't worry, we are both okay. It is the will of God, and we are bearing up to that, as He says we must.'

Morris and Barber caught each others' eye.

The next was not a connection they waited on, but an incoming call. Alan Barber took it. 'No,' he said, 'the parents are not available for comment.' He palmed the mouthpiece and, in an aside, told Michael it was from the Melbourne *Herald*. 'I'll take it,' Michael said.

'I want you to emphasize that people ought not to feed dingoes, here or anywhere else,' he said. 'There are notices prohibiting it, but people should be more aware of the dangers than they are.'

When he handed the telephone back to Barber, he asked, 'Was that all right?'

'Fine.'

Precisely how those warnings might countermand the will of God was a little difficult for Alan Barber to figure out, just now. And the phone rang again.

In his office at the Adelaide *News*, Reid's broad face lit up. 'He's on.'

The movements which followed involved the telephone passing from Reid to the pictorial editor, Scadden, across the table to DeLuca, and back to Reid. Scadden was promised photographs of the camps and of the abducted baby. DeLuca's request for a meeting at the Rock was deflected but not rebuffed. Reid hoped now to draw enough of the story from Michael Chamberlain to make the streets for the second edition. He signalled success with a huge and triumphantly erect thumb.

When Michael put the phone down he said to Morris, 'The press want to interview me.'

'What are you going to do?'

'I don't know how I ought to behave.'

But Morris was no expert either. 'Just act natural, I guess.'

Room 34 was still in a mess when Bobbie Downs got there around nine. The double bed was unmade and, where the boys had slept on the floor, blankets and clothing lay despondently over the carpet. Lindy wore dark glasses although the room was dim. She was slow-moving and tired. Bobbie saw the Valium pack, which she had delivered here last night, on the bedside table, unopened.

Bobbie began tidying, an activity designed as much to distract the forces of gloom as anything else. Michael seemed to have somewhat the same idea. They all now knew that the search for Azaria had begun again at first light, but the structure of tragedy had entered an administrative phase, and it was here Michael took up responsibility with a grateful urgency. The interest of the press called for decisions about the rights of the public to information. The requisition of clothing and blankets bearing the baby's blood called for adjudication between the police regulations and, for example, Aidan's need for his own parka, which on current examination was found to be spattered. And Frank Morris had produced a questionnaire, of inquisitorial length, requiring more detail than the life of a nine-week old baby had to offer. It was entitled 'Information as to Death'.

After the room was straightened, and when the boys were interested enough in paper and crayons fetched from the office, Bobbie looked about for something else to do. She found Lindy in the car outside, sitting in the passenger seat, the door open wide, her feet on the ground. Her cheeks were wet. Over her lap lay snaphots, all of the baby, and arranged according to a priority which had not yet made itself clear.

'The newspapers want photographs,' Lindy said.

'You don't have to, if you don't want.'

'I don't know. I think I want to, anyway.'

And there was a certain logic in that, as Bobbie's gaze ran over the snaps: Azaria with the family, in the arms of a stiffly seconded adult, or held precariously erect for the moment by a pair of hands amputated at the border. The baby was tiny, endearing, and amusingly mystified. This was a form of resurrection.

3

THE CALL came through the police switchboard in Alice Springs at nine. Gilroy, the district inspector, took it, confident that he already knew enough about the incident to give Frank Morris instructions, proficient and complete, without leaving his chair. Gilroy was an officer of unusual cut in the Northern Territory. He was slim, in a force of bulky men, liked to dress smartly, and kept his, now greying, hair well groomed. Gilroy was habituated to the force by circumstance as much as by experience: he had twelve years seniority in the Territory, was earlier a policeman in Ireland, his birthplace, and his Christian names were Michael Seamus. His authority now covered a half million square kilometres, and he was on call whatever the time of day. Last night, at home, he took a call from the duty officer. The switchboard had received a radio message. A dog, or a dingo, had taken a baby from camp. The child was Aboriginal. The transmission was bad.

The report now from Morris changed everything. Gilroy told the switchboard operator to get John Lincoln, the duty sergeant, on the line, and then to arrange a flight out to the Rock.

This sort of incident required thought and care. He wouldn't be surprised if the newspapers had hold of it already.

4

THE BAR-ROOM DOORS, which also do service around this time as the doors from the breakfast-room, opened to the morning's first release of tourists. Twenty or so Swiss, in sturdy middle-age and wearing enthusiastic boots, were today scheduled for a sight-seeing tour by bus. Conversations faltered enough, as they walked curiously around the couple standing with the constable on the path, to indicate that the news of the night was a breakfast-time topic.

'Bizarr,' said someone who did not expect German to be understood in English.

Michael and Lindy Chamberlain walked the path slowly back to the room. They should anticipate, so Morris had now warned, an interview here with the district inspector later in the day. They should not stray far. 'I don't know what we can do with the boys,' Lindy said. Behind them, the Swiss began an orderly and genial queue at the bus door, soon to set off for the west track and, as the destination-board noted, to Mt Olga.

It was among the Olgas that the Chamberlain family had once planned to pass this second, warm afternoon; to the slender gorges and the soft brook, their path in some earlier, and now cancelled, life.

5

GEOFF DeLUCA'S FLIGHT landed on the Alice Springs tarmac at one o'clock. The stream of passengers, making from the aircraft steps towards the mesh gate, were mostly holidaymakers by the look of them. But in this part of the country it was hard to tell. DeLuca's own shirt, printed with the colours of tropical foliage, flapped in the dry breeze. Bert Stanbury, the photographer on this job, carried items of camera equipment he would not entrust to the baggage hold. Anyone would take them both for tourists.

The grassy forecourt to the terminal building was so crowded that it was difficult to shoulder through. The throng here was only partly attributable to the link south with Adelaide. The flight from the south-east, out of Sydney three and a half hours ago, had also just arrived, and those passengers were waiting around for their baggage-call. The timing, for DeLuca's purposes, could not have been better.

Erwin Chlanda met them. Chlanda, stocky and dark, was a well-known figure. He flew gliders and powered aeroplanes, with a reputation for daring. Sky-diving with the local parachute team, he enjoyed the heady onrush of free-fall. On the ground he worked in the communications business, reporting for the *Centralian Advocate*, and freelancing in TV newsfilm. DeLuca considered him a good contact. It was Chlanda he had telephoned from Adelaide as soon as he knew the job was on, suggesting collaboration. A light plane now stood in a side bay, Chlanda said, loaded with movie gear, fuelled, ready to roll.

While they waited for luggage, DeLuca went for a stroll. Inside the terminal the shop-counters were doing a busy trade in postcards, beer-mugs, gaudy towels and T-shirts, many printed with cartoons amusing to heavy drinkers or to shooters of buffalo. At these DeLuca did not glance at all. Instead, he was browsing faces. There was none here he knew. They seemed to have the field to themselves so far. Good.

6

IN ORDER TO ESCAPE the forlorn room, Bobbie Downs sat in the yellow car and tried to amuse the boys. Bobbie, with her large spectacles and shy smile, looked ready for the part of playleader, but both boys were disposed to bicker, impatient for the return of their mother, and readily tearful. She tried guessing-games and rhymes, but no game was successful for long, and it was surprising just how few childrens' rhymes there were which did not somehow lead to associations with unexpected fear, gore, bones, or what little children are made of.

It was with some relief she was able to say, 'Here are your folks now.' Michael was carrying his camera, so some movement was afoot.

'All out,' he said. 'We're going on a bus.' The motel's assistant manager, Lytle Dickenson, had offered to drive the family to the Ininti store for a film, then on to the camp for a photograph of the tent. The *News* had asked for shots in monochrome.

Bobbie thought some sort of outing a good idea. She thought less of the newsmen at whose request it was made.

One of those newsmen was then in a light aircraft somewhere around three thousand metres above the dry bed of the Palmer River.

DeLuca, sitting to the right of the pilot, Chlanda, and Stanbury, heftily taking up a good deal of space behind, were finding the trip a little bumpy. This is a part of the country loved by people who set records in very lightweight sailplanes. These blue skies, hot ridges, and breathy currents, which make glider-pilots smile happily, are not so good for small-powered aeroplanes. But the nervousness in DeLuca's hands—gripping his thighs, then the seat, then the scuttle—had nothing to do with the turbulence. DeLuca's hands also grip things in automobiles, in bars, in offices. It is a symptom, endemic and recessive, and has to do with the familiar onset of excitement.

'How do you interview a Bible preacher, for Chrissake?'

'Not like that, pal.'

This was the constant topic. There must be an angle.

Journalists exist, as they firmly believe, only when they are onto a story. Geoff DeLuca had the feeling for some time now that the story for which he was heading was bigger than it looked from down south.

The boys were not enthusiastic about posing in front of the tent. Aidan directed a blank gaze at the camera, Reagan overplayed an interest in his finger. Michael lined them up with the tent and, as a back-drop, the Rock. He took five shots. An afternoon breeze was about. The tent, alternately slack on one side and swollen on the other, tugged at the ropes, which gave it a curious air of restlessness. 'That'll do,' Michael said. 'Let's go.'

Lytle Dickenson's bus took them to the old airfield, a sandy strip too close to the walls of the Rock for the safety of large aircraft and now relegated to lighter traffic. There they found a six-seater, painted with the words 'Opal Air', whose unfussed pilot agreed to deliver the film to Adelaide so long as it was after he'd had something to eat.

A small plane came in low. Reagan wanted to watch it land. It touched down, on a precisely synchronized spurt of dust, and taxied to the apron. The doors opened. The men who climbed out began to unload, and Lindy Chamberlain firmly ushered the protesting boys into the bus. On any other occasion Lytle Dickenson would have offered the new arrivals a lift, but this time he started the bus without a word, and they drove away, leaving behind them the newcomers and their growing pile of film boxes, tripods, camera cases.

Mischance was unmercifully abroad. Once back at the motel, Michael expected the arrival of Inspector Gilroy, and of the Alice Springs pastor, Bert Cuzins, any time now. The grass beside the swimming-pool might be a good place to wait. It was shady and offered a view of the gate. He and Lindy found it unexpectedly popular. A lecture on local fauna was in progress, and the guide delivering it hesitated as they entered, but carried on. Someone moved aside enough so that they could sit, and Michael helped his wife gratefully down. She looked tired and still wore her dark glasses. It was a moment before they understood, at much the same interminable instant, that the topic under discussion was the desert dingo. They sat it out.

7

FRANK MORRIS collected Inspector Gilroy and Sergeant Lincoln from the airport and drove them, in the police truck, to the camping-ground. On the way Morris filled them in as best he could. It made a complicated story, and it seemed that the exact sequence of the reports Morris had come by was not yet clear. 'You are keeping notes on all this?' the inspector asked.

'We've had more urgent things to do than paperwork.'

Gilroy shook his head. An investigating magistrate might not think that a fine excuse.

They drew up by the green and orange tent. The face of the Rock was in shadow. Morris indicated a nearby barbecue-stand and said, 'The parents were there.' He showed them the corner of the tent in which the baby had slept, and then pointed to the dune, sunny on the opposite side of the road. 'That's where the dingo took her, the trackers say.'

Searching had begun again this morning, as Morris explained, the trackers losing the trail on the dune then widening the search south to the plains. A party was still out there. 'Nothing so far?' Lincoln asked.

'Not a stitch. The rangers think we won't find anything now. If the baby hasn't been eaten entirely, they might find something buried.'

'And the parents?'

'Talk about the ways of the Lord.'

'What a mess.' Gilroy turned away. 'Let's get started,' he said. This, for Gilroy, involved walking about, taking in the feel of things: an impression of the space here, the distance from the barbecue, over the rail to the tent, the mother's quickening path, alarm, the vacant road. 'It was dark here last night?'

'Very dark.'

Paw-marks ran, as Morris showed them, along the right-hand side of the tent. At the far corner was an arresting print, heavy and without the appearance of movement. The muzzle of the beast that made it must have been very close to the fabric. In this corner was the baby's sleeping-place.

Something else took Gilroy's eye. On the side wall was a stain, a handspan, no more, from the ground. So fine was the nylon that the mark seemed fleeting, illusory. He smoothed the fold to better catch the light. The shape of a spray, the colour of blood.

The trackers came back from the plains, making a further traverse of the dune. They had been out since dawn, so when Frank Morris called them down to talk with Gilroy and Lincoln they were happy for the interruption. Because Gilroy plainly carried the authority for his group, Winmatti thought it proper to address the information to him. The old Pitjantjatjara squatted, levelled the sand with the sweep of a palm, and drew in outline the ridge, the camp, the ring-road, the Rock. Displaying all the while a marvellous disarray of teeth, as awry as the surviving pickets in a loose fence, he began to recount the events of the morning:

At daybreak the trackers gather, here, at the campsite. Winmatti himself, Barbara, Daisy Walkabout, Kitty Collins, and Nuwe Minyintiri. The morning is cold, cloudless. Beginning at the dragmarks, high on the dune, they inspect again the depression in the sand where that dingo had laid its burden. Clear the pattern of clothing, and clear the furrow, made by an arm or a leg. The trail climbs, is lost and found many times on the way up. And it is at the top, beside the water-tanks there, where the ground holds marks faithfully, that Winmatti sees they have somewhere exchanged the tracks of one beast for those of another.

They begin again at the tent, this time with a sharper picture of this dingo. He is big. One front paw does not tread the ground truly, an old injury. His changes of direction show the spirit in him, not of fear, but of cunning, like Kulpunya, the ancestor of all dingoes.

This time they trail him better. He takes them up the dune, beyond the marks of the baby, along the ridge and down again, over the plain in a wide sweep which will show him anyone who follows, towards the water at Mutitjilda, the Maggie Spring. He hurries, keen to eat, and runs on the roadway there. Often dingoes do this for easy travelling. At times he moves from the gravel into the scrub and back again, and this way he avoids the occasional approach of motor cars. It is, in the end, the winds of traffic which hide him. Like roadside leaves, his prints have blown away.

One aspect of the storytelling Gilroy noted with curiosity. Winmatti, elder and spokesman, was the custodian of all this information. When he told of the discoveries of last night, he spoke as if it were he who had made them. The unsettling fact was that Winmatti wasn't there then. The tracker was Nuwe Minyintiri, who now stood respectfully mute.

8

MICHAEL CHAMBERLAIN, carrying Aidan, and Lindy, holding Reagan, stood on the grass outside room 34. DeLuca tapped his microphone. Chlanda swung the movie camera until his shoulders were compliant and steady. Stanbury took stills with his flash.

'I've done some journalism at Mt Isa,' Michael said. 'I know what you want.'

DeLuca was familiar with church columns in the provincial press. They seemed eager and wordy. He began the interview with references to religion, and returned to it whenever the narrative lagged. So well did this angle work that DeLuca was able to break the interview midway.

'Do that line over,' he said, adjusting the levels for sound. 'Take Two.'

Michael knew precisely what was wanted. 'The loss of our baby is the will of God,' he said again.

'How did you identify the animal as a dingo?'

Michael was assured, talkative, a delivery aimed at the camera's eye. 'When we saw spots of blood in the tent, we realized it must have been a very quick event. The sharp, jagged marks in that thickly woven blanket, we knew it was a powerful beast with sharp teeth. It was more than a domestic dog that did that, and it was confirmed, in our minds, that it was a very powerful, sly and wily beast. It had probably stalked the baby, because we'd been there the second night. It had premeditated it, we think.'

His wife began confidently enough, undistracted by the fidgety boy on her hip. 'I just yelled. There wasn't time to go and tell people. I just yelled out loud, "Has anybody got a torch. The dingo's got my baby."'

But it was now plain, from the sudden disobedience of her lips, that the enactment had her close to tears, and Chlanda held, rolling, on a leakage of misery which would be extended a few frames further by the technicians who edited it for the networks of five capital cities.

'A rotten, horrifying experience,' DeLuca said, on tape, off camera.

They carried the cameras to the motel office, leaving the Chamberlains to their room. DeLuca caught Stanbury by the sleeve. 'There's something in this,' he said. 'They are weird, even allowing for religion.' Stanbury and Chlanda should fly the film out. DeLuca had decided to stick around.

9

AT AROUND FIVE, DeLuca, in an appropriated truck, set off for the camping-ground. The tracks were sandy. Even the sealed road gave up a fine plume. DeLuca was a fast driver, whatever the traffic, and here he expected to have the roads to himself. He was surprised that the most frequent users of the roadways at this time of day were dingoes which, at the sound of an approaching car, moved to the right like streetwise pedestrians.

He lined one up, and drove at it hard, but the changing note of the motor caused the dingo's ears to sleek, and it took to the bush. The next, a half kilometre closer to the camp, trod the gravel verge until the truck was close. It moved then, a little irritably, off the roadside to the plain, and DeLuca swung the wheel. The cabin bounced, the scrub splintered, but the dingo had somehow evaded DeLuca's accelerating lunges and, with appalled leaps, made for less penetrable ground.

Something of the same exercise was to take place at the campsite. When DeLuca got there, he found the constables Nobel and Morris, and the rangers Roff and Cawood, cooking at the barbecue. They were not off duty. Their loaded rifles lay on the table. Under orders now from the Conservation Commission, scavenging dogs and dingoes were to be shot.

In the course of the meal they bagged one dingo and two dogs. The dogs had come over from the Pitjantjatjara camp. A second dingo was giving unaccustomed trouble. Since these parks are also sanctuaries, the sound of gunfire is not a familiar threat, but this animal was evasive, staying close to cover. Unable to bring the dingo down with a clean shot, the rangers seemed embarrassed in front of DeLuca. It was an hour before that dingo became the fourth kill. Out here there was no reason to keep their marksmanship so sharp, they said.

10

THE FAMILY sat at a table in the dining-room with Alan Barber. Lindy and Michael picked at salads. The two boys were hungrier and went on to pudding. The menu in outback diners is restricted, not so much by the inefficacy of itinerant cooks, as by the preservative mode. Food commonly comes here either in cans or frozen. The choice at table is between warm and cold, and with a minimum of gradation in between. Michael's unnerving concern seemed to be his capacity to pay for it. 'On the house,' Barber said, happy to find a topic, 'and you don't cost much to feed.' The subject was not pursued. Among the members of a family which had lost its baby to a carnivore, their vegetarianism was not for discussion. They left the table as soon as the boys had finished.

11

INSPECTOR GILROY FOUND room 34 at the end of the path and knocked. Lincoln carried the tape-recorder. The door was opened by Lindy Chamberlain, and Gilroy told her who they were. She looked dark-eyed and weary.

'I'm sorry we have to interview you just now,' he said, 'but we have to know what happened to the baby.'

'It's all right.' She opened the door wider. 'It will probably help me to talk about it.'

She was alone, but for Reagan, and said that her husband Michael would return soon with their other son. They were at the clinic with Sister Downs. John Lincoln set the recorder on the bed. He spoke into the microphone, adjusting the sound. When the levels satisfied him, he spoke a line of identification, gave the date, and nodded to Gilroy. Gilroy turned to Lindy Chamberlain.

'When did you leave Mt Isa?'

'Ah, last . . . whether it was Tuesday night or Wednesday night. Wednesday morning, I think. Monday, Tuesday . . . Monday or Tuesday,' she said. But her confidence in that was short-lived. 'Or Tuesday or Wednesday.'

'Could you tell me how you all left Mt Isa to come here?'

'I beg your pardon?'

'Did you come in your own vehicle?'

'Yes,' she said with some relief. 'We came in our car. My husband and I, and our two boys, and the baby.'

It was not a fluent beginning. She pulled at her wedding ring and her eyes swam. It did not take long for Gilroy to decide on abandoning the usual form of police interview. Since she found his simple questions difficult, he would allow her to choose her own.

'Can you tell me when you decided to bed down for the night? Or prior to that? Or where you had a meal?'

The change in her was immediate. She began the narrative with the bathing of the children, described her preparations for the meal, gave the geography of the camping-ground and the sleeping arrangements she had chosen for the baby. By then she was running through the story at full tilt, doubling back now and then for some item of remembered detail.

'And my husband said to me, "Is that Bubby crying? Didn't she go to sleep?" And I said, "I don't know, I can't hear her", and I walked back up, and I said I'd go and see anyway, and I walked back towards the tent, and got halfway there, and it wouldn't be any more than the length of this room away from the tent, and I saw the dingo come out of the tent, and the light didn't show on the lower part of the tent because the bushes blocked it, and I saw the dingo from about, oh, shoulder up, and he sort of, he looked as if he'd got a fright and heard me coming. He was having trouble getting out of the tent-flaps, he sort of moved his head to get out, and I didn't realize he was in there, and the cry, the baby, he might have savaged it. The thought went through my mind because I had heard they bite, they had been biting around here, and then I, oh, I yelled at it to get out of the road, and it took fright, and ran in front of our car, which was parked next to the tent, but I didn't sort of keep looking at it, I dived straight for the tent, to see what had made the baby cry, and when I got in the tent the bunny-rug and the two thick blankets she had around her were scattered from one end of the tent to the other. Some of them were on Reagan, so the dingo must have walked on his feet, at least walked right past him. The baby was sleeping at his feet, in her carry-basket, and it must have walked right past him to get to the baby and taken the baby out. It was empty, there was nothing there, and I called my husband straight away. I came straight out of the tent and called him, and to next door, that the dingo had taken the baby, and to chase it. I chased it into the bush and followed it, and I got to the edge of the road. The light didn't carry any further than that. I was aware that it went into the bush, and oh, I realized it was no good, unless—And as soon as I called out to my husband that the dingo's got my baby, he came running, and he ran straight into the bush.

She had completed that part of the story with effort, but for the most part tearlessly. Gilroy thought her courage was clear and admirable. But he could see, watching Lincoln's face, no comparable expression of admiration there.

It was perplexing for Michael Gilroy that Lindy Chamberlain had seen nothing of the baby in the dingo's mouth. 'I didn't see anything in the dingo's mouth,' she explained, 'because that was below the level of the light. It sort of had its head down, and coming out of the tent, I thought it was just shaking its head to get past the thing. It was obviously because it had a heavy burden. She had a little towelling stretch-suit on, and often my other two used to wear towelling suits, and often when they were bigger, and crawling, I'd pick them up by the back. They're very strong, and it's quite easy to pick them up by the back and, in which case, the towelling stretches and the baby would be six inches from the mouth if he was carrying her like that.'

Lincoln was interested in more tangible evidence. 'Would you have any idea of the baby's weight?'

'She was weighed a week and a half before we came out here, and she was ten ounces under nine pounds. The way she is gaining, I would have said she'd be ten pound now. Ten pounds bare weight.'

'Bare weight, plus the weight of the clothing?'

'She had a little throw-away nappy, and singlet. They always weigh them in at three ounces. And a little stretch towelling suit, little pair of knitted booties, and a little knitted matinee jacket.'

If Gilroy was surprised at the mention now of a matinee jacket he gave no indication of it. Constable Morris had not referred to it, in the briefing he gave Gilroy, although it was Lindy Chamberlain's belief that she told the constable about it last night. In the scheme of evidence, as Gilroy was toting it up, a knitted jacket fitted well enough the sort of pattern Murray Haby had found on the sand dune.

Sergeant Lincoln was not so interested in patterns of clothing. His curiosity seemed to lie, for reasons not yet clear to anyone else, with the aggregate weight of a fully clothed baby.

Michael Chamberlain came in midway, trailing Aidan. He was identified on the tape. The topic was, at that time, the description of the dingo his wife saw at the tent. Michael had judged, evidently, that his own contribution ought to be of a theoretical nature.

'It looked to me,' Lindy went on, 'a youngish dog. It struck me as perhaps not being the one that was by the campfire, earlier, because that looked mangy, and this one was very young and very strong.'

'I thought it was the same dog,' Michael said. 'But it may not have been the same dog, now that I think about it.' He seemed suddenly overtaken by some troubling aspect of this. 'Not that I saw the dog,' he added.

When Lincoln asked how close to the tent Lindy was at the time the dingo made off, Michael said, 'See, the thing is the process of elimination, okay? If anyone says it is not a dingo, what would it be that could do that? That's my question. I believe it was. I didn't see it, my wife did. But what other creature would do that? Could we conclude otherwise?'

'As opposed to a camp dog? An Aboriginal's dog?'

'That's right.'

Lincoln left the next question hanging. 'Or a—'

'The alternative is too frightening. If there is an alternative.'

Bringing the conversation back to the corporeal, Lincoln asked Lindy Chamberlain if the baby was ever ill. 'No.' She allowed more than a little pride to show. 'She's been fit and healthy.'

'Tell me when the baby was fed, prior to her going missing.' She had fed while they were watching the sunset, Lindy recalled, at six-thirty, and for most of the following hour.

'You were breast-feeding her?'

'I breast-fed her and complementary-fed her. She would have had about 200 to 250 mls. She would have been full of food.'

A knock at the door took Michael away. They heard Bobbie Downs's voice outside. Michael carried a parcel which he set down on the dresser. 'A breast-pump,' he said, as if the police might expect disclosures of this nature. 'My wife is in some pain from the milk.'

The interview was coming to an end. Michael was accustomed to deliver, at the conclusion of any gathering, an encomium.

'I'd like to pay tribute to the people who went out quickly and so voluntarily,' he said, as if the recording were somehow to be made public. He thanked Constable Morris. His wife thanked Sister Downs. 'Everybody has been terrific to us,' she added.

The return to formality drew Gilroy back to standard police practice. 'Is there anything else you would like to comment about to finish off our conversation?'

'Yes,' Michael said. 'This is an observation. I have listened

very carefully to a lot of people about this incident. I wouldn't
be so unkind as to say that some would try to defend the dingo,
and consider you are a bit daft for suggesting it. But I have
noticed that some of the more authoritative people have been the
ones who try to knock the idea. Not openly. Through innuendo.
Well, not innuendo, but questioning. Whereas, when you talk to
people who live here and know the dingo, none of them have
been at all surprised.'

On the path outside Gilroy said, 'Well?'
'Too easy,' said Lincoln, and walked on.

12

THE LOWES, who were at this moment driving north
on Stuart Highway, would have been surprised that Lindy Chamberlain's interview contained no mention of them.

In the morning, they had driven from the grounds of the
Inland Motel, irritable after a sleepless night, and headed for the
camping-ground. Across the dune, squads of volunteers in shorts
and T-shirts picked through the scrub. 'So she's not yet been
found,' Greg said. The plain below looked desolate and hopeless. Greg saw Derek Roff, who was standing with a blacktracker
by the road, and pulled alongside.

'We've got the tracks of the dingo that took her off, all right,'
Roff said, 'but nothing else.'

They drove to the gas-station, fuelled, and pulled out. On
each side of the road the brush was limp and dusty, the trees
runted and birdless. Greg, in whom the need for escape was
irrefutable, drove past the administration signpost without slowing.

'Hey,' said Sally. 'We should leave our names and address.'

'No.' Greg kept driving. 'The baby is dead,' he said at last.
'Nothing is going to change any of that.'

They drove the four hundred and twenty kilometres, over
eight gritty hours, without breaking the silence more than a
dozen times. On one of those occasions Sally said, 'We can give
a statement at Alice Springs.' Greg said nothing.

It had not occurred to Sally that the Chamberlains might give
to the police an account unpopulated by witnesses, but she felt
there was something unsafe and deficient now in so sudden a
rush to seclusion.

The cleavage of Heavitree Gap came up ahead. There was passing traffic. Sally shifted on the Toyota's severe seat, holding a plait of her hair in one hand, and with the other, Chantelle, from whom she had not been parted for an instant in the last twenty-four hours. Dust from the desert road lay over the seats and over their clothes. It was like sitting in a room in which no one had spoken for a very long time, while the world outside went on with things she didn't know about.

13

THE HOUR IS LATE and the day has been long, but the police do not yet feel like turning in. Neither does Geoff DeLuca. They drink on in the bar of the Red Sands Motel.

The topic of conversation is, and has been for the past two hours, the propensity of a dingo for child abduction. Michael Gilroy sees no reason to doubt it. Frank Morris is quiet. DeLuca won't entertain the possibility for a moment. Lincoln is vehement. 'Not a chance,' is the way Lincoln puts it. 'Never happened before. There's a fact you can't beat. Never ever happened.'

'But close,' Gilroy argues, ''Attacks, savaging. Close.'

'On open ground. Not from a tent.'

'Roff is convinced. Roff warned the commission it might happen.'

Lincoln seizes the point. 'For Roff this is the fulfilment of a prophesy. His prophesy.'

'He knows better than anyone.'

'I've been in the game too long to wear a story like this. A camp full of tourists, but no witnesses.'

'The tracks don't mean anything?'

'The tracks mean something, all right. I am supposed to believe a dingo lifted the baby, took it out of the tent, and got halfway up the hill before any part of the body touches the ground. Not a chance. That baby weighed ten pounds. Do you know how heavy ten pounds is?'

They all know what is bothering him. It has little to do with Gilroy. Lincoln has more experience with quirky cases like this than anyone else here. He is fresh from six years in the crime squad. Before that he spent five years in one-man stations, some of them in tough towns. He is brawny, handsome, and tight-lipped, much accustomed to decisive and preremptory action. In his league, a cop does what he judges the moment calls for. This moment, the way Lincoln judges it, calls for suspicion and surveillance, for surprise road-blocks, interrogation, and searches without too much deference to the effete requirements of police regulations.

Lincoln turns and strides away, letting the swinging door fend for itself behind him, in retreat while his anger is still controllable, so it seems to everyone else. Frank Morris is at a loss for anything appropriate to say in the wake of his departed superior. Geoff DeLuca, as the only sceptic left in the room, says: 'The way the parents go on is what gets to me. Their reaction to publicity. It's weird. It's like the Light has shined upon them.'

The bar door opens. It is John Lincoln. He has in his hands a plastic bucket. It is full of red sand. He lifts it, takes the swinging handle between his teeth, and lets it hang. The weight of his jaw makes his jowls loose and canine. He cannot support it for anywhere near a minute. 'That is ten pounds,' he says, and insists the others try. They are a little disabled by laughter, and no one can do better.

Michael Gilroy is not impressed, but the joke has made some point. They are not so much judging the weight of a baby, as beginning to judge the weight of probability.

14

TUESDAY BEGAN, in room 34, with prayer. Aidan and Reagan knelt with their mother by the side of the bed, a tableau more familiar to the boys at night-time. Michael Chamberlain led this tiny congregation, standing. He chose to recite Paul, a comforter in bereavement the Christian world over, but avoided the usual passages from Thessalonians. He was not ready to taunt death. Its sting was aplenty; the victory of the grave anonymous but imperious. He chose, instead, Corinthians.

' "For the Lord himself shall descend from heaven with a shout, with the voice of the archangel and the trumpet of God, and the dead in Christ shall rise first. Then we who are alive and remain shall be caught up together with them in the clouds, to meet the Lord in the air. And so shall we ever be with the Lord." '

Lindy got to her feet, and the released boys tumbled on the bed. 'What are we going to do now?' they said.

It was a question Michael had considered already. So far as

he knew, the search had turned up nothing. No one, not the police nor the rangers, had thought to tell him of paw-prints leading from the tent, of drag-marks, of Haby finding a knit-imprint on the dune, of the trackers following a burdened dingo over the plains. Michael's decision was unimpeded by expectation or by hope.

'I think,' he said, 'it's time we all went home.'

15

WHEN THE POLICE Toyota drove through the gateway into the Aboriginals' camp, many of the adults, and a good number of the children, were out, already, at the search. This didn't displease Roff—who was then dismounting with Gilroy, Lincoln, and Morris—given the nature of the visit. Pitjantjatjara sat in shade under the still trees. Winmatti was there with Barbara. Small children looked on, curious. Roff began to take count of the camp dogs. He was concerned not to be too obvious about it, minimizing somehow the callousness of the impending task. Dogs lay in the angular shadows of houses, under the trees, by the fireplaces.

Winmatti climbed to his feet and walked over. His greeting included the words 'Old Derek', a form of address normally amusing to Roff when used by so old a Pitjantjatjara. 'I am sorry to tell you why we are here,' Roff said. Winmatti seemed already alerted to something, mystified perhaps because Roff had not crossed ground to join the group. Roff was not here as a friend.

'I have come to shoot the dogs,' he said.

The others loitered around the car. Roff ambled back to them. There was no hurry, best let the blacks get used to the idea. A child, somewhere behind him, began wailing. 'You can't expect them to like it,' Roff said.

Another car drive through the gate. Gilroy recognized the yellow hatchback and glanced at John Lincoln. Lincoln had seen it already. 'Look who's here,' he said. Michael Chamberlain pulled in close. He and his wife got out. The car was piled to the back window with clothing, bedding, utensils.

'We were told you wanted us to look at the camp dogs,' Lindy said. 'A sort of identification, maybe. We thought we ought to do it before we go.'

'Well, yes,' said Derek Roff, although he didn't recollect the instruction. 'Take a look around.'

Lindy walked further into the dusty compound. She was soon back. She shook her head. 'They are all bitzers, sort of hound-dogs, around here. Nothing like it at all.'

Michael asked Roff, 'You shot some dingoes? Last night, I believe.'

Roff agreed they had. Last night and this morning.

'Any chance of a photograph of one?'

'Of a dead dingo?'

'The jaws,' Michael explained. 'Someone ought to write a book about all this. My wife and I are thinking of writing one ourselves.'

It was a request about which Roff felt instantly uncomfortable, though reasons didn't readily come to him. 'No, that wouldn't be possible.'

Michael had another question. He had seen plaques set into the base of the Rock, memorials to the dead. Could the Chamberlain family provide one in memory of Azaria? 'I couldn't authorize that myself,' Roff said. 'You should approach the Conservation Commission.'

Perhaps his refusal of two requests prompted Roff to concede the third. It was for a photograph of the trackers. They stood, while Michael lined up for the shot, and shuffled more closely together: Winmatti in old bone slacks, the vast Barbara, Daisy Walkabout, and little Kitty Collins. Roff agreed to tack himself to the end of the line, all now intent on looking serious but pleasant.

Michael and Lindy Chamberlain climbed into the yellow car, nodded farewell, and drove out through the gate.

'We ought to search that car,' Lincoln said. But this was an old argument by now, and Michael Gilroy chose not to answer it.

16

LINCOLN WALKED OFF, followed all the way by Roff's uneasy gaze, heading towards the nearest of the houses. A Pitjantjatjara couple lived there, Toby Nanyinga and Ada Nangala, white-haired and frail, gentle people whom Roff much liked. The police had no authority to enter any of the dwellings here, but nothing in Lincoln's dusty, resolute footfalls indicated he was about to wait for an invitation. When he pushed through the door, Roff and Gilroy began to move.

They found him in the kitchen. He was emptying a trash bin, searching. Ada's face was as dark as a shadow, and the white hairs on her chin trembled. She was groping for a broomstick. Toby's arms were outstretched, giving the proportions of his indignation. 'You think I ate the child?' he cried.

Roff and Gilroy bundled Lincoln outside. He shrugged them off. 'I can't search a black's house now without a warrant, for Chrissake,' he said.

So far as Roff could tell, Lincoln's anger wasn't directed at anyone. It was something deeper, bewildering.

17

CONSTABLE MORRIS, driving past the Ininti store on an errand, saw the hatchback outside. He remembered then that there was something he needed from Lindy Chamberlain before she left. He pulled up and went in.

The Ininti was the only general store at the settlement. Its staple sales were in foodstuffs and in accessories for forgetful campers, but it also had a high turnover in film, postcards, and souvenirs. Morris interrupted the Chamberlains as they were being served. 'Not souvenirs, exactly,' Lindy was saying. 'Mementoes.'

'I'd forgotten something,' Morris confessed. 'A sample of the nappy Azaria was wearing when she vanished.'

'Sure,' she said, went out to the car, and brought one back. 'Here, you see? Plastic outer, absorbent lining, Johnson's. It's from the same pack.'

The constable was leaving when Michael said, 'And thanks for all you've done.'

'That's okay. It's what we're here for.' It was crossing his mind just then that mementoes of Ayers Rock would not be items attractive to him in similar circumstances.

18

BOBBIE DOWNS WAVED as they drove away. She stood in front of the clinic where, a moment before, Michael had insisted on taking her photograph. Although she was nothing of a religious practitioner, Bobbie understood what that photograph was about. It was part of the record of an event. That event was the passing of their baby into the arms of Jesus. Bobbie saw in it a tragedy of far more human dimensions.

CEREMENTS

1

SPRING IN THIS PART of the desert can arrive while botanical calendars elsewhere are still talking about winter. It might
happen anytime after the end of July. The most exciting characteristic of a good spring here is the astonishing profusion of
wildflowers. The phenomenon depends on winter rain. When it
happens on time, it is as if the land had water-soluble pigment
stored, waiting. The ground-cover, once brittle and fatigued,
now greens and softens. Come sunshine, it floats blues, pinks
and yellows, just above the surface as it seems, in mists of
quite unrelated colour. Pamphlets published by the office of
tourism commonly show, on a prominent page, a graph on
which the flowering of shrubs, herbs and grasses is seen most
likely to occur over August, September and October. A page
or two further on is another graph which, with equal authority,
discounts that likelihood by a significant factor, showing a
disappointing number of years in which spring did not occur
at all.

Since this is country where the rainfall collected over any
average year would not fill a bucket, most plants of the region
get through the unremarkable seasons by having a modest floral
display all year round. This saves moisture but allows them to
seed. They are, typically, highly competitive for moisture and
draw it quickly from the sand before it can evaporate or be used
by another. Indeed conservation and use of available water
accounts for the more important elements of design. The leaf of
the native fig revolves so the tougher surface follows the sun.
Spinifex leaves are rolled tightly so the plant breathes through a
tube. The witchetty-bush, an acacia, grows wide leaves to catch

dew, shapes them so the drops run to the stem, and then discards old foliage tidily enough to mulch its own roots.

A conservation device which wildflowers hereabouts find successful is diminution of scale. A daisy is a popular size to be. There are many variants, and wildflower fanciers find two or three species together called Yellow Top, with Poached Egg Daisy, Pink Everlasting, a vermillion Minuria, and White Paper Daisy, in a few minutes walk. The Bluebells are smaller. The Pink Peaflower, a herb more the colour of transparent lilac, is little more than a centimetre across, and the flowers of the Pink Verbine, particularly those near the tip of the slender wand, find difficulty making it past five millimetres, petals outstretched. It is as if these flowers are designed to beguile insects of pollinating size rather than anyone big enough to pick them, and tourists have trouble photographing the precise form and posture of single blooms.

At four in the afternoon of 24 August, a spectator intent on overcoming the disadvantage of human scale crouched over a low bush not far from the lichened bluff on the south walls of the Rock. The flower which had caught his eye was pale blue, transluscent. Its name was *Isotoma petraea*, its family Campanulaceae. The man's name was Wally Goodwin, and his family waited nearby. He squinted through the viewfinder of a neat 35 mm Paxette. A Super-8 movie camera lay carefully beside him. Wally was a keen photographer, outdoors. His solution to the problems of size and clarity involved a macro-lens and steadiness of hand. He brought the bloom into sharp focus and pressed the shutter. He was pleased with the shot. The bright-pointed Isotome on its crescent stalk reminded him of fireworks, a blue starburst trailing a green trajectory.

Wally Goodwin might not, at first blush, seem the sort of man likely to spend time in admiration of tiny flowers. He was strong, stocky, and had worked most of his adult life retreading automobile tyres. Now, at thirty-five, he managed a factory for Dunlop in Melbourne. But Wally's cameras had already accounted for a good number of snaps and panoramas over the four days since they drove in via Curtain Springs; thick albums stacked somewhere at home held photographs of a visit here four years ago, and of camping tours in snow country and in tropical rainforests. The Goodwins' Land Rover, which was parked back on the gravel road, was fitted with long-distance tanks, water-carriers, roof-racks, off-road radials, bumpers to fend off light-blinded kangaroos by night, and a mechanism for varying tyre-pressure according to terrain.

The Goodwins were heading for a gully at the base of the Rock, Wally following a track, Margot Goodwin keeping to high ground from which she could watch Philip and Joanne who were running about somewhere between. Philip found that he was now tall enough to catch the web of some ambitious spider full in the face, and squawked when it happened. They unwound him and pressed on. The track Wally trod was an animal path, dingo or kangaroo. Perhaps both. Foliage was denser here, the trees high. Taking this direction was his idea. Last night it had rained at the camp, heavily enough from four a.m. onwards to keep him awake for a half hour while campers with the Roadrunner bus parked next door packed up and shipped out. Rain hereabouts brings fresh blooms and lively birdlife, especially in a gully like this where watershed from the Rock multiplies the fall, maybe ten or twenty-fold.

Margot, from a boulder high to his right, saw something ahead. 'Look,' she called. 'What's on the ground?'

Wally caught sight of it at much the same time. He did not experience a second's puzzlement. Back at camp he had been told, in camp-fire conversations, that police were searching for the abducted baby's clothes: grow-suit, nappy and jacket, and he knew he was now gazing at some of it. The thought occurred to him that he might photograph this, but concluded then he ought not, in case some unreasonable rule of evidence required the confiscation of his film. He laid his cameras on the ground and walked closer. The nappy was shredded, the plastic torn. His immediate impression was that birds had pulled it apart. The towelling suit lay on bare ground nearby, crumpled. It was grubby and open from neck to crutch. The neckline was rusty with old blood. The feet took his attention. There was something terrible about them. They seemed stiff and substantial, as if some part of the baby was still in there.

He had forgotten, for a moment, the rest of the family. They were walking up behind. He called for Margot to keep the children back. Too late. Joanne turned and ran off, crying.

Wally halted the Land Rover outside a house which seemed to have been converted into a police-station by the addition of a sign at the gate. He found an office at the back and walked in. The duty constable, Frank Morris, was talking on the radio to a superior in Alice Springs. Wally leaned on the counter.

'We propose to call off any further search,' Morris went on. 'Evidence to hand is negative at this time. Correct. Nothing found at all.'

Wally Goodwin's thought was private and laconic: Boy, have I got news for you.

Morris, driving the police truck, followed the Goodwins back to the Rock and pulled up well off the road. Wally Goodwin guessed they were now about six kilometres west of the camp from which the baby had disappeared. He climbed down from the Land Rover and caught Morris at the edge of the brush. He pointed towards the gully. 'We go straight in.'

Morris scratched his head. 'We've been looking in exactly the opposite direction,' he said.

They joined the animal track and followed it, in single file, Morris behind. The bush thickened, darkened, twigs picked at their shirts. The sky was still overcast and the air a little humid. The great boulder, from which Margot had first seen the clothing, came up on the right. 'There's a dingo lair under that,' Morris said.

Standing so not to cramp Morris's first view of the clothing, Wally Goodwin looked about for anything he might have missed earlier. By the time he glanced back again the constable had the towelling suit in hand, turning it over. This small event caused Wally some surprise. It seemed to him an unprofessional thing to do in these circumstances, perhaps a laxity in investigative practice. At that instant, Wally regretted not taking a photo of all this when he had the chance.

In Morris's grasp, the body of the suit lay slack and inert. They would find no remnant of the baby in that part of it. But the feet were another matter. They swung to and fro. Wally watched Frank Morris's trembling fingers.

The first item Morris drew from the suit was a singlet, lank and smeared, which he draped over his forearm. His hand pushed deeper, filling out the leg, but the object with which it returned was no more than a tiny white bootie with yellow ties. He found a second in the other leg. His round face relaxed. He asked Wally Goodwin to fetch Gordon Noble from the station, and then to set up a roadblock to keep tourists away from the area until official photographs were taken. 'I'll arrange the clothing just as we found it,' Morris said.

You're real good if you can do that, Wally thought, and walked away.

Driving the rangers' emblazoned truck back from an afternoon at Mt Olga, Derek Roff opted in favour of the south route around the Rock and made a right turn at the ring-road. This took him past the climb. An endless belt of climbing and descending pilgrims hung from the summit to the plain. The car-park was crowded, but everything here seemed orderly enough, and he drove past. A kilometre or so further on he saw a Land Rover, disabled on the roadway. No, it was parked there as a barrier, for some reason. The man beside it flagged him down. Roff pulled up and said, 'What's going on?'

'I found the baby's clothes. The police are in there now.'

'Good man. Which way?'

'Straight ahead. The end of the gully.'

Roff strode through grass and low brush, joined the track and followed it in. There were several dingo lairs close by, he knew. In one of them, a recent litter. He reached the end. Morris, who had heard his approach, stood beside the torn nappy and the grimy jump-suit. Morris had been looking about for anything else of interest. 'This seems to be all there is,' he said.

Roff crouched on his haunches. The crust about the neckline was gore, without doubt. And the violent smears below. A vivid painting, poor child, the brush-strokes of her own death.

The nappy was pulled about, the pieces lying at random, and speckled with red sand. The baby might have been buried meantime, as dingoes will to a kill. But something about the demeanour of the jump-suit was not satisfying, as he looked down at it. An animal might be expected to bundle it more. Was that what was wrong? Or on the contrary, pull it further open. The sense of a garment discarded, abandoned, was not as strong as it should be if the last paws to touch it were those of a dingo.

Wally Goodwin climbed in behind the wheel. He rested his fingers on the ignition key. The children were quiet. Margot waited to be told what was unsettling him. 'It's really no business of mine,' he said, concluding some argument with himself, and started the motor.

2

EVENING HAD FALLEN. The offices and corridors of the police building in Alice Springs were brightly lit but calm, for this is a time junior officers are on mobile duty or on the drunks patrol, and administrators turn to paperwork. Inspector Gilroy sat at his desk. A neat entry in the book of memoranda, which then lay open in front of him, contained his precis of the directions given to Frank Morris by radio-telephone. This included instructions to search about Maggie Springs, with rangers and black trackers, and remit to headquarters the baby's clothes and anything else of interest they found. Apart, now, from notifying the forensic division of more work on the way, the file was abreast of the action.

The telephone rang. The operator had an incoming call from Mt Isa. The caller was Pastor Chamberlain. 'Put him through,' Gilroy said.

'We heard that the clothes were found,' Michael Chamberlain said. 'It was on the news.'

'Yes, around four this afternoon, I was told.'

'Are you sure they are Azaria's?'

'As sure as we can be at present. The jump-suit, a singlet, nappy. And little boots.'

'Is that all?'

'Nothing else was found.'

'Where was it?'

'Not far from Maggie Springs, I believe.'

In the pause which followed, Gilroy assumed the pastor was making the connection between this location and the Fertility Cave, where his wife had seen a dingo. 'Yes,' Gilroy said.

'There's another thing. One of the children's jackets has blood on it. It's here now.'

'Send it to me. The people in forensic will want to look it over, if you wouldn't mind.'

When the conversation concluded, Gilroy made a note of it on the pad. He checked his watch. The time was seven-thirty. Michael Chamberlain might have heard the broadcast at seven, if his source was radio. Perhaps six-thirty, if it was television. The information was first released to the newsrooms, from the sergeant's desk, before the parents were notified. This might account for the quality of terseness in the pastor's voice.

3

THE SUN WAS HIGH by the time the search began on Monday morning. This was the wiser timing, as the rangers considered, so that old Winmatti's eyesight could be given the benefit of even light. Frank Morris and Ian Cawood stood with the trackers at the gully's end. It was cool and shady. Morris pointed at the ground. 'The clothing was lying there,' he said. The trackers made no response. It was as if the signs were plain enough that the fact spoke for itself.

Morris explained the instructions he had received from Alice Springs. At the mention of dingo tracks, Winmatti rubbed his white beard and looked about him with polite care. 'Plenty,' he said, and smiled. 'Today track, yesterday track, old track. Many.' Behind him Barbara Winmatti and Daisy Walkabout stood stiff-legged and amused.

They searched west to the climb and back again, covering the verdant afforested rises close under the Rock, and the dry tussocked flat, without a discovery of any interest. Morris directed them east then, towards the Maggie Spring. On the way, Winmatti picked up some fragments of bone and handed them to Morris. 'Wallaby, maybe. Maybe something else,' Winmatti said. Morris dropped them into a plastic bag for despatch, later, to Alice Springs.

The barefooted women, in cotton frocks knee to shoulder, seemed to be finding the travelling easier than anyone else, and had moved ahead. The two police and the rangers were slow in the hot sun. Flies hung on their damp shirts like black sequins shot with green. Morris had ordered rest when Barbara Winmatti called him over. He followed her to a cave. He found, when his eyes had adjusted to the gloom inside, that Daisy Walkabout was there already. She was pointing to a low rock, on which he could now see stains. He felt his pockets for a clasp-knife to scrape away a sample.

'Blood?'

'Blood.' Although this was the Cave of Fertility, the possible origin of these stains was evidently not one Daisy Walkabout might have expected here.

4

THE CHANNEL SEVEN television network wanted to film the baby's clothing. Michael Gilroy found the Chamberlain's telephone number in the file and dialled it. His purpose was not so much to seek permission, as to warn the parents that the blood-stained garments might appear, in colour, in newscasts. Mrs Chamberlain answered. The pastor, she said, was not at home.

'Will he be back soon?'

'I don't really know. Is there something I can do?'

'I'll ring back later,' he said.

Gilroy's unaccountable disquiet was confirmed by her abrupt response. 'What are you holding out on me, Mr Gilroy?'

His denial did not mollify her for a moment. 'You shouldn't do this. You've made me angry,' she said, and rang off.

Gilroy put the telephone down slowly. He made a careful note for the file. He preferred to speak with her husband, and her irritation about that was a surprise.

Television bulletins carried, over succeeding evenings nation-wide, slowly panned footage of the reassembled nappy, the tattered and encrusted jump-suit, the streaked singlet, and the empty booties side by side, laid out on a bench and attended by a policeman in a laboratory coat. The sound track carried the voices of the parents. This was, in fact, a rerun of the recording made by DeLuca and Chlanda at the Uluru Motel a week earlier. 'When we saw spots of blood in the tent, we realized it must have been a very quick event. The sharp, jagged marks in that thickly woven blanket, we knew it was a powerful beast with sharp teeth,' Michael Chamberlain said, and the effect was that of a new commentary.

5

WHEN THE MELBOURNE TRANSMISSION of this bulletin ended, it took Les Harris a moment to identify what there was about it that puzzled him. He then located a contagious aftertaste of scepticism. It was as if the newsgatherers were now careful not to attribute the baby's death to a dingo, except by the parents own, unsubstantiated, claim. This sudden onset of editorial caution worried him. It suggested that some other, yet unexplained, supposition was afoot. He was, himself, a methodical thinker, more used to proceeding towards a secondary hypothesis only after the primary hypothesis was disposed of.

Harris was an aeronautical engineer. The walls of his living-room and his study were hung with pictures of imprudently delicate aeroplanes, caught in attitudes astonishingly at odds with gravity, because one of his two passions was the design and performance of ultra-light aircraft. But beside these hung photographs of dingoes, caught in alert poses, because the physiology and behaviour of these animals was his other passion.

His interest in the disappearance of the Chamberlain baby began with first reports a week ago. So far, the view he had of it was from his home in Kew, a muffled and leafy suburb of Melbourne, two thousand kilometres from the event. But his vantage-point was elevated to some extent by a solid understanding of dingoes. Harris was president of the Dingo Foundation. He observed and documented their habits in the wild. Others he tended in captivity. And, when this television bulletin ended and Harris reached to turn off the set, he moved with care enough not to disturb the two dingoes dozing on his living-room floor.

At six the next morning, the animals were waiting by the door of the cage in which they spent nights. A few minutes earlier they had heard Les Harris climb out of bed. He came through the gate carrying a pan and a whisk. He refreshed the water-bowl, and was rewarded by a gurgling growl from the female, which he understood to convey something like appreciation. Two clean rolls of scat lay on the concrete floor. He made a quick, diagnostic inspection and flipped them into the pan.

Although the fences outside stood higher than two metres, Harris was careful not to release the cage-gate until he had snapped the female to her long chain. The male had a malformed fore-leg, an old injury which denied him any useful leap, but the female could have made it over the top with a standing jump. When the gate opened, the male trotted peaceably out. The female took off as if she was unbridled. She accelerated right, turned this into a fast arc left, and came to rest at the bottom of the yard. The quadrant she had covered, in not much more than a second and a half, represented nine-tenths the perimeter of the yard. It was all accomplished without quite straightening her chain. This was a daily phenomenon designed, so it seemed, to exhibit speed and exuberance, and to show that she knew the length of that chain to the millimetre.

The animals were well settled by the time Harris was ready to leave for work. He walked, briefcase in hand, out of the front door and towards his car, pausing at the mesh gate. They were waiting there already for his passing. Nothing in the behaviour of dingoes is random and, as far as Harris could judge, they did not expect randomness in anyone else.

It grieves Harris that the dingo is so misunderstood in its own country. In an effort to set this to rights, he addresses around five meetings a month. He is a lean, energetic and voluble man, whose beard shows ruddy lights when he speaks. His voice has been scorched by many cheroots. He describes himself as moderately aggressive, and is not then thinking of the rough peaks of his personality so much as a fair descriptive average. In conversation, the circumstance most likely to release a bellow from Les Harris is any suggestion that the dingo is a dog.

The dingo, he says, is a wolf. Its ranking on the canine chart appears on the third pedestal down, below the major mountain, forest, and tundra wolves of northern latitudes, but on the level of the Indian wolf, *Canis lupis pallipes*, and the American Coyote, *Canis latrans*. So closely does the dingo resemble the Indian wolf that zoologists have difficulty distinguishing between them by eye. Harris likes to refer to the group as natural canids, to set them apart from animals more properly described as dogs. The conformation and behaviour of dogs have been influenced by human judgement. Natural canids have maintained strength and intelligence of an entirely different order, and according to far more utilitarian forces. The most significant of those forces is, as Harris sees it, the animal's need to make a kill every day of its life. Harris calls this 'the primary imperative'.

He caught the seven-thirty newscast in the car. A terse report noted that Azaria Chamberlain's clothing was found in scrub close to a dingo cave. Dingoes from that lair were to be shot, and stomach contents examined by forensic analysts. By the time he swung through the Commonwealth Aircraft Corporation gateway, his mood was grim.

Harris worked at the northern end of the airfield. The broad runways here have been silent for many years, for parts of Melbourne now lie under each approach and aerial activity is restricted to helicopters. But the amount of flying which takes place at the altitude of drawing-boards, testing-rigs, and the quiet chambers of the mind is prodigious. The vast factories and workshops are still in use. Here aircraft are designed, manufactured, repaired. Harris parked his car and walked to a building labelled Aircraft Factory One. It was a hangar with a narrow mezzanine of offices, suspended like a gallery at first floor level. The desk in Harris's office was little tidier than his desk at home. He was engaged, at this time, in writing operation manuals for the pilots and flight-engineers of certain defensive reconnaisance aircraft. Most days he found the task absorbing. This morning there was, on his desk, a newspaper clipping which competed insistently for his attention. The item, one he had cut from the Melbourne *Age* the Friday before, was headed 'Man Turns on the Dingo.' The last paragraph read: 'Unless evidence is found to prove otherwise, the dingo will carry the blame. Dingoes will be shot on sight until they realize it is no longer safe to scavenge for food.' Harris's duty to the operation manual held out until the coffee-break. He then reached for his phone and booked a call to the Alice Springs police headquarters.

He was put through to Inspector Gilroy. Gilroy seemed pleased enough to be talking to someone of authority on dingo behaviour. 'There aren't many around,' he said. But it was not in Harris's nature to wait on pleasantries. He started right in.

'Shooting those dingoes is an act of stupidity,' he said. 'These chaps don't know what they're doing.'

'The scientific branch wants the stomach contents,' Gilroy answered. 'If there's human tissue in there, they'll find it.'

'They'll find nothing. In less than twenty-four hours everything has passed through. After that they ought to be examining droppings.'

'A dingo might still be feeding on the remains.'

'Forget remains. There won't be any remains. Dingoes don't live like that. They'll take it all in one hit. A female might share it with a litter. But it will all go. We're talking about dingoes in the wild. They can't afford not to eat it all, right off. With small mammals, they eat the lot, fur and all. With birds, they eat the feathers. You had no longer than an hour to find remains, and twenty-four for stomach contents. After that, shooting the dingoes is destroying the most important observable evidence.'

'How's that?'

'It would have taken maybe four days. Observers and cameras. Dingoes are territorial. You could have plotted the territories, recorded the habits of all the dingoes in the area, and narrowed the possibilities down to perhaps four animals. Now you've got nothing.'

'We have the clothing. That is the thing we are interested in right now. Would you have expected a dingo to have eaten the clothing?'

'We're not talking about goats. Dingoes will unwrap meat pilfered from a box. They will eat a chocolate-bar and discard the foil. They eat what they perceive as food.'

'They perceive a baby as food?'

'Sure they do. Any small mammal is food. Wolves have eaten babies throughout recorded history.'

'This baby weighed ten pounds. Our people here say that is too heavy for a dog to carry off without dragging. There isn't enough sign of dragging.'

'Look. Inspector. You're getting it all wrong. Stop thinking dog, think wolf. Dingoes carry wallabies off, for God's sake. They drag kangaroos, they can carry twenty-five pounds of wallaby. Ten pounds is nothing. A dingo will run with ten pounds.'

Gilroy concluded the conversation with a promise to send photographs of the baby's clothing, but without a promise to call off the shooting of dingoes. Harris checked his wristwatch. The call had taken a half hour, but there was nothing about it to suggest that the police might now abandon, as an evidentiary benchmark, the familiar behaviour of dogs.

6

IT IS THE DISPOSITION of policemen to be attentive to rumour, and anyone spending time around the common-room or the water-cooler at Alice Springs headquarters would have heard, within four days of the clothing discovery, that the Azaria Chamberlain case might soon pass from Michael Gilroy to Graeme Charlwood. Charlwood held detective-sergeant's rank in Criminal Investigation. He was known as an especially vigorous young man. His gaze was habitually insistent. A dark crescent moustache, of the cut popular among Australian tennis-stars and cricketers, marked an interest in demonstrable success. An effortless and deceptive air of the laconic marked him as a tactician.

Charlwood had recently returned, after a few days away somewhere. There was yet no official comment about that. The betting was police headquarters, Darwin.

* * *

On Saturday morning, 30 August, a terminal in the telex-room at Alice Springs headquarters began the transmission of messages directed to motor registration departments in every state. The messages requested the names and addresses of motor-vehicle owners, and the registrations listed here numbered in the hundreds. All were vehicles recorded at the Ayers Rock camping-ground, overnight, on 17 August.

The telexes were authorized by Graeme Charlwood. Charlwood's assignment to the case began on Thursday, 28 August, although he had, with not untypical impatience, sent a subordinate to Ayers Rock for these registrations two days earlier than that. He should soon stop by at Gilroy's office to assume possession, officially, of the investigation. But that could await a proper time.

Inspector Gilroy was in his office. He had chosen Saturday to write up the file. It was a difficult task. He had been growing uneasy for some time now, and his notes reflected it plainly. Suspicion had engaged him more slowly than it had engaged anyone else, but this was the sort of case in which opinions could be changed by every new item of information. There was plenty now, and he wrote:

Azaria Chamberlain was born at 1.16 p.m. on Wednesday the 11th of June 1980 at Mt Isa Hospital, at a weight of 2880 grams (6 pounds 5½ ounces). The mother was reported to have repeatedly complained about the child being sick, stated that she was suffering from pyloric stenosis, an ailment which closes the sphinctum and causes vomiting. She would not heed hospital staff when they told her the baby was completely normal.

She allegedly told the staff that her other children suffered from the same complaint and that she had cured it herself when she had fallen down a hole carrying them as young babies.

It is reported that she appeared not to have cared for the baby, and at one stage did not feed it for over eight hours. Registration of the baby was never completed.

When bringing the baby in for a check-up she astounded the Sisters by having the baby dressed completely in black. A doctor who treated the baby said that she did not react like a normal mother.

The same doctor said that he looked up the name Azaria in a

Dictionary of Names and Meanings and found that it means 'Sacrifice in the Wilderness'.

On visiting the library on Saturday morning, I found that this book is in stock but has been mislaid. It is believed it should be available on Monday.

The parents appeared on the TV show 'This Day Tonight' on Channel Seven, on Friday evening, 29 August 1980. Mrs Chamberlain allegedly made the comment that the blanket which covered Azaria was a strong one and difficult to cut with a knife. (The blanket which we took possession of at Ayers Rock had numerous small cuts in it which, even to the layman, looked more like cuts from a sharp instrument than punctures one would expect from a dog's teeth.)

Gilroy had intended finishing the memorandum there, but carried on, instead, with an addendum designed to give some direction to the investigation.

To date we have actually not one witness who can say they saw the baby at Ayers Rock, but people who have assumed she was holding a baby when they have seen her holding a white bundle to her breast.

The impression given in her statement to me was that the two boys climbed the Rock with their father, and she was left at the bottom with the baby in the car. Later on in her statement, she states when she was at the Fertility Caves with the baby (when the dingo 'cased' it). The two boys were with her but the husband was not. They would appear to have descended by themselves. Where the clothes were found was not more than four hundred metres from there. Constable Morris was instructed to check out the floor of the caves for patches of soft earth, etcetera. Many tourists have visited them since, and he has, no doubt, contacted them. He is also reinterviewing the ranger who saw Mrs Chamberlain at the bottom of the climb that Sunday afternoon, who saw her holding the apparel of a baby.

7

THE SMALL ADMINISTRATIVE CEREMONY was done. Gilroy sat at his desk until the retreating door had closed. The file had gone with Charlwood. The building was quiet. The sergeant had chosen Sunday upon which to displace the authority of the inspector, a decision certain to reflect well his capacity for tactfulness.

8

COME MONDAY, Gilroy was ready to complete unfinished business. He made through the main doors, down the steps, and out to the wide footpath. The business of which he was thinking concerned the reports, from Mt Isa, presenting Mrs Chamberlain as an uncaring, and perhaps wicked, mother. It troubled him that the doctor who originated those reports was so carefully anonymous. In response to medical ethics, so he'd said. Michael Gilroy was now bent on checking that doctor's one verifiable claim: that Azaria was a cipher for sacrifice.

He turned south on Todd Mall, keeping to the kerbside, wide of shoppers and souvenir hunters, and on to the library. The Dictionary of Names and Meanings was waiting for him at the desk. He carried it to a reading-table and thumbed through the pages.

There was no entry at all for Azaria. But a masculine form, Azariah, covered twenty-five separate biblical entries. It translated from the Hebrew as 'Whom God Aids'. The nearest association with sacrifice was the name Azazel. He slapped the volume shut. Not even close.

Outside, he paused on the sidewalk. There was a small park, popular with girls in sunny frocks, with sleepy magazine-readers, and whirling children. Suspicion and intrigue seemed far from here, part of another, darker world. Gilroy drew a breath and walked on.

EVIL EYE

EVERY PART OF TOWN

1

SEVENTH-DAY ADVENTISTS in Mt Isa refer to their church as community-centre style. They mean by this a building used as much for instruction as for worship. It is made from plain concrete blocks. There is a hall, which does duty as a tabernacle, and subsidiary rooms for the meetings of elders and for classes in Bible, nutrition, and health. Michael Chamberlain was pastor here. He preached, he gave public classes in health. An anti-smoking campaign was his particular interest, as it had been in his parishes at Burnie in Tasmania, and Innisfail in Queensland. He was quite innovative about this, which did not surprise anyone who knew he was a convert to Adventism and at one time a smoker. The props he used included an articulate physician, a sorely anatomical movie in colour, and two pall-bearers who, at the end of proceedings, walked the aisle carrying a small coffin into which the congregation threw their cigarette-packets and lighters. Of all these. Michael Chamberlain thought the coffin the most effective.

In the hall, which takes up the front of the building, he brought his congregation to devotion. By August 1980 he had led them, in prayer and song, each Sabbath for seven months. The hall is spare and resounding, and is of intimate size as far as places of worship go, but the needs of this ministry are modest. Parishoners number around sixty adults.

2

MT ISA is no spiritual town. The high steeples here rise, not from churches, but from the furnaces necessary for smelting metals. The tallest smoke-stack is a disappointing thirty metres shorter than the Eiffel Tower but is tall enough that the nearest peaks of the Selwyn Ranges don't seem as spectacular as they once were. So not to ambush unwary aircraft, the chimney is white. The next most hazardous is painted like a barber's pole, conforming to the symbolism of an earlier age. The ranges stand off to the east and the west, and in the valley between lies the Leichhardt River, named for a German explorer who disappeared somewhere around here and died of thirst. His river divides the mine from the township, or as officials of the company say, divides the lease from the community. But this is something of an attractive myth. When it flows at all, the Leichhardt runs north, but most of the year the river-bed is bare. Mine and township are far more efficiently separated by the railway-track and the flow of ore. Mt Isa is the greatest producer of silver and of lead in the world. This might seem a performance satisfactory to the most avaricious shareholder were it not for the fact that its production of zinc is also prodigious and in copper its world ranking is tenth. Mt Isa Mines Limited uses as its sign the letters MIM, but an emblem which the twenty-seven thousand townspeople here find as memorable is a pennant of grey smoke flying, two hundred and seventy metres high, from a concrete staff. They can see it from any part of town.

The Capricorn parallel is three hundred kilometres south, so Mt Isa is classed as tropical, but this is a celestial technicality since the ground is hot and dusty underfoot, and stony and ungenerous under a plough. It rains here roughly half as much again as on the central desert, south. Mid afternoon temperatures in the winter hover around twenty-five degrees, but the summer seems to most people a longer season, and afternoons commonly get to forty. The company has been known to describe this climate, in recruitment brochures, as delightful. To ameliorate the delight a little, the company fits its office-blocks, executive automobiles, and staff quarters, with very efficient air-conditioning.

The round-trip to which hospitable families treat visitors commonly takes in a sports-ground or two, a swimming-pool, a gymnasium (in thundering use, the doors wide), and a tepid lake where the waters are choppy in the wake of speedboats towing oblique skiers across the path of an innocent sailboat (here someone points to the tall dam-wall built by Australian workmen after an earlier American attempt had fallen down, and laughs), the route then making back again to the level suburbs, to rouged bouganvillea and purple jacaranda facing the streets, where front lawns are moistened daily with water piped underground from the lake and soft hibiscus and yellow butterfly-trees make showy displays in topsoil trucked here from bends in the river-bed far away.

3

THE CHAMBERLAIN HOME is at number 3 in Abel Smith Parade. It shares an allotment with the church, opposite a busy strip of retail shops. The house is painted the colour of iced coffee, and piped with chocolate. It stands high on the foundation-stumps in an effort to stay cool all day long, although some earlier and utilitarian occupant has built an office underneath and lined the rest with open shelves. This is now Friday morning. The Chamberlains are at home. They drove in from Alice Springs yesterday. Lindy Chamberlain's parents, the Murchisons, are here from Nowra, and plan to stay for as long as they are needed. Cliff Murchison, grey-browed and bespectacled, is a long-standing pastor of the church. Another churchman, Harold Harker, who is Michael's superior, has travelled eight hundred kilometres from Townsville to be here. He may, if Michael is not yet up to it, lead the Sabbath services tomorrow.

Sympathetic friends have been calling in all morning, and now a journalist and a photographer from the Sydney magazine *Woman's Day* wait in the lounge-room hoping for an interview. The unpacking has fallen way behind. Gear and clothing is spread about the rooms, some still by the car under the house. Avis Murchison has taken charge of washing and storing the baby-clothes in order to disfranchise her daughter, who ought not be exposed to that chore. Lindy Chamberlain has taken charge of everything else, in order to disfranchise Michael who, so she believes, is not yet capable of making practical decisions. Never-theless Michael trails through the rooms, tidying, but achieving little more than the random rearrangement of things.

Jennifer Richards, Lindy's close friend, dropped by earlier and stayed on. Although she thought of herself as 'in a bit of a dither' in the face of the family's tragedy, it seemed that Lindy liked having her around. Yesterday, the best she could do was leave some food by the doorstep and retreat. Last night, she rang Lindy before midnight, and they talked until two in the morning.

Jennifer is long and lithe, in her thirties. In more normal circumstances she would call in, wearing a short white frock and runners, and take Lindy to tennis or squash. Now she stands in the space underneath the house, where gear has been unloaded from the car, while Lindy sorts through clothing in need of cleaning. A parka belonging to one of the boys is grubby and crumpled.

'It's Reagan's,' says Lindy. 'There's blood on it.' The stain has made the shape of a U. Michael, who seems to have caught something of this from outside, walks in and takes the parka from them. His reasoning is not apparent until he says, 'The police were interested in that,' and leaves, to put through a call to the Alice Springs police-station. His wife takes an exasperated breath. The implication Jennifer Richards gathers from this is that Michael's concern with the needs of the police might leave the rest of them bereft.

Lindy's tracksuit pants are spattered. Quite evidently they are nearly new. She hands them to Jennifer for despatch to Western Dry Cleaners in town. 'Would you be sure they get all the marks out?' she asks. 'I've worn them only once.' The stains look like blood, are on the legs below the knees, and remind Jennifer of a small splash. It is not the sudden proximity to Azaria's blood which now appalls her, but the realization that vivid mementoes of the baby's death will appear for some time yet, according to some persistent and pitiless schedule.

Jennifer follows up the stairs to the kitchen, to gather cans of milk supplement for return to Menzies' Pharmacy, then on to Reagan's bedroom. There is a quaint dissonance in the decoration here: at one end model planes, toy cars, a cricket bat, and a red heart-shaped poster anointed in bold crayon with the words 'Jesus Loves Reagan', and at the other end the beginning of a collection of fluffy toys, a greater use of baby-pink in the drapes, and a white bassinet. This room Reagan would have shared with Azaria.

Lindy takes from a drawer a crepe-paper parcel. She asks that Jennifer return it to the infants' outfitter in town, Playtime. There is no need for her to open the parcel now. Jennifer takes it and turns away, tearful. She was here the day it was brought home. It contains a dress, rich and colourful, the size a baby might grow into at around six months. For so premature an extravagance Lindy had arranged purchase by instalments. The final payment would not have become due until Christmas-time.

4

MICHAEL CHAMBERLAIN did not lead his congregation on the Sabbath-day. He looked tired and, as it seemed to Jennifer Richards and the Murchisons, seriously weakened in spirit. 'I'm not up to it,' he said. 'Prayer should come out of a pure and happy heart. I don't have that, just now.' His father-in-law took the service instead. The hall was crowded. Michael and Lindy sat with the boys in a row near the front. Cliff Murchison throught it wise not to preach too closely to matters of death and resurrection. He chose texts which spoke of the need for love and understanding.

Jennifer called around again on Monday. Indeed she called in every day that week. It was not an enjoyable time, dismal in fact, but she couldn't have stayed away. Lindy was a special friend. They confided in each other: when Jennifer faced problems, it was Lindy who helped to solve them. It was Jennifer's turn to be helpful, courageous, but it was not easy. This was no ordinary bereavement. It had become a public event. Of course this was all according to God's will, everybody here knew that, but it made the proper order of things so complicated. The family could not, now, retreat into sorrow behind drawn blinds. There was a meaning, doubtless to be made plainer to everyone at an appointed time, and, meanwhile, a proper path.

That it was an uneven path came clear when Aidan got home from school.

'What's the matter?' his mother asked.

'Nothing,' he said, but his eyes were evasive.

'Was school okay?'

'I guess so.'

'Something happened that you didn't like,' said Lindy, 'so tell me what it was.'

'Just some of the kids yelling something. They said, "Dingoes don't come into our house stealing babies." '

'Well,' she said, deciding that the moment called for Aidan's prompt promotion to adulthood, 'you can't expect children to understand these things so quickly, can you?' and took him off to find some sweet diversion in the kitchen.

She was soon back, this time to the ringing of the telephone, another call from a city newspaper. Since Sunday, and the telecasts of Azaria's forlorn clothing, the calls were coming in at the rate of six or seven a day. Avis Murchison, who generally managed to get to the phone first and identify the caller, held the hand-piece and whispered the reporter's name. Lindy took it over. 'Bill, what can I do for you? No more news, we're just waiting. We seem to be notified of developments by television, like everybody else. All the newspapers have called today. I don't think there's anything I can tell you that I haven't told them. My parents are staying a while. We're doing the best we can, like any close family. We put our faith in Jesus. And Aidan went to school again today. Fine, just fine. Yes, you could say that. Most people are very sympathetic.'

This was truthful, but a stony and literal truth. Certainly, mail was coming through in volume enough that the mailman carried it in a separate box. Much of it was from friends, or from slight acquaintances of long ago who now remembered the Chamberlains from press photographs. Some came from people moved to write by simple and direct compassion. Of any beginning, 'You don't know me, but . . .' it was not necessary to read much further before the writer's own bereavement made its sad appearance.

But today Lindy had picked out a sheet she had laid aside from the morning mail and handed it to Jennifer. It was very brief, a line or two, but Jennifer read it twice before she began to understand. The writer seemed to accept that a dingo had killed Azaria. It was the twist in the last sentence which was confusing. 'A two-legged dingo, like you.'

'Sick,' Jennifer said. 'Normal people don't behave like this.'

Jennifer was not then referring only to the letter. Michael Chamberlain had taken a telephone call from a woman who did not give her name, but said she had lost her six-year-old son in an accident. She found the Chamberlains' composure affronting. 'We have an inner serenity, I suppose, because Azaria is in the arms of Jesus,' Michael said, but when the caller accused him of being a liar he hung up. Suddenly regretful, he picked up the telephone again but she had gone. Lindy had taken a call from someone who thought the Chamberlains were treating their baby's death as if it were 'a big joke'. None of those conversations was as unsettling as the frequent phantom at the end of an empty line. The caller's silent voice resounded long in the mind.

5

FROM THE BEDROOM Avis Murchison could hear the girls chatting in the lounge. They were Lindy's friends, come to take her jogging. She was now in the adjoining bedroom, changing. Avis was pleased it was happening. The door opened, and Lindy came in holding her running shoes. She was crying. 'Even my runners have blood on them,' she said.

Avis took them from her. Some of the blotches were blood, although the rest she thought looked more like blackcurrant-juice. Avis was a tiny and energetic woman, not often defeated by a stain of any kind. 'I'll scrub these,' she said. 'Wear something else.'

Lindy headed for the bathroom. 'I'd better wash my face,' she said. 'Anyone would think I'm a child.'

6

THE ALICE SPRINGS police station rang through. While Lindy Chamberlain spoke, Michael and the Murchisons came from other parts of the house expecting news of a further find, but it was nothing like that, she said. Somehow the police had let witnesses leave the Rock without making a record of names and addresses.

'They don't have any?'

'Not a one. Or rather, they've got too many. Everyone is registered with the rangers. But they don't know who is who, or anything.'

'There must be hundreds.'

'The people from Esperance, the Wests, they wrote,' Lindy said. 'I can give the police the letter.'

'The little woman, from the caravan further along. With the Christian family. What was her name?'

'Amy something? From somewhere down south. Yes. Whittacker.'

'And the Tasmanian couple. She had a little daughter she held on her hip; he ran into the scrub, searching.'

'They saw a dingo. While we were cooking. Oh, I can't remember.'

Better, it seemed, to write down the information they could summon. It did not make an impressive list. While Lindy took it towards the phone, Michael uttered the strongest expression to which he was accustomed. 'My hat,' he said, 'this is all a bit late in the day.' Lindy dialled the number and was put through to Inspector Gilroy, who was, yet, charged with responsibilities of co-ordination. 'This is all we have, I'm afraid,' she said.

'It's a beginning,' he said. 'If the Tasmanian couple contact you, let me know straight away. Are they the people who saw a dingo around the camp?'

'I think so. Yes, I'm sure.'

'Then you understand how important they are to you.'

'I suppose they are important to everybody,' she said.

'They bear out your story, your sighting of a dingo.'

'There was a dingo.'

'Independent corroboration.'

'I can do that, anyway. One of the blankets still has a paw-mark on it. We have it here.'

'You have?'

'Sure. If you want, I'll send it to you.'

'No. Don't do that,' Gilroy said. 'I'll have it picked up.'

Lindy turned, when the conversation had finished, to the others. 'Now they're interested in the blanket,' she said.

Next morning Michael answered the door to Greg Brown, a constable from local headquarters. Brown's orders were that he take possession of a mat. Michael did not at first understand this, but invited him inside, to the lounge, where Lindy said, 'Oh, they mean the space blanket. We didn't expect anyone so quickly.'

Avis fetched it. Lindy explained that the name derived from garments developed for astronauts: blanket on one side, a shiny metallic weave on the other. They spread it out, pointing to a smudged corner, and held it to the light, showing fissures in the weave. Lindy said, 'There weren't any cuts in it before.' The young policeman might have wondered at the vigour of these demonstrations, since he was presently merely a courier, but when he left, everyone was satisfied that he now knew the importance of the item he carried to the police-car outside.

'There. That ought to put things straight,' Lindy said, and with this her mother was disposed, energetically, to agree.

7

CLOSE FRIENDS ARRIVED quietly at the Chamberlain home. They moved then from the house, across the grass, to the church. Pews there were already occupied by those who had gone directly into the hall. It was Wednesday. Some care had been taken with the invitations so that the gathering would not be mobbed by the press. The occasion was a memorial for the departed child.

The service was taken by the pastors Haker and Kennaway. Mervyn Kennaway was thin and lined, his cheeks shadowed, his fingers nervous. The congregation then facing him numbered close, he thought, to a hundred. No one here doubted that Azaria now dwelt with Jesus, but the parents seemed to him heartbroken. He had watched Lindy Chamberlain's intricate composure disassemble itself as the time for the service drew nearer. The blond boys beside her were pale-faced, and someone had told them not to be fidgety. And Michael, his long-time friend, his brother in Christ, could hardly stand upright.

The last time Mervyn Kennaway led prayer here was also at the invitation of this family. That was a happier day. He was then celebrating the birth of this very child, calling down the blessing of God upon her.

CURIOSITIES

1

EARLY ON MONDAY morning, at around the time the Chamberlains were preparing Aidan for his first day back at school, Western Dry Cleaners in town was preparing to open for business. It is the sort of shop where the air smells of warm steam and spirited compounds. Frocks and trousers make for the rear in dejected queues, and the chatty women who work on the benches despise those flimsy agencies where the toil of their trade is sub-contracted elsewhere.

Joan Hansell, allotted for the day to the spotting-board, found garments there already, the overburden from Friday and Saturday. She picked out a pair of tracksuit pants. They were green and not much soiled, so far as she could see. Laying them out she found the problem below the knees: small dark spots, dribbled downwards, a spattering on each leg. Beside the bench stood an array of solutions, in spray-bottles and coded with primary colours. Mrs Hansell had been working here for three years, and the routine was familiar. With a pad and a soap mixture she rubbed away in case these spots were water-soluble, as chocolate and cordials are. They were not. She took the green-labelled bottle, a preparation she knew to be useful for blood, sprayed the stains, and scrubbed with a small, bristled brush. The residue she vacuumed away. This had removed enough, she thought, to justify passing through the next stages of the regimen, and on to the presser. She was wrong. The pants came back, an hour later, to the board. The stains were faded but not extinguished. This time Mrs Hansell reached for the ammonia. She could think of nothing which would take so unyielding a hold on fabric like this unless it were blood.

2

DR HARRY HARDING was delivered a package from the Northern Territory Police, Darwin. Harding's laboratory was in Adelaide. The academy was the Institute of Medical and Veterinary Science. It was common for the forensic unit in Darwin to send items to the other side of the continent for analysis. The request he now held, from a Constable Myra Fogarty, called for the identification of eight fibres, possibly dingo hair, collected after vacuuming the floor of a tent. The reference was to Azaria Chamberlain Deceased. He had read of the case in the newspapers.

Harding's scientific interest was in hair. His doctoral thesis, completed ten years ago, dealt with the structure and growth of hair. He looked more a successful administrator than a biologist, a picture coloured by bright well-laundered shirts and shiny gold spectacles, and it was he who had established this institute as a centre of biological analysis.

The imprisoned fibres were distributed between two glass slides. Someone, he presumed it was Constable Fogarty, had numbered the slides 32 and 42, a choice which, fleetingly, made the intervening series intriguing. A search for the hairs of a dingo inside the Chamberlain tent was an obvious avenue of inquiry but already, with the slides held to the natural light, only five of the eight were serious contenders.

Harding focused them under the microscope, one by one. Each stood out in thick relief, like a bar across a brightly lit window. It seemed that Constable Fogarty's experience in the forensic unit was not extensive. She had sent Harding five human hairs and three strands of wool.

3

IN A LABORATORY not far from Harding, Dr Andrew Scott also received a consignment from the Northern Territory police. Scott, a fit fair-headed man in his thirties was head of the biology department at the Adelaide Forensic Services Centre. Scott's scientific specialty was the biochemistry of blood.

The parcels yielded Azaria Chamberlain's clothing, her two purple blankets, and a sleeping-bag labelled with her father's name. He took up the singlet. Making notes as he went, he saw it was inside out, judging by the position of the manufacturer's label, and heavily bloodstained. It was also damaged, grubby with red soil, and creased. The line of each crease was clean, so it seemed that the garment was doubled, here and there, before soil stained it.

But he saw then a contrary indication. The bloodstains from the neckline down were heavier on the inside, as he then held it, a condition he would not have expected unless the singlet was fitted the correct way when the blood flowed. No, it was too early yet to be sure. In either event, if the baby had worn a jump-suit over the singlet, the blood may have soaked right through to the skin.

The jump-suit was also soilstained. Scott laid it down, arms and legs outstretched, on the bench. So wretched a garment it seemed in this condition: blood all around the neck, over most of the body, the arms, the legs. It would take a lot of blood to do that. Plainly sufficient to cause death. Sometime he should be able to quantify the loss of blood. The collar was torn. Holes in both arms. Blood was heaviest, he recorded, about the neck. Much had soaked through the weave of the fabric, from one side to the other.

The cuffs around the wrists were designed to fold down, to cover the baby's hands like open-ended mittens. They were heavy with blood, particularly the right. The cuffs might have lain for a time in a pool. Or some small gesture might have caused it. Infant hands fumbling for the place of agony. Clearly, blood had flowed to the chest from somewhere above the collar, from the head or the neck. At that time the baby's head and body were upright. Near the end of the left arm he found a puncture and a smudge of bleeding, but otherwise he could not relate these holes in the clothing, with any sense of conviction, to the emission of blood. Evidently damage to the head, and damage to the suit, were caused by separate events.

Scott then picked over each garment, searching for animal hairs. He could find none. He turned to the remains of the nappy. The absorbent padding bore the residues of old urine, but no blood. The plastic liner was damaged, tears or punctures. This was someone else's technical field. But another feature of the liner caught his eye, a stretch-mark in the plastic. He held it up. The outline and the depth were familiar and provocative: the mark of a human thumb.

So far, Scott had caught nothing of a dingo in his, yet cloudy, picture of the baby's death. He had no experience of dingoes, but it seemed fair to expect signs of slavering over the clothing if the animal had carried the infant off as food. The difficulty was that no biologist in the world yet knew how to detect it. There were ready methods for showing the presence of human saliva, methods familiar to every forensic biologist because they were particularly useful in rape cases. But the matter they detected were enzymes, and this was a problem. Humans begin the chemistry of digestion at the moment food enters the mouth. Digestion is a function of the saliva enzyme ptyalin, and ptyalin is detectable. But dogs do not have it. Chemical digestion occurs, in dogs, below the level of the gulp. If dingo slavering is identifiable on this tiny garment, it must be through the presence of another component. A conclusion Scott would soon reach was this: since no method of detection presently existed, he must invent one.

4

TONY JONES was trying to invent an animal. The fragments of bone he was rearranging on the bench made no familiar mammal, however much he shuffled them. They certainly made no part of a human baby.

This laboratory was in Darwin, at the Casuarina Hospital, where Dr Jones was the pathologist. He had worked there eight months, the sole pathologist, after two years with the Adelaide Institute of Medical and Veterinary Science as a colleague of Harding. His duties now included forensic examinations at the request of government agencies. This one was made by the police department, and the pieces of bone were those picked from the dust by Winmatti, not far from the Cave of Fertility, after the baby's clothing was found.

Jones had fulfilled his part already, by determining that this could not be any remnant of Azaria Chamberlain. The reason his chubby fingers kept fiddling with them now had more to do with curiosity, and perhaps with some sort of scientific patrimony from his physicist father, than anything else. It had become an intellectual game, a puzzle, and the solution began, quite suddenly, to fill in. This was part of a skull. A small marsupial, an adolescent wallaby, perhaps. And here was something else for his brief report: not only was the morphology all wrong for human form, but these splintery pieces were profoundly dry. Traces of membrane or tissue were long gone. The surfaces were grey. This was the condition of bone after many months weathering, perhaps years. Not eleven days.

5

'   COLD STORAGE BINS at the Arid Zone Research Station at Alice Springs held the bodies of troublesome dingoes shot at Ayers Rock. Veterinarians in white smocks laid out the carcasses, slit the bellies, excised stomach and bowel, and drained the slurry. They were searching, on Sergeant Charlwood's instructions, for human bone and human protein. As Les Harris had predicted, they found nothing of the sort.

6

DOGS' TEETH, other than the molars, produce tears in clothing rather than cuts. The plates of the molars can sever fibres, by the action called shearing, but even this causes some crushing at the fibre ends. How cuts may differ from shearing makes for fine problems of definition, complicated by the tricky behaviour of dissimilar yarns and fibres. Nobody in the country was much skilled in the field, and Kenneth Brown, to whom Andrew Scott had delivered the Chamberlain infant's clothing, was doing the best he could. His resources included papers from odontological centres overseas and his eight years' experience as a forensic consultant here in Adelaide. He specialized in tooth-marks, until now those from the biting of human teeth.

He turned first to the singlet. Like Scott, Brown judged from the manufacturer's label that it was now inside out. Some small rectangles had been cut out already for testing in other laboratories. But here, about two centimetres below the front neckline, was an indentation, a deformity of the fabric as he noted it, as if something had been pushed into the weave from the outside with enough force to leave a permanent dent in the material. It did not seem to him consistent with a tooth-mark, since there were no other marks from adjoining teeth. Drying blood had helped to preserve the shape, so it must have been made when the baby's blood was still wet. Whatever instrument caused this, it occurred to Brown that the baby's body might not have been in it then. The dent seemed too deep.

On the back of the singlet he found two small perforations,

neither larger than three millimetres across. Had this been the bite of a dog he would have expected other marks close by. There was none. These holes exhibited a curious feature. Once the singlet was turned the correct way out, the holes seemed to have been made from the inside.

The nappy was in pieces, both padding and cover. A fragment of the plastic caught his attention. Here was a three-cornered rupture which might have been made by a dingo's teeth. No, the perforations around it did not correspond with the spacing of a dog's teeth. Brown was also well supplied with fresh nappies of the same type. When he tried now, using one of these, to duplicate the rupture, he found he could do it only by stretching the plastic until it burst.

The jump-suit collar was much damaged. On the right side, it was asunder in two places. Closest to the right shoulder, severance seemed to have begun at the edge, then changed direction by about a hundred degrees. None of the lower holes, on the body, the shoulders, or the left hip, was attended by the marks he expected from the full bite of a dingo's mouth. And the comparison of the singlet with the jump-suit was interesting. He could find no mark on the front of the suit to correspond with the dent in the front of the singlet.

Brown carried both garments to the microscope. He used one of low power for better perspective. All the fibres he examined showed the characteristics of cutting rather than tearing. The fibre ends were too abrupt. Brown then ruled out, as a cause of any of this damage, the bite of a dingo. He preferred an instrument with a slender, sharp point.

7

TWO PURPLE BLANKETS, which had covered the baby in her bassinet, arrived at Andrew Scott's laboratory in the Adelaide Forensic Services Centre. The weave was said to be damaged. It was again Kenneth Brown's job to determine if this was caused by tooth or claw, or by some other agency altogether. Using Scott's equipment this time, Brown brought the broken threads into focus under a microscope. Here too, the ends of the fibres were clean and precipitate. These were cuts, made by a sharp instrument, some manner of blade.

The next eyes to take a magnified view of those marks were, some time later, Andrew Scott's. Scott had begun by looking for blood, but made a small inquisitive diversion here, although these fibres were not strictly his concern. The strands were neatly severed, right enough. In fact the track here was steep-walled, bluffs on either side, and set back as if there was not enough bulk in the weave ever to have bridged it. Scott followed it along, a highway-cutting at this magnification, until it ran out. Here was a curious structure, tubulous and cosy. A fat cocoon. The discovery brought a swift smile. The blanket had been attacked, not by some wicked blade, but by the gobbling grub of a wool-moth, now alseep.

8

THE BLANKETS CHANGED laboratories, from Scott's to Harding's. The two biologists picked them over, searching for hairs. Some were plain enough to be removed with tweezers, other were lifted off with adhesive tape. Harding made a quick inspection and discarded those of human origin. He was left with fifty-five.

For the next exercise he used a comparison microscope, which allowed him to put a hair from the blanket next to a dingo hair, and control precisely the conditions of magnification and of lighting. Magnification for comparing size, lighting for comparing colour. He selected dingo hairs, from pelts flown down from Alice Springs, to provide a useful array of sizes, hues, and body locations.

Hairs from the blankets ranged in colour from white to brown. Some were banded. In shape they were characteristic of cat or of dog. Between these and the hairs from the dingo pelts there were some differences in structure, but minor in any fair judgement, too subtle to be relied on. Harding could not match any for colour, but the range was broadly acceptable. One could not, he decided, rule out the possibility that these were the hairs of a dingo, although, if he were asked, he guessed cat.

But many of these hairs were old and fractured, and nearly a quarter were, when Harding detected them, embedded in the fibres of the wool. This finding seemed to him far more persuasive than dissimilarities of shape and colour. It put the hairs in the blanket well before 17 August.

9

FOR SOME DAYS NOW, names and addresses had been coming through, list on list, to police headquarters at Alice Springs from vehicle registration centres interstate, identifying the owners of vehicles at Ayers Rock on the 17th. The telex machine rattled off the last and went on with other business. Sergeant Charlwood counted them off. One hundred and thirty one. How many of these might be of any use at all in an investigation like this? Six or eight, maybe. And he could spend weeks getting around the country, interrogating them all one by one, finding owners who had not registered changes of address, or people who had borrowed the vehicle for the trip. There was no lead here, for example, to the people whom the Chamberlains called 'the couple from Tasmania', assuming they ever existed. So Charlwood began to draft a questionnaire. All these people could be interviewed at local police-stations, as long as the questions he drew were, at the one time, wide enough and specific enough. Trouble was, he might still miss something important. It was not easy, interrogation by proxy.

The baby was a little more than three weeks dead. A less wily investigator might, by now, have confronted the parents, demanding explanations of the anomalies in their quite imperfect story, watching all the while for the cunning strategies of conspiracy and for the conceits of invention. Charlwood had other plans, and they were running, near enough, to schedule. He had booked a flight to Ayers Rock for 10 September, there to arrange two scale-charts of the topography, one of the Rock and the road system, another of the camping-ground, correct to the smallest desert oak. The Adelaide biologist, Harding, should join him there on the 13th, after Charlwood had again questioned the local constable and the rangers, and was on familiar terms with the location. Then he and Harding would search for blood.

10

CHARLWOOD CHOSE HARDING alone for this journey because both Andrew Scott and Kenneth Brown were about to begin novel experiments. The day before he left, Charlwood consigned to the freight-hold of Ansett flight 253 two cannisters marked for urgent delivery to the Forensic Services Centre, Adelaide. The temperature in the cannisters was minus one hundred degrees Celcius, and the weight was almost entirely made up by the solid burden of frozen carbon dioxide inside. The objects at the centre of all this heavy packaging were themselves as light as the lading docket pasted on the side. These were sterilized cotton tufts, used to swab saliva from the mouths of dingoes at Ayers Rock, now bound for Andrew Scott.

The materials Brown chose for his experiment were more easily come by: three Johnson and Johnson disposable panty-nappies. The experimental site: Cleland Park. Cleland Park is a wildlife reserve rather than a zoo, and here the dingoes live in landscaped enclosures, grassed and treed. Brown proposed to feed these animals, in place of their more usual evening meal, meat wrapped in nappies. This should simulate the marks made on the plastic liner, more reliably than did the dried dingo skull now mounted on his laboratory bench, when a hungry dingo stripped a nappy from an infant's buttocks.

NOTHING AT ALL LIKE TRUST

1

OF COURSE IT WAS SUNNY, and sunny weather makes for gay frocks and shirts and for a medley of bright voices in the street, even though the street was in Mt Isa and the weather was no surprise. Michael Chamberlain felt better than he had for some while. He was used to people thinking of him as a keen and lively young churchman, and now it was time he was seen out and about. Stories were abroad of his arrest. Here he was, shopping. His little car was parked at the kerbside, as clean as a buttercup.

He was heading for Western Dry Cleaners. This was the one errand of the day which could fracture his mood, but he shouldn't be in there for more than a minute. The bundle he carried inside and laid on the counter was Lindy's sleeping-bag. It was blood-spotted. The police had no interest in it. Lindy was right, he couldn't throw everything away.

He folded the docket into his wallet and walked outside, having forgotten already the date on which he should go back again. He had a couple of other calls to make. The footpath was busy. There was a time not so long ago when walking a busy street was not a complicated thing to do. Now it called for a series of judgements. He chose an earnest gait, after all he was not browsing. He caused no distraction among the faces advancing, as far as he could see, but did he leave a wake of backward glances? A month past, say, he might have expected the occasional pleasantry, but his memory of the way he lived a month ago now seemed disjunctive and invalid. He had gathered from Lindy that he was becoming vague.

The route took him beyond a news-stand. Tatty placards,

propped against the hoarding, hawked the headlines of the day. Banners from the morning presses held nothing to slow his pace. The weekly, *Truth*, headlined a story entitled: 'We Didn't Kill Our Baby'. Michael turned back, searching his pockets for change, his fingers suddenly inept.

He found Lindy in the kitchen. She recalled the interview clearly enough. The reporter, who telephoned her from Melbourne, had a list of stories he said were doing the rounds down there. Some she had heard already from the faithful Jennifer Richards. Some she had not heard about at all. Michael opened the pages across the table.

The mother of 'dingo death' baby Azaria Chamberlain has attacked rumour-mongers who have accused her and her husband of murdering their child. She bitterly denied gossip that baby Azaria had been taken to the top of Ayers Rock and slain as a human sacrifice. Mrs Lindy Chamberlain spoke out as teams of police continued their investigations into Azaria's strange disappearance.

'People are saying she was a spastic baby or a cretin, and that she should have died naturally in a few months. Others are saying she was a sickly baby and this was a good way to get rid of her. They are saying that her father did it and hid the body, and that her father is in custody.'

Mrs Chamberlain said anybody who knew her and her husband were 'absolutely shocked' and so were all genuine people around Australia. 'God has given us the strength to cope with her death but going down the street people are talking about us.'

She also hit out at rumours that she and her husband were linked to the cult that led to the Jonestown mass suicide in South America two years ago. She had heard rumours that Azaria had been sacrificed to atone for the sins of the 7th-day Adventist Church, and a memorial erected as part of a religious ceremony.

'You know what they've done,' Michael said.
'Anyone can see what they've done.'
'What they've done,' Michael said, as if she was not bringing her mind to the point, 'is use you to sell this rubbish, front page.'
'Well, it seemed right to talk to them at the time.'
Michael rang a supervisor at the telephone authority. The best they could do, she suggested, was programme the number for

operator-connection and turn away calls from the press. But he should understand that they were not infallible. A reporter who posed as a friend would get through. She thought they were cheeky enough to try it. Michael understood that, all right.

2

LINDY WAS RUNNING LATE. The kindergarten was out in a few minutes. There were the Richards' children she must pick up; Jennifer was shopping. By the time she got to the school-yard, mothers waited already around the gate, chatting. Children began to spill from the door, all of them at the age when boys talk to girls and girls to boys. They came on the adults like a merging flock, pushing between and talking still, at the level of hips and shopping baskets, drawn to their mothers' flanks by some method of perception not much to do with sight. The Richards' children hadn't come out yet. She caught, from a woman's voice not far ahead, the words '. . . if a dingo had taken my baby'.

'Everyone's different,' someone said. 'She's got a lot of courage.'

'She shows no regret. I saw her on TV.'

'Well, everyone's different.'

Not for a moment did Lindy Chamberlain consider concealment. She pushed through. 'That's me you're talking about,' she said. 'You shouldn't go on like this.' Heads turned, a face whitened, a hand flew to a mouth. Lindy gathered up the two tiny, surprised Richards, leaving behind her enough aftermath of silence that she could hear: 'Really, I didn't know she was there.'

3

THE AIR WAS CALM, the afternoon waning and fragrant. Lindy and Michael were in the rear garden. They looked around together as someone came by the side of the house. They had not heard the doorbell. It was no one they knew. She was wheeling a bicycle, a short woman in early middle-age. Her face carried heavy lines around the eyes and the mouth. 'You're the Chamberlain people,' she said. Perhaps Michael nodded. 'Good,' she said, 'I want a word with you.'

Michael was disposed to make some sort of courteous reply but, far too quickly for him, Lindy said, 'Well, what is it?'

'I'm here to help you,' she said. 'This trouble you're in. Awful. What you need is someone you can trust.' Her smile invited nothing like trust. 'Tell everything to. And discretion. Whatever you've done, you know what I mean? Nothing ever to pass my lips.' This she illustrated with a finger. 'I am a social worker,' she said. 'And a practising Catholic.' Michael was more interested in the behaviour of the bicycle, which, under her hand, had taken up a nauseating motion of its own.

It took a little time to turn her away. Lindy's lips were tight with outrage. Michael supposed he should put through a call to the local priest, in case the woman was in the parish. Although how anyone exercised pastoral control over drunks was not a skill with which he was himself familiar.

4

ON THE WAY HOME from school Aidan was followed. He well remembered that he was not to talk to strangers, but there seemed subtle differences between what he was warned of then and what was happening now. A well-dressed woman, old enough to be someone's grandmother, had left the bus stop at which she was waiting and caught him up. 'Tell me what really happened to your little sister,' she whispered, over his shoulder. He couldn't shake her off. 'You can tell me,' she said.

The others were rich with gossip. Jennifer had a friend who travelled a great deal and who passed time in the car listening to CB. 'What about?' Lindy asked.

Evidently Jennifer had decided that tittle-tattle could assume too much importance altogether. 'Oh, the usual stuff,' she said. 'Sacrifice, and things like that.'

5

AND MICHAEL had abandoned all hope that the aggravated tooting, from automobiles dawdling past the house, figured only in his shrill imagination.

6

THE SLEEPING-BAG ought to be ready at Western Dry Cleaners. Michael called in. Joan Hansell, rostered today at front-of-house, set it down on the counter. Michael seemed in no hurry to unfold it. 'The bloodspots came out?' he asked.

'Well, it didn't have any special treatment.' Mrs Hansell checked the ticket. 'Only a general clean, it says here. I guess that's what it got.'

'But I'd like it cleaned properly,' Michael said.

'It's cleaned properly, if you mean it that way. Only, blood should come to the spotting-board. Any spots on it now won't be too noticeable. It's not dirty, or anything like that.'

But Michael shook his head. 'It is the blood of my daughter Azaria,' he said, and picked up the docket. He caught the door as it closed after a departing customer, a woman about whom there was something a little odd. She had waited quite patiently throughout the whole of his conversation there, and then walked off without transacting any business.

7

MICHAEL PUT THE PHONE DOWN. Lindy sat in a lounge-chair, mending socks. 'That was a detective, Morris,' Michael said.

'From Ayers Rock?'

'No, another one. Here in town. He says a baby under six months has peculiar blood, and they can't identify Bubby's unless they have ours first. We have to call in to the hospital.'

'When?'

'Soon. He says it's all just a matter of routine.'

FACES IN THE BLOODSTREAM

1

PREJUDICE AND BIGOTRY are processes familiar enough, but you wouldn't expect them to be studied in a chemistry laboratory. The terms have a soft-science ring. They seem to belong in social commentaries and in papers on group behaviour. Pick up a lexicon of the hard sciences, a biology dictionary, for example, and typically the entry after biennial is bilateral, and after preformation comes premaxilla. Bigotry and prejudice are exempt. But they're there in translation, right enough. The words biologists use are immunity and resistance, although what they are often watching for are prejudices, the acts of discrimination of one group of particles against another. So important are they that these days every diagnostition and every haematologist is part immunologist. It is discrimination which allows biologists to group blood according to type, and to distinguish the blood of an infant from an adult. For there are in human tissues, and particularly usefully in blood, the strains of a complex and predicatable talent for bigotry.

Blood is a tissue, as biologists adamantly affirm, vigorous, mobile and well populated. They mean by tissue a system of cells living together in some sort of framework. For blood cells the framework is plasma, a fluid, and an advantage for tissue which has to go to work at the double. Blood goes to work on the run, in step with a drum-beat far away, every pace forward but no pace back, retreat forbidden by muscles lining the corridor, flexing.

The way of life here is hard-working and crowded. Nearly half the volume of whole blood is occupied by the cells. Most are red, tight with the pigment haemoglobin, and more or less evenly distributed through the plasma. Red cells work all the time, moving oxygen and carbon dioxide about, and life expectancy is only a hundred and twenty days. Someone with a mathematical bent has calculated that they die and are manufactured, in the adult body, at the rate of two and a half million every second. In a healthy bloodstream, red cells outnumber white by about five hundred to one. White cells are colourless rather than white and, though they are not all of the same family, are all poisoners of foreign microbes, generally inactive until there is something to do. They have an astounding capacity for leaving the slim capillaries, whenever they are needed elsewhere, by squeezing through the walls, a contortionist's trick that red cells aren't able to pull off. Small discs, platelets, float along between the larger cells. These are fragments shed by cells in the bone marrow, and their work has to do with sticking together in dangerous times, releasing the hormone serotonin to contract a damaged blood vessel, and keeping fluid loss to a minimum by clotting.

Some of the smaller voyagers in the bloodstream, salts and glucose for instance, are tinier than the molecular mesh of the side walls. They could simply flow through the weave if it were not for the plasma proteins, particularly albumin, whose duty it is to keep smaller molecules in place. This it achieves by the influence of osmosis, a chemical expression of sympathy and compassion: albumin needs salt and glucose more than does the tissue outside, so they stay around. The labours of other plasma proteins, like haptoglobin, globulin and fibrinogen, are more various. Haptoglobin sweeps up free haemoglobin from around leaky red cells before it becomes toxic. Globulins transport antibodies with which to fight disease, but are prone to overenthusiasm and often create allergies as well. Fibrinogens stay in solution in the plasma until summoned by platelets nearby. Injured platelets give out thromboplastin, an enzyme which fibrinogens interpret as a scream of distress. Fibrinogens come out of solution then to produce threads, a sticky net, tying together platelets and other cells as they come past, a crimson sargasso, drying to brown. This is a scab.

Other inhabitants of the plasma are not often of much interest to the forensic analyst—the inorganic chemicals, the soluble gases, tissue debris, and so forth—beyond provoking a cheery and persistent wonder at the multitude of intricate systems operating in the bloodstream of the most unremarkable human being.

As if to keep that sense of wonder going awhile, individual

differences occur in the way those intricate systems work. There
are alternatives available. Charles Darwin joyously attributed all
tendencies towards variousness to 'the nature of the organism'
and so redirected inwards the search for the meaning of life.
Gregor Mendel found rules of heredity growing in his garden and
bred a first generation of pondering geneticists. Somewhat as an
attenuated by-product of all this, the forensic biologist now
chooses from an array of fourteen blood classification methods,
and can predict the range of groups available to a yet unconceived
child.

The texture of the casing around red blood cells is not the
same in all of us. Neither is the molecular recipe for the
haemoglobin they carry, nor the structure of proteins floating
through the plasma. The variations are many and the possible
combinations many more, but the particles are all tiny, and the
molecular variations tinier still. They are detectable in the
laboratory only because the particles themselves recognize their
differences. Proteins appear to believe deeply in the rejection of
foreigners, however well meaning the newcomers might be. At
times this borders on the irrational, and makes a transplant—say,
a transplant of a donated heart—something of a risky exercise in
persuasion. Blood is not a gregarious tissue. Brought to close
quarters, protein from one blood group will react against certain
protein from another with antagonism, vehement and predictable.

A laboratory analyst, with a sample of blood for grouping,
will normally head for Landsteiner's ABO method, an old
technique and still the most popular. In its simplest form it
distinguishes four blood types: A and B and AB and O. It relies
on the reaction of some proteins, the antibodies in blood plasma,
against the red cells of another. In place of plasma as a test-
pond, the method calls for serum, a clear yellow fluid, which is
plasma after fibrinogens and other agents are cleared away.
These days ready-made serum is sold off the shelf, certified to
contain vigorous antibodies, and called antisera to emphasize its
undeviating ill humour. The analyst takes antisera with antibodies singlemindedly hostile to any A cells, and antisera hostile to
B cells, and anoints a laboratory plate, or a glass slide maybe,
with a glistening bead of each. From the blood-sample to be
tested, the analyst draws off red cells—separated by now from its
own plasma, through a handy centrifuge most likely—depositing
a tincture of red in each bead of antisera, and carries the slide to
a microscope.

A red cell is shaped like a life-raft, roundly inflated and with a membranous floor, the same whichever side is up. This is the best possible geometry for a carrier of haemoglobin, which needs, at the one time, surface area and volume to move oxygen and carbon dioxide about. On the surface are the trade-marks of genetic manufacture, the molecular patterns. The configurations here are recognized by antibodies in the ponds of antisera. Antibody hostility causes clotting of the red cells. They seem to draw together into a defensive formation, plain under the microscope.

The number of reactions available is four. Clotting in the anti-A pond, but not in the anti-B, indicates that the visiting cells are of group A, since the antibodies there will be agitated by nothing other than the appearance of A cells, specificity as it is called. Clarity in the anti-A pond, with clotting in the anti-B, indicates group B in the red cells, plainly enough. Clotting in both ponds shows that the red cells are stamped with the patterns of A and B together, indicating the grouping called AB, the one permissible amalgamation. The remaining possibility now, clarity in both ponds, demonstrates that the visiting cells show neither A nor B patterns, purely or intertwined. It is an unruffled blank, for the purposes of this method, the cells unrecognizable as foe by the antagonists either of A or B, and called by Landsteiner O.

There might be, in the molecular deep of the blood, unique matter identifying the tissue with an individual, rather than a class. Some biologists think so, but science has not yet got there. Landsteiner's ABO system provides a coarse grid intended, first of all, to save from death patients in need of transfusion, and not so much to give law-courts proof of furtive paternities or blood-spattered felony. Although only three or four per cent of people in this country can claim the blood group AB, about ten per cent have B, forty per cent A, and forty-six O.

The best science can do right now is narrow the field by submitting one blood sample to several methods of classification. It is not considered of much use to choose more than one red-cell grouping system. Using the same sort of reasoning as a navigator fixing position by reference-points as dissimilar as possible, a biologist will usually make now for another mark in the blood-stream, an enzyme or a protein, haptoglobin, perhaps.

Haptoglobin, the street-sweeper, takes up crimson haemoglobin leaked from ruptured red cells and holds it harmless until recycled in the liver. Haptoglobin is a protein. The amino acids of which proteins are made carry an electric charge, and the convenient thing is that they are charged differently. If pushed in the same direction, by an independent current, some will travel faster and further than others, a process of separation called electrophoresis. This is not unlike certain races in which everyone starts from the barrier at the same time, and results are determined by the placings along the track when the race is called off. A few drops of serum, containing the proteins to be separated, are drawn from the sample blood and squeezed into a hole, a well, made in a plate of gel. These plates are often no larger than a cigarette-paper. Because only some proteins are positively charged, and the test requires all negative charges, the gel is chemically arranged to move all values as a block towards the negative, without distorting the relationship between them. All proteins will then start down the track, in the same direction, as the test begins.

When the current is disconnected and the plate taken up, each protein has travelled in the direction of the anode with varying efficiencies. The stained plate now shows each protein as a bar across the track, successive brush-strokes like a cartoonist's impression of a shudder. The furthest is albumin, a fast mover because it has the greatest negative charge. The gammaglobulins are not so energetic and don't get far from the well. Haptoglobin will show up, in one of the three forms available to the human bloodstream, allowing itself to be grouped into Hp 1 or 2-1 or 2, as these classifications go, according to the position it made before final flagfall.

A simple foot-race like this will identify matter other than protein, and it makes good sense for a questioning analyst to turn now to a blood component of a quite different order, to an enzyme, say. Phosphoglucomutase—PGM is easier—is an enzyme present in most bodily tissue, including the red and white cells of the blood. It is there to help with the metabolism of glucose. PGM is a genetic marker: the forms in which it is available to the human body are determined by parentage. These groups are known as PGM 1, 2, 3, and in an effort at finer tuning a plus or a minus indicates the graduations between. In electrophoretic testing, the sample to be identified is run alongside known samples, all on the one plate but in separate lanes, and when the current is switched off the bars made by PGM in the unknown sample are compared with those in the known. PGM 3, with smaller molecules, wades more quickly through the soggy gel and makes it well up the track. PGM 1 is always the laggard.

A biologist might use the same sort of test to separate various forms of the pigment haemoglobin, just as Andrew Scott now does on a day in mid September, drawing off red blood cells from a sample, brutally, bursting red cells to free enough haemoglobin into the serum. Haemoglobin moves well under electrophoresis, and shows clearly any unusual forms. A plate Scott disconnects from the current shows two bars where haemoglobin has come to rest. This sample he had soaked earlier from Azaria Chamberlain's jump-suit. The two bars here are adjacent. They constitute, more accurately, an overlap. The first is in the position Scott would expect of haemoglobin A, the normal adult form. The second lies slightly behind and is less vivid a band. This is undeniably haemoglobin F, the form dominant in the blood of a foetus, a vivacious charmer of oxygen from a mother's bloodstream, but short lived. It normally drops to one per cent or so by the age of six months. The vividness of this stain works here as an indicator of its volume. To Scott's eye, around twenty-five per cent of the haemoglobin here is foetal, the remainder adult. This is a pleasing, but not unexpected finding. The blood of a ten-week-old baby ought to contain the two haemoglobins in about this proportion.

Phials standing in a rack on Scott's laboratory bench on 15 September 1980 hold extracts of bloodstains taken from two blankets, a sleeping-bag, Reagan's jacket, and the baby's clothing, each classified according to the HBO system, and by phosphoglucomutase, and by haptoglobin. Scott has, today, carried out the same tests on two later arrivals. The first, a blood sample from Michael Chamberlain, he classes PGM 1, Hp 1, and group O; the second, from Lindy Chamberlain PGM 1, Hp 2, and group A.

Any child of these parents, as Scott concludes, must inherit PGM 1, Hp 2-1, and either group A or group O. Blood he has extracted from Azaria's clothes shows PGM 1, Hp 2-1, and group O.

Blood on Reagan's jacket and on the bedding gives the same answer. This does more than simply identify the blood of the missing baby. It should also put to rest a piece of new gossip, current around Sydney and Melbourne: the child killed at Ayers Rock was not a child of the Chamberlain couple, but the result of a stealthy and adulterous union, so this rumour runs, a story retold at dinner-parties, taking on convincing and incremental detail as it moves along.

PARTISANS

1

JENNIFER RICHARDS was showing her grit. Other visitors to number 3 Abel Smith Parade were now not so numerous, and this seemed reason enough for Jennifer to call by more often. She didn't feel the need to display an excuse, but suggestions of tennis or squash came conveniently to hand whenever easy chatter began to run out, or Lindy had to be diverted from some thought that had arrested her in mid conversation. It was the unusual duality of Jennifer's role which made her uneasy. Steadfastness in a friendship held no problems for her, although she would not have thought herself more resolute than she judged every Christian ought to be. It was as a gatherer of tidings she felt increasingly uncomfortable. The tidings were so malevolent. People Jennifer spoke to were surprised that Michael Chamberlain was at a meeting in Townsville and not in jail, as they'd heard tell. She knew, from her travelling friend, that the CB wave-bands were still considered the established conduits for information. And to the popular inventory of rumour had been added another, now, that Azaria was injured in a fall from a supermarket trolley, and denied medical treatment (often described as a blood-transfusion or as essential surgery) by fanatical parents. This version exhibited some confusion between Seventh-day Adventism and some other group, Jehovah's Witnesses very probably, but this didn't make the rumour any easier to subdue. Was the world so ignorant of Adventist surgeons and nurses and hospitals as this? Indeed the kernel of the story was true, Azaria had fallen from the trolley. Lindy had taken her to the hospital, although nothing appeared amiss. The doctors pronounced the baby unharmed. Gossip pronounced her irreparably damaged, retarded, and later despatched by her father because of it.

It seemed to Jennifer that the mere recounting, even to Lindy Chamberlain, of whispers like these gave to them a certain shameful credibility. Her solution was to keep such things more and more to herself, until the winds of scandal blew themselves out. Meanwhile she should stay fast by Lindy, especially on evenings when Michael was not there. But what sorts of times were these, when the happy conversation of gentle friends is suspended by the siren of a police-car far away?

2

MORE MAIL CAME IN than Lindy could possibly answer. Close to five hundred letters by now. She read every one, sorting them then into neat bundles. The genuinely sympathetic out-numbered the cranks, overwhelmingly. The cranks she filed separately since they deserved no reply.

Not all were so easy to classify. There was a middle ground. Some, quite heart-torn writers, were plainly silly about it. Take, for example, one late in September. It was prompted, evidently, by a report in a southern newspaper captioned 'Mother Murders Baby?' This had so upset the couple—it was signed by a husband and wife—that they spent the first vivid paragraph describing their sense of affront. 'We trust you are able to ignore those slanderous statements,' they wrote, for which sentiment Lindy Chamberlain was grateful, but they went on to a suggestion of public support and a donation towards the cost of a memorial. Endearing though it was, the offer of a public statement by two people unconnected with the events seemed to pitifully misjudge the way the world worked. On re-reading, perhaps it was stimulated by no more noble a motive than publicity-seeking, and best not encouraged by an answer. Lindy Chamberlain noticed nothing familiar in the Hobart address at the top of the page, nor in the names Greg and Sally Lowe, and made no connection with the couple she had described to Inspector Gilroy a fortnight ago as 'the people from Tasmania.' So she filed the letter away with the cranks.

3

THE MEETING, for which Michael Chamberlain was then in Townsville, was of ordained ministers. During registra-

ion and induction, pastors who had known him in earlier days
offered sympathy, tactfully brief, and the sessions got underway.
It was something of a relief to be given over to the familiar
demands of proposal and argument, and of compromise and
consensus, while the concerns of a less ordered world went on
elsewhere. The conference was scheduled to run for three days.
It was after the conclusion of a session on the second day that a
minister of the host group took him aside and said, 'You ought to
know what's being said in Townsville. The word is strong, here,
that you are about to be arrested for the murder of your
daughter.'

Michael conceded that he had heard something of the sort
himself. The rumour was remarkable, not so much because it
had travelled to a seaboard city seven hundred kilometres from
home but because it seemed to have carried with it a curious
measure of authenticity.

THE RAREST SPECIES AROUND

1

THE WAY THINGS WERE GOING, the investigation was currently occupying more laboratory time in Adelaide than anywhere else. This didn't surprise anyone who understood how much of the country's arid centre is shared between the Northern Territory and the state of South Australia, or those who knew how similarly outflung their small settlements are, or how alike their styles of police administration. Recruitment to the police force of one region from the other runs high, and not only at junior levels. The most spectacular example is the present police commissioner for the Northern Territory who was recruited from his post as chief superintendent of police in South Australia.

Co-ordination of laboratory tasks in Adelaide was the duty of Sergeant Barry Cocks. Forty years a policeman, Cocks still walked office corridors with the rolling gait of a big cop on the beat, arms trailing, his belt-buckle leading the rest of him by a healthy margin. The last thirty years he spent in the administration of forensic scientists, and it had not taken Cocks long to conclude that Azaria Chamberlain's clothing might yield more material evidence than punctures, blood and hairs. The punctures he had allocated to Brown, the blood to Scott, and the hair to Harding. Used to filling in, himself, in the absence of an appropriate scientist, Cocks was already planning to carry out tests of his own devising, to reproduce the long rupture he found in the baby's jump-suit collar. He had dismissed the teeth of a dingo as a possible origin. He had in mind razor blades and knives.

But Cocks was primarily an administrator, and his present concerns were with plant fragments and dirt on the baby's clothes. These should be identified by a botanist and a soil analyst. He had someone already in mind. Looking now at the jump-suit, it occurred to Cocks that there were more pieces of leaf and seed bedded in the weave than he would have expected if the baby were carried by a dingo over a plain. And another curious thing: there were fragments inside the clothing which could not have got there if the baby was then wearing it. Someone had deliberately rubbed the empty garment into the vegetation.

2

ON 18 SEPTEMBER, Sergeant Cocks took the clothes to Kenneth Brown's laboratory. He met Brown and the botanist Rex Kuchel there. Cocks carried with him, in small plastic bags, fragments he had already vacuumed from the garments using a series of gauze-paper filters. The fragments he gave to the botanist. He then laid out the singlet and the jump-suit on a bench. Brown and Kuchel began to pick over them, lifting more pieces of crushed leaf, stalk, and seed out of the weave.

Brown's part in this team owed more to his enthusiasm than anything else. His notable interest in the Chamberlain investigation had caused some perplexity in police circles already, for this small eager man was himself a Seventh-day Adventist. But Brown's training was in teeth, and it was upon Rex Kuchel that the authority of this afternoon's exercise depended. Kuchel was around sixty years old. Curretly a consultant to the Police Department, mostly identifying plants in drug cases, he was for sixteen earlier years with the Adelaide Botanical Gardens. He had become assistant director there by the time he retired. His demeanour was now reflective rather than vigorous, although, looking at his wide tanned face, it was still easy to imagine him leading a field-party of botanists through remote territories with compass and map.

Kuchel held up the jump-suit and shook it over a sheet of brown paper. The soil he collected this way would be sent to an analyst for identification. He turned to the plant fragments and separated the seeds from the pieces of leaf, using shallow Petri dishes to hold them. He discarded stalk along the way. Stalk is not so distinctive. After several stages of sub-division then, each increasingly fastidious, he was left with four dishes of seed and three of crushed and desiccated leaf. Already Kuchel was able to see that the seeds were not kindred to the leaves. So there were now representatives of seven species of plant.

Here were seeds of *Brachyscome ciliaris*, a daisy, typical of the arid plains, sometimes around the bases of the sand dunes, more rarely close to the Rock. And pieces of leaf from the hollyhock-hibiscus *Abutilon*, devoted to water-courses on the plains, and closer to the Rock, suited to the sort of micro-region where the clothing was found. A saltbush, of the Chenopodiaceae, here only the seeds, Kuchel thinks of as quite common all over. The family Boraginaceae. was present too in seeds, locally called a potato-weed, he remembers, common close to the Rock, but he has seen it growing out on the plains. Here were seeds of a speargrass, belonging to the *Aristida*, or perhaps *Stipa*, it was difficult to tell, but in any event one of the grasses hardy enough that it can be found in most places during wet years, as is this next specimen, *Caliotis hispidula*, a small daisy. And *Parietaria debilis*, a nettle, which grows only in moist shaded soil, a green annual he would expect to find close to the Rock rather than anywhere else, sprouting whenever there is added run-off after rain. There was a nice coincidence about Kuchel's ready identification of this last specimen. It is listed as a rarity in the desert. But he had recently worked for a South Australian publisher on its field guide to the Flinders Ranges and had illustrated for it *Parietaria debilis*.

Of these seven plants only two were not widespread. The potato-weed Boraginaceae was recorded as an inhabitant of the plains and the flats close to Ayers Rock, never in the dunes. And the uncommon, moisture-seeking Parietaria, not unlike a deep green grouund-creeper, grew only in the sort of nook where the clothing came to rest.

So the garments had taken up fragments of plant from three regions through which the baby was dragged, if it was dragged by a dingo, over dune, across plain, to the Rock. Kuchel had performed something like a man-hunt in reverse. Instead of traversing the terrain, picking up pieces of clothing, he had traversed the clothing picking up pieces of the terrain.

'The strange thing is,' he said. '*Parietaria debilis*, the rarest species, outnumbers everything else by about fifty to one.'

3

THE DESIGN of a saliva test was complete. Andrew Scott had spent time looking about for a model. His fancy lighted, in an unlikely corner of laboratory endeavour, on a test used for the identification of species of fish.

The swindling of housekeepers and restaurateurs by sly fishmongers—notably in the substitution of plausible imported fillets for the native barramundi—was long in odium around the fishmarkets of the south, and national outrage had given the scientific identification of fishy tissue a boost. Now scientists could compare those delicious proteins with one another, by setting the genuine against the suspected along electrophoretic paths on laboratory gel-plates. This development was called isoelectric focusing. It had occurred to Scott that he could isolate proteins in dingo saliva and compare the known with the expected in just the same way.

Like anything borrowed, the technique had certain shortcomings in its new context, which Scott recognized right away. The concentrations of saliva must be high. He could meet this requirement by soaking fragments of the Chamberlain clothing, and heightening the intensity of whatever came away by sieving the solution through a membrane. The more serious difficulty was locality. There was no screening-test, as there is for blood, to show him where best to search for saliva. Testing the whole suit was out of the question. If the correct proteins were not found in lodgings around the holes in the garments, where next should he look?

SPELLS

1

MICHAEL SUSPECTED SOMETHING was amiss as soon as the shopgirl at Western Dry Cleaners called for the manager.

Lindy said once again, 'We've come for my sleeping-bag,' and added this time, 'Has anything gone wrong?'

'Not wrong, exactly,' the manager said. 'It's not here any longer.'

Michael produced the tab. 'But here's the docket.'

'I'm sorry to be the one to tell you this. The police took it away.'

'How can they do that?'

'They had a warrant.'

'But they didn't want it, earlier.'

'There was nothing we could do. It's the law.'

Lindy seemed more aggrieved by the churlishness with which the law exercised its privileges, than by any discernible threat. 'They only needed to ask us,' she said.

2

REAGAN WAS PLAYING TRAINS. He set up his model railway on the carpet in the lounge-room, kneeling between the easy-chairs where his grandparents sat and the couch where his mother was. He had no interest in what they were saying. Their conversations passed over his head. The game he devised called for a locomotive and one carriage, which was all the rolling-stock he had. He pushed them around in a circle, an-

nouncing in a stern voice the places of importance passing by. It
had begun with too complicated a form. But the words became
simpler and simpler, taking on rhythms of their own, repetitious
and insistent, like the clacketty-clack of the railway-track. Around
and around:

'There's your blood,
There's your blood,
There's your blood,
And the big black dark.'

So bewitched was he by the power of the chant that for some
time he did not know the adults had fallen silent, watching. Then
someone laid a hand on his shoulder.

3

NEWSREPORTERS were the first people to hear about
anything important, and Lindy Chamberlain was altogether sick
and tired of it. A journalist from the *News* had telephoned to tell
her that scientists in Adelaide found no dingo saliva on Azaria's
clothes. 'I don't understand that at all,' she said, 'but thanks
anyway.'

She dialled Alice Springs police headquarters. Michael stood
close by to hear what he could of the conversation. She asked for
Inspector Gilroy. 'It's Mrs Chamberlain calling,' she said.

It was not the inspector who answered the extension. 'I asked
for Mr Gilroy,' she said.

'Detective Sergeant Charlwood, Mrs Chamberlain. The matter is my responsibility now.'

'Oh,' she said. 'Well, the newspapers have been on the
telephone. They say Azaria's clothes have been examined for
dingo saliva.'

'Do they?'

'They say there was no saliva, anywhere. Is that true?'

'It's probably true, if they say so. I'm still waiting for the
report.'

'How would they know before you?'

'They've got their methods. There's nothing I can do, I'm
afraid.'

She replaced the hand-piece and turned to Michael. 'There's
a new man in charge.'

'What did he tell you?'
'He doesn't seem to know much.'

4

'I DON'T WANT ANYONE TO KNOW I've spoken to you,' the caller said.

Michael knew him well. He was with the *Courier-Mail*, a Brisbane daily.

'Okay,' Michael said. 'Go ahead.'

'It's just that I don't like the way things are going on around here.'

'I see. I'm very grateful,' Michael said. 'What is it?'

'One of our editorial people was at a dinner. Sitting near a police chap, an inspector. And he got the tip-off that we should be ready to open up on the story again. You are the story, Mike. You're going to be arrested.'

'I've heard that before,' Michael said, 'and I'm still here.'

'I'm telling you, we've scrambled a team, and they are ready to go. This time it's really on.'

'When?'

'That's the point. It's any day now.'

5

THE FAMILY WAS WORRIED about Reagan. He was having the same nightmare over and over. His mother lifted him from his troubled bed. He seemed deep in some dread predicament, and was difficult to wake. She laid him in the double bed between herself and Michael. 'All gone away,' she said softly, 'all over now.' The hand was as caressing as the voice, and his breathing came easier. As far as she could gather, the boy's dream had to do with unaccountable lights burning in the night, and the slow passage of a beast over his breathless and enchanted body.

THE PROPER MANAGEMENT
OF SORROW

1

AN UNFAMILIAR SEDAN stood at the kerb outside the house. Lindy Chamberlain pulled around it and parked the yellow hatchback in the drive. This was 30 September, a sunny morning around ten o'clock, a faint breeze. Walking across the lawn to the front staircase she shook her hair so that it floated free at the nape. It was a Tuesday, and she was just back from the hairdresser.

Jennifer Richards met her at the door, uncertain and uneasy, as if Lindy were a visitor calling at an inconvenient moment. 'Oh,' Jennifer said, 'the police are here.' They walked into the lounge. The policemen were standing politely in front of recently abandoned chairs.

'Hi, I'm Lindy Chamberlain,' she said in the manner of a general broadcast, since it was not immediately plain who she was expected to address. It came clearer with the manner of introduction. The sergeant who identified himself as Doolan of Mt Isa headquarters, and Constable Graham beside him, were evidently subsidiary to the slim detective with a neat horse-shoe moustache, presented to her now as Graeme Charlwood, a sergeant from Alice Springs. The suggestion of trimness, of dressiness about him, was not at all out of place here. In the part of the world she knew best, young men were proud to look clean-cut and smart.

'I spoke to you on the phone,' she said.

'Yes.'

'Now I can put a face to the voice.'

They sat. Charlwood crossed his legs and leaned back. The mood was unexpectedly relaxed. 'It's my job to gather information for the inquest,' he said. He appeared to be both confident and easy-going, an attractive combination. She liked his smile.

This was a moment for which Charlwood had prepared with some care. After the days he spent at Ayers Rock from 10 September onward, walking the locations of significance, he was more knowledgeable about those places than were the Chamberlains. He was now familiar with their clothes, their bedding, and the camping-gear. He had picked over the statements they made to the press, spoken to journalists who met them face to face, replayed the tape of their conversation with Lincoln and Gilroy at the Uluru Motel.

On Sunday, here in Mt Isa, he had passed the afternoon in a theatre at the television station. There he watched footage of the Chamberlains speaking to the telecameras. It was a private viewing. His attention was only partly on the dialogue and their response to difficult questions. He was as interested in the manner of delivery and the stories told by eyes and hands. He ran the tapes several times. This pert little brunette and her harmonious husband were, at the one time, bold and implausible. Charlwood didn't believe in that religious fatalism for a moment. Their unquenchable talkativeness he saw as a welcome sign of overconfidence, and a failing he would now do much to encourage. Familiarity had become Charlwood's competitive advantage: he had known Lindy Chamberlain longer than she had known him.

'What else do you need?' Lindy asked. 'I thought you'd got everything, one way or another.' She was still piqued by the preemptory seizure of her sleeping-bag from the dry-cleaner.

Charlwood asked for anything inside the tent at the time the baby disappeared. 'The cot?' he said, 'other bedding?' There were, indeed, mattresses and blankets she could give him, and yes, Bubby's tiny pillow. He had the grace to pause, she noticed, for her agreement to each item before he went on to the next. These were not demands. He seemed to be asking her, and she felt disposed to consent. Charm was his long suit, as the saying runs.

She was without her husband, a good enough reason to move the topic on to the events at the barbecue. It was Charlwood's belief that this investigation would have been much advantaged if Gilroy had excluded each of the Chamberlains while the other was questioned. An early mistake, now to be rectified.

She wrinkled her nose. 'I went through all that with the inspector at Ayers Rock,' she said.

He knew of that interview, he explained, but it was less detailed than he needed, and was on tape rather than a written record. 'What I'd like is a more formal interview at the office in town, maybe later this afternoon.'

'Anytime you like,' she said.

Meantime, while he was here, if she wouldn't mind running through something of what she remembered, so he was more familiar with it all?

The account she began followed broadly the substance of the Gilroy tapes. The sequence of happenings was, if anything, a little more credibly ordered. Was this because she had more time to rehearse, or because she was free of her husband's influence?

At that moment Michael Chamberlain walked into the lounge-room. The event called for a fresh round of introductions. The pastor's handshake was firm and brief. It was striking how truly the press photographs represented him. His face was tanned, boyish, and symmetrical, the blond hair groomed. He was fit, but there was some capacity for indulgence here. Without exercise he could run to fat in a month. Throughout the conversation now, his eyes held an appropriate measure of intelligent concern. Pastor Chamberlain was what you expected of him. Indeed that quality, the fulfilment of expectations, was disturbing, unconvincing. It was as though he had always a clear picture of himself, full face.

Lindy Chamberlain brought in the baby's cot and bedding. She held the cot by the hoops. It was white, basket-woven, and creaky. Evidently it had seen earlier duty when the boys were infants.

'Is this all you want just now?' she asked.

'The mattress. The pillow.'

'They're all here.'

'So,' he said, 'can I collect you around one o'clock?'

'Fine,' she said.

He turned to her husband. 'And you sometime tomorrow?'

'Yes. Tomorrow, yes.'

They moved for the door. Charlwood again scanned the room. Here were the conventions of a happy home. The dining table near the kitchen door shone with polish. The lounge-suite was bright and plump. The Chamberlains were fond of family portraits. A glazed photograph on the sideboard held intently pleasant children. Another showed their smiling mother on her wedding-day. She had jonquils in her veil.

2

BEHIND THE WINDOW, Lindy Chamberlain watched them load the police-car. They swung open the doors and climbed inside, Doolan the front passenger, Charlwood in the rear, talking already. It was a movie without sound. The constable swung the wheel, Doolan turned askew in his seat so better to speak over his shoulder, Charlwood reached into his pocket as if for a cigarette, and they drove out of her view.

Charlwood's fingers were not at that moment probing for anything like a cigarette. The object he withdrew from his pocket was a slim tape-recorder. At the house it had been running all the while. He rewound, and pressed play-back.

3

THE POLICE BUILDING was in Isa Street. Charlwood held open for her the door into the foyer. This was the standard of gallantry she expected, made pleasantly less extravagant because her arms were occupied by a doll, some of Azaria's clothing, and rugs. The doll she had plucked from the childrens' room as she left. Charlwood carried her running shoes. 'Which way?' she asked.

'Up the steps.'

Leaving her in an upper level corridor, he disappeared through an office door for a moment, then called her in. With Charlwood was a Sergeant Morris, whom she knew was stationed at Mt Isa, a Queensland policeman, and John Scott, a detective from Alice Springs. She looked about. Here were filing cabinets, desks, chairs. Azaria's cot lay on the floor. Still seated, at the time she'd walked in, were two other local policemen. They looked at her with some interest, but evidently were not to stay. One said to another, 'Want to come for a walk?', and together they made to leave. Charlwood called, 'Close the door', over their departing footsteps. Morris took a chair, and motioned Lindy Chamberlain to another. Charlwood sat on the other side of the desk. He arranged his file. He closed a drawer. She drew a breath and waited.

Charlwood was careful not to close the desk drawer too far. The tape-recorder was running in there. It was preferable that she did not think this conversation important. He chose a casual beginning. 'What I'll do first, I'll just get you to go through what happened from here to the incident,' and here he sounded almost confused, 'so that I—'

'From the time we left here?' she queried.

'Well, just very briefly.'

'Fine. Okay.'

'So we can work out, leading up to Ayers Rock, then in some depth there. Just so that I can get a clear picture of what happened, and then we can get another statement.'

'Yes,' she said, 'all right.'

But the lack of conviction in her tone was worrying. If inspector Gilroy's file-note was correct—that not one witness had seen the baby alive at Ayers Rock—then the child might have been killed anytime, even days beforehand. It was part of the investigators' task, now, to have her account for that time, and preferably while she did not suspect their interest in it.

'We could start on the statement first,' he said, 'but then things could get out of sequence, I guess.' He made a point of arranging pencil and notepaper. 'During this, I'll just make some notes, so my memory's clearer.'

She seemed satisfied with that.

'So, you left on what day?'

'I was just trying to work it out,' she said, twisting her fingers as if they should be limber for the counting of days. 'We left Wednesday morning. We would have left Tuesday, but the dry-cleaner's had the blankets, and we had to wait till the following morning. So we left here, I suppose it would have been about nine, and we headed more or less straight through. Stopped at Tennant Creek for a while, had a look around. Camped at the Devil's Marbles that night.' She clearly assumed Charlwood knew the Devil's Marbles, clusters of rough granite, huge and precarious, near the Stuart Highway. 'We actually camped out that night.' Her quiet gaze was on Azaria's cot and the rugs. 'She slept in the car.'

* * *

'And the following day on to Alice Springs. Stayed at Heavitree Gap, in our other tent. Looked around town that day, and we had a petrol-pump fault which we had to get fixed. Fixed it up on Friday,' she said, still counting. 'Stayed there that night. We were going to stay the following night, but the rodeo was on and it was rowdy, so we decided to take off. We left, probably about lunch-time Saturday. We got there just after sunset. We tried to beat the sunset, to get the sunset on the Rock, but we missed out that night. We pulled in at the ranger station. I suppose it was three quarters of an hour after the actual sunset by the time we got there, at a guess. It was dark, anyway. You know, the glow had gone. The camping-ground was crowded out. There were, I don't know how many, bus-tours. It could have been anything up to eleven of them there, I guess.' They had driven around, circling two or three times, before finding a space suitably far from the buses.

'The next day my husband got up with the sunrise. And then we took off around the Rock at about, I guess, ten by the time we started. Maybe it was a little bit later than that. We went around, had a look at the Brain.' Charlwood knew the Brain, a cellular cavity on the north face. 'That side around,' she said, tracing their path anticlockwise with an airborne finger. 'We came back. No, we stayed, went up the Climb. My husband went up the Climb, and I waited down with the kiddies. Then he took Aidan and Reagan up. Then we took some photographs. No, the photographs we took of Azaria were in between him coming down and the boys going up.'

Charlwood had a copy of one such photograph in his file. This had been published, in colour, by the magazine *Woman's Day,* and in monochrome by the *Sun-Herald,* a Sydney paper where someone in Graphics managed to print it back to front. It was taken by Michael Chamberlain. The part of the Rock he chose for the foreground was fiery-red and steeply oblique. An inappropriate sky hung like a dark indigo wash, the result of some filter or other. The slope underfoot had confused him, so the rim of the plain was not as horizontal as the earth is. His crouching wife, smiling and girlish, wore a roomy frock above calf-length tennis socks and runners. She was holding Azaria, whose gaze seemed to be on something close to the tip of her nose, firmly by the elbows. The baby appeared to be standing.

But, on close inspection, there was no strain on those chubby legs. It was a proud pantomime.

This snapshot was of interest to the press for reasons to do with increased circulation. They had billed it as the last photograph of Azaria alive, and sold plenty. It was of interest to Charlwood for quite other reasons. This baby's hair was very light, and she was, by comparison with Lindy's adjacent limbs, unaccountably tall. On all reports, Azaria's hair was dark, and she was quite tiny. The heady supposition came to this: the infant in that happy scene may not be Azaria at all.

His quick decision was to establish the chronology now. He could come back to identification later.

'So about what time was that?' he asked.

Between three and four-thirty, she guessed. Michael had climbed the Rock alone first, then with the two boys, who separated, she recalled, so Michael climbed again. Aidan meanwhile had formed a descending party. 'Then he came down—so we all came—Reagan was down there with me.'

The phenomenon of a scattered family was plainly not new to her, and they should all regroup in her memory on the tapping of her forehead with a finger. But somewhere in there she had temporarily lost her husband, who then turned some corner of her recollection and came back. 'He'd had it, by this time, because he climbed the hard section three times in the one day. He was feeling tired. And on the way home I said to Michael I'd promised the kids they could have a look at the water out there, because they reckoned there wasn't any. We were going into Maggie Springs, and we were sort of looking to see where it was, and we saw the bus pulled in just ahead of us. No, it pulled in just after us. We pulled in, saw the sign, then the bus pulled up, and actually they got into the Echo Cave before we did.

'And there were some tourists there, and a couple about, I suppose, mid forties, with a child of, I'd say, eight, and another about ten or twelve, walking around the rocks. We met them at the back of that Fertility Cave, and we were standing there talking and looking around, and wondering what the Aboriginal legend of the rock above was, and where the Echo part of it was. And I looked—I sort of sensed as though I was being watched— and I looked up. I would have been standing about where the corner of this desk is, I think. On a rock, just above, there was a dingo looking down over the top at us.'

Charlwood was suspicious of this entire episode. It had made an appearance in Lindy Chamberlain's conversation with Inspector Gilroy and next in her statements to pressmen, always with an imprecise description of the tourists she said were there, always too skimpy to be checked out. It was altogether too convenient.

'This is, what?' he asked, 'sort of right at the back of the Fertility Cave?'

'Yes.'

It was inside this gloomy sepulchre that Charlwood had taken samples of dried blood on 13 September. A copy of Andrew Scott's analysis of that blood was now inside the file on the desk. He left it, for the present, right there.

'Well, you could get in it either way. But we had come through the cave. Half of us went through, and half of us went back again. Michael went back around the other way, and the kids wanted to know what the cave was.

'And I said, "Look what's watching us." And we all stood there for at least four minutes, maybe longer, watching this dog. There was a crevice just beneath where it was, and Reagan was moving around, and it struck me at the time it was odd, because he said, "Where is it, Mummy, I can't see?" The dog would usually follow movements with its eyes, but it didn't seem to take its eyes off me. It made me feel a bit creepy, which I thought of after. Azaria was with me at the time. She was with me—unwrapped and awake—sitting across my shoulder, looking about.'

Because Michael was tired they'd driven back directly to the campsite, she recalled. 'And I bathed the kids.'

'What time was that,' Charlwood asked.

'Sunset was six-thirty. I would have been bathing them somewhere between quarter to six and six o'clock, I should think.' They had made it out to Sunset Strip in time for photographs. When they got back, Reagan was already asleep. She slipped him into a sleeping bag on his mattress in the tent. 'Meanwhile Michael started to look after tea. Then I picked the baby out of the carry-basket in the car, took the carry-basket into the tent, and then carried her down to the campsite. She had wind. I was patting her, walked around with her for a while.'

'And what time was that?'

'It was dark. Between seven and eight. She finally went to sleep. At a rough guess, she would've been asleep half, or three-quarters, of an hour before I put her down. Another young couple arrived there and were using the opposite stove to cook their tea on.'

'This is in the barbecue area, directly down from your camp?'

'Yes. They had a little eighteen-months-old baby girl. And there was a dingo in the area, actually. It had been there the night before. We'd been talking a bit about them, because the hikers that had been camped around there the night before said to us, "Don't leave any food out, because they scrounge for it." And we'd read the notices in the toilets, and I'd only seen them that afternoon. We were actually watching this dingo, when Aidan spied some sort of animal. He didn't know what it was. It turned out to be a little kangaroo-mouse. The husband of the young couple was sitting on the fence, about that far from the railing that goes around it.'

She gestured to indicate just how astoundingly close that really was. Charlwood nodded. 'Yes,' he said.

'There was a post in between us. And all of a sudden he said, "I think that mouse is here by this post." Before Aidan got there with the torch, this dingo pounced in, right between us. Say, so far from his feet and so far from mine. We'd had no idea it was there. It was so quiet, and was gone. About a quarter of an hour after that, Michael and Aidan had both finished tea, and Aidan said he was tired and wanted to go to sleep. I hadn't had my tea; I wasn't very hungry. Michael said, "You'd better put her down and have your tea." So I said to Aidan, "It's time I put Bubby down." I was thinking to myself, I'll spoil her. He said, "I'll come up with you." I had the tent zipped up with Reagan there, because of what they'd said.'

The incident she began to describe did not seem to have much relevance to the story so far, until it came clear as some manner of corollary, and likely to fall into sequence if Charlwood let her run on. 'The day before,' she said, 'we'd had a rubbish bag beside the stove, and we'd gone away to get something or other, and come straight back. And an animal, a camp dog or a dingo, I don't know which, had tipped it all out, spread it all over the ground and made a real mess. I'd got a plastic bag, so I jammed it as tight as I could in a sort of open-fireplace by the tent.'

'Ground-level?'

'Yes. Over by that concrete . . .'—here her questing fingers weren't able to grasp anything like the precise term—'thing'.

The short-fall in her powers of description called for some response from him. His familiarity with the cooking facility at the campsite would show he'd been there lately. No matter. 'Yes,' he said.

The refuse bag with which she was now concerned had held Azaria's soiled nappies. She wanted to fill the bag before throwing it out, so had pushed it deep into the fire-box. But, when they got back to camp, the nappies were shredded, the debris everywhere. 'Michael said he'd seen a dingo the day before doing the same thing to others. We picked all that up and put it back. Of course, because of this I thought, Well, they're scavenging for anything. If they go for nappies, you know?

'The kids' shoes were all along the front of the tent. Reagan was inside. I zipped it up. When I came back, I walked up with Aidan. We both climbed in the tent. And he got his parka off and dumped it near the door of the tent, where Reagan's was, and started to get himself into bed. I put Azaria down and tucked her in. I put her down in the things I had her wrapped in, and just put a blanket over the top.'

'She was, at that time, wearing what?' Charlwood asked.

'The clothes or the blankets?'

'Clothes.'

He knew already the inventory of that tiny wardrobe by heart. It was listed in the Chamberlains' interviews with Michael Gilroy and in several with the press. But none of the clothing showed any evidence that it was ever carried in a dingo's jaws, as the reports here in his file attested. An outer garment, the absent matinee-jacket, could account for that. Charlwood was suspicious of that jacket. It had the character, laggard and defensive, of an afterthought.

'She was wearing a throw-away nappie, a singlet, white stretchsuit—it was all white, with white booties underneath—and a little white matinee-jacket, with very pale lemon edging around the collar and cuffs.'

Because the jacket had not been found—or as Charlwood suspected, to underscore plausibility here—she pressed on with it. 'It was one of those matinee-jackets that's just got two or three buttons on the yoke, and then none coming down, and the buttonholes were a bit loose. She was wrapped up as I showed you this morning, the blue bunny-rug and the larger of the two blankets. She slept with her arms up, and her head on the side, and her arms would be this angle, and her head back that way.' Her face lay, now, between her forearms, and gently she inclined it to express slumber.

'She had her arms level with her head?' Charlwood asked, concerned with making her posture intelligible in the tape-recording.

'Yes, or slightly back a bit.'

'And then Aidan said, "Is that all the tea I'm getting?" He's at that stage, where, periodically, he decides he's got hollow legs, because he eats a huge feast, and he's still hungry. So I said, "Well, I'll get you some more. What would you like?" He didn't know. He rather likes baked beans.

'So I went out to the car—which reminds me, Michael had a slide taken about midday, that day, with the car parked where it was, and the tent set up—yes, I went back to the car and got the baked beans out, came back to the tent. Actually, the car door would hit the tent, so I was right beside the tent at that stage. I saw nothing in the area. Anywhere. There was not a sight or a sound of a thing.'

With Aidan, she left the tent for the barbecue. 'For some reason or other, I didn't zip the tent up again. I was planning to get his food and then bring back the tray with me and let him have it in the tent. I had decided by then I didn't want anything much, probably just watch him, and then go straight to bed. And I walked back to the barbecue area. I can't remember now if we climbed the fence, but I think we might have. I was going to chase him, and he went one way, and I went the other, to see who got back fastest.

'We climbed over the fence, on the right side of the gas bottle. Walked around on the side where we had our things, and the can-opener was sitting right on top. I put the can of beans down, picked up the can-opener. And my husband said to me, "Bubby cried." I sort of paused, and said to him, "Are you sure?" She was sound asleep. He said, well, he heard a cry. And the other fellow sort of indicated that he'd heard something, whether he heard a cry or not I don't know. So I said, "Well, I'd better go and see." I put the can-opener down, walked back across the gas bottles, climbed the fence, and I was halfway between the fence and the post, on the way to the tent, and I saw the dingo coming out of the tent. And it had its head down, and it was in the light from about there up.' She indicated half face, with impenetrable fingers. 'Because the tent was being—'

But the amount of light shining on the tent, about which Inspector Gilroy had questioned her closely, was not evidently best described the way she had begun. She looked about for some sort of assistance, and found it on the desk, where Charlwood had a sketch of the camp. 'You've probably got all the measurements, but say the tent was about that far back from the post-and-rail fence, and the bushes came right up to the fence, and standing back further, you could see into the tent. When you got close up, the shadow was shining right down to the front of the tent, from this post-and-rail. It was sort of obscuring the view just where I was standing then, because there was this biggish bush in front of me. And, when I saw it, it was going like this to get out.' Her head now shook from side to side, irritable and determined.

'And I thought, It's got Michael's shoes, because his shoes were right beside the door. It was a young dingo, and my first thought was either it was a young one, or still a puppy.' She waved a hand about, level with her seated thigh. 'It would've been so high at the shoulder. Gold. Its coat was in beautiful condition. It wasn't one of the mangy ones around there. The light was blinking on it, so it must have been a shiny coat, and it wasn't dusty, or anything like that. Around its neck it was, I'd say, like a rust. It put its head down.'

In the account she had given to Michael Gilroy, the dingo was already on its way out of the tent, pushing between the flaps, when she caught sight of it. Here now was an opportunity to test the point again. Charlwood said, 'When you first saw the dingo, it was still inside the tent?'

'It was still inside the tent, its head was out, and it was trying to get something through the doorway and swinging its head around, now with its head down. That's what made me think it was a shoe, and I thought, He's got it by the shoelace, and it'd be swinging, and he can't get it through the door. The dog wanted to get out. It was unzipped, not only down the middle, but at both sides, across the bottom.

''And I yelled at it, because I thought it would drop the shoe. As soon as I saw it, I started to run. And I yelled. I can't remember what I said. But I think I said, ''Get out.'' Or, ''Go.'' I think I said, ''Go on,'' to it. Sort of yelled, ''Go on, get out.''

'Then I realized. I thought to myself, The kids. There's no food in there. The shoes. And I thought, Well, she cried. So he must have disturbed her. And then it sort of flashed through my mind that they're wild. When she first went to sleep, she would sleep very heavily, and he would have to actually touch her to disturb her. I thought, Well, a wild dog. It could have bitten her. The only thing visible is her head. She'll need, she'll need, first-aid. As soon as I reached the front of the tent, I could see the blankets scattered. Instinct told me that she wasn't there, the dog had her, but my head told me it wasn't possible. Dingoes don't do such things, and this was, you know, just beyond the realms of reason. And I dived into the tent just to make sure. I could see from the door that she wasn't there. But my mind wouldn't accept it. And I dived in, actually felt in the cradle for her, to make sure she wasn't there. And as I backed out of the tent I felt with my hands, in the blankets that were scattered, and the sleeping-bag, just in case I frightened it off, and he dropped her, and one of the blankets was completely covering her. Being so tiny she didn't make much of a bundle. And if he dropped her? Anyway, and I briefly glanced at Reagan on the way out, and he had his sleeping-bag hood up. No damage to the sleeping-bag. There was no skin showing anywhere on him, and I remember it flashing through my mind, Well, he's all right, because the dog couldn't see anything of him.

''And I backed to the door of the tent, feeling as I went, and as I stood up in the opening, I called out to Michael that the dingo's got the baby. And as I was calling this, I started to run in the direction that the dingo had gone, because as it came out of the tent—as I was running towards it—it went out the tent and across in front of the car, which from my direction was right, and ran off into the darkness. It was under the shadow of the fence at that stage, and I didn't look at it again. My interest was what was in the tent, because immediately my thought was to get out after it. I felt within myself that she was dead, because if she was alive I'd have heard a whimper, or a cry, or something, unless by some miracle she was unconscious and still alive. And Michael called to me as I was running across there and said, ''What?'' So I said *something* to him. And again, ''The dingo's got the baby, quickly!''

'And that was all in the matter of the time coming out of the tent and around at the other corner of the car. The dingo was standing in the shadow of the car, at the back, the back left-hand corner of the car. And as soon as I peered around the corner, it took off. It was standing with its back to me, with its head slightly turned at that stage. I couldn't tell you whether it had anything in its mouth or not. My mind refused to accept the thought that it had her in its mouth, although I knew that must be it. I didn't know what I was going to do when I caught it, but I was going to.'

'At that stage,' Charlwood said, 'you could only see the back of the dingo and its head, when it was at the back of the car?'

'Well, I could see all the dog in the shadow. I was standing here, and it would have been slightly on an angle, with its head partly turned, and it took off at an angle. Say that's the car, here. I was coming around here.' She converted the desk into a car with an effortless wave. 'It was there. The road was here. It took off across there.' The dingo disappeared somewhere behind Charlwood. 'I took off, up this way, and when I got to here, in the meantime Michael came from the barbecue, straight through this way'—evidently close to her right shoulder—'and caught me: "Where?" And I said, "That way!" And he went up in the dark, and he ran out without his torch. I'd stopped, because I realized there was dead silence. You couldn't see a thing, you couldn't hear a thing. The light from the barbecue didn't show anymore, there. I realized that there was just no hope of finding it. We needed a torch. We'd searched for ours earlier. Couldn't find the little one we were using. We went to get our big one out. We've got one of those Big Jims. Something had been packed on the button and flattened the battery, and the one we had was just about flat. That's why we were looking, because I realized that our torch was useless, and it sort of went through my mind, Nobody's going to believe me. They'll all think I'm either drunk or I'm joking if I go to the tents and tell them to come. It's just going to take too long. I need help now. So I just stood there and yelled as loud as I could, "Has anybody got a torch?" because the dingo had the baby. "Has anybody got a torch!"

'It was almost as if people had them on their laps. There were three torches that came almost immediately. They must have been sitting beside their torches, came out and called to me as they sort of ran towards me, "Which way?" And I said, "It's gone in there," and pointed to the direction as they went in. Michael realized he couldn't see and rushed back to the car. By this time, the lady in the tent beside us called out, "Have you gone for the police?" And I said to her, "No, it's only just happened, and we need a torch. We've got to look for her, if someone could go?'' And she said, ''Well, would you like my husband to go?'' And I said, ''Yes.'' And she ran back for her torch and for her husband, and she came back and she said, ''He's going straight around for the police and ranger.'' Michael was back by this time, and we offered him the torch. It was one of those fluorescent ones. And the only thing that did penetrate into his mind at the time was that they don't give enough beam. They shoot around, but it's not a beam. And we went to our car and looked for a torch, and asked people if they had torches could they go and look.' Michael, she recalled, ran to the other tents while the Tasmanian man found a torch in his truck. 'About that time, Michael went back out, with a torch. They would've spent, I don't know, quite a few minutes out there. Say ten, fifteen minutes. Then the police arrived and the ranger was there within two or three minutes after him.

'By this time, there would've been anything from thirty to fifty people out with torches, looking. Then the police went around and got more, and they just kept coming from the bus tours. Within the hour there would have been about two hundred or more, out in different directions.

'And Michael said, ''Did you check to make sure she's not there?'' And I said, ''Yes, she's not there, but do you want to come back and look with me, just to make doubly sure that there's nothing I've missed?'' And we checked the tent again. And as we were crawling out of the tent the second time—he had the torch this time, and he was using it everywhere, just to make sure that there was nothing—he shone the torch on the end of his sleeping bag, and I saw the drops of blood which I hadn't seen before.'

Since Lindy's sleeping bag, the one Charlwood had requisitioned from Western Dry Cleaners, no longer showed anything in the way of bloodstains, these new drops were of some interest. They may be disprovable. 'This was on the one that he was sleeping in?' he asked. 'His sleeping bag?'

'His sleeping bag,' she agreed.

This answer could not have been better. It was worth nailing down. 'On Michael's?'

'There were only half a dozen of them or so. We didn't see anything else at that stage, and he said to me, ''Look, Honey, she's bleeding, so I don't think there will be any hope.'' She also had a very—a very—tailend of a cold. She was just sniffling, and it had been very, very cold when I changed her nappy earlier on. Because of the cold she had, and the temperature—which had frozen the water around—we had a saucepan half full of water the night before, and it had frozen ice on the top of it. I said to him, ''With the cold she's got, if she's alive anywhere, we've got maybe three-quarters of an hour, an hour and a half, for them to find her, or she'll be—she'll be either—have very bad pnuemonia, or she'll be frozen to death, with no blankets on or anything. After about two hours we just hoped that we would never—We initially said to the police if they found anything of her, it didn't matter what it was, we wanted to see her. Then we decided that, if they found her, we'd like to see something of her clothes, but we didn't particularly want to see her, in a morbid state at all. As the night wore on, the ranger said he felt that they wouldn't find anything. He said we'd be very lucky to find clothes; it'd probably taken it back to its den. Very occasionally they would savage without killing. Then he was asking heights—'

Here she seemed to be talking about the size and configuration of the animal she had seen, the first true indication of rambling she had shown since the interview began. '. . . and I said to Michael that I had no reason to say that, except for a mother's instinct that I felt it was a female that had taken her, that it was like the first dingo we had seen at Maggie Springs that afternoon. And Michael said to me, ''Now listen, you be careful. It's one thing to say what you saw, and it's another thing saying what you suppose to be. If you go around saying it's the same as that dingo, there seem to be dozens of dingoes around here, and they all look alike, you know. You're getting into the realms of probability.'' So I never said anything about that then. Although the next day, when Inspector Gilroy came and talked to us, and he asked me to describe the dog at the barbecue, I said to him, ''Well, it was so like that one I'd seen at Maggie Springs, even when I saw it coming out of the tent, I thought, Oh, you're the rascal we saw this afternoon. But it's a bit far away, I guess. They're too alike, around here. And when they said, afterwards, that they'd found the clothes near Maggie Springs, I said to the inspector, ''Can you tell me if they were found just behind the opening of that cave?'' '

She broke from the story to ask Charlwood, 'What do you call this cave?'

'The Fertility Cave.'

'And the inspector said, ''Oh, it wasn't far from there, as a matter of fact.'' He said, ''You're thinking what I'm thinking. I remember you saying to me that it was so like that dog, and your husband shutting you up.'' And then afterwards, discussing different things with the ranger. He was talking about that, the different habits, the different heights, etcetera. To my mind it was a female. Of course, you know, it's supposition.'

The long narrative was beginning to take its toll. She dropped her gaze. 'Of course, you probably know more about that than me, by now.'

This was a point Charlwood was happy to lose. 'No. I don't know a great deal about the dingo.' He searched for a topic which might give the lead back to her. 'What, then, was the baby wearing when it was taken from the tent?'

'I already explained to you, before,' she said. 'The booties, stretch-suit, the singlet, a throw-away nappy, and the matinee-jacket.'

'The matinee-jacket.' In the tactical scheme of things, it might be useful if she now suspected that he didn't necessarily believe in the matinee-jacket.

'They've got them all back,' she said, 'except the matinee-jacket, and it wasn't a tight one. It had light elastic around the wrists and the buttons were loosish. So there is as much chance of it being off on a bush, on the way from the Rock somewhere, as there would be down a den, and left away from the other clothes, I should think.'

This was delivered in assertive tones. She sat forward on the chair, quarrelsome, expecting a direct challenge, right now. She could wait.

They took a break. Lindy Chamberlain asked for the wash-room. When she came back into the office, Charlwood was chatting with Sergeant Morris, and she caught the word, 'inquest'.

'When will the inquest be?' she asked.

'The coroner hasn't fixed a date yet,' said Charlwood.

Sergeant Morris leaned forward on his chair. His gaze was serious. He asked her, 'You know what the finding will be?'

Judging by the moistness of her lashes, she had freshened her face in the wash-room. Her hair was combed. But whatever these swift renovations had done for her vitality in the mirror there, it was not enough to help her venture an answer now.

'So,' Charlwood said, looking through his notes, 'on the Sunday night?'

'Michael said, by his watch, when it happened it was about eight-thirty.'

'So the searching went on into the night. At midnight the ranger came back and said, "I feel that there's not much chance of finding her." What went on from there?'

'Was it the ranger, or the police? I don't think we saw the ranger again that night at all. The police came back two or three times. We didn't see the ranger until the following morning. We'd seen both police, off and on, and they said that by the habits of the dingoes in that area there wasn't much hope of finding her at all, and it's cold.

'Now, Aidan—which I missed out, before—Aidan, as I came back to the tent, I hadn't realized that he was following her, following me. But as I saw the dog, I'd glanced back to the others as I told them. They looked up, and I said that a dingo was in the tent, and I glanced back, and noticed Aidan was four foot, six foot, behind me, following me back. Where he went then I don't know. He wasn't near the tent. He must have been coming, but he didn't get into the tent when I was there—'

        The memory she wanted was lost. She entered the present tense, searching. 'Reagan is still there.' It was as if she must visit the scene, in the dimension of its own time, to retrieve the fugitive event and carry it back with her into this room's brighter light. 'Reagan is still there—and—I knew Aidan was there, and—he came running out from around the car. He must have been near the tent, or looked in the tent. I don't know. As I came back, these people were starting to come everywhere, and he arrived, to me, just before the lady who asked if I was sending for the police.

'Aidan is actually the type of child that when, well, if he cuts his foot he goes hysterical, and he didn't that night. In fact, it amazed me. Shock, I suppose. He came running out, and he screamed at me and he said, "Mummy, don't let the dingo eat our baby!" He put into words what my mind wouldn't accept. There's no doubt in my mind that he was quite aware of what had happened, and what was going on. I explained to him, then, that I wanted him to stay back. I didn't know whether to stay with him, or go and look for her, or what. And the Western Australian lady said to me, "Don't worry about him. I'll look after him. If you want to go out with your husband and look, you can." And we went looking, and Aidan was still standing around there, but I was cold, and he had taken his parka off to go to bed already, and I said to him, ''I want you to go and get into bed,'' and I told him what was happening. And I said, ''There is nothing we can do, the policeman's coming soon, get into bed.'' Because if Reagan woke up he would be frightened. Reagan slept through the lot. And I said, ''I want you to be there so Reagan's all right, because he knows you.'' Aidan didn't want me to go away, so I said, ''I'll be just out there, where I can see what's happening. If I go away, the other lady is going to stay right there on the fence, where you can see.''

Someone had set up a comforting light outside, but Aidan stayed awake. 'Well, he was still awake around the twelve o'clock mark, I should think. I thought he was asleep a couple of times, when I nicked in to get tissues and all, popped back and checked him each time.

'I went out with Michael. We both went together, looking, and we came back about every half hour to check if the police had come back, or if anybody had found anything. And we stayed close then, in case they wanted us, back and forth. We could hear them. People were doing other things. We were out by ourselves.'

The Ayers Rock head ranger was, as Charlwood remembered, surprised by the way Lindy Chamberlain and her husband had spent time waiting by their tent while the search was on. Roff's was an observation made more striking by an odd paradox, because Roff believed the baby was taken by a dingo. But, back on 26 August, he had said, 'I must admit to feeling that the parents in this case were so overcalm, and that really confused my thinking altogether. Obviously, the ways shock takes people are different, but, this is the thing, the conduct of the parents in this case was quite amazing.'

Charlwood agreed. Prayer and contemplation, the proper management of sorrow, the Divine Purpose, it was all far too orderly. Nothing here spoke of anger, desperation, of explicable human emotions. If the child were his, he would have been somewhere in the thick of the search, no risk.

'How long were you out looking on the Sunday night?' he asked.

'We stayed out, ourselves, until somewhere between eleven

and eleven-thirty, if not longer. But we didn't want to look any more after that. Michael said, ''I'll quieten down, someone else might, but I don't want to.'' I think perhaps too, the initial shock was wearing off, and he sort of realized just what he might find, and didn't want to, so he stayed and sat on the fence. Then Bobbie, the nurse, went around to find a motel room for us.'

'When did she arrive?'

'When?'

'Yes.'

'Could have been anything between nine and ten o'clock. That's a wild guess. She stayed with us for a while and then she went away.'

'Where had she gone?'

'She went somewhere, to the motel, I think. Then she came back, and she said she had a place for us. And the policeman was coming over to pick up our stuff. I think it was quite a while, somewhere between twelve and twelve-thirty we packed up. We decided to pack the lot. I went with the policeman, and took some things in the back of his car, and the rest we just threw in the back of our car. I took the kids in their sleeping-bags. And Michael grabbed the last few things, and came in our car. The Western Australian lady, and the other lady, said they would tidy up our dishes at the barbecue for us, and send them over in the morning. They sent everything back except the tin of baked beans, which I thought was rather diplomatic of them. And I think we finally settled, by the time we were all ready, at about half past one, or just before. I was the last one. It was half past one when I looked at my watch, just before we climbed into bed.'

'So you went to the motel, and the following day, on the Monday, what did you do?'

But she was not done yet with her account of the night. 'We decided that we would need to ring my parents, and Michael's parents, and Michael's boss, as soon as possible, and we'd ring before eight.' Motel staff had told them the radio-phone transmission was poor until then. 'So I went back to the kitchen that night, and asked if we could use their phone, and went to bed after that.

'The next morning, with the sunrise again, I was cold. We got out and got dressed. We thought, hopefully, we'd be out and back before Reagan woke up, which we didn't manage to do. Aidan woke up. He could hear the taps running in the bathroom, and we told him what we were going to do. Right, he'd woken up, put his clothes on. Reagan was asleep. If he woke up, I said, tell him it's all right, Mummy and Daddy are ringing up, and we'll be back in a minute. Michael went to have a shave. I'd told him if he had a shave it might help him to feel better. Reagan woke up in the meantime.

'We informed our parents, and Michael's president, before eight a.m. We had our meals in our rooms, and spent most of the morning on the phone, talking to the press, as the police had advised us it would be better to talk to them, rather than avoid them. We drove to the airport, and back around the campsite, to take photos of the site. The area was nearly deserted. There were only two tents. A number of the bus-tours were also gone. We spent the afternoon around the motel, and spent quite a bit of time talking to an Ansett employee who had been out searching all night and who had done a number of safaris with Harry Butler. Our minister came out from Alice Springs. And then we more or less spent the rest of the day, in between phone calls, talking with these men.

'We had tea there that night. We went up to the dining-room with the motel owner. We'd invited him to come up and have tea with us. Or was that the next day?'

'Perhaps the Monday,' Charlwood volunteered.

'Yes. I'm just trying to work out the date in my mind. We spent Wednesday night in Tennant Creek, and the night before that in Alice Springs. So, Monday night. We had tea in the dining-room together, and then we more or less spent the morning with them, until we packed up and we left around about lunch-time.'

'Was that on the Tuesday?'

'That was on the Tuesday. Yes, before we left, we went and saw the ranger.'

'Frank Morris, or the ranger?'

'The ranger.'

'Derek Roff?'

'Derek Roff. Because we wanted to ask him, before we left, about a memorial to put up by the Rock. He was in the Aboriginal camp. And we knew the trackers had been out, and we thought we'd like to thank the trackers before we left. So we went across there, and both policemen were there, and the ranger, and I presume it was another ranger. There were about four or five of them.'

'Yes?'

'The ranger took us all around the Aboriginal camp, and we

had a look at all the native dogs to see if I could identify any of them. But they were all different sizes and shapes, and complete bitzers. Sort of hound-dogs. Black, like brindle, mostly. Long trunks, odd-shaped, everything.'

'There was no resemblance to the dog you saw?'

'No. And he asked me again, could we describe it to him exactly. The height: Was it so high? Or, so high? The shape of its face, the shape of its ears? He asked me if I saw his feet—of all things! And whether I'd noticed if it was a male or a female. If I was a better drawer, I could draw it.'

'What's that?'

'The dog.'

So vivid a picture of that dog did Lindy Chamberlain claim to have now, that Charlwood might not have shown much surprise had she attempted a sketch, then and there. It had seemed, in the telling, a damning example of recent invention. But the person who unexpectedly weakened this suspicion was Roff. Since she was persuaded by him to recall those details, so exactly that Roff would recognize the dingo himself, her current claim might betray no more than an obliging and impetuous imagination.

'And just before we left we wanted to pick up some T-shirts, and I wanted to get some cups with Ayers Rock on them, for my young nephews, and we called at the store, and just before we left Frank Morris came around again, and then I asked him if he wanted any of the clothes, like those she had around her, and he said, would we have one of the nappies? And I got a nappy out of the car, and showed him the same type of thing that Azaria had on.'

Ready, now, to take her to a topic of rather greater importance, Charlwood sat more closely over the desk. 'When did you first notice the blood on the clothing?'

'That was—' she began, and broke off as Morris, the sergeant here at Mt Isa, came through the door. This was a minor distraction for he had been in and out, often. She waited until the sergeant had lowered himself on a chair, and everyone was again ready. She clearly assumed that there was no purpose in talking unless someone was taking it down. Charlwood smiled at her courtesy.

'Right,' he said.

'Well, I noticed it on the parka. Which reminds me, did you find out whether there's a parka in Alice Springs as well as here?'

'Adelaide.'

'They've got two?'

He nodded.

'Right, well, the second one has some blood on the sleeves here,' she said, patting her own cuffs, 'and when Aidan went to put it on the next morning, I noticed it and showed Michael. And then Frank Morris came to get the blankets, and we showed him. We'd found it with the blankets, a couple of spots of blood on it, and a couple of other tooth-marks, rips, that hadn't been there before. I showed him the parka, and he said he wanted everything. And I said, "Do you have to take their clothes?" And he said to me, "If we could have the sleeping bag and the blankets, that would be enough." But Aidan wore it all the way home, and it was a little bit wet on the sleeve, just a couple of little splashes.

'When Mum came on Friday—was it Friday? My Mum is a bit like me, it's the things I don't know that worry me, but if I know what I'm doing, I can cope with it. It's just the unknown that's rather more hard to cope with. And I said, "We have got some things here, do you want to see them or not?" The girls grabbed everything that morning—we'll wash this; we'll wash that; we'll wash something else—and one of the parkas I'd put away, as it wasn't dirty. We more or less glanced at it. I grabbed everything else for dry cleaning, including my tracksuit. Wasn't that washed that day? My dress, I only had one dress with me that's suitable for colder weather and I'd washed it, wore it, washed it, wore it all the way home. But—'

This was too much for Sergeant Morris. The path of her recollection was about to meander beyond the tracksuit, as though it were a curiosity of only passing interest, and ramble on elsewhere. It was Morris's local squad to whom news of the spattered garment had first come, and who then arranged the warrant of seizure for her sleeping bag from Western Dry Cleaners.

'What about the tracksuit,' Morris said.

'Right. That night it was cold, so I stuck the tracksuit on underneath the dress, and then the jacket, and then my parka

over the top, progressively, and I had those shoes on that I gave
you.'

'Running shoes,' said Charlwood, by way of clarification for
someone or other, although the shoes were there in the room.

        Although she might stray about between the ramshackle
details in her memory, she seldom quit for long the neighbourhood
of the general topic. She seemed intent on recounting meticulously
each new discovery of bloodstains, once she'd got home to Mt
Isa. Her running shoes, she said, were smeared with 'what
looked like just blackcurrant', but when friends came by to take
her running she had looked at the shoes more closely. 'There was
blood. I must have crawled through a pool of it somewhere,' she
said, turning her mind now to her path through the disordered
tent. Both boys' parkas, which had been 'spread-eagled right
near the door of the tent', now showed stains. Aidan's more than
she'd at first thought, and Reagan's with 'blood all up one arm',
on the hood, and over the other sleeve.

On her own sleeping bag, taken from a wardrobe one cold
night when the boys were to watch a late television programme,
she found 'two or three spots of blood across the flap' and
milkstains where she thought the baby must have 'vomited a
little bit' as the dingo took her. 'The drops were this shape with a
splash-tail,' she said, outlining in the air a fat tadpole. When she
told local police the sleeping bag was stained, 'they said they
didn't want it', a fact she remembered because she had delayed,
until then, sending it off for cleaning.

The early reluctance of police to accept offers like this was
now an emerging refrain. She shrugged away her irritation for
the moment and made an effort to smile, but she had not done,
yet, with her complaint.

'We were actually looking, my sister and I, for blood on the
space blanket because we remembered it had been over Reagan,'
she said. Her mind was evidently following the possible path of
a dingo. 'It must have sort of walked over his head, and walked
around. We turned it the opposite way to the light, and you could
see all the rip-marks through it. But you could see a dusty
pad-print on the thing, once you realized what it was.'

That seemed to complete the inventory of items she could
recall pressing on indifferent policemen. 'And I'd more or less
gone through everything then, although I kept wondering why
they didn't ask.'

No one here was about to justify omissions of that sort. If there was one premise these detectives shared with Lindy Chamberlain, it was this: it seemed that all shortcomings so far lay with Gilroy rather than his successor, in this investigation. Charlwood was here to straighten things out.

'I had a good look at the cot.'

'Yes?'

'I think it was last Thursday I looked at it. It occurred to me when I was sitting in bed the other night, and I thought, Well, there was nothing on that track down there when I was coming out.' Her mind, it seemed, was back in the tent. 'Without there being two lots of paw-marks, it either walked in over the mattress and out over Reagan, or walked in over Reagan and out over the mattress. So I had a look, and I found those.' She gestured towards the stained mattress, which lay humped over a wicker side of the disordered cot.

'They were big-looking marks. Whether the kids had spilt their milk in the car or not, no, it would have had to happen in the tent, come to think of it. But I don't recall seeing it on the mattress before, anyway, and as far as I know there was nothing else—'

Her voice trailed away. She had reached the end of her story, the end of her effort. The detectives exchanged glances. Charlwood checked his watch. She had been talking now for more than two hours. Counting their time at the house, more than three. 'So,' said Charlwood, 'we're ready to begin the interview.'

Tactical decisions were necessary, now. It is a peculiar irony of police investigation that the closer you get to a solution, the less advantage you have. The way police see it, the fault lies with the rules of interrogation. The moment Charlwood concluded that this woman was guilty of a crime, he was required to caution her, to advise her that she was not required to answer questions. She might then do just that. So there is a time in every conversation with a suspect at which the interrogating officer has to examine the fibre of his own belief, and that time had arrived.

Sergeant Morris aligned the pages in his typewriter. 'What are your Christian names?'

'Alice Lynne.' She spelled Lynne for him. Charlwood pulled back his chair so that he could read the lines as they came up on

Morris's page. Morris typed the heading, beginning with the words 'Record of Inteview', and noting the time as 3.20 p.m. It was his practice to number each question for easy reference in court. He typed Q1.

Charlwood looked across the desk at Lindy Chamberlain and said, 'I am going to ask you a series of questions about an incident that occurred at Ayers Rock in the Northern Territory on Sunday 17 August 1980.' He held up his hand to indicate that they should wait while Morris's fingers were busy.

There was, in this opening, nothing to show they had ever discussed the topic before, but Lindy Chamberlain gave no sign of perplexity. She recited again her full name, gave her address, the dates and places of her own birth and of her daughter Azaria. Morris returned the carriage of a fresh paragraph, and typed Q8. He paused. If Charlwood had decided to administer the caution, he should do it now.

'Can you tell me the date on which you and your family departed Mt Isa to travel to Ayers Rock?' Charlwood said.

The moment held no significance for Lindy Chamberlain. She asked for a calendar. It was in Charlwood's ready hand.

By five-thirty they had progressed through seventy-one recorded questions and answers, but, slowed by the detective's pursuit of detail, were not yet beyond that point in the narrative at which the family was preparing dinner at the barbecue. Charlwood halted the interview there for the day. They began again at ten-fifteen next morning. This session produced Lindy Chamberlain's first clear departure from her earlier story. Describing the emaciated dingo she saw scavenging mice by the camp-fire, she said, 'Aidan asked me if the dingo would take our baby. I told him no. Mummy wouldn't let him. She was safe with us. They wouldn't come close, or go in our tent.' This seemed like a decoration, fancy and overimaginative, made of a more transparent fabric than truth.

It was after midday before Sergeant Morris's laborious typewriter had captured, to Charlwood's satisfaction, enough detail of the plundered tent, of the long and hopeless night, and the return of the depleted family to Mt Isa. These were now anniversaries Lindy Chamberlain had commemorated for them three times in the last two days, but Charlwood yet had no reliable clue to suggest to him just when the infant's body may have been hidden, or the clothing laid out in the gully far away.

'Was it the policeman, or the ranger, who inspected your tent at Ayers Rock?'

'The policeman,' she recalled.

'What time did the nurse arrive at the campsite?'

'I can't remember—Somewhere between ten and eleven. I don't really know.'

'Was there anyone with you and Michael when you were out searching?'

'There were others in the area, but not with us.'

'On the Monday, how did you travel to the airport and around the area?'

'We went in the motel bus. The bus driver had a funny name, too—'

But she could not recall it.

The strength of the bond between mother and child is an intangible of a sort from which detectives like to keep well away, but there was a sentence in Inspector Gilroy's memorandum which called it, in this case, unavoidably into question. It ran, 'It is reported that she appeared not to have cared for the baby, and at one stage did not feed it for more than eight hours.'

Charlwood asked, 'Had you been breast-feeding the baby since birth?'

'No, I actually started when she was about two weeks old. I fed her one day, stopped, and started again,' she shrugged. 'I was still comp-feeding her a little bit with the bottle,' she added, as if the information might be of some practical, if abstruse, importance.

Charlwood took from his folder a copy of a magazine. He laid it on the desk in front of her. The cover-page showed the snap Michael had taken while she dandled her baby on a low reach of the Rock. She had spoken of it earlier.

'The photograph which appears on the front of the latest edition of *Woman's Day* shows the baby's hair as being blonde,' he said. 'Is that a true representation of the hair colour at the time the photo was taken?'

'Are you sure it shows the hair as blonde? Doesn't it look slightly ginger?' She studied it awhile. Azaria's artless feet touched the slope. The air was warm and still. The baby's round head was bright with sunshine.

'I suppose you could say that it's blonde,' she said eventually. 'I would say it had a gingery colour in it. Her hair was, actually, medium to dark brown, but was beginning to lighten, and had almost a ginger sheen in the sun. The picture actually looks lighter than it really was. The base of the hair, at the back, was quite dark, still.'

She put the photo back on the desk, face up. Charlwood left it where it lay.

'Did either you or your husband, or either of the two boys, suffer any injury while you were at Ayers Rock?'

'Only a few prickles in the feet. Reagan had a chafed bottom, from sliding down the Rock on it, but it hadn't bled.'

'Do you, or have you had, any pets in your household?'

'We've had three siamese cats. The last one was stolen here in Mt Isa, when the baby was two weeks old. We also had a collie-labrador cross when we were in Tasmania, and a small terrier pup when we were in Bowen, which we returned because it was vicious and bit. Aidan was terrified of it.'

Charlwood stood and walked to a corner of the room where lay a heap of paper and plastic bags, camping gear, clothing. He piled it closer to the desk.

'Do you recognize this sleeping-bag?' Charlwood held it up.

'Yes, it's mine. From the dry cleaner's, isn't it?' she said. 'It is inside out. Can I look at the blood Michael reckons is on it?' She reached over the desk. 'He made enough fuss about it.' The fuss was not justified, it seemed. Nothing remained of the stain.

'Can you tell me if you recognize this parka?'

'That one is Aidan's parka, because it's got three badges on the sleeves.'

She hadn't shown any sign of discomfort so far, but they knew she was smart enough to guess the sequence was building up to something.

'Can you tell me if you recognize this piece of clothing?' The item he laid on the desk was a singlet, small and limp, bloodied at the straps.

'Yes,' she said. 'That's the singlet Azaria was wearing.'

Next to it he spread the suit.

'Can you tell me if you can recognize that piece of clothing?'

She picked it up and slowly turned it over. Brown smears at the neck and the cuffs were as powdery as flaking rust. Craters cut in the weave were plainly the recent excavations of laboratory implements. The collar flopped. Not so long ago it must have been stiff and scabby.

'Yes,' she said. No one else spoke. Something more was required of her. She added. 'That is the jump-suit Azaria was wearing.'

'Can you tell me if you can recognize this disposable nappy?' She made no effort to reach over. The precise and burdensome formalities of identification were now beyond her.

'Yes, that's it,' she said quietly.

'Is that the nappy that Azaria was wearing on the night she disappeared, on the night of 17 August 1980?'

'Yes.'

She averted her face. Morris stopped typing. For Charlwood, this was no time to let up. 'Would you have a look at these baby's booties,' he said, 'and tell me if you recognize those?'

'Yes. Azaria was wearing them, too.'

'Is there a comment you would like to make, in relation to the clothing?'

'None that I can think of.' Responding then to the lengthening silence she said, 'I did notice that the hand-pieces were still turned over.'

'Would you like to have another look at it?'

She accepted the garment with dull hands. It hung like a rag. Selecting a cuff, she straightened it slowly, avoiding the blood. 'That cuff, there, was turned over,' she said, spreading it flat on the desktop.

'And that cuff now, is that how it was?'

'Yes.' But her gaze and her hands were together somewhere in her lap. Drops fell, unnoticeable until they blotched her skirt, large and irregular, like the first few spots of tepid rain. She searched for a tissue. The ragged one she came up with, from her sleeve, would have to do. 'Basically, the same as it was,' she said.

Morris pushed back his chair. 'We'll wait awhile,' he said. 'There's no hurry.'

There was good reason to hurry. Michael Chamberlain was due to arrive here around four o'clock, only an hour off now. Charlwood wanted every piece of information from Lindy Chamberlain squared away before he started on Michael. Whatever she said in this interview, Charlwood could use in the interrogation of her husband.

It was time now to show her just how untenable her story was. He cleared the desk of the clothes and camping gear, and set out his files. The reports made an impressive pile.

'Certain forensic tests have been carried out on the clothing, and one of those tests was to determine the presence of dingo or dog saliva. The results of those tests were negative. That is, there is no dingo or dog saliva present.' This sounded wordy and stilted, but it was the sort of language courts of law seemed to prefer. 'Have you any comment you would care to make?'

'None that I can think of,' she said. 'it just makes me wonder how.'

'Would you have expected saliva to be present?'

'He would have to use his mouth, I should think.' If this was her opportunity to use the absent matinee-jacket as an excuse, she missed it. 'I would have expected to have some on it. I presume dingoes have saliva.'

'Further forensic tests have been carried out in respect of the holes present in the clothing. The results of these tests indicate that the holes were not made by either a dingo's or a dog's teeth. Is there any comment you would care to make?'

Her comment was not one he expected. 'Do your tests show what made them?' she asked.

'No, not conclusively. At this stage.'

'Are you trying to say that somebody murdered her?'

It was the detective's job, rather than the suspect's, to ask the questions in this forum, but she was angry now, the tissue was rolled into a ball inside her fist, and it was clear they wouldn't get far unless he gave some ground.

'I'm just putting to you the facts I have,' he said. 'I am looking for answers.'

'Would saliva wash out in the rain?'

'I don't know. There was no rain at Ayers Rock at the time of this incident.'

She didn't accept this for a second. 'Inspector Gilroy told us that it had rained on the clothes,' she said. And there was another thing. 'What about the space blanket?'

'It's still being tested at the moment.'

'I find it most incredible,' she said, 'that the forensic tests were leaked to the press. You,' she said, irritated by the recollection, 'didn't know the results when I spoke to you.'

Sergeant Morris was typing all this on the record. Charlwood said, 'At the time I spoke to you, I didn't know the results?'

'What you've told me, that's exactly what the press told me,' she said, peevish.

The entire subject was best left alone.

* * *

'I have here a report from the forensic biologist, which I received here, Monday afternoon, last. Would you care to read that report?' She certainly would. It was from Dr Andrew Scott of the Forensic Sciences Centre in Adelaide, a summary of his blood analyses. Some passages she seemed to skip through, as if they were not of much moment. A paragraph describing the identification of bloodstains, which Charlwood had scraped from rocks inside the Cave of Fertility, took more attention. She read it twice.

When she handed the report back, Charlwood held it up with his finger on that paragraph. 'Can you explain this one to me?' he asked.

'So,' she said, as though not too sure of the point he was making, 'there is blood on that rock with the same blood-grouping as me.'

'A little more than just the same group as you.'

'Identical group?'

'Not identical,' he conceded. 'But coming from fourteen per cent of the population.'

'Oh?'

Charlwood required a response more generous than surprise. 'Is there any comment you would care to make in relation to that report?'

While Sergeant Morris caught up with the typing, she thought it over. 'The findings almost seem incredible to me,' she said. 'I am to consider that it was done by something other than a dingo. That brings in such a range of coincidences, with split-second timing, that it seems impossible.' She shook her head. 'Reading about the blood-group on Ayers Rock, the same as mine, almost sounds like a well-planned, well-thought-out—fantastic plan to set me up.'

This was better. An answer like that, in the experience of every investigator, leaves the suspect with nowhere to go. Maybe she was getting to that point, now.

'If that is the case,' he said, 'do you know who would want to do such a thing?'

'I have no idea.'

'I've got a further forensic report here, in relation to the hair examination. Would you care to read that report?'

The hairs of which he was talking were those Harry Harding had found on the blankets, at the Institute of Medical and Veterinary Science. Lindy Chamberlain did not take long to read his summary. Harding believed the hairs were those of a cat rather than a dingo, although he could not be sure.

'Yes,' she said, rather more engaged by this report than she was by Scott's. 'Obviously the space blanket, with all the cuts down the end, is going to be very interesting when it's done. The pad-marks on the blanket were very distinctive.' Then she added, challenging his gaze directly, 'And a number of people saw them before it was given to the police.'

'Who were the people who saw the pad-marks?'

'I think we all examined it. My mother, who drew my attention to it, my sister-in-law, and myself. My husband, father, and brother all saw it. Also my mother-in-law.'

'Is there anything that you haven't told us in relation to this incident?'

Omnibus questions like this are formalities of police practice, and generally signal the end of interrogation. She could volunteer nothing of importance, and Charlwood did not press her. He checked his notes. 'Yesterday you supplied me with a pair of Rockettes running shoes that you said, when you returned from Ayers Rock, had blood on them. Can you tell me how the blood got on the shoes?'

This was an easy matter. They had been over the same ground before. She could answer faster than Morris could type. 'The parkas were right inside the door. I think there must have been a pool of blood on them when I crawled in the tent, because the blood was on the top side. I thought it was blackcurrant next day. When I got them out, several days after I returned home, I realized there were two different coloured stains on them, and it looked like half blood and half blackcurrant.'

'I have received information that the navy blue and green tracksuit submitted recently to the dry cleaners had bloodspots on the legs. Can you give an account as to how the bloodspots may have got there?'

'I think I put them on after it happened. I presume it would have come off my shoes, or the parkas, when I crawled in the tent the second time.' Something about these slacks was irritating her. 'Does Michael have to know there is blood on them at this stage? He has a tendency to burn everything that has blood on.' This was delivered as though in parentheses, and she turned back to the mainstream of the answer. 'I got the slacks out of the tent to put them on, because I was wearing the coat, but I didn't put the slacks on until after, about nine o'clock or so. Until after it happened, anyway.'

'Do you know what happened to Azaria?'
'From the information you are giving me I'm beginning to wonder if I know anything. But I feel certain within my own mind that it was a dingo.'

One other task remained.
'How do you want me to do this?' she asked.
'Exactly as Azaria was wrapped,' he said. 'I want to have it photographed.'
Detective Scott lifted the bassinet to the desktop. Charlwood handed her the doll and bedding. The doll was plump-cheeked and had black hair at the crown. A high forehead and lowered eyes gave an impression of drowsy surprise. The legs were endearingly bandy.
She wrapped it in a doubled blanket and laid the bundle full length in the cot, slipping the pillow under the head. The small fingers rested obediently over the temples. Another snug layer took from view all but a suggestion of dark downy hair. Tightly the remaining rugs were tucked in, side to side, impermeable to the cold breath of night, warm and safe.
'There,' she said, turning her back on them all, walking away to become a silhouette at the dizzy window-pane.

4

MICHAEL CHAMBERLAIN was sitting in an ante-room. He had been waiting nearly half an hour. The detectives had not contrived this, it was simply that questioning the wife had taken longer than planned. When Sergeant Morris took Lindy Chamberlain to another office, Charlwood brought Michael into the questioning-room. Doolan was at the desk.
'You remember Sergeant Doolan?' Charlwood asked.

'Of course,' said Michael, affably. 'Now, where would you like me to sit?'

'Before we start, did you bring your car?'

'Yes. I parked it just outside.'

'Do you mind if I get someone here to take a look at it?'

'Not at all.' Michael fished in a pocket for his keys. 'I've taken all the camping gear out. There's nothing much to see.'

'It shouldn't take long, then,' Charlwood said.

The keys despatched with a local constable, they sat around the desk, Doolan behind the typewriter.

'I'm going to ask you some questions in relation to a missing child Azaria Chantel Loren Chamberlain who went missing at Ayers Rock on Sunday 17 August 1980,' Charlwood began, sufficiently slowly that Doolan could keep pace. 'You do not have to answer any more questions unless you wish to do so, and anything you do say may be taken down and later given in court. Are you fully aware of what I am going to speak of, and your rights?'

'Perhaps not as fully as I ought to be.'

'Briefly, you have the right not to answer any questions if you don't want to.'

So formal a caution seemed to cause Michael only fleeting surprise. He smiled. 'I understand,' he said.

Charlwood's questions followed much the contours of inquiry he had followed in the interview with the pastor's wife. When those answers are set side by side, a task due for some later time, irregularities ought to come into clear relief. This was the correct interrogatory principle, in the absence of an accomplice's confession, tried and true. The trouble was, this natty and well-modulated clergyman rambled so. His attention was diverted equally by specious detail and considerations of moral sensibility. He was both tirelessly indirect and dauntlessly eager, like a young preacher not often exposed to an unsympathetic audience.

His first attempt, now, to account for the day on which his daughter disappeared, was this:

'I awoke, the following morning, perhaps later than I should have, according to my wife who said that I had missed the best part of the sunrise, and as a result moved hurriedly with my camera equipment to the sandhill to the east of the tent, where I believed a good view could be obtained. I spent perhaps half an hour or more shooting thirty-five millimetre film, then after everyone else had gone, decided there was little reason to stay, and moved directly back to the tent where my wife and children were still getting up. We had breakfast. After we got washed I walked around the southeastern area, via the road, to see if I could get any other worthwhile pictures, at that time, of the Rock. After cleaning up, we then proceeded by vehicle, later in the morning. I cannot remember whether we had had lunch or not, as I was very keen to get as much of the scenery on film as possible. Stopped. We took pictures of the Brain. We went out to the airstrip, returned, and moved slowly around to the main, official, Ayers Rock walkway. After gathering camera equipment—'

He paused here and raised a finger, as if calling attention to an aside. 'Excuse me, do you wish for me to relate primarily what I did, or what the family did in general, here?'

'You can relate anything to me that is in your specific knowledge,' Charlwood said.

'The reason for my question, I believe, is because you asked me to relate briefly.'

'You can certainly go into as much detail as you want to.'

The pastor coughed, frowned, and folded his arms. 'I was amazed at the beauty and stark contrast of the colour of the Rock, especially through the filters I was using, and firstly took a wide-angled shot of the cars, tourist-buses, and the Rock together. Lindy and the children scrambled up Chicken Rock. I then left them and moved quickly to the top of the Rock. I took several pictures using various filters and lenses, had another tourist take a picture of myself leaning against the monument, I suppose. I'm not sure what it is, at the top. It had a book in it which I signed. Then I proceeded, even more quickly, back down to the children and my wife. Aidan and Reagan wished to climb part of the Rock also, and this we did. On returning, we then travelled by our vehicle around to what is known as the Maggie Springs area, where my wife and children, with a coach-load of young people, surveyed the area. It was getting reasonably late, about four-thirty or five o'clock I would imagine, and we then, after I had taken some photographs of the paintings, proceeded by car back to the camping area. We prepared tea while talking to some people from Tasmania. I cooked, my wife attended to the baby. When we had eaten, it was approaching eight-thirty, or thereabouts, when the tragedy occurred.'

This was not as cogent or detailed an explanation of the

baby's disappearance as the detectives had in mind. Charlwood took the story back to the happenings at Maggie Springs, and they started again from there.

'When you were in the area of Maggie Springs, did you sight any dingoes?'

'No.'

'Do you know if your wife, or any of the other parties that were there, did?'

'Could you repeat that question?'

Sergeant Doolan stopped typing and read the question out again. 'Do you know if your wife, or any of the other parties that were there, did?'

'Yes.'

'Was that sighting related to you?' Charlwood asked.

'Yes.'

'Could you tell me who told you, or what they told you?'

'My wife sighted what she considered a beautiful looking dog, possibly a female. And it was close enough to cause some apprehensiveness. I considered that she may have been unreasonably frightened, as I had not thought of dingoes particularly a creature to be feared.'

'When did she relate this sighting to you?'

'At the time, as I recall, at Maggie Springs. But I cannot be sure.'

This incident still lacked any independent tone of authenticity. There were no verifiable bystanders about, an absence more striking in Michael's version than in his wife's. This was true too of the busy scene later at the barbecue. When Charlwood took him again through the preparations for the evening meal, it was clear there was no one close by whom Michael could now identify.

'At or about eight-fifteen, or eight-twenty, we all saw what we considered a rather mangy forlorn specimen of a dingo, lurking just outside the barbecue enclosure. It appeared to be looking for food. It went into the shadows, and then without any warning came back into the light of the barbecue area, next to the gas bottles, and pounced with frightening agility on a small, I guess you'd call it a field-mouse, which we had sighted a few minutes earlier. This had been seen by the Tasmanian people as well as ourselves. My wife, who had been nursing Bubby, then took her to the tent to lay her down to rest. I prepared some food for her while she was putting Bubby down, as she had not eaten much prior to this. She returned, to have something to eat, and, as she was eating I think, I thought I heard a faint cry from the tent. I think my words were, "Is that Azaria crying?" My wife said she would check it out, and as she was proceeding back, and into the tent, her voice startled me when she cried out in horror, "The dingo's got my baby." I was stunned and raced with the other man madly towards and into the tent to see if this was so, that is, if the baby was missing.

'The sequence of events following this for some minutes is a little unclear. I was in a severe state of trauma. I felt useless. I raced for my torch, I think, and it would not go. I think that I ran into the bush, madly hoping that in the darkness I might find either the dog or Azaria. I remember feeling very angry and frustrated because normally I pride myself with having very effective lighting, and also, because my keys were not in my pocket, I could not switch the ignition of my car on in order to use the one hundred watt searchlight that was in my glovebox. My Tasmanian friend, who had somewhere got hold of a torch, had raced out into the bush in front of me and searched feverishly. I cannot remember much at the time, for a few moments, except that I came back to the tent in the hope that our eyes were playing tricks on us. In other words, that the dog might have left Azaria somewhere in an unlit corner, under a rug, or bag, perhaps. But not so. The moment of truth, that she really was gone, hit me, and realizing now that I could do nothing alone, cried out, "Oh God, help me"—it was probably a silent cry—and raced along the southerly section of the road to alert any other campers that I could see, to—if they had a torch—get out and start searching. I was led towards a tent, on the end of the road, where I had heard Christian music. I raced unceremoniously to the tent door, and said two things. "A dingo has got our baby, if you have a torch please come out and search. If you haven't, please pray." '

After another hour and a half, which took the interrogation to seven-thirty, Michael became visibly weary. They took five minutes rest. Nothing of their conversation, during the break, was typed into the record.

'Do you know Azaria's clothing was found folded?' Charlwood asked, by way of conversation rather than serious inquiry.

'No.'

'And wedged between rocks?'

'Yes, I did hear that.'

'See, it's evidence like this we have to look at.' He watched Michael closely. 'There were no dingo hairs on any of the clothing, and none on the camping-gear.'

'When do dingoes moult?' Michael asked.

'August and September. They were moulting when Azaria disappeared.' Since there was no response he said, 'There was no saliva on the jump-suit, either.'

'I'd have thought desert creatures might not salivate much at all.'

'They're just dogs,' Charlwood said.

By around eight-thirty, Charlwood had enough detail of the long Sunday-night's events to compare the husband's account with that of the wife, and with those he had from the rangers and the local police. It took another hour before the Monday was sufficiently accounted for, and the journey home to Mt Isa was completed.

'Have you seen a copy of this week's *Woman's Day?*'

'Yes. I read it cursorily.'

'Does the photograph on the front cover of that issue, dated 1 October 1980, show your wife and daughter Azaria?'

'Yes.'

'Is that one of the photographs taken by you of the child?'

'Yes.'

'The hair colour depicted in the photograph of the child, would you say that it was a true depiction of the colour of her hair at the time?'

'Not quite,' Michael admitted.

'In what way does it vary?'

'It was a little darker than that, and did not look as reddish as the picture portrays.' His polite fist closed around a small and unnecessary cough, a gesture he often made at the approach of confusion or embarrassment. 'I might add that I had been experimenting with a fluorescent filter, light pink in colour, and at the time of the photograph had forgotten to remove it, as I usually only used it as a contrast with my polaroid filter to shoot landscape, and the Rock.'

'Had Azaria undergone a hair colour change since her birth?'

'Her hair was fairly dark at birth, and had got fairer as she grew.'

'Whilst at Ayers Rock, did either you, your wife, or either of the boys suffer any injury? That is, physical injury?'

'No. Excepting the fact that when I ran down Ayers Rock my two toenails, which were a little long, had dug in and at the bottom of the Rock, after the first time I climbed it, I was forced to cut my nails to relieve the pain, and to remove my socks.' This seemed to be all the serviceable detail he could come up with. 'There may have been scratches on our children, but none treated by the nurse. I don't recall. I think Reagan might have needed a Band-Aid, I'm not sure.'

'Do you currently have any animals in your household?'

'No.'

'Have you ever had any animals in your household?'

'The last animal that we had was earlier this year. She was an eight-week-old chocolate, or seal point, siamese kitten,' Michael said. 'Purchased for twenty dollars, which for a time lived in our home.'

'When did you last have that?'

'It went missing, as I recall, sometime just prior to Azaria's birth.'

'What about animals prior to that?'

'The last animal before that was a very beautiful looking collie-laborador cross, black in colour,' he said smiling, evidently remembering it with some affection. 'This we had while we were in Tasmania during 1970, 1971 and I think 1972. We bought it at an auction at a church tea, and had nursed it and had much joy from it during its adult life.'

'When was the last time you saw Azaria alive?'

'The last time I saw Azaria alive was in Lindy's arms while nursing it sitting on the bench-rail at the barbecue, just prior to putting her to sleep.'

'Did anyone else see her at that time?'

'Yes. The two people who were mentioned, who we had spoken to from Tasmania, and who had shared stoves with us.' Then he added, as if to complete the identification with absolute precision, 'As well as conversing.'

'Do you know what happend to Azaria?'

'No,' Michael said. He pursed his lips and frowned, a demonstration of deep seriousness, a very boyish characteristic. 'Except on the evidence we have given you, I do not know.'

'Is there anything at all that you want to tell me in relation to the disappearance of your child?'

'No. Except for my continuing observation, and strong feeling, that she was killed by a dingo or wild animal. What other alternatives? God only knows,' he said nodding, an indication that he thought this remark should be taken literally.

'The booties are dirty,' Michael went on, 'regardless of some evidence which seems contrary to dingo attack.' He waved a perplexed hand. 'To my untrained eye, I still believe she must have been dragged somehow, some way, by an animal. But I only wish we would ever know for sure.'

'When the clothing was found, the booties were still inside the feet of the jump-suit,' Charlwood said. 'Is there any comment you would care to make about that?'

'No,' Michael said. 'It does seem strange. But then again, it seems that we are dealing with a number of intangibles. But not enough is known perhaps about the wild, and only time will tell the answer.'

The interview was done. Doolan sat Michael Chamberlain at a corner of the desk and handed him, for page-by-page reading, the typed record. Michael was a meticulous reader, and his examination of these fourteen sheets took another half hour. He signed it and stood up. 'Well, I suppose that's it,' he said.

'I'm not sure about that,' Charlwood said. 'There's still scientific work to be done. We can't yet be sure it was a dingo that took your baby. If you or your wife remember anything you haven't told us, you know, or think of any other possibilities, you should call me straight away.' He smiled. 'It would be helpful.'

'We certainly shall,' Michael said.

He handed Michael the keys to the yellow hatchback. The two local police who inspected it had found nothing. There was no purpose in making a comment about that at the moment. 'And thank you for your co-operation,' Charlwood said, instead.

5

REVIEWING THE DAY'S WORK, a certain amount of short-fall had to be faced now. The goal of every interrogator, in the questioning of a suspect, is a confession. Charlwood knew he was no closer to a confession, from either of the Chamberlains, than he was when he began. He had formed no firm view, yet, about when the baby was killed, or where her body was now hidden, or when the parents had disposed of her clothing. And, until the details of Lindy Chamberlain's one hundred and sixty-five answers were matched with her husband's one hundred and thirty-three, it was too early to judge the volume of opportunity. The scientific investigation—once considered to be his fall-back position—was as important now as ever it was.

But there was enough in the work of these two days to prove, for Charlwood, one essential. The behaviour of the parents was not consistent with innocence. The highlight, as it happened, had come at the very end of his interview with Lindy Chamberlain. It was not recorded. When she was ready to leave, he said, 'Those few seconds, there, when you saw the dingo at the tent, are very important, you understand?'

'I know that,' she said.

'But some details you can't recall.'

'I didn't see my baby in its mouth, if that's what you mean.' She then repeated the explanation she had given earlier. 'My mind refused to accept what was happening. Perhaps I have just blanked it out.'

This was precisely where the detective was leading. 'Maybe we can do something about that,' he said, 'if you were willing to undergo hypnosis for an—'

'No.'

'It's not as unusual as it sounds. Not so long ago, in a case in South Australia, the police there used it and with some success.'

'No,' she said. 'Giving up one mind to the control of another, it's forbidden. The power of the devil. Under no circumstances would I even consider such a thing. The church wouldn't allow it and I wouldn't do it. God slew Saul for that. Do you know Saul and the Witch of Endor?'

Sergeant Charlwood didn't know Saul or the Witch of Endor, and so vehement was her repudiation that he could not press the question any further. But, one way or another, he'd got a useful answer, one which failed the demands of credulity, part of a richening fund.

A GRAVEYARD, FLOODLIT

1

THE PEOPLE who run newspapers like to print news gathered by their own reporters. When an item reaches the newsdesks from a staff journalist and, at much the same time, from an agency like Reuter or AAP, the staff report stands the better chance, however less informed it may be. Editors very much dislike taking, or 'picking up' as they say, items already published in rival newspapers, although nearly everyone keeps some part of the day free in which to do nothing else. On 3 October, metropolitan dailies picked up, from the Adelaide press, new of the laboratory tests carried out on Azaria's clothing. Some then combined this item with material of greater age, and produced a pastiche which read as if it were substantial and contemporary.

The Melbourne *Sun* ran it this way:

Report on Clothes in Dingo Baby Case

Police are studying a forensic report which will be vital evidence at the inquest into the death of Azaria Chamberlain. Police at Alice Springs would not comment on the contents of the report. Reports from Adelaide yesterday said it was understood the report said there was no evidence of dog or dingo saliva on the baby's clothes.

Animals had apparently been near the clothes, but this could have happened after the baby was killed.

Inspector Gilroy, who was handling the police investigation, said the report was confidential.

Inspector Gilroy said he had never known a case which had attracted so many rumours and assumptions and conjecture.

'Ninety per cent of the stories I have heard are completely without foundation,' he said.

Last night three Alice Springs detectives returned from Mt Isa, after interviewing Michael and Lindy Chamberlain.

The disturbing aspect of all this, so the Chamberlains considered, was the speed with which the press had found out about their interrogation. It looked as if the reporters in Adelaide had been told last night, before Michael had yet left police headquarters.

2

SO OCCUPIED WAS THE PRESS with what was happening to the Chamberlains at Mt Isa that it missed what was happening further south. While detectives questioned Michael Chamberlain, the odontologist Kenneth Brown and biologist Andrew Scott were just arriving at the Adelaide zoo. It was dusk. The zoo was closing for the night, but Brown and Scott were expected. They walked with a small party of zoo-keepers to an enclosure, bushy and high-walled. It held a lone dingo, beige-coated and in fine condition, which sniffed the air, ran the boundary, lay down, and stood up again. The reason for its agitation was the approach of food. It had not been permitted to eat anything in the past five days. The scent came from the gamey carcass of a small beheaded goat, which was being costumed, as Brown and Scott watched, in an infant's singlet, a Johnson's disposable nappy, and a Bond's towelling jump-suit. The outside studs, from the knee to the throat, were snapped shut, and the completed mimic was held aloft for the inquisitive spotlight of a video camera, which was there to record the experiment faithfully for the coroner's inquiry. But when the bundle hit the ground inside the enclosure the dingo stayed where it was, prowling behind the bushes. Somebody called for the cameraman to swing the spotlight away for a moment, but not much of that moment was needed, and the beam swept back again just in time to catch the dingo's diminishing shadow. The small white figure was gone.

This was the third field-trial Kenneth Brown had arranged. The first, a fortnight ago now, was at the Cleland wildlife park. There he watched three dingoes tear apart babies' nappies he had stuffed with food. By the time he retrieved them, the nappies were in shreds, the plastic covers nipped and tattered, a magni-

tude of damage incomparable with the marks on the nappy from
Ayers Rock. Then he laid out a nappy baited for crows, since it
had been suggested in the press that Azaria Chamberlain's
looked as though it had been attacked by birds, but no crows
were obliging enough to come near. So now the experiment here
at the zoo was designed to provide three discrete categories of
physiological evidence at the one time: tooth-marks for Brown,
saliva for Andrew Scott, and hair for Harry Harding. They came
back to the zoo early next morning, before opening time, and
lined the coop wall. The dingo lay in plain view, fluffy and
contented. When it arose and trotted closer, this was plainly out
of inquisitiveness and not in the expectation of another gift.
From where Brown and Scott stood, there was nothing to be seen
of the night's meal. The keepers entered the pen, scanning the
ground, but keeping the restless dingo fairly in sight. A dusty
piece of the goat's viscera was easily found, and another. A
keeper noticed a patch of fresh digging. He soon exhumed the
singlet. Then the jump-suit, the nappy, and a hunk of uneaten
carcass were found, all from separate graves.

This nappy was still whole, but when Brown turned it over
in his hands it showed some of the same small perforations
which he now associated with nipping by the front incisors. The
singlet was dirty and seemed to have been chewed with the
molars. The jump-suit was torn about the legs and body, by the
sharp canines probably, and chewed about the collar.

But the fastenings in the jump-suit exhibited the most curious
feature. Nearly all of them were still done up. This brought to
mind the report Constable Morris had made at Ayers Rock. To
Morris's recollection, only four press-studs at the top of Azaria
Chamberlain's jump-suit were open when he first saw it, so
everyone thought it implausible that a dingo could have stripped
the child. Here, the dingo in this pen had done far better than
that. The garment Brown held was still fastened except for two
studs close to the throat.

3

AIDAN WORE SCHOOL SHORTS and a open-necked
shirt for his interview with Detective Scott. His mother introduced him and then stood a few paces off, as if she were
presenting her six-year-old son for an entrance examination at a
reputable private school, and he must be seen to succeed here on

his own merits. John Scott sat at the typewriter, an impartial examiner, not expecting too much of this white-haired, quizzical child. The boy was, for the most part, unhesitant as he dictated his simple piece, looking to his mother only once or twice for reassurance. The one novelty he had to offer, beyond his mother's account, was a recollection that the foot of the tent-pole was found knocked out of its cup when his sister had gone. After two pages and very little of a third his memory was exhausted, but the detective said he had done just fine.

The boy printed the word Aidan in serious and tidy letters at the bottom. In the style of essays which children are asked to compose when they come back to class after a happy vacation, it began, 'In the August school holidays, I went to Ayers Rock with my Mummy, Daddy and Reagan, and bubby Azaria.'

4

THE SEARCH INTERSTATE for campsite witnesses had begun to pay off. Sergeant Charlwood's circulars and questionnaires, despatched through local police stations to vehicle owners registered with the Ayers Rock rangers' office, had two functions: to find who the campers were, and identify those who were closest to the events. After a slow start, they were now beginning to make contact with people in the second category.

Murray Haby, who had read press reports of the investigation with some disquiet, came home from a day teaching school determined that it was high time he put in a long-distance telephone call to the Alice Springs police. Haby lived in Box Hill, a quiet residential suburb near Melbourne. It was he who had found paw-prints, drag-marks, and the imprint of a knitted garment on the side of the dune, during the search. Puzzled because no one from the police department was yet in touch with him, he wondered if those discoveries held any significance at all for the investigators. While he was talking this over with his wife Diana, the phone rang. It was the Box Hill police.

Not ten kilometres from the Habys' was the suburb in which the Whittackers lived. At Ayers Rock, their camping site was separated from the Habys' by less than fifty paces, but the two families had never met. Amy Whittacker had spent more time than anyone else with the Chamberlains during the night of 17 August, while Max Whittacker and their daughter Rosalie tramped the plain and the side of the dune with other searchers. Because the family had registered at the camping control office, and because Amy had sent a consoling letter to Lindy Chamberlain, they thought that if they were needed someone would let them know. It happened one afternoon. Amy was not long home from her work as an almoner when a constable knocked at the door. He asked if she could attend the police depot to give a statement. She had rather expected him earlier.

On their farm, not far inland from the remote southern coastline of Western Australia, Judy West took a phone call from Sergeant Sparks. Sparks ran the small police station as Esperance. Judy thought the sergeant a good, humorous man, and knew him as Ron. 'I'll drop by in the next couple of days,' he said, as if the detour, over fifty dusty kilometres of swaying wheat and barley country and hard cattle-range, might be accomplished routinely on the way to somewhere else. In fact, he drove through the gate to the homestead next afternoon, and helped Judy and Bill piece together something of a coherent statement. Ron Sparks seemed to have instructions to question the family particularly about Azaria Chamberlain's appearance, about 'the way she was when they looked at her,' as he put it. 'She was the image of her father,' was all Judy could think of, which caused the sergeant to laugh. 'But that's not admissible in court,' he said. The following week the Wests made the journey into Esperance for another interview with a detective from Criminal Investigation, but the afternoon ran out before the interview finished. Sergeant Sparks and the detective drove to the farm again a day or so later. They were then on their way to Perth, and short of time, so Judith agreed to sign along the bottom of a blank sheet of typing-paper on which the detective would copy her earlier statement. Lying in bed that night, Judith rolled over and asked her husband if she ought to have put her name to an empty form. 'I think it's okay the way the police are around here,' Bill said, 'but in the city you wouldn't risk it.'

West Moonah, where Greg and Sally Lowe lived, was a popular suburb in days when Main Road, which still runs through it, was the principal route north out of Hobart. It is no longer. A multi-laned highway now passes it by, so West Moonah has its share of old roadside shopfronts and fibre-sheet bungalows, but from houses high on the hill you can still see the grey broads of the Derwent River. People here like to spend Saturday afternoons in wintertime at a football game and the evenings watching televised replays of league matches on the mainland, sometimes drinking a beer or two whenever the action is a little slow. Greg Lowe was preparing to pass the first Saturday in October just this way when he answered the doorbell to an excited reporter from ABC television. The reporter was after an interview. Greg refused, but the reporter was civic-minded enough to tell him about a nation-wide appeal, made by the Northern Territory Police Department, for witnesses to Azaria Chamberlain's disappearance. He had located the Lowes by following up an interview with Sally published in the Hobart *Mercury* a week before. Greg and Sally drove then to the police-station at Glenorchy. There they were told to come back in a few days, by which time Glenorchy's communications should have bridged the two thousand and five hundred kilometres which separated them from Alice Springs. It didn't take nearly that long. Three hours later a constable arrived on their doorstep. 'You're the ones they want, all right,' he said. He came back on Monday with a questionnaire. His questions, so Sally thought, were directed more to the blood she saw inside the Chamberlain tent than to anything she witnessed outside it.

5

SOMEONE HAD THOUGHT to alert the media well beforehand, so when the police aircraft came in for touchdown at the western end of the Ayers Rock airstrip a television crew was there already, filming. The plane rolled to the end of the sandy runway, and taxied over. Graeme Charlwood, who had himself flown in two days earlier, climbed out of the waiting police truck. He wore white cover-alls, crisp and unblemished, which made him look more like a navy flyer than a detective. A cameraman, until then occupied with the dry blue sky and red-ochre bluffs familiar to television viewers, swung the lens towards the opening hatch as Charlwood welcomed the emerging Kenneth Brown and the botanists Kuchel and Carroll. The commentary to be spoken over this scene began: 'Doubts have been expressed about the dingo theory, but police still have not dismissed the possibility that it was a dingo which carried her off.' The scientists unloaded luggage uneasily from the cabin in the background. Charlwood faced the camera and said: 'We have forensic botanists collecting samples of soil and vegetation. I think we will find something to reinforce what we have at the moment.' He waved the camera away. 'That's all I can give you right now,' he said.

The interviewer, who was evidently wondering how to richen this bare offering a little further, asked: 'The dingo trail the trackers followed was heading in the opposite direction from where the clothing was found. Can you say anything about that?'

Charlwood grinned but shook his head. 'That's a matter for the coroner.'

'Can I say that?'

'Yes, I guess you can say that.'

Rex Kuchel was anxious to begin the botanical work of the day. They loaded baggage into the back of the police-trucks and headed, first, for the camping-grounds. The Chamberlain site was fenced around with rope and stakes. The party, which included the local constable Frank Morris and several other uniformed police, followed the botanists. Kuchel, tanned and good-humoured, strode about like an expeditionary leader, staring hard at the soil underfoot, crossing the road to the scrubby plain, and on to the dune. He scooped mounds of sand into small plastic bags and coded them according to the locations from which they had come. He rubbed earth between finger and thumb looking for seeds. He noted the incidence here of the plants of which he had found fragments in Azaria Chamberlain's clothing. The daisies and the saltbush were abundant enough, but the potato-weed Boraginacea, and the speargrasses *Aristida* and *Stipa* were gone, having died back over the intervening eight weeks, perhaps.

They drove next to the ring-road, under the southern heights of the Rock, and pulled off the road to the plain. Little more than a hundred metres away, in shadow, lichen stained the ascending cliff. On foot they followed Morris and Charlwood deep into the gully, to the cramped space where the clothing had been found. Morris pointed to a lair underneath a boulder to their right. 'A dingo bitch with a litter lives under that,' he said. No one seemed interested in the information, and he did not press it

further. Kuchel was occupied with the vegetation. Here were
some specimens of the daisy *Caliotis*, and the saltbush Chenopodiaceae, and the speargrasses, all of them plants he would expect
to find on plains, near dunes, and close to the Rock. But the
nettle *Parietaria*, the one plant specific to damp gullies like this,
was nowhere as abundant as he would have thought, and the
examples he could see from here were poor. The life-span of this
small annual must, in this habitat, be as short as three months.

Kuchel turned his attention to the earth. He gathered handfulls
of the red soil, an arm's-length on either side, and fed it into a
fattening sample-bag. There was something quite striking about
the sand now running from his palm. He held it up to better
light. The grains were speckled with black. These were particles
of charcoal, the residue of a bushfire in this gully, sometime. He
looked about. There was no sign of charring anywhere aboveground,
the trees were smooth-barked and clean. Carbon had mixed with
the soil here a good while back, but the sand he had shaken from
the Chamberlain jump-suit in the laboratory showed nothing of
it. So, if the clothing had been buried somewhere, it was not
around here.

The sun set that evening on rosy clouds high above the
plains, and overnight it rained. At daybreak the Rock's alpine
cloughs were stiff and glassy. Rain had smoothed the sands,
seeded the spinifex with trembling pearls, and shined every
green leaf so that the random scrub now seemed part of a
thoughtful arrangement of handsome trees and charming shrubs.
Delightful though this magic was, it sent the botanists back to
Adelaide ahead of time. Kuchel and Brown had planned a further
exercise, but the one circumstance which could invalidate it was
rain, and there was no purpose in staying around now.

The ground and the foliage took some days to dry. Then
Constable Morris drove out to the campsite. It was dark. He had
with him a Bond's infant jump-suit. Carefully he packed inside
it, following Kuchel's instructions, several tightly rolled towels
to simulate the body and limbs of a baby. When he had finished,
the arms held out a little more rigidly than might those of an
unconscious child, but otherwise he thought it not a bad job.
Holding it then by the shoulder, he stooped low enough that the
white doll hung stiff and horizontal at about the height of a
dingo's head, and set off towards the dune, brushing the figure
here and there against grass and bush. The constable's lonely

path through the night scrub was made the easier by mobile floodlights carried by the Channel Nine television crew pacing alongside, whose record of the event would go to air just as soon as they could get it back to the studio.

6

METROPOLITAN DAILIES were notified of the experiments at the Adelaide zoo and Cleland Park, and, because rumours were strong that the inquest date would be set any day now, most newsrooms ran the two stories together without attributing a source to either of them. An Adelaide reporter managed to get through to the Chamberlain household by telephone and wrote:

Nothing To Fear: Parents

The parents of baby Azaria said at the weekend they had nothing to fear from an inquest on their baby. Azaria's mother, Mrs Lindy Chamberlain, said, 'We have nothing to fear from the outcome of the inquest despite what some people might be saying. Losing Azaria was a tragedy.' The baby disappeared from a camp at Ayers Rock on August 17th. Baby clothing believed to be Azaria's was found a week later in a crevice, four kilometres from the family tent.

Doubts have been expressed on whether a dingo took the child. Details of a secret test at the Adelaide zoo conducted on behalf of Alice Springs police were made public last week. In the bizarre test, a young goat was dressed in clothing similar to that worn by Azaria, and fed to a wild dingo at the zoo. Its reaction—which included eating parts of the goat and leaving the carcass—was filmed to further the coroner's understanding of how wild dingoes handle their prey.

Mrs. Chamberlain said she was surprised at the zoo tests. 'We are conducting some of our own too,' she said. 'We have sought information from experts who have observed dingoes in the wild for many years. Doggers and trappers, who know dingoes well, tell us Azaria could quite easily have been taken by a killer dog.'

7

AIDAN AND REAGAN ran into the lounge-room at their mother's call and pulled up, suddenly quiet. It was time to close the day with prayer. Everyone knelt. Avis Murchison clasped her devoted hands high. Michael Chamberlain bowed his head along with the others, for this short service would be led by his father-in-law. Cliff Murchison, who steadied himself against the arm of a chair, was getting on in years although his broad face didn't show as many of them as there were. He knew he might stumble sometimes over the longer passages of worship. He suffered a malady which, as he would often explain to visitors, now constricted the blood supply to his head and impeded the ready flow of words. But he was considered a fine preacher, with a preference for simplicity, and no one seemed to mind an occasional pause.

'Lord, we give thanks for the joy of daily blessings, and for the strength to cope with daily tribulations.'

'For the strength to cope,' repeated his wife, supporting the most affecting words of the prayer, in the way Adventists are used to.

'Help us to remember that the life You choose for us is not always the life we expect. Whatever You choose for us, is best for us. And we will follow Your Mysterious Path, safe in the love of our Friend and Saviour, Jesus.'

'Yes, our Friend and Saviour,' Avis said.

The tone of the pastor's supplication was prompted by something Avis had spoken about earlier. It was Avis's habit to search for bright objects of faith in dark times. God's ways, as she well knew, are mysterious only because He sees things from where He stands that His people cannot. The world is full of unexpected terrors; you only have to read the newspapers, and like other questing Christians the family believed their problems were best solved by closer scrutiny of the design behind the event. It had occurred to Avis that the Lord might permit the early death of a tiny child to prevent some greater evil. Suppose, just for the moment, that God foresaw in Azaria's destiny some awful predicament, in her teens, say, rape or torture and a horrifyingly slow death. Such things happen. No family could bear a tragedy of that magnitude. Might not the Lord, displeased with that future, dispatch a beast to pre-empt the triumph of evil? This way, Azaria is sent to Jesus in a state of innocence, no one has sinned, and you couldn't blame the animal since it is the agent of God.

Avis would not have been at all surprised if the truth turned out to be something just like this, clever and compassionate. It was a comfort.

USE THE WORD: MERCIFUL

1

THREE WISE MONKEYS sat askew on a carved log, next to a pencil-stand, on Denis Barritt's desk. Altogether there were nine sets of figurine monkeys around the room. As a popular comment ran, this was the heaviest concentration of wisdom for thirteen hundred kilometres in all directions. The collection began when Shiela Barritt gave her husband the first set at the time he was appointed to the Bench here, three years ago. Now, when any one of the family happens on a set in a bric-a-brac shop anywhere in the country, it is parcelled off to the magistrate's chambers at Alice Springs. For Barritt, these are less comic conversation-pieces than some sort of jurisprudential motif. The monkeys repudiate evil. Because they are sages, their exposure to it is daily. Their plaintive and nervous fingers cover the eyes, the ears, the mouth. It is as though evil is an infection, contagious and debilitating.

The magistry was Barritt's fourth career. In his teens he joined the Air Force as an apprentice and made instruments. He was a Catholic boy from a large family, and built into boys like this is a deep need to get on in the world. When he discovered that technicians in the defence forces don't often get very far, he transferred to a job where Catholic boys have been known to make it all the way up, and become a cop. But he found that increments in seniority came slowly and had more to do with the passage of time than the expenditure of effort, so he took to law school part-time and after seventeen years 'in the job', as Melbourne cops say, he turned in his sergeant's badge to try advocacy in the criminal courts. There he avoided taking on the carriage and inflections of young barristers who aspire to careers in the higher jurisdictions. He was older than his new contemporaries by ten years, but it didn't bother him. He had a truer vision of the possibilities of life than they did. When, at round nine-thirty in the mornings, young counsel in dark suits spilled from the foyer heading for junior cases in company law or probate in the grand brown-stone court-house just across the street, Denis Barritt set off for the Melbourne police courts in blunt shoes carrying his books in a heavy satchel which may also have held his lunch.

The Administration of the Northern Territory appointed him in 1977 and at the time it was a good deal for both parties. The Territory got a tough-minded lawyer who, by then, was experienced in summary courts and in jury trials, who knew how the police worked and how the defence lawyers worked. For Barritt's part, it was an opportunity not open to him elsewhere. Melbourne magistrates were chosen, in those days, from among officers in the state's law department. Although Barritt may have been offered an appointment to a superior court if he remained an advocate, his prospects were not as bright as were those of his peers who had taken to law earlier, so waiting it out was risky.

He liked it here in Alice Springs. It was a frontier. Of his five children, the two oldest boys were independent enough to choose for themselves where they wanted to live. In the event, both chose Darwin, which was considered not far away by local standards. Shiela, who worked as a mothercraft nurse for years before their marriage, set up the household here with off-hand efficiency, took up teaching religious instruction at a local school, and went about designing her own business-card, which read: 'Shiela Barritt, mother, wife, housemaid, cooking a specialty, discount rate for family.' This wording reflected a growing dissatisfaction over the amount of time her husband was able to spend as part of the family. Denis Barritt was out of town a great deal, travelling hundreds of kilometres every month by light plane to conduct hearings in outback towns and Aboriginal centres at Papunya, Warrabri and Yuendumu.

Sooner or later, a magistrate is judged by the way the court deals with 'the Aboriginal problem', as much of the white community here calls it, and trouble was not long coming. The phrase 'a Stone Age people' made him angry. That the wheel was absent from traditional Aboriginal life seemed to him to have no place in any well-considered argument. As he saw it, the desert people had embraced the wheel when it was time to embrace the wheel. 'What's the use of a cart without a horse?'

he said. Horses came with the European. So did alcohol, and he spoke disrespectfully of those liquor companies which manufactured bad, oversweet port wine for the sugar-deficient Aboriginal market.

After a few months in this jurisdiction, he saw that Aboriginal people typically came before his court on charges to do with alcohol or with motor cars, or both. Most highway deaths and injuries involved one car and an open road. Many thefts involved one car and a flagon of port wine. At the beginning of his term, Barritt's method of calculating fines for simple theft or for brawling accorded with the offender's means of paying it, so those who earned more paid more. He came to believe that this was going about things precisely the wrong way. An Aboriginal who couldn't pay his fine, as Barritt noticed, was often helped out by an older relative, and then both disappeared back to their clan. He spoke to some black elders about that. Thereafter, the fines in Barritt's court became astonishingly tough. A conviction which once had brought a fine of fifty dollars, now brought hundreds. This seemed to many whites a step in the right direction, long overdue. But what was happening here had nothing to do with punishment. Barritt, and the elders who had advised him, were set upon quite a different plan. An Aboriginal who got into trouble in town had generally first broken with his family, so Barritt fined him a sum that only the family could pay. A deputation, most often of uncles and aunts, then came to town, cleared up the fine, and took the offender back home to work the loan off. Barritt saw this as a way of using the tribal support system. In criminological terms the rate of recidivism dropped, as he estimated, to about a tenth that of the white rate. But it was not a universally popular remedy. Aboriginal legal officers thought the fines too harsh. Local whites took little time to conclude that not so many blacks were going to jail.

Barritt thought his solutions were working perfectly well. Although his two youngest boys sometimes came home with stories of unkind sallies made at them in school, he believed that his judicial style would win out, so long as it was well enough explained. These things always took time. If that was a pragmatic and hearty view of the world, it was because he is himself pragmatic and hearty. He is one of those people whose appearance suits, in some emphatic way, his personal philosophies. Barritt is a big man, with a broad bluff face and burly ears. He was not about to be intimidated by any ill-considered and short-term criticism, although he was once heard to remark at home that the government might consider moving him to Gove. He was making a joke, but it caused Shiela to give him a black look and to light another cigarette from the tip of the last. Gove is a mining town on the northern tip of Arnhem Land. It has a population of three thousand souls.

The second magistrate was on leave in December, so Barritt had to fulfil the demands of both rosters himself. He did this through a system of case-listings which seemed, at the one time, both complicated and ad hoc. On busy days he opened court a half hour earlier than usual and got through the drunks and vagrants first. No one, not police or lawyers anyway, objected to working a little harder in the cooler part of the day. They were more disgruntled if the list threatened to run late. Traffic offences and simple criminal charges, the fights and dishonesties, then took up the hours until lunch-time. Preliminary hearings, in which Barritt had to decide if a prosecution case was solid enough to be sent for trial to a higher jurisdiction, and civil summonses, in which citizens claimed redress from one another and sometimes concealed elaborate disputes of honour, were fought through the afternoon. If a local lawyer or a police prosecutor was unhappy about the length of the legal day, the complaint would more likely be dealt with in an off-duty way, over an evening drink at the Lawn Bowls Club where Barritt was president, than as a formal complaint in the courtroom.

A magistrate here is also a coroner, and when Sergeant Charlwood applied to Barritt for a hearing date for the inquest into the death of Azaria Chamberlain, Barritt chose 16 December. He guessed this would allow five full days before he should go back to the ordinary business of his court to clear the backlog there before Christmas. The rest of the inquest would fall into early February, the beginning of the new legal year. Just how much evidence would go into February came clear as soon as he looked through the file. A coroner is alone responsible for the way an inquest is run, and the list of witnesses numbered nearly forty, if he chose to call them all. It was all here, the statements of holidaymakers and campers taken by policemen who where two-finger typists, and stern reports under the letterheads of forensic laboratories. There was a full day's reading in this file, before he could decide which testimony ought to be delivered from the witness-stand, under oath.

*   *   *

The law department chose Ashley Macknay to 'assist the coroner' as such a brief is entitled, which means, in this jurisdiction, that it would be his responsibility to present the evidence and an array of justifiable conclusions. Macknay was a barrister from the south who now lived in Alice Springs, a careful man with a neatly clipped beard and a well-mannered courtroom style. Barritt, who had no hand in the selection, thought him a good choice. In a delicate case like this, the last thing they needed was some sort of glorious hothead.

They sat together in Barritt's office. It was air-conditioned and comfortable, although the afternoon temperature on the street outside was nearly forty degrees. Barritt wanted to talk about the order of witnesses. Coroners are empowered to arrange the witness-list as they like, but the sequence is more important than it sounds. A coroner concerned with a fair hearing will not compel to the stand any witness who may be charged with the homicide before the inquest is over. So it was Barritt's duty, the way he saw it, to exempt the Chamberlains from testifying if there was enough material already to hand which may justify sending them to trial.

He took two cans of beer from a small refrigerator, set into the bookcase behind the desk, and passed one to Macknay. Then he put the question straight. 'Are you proposing to call the parents?'

'Yes,' said Macknay, 'and I think they should be called first.'

Barritt nodded. Both of them knew that Barritt might just as well have asked Macknay his opinion of the police case.

2

NEWS TEAMS AND TV CREWS began arriving on flights inbound from the south and the east three days early. Camera operators walked the footpaths filming bright crowds, desert oaks, Aboriginals on street corners, the police headquarters, and unidentifiable officials entering and leaving the doors of the court building, so that the city networks had something with which to fill television screens when the early bulletins began. Accommodation was booked out all over town. So newsworthy an event reunites old friends in the press business, and, as some sort of rowdy by-product of national communications, each of the hotels favoured by journalists had already taken on the

clubby air of a convention centre. At the airline counters, so it
was said, some clerks had been given a few dollars and a chance
for more if they promised to alert the press the minute a
passenger-list came through with the Chamberlain name on it.
But they must have taken the money and run, because only those
reporters who staked out every flight got the pictures they
wanted, of a serious and abbreviated wave from the pastor and a
defiant smile from his pretty wife.

On Monday morning, at nine-thirty, before the inquest began,
such was the crush of journalists at the court-house doors that the
photographers had trouble keeping enough clear distance between their gawking lenses and the striding Chamberlains for
full-length shots. The coroner had prohibited the taking of
photographs inside. So the best they got was of Lindy Chamberlain during the morning break, talking to her lawyer Peter Dean.
They were arguing about something. Lindy had her hands
planted on her hips. Her handbag swung from a shrugged
shoulder. She looked attractive and bossy, three-quarter face with
upturned nose and pert mouth, a young woman who was well
used to calling the shots even to her lawyer, and editors ran it
front page all over the country.

3

THE COMPROMISE between majesty and utility accounts for a good deal of public expenditure in law buildings
anywhere, and in Alice Springs much of it was accounted for by
high ceilings, polished furniture timbers, landscape paintings,
soft carpeting, and electronic recording and loud-speaking de-
vices. Inside no. 2 courtroom, where Barritt had listed the
Chamberlain inquest, the judicial bench took up the greater
width of the southern wall, elevated by a metre of timber panels.
The bar-table and witness-stand were separated from the pews in
the public gallery by a refractory railing beyond which access
depended on the judgement of an official stationed at the gateway. The gallery seated around sixty onlookers. Denis Barritt
walked to his seat on the bench from a door in the wings, at ten
a.m. on the dot and determined to begin on time. The gallery
was full. Everyone stood until the court-crier completed the
salutation to the Queen and then sat again. Barritt could see that
the constable guarding the doorway held off a queue of spectators
which stretched well back into the foyer. The first two pews,

reserved now for the press, were jammed tight. Two pews were not nearly enough; he may have to do something about that later. The jury-box was empty, and it occurred to Barritt that he might have to use it as a press-box. On a seat by a side wall sat a gentle and elderly man, fit and well tanned, fiddling with a shiny microphone he had set up on the rail close to the witness-box. This was Bert Cuzins, pastor of the Seventh-day Adventist Church here in Alice Springs. Barritt had given him permission to tape the evidence as long as it didn't cause any distraction. The Chamberlains sat on chairs drawn up behind Peter Dean. Police officers, among them Charlwood, sat behind Macknay. Both Macknay and his assistant were bearded, a coincidence which was worth a comment or two in the press-pews. Beards were always more popular in the Territory than down south. This was not a matter of fashion here so much as a mute association with the outback as a frontier, even among desk-bound professionals. The law department officer Mick O'Loughlin, who sat opposite Macknay, wore both a beard and long hair, and tattoos on his forearms evidenced an earlier career as an overland truck-driver.

When the crier declared the inquest open, Dean got to his feet and said, 'May it please Your Worship, I seek leave to appear on behalf of Mr and Mrs Chamberlain.' Dean put it this way, seeking Barritt's permission, because no one has the right to representation by a lawyer at an inquest until the coroner grants it. Coroners generally allow representation to those who have a legal interest in the hearing. This includes the relatives of the deceased, who have an interest in bringing to light the true cause of death. It also includes anyone implicated in the death, whose interests may be served best by hiding their light under a bushel of objections. The Chamberlains might have qualified in both categories, the way the police brief presently stood. Barritt was glad he didn't have to make that distinction right now. Dean's choice of words was happily ambiguous.

Macknay wanted first to lay claim to jurisdiction. An inquest, he said, is an inquiry into a death, and the coroner ought first determine that Azaria Chamberlain was dead, and her remains 'have been destroyed or are in a place from which they cannot be recovered.'

Barritt could see, from the shuffling in the front rows of the gallery, that the reporters thought this was leading towards the arcane, and of no use to readers of lively newspapers. But he knew what was coming, and knew the uninterested journalists to be quite wrong.

'The deceased lost approximately twenty per cent of her blood volume,' Macknay was saying, 'that being a minimum figure based on calculations of blood, consistent with coming from the deceased, which was found on the deceased's clothing.' He summarized the scientific reports and drew conclusions which, he said, he drew now only to establish jurisdiction. 'Firstly, the deceased was removed from her clothing by a person rather than by a dog or a dingo. Secondly, the damage to the clothing was more consistent with having been caused by a person rather than a dingo. Thirdly, the state of the clothes suggests that the clothes were put in the place in which they were found, by a person rather than being dragged there by a dog or a dingo.'

Barritt knew he could have decided the argument then and there. He might determine that there were only two alternatives open on the material in the file: death by animal attack, and death by homicide. In both cases the body was now destroyed or irretrievable. For the purpose of his claim to jurisdiction, that was all he had to decide, at the moment. But he was not a man for whom the easy course was the most attractive. The reports from Scott, Harding, and Kuchel, which he had read several times sitting alone in his office, had impressed him. When the time came to decide just how the baby had died, he would need to see those scientists in the witness-box, delivering their findings under examination, but for the present he was empowered to rely on the material as it was. If he thought the opinions of those scientists useful, shouldn't he say so? Disposing of the argument on some other, limited, ground which disguised the way his reasoning had begun to run did not seem to him a fair exercise of his authority.

'I find on the question of jurisdiction,' he said, listing in parentheses the points Macknay had made, 'that death has occurred.' Then he leaned forward on the bench, reading from notes he had taken as the argument went along. 'I agree that because of the nature of the damage to the clothing and the manner in which the clothing was found, it would indicate that there has, at some stage, been human intervention in the disposal of the body, and that the body cannot now be found. I find that the body is in a place from which it presently cannot be recovered. On those grounds, I find that I do have jurisdiction.'

There was movement in the public gallery. The words 'human

intervention' had caused radio-news reporters to head for the telephones outside, while the press journalist scribbled into their notebooks. Barritt waited for the courtroom to quieten. He wondered how many of them had got it down right.

Within two days it was clear that the honours were about evenly divided between those reporters who had understood the finding, and those who thought the whole matter inexplicable and not worth mentioning at all. As one newspaper managed to report it, the coroner had decided already that Azaria Chamberlain was murdered in the tent.

Macknay called Lindy Chamberlain to the witness-box. Spectators, most of whom were dressed appropriately for a day at the seaside, craned for a better view. They had not expected the highlight of proceedings to be scheduled so early. The journalists, whose links with the police were friendly and symbiotic, were not at all surprised.

She stepped up into the stand and took the oath in a small but deliberate voice. When she was asked by Macknay to recite her address she gave it as Avondale College, Cooranbong, which confirmed rumours around town that the Chamberlains had fled Mt Isa because their house there had become a tourist attraction. The hand she now laid on the rail was trembling. She wore dark-glasses through which it was impossible to judge the expression in her eyes.

Macknay took her through her account of the disappearance of her baby, an account made the slower, the closer she came to the end of it, as her words were lost in tears. When she then removed her sun-glasses, her eyes were dark and lined. Barritt was as interested in her demeanour as was anyone in the courtroom. It was part of his evaluative task. She was described by the press as emotionless, and now seemed oddly unsettled by these tears, as though they represented some sort of inconsistency. It struck Barritt that, guilty or guiltless, she was in danger of being constrained by her own notoriety.

While she listened from the witness-stand, Mackay read through the scientific reports. All suggested the damage to the baby's clothing was not caused by a dingo. Then he got to the dentist Brown, and a description of holes in the singlet. These, so Brown thought, were made when the singlet was 'inside out'.

She pulled Macknay up, right there. 'I beg your pardon,' she said.

'Inside out,' Macknay repeated.

'Did you say the singlet was inside out?'

'Yes. Assuming it was,' he said.

'Well, it wasn't.'

'You are absolutely certain about that, are you?'

'Yes, I am absolutely certain about that. I never put my children's clothes on inside out.'

'You have never, on any occasion, put a child's singlet on inside out?'

'Yes, I can say that with certainty. It is one thing that extremely annoys me.'

'You dressed the baby in the ladies' toilet, did you not?'

'I don't know that I did dress her in the ladies' toilet. I think I dressed her in the—I at least half dressed her in the barbecue area. From memory, I don't know whether I put any clothes on her at all in there. I carried her out in a towel. She may have had some—She certainly did not have a nappy, or jump-suit, or matinee-jacket, or booties on. Whether I put her singlet on in there or not I don't know, because there was nowhere to lie her down, and I had not taken her change-sheet into the toilet. I can remember holding the blankets up around her, to keep the wind away from her, while I dressed her in the barbecue area. But I could not tell you whether I put some of her clothes on in the toilet or not.'

'You remember that you put the singlet on the right way around, but you cannot tell me where you put it on?'

'That is correct.'

'This is what, sometime before six o'clock?' Macknay asked.

'Yes, it would probably have been somewhere between five and five-thirty.'

'You were in a hurry, were you not?'

'When I was bathing the baby? No.'

'You were in such a hurry,' Macknay insisted, 'that you went straight from the toilet to the car, to go and watch the sunset. Is that right?'

'That's correct, but that was after I had bathed the boys. Not after I had bathed the baby. I did her first, and there was a time-lapse in between bathing her and bathing the boys.'

'So you can remember that, can you? But you cannot remember where you dressed her. Is that your evidence?'

'That's correct.'

'If I suggested to you that this singlet was found inside out, among the clothing when it was located, what would you say about that? That the dingo had turned it inside out?'

'I would only be surmising what had happened to it.'

'What is your supposition about it?'

'I don't know that I have one at the moment, and it would be only a supposition. I prefer to deal in facts,' she said. This was a clear reference to something she had said earlier, when she criticized Brown's report for dealing in the inflated currency of hypothesis.

Macknay, as best he could, gave her an outline of the experiment Brown conducted at the Adelaide Zoo. 'Now,' he said, 'if it were the case that the clothing located at Ayers Rock did not have any consistent features with those taken from the zoo, would you then accept that the damage to the clothing at Ayers Rock was not caused by a dog or a dingo?'

Lindy Chamberlain evidently considered this conclusion critically premature. 'I would like to question what differences there are between domesticated dingoes and wild dingoes.'

'If the forensic dentist told you there were no significant differences between wild dingoes, tame dingoes, and dogs, insofar as the present purposes are concerned?'

'Have tests been done on wild dingoes?'

Denis Barritt, who was himself interested in the answer to this question, leaned forward. The police brief was, he believed, a little short of evidence about the behaviour of dingoes in the wild. And he wondered how Macknay liked being interrogated by a witness.

Macknay offered her, instead, another assumption. 'If we hypothesize that the forensic dentist knows what he is talking about—'

'You are still hypothesizing,' she said. 'I was just asking, "Have there been any tests done on wild dingoes?"'

There was no answer available, a concession Macknay made plain by changing the subject. Barritt took a note to discuss with Macknay the need to call evidence from a zoologist with field-work experience, if they could find one.

'Well,' Macknay said, 'is it not the case that you did some sort of thesis on dingoes?' The question caused a rustle of interest in the press-pews. The suggestion that Lindy Chamberlain had made a study of dingoes at college, and therefore knew more than she was prepared to admit, had first made its appearance about a fortnight after the baby disappeared. No one seemed to know just where the information had come from, but some city tabloids had printed it anyway.

'No, it is not the case,' she said, with more than a little scorn. 'That is a press invention.'

'It arose out of the *Woman's Day* article?'

'I wouldn't have any idea.'

'You did not read the *Woman's Day* article?'

'Yes. But I didn't gather that from it. I thought it came from a newspaper.'

'Was the *Woman's Day* article an accurate one?'

'No. It was an extremely inaccurate one. In fact, it was the most inaccurate article of reporting perhaps that there has been. Or, at least, that I have read so far.'

'Were the parts marked in quotation marks accurate?'

'No. There were actually only two or three small paragraphs that were accurate out of the whole article. In actual fact, there are only about five reporters who actually write exactly what you say. The rest of them use a little bit of licence.'

'I just want to read part of page twelve of that interview, which is contained in quotation marks apparently quoting you. And firstly, can you tell me whether this is what you told them, or not: "I was cuddling Azaria all the time, kissing her toes—"'

Macknay pronounced the name as if it were spelled 'Azairia', a mistake he had made throughout. This time, Lindy Chamberlain did not let him get far.

She made a face. 'Excuse me, would you mind calling my daughter Azaria,' she said, stressing the R-sound of the second syllable. 'It does annoy me when you call her the wrong name.'

'I'm sorry,' Macknay said, and began the passage again. ' "I was cuddling Azaria at the time, kissing her toes and thinking what an incredible baby she was. I think Michael said, "You must put her down sometime, you're spoiling her." Did you tell that to the reporter?'

'Pure invention. If you stop to think about it,' she said, as if it were high time Macknay did just that, 'cuddling a baby and kissing bare toes in those temperatures is absolutely ridiculous. But it does sound good for the audience that the paper is specifically written for, and I think that the Liz, whatever her name was, who wrote that particular piece, wrote in a way that she thought would be as kind as possible, and get the message over to her readers, without necessarily being correct.'

Macknay brought his line of examination back to Kenneth Brown's reports of damage to the baby's blanket. It was Brown's opinion, at the time he wrote the report, that the blanket was damaged by some manner of sharp implement.

'Perhaps I could just read something out, and see if you are prepared to accept the accuracy of what I read, in relation to those blankets,' Macknay said. ' "There were several small cuts in the blankets but there was no evidence of tooth-marks." '

'Well,' she said, 'teeth cut, don't they? Teeth cut, knives cut, scissors cut, several things cut.'

'The fact that the forensic dentist has concluded there was no evidence of tooth-marks on that blanket does not cause you any concern at all?'

'It does cause me concern. The fact is they cannot tell what it was done by. And, if they can be so accurate in one thing, why can they not be so accurate in stating what it is?'

'I see. So you are not prepared to accept the fact that he may be able to exclude some cause, but not necessarily pin-point a particular cause?'

The distinction was not lost on her; indeed this was clearly the argument she was pressing. 'I am prepared to accept that he knows, in a certain field, what has happened, yes.'

'You are not prepared to accept his expertise in saying that there were no tooth-marks?'

'I am not saying that at all. I am saying that I would like a full answer, not a partial answer,' she said. 'I would like to know more, perhaps than anyone else, what happened to my daughter—'

When Lindy Chamberlain stood down from the witness-box, she looked tired. Her examination had run into the second day. In Denis Barritt's estimation, Macknay had got no further with her than had Sergeant Charlwood, judging by the record of interview now in the file. Macknay had not shown her to be a mother with the inclination or the propensity to murder her own child. He had shown her to be capable of sorrow, bewilderment, humour, anger and scorn. And, perhaps more clearly than anything else, a surprisingly tenacious fighter.

*   *   *

Michael Chamberlain revealed nowhere near his wife's array of emotions. He sat in the witness stand, handsome and serious, one of the few men in court to wear a tie. He sat as erect as he might in church. He folded his hands in his lap. His answers were deliberate and composed, as though his task as a witness had as much to do with the accuracy of sentence construction as with the accuracy of memory. This was a mannerism Barritt had seen before in preachers. And its importance for Michael Chamberlain suddenly came plain: no one here addressed him as pastor. Now, in this public predicament, he reaffirmed with every quiet response, his standing as a man of God.

He was still in the witness-box when the afternoon session began. It was Barritt's practice to remind every witness, after an adjournment, of the continuing mandate of the oath before the evidence resumed. Barritt waited until the courtroom was still. He wanted no distraction from the exercise he had in mind.

'Pastor,' he said, allowing the title to stand alone for a moment, 'you have already been sworn and are still on oath.'

Michael Chamberlain bowed his head. His hands covered his face. When he removed them his cheeks were wet. Macknay asked him a question he did not hear. 'I am sorry. I have had a lapse,' he said. 'If you would just like to repeat the question for me.'

The switchboard-operator in the court-house office took an anonymous call. 'I'm going to blow that bitch away,' the caller said. 'You can tell her that for me.' He was talking about Lindy Chamberlain. It was not the first message to come through that way, but it was the most unambiguous. The operator rang through to the police room.

In the courtroom, proceedings had slowed while Macknay listed, for the court record, a series of photographs. A policeman walked quietly to the bar-table where Peter Dean was seated, and delivered a note. Dean paled as he read it. He passed it across to Macknay, who paused for long enough to scan it and then halted altogether as if he were not sure what to do next. Dean got to his feet and asked Barritt to grant a short adjournment. 'I support his application,' Macknay said. Both counsel were now on their feet at the one time, a breach of court etiquette of which each seemed oblivious, so Barritt gathered something serious was in train. He adjourned for five minutes. As he walked from the court, he saw

Dean turning towards the Chamberlains. Macknay waved away the mystified journalists.

Dean and Macknay headed upstairs for the magistrates' chambers. By the time they got there Barritt had the news already. 'I've ordered the police guard doubled,' he said, pacing the room, 'but what else can I do?'

'My clients need protection while they are away from the court,' Peter Dean said.

'Yes,' Barritt said. 'What do you think, Ash?'

Ashley Macknay suggested Barritt might make some sort of statement from the bench to dampen passions. 'What worries me is the way the press could handle this,' he said. 'We'll have trouble with every crank in town.'

Barritt had more news for them. 'The way the caller spoke, the switchboard girl thinks he's been sitting somewhere in court.'

'Christ,' Macknay said.

'You'd better make an application to me in open court,' Barrritt told Peter Dean as they left.

When court resumed and everyone else sat, Dean stayed on his feet. 'If Your Worship pleases,' he said, 'the reason I sought that short adjournment is that it's come to my attention that there have been a number of phone calls made to the government switchboard here, and they've been—certainly just recently—of a somewhat threatening nature towards my clients. I have now discussed the matter with my learned friend, and I understand that they may be able to seek some assistance. I ask Your Worship to do what can be done to protect my clients.' The reporters in the front rows, who by now knew precisely what was afoot, were intently poised. Barritt cleared his throat. 'Yes,' he said. 'I understand steps have already been taken to ensure that the situation will be kept under control. The nature of the phone calls has been brought to my notice, and I think it is appropriate that I ought to point out that an inquiry such as this is a judicial inquiry. The basis of our judiciary in Australia is to inquire impartially into circumstances surrounding whatever particular case we may be engaged in at the time. It is one of the cardinal principles of such an inquiry that the person making the inquiry maintains objectivity through all the evidence.'

He turned his gaze to Peter Dean and the Chamberlains. 'It may seem at times that suspicion or innuendo refer to your clients, Mr Dean, and of course in other parts of evidence that have been called, and no doubt other parts of evidence that will be called, there will be quite countering, and significant, pieces of evidence. It is certainly not my role to make any judgement until all that evidence is in, at the conclusion of this inquiry. I would certainly ask that the public adopt the same attitude, that they ought not make any such prejudgement of the situation.' Barritt then delivered a plea for fairness and compassion and turned his attention to the role of the press. 'I ask the public at large to reserve judgement in this case until all the evidence is in. And they must also remember that a lot of evidence is given in a court that cannot physically be transferred by the media into the media outlets. It is a physical impossibility. A lot of evidence must, of the very nature of its volume, go unmentioned to the public. So it is very difficult, at any stage, for the public to give a proper judgement. I will say this, that at the conclusion of this inquisition, I will give as detailed a judgement on all the evidence as I can, and I would at this stage ask the media to give as much publicity to that as possible, so that the public at large, who no doubt are concerned, and some of them irrationally concerned apparently, might have the opportunity of appreciating all the facts of the case.'

He surveyed the faces in the public gallery. Who could tell what was deep in any human heart? Set into the panelling under the bench, next to his right knee, was an alarm button. It was said to be connected directly to a siren in the police room. Any time he had accidently pressed it in the past, nothing seemed to have happened.

4

THE HEAD WAITER looked around for a spare table. Wally Goodwin caught sight of Greg and Sally Lowe sitting with the Chamberlains, and headed over there instead. The Chamberlains he recognized from press photographs. The Lowes he had met on the plane, coming up from the south late this afternoon. They expected, as he did, to be called to the witness-stand sometime tomorrow.

They made room, and Sally Lowe introduced him around. 'What are you a witness to?' Michael Chamberlain asked.

'I found your daughter's clothing,' Wally said.

The waiter gave him a menu. Lindy Chamberlain told him, 'We've ordered already. You go ahead.' Wally saw that the Chamberlains were drinking fruit-juice, but Greg Lowe had a beer so Wally ordered a beer for himself.

'Something I've wondered about,' Michael Chamberlain said. 'We were told the clothes were found jammed between rocks. Is that true?'

'Nowhere near rocks. They were lying on the ground. The nearest rocks were yards away.'

'You can't believe everything you hear.' Sally Lowe said. 'I can't wait to read the newspapers after I give evidence, to see what I'm supposed to have said.'

Lindy Chamberlain shook her head. 'I don't think Graeme Charlwood would tell us a deliberate lie. He thought they were found in a crevice.'

'Well, he'll know soon enough, if he doesn't know already,' Wally said. Greg Lowe rubbed his stumpy beard and then drained his beer, as if he had suddenly decided against saying anything.

5

THE ORDER in which Macknay and Barritt chose to call the witnesses now reflected, as conveniently as airline schedules would allow, the chronology of events as they happened at Ayers Rock. It reflected also a growing concern with the presentation of the evidence to an attentive but readily confused nation. The clearer the evidence was for reporters, the clearer it might be for readers. Barritt had sketched four broad categories of events: Azaria's disappearance from camp, the search, the police investigation, the scientific investigation. It was a format he was keen to preserve. If he ran his court to schedule, he might have taken evidence from the campsite witnesses, and from those involved with the search, all by the time he should adjourn the hearing for the Christmas break. This would leave the police and the scientists to February.

Now, sitting in his chambers at the end of the third day, he felt satisfied with the progress so far. He was working through transcripts of the testimony, noting important points on a runningsheet, a procedure which made things easier when the time came to make a finding. He had taken testimony from Judy and Bill West and from the Lowes, all of whom were close to the aciton when the cry went up, from the gentle Florence Wilkin who had nursed the baby for a moment at the base of the Rock while the Chamberlains went higher, and from Wally Goodwin who had found the clothes a week later. This completed the appearances of those campers Barritt considered should give their evidence on oath. So well did the proceedings run that Macknay finished with Bobbie Downs, the bush nurse, during the afternoon, and was dealing with the head ranger Derek Roff when the day ended.

It was already clear to Barritt that the early police reports were cruelly misguided. Lindy Chamberlain did not take to the Rock merely 'a white bundle' she held to her breast. The baby whom Florence Wilkin held was alive and wailing. The photograph Michael Chamberlain took while his wife dandled the child in front of the camera was not of a borrowed baby, but their own, a tiny infant whom the Lowes later saw. Azaria was not already slain when her mother laid her down for the night; Sally Lowe heard her cry from the tent. Lindy Chamberlain was not a harsh and uncaring mother but tender and loving enough to be admired for it by everyone who saw her there with the child. There was no ritual killing. If the baby was murdered, the felony was of a different quality altogether.

So disturbed was Barritt by imperishable rumour that he had interrupted the hearing today to read out a report sent to him by a researcher in Hebrew Studies from Sydney. The name Azaria, the report read, had nothing to do with sacrifice. That was a confusion with the name Azala. Azaria translated, 'with the help of God'. Barritt had read it out, in a loud and measured voice, directed at the public gallery and the press-benches. He wondered if it would make any difference.

Now, sitting at his desk, he made a note to repeat the definition in his finding. He tidied his papers and decided to go home. Outside, the air was soft and blue. Street-lamps were switching on. A newspaper photographer sat on the steps. He was waiting, most likely, for his reporter to finish phoning copy through to a city newsroom somewhere on the seaboard. Others were doing the same thing from motel foyers and hotel rooms about town. At the kerbside, young men in jeans and T-shirts loaded television cameras and coils of cable into a van.

This was what worried Barritt about the case more than anything else: the disproportions, the distortions of publicity. Everything was larger than life the moment it hit front page. He was conducting an inquest, but the nation was watching a public trial.

Winmatti spoke through an interpreter. He stood proudly, in open-necked shirt and pale shorts. Barritt took it as a mark of respect that the old man was wearing sandals. The language Winmatti shared with Mrs Harmer, who stood by his side, was Luritja. He had also a little English, and sometimes he began to answer Macknay's question before Mrs Harmer had finished translating it.

In spurts which were seldom more than a sentence long, the tracker took them from the first dingo-prints beside the Chamberlain tent, east to climb the dune, past the smudges of a small bundle on the sand where he could 'see him put it down', up to the ridge where the tracks were obliterated because 'too many have gone there at night-time'. He picked up a track which went away over to the east into flat spinifex country before he decided it was the wrong one, backtracked, and picked up the more familiar trail, an animal hungry and thirsty with 'the same like it, the paw', near the Maggie Spring. Along the way, the detours were as much semantic as geographic. No one in court was sure where the search had taken them.

Barritt's interest in the chase waned. He was now more concerned with the Aborigine's belief in the propensity of a dingo to steal away a child. He knew of no black baby taken from camp, at least there was none on record. But the Aborigines had their own method of recording events long past. Often they made an appearance in mythology, in the legends of the dreamtime.

He asked, 'Using Luritja dreaming, could you tell the court the Luritja dreaming of dingoes and children?'

Mrs Harmer was unhappy about the question. 'This would be hard to say in Luritja, but I know for myself.'

'See if he can recall the Luritja dreaming of dingoes and children,' Barritt insisted.

She translated the old man's answer, uneasily and with downcast eyes. 'For an Aborigine to have twins, who both die, that is taboo. So they keep one baby, the strongest one. And the dreamtime story is that children who leave the camp, the Dingo Spirit will get them. So they leave the weaker twin out bush. For the dingoes.'

During court recess, Pamela Harmer ran upstairs to Barritt's chambers. She stormed inside. He should not have asked Winmatti the questions he did, she told him. The Dingo Spirit dreaming was a forbidden subject. He had now shamed the old man and his clan. Outside the room, court staff could hear her indignation two corridors away. Barritt promised an apology and ushered her out.

Nevertheless, he could not think how else he might have handled the topic. The way the evidence was shaping, it was the desert people, the rangers, and the Ayers Rock police who believed a dingo was capable of the abduction. The sceptics were people of towns and cities.

6

LES HARRIS was thinking along similar lines. His appreciation of the way the inquest was shaping was drawn from the Melbourne daily, the *Age* and from television bulletins. Mornings, he snipped the reports from the pages of the newspaper during his coffee-break at the aircraft factory, underlined and annotated them. Evenings, he caught the television bulletins as he sat in the lounge-room at home taking notes, very often while his own two dingoes lay at his feet. Daily, he heard city people say that no dingo would carry off a child. It made him angry, every time.

Before the inquest had opened, Harris wrote to the Alice Springs coroner. That was in December. He had addressed it to the wrong magistrate, as it turned out, so he rang the court-house to make sure that the letter was redirected. The information in it took him some effort to compile. It took more effort to convince the members of the Dingo Foundation that it should go under its official letterhead. Some thought it should not be involved at all. Harris was, at the time, president. If it was not the foundation's duty to offer accurate information about dingoes, Harris wanted to know what it was here for, so that was that. He wrote:

1. Search for remains
Observations show that a mammal weighing ten pounds would normally be totally consumed in less than twenty minutes by a solitary dingo eating in the most leisurely fashion. A mated pair would probably consume the same mammal in less than ten minutes, there being a finite hierarchical order of food sharing with mated pairs. Two or more immature dingoes (less than two years old) would consume it in four minutes or less, there being

vigorous competition for food, unhampered by considerations of adult hierarchy or mated pair behaviour. Mammals are usually consumed entirely; nothing is left. It is difficult to identify a spot where a mammal has been consumed for this reason.

Comment: If the baby was taken by a dingo, it is improbable that any trace would be found more than thirty minutes later.

2. Stomach analysis

Observations indicate that food is digested and the waste excreted in ten to twenty-four hours, depending on the nature of the food and the age of the animal which consumed it. When added to the above notes on consumption time, it can be seen that by about eight p.m. on the following night the waste would normally have been excreted, and nothing could be learned by examining stomach contents later than that time, and probably to twelve hours earlier than that time.

3. Speculation on the strength of dingoes

There has been much speculation as to whether a dingo could carry a weight of ten pounds and, if so, how far it could be carried. Observations show that mammals of about twenty pounds can be carried over long distances with considerable ease, e.g. an adult female dingo was observed carrying a wallaby of approximately twenty pounds; it was carried by the middle of the back with only the tail touching the ground. The distance over which she was observed was about half a mile, for which distance she moved at a trot with no indication that the load impaired her in any way.

An adult male was observed carrying a very large hare up a slope of some thirty degrees, over a distance of about six hundred yards. On detecting the presence of the observer, he stopped motionless for some two to two and a half minutes whilst he assessed the situation. During this time he stood in the characteristic neck-up attitude with the hare in his mouth. The weight of the hare appeared to be of no consequence. After satisfying himself that there was no danger, he moved off up the slope and disappeared into the trees.

Comment: A mammal weighing ten pounds is smaller than the game regularly caught, killed, and carried over various distances. Such a weight would offer no hindrance, and it can be reasonably presumed that it could be carried over a long distance with ease.

4. Condition of the baby's clothing

There has been considerable speculation as to whether a dingo could have removed the baby's clothing and, if so, how it would be done. The manipulative ability of dingoes is extremely high but this ability is very difficult to quantify and can only be done anecdotally.

a) I have on three occasions left parcels of meat within reach of my tame six-year old male dingo. On two of these occasions, the parcel was unrolled and the meat extracted from the plastic bag. The paper was torn minimally and only at the point at which the unrolling commenced, and the plastic bag was not torn at all. On the third occasion, the end of the parcel was opened and the meat was extracted. This parcel was wedged in a box along with other parcels and he performed the extraction in situ. Only the end was opened.

(b) A tame three-year-old female has been observed to open a domestic refrigerator, pull out the meat tray, and help herself to the contents. Whilst the refrigerator door did not have a mechanical lock, it nonetheless required a hefty pull in a finite direction to open it. In order to exert the amount of leverage in the required direction, she stood on her hind legs to one side of the door, braced her forefeet on a cupboard, leaned sideways, took the door handle in her teeth and pulled it open. She then changed position, stood on her hind legs again and pulled the meat tray out, again in one finite direction.

(c) During the mating season, I had my six-year-old male and a four-year-old female chained to a post. The female was on a chain twice the length of that of the male. Although the female was then post oestrus, the male was still strongly motivated to mate, but the female deliberately stayed beyond his reach. (The females are in oestrus only once a year and the males are sexually active for about six weeks spanning the female oestrus period.) After failing to entice the female within his reach, the male reached forward and took the female's chain in his teeth. He then gave a mighty heave on the chain, taking the female unawares, and tossed her back well within his reach. As she was still scrambling to her feet, he pounced on her and mounted her.

I am considerably handicapped in making any significant comment on the state of the baby's clothing as my only information was a very brief TV news film-clip of the clothing laid out on a table shortly after it was found. I therefore cannot draw any conclusions, but point out that I judge the manipulative skills and the cognitive abilities of dingoes to be very high, far higher than dogs, and probably as high as that of a young primate. If the baby was taken by a dingo, the presence of soft, pliable, and probably loose garments would not impede them, and I can well visualize that they were peeled off without difficulty. Macabre as this comment may sound, dingoes are usually fastidious eaters and tend to reject foreign matter from their food. From the brief view that I had of the clothing, the amount of blood around the neck of the garments would be commensurate with the observed tactic of killing small mammals by seizing them by the nape of the neck and giving a very fast and powerful shake; if the baby was carried for some distance with its heart stopped, little bleeding would occur.

5. The zoo experiment

The results of the experiment where a kid goat was dressed in baby's clothing and given to zoo dingoes would be valid for that situation only, and could not be reasonably extrapolated as being indicative of the behaviour of naturally occurring dingoes. The pressure to compete for food is very much diminished in zoo and sanctuary predatory carnivores, simply because very palatable food is delivered to them in abundant quantities every day without fail. Since they have never had to exercise the very demanding hunting skills on a daily basis in order to survive, these skills never develop to more than a miniscule fraction of their wild counterparts. Whilst I have myself, in the course of these notes, made some comparisons between the eating habits of wild and tame dingoes, I could not in any conscience draw any conclusions from this particular experiment.

It is an unfortunate but inescapable side effect on zoo animals that they are natural animals in physical appearance only. In such an experiment, dingoes which have lived their entire lives in an area the size of a couple of tennis-courts, and who have had their food supplied each day, are not going to act in the manner of, or with the determination of, naturally occurring dingoes which must stalk and kill prey every day of their lives in order simply to stay alive.

Comment: The zoo experiment would not reveal any results which could be reliably extrapolated to naturally occurring dingoes.

6. Saliva on clothing

Observations indicate that dingoes are tidy eaters and, in conditions of adequate supply, do not appear to slaver when eating. In the common sociologically stable situation of the mated pair, food is shared on an unhurried basis. The tearing apart and gulping down of a mammal could occur in certain situations, e.g. in times of dire shortage of prey, or when the available food is being consumed by a number of immature dingoes of equal social status. In the latter situation, an overabundance of saliva could be promoted by hunger or competition. Direct observation of wild and captive dingoes in a stable social order show that consumption is unhurried, the lips are well drawn back when the carnassials are used in the shearing mode, slavering appears to be absent, and food is not scattered about. In the cases quoted earlier, where one of my captive dingoes opened meat parcels, there was no sign of the wetting of the paper by saliva.

Comment: Saliva would not necessarily be present in discernible quantities on the clothing.

Harris dwelt awhile on the exploits of his own dingoes, and concluded:

Comparisons between dingoes and domestic dogs are not particularly valid, tempting as they might be. The dingo is a natural canid (in fact a wolf, not a dog) which has to practise its hunting skills on a daily basis and at a very high level of efficiency in order to survive. In terms of strength, speed, agility and reasoning power, they compare more readily with the natural felines, i.e. tigers, leopards, *et al*. It is easier to underestimate the capabilities of dingoes than to overestimate them.

The Ayers Rock dingoes are atypical in one respect of natural behaviour. They have had very close contact with tourists for a long time and have been fed directly and indirectly by tourists. They have maintained all of their hunting skills, plus extended their abilities to acquire food from tourists and their campsites, and you are no doubt aware that they often raid tents in their search for food. Humans, their accoutrements, their tents and caravans pose no threat, and pillaging is not uncommon. This has resulted in a very dangerous situation wherein they are not tame and they are not wild.

In considering the questions:
1. Could a dingo have taken the baby?
2. Could a dingo or dingoes have removed its clothing?
3. Could a dingo or dingoes have totally consumed the baby?
my answers, based on many years of observation of dingoes in their natural habitat and in captivity, would be:
1. Yes, with ease.
2. Probably yes.
3. Yes, without any doubt.

Harris had posted his letter early in December. There was no reply. This was not a silence he was happy about. He read that the Chamberlains' lawyer was Alice Springs solicitor Peter Dean. The newspaper also reported the date on which the Chamberlains had engaged him. That was the Friday before the inquest opened, and gave the lawyer only three days to prepare. Harris thought this betrayed either worldly ignorance or religious bravado. He was impatient of both. He rang Dean in Alice Springs and then posted him a copy of the material sent to the coroner. His covering letter to Dean made the boundaries of his interest plain. 'I have no sympathy for the Chamberlains. I cannot think of any more damaging statement than to attribute this tragic matter to divine direction. Great rationalization, but bad news in court.'

The bad news in court worsened when the inquest resumed. Harris, who had written again to the court during the adjournment, watched for some sign that the nature and capabilities of dingoes might yet receive some serious scrutiny. None came. Instead, the procession of evidence now comprised suspicious detectives and scientists who were looking for the wrong answers in the wrong directions. Harris was not impressed by the findings of Kuchel, Scott, Harding and Brown, because they didn't know what they ought to be finding.

The other news was this: the Chamberlains had engaged another lawyer.

Peter Dean stayed on the case, but was led now by an Adelaide barrister, Phillip Rice. Rice was described in the newsreports as a Queen's Counsel with a specialty in criminal law. Harris thought no one called in an advocate of that calibre unless they were losing the argument, so the event confirmed his growing fears.

Harris rang Rice over the weekend. Rice sounded warm and receptive. 'Send me anything you've got,' he said. Harris spent Sunday compiling another dossier of facts and comment. It contained a new topic, prompted by evidence given by Kuchel, the botanist. It was Kuchel's view that the baby's clothing was rubbed in the nettle *Parietaria debilis*, near where the clothing was found, to give the impression that she was dragged there by dingoes and eaten. Harris did not see it that way at all. He wrote:

I confirm and extend the comments I made on the phone regarding the propensity of dingoes to investigate objects of interest to them. I have seen both naturally occurring and captive dingoes exhibit considerable interest in strange objects. They will paw, nose and mouth, hold it with one or two front paws and carefully manipulate it with incisors or canines, and finally pick it up and shake it very vigorously. During the process, the object is invariably moved from its original location. I have also observed dingoes urinating on, and/or rolling on, such objects. The rolling can be very vigorous, to the degree that the rolling can change the configuration and the location of the object.

He typed it out and sent it away. The exercise had given him heart. Now they might be getting somewhere.

Next day the Melbourne *Age* carried a report which Harris read through in his office, then folded away in his briefcase. He needed to think about it. Coroner Barritt had asked the public to send him 'reports of dingoes attacking children'. Barritt cited as an example 'the disappearance of a two-year-old child from a verandah near Gympie about a hundred years ago'. This plea might, some weeks ago, have given Les Harris a measure of satisfaction. But now, at this stage of the inquest, there was something disturbing about it. He read the report again at home, with the paper spread out over the busy table he used as a desk, and began to make notes. The task was to make clear, to himself, what was going wrong here.

This morning, Tuesday.

The *Age* carried an item headed 'Coroner Asks for Dingo Leads', stating that he is seeking information about attacks on children.

I debated with myself whether I should prepare yet another set of notes, and the decision was No. I have the feeling that I have been volunteering information which is only half relevant because my source of information—the media reports—is only half accurate. This is likely to be true in the case of these notes also.

I will confine myself to stating that:
(a) any adult dingo would be fully capable of taking and consuming a ten-week old baby, and,
(b) the probability that this is what happened at Ayers Rock (and only at Ayers Rock) is extremely high.

The justification for the first statement I have already given in previous notes.

The justification for the second, although very clear to me, would require many, many pages of reasoning to make it clear to anyone who has not lived with dingoes for long enough to understand their capabilities.

It is my belief that the coroner doesn't realize that the dingo is a highly intelligent, fast thinking, fast acting, strong and capable carnivore. Because he doesn't know this, he hasn't taken any evidence on the subject. Because he hasn't taken any evidence on it, he doesn't know anything about it.

Classic *Catch 22* situation.

And the information I have volunteered hasn't broken the *Catch 22* circle.

Now the coroner is calling for narrow, specific, even minuscule information, but still without having tried to establish the basic facts from which such information must be evaluated.

I think I have come to the end of what I can do.

I give up.

7

IN THE COURTHOUSE MAILBAG Denis Barritt got twenty-seven accounts of dingo predations on adults and children, four opinions that dingoes are incapable of such behaviour, a story about the abduction of a baby from a farmhouse by a disgruntled pig, and a finely wrought scenario for murder concluding with Lindy Chamberlain feeding to a punctual dingo the remnants of her daughter which were then disguised as table-scraps from the evening meal.

A sincere search for information was only part of the reason Barritt made his appeal. The gesture was as important. He wanted to throw open the public mind, somehow, at least until all the evidence was done. Again, a demonstration of his own open-mindedness was the best ploy he could think of.

Events the Friday before made it all the more urgent. That day, the manager of the motel in which the Chamberlains were staying asked that they leave. No one argued with his reason. A caller to the motel switchboard had threatened to blow the place apart with a bomb. The chances that it was a hoax were high, for the date was Friday the thirteenth, but the police moved the Chamberlains away and kept their destination secret.

8

FROM THE MOMENT he stepped into the witness-box, Dr Newsome was chary about questions he considered undisciplined. Macknay, who was then taking Newsome through the preamble necessary to prove him an expert ethologist, asked if he had studied wolves and coyotes in America.

'Yes.'

'Wolves and coyotes do bear some relationship at least to the Australian dingo?'

'They all belong to the same genus,' Newsome said abruptly. '*Canis*.'

So do domestic dogs, which was the point Newsome was making, so Macknay left it at that and went back to Newsome's long list of qualifications.

The length of that list was the reason Barritt had chosen Newsome to testify, rather than his colleague Lawrence Corbett, or Les Harris. Barritt's interest was especially prompted by Newsome's ten years as leader of a field team of zoologists studying dingoes through Central Australia and Victoria. Newsome, confident and expansive, looked like a young man well used to some esteem wherever he was, inside university halls or on a sports field. Other scientists at the Wildlife Research Division in Canberra, where Newsome worked, were said to hold the ebullience and gusto of the dingo specialists there in high, if astonished, regard. Now, his disobedient dark curls and irreverent smile gave that gossip a measure of credibility.

Recalling the time his team released dingoes to which they had fixed radio transmitters and then tracked the signals over the plains, Newsome said: 'We had believed, until then, that dingoes lived essentially by themselves, that they were loners. We were surprised to find this was not so; although individuals were mostly found by themselves, in fact they belonged to groups which met infrequently, but sufficiently so that these groups knew one another, and kept their entity.'

This topic, action in concert, Macknay kept coming back to. 'The growl that Mr and Mrs West heard,' he reminded Newsome, 'could you tell us whether dingoes growl and, if so, under what circumstances?'

'Yes. They do growl. We would expect growling mostly as a warning signal to other dingoes. That would be the most usual circumstance.'

'So you think that the growl, if it was from a dingo, most likely came from a second dingo?'

'Yes,' Newsome said.

And again later: 'I think,' Macknay said, 'you drew some possible significance from the growl which the Wests heard shortly before the alarm was raised, and the fact that there was a dingo seen which was standing still immediately after the alarm was raised. I think you considered, as a hypothesis from that, the possiblity of there being two, rather than one?'

'I expected, from the growl, it would be more likely than anything else for that to be an interaction between two dingoes. How the one seen behind the tent, and the one seen emerging from the tent, might have conducted themselves in that way with the tent between, as it would appear, I don't know.'

'But you considered there was some significance in the growl, and the fact that a dingo was seen so close to the tent, but standing still and not fleeing?'

'That it was not the animal which came out of the tent, was my first response on reading it.'

'They commence moulting, or heavy moulting in comparison to the other months of the year, around about August-September?'

'That is the peak of it.'

'If a dingo had carried a child in clothing for a minimum of five kilometres, would the moulting be sufficient, do you think, to transfer a large number of hairs, or any hairs, to the clothing?'

'If the transport was entirely in the mouth, then the moulting on the body is not likely to affect it. If dragged, I should think there might be some hairs on it.'

'In relation to saliva, you have told us there is a pint lost a day?'

'That includes urine and faeces too, but it is losing a pint of water or fluid.'

'Given the prevailing conditions of a very cold night, and perhaps assuming that a dingo takes the shortest route and takes it in a leisurely fashion, would you have expected that any large amounts of saliva would be transferred to the clothing?'

'I would have expected some saliva.'

'In whatever fashion the child was being carried?'

'More so, of course,' Newsome said with a smile, 'if in the mouth than any other way.'

Macknay wanted to know what the chances were 'of a dingo having removed the child from the tent, having disposed of the remains in some way, and depositing the clothing somewhere.'

The question made Newsome frown. It had more to do with the philosophy of experience than scientific probability. He mused, by way of a quiet protest, 'Any one of those parts has to be a long-shot, but there is no way of demonstrating it could not happen.'

'And irrespective of how the clothes were removed, and irrespective of where they were placed, do you consider it consistent with the behaviour of crows and eagles, for instance, that you observed in your time in the bush, that they pick up things like clothes and may drop them elsewhere.'

Eagles and crows they had talked of earlier. 'I can't remember an example immediately, off-hand,' Newsome said, 'but it is the sort of thing crows may do.'

This was too much for Barritt. Macknay had finished with the witness, but Barritt broke in before Rice could get to his feet.

'Would it be consistent with your understanding of dingoes that, having taken the clothes off, the singlet would be put back inside the jump-suit, and left in a little bundle with the nappy, covering an area of no more than eighteen inches in a little square?'

'There are clearly things which are very difficult to understand about that,' Newsome said.

'Do I take it you mean, from what you said to Mr Macknay, that you could not understand a baby taken out of the bassinet in the tent? He put to you three propositions in one, and you said that you cannot understand the earlier propositions.'

'I was tending to put aside the problems of transport of clothes, and think about an act of predation. You see, every one of the events, for it to have occurred naturally, seems to me of a very low probability.'

'I am asking you to cast your mind only to the first event, the taking of the child. Disregard the subsequent events,' Barritt insisted. 'Just that first one.'

'The odds must be very long on such an event happening, but I do not see how its possibility could be dismissed.'

Every possibility killed the baby afresh. Barritt wondered how long the parents could stand it. He had taken to keeping his gaze from them, but knew that they sat closely enough together that their arms touched and the pastor held his wife's hand while the evidence spoke of entrails and viscera and the peeling of skin. The dead rise again for an inquest. It put Barritt in mind of the coroner's court in Melbourne, a building he thought the gloomiest on earth, where inquests were held upstairs from the autopsy laboratories, and melancholy perfumes drifted the corridors like wraiths.

Barritt had seen Phillip Rice work before. Rice had been around criminal courts for many years now. His style of advocacy made good use of charm and the authority of age. In his white shirt and pale trousers he might, with the addition of a bow-tie or cravat, be taken for someone who liked to spend a day in the members stand at the race-track and enjoyed water-colourists of the English school. He ran a hand over his grey hair. He was about to bring Newsome to a topic of some difficulty.

'You know, do you not, that the digestive juices of a dingo are not unlike the strength of the digestive juices of dogs?'

'I have assumed that to be so.'

'And you know that they are exceedingly strong, and capable of digesting bones?'

'Not all bones,' Newsome demurred. 'Parts of them.'

'But postulating for a moment—as much as I don't want to conjure it up as an example—the bones of a ten-week-old baby of course would still be in a supple state, relatively speaking, and would be capable of being digested relatively easily by an adult dingo, would they not?'

Newsome seemed to think this an unnecessarily gory question. He turned away from Rice, behind whom the Chamberlains sat. 'One is inclined to use the word "merciful",' he said quietly, 'in not knowing very much about that.'

A movement caught Barritt's eye. Michael Chamberlain had lowered his face to his hands. His wife replaced her dark glasses and sat upright. The press had caught it too. Those sitting in the jury-box had the better view, though they had to look sidelong which made them seem somehow aloof and distrustful.

Then something occurred to Barritt he had missed until that moment. The press was sitting on the seats of judgement. No point in moving them now. But the unlucky metaphor was, like some sudden unpardonable remark, far too apt.

* * *

Another part of Newsome's evidence was bound to cause trouble. Newsome thought the Ayers Rock dingoes ought to be shot. And Dr Corbett, who had worked with him on the research team, thought so too.

The problem, as Newsome saw it, was peculiar to dingoes which were neither tame nor wild. The tame obeyed, the wild stayed away. Ayers Rock dingoes did neither, and people were bitten. He could think of one feasible solution: begin a fresh generation of dingoes there, then keep them wild.

'Those difficulties were present in your mind before this matter'—and here Macknay meant this case—'ever came to your attention?'

Newsome agreed, nodding.

Barritt's duty as a coroner required him to consider human safety at Ayers Rock. But, offhand, he couldn't think of a resolution which could make him more unpopular.

By four o'clock, Barritt knew Macknay was stalling. Dr Harding was in the box. Macknay's questions, about the methodology of hair comparison, had taken a half hour. They should have taken ten minutes. Barritt asked if Macknay wanted to adjourn.

'Actually, Your Worship,' Macknay said, 'there is a matter my learned friend and I would like to raise with you in chambers.'

Barritt waited for them in his office. Whatever was wrong now had to do with Harding. His report presented something of an enigma already. On one hand, he had found animal hair on the baby's clothing. On the other, he found nothing but old hairs on the blankets. Something about that did not add up.

Barritt checked the refrigerator for iced water and beer, leaned back in his chair, and drew on a cigarette. As he was persuaded by the testimony so far, the campsite witnesses were honest and reliable observers, every one. They supported the Chamberlain account, to an extent which must by now have surprised even the investigators. Yet the scientists stood together, an outpost of disbelief. On their testimony, human hands disposed of the clothing. Who might have had reason to do that? The parents, if the police were correct. Otherwise, someone responsible for the safety of campers? Someone whose pet the animal was? In Barritt's experience blacks came under rapid scrutiny at a time like this. But why did the local whites take care to search under their houses and around the sheds? If the clothing was damaged by scissors rather than a knife the instrument is handier and more familar to European fingers than Pitjantjatjara. The laboratory evidence, as it presently stood, set an unpersuasive direction, anomalous to the likelier course of events, but it was not Barritt's job to ignore inconvenient testimony. The task was to find a hypothesis which fitted all the facts equally well. So long as the scientists could demonstrate that a dingo did not dispose of the clothing, Barritt would have to search out a solution which took precise account of that.

When Rice and Macknay walked in, he asked, 'Is there a problem with Harding?'

'He wants to change his opinion,' Macknay said. 'When he examined the child's blankets in Adelaide, the only hairs he found were all embedded in the weave. Too old to be relevant.'

'And now?'

'Now we find that the blankets were vacuumed at the forensic unit in Darwin before they were sent to him.'

'Do we know what was picked up?'

'Hairs, all right. White, and, so far as he can say at the moment, maybe from around thê face or the mouth.'

'Possibly dingo?'

'Possibly,' Macknay said. 'Or cat, or dog. Animal anyway.'

'Where's the problem?'

'Because they were vacuumed off, he can't say if they were of recent origin or not.'

'They might well have got there the night the baby disappeared,' said Rice, by way of underlining the point.

It was clear why Macknay was annoyed, while Rice had an air of comfortable satisfaction, but Barritt couldn't see any difficulties for the conduct of the hearing. 'If that's Harding's opinion now, he can give it in evidence,' he said. He rather admired someone who changed an opinion to align with the facts.

9

BARRITT'S FIRST IMPULSE was to laugh. He stood up from his desk and turned towards the window. 'Unprecedented,' he said. 'I don't know of a case where it's been suggested to a coroner before.'

Gary Tait had just asked permission to televize, live from the courtroom, the coroner giving his findings. Tait was with Channel Seven, the head technician. He was broad-chested and stocky, shirt-sleeves rolled to the biceps, with fair curly hair. A muscular cherub Barritt had seen outside the court-house fussing with cables and monitors. Barritt guessed he doubled as some sort of team leader, and carried both jobs with energy to spare.

'There's never been a case like this before,' Tait said.

Taking the easy way out for the moment, Barritt said, 'Well, how do you put your argument?' He sat, found paper and pen.

Evidently Tait had rehearsed. 'Basically, this is the only way you can avoid being misreported. By anybody. First, by the print journalists. There's not one of them knows how he's going to be edited, even if he gets it right this end. Can I ask what you think of the newspaper reports so far?'

'No. Go on.'

'Second, radio. They're on air in a flash. Coming ready or not. And most of them have got two minutes airtime, some three, it depends who. Third, television. If we lay it down from outside the court, we have the same problems, getting it right, getting the balance.'

'You can wait for the transcript. An hour, perhaps half.'

'We can't wait for anything. It's big competition out there. Everyone is hot to be first off. But if we can roll it live, inside the court, we give it to viewers in every state, no mess, no mistakes. From you to them.'

'No editing?'

'No editing,' Tait said with emphasis. 'I'm here to tell you we'll run it start to finish, no breaks.'

'If I was to send,' Barritt paused, 'anyone for trial, the finding would be short. If I don't, it could be long.'

'We know that.'

'Okay.' Barritt lit a smoke and said a little puffily, 'Why should it be Channel Seven?'

Tait grinned. 'Because we asked.'

Barritt thought, Every time a newspaper messed a report, Gary Tait was watching me. He laid his pen on the desk-set where Three Wise Monkeys saw, heard, spoke no evil. He pushed back his chair.

''I'll think about it,' he grunted.

* * *

Macknay was against it.

He waved away the arguments. 'It sets a bad precedent,' he said. 'You'll be criticized, however fine your intentions are, for not upholding the dignity of the court.'

'I'll bring it up for discussion in open session,' Barritt said. 'You can have your objections recorded in the transcript.'

'Listen, Dinny,' Macknay said, using the familiar to show how deep his concern was, 'there's something I can't put on the record yet. I will be making some criticism of the police forensic science unit.' Macknay was referring to the time of his submissions to the coroner, to be given when the evidence closed. 'They made mistakes right from the start, and I'm not going to pull any punches. These are criticisms you will have to deal with openly. How is the department going to like that, on television in every living-room in the nation?'

Barritt examined the ends of his huge fingers. Macknay was courageous enough to buck the government that hired him, but he was no fool either. 'Ash,' Barritt said, 'I hear what you say.'

* * *

The hearing began again at nine the next morning. When Barritt took his place on the bench, spectators were still filing into the seats in the gallery. The early start reflected Barritt's hope that, with any luck, they could complete all the testimony before the end of the afternoon. Dr Harry Harding was already part of the way through his evidence after which only two brief witnesses remained.

Harding was not yet in court. Evidently Macknay planned to interrupt his testimony either with Constable Fogarty or Dr Milne. Myra Fogarty, from the forensic science unit in Darwin, had examined the Chamberlains' tent and bedding sent from Ayers Rock. Since she had missed the sprays of blood there were to be seen on the walls of the tent, mistaken the animal hairs she had found for other fibres, and tested samples of soil for blood when they should have been tested for saliva, Barritt knew she was in for a tough time from everybody when she got to the witness-box.

Macknay announced he would call Dr Irene Milne.

'Very well,' Barritt said. He knew this witness wouldn't take long. Dr Milne was an obstetrician at the hospital in which Azaria Chamberlain was born. She was first put on the witness-list to prove the baby's weight. Now, she was being called for a

more important reason. Dr Milne's report showed that Azaria
was a normal healthy baby girl. With this testimony, so long as it
was well reported in the press, the last delinquent rumour would
be put down.

'Before I call the next witness,' Macknay said, 'I
noticed in a local newspaper this morning, an article which
is unfortunate, in my opinion, to say the least.' He shook his
head, nonplussed. 'The general tenor of it is to give apparent
credence to a rumour, and then provide comment to discount the
rumour—'

On the table in front of him lay the morning's copy of the
Star. It reported a story 'circulating the town', which attributed
the baby's abduction to a Kadaitcha man, an Aboriginal execu-
tioner who vanishes leaving behind him only the tracks of a wild
animal.

Barritt read the piece through. He was struck by the similari-
ty the story bore to those going around about the Chamberlains.
They seemed to be saying: Evil happens, not because we believe
in evil, but because others do.

'Someone has a fertile sense of imagination,' he said.

Thank God it was all nearly over. At a certain point, he
thought, you simply lose the capacity to deal with the volume of
superstition.

FOR ALL THE GOOD IT WILL DO

1

BY NINE O'CLOCK on Friday morning the court-house foyer was crowded and noisy. When an orderly opened the door to the courtroom, at nine-fifteen, the public gallery filled without appreciably lessening the crush outside. Reporters crammed the press-benches and the jury-box, and jostled for room enough to use their notebooks. A television camera stood on a tripod close to a side wall. The crew seemed to be taking instructions from a voice they heard through their earphones. The camera pointed at the clock on the wall. At 9.25 a uniformed sergeant held his hat aloft by its wide brim to quieten the gallery. He announced that anyone talking after the session began would be removed. In the following lull an elderly woman on the third bench went into a coughing fit which she couldn't stifle with a billowing kerchief, and a duty-constable helped her away.

Ashley Macknay leaned on the bar-table talking in low tones with two detectives. Rice and Dean pushed through the crush at the door trailed by the Chamberlains, who took their seats without responding to the sudden murmur from onlookers, beyond a brief nod from Lindy Chamberlain to someone in the front row. Two orderlies, women in black skirts and white blouses, stood together like nervous sentinels, their backs to the Bench.

Cables from the television camera ran across the floor, through the foyer, and outside to a van on the footpath where Gary Tait was busy watching a monitor. Tait had problems. He was not pleased with the quality of the test transmission. The signal went from the van to a communications dish which stood on a hilltop to the north of town. Something was wrong with the link here. It occured to him that he might send a clearer picture by bouncing the signal off the glassy facade of a building further along the street, and on to the dish like a snooker shot. He tried realigning the antenna. It did work better that way.

His other worry now was timing. Since the network was to go live to air as soon as court began, it must be precise, to parts of a second. No amount of synchronizing watches could provide that measure of accuracy. What they needed was a central timepiece. Tait had realized that there was one: the clock high on the courtroom wall. So he had instructed the camera crew to focus there. The clock-face doubled as his test picture and, as if time itself got stuck between strokes, counted down their common seconds with a hesitant hand. It was watched now on monitors by coordinators who were thousands of kilometres away, and by Denis Barritt who was standing behind a partly open door, just offstage.

The instant the wand touched zenith, technicians in control rooms in every state switched picture and sound to air, the camera framed the Bench, the crier called for the court to rise while Barritt walked on-cue and on-screen to his seat and, at the van outside, Gary Tait wiped his face with the sleeve of his shirt.

2

ONCE THE COURT was seated, the camera locked in on the Bench and stayed there. This was part of the deal. It was not to go roaming faces in the room like a newshound. The composition included the escutcheon of government mounted on the wall behind, a shield representing the resources and authority of the Territory framed by an eagle and two dignified kangaroos, and, head and shoulders in the foreground, Denis Barritt in the white short-sleeved shirt which Shiela ironed for him freshly this morning, his considerable brow serious and wrinkled, as if reading his notes without being beguiled by the eye of the camera might take particular concentration.

'On the thirteenth of August 1980, Pastor and Mrs Chamberlain and their three children—Aidan Leigh, six years, Reagan Michael, four years, and Azaria Chantel Loren, then nine weeks—left their home in Mt Isa for a holiday,' he began, smoothing his tie away from where it had nervously fallen across the page.

3

THE JOURNALISTS WERE RESIGNED to a slow beginning, fulfilling some need for historical and legal perspective. They expected the coroner to lay out the full sweep of testimony, take his choice from it, and conclude with a finding. It was the way courts most often worked. But it was suddenly plain that this was not happening here.

Barritt was saying now, 'From there she saw a dingo standing at the rear of the car, she yelled, and it made off into the adjacent sandhill area. It was this observation of the dingo that caused the subsequent search to be directed to the south and east of the campsite.' Barritt had decided to make his choice clear, without wasting broadcast time. And his choice was this: What the Chamberlains said happened, happened in fact.

'Mrs Chamberlain's movements from the time she had been seated on the rail at the cooking area were observed by Aidan, who had accompanied her to the tent when Azaria was put down for the night, and also by the witnesses Mr and Mrs Lowe of Hobart, Tasmania. Mrs Lowe described the baby kicking her legs while she, Mrs Lowe, was talking to Mrs Chamberlain. This evidence was further corroborated by Mr and Mrs West of Esperance, Western Australia. They occupied the campsite adjoining and to the north of that occupied by the Chamberlains. Immediately before she heard Mrs Chamberlain cry, ''My God, my God, the dingo has got my baby'', she heard a canine growl outside her tent. This evidence raises a very strong possibility, indeed almost a certainty, that there was more than one canine in the vicinity that night.

'My impressions of Mrs Wilkins, Mr and Mrs Lowe, and Mrs West, were that they were straightforward, truthful people, accurately relating the events to which they have attested. It would be hard to imagine more independent witnesses. The nearest any of them lived to each other is about one thousand kilometres, and none lived less than fifteen hundred kilometres from the Chamberlains. They met in passing in a remote area, and apart from this tragedy would, no doubt, have quickly forgotten each other. One came forward at the behest of the media. The others were painstakingly traced by the efforts of Detective Sergeant Charlwood from motor vehicle registration numbers recorded by rangers at Ayers Rock. Each was interviewed by the police force at their home states. The written accounts they gave to the police, and subsequently attested to in court, do not vary in any material substance. I confidently rely on each of their words.'

4

OUTSIDE ON PARSONS STREET, Gary Tait watched the flow of traffic move along the roadway. He thought it may account for the interference on his monitor. What worried him most was the effect on transmission. More heavy vehicles were about now than when the broadcast began. Every time one drove past, Barritt's face ghosted over the screen.

Tait buttonholed a constable who was emerging from the police headquarters doorway and explained what was going on. The constable did not immediately see what it could have to do with him, so Tait quoted a section from the Broadcast Act which made it an offence to interfere with licensed transmissions. The legislators who passed it had in mind saboteurs and pirate stations, rather than diligent trucks and buses, but Tait wasn't going to bother with fine distinctions now. The constable fetched a colleague, and together they diverted traffic around the block. Tait walked back to the monitor. Barritt looked just fine.

'Another occurrence of significance occurred when Peter John Elston, a charter air pilot, and Richard Daldy called at the Cawood residence during the night, after completing their part of the search. Elston stated, to police, that they remained with Val Cawood for a short time while she and her children looked around the property, because their view was that a dingo does normally bring its prey around the house. Her husband did not support this theory when giving evidence, but did state he had learned that the surrounds of all the houses had been searched that night, at some unknown person's behest. It would appear that at least one, unknown, person held a belief in that, supposed, behavioural habit of the dingo.

'I should state here that I accept Mr Cawood's evidence, and do not in any way suggest that either he or any member of his family became involved with the disposal of Azaria's body.'

5

'SEARCHING WAS FINALLY ABANDONED, and it was not until the following Sunday afternoon that Mr Goodwin of Dandenong, Victoria, discovered the baby's clothing near the southwest end of the Rock.

'Again, upon the police being advised, commendable efforts were made to preserve the scene of this discovery. It was the opinion of all who observed this scene, on that afternoon, that the clothes had been deliberately placed in that position, and the surrounding growth had not been disturbed.'

Wally Goodwin, watching this on replay at home in Melbourne, shook his head. Police efforts to preserve the scene had not impressed him at all, and it was not his opinion that the clothes were deliberately placed there. He'd have felt a lot better if he had taken a photograph when he had the chance. It irked him that people talked of the clothing as if he'd found it in a bundle. But it was a small point, one which didn't seem to matter a lot now.

6

THE TELEVISION CAMERA annoyed the print journalists, most of whom thought that television reporters had too easy a life as it was. The camera annoyed Malcolm Brown, who was with the *Sydney Morning Herald*, enough that he was considering making some sort of official protest afterwards. Meantime, his job was to report better than his competitors, television reporters or anyone else. He had a competitive edge, as he saw it, since the television people couldn't tell chaff from grain. A big, grotesquely shy man, Brown despised the use of court transcripts and relied instead on furious shorthand. As he went along, he marked in his spirax the quotations which best synthesized the path of Barritt's reasoning. It was the sort of good copy he had been waiting for.

'The fact that damage to the jump-suit was slight, that no blood or tissue was found inside it, no dog or dingo saliva adhering to it, appeared inconsistent with the controlled experiment conducted at the Adelaide zoo.

'In accepting these inconsistencies, it would appear there are two alternatives: either Azaria met her death by a cause other than a dingo attack, or else the dingo's possession of the child ended abruptly before it had time to set about devouring the child.

'After the December portion of this hearing, and before its resumption last week, Dr Scott was finally given the tent to examine bloodstaining on its walls. These stains had been observed by several members of the police force on 18 August 1980, the day after the tragedy. These officers were unable to determine whether the stains were on the outside of the thinly woven material constituting the walls of the tent, or on the inside. No doubt to ascertain this significant information, they packaged the tent and forwarded it to the specialist group, forensic science section, Darwin. There the tent and its contents were examined by policewoman Constable Fogarty, who stated she did not observe the presence of any bloodstains on its walls. Dr Scott's examination of the tent walls revealed three stained areas, of what was described as finely sprayed blood. The three groups of stain came from the outside of the tent. He was unable to determine the origin of the blood, whether human or animal, but was inclined to think it may have been animal. He described each spray group as it would have appeared at the campsite. Two spray stains appeared on the southern side wall: one at the western end, and one about the centre of the wall under the guy rope. The third appeared on the northern end of the rear, or eastern end, of the tent.

'Although he felt there was sufficient blood in each group of stains to classify the group for type, Dr Scott's efforts in this regard proved unsuccessful. Dr Jones, however suggests an explanation may well be that chemicals, associated with the waterproofing of the tent, destroyed the protein content of the blood.

'On all the evidence pertaining to these stains, I am satisfied beyond reasonable doubt—to the highest degree of proof recognized in law—that the sprays of blood on the exterior of the tent were sprays of arterial blood coming from Azaria's head or neck.

'The evidence of Dr Brown, an odontologist, was called to show the possible correlation between the bite of a dingo and marks on, and in, various items of clothing. I am satisfied that Dr Brown, an acknowledged expert on the bite-marks of humans, used his best endeavours to learn what he could of what had been—until the request had been made for his assistance in his case—an unknown field both for himself and indeed for anyone else. In the light of his straightforward admission that he had no experience in examining bite-marks in clothing, I feel it would be dangerous to rely on his evidence in that regard.

In any event, I accept the evidence of Dr Scott, that the singlet Azaria was wearing, on the night of her death, was being worn correct side out. This fact alone disposes of Dr Brown's evidence.

'I conclude, from the absence of dingo saliva on the jump-suit, that Azaria was being held by the head or neck at all times when possessed by the dingo.

'I accept the evidence of Sergeant Cocks, that the cuts to the sleeve and neck of the jump-suit were caused by scissors whilst the clothing was under tension. On the probabilities, I find that at Ayers Rock a scissors would be a tool used by a white person rather than an Aborigine. From the evidence, the lack of damage to the clothing—particularly the singlet, which would have been a difficult garment for a dingo to remove undamaged—and the absence of dingo saliva or any large number of hairs, I find that the dingo's possession of Azaria was interrupted by human intervention on the night of 17 August 1980.'

7

SHIELA BARRITT was watching her husband on a screen in the living-room. The ash-tray beside her was full. Shiela knew what was soon to come. The passages of which she was most apprehensive were his recommendations. They criticized people he had a lot of contact with, and this was a small community.

The first one wasn't too bad. He placed responsibility for human safety on the Conservation Commission, and rounded off:

'Lessons ought to be learned from this inquest, and applied. The death of this babe in an area where previous attacks causing bodily injury, or potential bodily injury, is too high a price, and a totally unnecessary price to pay in the cause of conservation. I recommend that all animals dangerous to man be either safely enclosed, or else eliminated from areas of national parks likely to be frequented by man.'

This fell short of Newsome's advice that the dingoes ought to be shot, but ought to help Derek Roff, who had wanted the camping-grounds secured long before the baby vanished. All in all, Shiela thought, it could have been worse. Then she watched Denis cross his arms, clear his throat, and begin a detailed castigation of the police forensic science unit.

'Police forces must realize, or be made to realize, that courts will not tolerate any standard less than complete objectivity from anyone claiming to make scientific observations. This standard must be attained, and maintained, whether the examination in question is of a simple or complex character. Any standard less than the highest attainable, where the rights and interests of suspect and prosecutor alike are protected, negates the credit of such a section, and renders the probative value of its conclusions useless.

'Constable Fogarty had only been working in the examination section, of the forensic science section, for three months, which I find surprising. I agree with Mr Macknay,' he said, talking of Macknay's submissions made to him in court yesterday, 'that supervision within the section must be negligent in the extreme. That she had been taught none of the principles of scientific objectivity is even more alarming, although understandable when her superior appears to be also ignorant of such a basic quality.

'This inquest had demonstrated very clearly the resourcefulness, initiative, and determination of members and officers of the Northern Territory Police Force in the field, to intelligently organize every resource conceivable to achieve success in such a complex investigation. The non-observation, or non-reporting, of the sprayed bloodstains on the exterior of the tent resulted in this investigation being diverted in the wrong direction, with subsequent loss of police resources and considerable public money, not to mention the added trauma caused to each member of the Chamberlain family.

'No meaningful liason appears to exist between the members of the forensic science section and the police officer in the field. From my observations of this section in this inquiry, and other cases in the past, I recommend that consideration be given to it being re-established on a proper, forensic, scientific basis, with operatives prepared to achieve and maintain the highest standards of efficiency.'

It seemed to Shiela that at times he seemed hell-bent on making himself unpopular. She was married to a man who thought he was here to rectify all the ills of the world.

'To you, Pastor and Mrs Chamberlain, and through you to Aidan and Reagan, may I extend my deepest sympathy. You have not only suffered the loss of your beloved child in the most tragic circumstances, but you have all been subjected to months of innuendoes, suspicion, and probably the most malicious gossip ever witnessed in this country.

'I have taken the unusual step of permitting these proceedings to be televized today in the hope that, by direct and accurate communication, such innuendoes, suspicion, and gossip may cease.'

8

'I DOTH FIND that Azaria Chantel Loren Chamberlain, a child then of nine weeks of age and formerly of Mt Isa, Queensland, met her death when attacked by a wild dingo whilst asleep in her family's tent at the top camping area, Ayers Rock, shortly after eight p.m. on 17 August 1980.

'I further find that, in attempting to remove this babe from the tent, the dingo would have caused severe crushing to the base of the skull and the neck and lacerations to the throat and neck. Such injuries would have resulted in swift death.

'I further find that neither the parents of the child, nor either of their remaining children, were in any degree whatsoever responsible for this death.

'I find that the name Azaria does not mean, and never has meant, sacrifice in the wilderness.

'I find that, after her death, the body of Azaria was taken from the possession of the dingo and disposed of by an unknown method, by a person or persons name unknown.'

9

FIRST OUT THE DOOR were the radio journalists, sprinting for telephones, some heading for the booths in Hartley Street, all of them composing copy on the run. Newspaper reporters with morning deadlines split into two groups: those from the east and those from the west. The westerners might make the late edition and looked for cabs to take back to their hotels, while easterners cursed the time-zone which put them behind. Reporters who had yet some hours writing-time eyed the door to the conference room through which the Chamberlains had disappeared with the lawyers. Malcolm Brown, whose *Sydney Morning Herald* did not go to bed until midnight, looked about for his colleagues from the same group, but couldn't see them anywhere yet. Brown thought he had the chance of an exclusive interview with the Chamberlains later. He decided meantime to stay around, listening to the comments of the crowd, which was now pushing through the doors to the footpath, slowly, like movie-goers after a show, into the stunning sunshine.

Gary Tait would up his transmission. He felt the strange discontentment of triumph. There was still mopping up to come, interviews and post-mortems, but the real feat was done, and the moment was past.

The throng outside the court-house was reluctant to leave. It was waiting, perhaps, for some sort of epilogue. At the corner, the constable was still diverting traffic. Sweat hatched the back of his tawny shirt. Tait walked across and nodded his thanks. 'It's over,' he said.

'Good,' the officer said, waving the traffic through. 'Now, maybe this town can get back to normal.'

10

PETER DEAN SENT a message to the reporters outside. Pastor and Mrs Chamberlain will answer questions, on the steps of the court, once the crowd thinned. This brought the press photographers from a side entrance where some misinformer had suggested they wait, and the television crews changed batteries in their bandoliers like waiting infantrymen.

The Chamberlains walked through the doorway, smiling, in an instant surrounded by microphones. It was difficult to make out the questions. Brown hung around the periphery. The sorts of questions voice-reporters asked weren't of much use to him.

Someone asked a question about bitterness.

'People who spread rumours have not understood the facts of the case,' Lindy Chamberlain said. 'They will have to make peace with their God.'

'What plans do you have for the future?'

'Well, to begin new lives, look after our children, and take a holiday. We hope the children can settle down and lead normal lives.'

'Do you agree that dingoes at Ayers Rock ought to be shot?'

This was a trick question, antagonistic, flagrant. The pastor fielded it as if the faces in front of him were the faces of his congregation. 'Dingoes remain beautiful creatures in their own habitat. But men's lives are above dingoes' lives.'

'Perhaps the humans could be fenced in,' Lindy said. 'If the camping area was safe, things would be completely different.'

'Michael, why have people been so keen not to accept that a dingo took the baby?'

'Perhaps because it's the first in Australia, documented.'

'What has accounted for your strength and stoicism?'

'The Lord Jesus Christ is a very dear friend of ours, our saviour.' He gazed around the circle and added, 'The peace of God has kept us from being very foolish in our own lives.'

Slowly they understood that they, and the scandalizing world at large, were being judged, and found wanting. No one seemed to have the stomach for another question.

Michael was not yet ready to let them go.

'Gentlemen, we have something here you may like to see.' He held aloft a paper cylinder. 'This is a picture of Azaria as she really was, the most beautiful baby.' It was opening into a portrait, babe in arms, poster size. He unfurled the infant's glossy cheeks, her deep and serious eyes, then the mother's face, proud and indisputably tender. A second or so of incredulity passed before the cameras got going again.

Malcolm Brown walked away. He'd had enough of being rebuked.

11

PRESS RELEASES WERE OUT within twenty-four hours. They made all the Sunday tabloids. Denis Barritt opened a beer and spread the papers over the couch in the living-room. He read that the Tourist Commission called his recommendations about safety 'impossible to implement' and drew what justification it could from the predations of grizzly bears in the game parks of northern America. But Barritt knew that the fence around the Ayers Rock camping-ground was going ahead anyway. The police department had come out in a swinging, two-handed defence of its forensic science section but confessed, by the end, that moves were afoot to reorganize it. Dr Kenneth Brown, who was described as having 'left the court quickly and under a cloud', reasserted his belief in odontology as a practice with much to offer the processes of law, and the Adelaide branch of the Forensic Science Society scheduled a review of the case for the next meeting.

Barritt saw from a piece in the *Sun-Herald* that the Chamberlains were planning a holiday in New Zealand. He wondered how familiar their faces might be over there to people who saw them pushing the boys on swings in a park or spreading a picnic cloth on the beach. The same newspaper carried a photograph of Barritt on his way to court and predicted that his use of television would cause a jurisprudential furore. As a prophesy it was a little behind time. Other newspapers began on Friday to run criticism like this and, on radio, legal commentators and academics were already coming out strongly against him. If he was to achieve anything by way of day-to-day justice, he supposed, these were the sorts of antagonists he ought to be proud to have. His own motives were unsoiled. He had made his judgement. He had spoken his mind. He had done the just and honourable thing.

THE SECRET ASSUMPTIONS
OF SCIENCE

SANCTUARY

1

A PARTY OF ADVENTISTS came by train to Cooranbong in the autumn of 1894. They were looking for somewhere to begin a community of missionaries. Ellen White was with them. She was then sixty-seven, long widowed, and in her third year of the Lord's work in New South Wales. She wore a full-length dark skirt, and a black clerical jacket with white lace at the throat. She kept her grey hair sternly short, a stout woman with an anguished mouth and unrelenting chin. She seemed to be asleep on the creaking seat.

The nearest siding to Cooranbong was at Dora Creek. They were close, now. The woman beside her took Ellen White's hand and patted it. The hand was withdrawn before the eyes opened. 'I have had a vision, Sister,' Ellen White said.

This did not cause so much as an intake of breath among the party with her in the carriage. Ellen White was a child of thirteen when God bestowed her first prophetic vision. This was in Portland, Maine, two months after the Great Disappointment. The trembling girl saw the people of God walking a soaring pathway into the heavens, to the golden domes of a city bathed in divine light. A week later she was given another, in which God bade her act as His courier. She thought this a fearful responsibility and prayed for death. But when the Advent preacher William Miller died she was twenty-two and well committed to her task as messenger to the elect. Now those messages came daily. No one in this carriage was surprised that she did not deliver the text immediately. Frequently, after she returned from the company of Jesus and the Angels, she was unable to utter the vision she brought back until the time was apt and the scene rose in her again.

From the Dora Creek siding they took a waggon to Cooranbong. This was a land of forests, somber and moist, with bright glades between. The countryside did not please two elders who were travelling with the party. They were from Iowa and found that the leaves of the forest here were harsh, rather than succulent. The timber, under the blade of an inquiring knife, was all hardwood. Sister White said nothing. She was looking for land from which they could hew a farm, where they would raise animals and build dwellings, a school, places of worship.

They left the waggon and walked. The holding here was fifteen hundred acres, wooded rises and creek flats. The Pacific Ocean was not far east. Sydney town lay ninety miles south. The ample rain fell in no season more than in another. Three brooks flowed through. The price at which it might be purchased was fixed at five thousand pounds, clearly beyond a community which yet numbered less than five hundred.

A dubious trail wound into the forest. Sister White led the way. In the eyes of her party she seemed to tread the ground with familiarity. Soon they came to a clearing. Around it stood a palisade of tall timber. The leaves were still. No beast was upon it, and nowhere was the grass nipped or the soil pugged. At the centre was a scar in the soft earth. It was a furrow, two full paces in the length and a quarter in depth. The clods were freshly turned, but no one could find the tracks of plough or plowman. The Iowa brothers bent over it. They rubbed soil between finger and thumb. They put it to the tongue and spat. This is sandy and poor, they said, and sour to the taste.

Ellen White's face darkened. 'False testimony has been borne of this land,' she said. The vision rose in her again, and she uttered it. She had trod the path in her dream and entered upon the clearing. The furrow was there, two paces long and a quarter deep, and the cut was fresh. An Angel of the Lord appeared beside it and explained to her the properties of the soil, which were true and munificent. 'The Lord will provide his people a table in the wilderness,' the Angel said.

The brethren from Iowa, who could quote no comparable authority, were routed and walked away. Everybody inspected the soil, and touched it, and knew it was God's gift, and good. And a great gladness lifted them.

With this miracle was associated two others. When the party returned to Sydney, Sister White called for a meeting of ratification. The hall was full. The bretheren from Iowa spoke against the land. They spoke with the wiles of the evil one, and many were duped. Brother McCullagh spoke in favour. But he was consumptive, and many times were his arguments interrupted by coughing and shallow breath. His words were courageous but weak. Sister White lifted her face and her voice to the Lord and pleaded for their Brother. While she prayed, Brother McCullagh's coughing stilled. He stood firm and upright. Then his voice came clear and strong. Together everyone gave thanks to the Lord for the sign and for the land.

Their acceptance of God's gift was not yet without problems. The Adventists had not the money to pay for it. Only Ellen White was unworried. She encouraged Adventists everywhere to travel to Cooranbong to see the land He had provided. Many came from Melbourne. Some sailed from over the seas. The Wessel family travelled from South Africa. They brought with them their daughter Anna, a pale and sickly girl who had married into a fortune but remained devoted to the scriptures. They walked the wooded paths and over the glades. Although they covered much ground, Anna did not tire. Sites for the school and a church were already marked out. Anna's eyes shone. They were told the miracle of the Angel and the furrow, and of Brother McCullagh who was now hale. Anna raised a shaky hand to her brow, and the others stood still. When her eyes opened, she pledged five thousand pounds, moved by the spirit of God. 'Thus does the Lord begin preparing for us His table,' Sister White said, and they saw it was true.

2

THE ANGEL was quite right about the soil. It grew burdened fruit-trees, lusty vegetables, and sweet green pasture. Hardwoods from the forest built lapstrake dwellings, schoolrooms, commons, and a chapel. In early photographs, taken a year apart, it seemed that the forest fell back of its own accord to make more space for orchards, garden beds, and a herd of milking-cows with ballooning udders and sappy-mouthed calves. Barns and store-houses appeared, as though fully grown, without the benefit of scaffolding or carpenters.

Those years turned like the pages of an old album, beginning in sepia, with the smoky timbers and small misty windows of the early dwellings and halls, moving to crisp monochrome with the arrival of white paint on the cladding and black to the eaves, and on to colour, mainly Ektachrome browns and russets when the Sanitarium health food factory was built, and the buildings turned to brick. Along the way, the greater part of the land holding, called the Avondale Estate, separated from the academy, called the Avondale School for Christian Workers. From the square mile of the campus most of the forest had gone. The table the Lord had prepared for them was of a size that abolished the wilderness.

Ellen White had left in 1900. There was trouble brewing at the Battle Creek College, in the Dime Tabernacle, and the Sanitarium Corporation, where John Kellogg was urging secularism in education. The doctrine of the Lord's withdrawal into sanctuary, heavenly preparations for Advent, and her own standing as God's messenger were all under attack, and her remaining years would be spent fighting evil angels in human form within the church.

But there was none at Cooranbong. The curriculum remained a curriculum for church workers, although the missions for which they were bound were not necessarily places far away. The school despatched Adventist missionaries into the territories of business, health, farming, manufacturing, education, science, and the arts. The words carved in marble on the portals changed in 1911 to read Australasian Missionary College, and in 1963 to the simple Avondale College, but all students still took lectures in biblical themes, the apocalyptic, prophetic guidance, Christian home and family life, and instruction in the works of Ellen White. They still began and ended the day with prayer. Courtship between students was encouraged, if rigorously platonic, and so was marriage, although students who married during semester were expelled. The guiding Elders liked young people to be healthy and happy in Jesus, so the world here seemed filled with energetic and smiling adolescents.

Although the incorporeal has not changed much in the time since Ellen White's departure, the facilities kept growing. A photograph taken in the spring of 1969 facing south from somewhere outside the physics building fits in most of the other science schools on the right, but misses the great residential halls and sports pavilions on the left because of the size of the administration complex and library, which the central roadway circles. The old white-painted chapel is out of sight from here but centre, background, stands the Sanitarium health food factory, as tall as any cathedral, the grain-silos round and strong like the columns of an unfinished temple, but grimy now, as if waiting too long for the lintel to be set. Mid ground, boys and girls in their late teens and early twenties seem to be carrying books from the library towards the commerce school, diligently keeping to the path rather than treading the grass. The roadway is black and shiny, so it has been raining, but the boys walking in the opposite direction wearing white and carrying racquets expect the tennis courts to have drained enough to play. Two unconnected joggers, arrested in springy midstride, each keep to the asphalt, an indication that the fields are under water and the grass verges are sodden, as sometimes happens here in springtime. The runner approaching the camera is nobody we know, but the diminishing figure is blond-haired and athletic. Since the year is 1969, it would do history no harm to replace whoever the snapshot caught with Michael Chamberlain, who ran the grounds daily over the four years of his course and was due in a month or so for graduation and soon after that for marriage.

Often he ran quite long distances. His degree was in arts with theology, and the teachings of Ellen White were clear about the importance of health in religion. Running was a bodily and spiritual discipline. Apart from that, he liked it. He liked Avondale, he had from the start. The college handbook made student life sound a little like compulsory joy, but that was not a criticism he found to be true. He enjoyed the community here, although he was older by five or six years than most other students and was not born to Adventism. His family, and they all lived in Christchurch, New Zealand then, were Protestants, his father something of a Methodist and his mother entirely Baptist. After his mother converted to Seventh-day Adventism, so did he, celebrating his majority and his conversion together by being newly baptized on the day he turned twenty-one. He applied for Avondale. Running now beyond the campus, down the access road leaving the watery meadows to his right and with the Charles Harrison homes for elderly folk looming on the left, he passed the cemetery. The tombs said something about the glory of Ellen White's vision. All those who waited on the coming of God shared a home of the spirit. At the gates he turned and ran back again.

3

WHEN MICHAEL CHAMBERLAIN came back to Avondale College with his depleted family, it seemed that little had changed in ten years, although now they were allotted married quarters, a house with lawn back and front and a garage. Michael enrolled in a summer course. Once the inquest was over, and they returned from their holiday in New Zealand, he registered for a master's degree, arts in religion. The boys went to church school. Lindy talked about taking a diploma in education or applied art. She wanted another child but that should wait until the boys were settled. They swam and played tennis. Michael ran daily, a little slower now but well for a man of thirty-eight, often with one or other of his old classmates who were now on staff. Here was the spirit of community, the deathless guidance of Ellen White, the governance of elders, and a sense of the proper continuance of things. Bells rang for morning and evening prayer, for Friday night vespers, for Sabbath school, for Divine Service, and this way life could go on and on and on.

4

FROM HIS ROOM at the Adelaide *News*, Geoff DeLuca put through a call to Paul Everingham's office in Darwin. Everingham was the chief minister, as the head of government is called there, and doubled as the attorney general. DeLuca knew him well. Everingham often had a beer or two with influential reporters when they were in town, such was the style of things in the Northern Territory, so there was no sense in not going right to the top.

Someone at the other end told him Everingham wasn't available. DeLuca said he would talk to anyone who would talk to him, and hung on.

It was 16 September, a Wednesday. DeLuca had a tip-off he wanted to check out. The forensic science file on the Chamberlains had moved from Adelaide to Darwin. This made DeLuca wonder if something fresh was afoot. A voice came on the line, a press secretary of some sort, one of the palace guards as someone had dubbed them, who said there certainly wasn't anything in the story, but managed to convey by way of the same words that if DeLuca bided his time he would not be forgotten. DeLuca replaced the phone. He headed for the editor's office.

NEWSFLASHES

1

IT WAS SABBATH. On the Avondale campus the seventh day was compulsorily for rest and worship, but no one needed to be reminded by regulation. So central is Sabbath-keeping to the beliefs of Adventists here that they describe it as the Great Test of Loyalty. When it came out in the newspapers that the Chamberlains had driven to Ayers Rock on a Saturday, Michael Chamberlain got letters from folk who attributed all his subsequent troubles to Sabbath-breaking. He couldn't help thinking that it wasn't as silly as it sounded. Ellen White had equated Sabbath-breaking with the Mark of the Beast and 'the same shall drink of the wine of the wrath of God'. Revelations, 14:10.

There was a knock at the door. The hour was early, around ten past eight. Aidan ran to answer it. Perhaps this was someone come to walk them to Sabbath school later. He left the door open and came back to fetch his father. On the porch stood Charlwood and five other policemen. They had a search warrant.

They followed the pastor into the lounge-room. 'Do have a seat,' he said, but no one sat. 'What is it you want?'

Sergeant Gilligan was from the New South Wales police force. Since this was his jurisdiction, he displayed the warrant. Charlwood said, 'Some fresh evidence has come up. The chief minister has authorized further investigations, and this is the start of them. We need everything you still have that you took to Ayers Rock.'

'I'll get Lindy. I've got a prayer meeting of elders, shortly. But we'll do what we can.'

'I think you should pass up the meeting, Michael,' Charlwood said.

2

CHARLWOOD'S INTRODUCTION had stretched the truth a little. This was not the start of investigations. Soon after the inquest closed a new police task group was formed. Its members chose the name Operation Ochre. On 27 May they despatched a parcel air express to Adelaide. It was picked up by the dentist Kenneth Brown. Brown, who was to attend a forensic science conference in Europe, made a stopover in London. On 8 June he took the parcel, which contained Azaria Chamberlain's clothing, the clothing he had used in the zoo experiments, and the skull of a dingo, to the London Hospital Medical College where James Cameron was the professor of forensic medicine. With Cameron was a forensic odontologist, Bernard Sims. They examined the clothing, and had it photographed under ultra-violet light. When Brown returned with the clothing from London, he had with him a report from Cameron and Sims. The report was sent on to the Northern Territory police department. On 27 August Police Commissioner McAulay, who had cleared the action so far with the chief minister, gave Charlwood authority to proceed. On 8 September Charlwood flew to Adelaide, and took the baby's clothing back into police custody. By the 10th he was in Brisbane. He met there Minister Commissioner McAulay, who had flown in from Darwin, and Professor Cameron who arrived on a flight from London. The occasion was important enough to call for the presence of Chief Minister Everingham. Their meeting was held in Brisbane because there were lawyers here whom the government wanted, early, on the case. Michael Chamberlain might now have suspected something serious was in train had he asked to read the grounds endorsed on the warrant which Sergeant Gilligan held. The grounds disclosed an investigation into a murder.

3

LINDY CHAMBERLAIN CAME into the lounge-room. She didn't seem pleased by the intrusion. Charlwood made the introductions. Sergeant Plumb and Constable Metcalf were from the Northern Territory, and the three others from the New South Wales force. 'What can we do for you?' she asked.

'We have further scientific evidence now,' Charlwood said, 'and I've got a warrant to search the house.'

'What sort of evidence?'

'I should execute the warrant first, before I tell you that. We want to start at the back of the house.'

'Start anywhere you like,' she said, and led them down the hall.

They cleared the kitchen, to use as a counting-house, and began the search at the back door. They emptied the narrow cupboards there, which immediately yielded a tent, a tent-fly, and poles. They felt behind the water-heater and pulled out the drawers in case anything was secreted behind them. Hats, raincoats, torches, a backpack and a diver's knife were carried into the kitchen where Michael Chamberlain stood by with his hands in his pockets. He seemed willing enough to identify the items taken to Ayers Rock. They were laid out on the kitchen table and Constable Johnston photographed them. Metcalf loaded everything into plastic sacks, tied the tops and labelled them with a felt pen. They went on to the laundry. The two boys watched from the doorway.

Charlwood took Michael Chamberlain outside. He wanted to search the garage and the shed. He found a tent stowed in a bag, and beside it the poles. The tent was orange and green, the tent the Chamberlains had pitched at Ayers Rock. Charlwood asked for the pegs.

'I don't know where they are now,' Michael said.

'They were given back to you.'

'We've moved house since then,' Michael said. 'If they turn up, I'll let you know.' But Charlwood was, for some reason, interested enough to keep looking.

Charlwood pulled up short. At the back of the garage lay a child's coffin. It was about a metre long with neat clasps and handles. It was empty.

'What's that for?'

'I used it at public health lectures,' Michael said. 'Anti-smoking.'

'Why do you keep it?'

'It might be useful again, sometime.'

That answer meant something different for each of them.

* * *

They walked back into the house, to the study. Charlwood went through the desk. He took a small bone-handled knife from a drawer and a larger one from the desktop. He picked over the photographic gear. There were two camera bags, an aluminum and a vinyl. Charlwood asked if both of these had made the trip to Ayers Rock.

'No, another one.'

'Where is it now?'

'It's in the Torana.'

Since the Torana was with a repairer at nearby Morisset, Charlwood said they would get it later and turned to a collection of photographic slides. He flipped them through. Those of the Rock or of the baby he laid aside. He chose about twenty-five. Here was a shot of the lichen growing on the south face, not too far from the gully in which the baby's clothing was found; incontrovertible proof that the family had been around there, although, judging from the volume of snaps, they'd been just about everywhere.

Michael Chamberlain walked back into the room. He was carrying a black camera bag. He looked pleased to have found it. It was, he said, the one he had taken to Ayers Rock. He seemed to find some measure of satisfaction in being helpful. He was a difficult man to figure out.

His wife was the prickly one. She didn't like the police being in her house, and clearly she couldn't bear Metcalf. This was a difficulty, since it was Metcalf's job to pack and list everything. Metcalf had a lumbering presence, and when the search began he seemed to find something in the task humorous, which his round cheeks did their best to suppress.

Lindy Chamberlain came into the kitchen carrying a plastic bag. 'You might be interested in these,' she said. From the bag she took two army hats, floppies, flecked with brown and grimy. The spots were blood, she explained, because they were on the floor of the tent. She ignored Metcalf's expectant hand, dropped them at his feet, and walked away from his suddenly surly face.

Metcalf was interested in scissors. He had searched the bathroom and the kitchen, and now held a pair he found in a kitchen drawer. He asked Lindy if there were others she had taken to the Rock. 'Only those I used to cut my hair,' she said. She went to the study and came back with two pairs. 'While you're at it, why don't you check Sergeant Morris's knives and scissors,' she said, piqued.

By the time they finished with the bedrooms the total of items seized reached, by Metcalf's list, beyond three hundred. They loaded replete sacks into the waiting cars. The time was twelve-thirty. The search had lasted almost four and a half hours.

Johnson, one of the New South Wales police, said to Charlwood, 'Have you searched the garage?'

'Most of it.'

'What about that?' Johnson pointed to the top of a wardrobe where a blade of some sort lay. He pulled down a machete.

'We'll take that,' Charlwood said.

The boys were intent on all this. Aidan said, 'I'll get you another one,' and climbed the rafters. He came down with a cane-knife.

'We'll have that too,' Charlwood said.

'And there's more up there.' Aidan pointed to the roof gutter above the back door.

'What sort?'

'A plasterer's knife.' Aidan said, deadpan.

Charlwood made no answer. The boy was sending him up.

Lindy went off to find a baby-sitter. Charlwood wanted to take statements from the Chamberlains at the police-station at Toronto, but by way of Morisset where the detectives would make their claim to the yellow Torana.

While they waited, Michael took the detectives out into the garden where they sat in the dappled shade of a tree. This part of College Drive was lined with small suburban houses and from where they sat the quiet gardens stretched far. High in the still air, from somewhere to the south, came the sound of a small aeroplane.

'You'll be glad when this is all over,' Plumb said.

'I'd hoped it was over by now.'

Michael rather liked Charlwood and Plumb. Both were tidy of mind and well mannered. They displayed a common sense of sureness about what they were doing, and attractively underplayed it. The work demanded of them by the community in which they lived might be familiar and repetitious, but they were not dulled by it. These were things Michael understood.

A man walked into the garden from the side of the house and took Michael aside. Michael came back and said, 'The college switchboard is jammed with calls from the press. Do you know what's going on?'

Plumb and Charlwood exchanged glances. It was Charlwood who spoke. 'I was going to tell you about that. The chief minister is making a press statement today.' He looked at his wristwatch. 'I guess he's done it already.'

'What do you think I ought to do?'

'If you don't want to talk, ignore them.'

'Yes,' Michael said, passing a hand over the back of his head. 'I think that's best.'

He went inside to phone the switchboard. He was soon out again. The small sound of an engine in the sky had become a resonant beating of the air. 'Is that a helicopter?'

Charlwood had seen it already. It was coming in low. 'Channel Seven,' he said. Any hope that it would overshoot was soon gone. The cars in the street gave the house away. The boys held their palms over their ears and grinned. The helicopter banked and circled the roof. The glittering barrel of a telecamera, mounted beside an open hatch, pointed down.

'What do you think I should do now,' Michael shouted.

'Do you want to talk to them?'

'No. I've had enough.'

Plumb and Johnson led Michael and the boys to a car at the kerb. They pulled the doors closed and drove off. Charlwood waited with the others at the house. The helicopter peeled away, looking for somewhere to land.

Charlwood took a tape-recorder from his pocket. It was running while he had talked to Lindy Chamberlain, before she left the house. He played it back. It produced only nonsense. The sounds were like voices bubbling underwater. He would try again, later.

4

THE BABY-SITTER ARRIVED and led Charlwood to the college administration building. He found Lindy Chamberlain waiting in an office. She wouldn't go back to the house while the press was around. But that was only part of the story. She had been in touch with a solicitor. 'He's told me not to say anything unless he is with us,' she said.

An interview with a lawyer present was not an option Charlwood found attractive. He checked his watch. Michael and the boys should be at Toronto by now, even allowing for a delay at Morisset to impound the Torana.

'I guess we should go there anyway,' he said.

They used her car. Charlwood drove. 'I can lose the press if they find us,' he said.

They drove out to the highway. Lindy called the turns for him in a precise and ungenerous tone, but otherwise stayed quiet.

'Look, I know your solicitor told you not to say anything,' he said, 'but there's one question, particularly, I'd have asked you, if you'd agreed to talk to me.'

Since this provoked no response from her side of the car he said, 'I'm intrigued that you haven't asked me yet why we're here.'

'No, I haven't, have I.'

'Why not?'

'It's fairly obvious why you're here.'

'But don't you really want to know?'

She faced straight ahead. 'Okay. Why are you here?'

Charlwood paused, as if the question had caught him off-guard. Then he said, 'I'm not supposed to tell you this, but I feel you ought to know. The baby's clothes have been examined by Professor Cameron, in London. He is a highly rated forensic scientist, number six in the world,' he said. 'Are you interested now?'

'Of course I'm interested,' she said flat-voiced.

'He confirms there was no dingo involved in the disappearance of your daughter.'

'I didn't know there were any dingo experts in London.'

'He doesn't profess to be a dingo expert. The baby was decapitated.'

'And there is a handprint,' he said, 'from someone whose hand was wet with blood. A print consistent with a female hand. You know what that means?'

'It's obvious what that means.'

'It puts you right in the hot seat.'

'What about everyone else?' she said. 'The rangers, the policeman, the people who cleared up when we had gone.'

'What about them?'

'You should be investigating everybody. Otherwise the same thing that happened last time will happen again. You're trying to make a jigsaw puzzle up, with half the pieces.'

She was angry. 'Anyone could have tampered with the clothing. Nobody has any idea what Frank Morris did with the clothes. There was some twenty minutes in there when he was alone. He had told them not to touch the clothing until it was photographed, yet he had done it himself, and not told anyone he had done it. Except that Mr Goodwin had seen him do it.'

'You seem to have missed the point,' he said. 'The handprints on the clothes are the same blood as your child's and were put there when the blood was still wet. The clothes were found a week later.'

'Did you kill your child?'

'You've asked me that before.'

'I've never asked you that before. I've asked you if you knew what happened to her.'

'What are the implications if I tell you?' she snapped. 'You've broken your word before.'

'What do you mean?'

'Last time we spoke like this, it was about hypnotism. Then you got to the inquest and threw it up at me. What guarantee have I got that you won't throw this up at me in court?'

'It depends on your answer.'

'You don't think if I did, I could have carried out this charade all this time.'

'You're selling yourself short.'

'Oh, come on. You're crediting me with the brains to commit the perfect murder and get away with it.'

'I mean it. You are an intelligent woman. Don't sell yourself short.'

'Ask my friends. They'll tell you I can't tell lies.'

'You haven't answered my question.'

'No, I haven't, have I.'

He swung the car into the driveway of the police depot and pulled up. She got out.

'No, of course I never killed my child,' she said, and slammed the door.

5

CHARLWOOD FOUND an unoccupied room and left her sitting there. It was an opportunity to check his tape-recorder. This time there was nothing. It hadn't rolled at all.

Plumb was talking to Michael in another office. Plumb said, 'Look, we want to help you as much as we can. If there's anything you want to tell me, feel free.'

'I can't think of anything.'

'Just don't assume we're enemies. I'm human,' Plumb said. 'You ought to know there could be a new inquest.'

'Under Barritt?'

'No.' Plumb shook his head. 'Not Barritt.'

They brought the Chamberlains together. The tone Charlwood assumed now was formal. He said, 'I understand that your solicitor has told Mrs Chamberlain that you should decline to be interviewed unless a lawyer is present. Do you decline to be interviewed?'

Lindy said firmly, 'Yes we do.'

'The baby's clothing has been scientifically examined in London. That examination found the print of a human hand. It also shows that the baby was decapitated.'

'But who would do something like that? What sort of person?' Michael said.

'Are you prepared to give me your handprints? Before you answer that, I want you to understand that the giving of them could be a means, not only of tying you to the prints on the clothes, but of also excluding you.'

Michael Chamberlain looked at his wife. 'Not until our solicitor is present,' she said. 'Can I call him?'

She tried to ring through on a desk-phone, but there was no answer. She hung up. 'Do you want to call us in a few days? I'll ring him Monday.'

'You won't provide them now?'

'No,' she said.

Michael shrugged. 'This is all a bit confusing to me,' he said, and slowly turned for the door.

6

THE PRESS was having an unexpectedly hard time of it. Avondale College switchboard would not connect calls. Re-

porters, who knocked hourly on the Chamberlain door, were
turned away by someone with a tireless capacity for uttering
nothing news-worthy. A television crew was pushed off the
footpath by angry neighbours. A short note of refusal written by
Michael Chamberlain made the front page of the Sydney *Sun*,
and the reporter who obtained it was commended by his editor.
Photographers, who shot film at the merest quibble of a curtain,
fell to playing cards in their cars. The house went dark. It rained
for days.

They fared better elsewhere. Police Commissioner McAulay
issued a statement explaining that this investigation was begun
six months ago, soon after the inquest concluded. Someone in
Darwin gave a summary of Professor Cameron's examination to
a Channel Seven newsreporter who then spent successive nights
releasing it. This brought a terse statement from London where
Cameron was reported to be unhappy with the term 'decapitation',
and this sense of fine distinctions was played up by every
newspaper which had missed the scoop. The *Sydney Morning
Herald* announced 'a break-through in the case after a forensic
examination in Sydney', but the police who supplied the information identified neither themselves nor the breakthrough. From
Adelaide, Geoff DeLuca made front page all over the country.
He broke news of imminent searches for the baby's body, one
alongside the highway where a car like the Chamberlain's was
seen resting on the way back to Alice Springs, and another in the
slurry of the septic tank at the Uluru Motel where the Chamberlains had stayed overnight. A police team carried out those
searches the following day.

Any suggestion of cunning in the way this material found its
way to the press was dispelled by the chief minister, speaking on
state-wide radio. Paul Everingham, who was best known as
Porky to his constituents, ran a weekly talk-back show, an
obedience to his duty to communicate with the people. A
publicity shot taken in the Darwin studio shows him sitting in
front of a desk microphone, wearing an ample T-shirt, earphones
pulled down over his baseball cap. On this occasion, which was
30 September, a caller asked him what he thought of the
Chamberlain investigation so far. 'The media's acting like a
buncha vampires,' he said.

7

ON 16 OCTOBER, Everingham held a press conference in Darwin. For the occasion he wore Territory rig, an open-necked white shirt, shorts and long socks. The assembled journalists expected to hear something important. As it turned out, he wanted to tell them to hold off awhile.

'I hope to be in a position to say something, probably not next week, but the week after,' he said.

No one could believe this was all they were here for. Someone asked, 'Will there be another inquest?'

'I've got no comment about that.'

'Why is Brian Martin going to Alice Springs?' Martin was the Crown solicitor, the head of the law department.

'He's just making a stopover on his way back from Canberra.' This raised a laugh, since the flights from the east carry on to Darwin after a half hour on the ground, and the reporters knew that Martin was booked into an Alice Springs motel overnight.

'The Chamberlain car was examined in Sydney and flown to Alice Springs in an Air Force freighter. It's now under police guard. What can you tell us about that?'

'I can tell you it's in Alice Springs.'

'Is it there as an exhibit for a fresh inquest?'

'Well,' he grinned, 'we've got better facilities for examining it elsewhere. You'll have to draw your own conclusions.'

8

THE CONCLUSIONS the press drew were fortified by rumour. Police had dismantled the Chamberlain's yellow Torana. They had indisputable evidence of murder. When the *Sydney Morning Herald*'s Malcolm Brown heard it, he rang around, checking it out. The answer was the same everywhere. The car was awash with blood.

9

RADIO BULLETINS REPORTED that Denis Barritt had been called, unexpectedly, to Darwin. An interviewer asked him, 'Does this have anything to do with disciplinary measures, or with the Azaria Chamberlain case?' His irritable denial didn't noticeably dampen speculation, although the magistrates' schedule, published for months now, rostered him for duties in Darwin from 17 October, and this was the 16th.

Barritt was recently in the news for another reason. Yesterday he gave his finding in an inquest into the deaths of Nafarula and Charlie, local Aborigines who died after drinking—with a riverside party of fourteen others who later recovered—from a flagon of sherry which someone had left conveniently close by. The flagon was spiked with strychnine. White townsfolk here favoured a finding which might leave open the possibility of accident. Barritt found murder by persons unknown. It was not a popular decision.

Shiela drove him to the airport. They parted in the crowd at the gate to the tarmac, and Barritt walked towards the shimmering aeroplane swinging his briefcase. Shiela caught sight of a news photographer lining them up. 'What big story can you make out of this?' she said. Despite the heat she waited at the rail while the aircraft took off and she leaned there, tired and frail, until the ascending vapours faded from the sky.

10

SO FAR AS THE JOURNALISTS could determine, the most likely next step should involve the quashing of Barritt's finding. They checked the law lists daily, and spoke to the desk staff in the registry each morning and afternoon. Peter Dean, who confirmed that he was still representing the Chamberlains, said he didn't know anything either. A reporter for the Sydney *Sun* was given a tip that a Crown application was soon to be made to the Darwin Supreme Court, but the lists disclosed nothing of the sort and an aide in the chief minister's office displayed his surprise so genuinely that the reporter pressed no further.

The application was heard on 20 November, a Friday, in a closed session in chambers, by Mr Justice Toohey. The applicant was Chief Minister Everingham, in his capacity as attorney-general. The other party represented was Denis Barritt, whose main concern was that the Chamberlains should be notified and permitted to take part. Barritt's lawyer lost that argument early and withdrew from the proceedings.

Friday afternoon is not an easy time to find journalists who are still on duty, but the chief minister's staff gathered as many as it could, happening on a good number in the sunny beer-garden of the Darwin Hotel, and distributed among them the court order and a summary of the judge's reasons for making it. The order quashed the first inquest and empowered a second. It disclosed that police had given evidence of persuasive new material, but the documents here were careful to give no indication of what that material might be. It directed responsibility for the next inquest to Chief Magistrate Gerry Galvin.

11

THERE WAS NOTHING now to keep them in Darwin. The air service to the east and the south on Saturday left at one-thirty in the afternoon. It was already a crowded flight, and evacuating newsreporters and television crews took up the unbooked space. Many spent an hour or so in the airport bar before boarding time to make sure of their seats. The route ran Brisbane, Sydney, Melbourne. The first leg pushed against the sun and took four hours flying time, so when they climbed away from Brisbane it was into a violet sky above a gathering dusk. This part of the flight had come to have more in common with the last hours of a successful party than with a journey. Someone who sat next to a holidaying stockman began to pass around warm cuts of a recently slaughtered scrub bullock. The peevish stewards had been discarded, and drinks were served from the bar by a cameraman now wearing an apron.

In a row near the aft of the aisle sat two reporters, sharing whisky. Both of them had been in the news game a long time, one in dailies, the other in radio. The newspaperman had slack loops under the eyes, the broadcaster was tough and tubby. They were talking about tips they had from friendly policemen, and had drunk enough that the bonds of confidentiality were loose. In this way they discovered that the same piece of secret and compelling information had been bestowed on each of them. During the search of the Chamberlain's house at Avondale the detectives had discovered a Bible in which a passage, marked in the Old Testament, described a ritual slaying inside a tent. The weapon was a tent-peg. The victim's head was cut off. The story was outlined in red.

The passage which excited the detective who found it was in the Book of Judges, chapter four. Verse twenty-one read, 'Then Jael, Heber's wife, took a nail of the tent, and took an hammer in her hand, and went softly unto him, and smote the nail into his temples, and fastened it into the ground: for he was fast asleep and weary. So he died.' Not only this verse, but the page was stamped with red. The detective might have missed the passage altogether if it were not for a melodramatic illustration of the story on the opposite leaf. He closed the book and left it where it was.

Apart from the presence of a tent in the narrative, there was not much to connect it with Azaria Chamberlain. The slain was a charioteer, the captain of an invading army. He and the slayer, Jael, were strangers, and their clans were enemies. The captain was not decapitated after death, even if, as the police supposed, Azaria was. For all that, the story was to enjoy an exalted currency in pressrooms and around police depots. The one particular which did not change in the retelling was the vivid and convincing detail that the passage was coloured—in some versions it was underlined—in red.

12

THE BIBLE, while the reporters on flight 61 were talking about it, still lay in the Avondale lounge-room. It sat in the centre of a coffee-table, a display piece. The house was empty. The Chamberlains were at Divine Service. Dusk meant the close of another Sabbath.

It was an old Bible, with clasps and cusps of brass, published during the nineteenth century in London, by K.C. Murdoch of Castle Street, Holborn, and included the famed commentaries of Scott and Henry. It had been in Lindy Chamberlain's family, according to an inscription on the fly-leaf, since 1884. In keeping with the fervour of the times, the stories were generously illustrated, with a process not much different from etching. This is not now a popular technique because it breaks down, and transfers colour to the opposing leaf.

EFFIGIES

1

THE FEELING ANDREW KIRKHAM carried with him into the Alice Springs courtroom was a growing unease. He had been working on the Chamberlain brief, together with Rice, for more than a week, but when he looked now at the journalists filing into the press-benches he suspected that some of them there knew more about the police case than he did.

The inquest was due to begin at ten, in fifteen minutes. So far, the constable guarding the door was letting through only officials and press. Kirkham laid his books on the bar-table. He was not unused to nervousness at the start of a new case. Fourteen years as an advocate had accounted for a great number of criminal cases, and he was jumpy at the beginning of every one. Back in the days of law school at Melbourne he was renowned on the track for very fast times as a quarter-miler and now, lean and boyish at forty, he looked as if he could still clear the blocks quickly. A personality of this sort carries keen pangs of its own, and he hoped the mood would pass.

Pastor and Mrs Chamberlain followed Phillip Rice into the court. With a gallantry which no younger man could have carried off half so well, Rice ushered them to a pew. They sat with their backs to the press benches. Michael Chamberlain sat erect and silent. Lindy turned to nod at Malcolm Brown who was close behind. 'Well,' she said, 'here we are again.' The seat beside her was taken by someone from the Adventist community here, a slim proud woman whose hair topped her grey head in a tight bun. A friendly face, and Kirkham couldn't see too many around.

*   *   *

The duty-constable began directing spectators into the public gallery. Rice and Kirkham pushed out into the crowded foyer. They were looking for Des Sturgess, the barrister from Brisbane briefed to assist Coroner Galvin. They found Sturgess in a small ante-room which, by the addition of a handwritten note pasted to the door, was converted into a conference room.

They wanted an outline from Sturgess of the evidence they had to face. It was a usual enough procedure. Mostly, barristers who were representing some participant in an inquest were given the statements of witnesses beforehand, so that it couldn't be said that anybody was taken by surprise. But for some reason this inquest was being played differently. A fortnight ago, when Coroner Galvin held a short session to announce when the inquest would begin, Rice complained about the secrecy with which the law department was treating its evidence. Galvin said he had no power to interfere, and so far Rice and Kirkham had got nothing.

Sturgess knew what they were here for. He shook his head. He was tall, round-shouldered, and spoke with a heavy smoker's croaky voice. 'It's out of my hands,' he said. 'I've got my instructions, and I can't help you.'

Kirkham wondered who those instructions came from in the first place. Des Sturgess was the law department's adviser on this case and, according to newspaper reports, had been calling the shots for three months now.

Rice said irritably, 'You're forcing us to go on blind.'

'Your clients are to be treated as witnesses. That's what they are here for. It's perfectly proper. They are not charged with anything.'

Something about the way Sturgess said this worried Kirkham. 'When will you call them?' he asked.

'Look, I control the order of witnesses.'

'They should be called last. You wouldn't call them before they had heard the evidence.'

'I propose to call them early, following the order of events.'

This seemed to Kirkham an unfair, if neat, trick. The tactical reasoning it reflected was this: the Chamberlains were not charged with a crime, they had none of the rights of an accused, they could be examined in public, and examined before they knew what the evidence against them was.

'If you want to argue it out,' Sturgess said, 'I'd suggest a closed session.'

Kirkham checked his watch, and made for a telephone. There was some case-law he needed sent up from Melbourne. Sturgess couldn't get away with this.

Gerry Galvin took his place on the bench, and the session opened. It made a slow start. Sturgess, whose task it was to organize the testimony, began by tendering, item by item, all the evidence from the defunct inquest. It was a process as laborious as moving old furniture from one roo.n to another. Galvin, a slight man of quiet but insistent voice, who kept fingering his neat moustache, allotted a new number to each exhibit like a careful storeman. The public gallery quietly emptied. Kirkham didn't mind the delay at all. The case-law he wanted from Melbourne was caught up in a mail strike. Copies were on the way by air-freight. He needed the time.

2

THE TROUBLE STARTED next day. Sturgess put Sally Lowe in the box. Sally's plaits had gone, and the curls which replaced them trembled. She was nervous because she thought she was in for the sort of questioning she had been through in conference with Des Sturgess yesterday. Sturgess spent that interview asking about her recollection of the baby's cry from the tent. They both knew the importance of it. The police said the baby was already slain. Sturgess had put the competing alternatives to her: that she had heard the cry of her own child, the cry of a bird, one of the dark cries of the night, or finally, a tape-recording which Lindy Chamberlain might have activated to provide an alibi. After two and a half hours Sturgess gave up.

The questioning here turned out nothing like that. Sturgess was putting her through in quick time. He asked that she identify a statement she had made to the police on 19 September, which was, as Kirkham noted, the day of Charlwood's raid at Cooranbong. Sturgess passed a copy to Rice and sat down.

This was the first Rice had seen of it. He stood up and hitched his trousers. The copious folds in those trousers were a delight to the Melbourne cartoonist Arthur Horner, who was sketching him from the back of the court. 'I will make an observation which might help the general conduct of the proceedings before Your Worship,' he said. He objected to the absence of a list of witnesses and protested against the secrecy of the testimony to come. 'Mr Sturgess, for reasons best known to the authorities who instruct him, is proposing to simply call witnesses without giving a summary, even to Your Worship at this stage, of the nature, extent, or their purpose in being called.'

'Mr Sturgess?' Galvin said.

Sturgess said, 'I will bear that in mind and see what I can do.' So that Kirkham could read her statement, he conceded that Sally Lowe might be stood down for an hour or two, but no later than the afternoon session. 'I know that the lady is booked to return to Tasmania and to her family tomorrow,' he said.

This was news to Sally Lowe. She broke in. 'I have an open ticket,' she said loudly. 'I'm willing to stay as long as it takes.'

At the bar-table, Kirkham lowered his head to hide his grin.

'I now call Michael Leigh Chamberlain,' Sturgess said.

Kirkham was interjecting before he was fully out of his chair. 'Your Worship, we object to the calling of Mr Chamberlain at this point in the proceedings.' He laid out the technical form of his protest, which had to do with the rights of a witness to refuse. But his case-law was still somewhere between Melbourne and Alice Springs. 'I will be in a position to put authorities before you, I believe, this afternoon. I have arranged to have some unreported decisions, recently made in similar proceedings in the Victorian Supreme Court, flown up.'

Because Galvin was not drawn by the pause which followed, Kirkham kept on. 'In as much as they have the choice,' and here he meant the Chamberlains' choice to testify or not, 'it can only be a real choice if it is known what evidence is going to be called. We don't know the nature or extent of the fresh evidence to be put before you, and neither of the parties we represent is in a position to effectively exercise their rights without knowing the nature of the evidence to be called. The fairer course would be to call the evidence, then call the Chamberlains and allow them to make an election, or to make submissions as to their rights, on the basis of what has gone on before.'

Galvin said, 'Do your authorities cover this point?'

'They do indeed.'

'On fairness, you say?'

'Not on fairness alone. Their common law rights as well.'

Galvin called on Sturgess for a reply.

'Your Worship,' Sturgess said, hunching over the lectern, 'I did invite my friends to make an application in closed court.' Reporters in the pews behind craned forward to catch his unexpectedly moderated voice. 'They said they would prefer not to do so. In view of the attention that this matter is receiving, publicly, one must be very careful how one chooses one's words.' He chose his words to convey to Galvin that he proposed to call the Chamberlains first and other evidence afterwards. 'I am subject to Your Worship's direction but, apart from that, I control who shall be called, and when they shall be called, and the order in which the evidence is presented, not the witnesses themselves.'

Galvin let the argument run awhile, then said to Rice and Kirkham, 'All I say is, if they are the authorities on which you are waiting I am prepared to postpone the inquest until you argue it. But otherwise I am prepared to go along with counsel assisting. Your clients should be cautioned, and they must elect to answer or not. But, if you have got your authorities, I am prepared to postpone it.'

It was, as it seemed to Kirkham, a grudging concession. They were, after all, only asking for time. This was going to be harder than they'd thought.

When the court adjourned, Rice and Kirkham led the Chamberlains into the conference room. Stuart Tipple followed them in. Tipple was a young and neat Adventist solicitor from Gosford, near Cooranbong. He had been on the case since the time of Charlwood's raid. Rice closed the door. 'Well, you can see the way it's going,' he said.

Peter Dean arrived. He had called his office. There was yet no parcel from Melbourne. 'I'm not sure it would make any difference,' Rice said. 'In any event, Gerry Galvin won't let us wait forever.'

Dean had worse news. A radio station was reporting already that Michael Chamberlain had refused to give evidence 'so not to incriminate himself.'

This upset Lindy Chamberlain more, evidently, than being forced into the witness-box early. She sat on the edge of her chair. 'It's very important to us how we behave,' she said. 'We want to give evidence. We don't want to look as if we've got something to hide.'

'I know,' Rice said. 'I know.'

Rice and Kirkham were worried most about the rumours around town of blood in the car. Current stories identified the blood as foetal, and splashed it about the car as far as the fire-wall near the passenger's feet. The Chamberlains had met this information so far with plain disbelief, which left the lawyers with little to go on either way.

Rice recited the alternatives. 'If you refuse to testify, the only ground available is self-incrimination. You would have to repeat that after every question. If you do testify, you'll have to answer all sorts of questions and without knowing what you're up against. Only you can make the decision.'

'Mr Rice, the answer is out there.' She waved a hand in the direction of the crowded foyer, the reporters, the bug-eyed cameras. ''We give evidence,' she said, and Michael nodded.

Rice was not finished yet. So great were the dangers that he wanted a declaration that they were properly advised. Dean had it typed out. The final sentence read: 'We confirm that we consider we have nothing to worry about, and that we wish to give evidence, and intend to give evidence.'

After Lindy Chamberlain signed it, she laid a hand lightly on Kirkham's sleeve and smiled. 'It'll be all right,' she said. 'Really.'

Rice sent a message to Galvin, conceding the absence of their authorities, and the session resumed.

Sturgess dealt with a geologist who had examined soil from Azaria Chamberlain's clothing, and had found much of it like soil taken from around the campsite, and some of it like the soil where the clothes were discovered. None of this excited Rice enough to cross-examine. Andrew Kirkham then had a fine time questioning Sally Lowe. He took her through her recollections of the baby's sleepy movements, and of Lindy's motherliness, in case they still had to meet some suggestion that the child was already dead, or that Lindy had planned to get rid of her all along. She described the baby's cry again, the shock and sorrow of the night, and the blood she saw later in the tent. By the time Kirkham sat down, he was sure he had displayed Sally Lowe as an observant and truthful witness.

It had occurred to Kirkham that Sturgess might plan to call no one else who was nearby when the baby vanished. Of the events at the campsite, Galvin would then have the testimony of bystanders only on the inert and passionless page.

Rice got to his feet as soon as Michael Chamberlain was called, and before he took the oath. 'Your Worship, we repeat our submission regarding Mr Chamberlain being called at this state. We have no control over his being called now. We would have thought it far fairer to have called him after other evidence which the authorities have, which they claim changes the aspect of things. I merely mention this, because we cannot in any way control the time when Mr Chamberlain, or Mrs Chamberlain, can give evidence. And to that extent, I rise in protest knowing that I am impotent to do anything about it.'

From the beginning, Michael Chamberlain was quiet and careful. He clasped his hands, pursed his lips. He paused before he answered any question, drawing first on some small provision of self-assurance. That provision ran out quickly.

Sturgess was interested in blood on the sleeping-bags. 'You have identified exhibit 20 as your sleeping-bag?'

'Yes.'

'And do you say that you did, subsequently when in Mt Isa, notice there was bloodstaining of your sleeping-bag?'

'I know there was bloodstaining. I seem to recall there were bloodstains on both bags.'

'Well, I am dealing with exhibit 20, and the question related to that. Is it your recollection, now, that in Mt Isa you noticed there was bloodstaining of exhibit 20?'

'It may have been pointed out to me. I cannot recall whether it was that bag, or not, that I saw it on.'

'Did you make any attempt to have exhibit 20 cleaned when you got back to Mt Isa?'

'If this is my bag.'

'Well, it is your bag, is it not?'

'Yes. Then I think I did. Yes.'

'What do you mean by saying you think you did?' Sturgess said, heavily. 'Don't you know whether you did or didn't?'

'Sir, I have been under a considerable amount of stress since the beginning of this, and a lot of things that have happened to me make it difficult to recall at times.''

*   *   *

Soon it was time for Rice to help.

Sturgess was saying. 'Can you tell me this: what was the nature of the bloodstaining upon the bag that you took to the dry cleaners, Mr Chamberlain?'

'There was blood, I think, around the collar area. And there may have been blood elsewhere, I can't recall. But I know there was blood on the bag. Probably around the collar area.'

'And this is the situation, correct me if I am wrong: you think that bag is exhibit 20, your bag, but you cannot be sure?'

Michael Chamberlain frowned. It seemed to Kirkham that Michael was now so confused that he didn't know if he was being asked if the bag was his, or if it was exhibit 20.

'Well,' Michael said, 'if you say that is exhibit 20, that is my bag.'

Sturgess's voice was slow and scathing. 'Yes, but that does not really answer my question, does it.'

'The question was ambiguous, Your Worship,' Rice interjected. 'And I rise simply, if I may, to make the observation that my learned friend, here, is to assist Your Worship. He is not prosecuting.'

Rather than answer the accusation, Sturgess chose to rephrase the question.

Rice and Kirkham were as interested in Sturgess's questions as they were in Michael's answers. They were listening for clues.

'A towel is something you would have used?'

'Yes.'

'Before you got to Mt Isa?'

'Yes.'

'And on the occasion of using it, did you see any bloodstaining on it?'

'Not my towel.'

'Any other towel.'

'Not that I recall.'

Kirkham thought, So somewhere there's blood on a towel.

'You would have travelled quite a few dusty roads, I take it, going from Ayers Rock and returning.'

'Yes.' Michael smiled at what seemed to be a more pleasant

turn in the questioning. 'We tried to avoid as much dust as possible, but we had to.'

'But the situation is that, back at Mt Isa, you had to clean the car, outside and inside?'

'True.'

'And you did not notice any bloodstaining on the outside or the inside of the car, when you so cleaned it? Is that what you say?'

'That is correct.'

'Is this the situation: apart from the bloodstaining that was inside the tent, you did not see any other bloodstaining, whatsoever, that could possibly be associated with this matter?'

'No, I don't recall having done.'

And Kirkham whispered to Rice, 'There's blood in the car, all right.'

'Have you been in any road accidents in the car?'

'Yes.'

'Many?'

'I think probably three.'

'Had anybody been injured?'

'No.'

'Had anybody suffered any injury in the car which caused bleeding?'

'Yes.'

'Who was that person?'

'There were several. There were my two sons, I recall. Reagan had bled in the car. I think Aidan had a nose-bleed in the car. And we had at least one occupant in the car who had bled quite profusely as a result of a road accident, who we picked up and took to hospital.'

'Who was that person? Do you know?'

Michael didn't know, but had a note of the date somewhere. He gave it as 16 June 1979. He and Lindy were trained first-aiders, and had taken the man to the Cairns Base Hospital.

'And he travelled in the back seat? Front seat? Or where?'

'As I recall, he was in the back.'

'What about Aidan, now?'

'Aidan had a nose-bleed. I don't know where in the car he would've been put. I might add that I think there were others in the car who also bled. Pathfinders, from time to time.'

'I beg your pardon?'

'Pathfinders. Young people in the church. That we would fix up.'

'What, young boys and girls?'

'Yes.'

'You say Aidan had a nose-bleed. What happened to him?'

'I do not recall about him so much. It was mainly Reagan, who bled from the head.'

'Did you take him to the doctor in the car?'

'Yes.'

'Where was he, front or back seat?'

'I think he was probably in the front seat.'

'Can you tell me anything else about possible contamination of the outside, or the inside, of the car by blood?'

'Not within my memory, at this stage. No.'

'Well, certainly we can be sure of this. There was no bleeding of the baby in the car, was there, that you know of?'

'Not that I know of. No.'

The last question interested Rice and Kirkham most. They had to face more than blood in the car. Certainly now, the blood was thought to be foetal, blood from a tiny baby.

'The police came to see you in Sydney, is that correct?'

Michael did not argue that it was Cooranbong, not Sydney. 'Yes.'

'And did you give them the camera-bag you had at Ayers Rock?'

'Yes. Yes, I had several bags out there, actually.'

Sturgess held one up. 'That is the bag you gave to the police?'

'Yes.'

'In that bag, then, you would have carried various parts of the camera, and the camera, packed in separate bags.'

'Yes.'

'Anything else?'

'Probably a cleaning-cloth.'

'Would you describe the type of cleaning-cloth?'

'Well, it was a soft sort of glass cleaning-cloth.'

'One of those, so called, lint-free cleaning-cloths?'

'Yes. You could call it that.'

'So, we have got the camera gear packed in the bags, and the lint-free cleaning cloth. Anything else in the bag?'

'There would have been, probably, a foam base to the bag.'

'Was there anything else,' Sturgess said, dissatisfied. 'I will ask you the question again. Apart from what you have described, I would like you to be as particular here as in any other place.'

'Well, it wasn't always used for camera gear, that bag. Not

since Ayers Rock. But I put various things in there. Other types of clothing. That sort of thing.'

This answer caused Sturgess some pause. 'I did not quite hear what you said.'

'Other clothing.'

'Before that please, Mr Chamberlain. You said it wasn't always used for camera gear.'

'It wasn't always used for camera gear. It was being used for camera gear out at the Rock, but I did put other things in it from time to time.'

'Yes? What type of things?'

'Clothing, usually.'

Sturgess thumbed through his notes on the lectern, as though looking for something, a sure sign in an advocate that the last answer came as a surprise. He had, Kirkham noted, twice used the term 'lint-free' talking of the cleaning-cloth. So it was a fair bet they'd found lint of some sort in the camera bag, and wanted to use it. Disposable nappies might shed lint, was that it? But it was the word 'clothing' with which Sturgess was unhappy. Clothing in the camera-bag wrong-footed him, somehow.

'Where did you carry that bag when you were on your trip to Ayers Rock, and while you were at Ayers Rock, with the gear in it? The back seat? Or the front seat? Or under a seat?'

'Well, usually I carried it underneath my feet during the trip. Mainly so I could get at it quickly, if I saw something on the side of the road. It was just so I could have very fast access to the camera.'

'Under your feet? Between the front of the front seat and the pedals?'

'Yes.'

'You did not find it somewhat inconvenient there? Interfered with your access to the pedals?'

'No, not really. When you weigh up the factor that you like taking pictures at a very smart rate, I was willing to forego that small convenience.'

Sturgess called for a copy of the statement made by Bobbie Downs. 'Roberta Downs, Bobbie, as she called herself, you say travelled with you from the campsite back to the motel. Is that right?'

'Yes.'

'Do you remember her calling your attention to this camera-bag?'

'Yes.'

'And offering to take it from you?'

'Yes.'

'Saying that it appeared to be inconvenient, or something like that?'

'Yes. I remember that.'

'She offered to hold it?'

'Yes.'

'But you refused that offer. Is that correct?'

'Correct.'

And Sturgess left the issue hanging there.

'Mr Chamberlain, on the Monday you set out to get some photographs of the tent-site. Is that so?'

'Yes.'

'How did that come about?'

'Well, I was rung up by a pressman from Adelaide.'

'Do you know his name?'

'Yes. I seem to remember it was the name of Scadden.' Michael spelled it. His voice was getting weaker.

Galvin said, 'Before you go on, if you wouldn't mind keeping your voice up a bit.'

'Was this man known to you, Mr Chamberlain,' Sturgess continued, 'or was he a total stranger?'

'No.'

'A total stranger?'

'A total stranger.'

'And when was he in touch with you about this matter? In the morning or in the afternoon?'

'Sometime Monday morning.'

'Can you be more precise than that? Was it fairly early in the morning? Or getting towards midday? Or when?'

'I can't really recall. I think it was mid morning, late morning.'

The courtroom stance Sturgess often adopted resulted in the lectern supporting much of his weight. It had nothing to do with nonchalance. It usually indicated the importance of an imminent question.

'Did you know that people were still out there, searching, at that time?'

'I'm aware that there was still some small search going on.'

'You decided to go and get these photographs, to oblige this man? Is that correct?'

'Yes. As I recall, I was fairly reluctant, but he pressed me, and tried to—well, "do it at all costs" sort of thing.'

Taking time over the sentence, Sturgess repeated it. 'Do it at all costs.'

'I think that was the general tenor.'

'You had quite a lot of film with you. Is that right?'

'Used?'

'Unused?'

'I didn't have much unused film left.'

'Anyway, you decided to get a black and white film. Is that right?'

'Yes.'

'Why was that?'

'Well, the press, as I understand, don't appreciate trying to use colour films in black and white newspapers.'

This was enough for Rice. He climbed to his feet. 'This has all been gone through before in the previous sitting, Your Worship, it is all on record. And it is taking on the semblance of a very dexterous, inquisitorial, cross-examination as to why this man did not go out searching—as one would have expected, perhaps—by the cross-examiner. This is entirely in Your Worship's hands, but I do not see this as assisting Your Worship.' Rice used the phrase 'assisting Your Worship' to convey, in a legal manner, the fairness and even-handedness he expected from a coroner's assistant. 'It is, more or less, to impute some impure motive, or at least to impute some sort of guilt to Mr Chamberlain. And I object.'

'On what basis?' Galvin asked. 'On the matter that it has been gone into before?'

'On all aspects. The fact is that it has been gone into before.'

'Can we get this one straight, Mr Rice,' Galvin said, in the loudest tone he had used until now. 'As far as I am concerned this is a new matter. And I would have thought I had to see the witness.'

Rice might have been more satisfied with that answer if Galvin chose to see all the witnesses, including those at the campsite favourable to the Chamberlains. So heated was the exchange becoming that both he and Galvin were speaking at the one time. Rice won. 'But is my friend alleging the commission of some sort of offence by Mr Chamberlain? You see, we know nothing. He has gone into the witness-box at this early stage without any notice to us at all. Now, we have been very patient. But I do object. If my friend is going to suggest that he has committed some offence, why has he not been charged? And the normal processes of justice allowed to proceed, instead of putting him in the witness-box and cross-examining him—under the guise of an inquest—with a view to building up a case when presumably this other evidence, this other undisclosed evidence, does not seem to have the fibre?'

'Well,' Galvin said, 'if I can perhaps paraphrase your argument, your objection is on the second leg, rather than the first?'

Rice conceded that. Galvin called on Sturgess.

'Your Worship, I seek to examine the conduct of Mr Chamberlain during the hours shortly following the raising of this alarm, what his conduct was on the Monday.'

'With a view to what?'

'With a view, really,' Sturgess said, as if searching for better words, 'just to making a full examination of it at this stage.'

'Would you then say that the objection—that that becomes an inquisitorial matter?'

'If Your Worship pleases, a coronial inquiry is an inquisitorial matter,' Sturgess agreed. 'One seeks to determine what occurred that is relevant to the matter being inquired into. Now, evidence that will be given might strongly suggest that some person or persons, subsequent to the alarm being raised on the night of the 17th, did certain things with the clothing that the child had been dressed in, and put it in a certain place, that there was human interference in relation to that matter. In those circumstances, I would submit that we have to be very much concerned with the conduct of the persons who were closest to this matter. I am seeking to examine what his conduct was on that Monday, and to examine the reasons why he went back to the campsite. We have, in the other proceedings, evidence of a return to the campsite, and an explanation for it, and I am seeking to examine that side of things, why he went back there and what occurred, and how long he was back at the campsite. And this is conduct that is very, very close to the occasion in question. I would submit that it is a matter of considerable materiality.'

Galvin leaned back in his seat. 'At this stage, I say that it is relevant to the—' he trailed off, substituting a wave of his hand for the rest of his adjudication.

'Thank you,' said Sturgess, turning back to the witness.

* * *

After the overnight adjournment, Rice made another attempt to have Galvin restrain Sturgess from acting, as Rice put it, as if it were a trial. This time, Rice asked that Galvin lay down some clear 'ground-rules'.

'I decline to do so Mr Rice. I think counsel assisting, in my view of the law, is entitled to ask leading questions, and to conduct an inquiry as such. If you wish, I agree that there may be questions of natural justice, and I think you are going to have to take objections to questions as they come, and I will rule.'

This was all Rice could hope for now. He conceded, and sat down. Clearly, it was just no use.

Kirkham was astonished. He had appeared frequently here in Alice Springs and in Darwin courts, without striking anything like this before. The thoughts which were moving him to anger were not at all complicated. This was an ambush. Galvin was not going to put a stop to it. Perhaps, he thought, he should have tried to dissuade the Chamberlains from testifying, looking back on it now. A chastening mirror, hindsight.

The spectators on the public-benches are growing louder. Reporters sitting in front can hear them clearly. Galvin's decisions are popular back there. When Rice sits down, defeated in the last exchange, someone in a large primrose smock says, 'How sad.' From the sniggering nearby, she seems to be held in high regard. On the witness-stand, Michael Chamberlain is handed a child's sleeping-bag and asked to identify it. His nervous fingers can't loosen a knot in the cord, and he asks for help. 'Poor thing,' she says. The reporters turn to look. They know her. She is the mood of the town.

The car is a main attraction for Sturgess. The questioning visits it time after time.

'Do you recall washing the carpet?'

'The carpet?'

'Using soap or detergent, or something of that nature?'

'No. I don't.'

'Do you recall cleaning blood off the seats?'

'I cleaned the seats fairly regularly. But specifically blood, I don't recall actually, specifically, cleaning blood.'

'You say you do not recall. If the seats, or some of them, become badly stained with blood, and you clean them, you would recall that. Would you not?'

'The fact is, Mr Sturgess, the car's interior is black, and it's very difficult to see dark things in that car.'

'Yes, I accept what you say, but I am trying to direct your attention to this: did you—at any stage—discover enough blood in the car that you required, as a quite separate task, to set about cleaning the blood off? You understand, off the seats?'

'Yes. No, I don't recall that.'

'If that had happened, it is a matter you would not quickly forget, surely, Mr Chamberlain.'

'I beg your pardon?'

'If that had happened, that is a matter you would not quickly forget. You have got enough blood in your car—on the seats and that—that you have got to set about attempting to remove it.'

Rice was climbing to his feet more slowly now, as if his energy had diminished with the fate of earlier objections. 'He has answered that question, Your Worship, and he does not specifically remember any such occasion, that is all. And he has answered. The rest becomes argumentative.'

'I will allow the question,' Galvin said.

'The question is this,' Sturgess said slowly, his hands perching on the lectern. 'If the car had so much blood upon it that you then set out to remove that blood from the car—that was your task, not just a general clean up of the car—you would remember that, would you not? Bearing in mind that you only purchased that car in December of 1977?'

December of 1977 was four years past. Michael Chamberlain shook his head. 'There are a number of instances when blood was in that car, as I remember, but I cannot specifically recall setting out to clean any of it up.'

'Have a look at these scissors, please.' Sturgess handed them up. They were small nail-scissors which someone had evidently dismantled for examination. 'You will see that the rivet, or the screw, has been taken out, so they present as two separate articles. Those scissors were in the console, were they not?'

'I believe so. Yes.'

'They weren't in that condition. They were screwed together, is that correct?'

'Yes.'

'Ordinarily, you kept those scissors in the little pocket of the console, is that correct?'

'Well, they are toenail scissors. I think they were not always in the car I think they might have been at home in our house.'

'But you frequently carried them in the car, is that correct?'

'Well, they were in the car sometimes, and other times they weren't.'

'They were certainly in the car when the police took possession of it?'

'Yes.'

Since Michael Chamberlain couldn't remember which scissors he had in the car on the trip to Ayers Rock, Sturgess came at it another way.

'We agree upon this, do we, that ordinarily you used to carry a pair of scissors in the Torana?'

'At least one pair. Yes.'

'At least one pair, and in the little pocket of the console?'

'That's the lift-up?'

'Yes, that one.'

'Usually, yes.'

'What about towels? Did you ordinarily carry towels in the Torana?'

'Yes, I did.'

For the next question Sturgess turned from the witness, an advocate's mannerism which anticipates the inevitable and damning answer.

'In the well, at the back?'

'Yes,' Michael said, apparently relieved that this was all there was to it. He was unshamed by the well at the back.

'Where the spare tyre is?'

'Correct.'

'You ordinarily carried a towel there? Did you?'

'At least one.'

At the bar-table, Kirkham's list of items on which the police might have found blood had grown by a pair of nail scissors, and a travelling-towel. And there was an attempt here to represent the towel as hidden in the wheel-well. Kirkham permitted a smile. he had carried a towel in such a place himself, on occasions.

* * *

'I have no further questions of Mr Chamberlain, at this stage,' Sturgess said.

The qualification brought Rice to his feet. 'When my friend says "at this stage", I understand that he does not have any present intention of asking any more questions, or he does not want to have him recalled. I really want to know whether he has any present intention of having Mr Chamberlain recalled.'

Sturgess said, 'I can answer that. Your Worship, much further evidence is going to be adduced, and I will at all stages, subject to what Your Worship requires me to do, give Mr Chamberlain the very fullest and the most complete opportunity to return to the witness-box and discuss any of the further evidence from that position.'

It wasn't the 'complete opportunity' of which Sturgess spoke that worried Rice and Kirkham, but the words 'at all stages'. They were facing a novel form of inquest, perhaps a running interrogation.

3

THE COURT took a short recess. No one left the public gallery, for fear of losing a seat. Michael pushed through into the foyer, wiping his hands on a wilted kerchief and headed for the wash-room. He was followed in by two radio reporters who hoped to provoke some quotable remark. The ploy was foiled by a power failure in that part of the building. The wash-room was in total darkness.

The spectators had to wait, as it turned out, until the afternoon session to see Lindy Chamberlain in the witness-stand. Rice won the postponement because he'd been told a carrier had arrived with Kirkham's case-law aboard. But when court resumed, he was still empty handed.

Galvin said, 'If I can just indicate that I see no reason to change the ruling or the nature of the questions.' He looked down at Rice. 'I do not feel I am doing anything wrong.'

4

LINDY CHAMBERLAIN'S VOICE was faint and unsure, but she seemed to have a better grasp of memory than her husband. It was not long before Sturgess moved to turn this to advantage. He began to confront her with Michael's answers.

'You were present in court here today when I was questioning your husband. Is that so?'

'That's correct.'

'And do you recall me asking him about a number of visits to the dry-cleaners?'

'Yes.'

'As though he was searching for a parka.'

'That's right. We were.'

'That had been lost?'

'That's right, we were.'

'Do you know anything about that?'

'Yes. When we had our interviews with the police, they wanted to know where Aidan's parka was because they hadn't received it, and it had been posted across to them. And it seems that there was some hold-up in the mail, or in some department, and it subsequently turned up after several inquiries.'

'I may not have heard what you said. You said "subsequently turned up" did you not?'

'Yes. The police had it.'

'The police had it?'

'The police had it. Here in Alice Springs.'

'Well, do you know anything about inquiries, and a number of them being made to the dry-cleaners in Mt Isa, about the whereabouts of a missing parka?'

'Yes. They asked us to inquire every place we could think of, just in case it had been mislaid—'

Sturgess interrupted her here. 'Those inquiries were made at the suggestion of the police, you say?'

'Yes. We knew a number of things had been to the dry-cleaners. And we thought that, by mistake, my husband's memory was rather bad, and I wondered if he had taken it to the dry-cleaners instead of to the post office. But it turned up eventually.'

At the police-station, which seemed to settle the matter.

Sturgess called for the jungle hats. 'That is an army hat, commonly called a giggle hat, Mrs Chamberlain, is that correct?'

'I understand the other one is a giggle hat. This is just an ordinary army hat.'

'That is your husband's hat, is that so?'

'No. It's my hat.'

'Your hat? Is it?'

She nodded.

'May I see it please?'

'My husband did identify it as his hat, but it's mine.'

'Very well. He made a mistake, you say?'

'That's right. He quite often borrows mine, and consequently thinks it's his.'

'And the other one? You saw it being produced yesterday. You may as well have a look at it again. That one is his, in fact, you say?'

'That's Michael's hat. Yes.'

'You gave those hats to the police in September of this year, is that so?'

'That's correct.'

'That is, when they were down there with a warrant?'

'That's right.'

'And you suggested they had better have a look at them, is that so?'

'That's right.'

Kirkham made a note about the army hats. So far, Sturgess had spent most time on clothes and bedding from the tent which were free of blood. Clearly the implication was to be that a dingo would have bloodied these items more. Now Kirkham was watching a curious reversal of tactics.

'What was it that you wanted them to look at?' Sturgess asked.

'Well, they were asking for anything we had in the tent. Particularly anything that may have had blood on it. And I suggested that these items, to my observation, had blood on them. Although they had rejected them for the last inquest, I thought they should be looked at again, if they were going through everything.'

'Pick up your hat, to start with. The one that is yours. Just indicate this stained area. Show it to His Worship. What about on the brim, underneath the brim.'

She let the hat dangle from her fingers and pointed. 'Through here, and also on there. And I think that area.' Most of it, red and brown spots, seemed to be on the left brim. 'I know the children did get hold of it at one stage, and throw some mud on it, and I think this side is the mud.' She looked it over. 'But I'm not sure which was—'

Sturgess turned to the bench. 'Has Your Worship had the opportunity to look closely at the hat?'

Galvin waved it away. 'I saw it yesterday,' he said.

All this was like walking through quicksands by night, but the more devious the route became, the more sure-footed she seemed to be.

'The next item, please.' Sturgess handed her a baby's rug. It was small and fluffy.

'It is a bunny-rug,' she said.

'Was that in the tent on 17 August?'

'No.'

'Was it at Ayers Rock?'

'Yes.'

'Whereabouts? Was it in the car?'

She was very pale. 'Yes. It would have been in the car. I think it would have been in the dirty clothes bag.' She made an attempt to say something else, failed, and began again, 'because I had used it the first two days of the trip.'

'The police took possession of that also in September of this year?'

Palsy, which had begun as a trembling of the hands, now had her about the shoulders. She held the bunny-rug, tightly. Her helpless wail of assent was barely audible.

Sturgess said, 'I may require an adjournment, if Your Worship pleases.'

Galvin called a recess. A court orderly, a well-tanned woman who was stationed alongside the witness-box, walked over to join the duty-constable guarding the door. 'It was the blanket,' the orderly confided. 'She had seen the other things in court before, but not the blanket. I was nearly in tears myself.' But her sympathy was not contagious, judging by the faces in the public gallery.

She revisited, in questioning, the car and the tent without further event. She had resorted again to dark glasses, but her voice grew stronger. By the time Sturgess got her as far as her interrogation by Sergeant Charlwood, she was tetchy.

'Now, let me proceed with this account,' Sturgess said, meaning Charlwood's account. 'Did Mr Charlwood say, "Mrs Chamberlain, did you kill your child?"'

'He said that was one question he hadn't asked before. He had asked me before what happened, but never had I done it.'

'Did you say this, or something to this effect, to him, "Well, what are the implications if I tell you?"'

'That's correct.'

'Did he say, "It depends on your answer?"'

'That's not correct. I said that he had promised to keep conversations confidential before, and he had broken his word. He asked me, "What conversations?" And I said that he asked me about hypnotism, and then in the box, last time, he maintained that it was an "official request", when there was no indication of that given. I said to him, "If I speak to you again like this, what guarantee have I got that I don't have this thrown up at me in court." Which obviously I am having. Right now.'

This was the current danger, as Kirkham saw it. Not that she might be disabled again by tears, but by losing her temper.

'Why,' Sturgess insisted, 'did you ask him that question, "Well, what are the implications if I tell you?"'

'Because I had told him that our legal advice was not to give an interview. And although I've learned very fast how far to trust the police, I was still expecting them to honour their word. And I was not sure what he considered an interview and what he didn't. And as I had no legal advice there, I was asking him the question. Unfortunately I was given the wrong advice.'

'Now, you understand what my question is. Why did you say to him, "Well, what are the implications if I tell you?"'

'Yes.' She shook her head. 'I've just explained why I asked him that.'

Sturgess's voice was derisory, the one sure way of making Lindy Chamberlain stubborn. 'Is that your complete answer on the subject, Mrs Chamberlain?'

'That's all I'm prepared to say right now.'

'Perhaps I can shorten this,' Sturgess said. 'Did he ever at the police station ask you if you were prepared to give him your handprints?'

'No. He said one of the things they would have liked to have done, if we had agreed to an interview, was to have taken our handprints, and we told him that was fine by us, provided they got in contact with our lawyers, and any interview, or handprints, took place with the lawyers, then we were quite happy about it.'

'Did he say something like this to you: "Being fully aware of what I have told you of the forensic findings, are you prepared to give me your handprints? Before you answer that, I want to understand that the giving of them could be a means, not only of tying you to the prints on the clothes, but of also excluding you?'' Did he say that, or something like that?'

'Yes.'

'Did you say this, or something to this effect: "Yes I realize that. I am prepared to let you have my handprints, but I would like to talk to my solicitor first?'' '

'That's correct.'

'And he said, "Yes, that's all right." Is that correct?'

'That's right. And he promised to contact us the following day. We haven't heard from him since.'

Sturgess wasn't prepared for this level of vehemence. 'Steady on,' he said.

He waited for the court to quieten.

'Mrs Chamberlain,' he said, 'would you be prepared to give, to the police, your palmprints?'

He meant now.

Rice leapt up. 'Before any answer is given, Your Worship,' he said, 'in the light of the previous evidence, no suggestion of any—' He readjusted the position of his chair, and stood behind it, slowing the pace of things, trying to break the bewitching drama of the moment.

He began again. 'I have not cross-examined at all on the "voire dire",' which was his shorthand way of saying that he had not yet questioned Charlwood about this interrogation, 'but Your Worship will well know that whatever was said by Mrs Chamberlain to Charlwood was against the background of her declining to say anything at all. For my friend to now suggest that she comply with any request of his is to deny a person the rights they have. They are not here to assert anything. They are not here to volunteer any evidence. They have the right at all times, a right she has exercised at the police-station, to refuse, and I would have to protest. I think the particular answer, one way or the other, is contrary to the conduct of a fair interview, let alone the examination of a person in the witness-box.'

It rankled with Rice that Charlwood had so arranged things that he would take a copy of Lindy Chamberlain's palmprints only if her lawyers were absent. It made Rice suspicious. Why did the law department deny him a copy of the handprint on the clothing? And here was Sturgess now, demanding either her handprint or a public refusal. The question was: how far would Galvin allow it?

So far, Galvin was not drawn. He rested back in his chair. From the floor of the court the bench obliterated all but his spectacles and receding forehead. Rice decided he'd better keep going. 'I don't care for this line of questioning,' he said, resuscitating earlier arguments, 'for this sort of request to be conducted. No one is obliged to comply with that request, and refusal, of course on advice, can be misconstrued. My advice would be not to allow Mrs Chamberlain to respond to that request, irrespective of what her state of mind would be.' That last sentence was directed as much to the witness-box, where Lindy Chamberlain was watching events from somewhere behind her round sunglasses, as it was to the coroner. But it brought Galvin leaning into the argument.

Galvin said 'That is a different issue to the question being put, is it not?'

'I do not think the witness ought to be asked the question.'

'Why?' Galvin asked. 'I'm sorry, I do not think I am quite with your application.'

'Simply on the grounds that a person is entitled at law to decline to answer anything, on any ground at all.' This was true of a police interview, though a little wide for application in a court. It betrayed Rice's firm belief that what Sturgess had in train here was a police interrogation rather than an inquest. 'The fact that she is in the witness-box does not elevate her, in any way, to a position different from that of her ordinary rights and entitlements. The advice any lawyer would give any client would be to decline such a request. Therefore she should not be exposed to the position of embarrassing herself because of the lawyer's advice not to answer the question.'

Kirkham, who had been scribbling a note, pushed it along the table. Rice didn't need to read it. He was there already. 'In any event, we would have to give her advice before any question was asked of her.'

'That is why I wanted you to delineate your argument,' Galvin said. 'If you want time to advise your client, you can have it.'

Inside the conference room, Lindy pulled off her sunglasses and said, 'What do we do now?'

'Gerry Galvin is going to let Sturgess run on,' Rice said

heavily, 'so the choice is refusal or agreement. Mr Kirkham and I advise refusal.' He looked at Kirkham. Kirkham nodded. 'We don't know enough yet to advise any other course.'

'The thing,' Kirkham said, 'is a double-bind. If your print is too big, they can say the mark is of only part of your hand. If it's too small, they'll say the clothing was bunched.'

'Okay. How do I say it?'

Kirkham let out a quiet breath. He had feared she might decide to go her own way about this.

'What was it you said to Charlwood?'

'I told Sergeant Charlwood, and I say the same thing again. I would have been quite happy to provide my palmprints to them, providing my lawyers agree. They do not agree that I give my palmprints at this stage. They know I'm quite happy to give my palmprints.'

Sturgess said, 'You are not prepared to give, to the authorities, your palmprints so they can be compared with—' He did not describe what they could be compared with. He gathered his notes and sat. Galvin stood Lindy Chamberlain down.

5

GOD ONLY KNEW where Kirkham's parcel of case-law was now. The mail strike, which had immobilized the first batch he sent for was bad enough. But there was also rain. The day before the inquest began, the town was hit by the heaviest cloudbursts seen for decades. One storm delivered fifty millimetres in two hours. The desert all around was a slurry. Sandy streambeds filled and the banks broke. The casino moved tourists in and out by helicopter, so wide was the Todd River. The front page of the *Centralian* carried a photograph of a delighted Aborigine, wearing a suit and tie, riding the current barefoot on a surfboard. The roads were cut. Air cargo coming up from the south was now displaced by more urgent supplies. Deliveries of anything else could take days yet.

In Rice's hotel room they had an evening drink and talked things through. The judgement for which Kirkham was most anxious, called Alexander's case, wasn't available anywhere but Melbourne. There, a judge had prevented a coroner from forcing a witness to the stand the way Galvin had compelled the Chamberlains, but nothing could be done about it now.

Second-guessing Sturgess's tactics, it seemed likely he planned to cross-examine the Chamberlains after each new piece of scientific evidence, and before they knew what was coming next. Plainly, the Chamberlains must refuse. The difficulty was publicity. The press would be merciless. Rice favoured making a refusal before the Chamberlains were called on again, and in writing rather than in open court.

The real task lay in the presentation. It had to be confidential and restricted to the law department, Sturgess, and Galvin. Making it public would prejudice the Chamberlains, irremediably, in the eyes of the nation. It had to be worded so that no one would risk pulling a trick like that.

They worked on it into the night.

6

THE POLICE COMPOUND, in which the Chamberlains' sedan was stored, was five minutes drive from the courthouse. Galvin convened the hearing inside the main shed. It was Sturgess who called the press together to lay out the rules. He had no trouble speaking over the heads of those in front.

'Be in no doubt about this,' he said. 'Anyone who doesn't do as he's told will be sent outside. I'll give you a few minutes to look at the car and take photographs. Don't touch anything. You may photograph what you will, but the moment the hearing starts you must move away, and then maintain complete silence. While evidence is taken, the use of cameras is prohibited.'

The compound was a wire-mesh cage with a gate, now ajar. The fence reached nearly to the roof of the shed. All this was built, so press-releases said, especially for this exercise. The yellow hatchback lay inside it, disabled, empty of engine and gearbox. The doors on each side hung open. Two seats lay on a nearby bench. The engine hood was propped against a wall.

The press photographers lit the passenger compartment with flashlight explosions. Three TV crews, with shouldered telecameras, filmed the car and filmed each other filming it. Then Sturgess walked in, leading Galvin, the Chamberlains and the lawyers. He waved the newspeople outside.

A court-reporter held a microphone close by while Metcalf

showed Galvin over the car. So big was Metcalf that, when he leaned inside, it seemed clear the vehicle was designed for a smaller race of people. He pointed here and there. Chalk marks made rough circles on the lining of the doors and on the carpets, where he had found blood. The nail scissors were found in a pocket of the console, between the absent front seats. A chamois was behind the driver's seat, a towel in the wheel-well. He had come upon blood on the brackets which held the front seats to the floor, on the hinge, and around the bolt-holes.

He held up a steel plate. This he had cut from the roof of the front footwell, on the passenger side. He had found blood there, the shape of a fine spray. He heaved into the passenger side, on his back, and lay with his head in the footwell. He pointed up. The vivid inference was this: the baby had been held down there, under the dashboard, still spurting blood.

7

STURGESS BECKONED JOY KUHL over to the car. She clipped across the concrete floor on quick high heels, a dark-haired little woman in a pink dress. She laid a fresh white handbag on the bench. She was both excited and confident.

Mrs Kuhl was a biologist with the Health Commission in Sydney. She had worked there for four years, in the forensic science section. When the Northern Territory police moved the Chamberlains' car to Sydney, it became her job to examine it for blood. She worked with Metcalf. He gave her the nail scissors, the camera-bag, and two army hats. They swabbed the inside of the car, and parts of the outside, then Metcalf dismantled the seats, and they examined those and the carpets. Wherever the stains were sufficient, she tested it for human character, for foetal haemoglobin, and made an attempt at grouping.

The way the tests came out, she identified traces of blood in both inner compartments and the zipper of the camera-bag. The army hats bore none at all; those stains were something else. She found more in the console in the car, on both door-handles, the seats, and carpet. On the driver's side, the carpet showed the presence of blood, but also the presence of soap, disqualifying it for further testing. But there was an edge of this carpet which gave up foetal haemoglobin. So did the towel, the plastic container in which the chamois was stored, and scrapings taken from under the passenger side glove compartment.

Beneath the passenger seat, and on a ten-cent coin she found there, the blood was human and foetal. There was enough volume here for an attempt at grouping, which suggested group O and PGM1 +, but only on the probabilities, before the sample ran out. She was able, in a separate test, to dribble blood from that seat on the mounting underneath, producing the pattern she had found there earlier. To make it work, she needed five millilitres, and someone had to be sitting in the seat at the time.

Mrs Kuhl had, throughout, instructed Galvin and the lawyers in a straightforward tone, although Kirkham noticed that the tests on which her conclusions relied did not figure much in her explanations. Kirkham was familiar with this style of scientific testimony. The absence of the middle steps, the laboratory techniques, made the evidence seem more like fact, and less like opinion. It gave the illusion of infallibility.

She led the party from the car back to the bench, where the seats lay. This was a surprise to Kirkham, because it was here that the demonstration had begun. She lay the passenger seat on its side. Parts of the black upholstery were ringed with chalk. She scanned it with busy eyes.

'I could probably illustrate the strength of the blood reaction,' she said, 'even though I've swabbed most of it off.'

In a case already on the bench she found two small chemical bottles and a white pad. The pad was the size of a cocktail-coaster. She swabbed part of the vinyl seat, laid the pad out flat, and held up the bottles.

'I'll see if it will still work,' she said. Kirkham couldn't believe she would risk a finale like this unless she was sure. The reporters crowded in more closely, a trespass which Sturgess didn't seem to mind.

She applied a few drops of chemical. 'Other contaminants will give a first-stage reaction.' She waited a moment, but the pad remained truthfully white. 'Blood gives this two-stage reaction, an immediate bright blue.' She poured on a little of the other and held the pad aloft. It began to shade near the centre and darkened, at first a swelling jewel, now a turquoise butterfly, vibrant and magical. She smiled.

It was that simple.

8

THERE MOVED THEN, through the witness-stand, a procession of testimony which gave Rice and Kirkham the best indication so far how busy the police investigation was while the oblivious Chamberlains were engaging in campus life at Avondale. Botanists and minerologists had flown to Ayers Rock to collect samples of vegetation and bags of arid sand. Technicians in Sydney and in Adelaide dug holes in baby-clothing with knives, scissors, and teeth from the jaws of dried dingo skulls. At the south face of the Rock, an entomologist watched, for hours, the behaviour of desert flies as they crawled over a cloth he had moistened with blood.

Cocks, the portly sergeant from the Adelaide police laboratory, had come up with two methods of cutting a baby's jump-suit which approximated the damage to Azaria Chamberlain's. He demonstrated this to Galvin. He folded part of the fabric in four, another in two. He used a pair of curved scissors, cutting this way and that. He let the folds fall and displayed the damage proudly, betraying the amount of time it must have taken him to perfect the design.

In a loud aside, made from the bar-table, Rice said, 'Any grade-two child could do that.' It put him in mind of paper figures joined at the fingertips.

Then Sturgess asked, 'You noticed that when cuts were made, little particles of thread and fibre fell off, is that so?'

'Yes,' Cocks said. 'The top surface has a looped pile. And those loops, when a scissor-cut is made into the material, cuts through the loops, a number of these little loops will fall off.'

'In the vacuumings from the Chamberlain car that were handed to you, you discovered similar looped particles?'

'Yes.'

'And subsequently, the camera-bag was vacuumed?'

'I had previously vacuumed the camera-bag. I then looked at the vacuumings, and I found three particles of thread. Little tufts of thread.'

In cross-examination Rice went in hard. He held up the Chamberlains' nail scissors. They were small and old. 'Were those the scissors you attempted to use in your first cutting tests?'

'Yes,' Cocks said, 'and they came apart.'

'They were wobbly to start with?'

'Yes.'

'And they were weak, were they not?'

'They hadn't been put together properly,' Cocks complained.

'Whether they were or not, they were weak.'

'Yes.'

Rice moved on to the scissors Cocks had used in court. 'The pair of scissors you eventually used, the ones you made your demonstration with before His Worship, you call that a similar pair, do you?'

'I could not get an identical pair.'

'Do you call it a similar pair?'

'The nearest I could get.'

'They are larger in size, for one thing?'

'Yes.'

'Greater in strength, for another?'

'Yes.'

'And far more efficient for your purposes?'

'Yes.'

The tufts of fibre found in the car and in the camera-bag represented a greater challenge.

'Mr Cocks, your theory is that scissors were applied to the garments after bleeding?'

'Yes.'

'And that the areas affected were heavily laced with blood?'

'Some areas, not all areas.'

'Well, you had better define which areas.'

'Areas of the collar were, heavily.'

'Laced with blood?'

'Yes,' Cocks conceded, 'but the arm was not. Only in what I would call discrete areas—most of it was unstained—on the arm.'

'Most of what was unstained?'

'Unstained of blood. The area through which the holes appear where the cutting has occurred is unstained of blood.'

'But certainly not so in the collar, is that right?'

'No, that is stained.'

'Very heavily?'

'Yes.'

'What about the tufts, as you call them, from the black camera-bag. Were they examined by you?'

'Yes.'

'And there was no trace of blood on any of them?'

'No.'

'That's right, isn't it?' Rice said, by way of underlining it for Galvin.

Cocks nodded. 'I could not detect, by the presumptive test normally conducted, the presence of blood.'

When Rice sat down, he settled back, pleased. He'd not had so much fun in a long while.

9

THE BEST PLACE Malcolm Brown could think of, searching for Professor Cameron, was the casino, since that was where Sturgess was staying. Word was about that Cameron would testify tomorrow morning. Sturgess would keep him close by. Brown wasn't after an interview, and he knew better than to hope for one. Brown wanted to see Cameron somewhere other than in court. He wanted to get a feel for the man.

He paid off the cab and went inside. Most of the crowd in the busy foyer was making for the restaurants and the gambling rooms. Brown headed in the other direction, to the cocktail bar where the house-guests drank. It was gilded and plush. Sturgess was there already, on a stool at the bar. Brown chose a corner table and ordered a double scotch. A double scotch represented, for Brown, four gulps. He was uncomfortable in places like this and now he was the only man in the room wearing a suit. A baggy pocket yielded a copy of the *Sydney Morning Herald*. He opened it out.

He was through his second drink when Cameron walked in. The professor was thick-set, balding, and shorter than photographs suggested. His ruddy tan indicated that he might spend a good deal of time in places other than the British Isles. He said something at which Sturgess laughed. Cameron looked pleased. It was Brown's guess that Cameron would be considered a fine raconteur.

Brown had already researched something of Cameron's standing as a forensic pathologist. The man had a classy reputation. He was professor of forensic medicine at the University of London, director of a similar department at the London Hospital Medical College, and a consultant, it seemed, everywhere else. He lectured to police trainees in London, Bristol, Sussex, Kent, and to military police. He was a specialist in the injuries of battered babies and infantile deaths. His frequent papers were widely published. And all this was probably not the half of it.

There was a suggestion, Brown remembered, that Cameron liked celebrated cases. He was thought a skilful witness, wily and resistant to cross-examination, and Brown now found that easy to understand. Sturgess listened while Cameron did most of the talking. When Cameron laughed, the eyes remained hooded and remote, the smile did as it was bidden. There was a strong coincidence, here, of the urbane and the competitive.

Brown folded his newspaper and walked out. Tomorrow, he could expect some excellent copy.

10

CAMERON sat in the witness-box, crossed his legs, and leaned with an arm on the rail. So long was his curriculum vitae that Sturgess handed a typed copy to Galvin, rather than read it all out. Then Sturgess said, 'I would like to pass on to your sources of information. On 8 June 1981, at the London Hospital Medical College, did you receive from Mr K.A. Brown of Adelaide, a forensic odontologist, certain items?'

'I did.'

'Now, as I proceed, you will wish to refer to notes, and reports you have made, and also photographs you have had taken. Is that correct?'

'I would like to,' Cameron said. 'Yes.'

This was a moment for which Rice was well prepared. He and Kirkham hoped they had found a roundabout way to flush out, from Sturgess and Galvin, copies of the scientific reports which would, in any other inquest, have been provided at the beginning.

'Your Worship,' Rice said, 'I have seen nothing at all, as usual in this case, by way of reports. I know my friend's stance on this. He is under instructions not to reveal anything to me. But I now reiterate my former requests that I be, at least at this stage, apprised of the reports on which the witness proposes to rely.'

Galvin called on Sturgess.

'Mr Rice will have everything made available to him at the appropriate time,' Sturgess replied. 'As Your Worship well knows, in a coronial inquiry the information is revealed to the court.' By this he meant that the information is not made available to witnesses, an interpretation which caused Kirkham to sorrowfully shake his head. Sturgess went on, 'The very proper practices of the court will be strictly adhered to.'

Looking down at Rice, Galvin said, 'Do you want to take the matter any further?'

It was a source of frequent wonder to Kirkham that Rice remained courteous in trying times like these. Not that Kirkham would himself have lost his temper, boyish though he looked. Advocates learn early not to upset the tribunal on whom their clients rely for a just decision. Nevertheless, charm was another thing altogether, and Rice had an inestimable amount.

The argument Rice was putting rested on his right to examine a document which a witness needs to prompt memory. As the legal rule has it, a witness should exhaust memory first, and then ask for permission to refer to notes. The notes must be contemporaneous, which is generally interpreted to mean that they should have been written closely enough to the time of the event as to be reliable. An advocate in Rice's position is entitled to examine them, and examine the witness about them, to make sure these conditions are met. The procedure slows the progress of a hearing, and Galvin was now being warned, in stylishly polite terms, that this was a stunt Rice could pull every time a witness asked to rely on notes.

'I do not wish to do so,' Rice said with a pleasant smile, 'but I must ask that if the witness is going to refresh his memory by reference to notes, may I have the opportunity of looking at the notes to determine what my attitude will be?'

Kirkham watched Galvin to see how he would take this. The coroner fingered his moustache. He'd got it, all right. He turned to Sturgess. 'Mr Sturgess, we are going to have to meet this, at some stage.'

'Yes,' Sturgess said. 'If Your Worship pleases.'

'I agree that I do not have the power to interfere, but I think we are coming to a stage where surely something should be made available.' He paused. 'Otherwise I am going to be forced to run a technically correct course.'

'Your Worship, all these reports will be made available to my friend's inspection. I will give him a copy of the report, but the complaint is that he has not received these reports days, or weeks, beforehand.'

But this did not meet the obvious and immediate point. Galvin said, 'What is going to happen now?'

'He can have a copy of the report.'

Cameron called for Azaria Chamberlain's jump-suit. He turned it over. 'Given a normal opening of a canine mouth, and working from the dingo skull in my possession, I found difficulty in finding an area of skin exposed in a child that remained to be grasped without damaging the material of the neck of the garment. Examination of the jump-suit, which I was presented with, confirmed that bleeding had occurred when the jump-suit was buttoned up to the top, and that the neck had been cut, at or about or shortly after, by a cutting instrument such as scissors or a knife. But on closer examination, it's more consistent with scissors.'

'One of the interesting features was that I could not detect any evidence of dragging on other areas of the jump-suit, which indicated to me that it was not a member of the canine family that had carried the child, or if it had been a member of the canine family, it would have to be a large member of the canine family, such as a Great Dane. For to carry a child of this size by the head or neck, without dragging, would necessitate the body being held at least twenty inches or more off the ground. In other words, if it had been grasped by the neck, the feet would have dragged, and I would have expected drag-marks in the form of tearing or marking on the feet, in the jump-suit particularly, on rough terrain.'

Kirkham scribbled a note: Sand is rough terrain?

'This garment was subjected to exposure to the sand, or the dust, that is found on it, and that staining is uniform. It's not as if it was done after the garments were folded. It's done when something was inside that garment.'

'So assuming that the garment was buried,' Sturgess asked, 'your opinion is that the body of the baby was in the garment at the time it was buried?'

'It would have had to have been.'

A court orderly set up a projection screen. Sturgess had the courtroom darkened. A stills projector stood ready on the bar-table, and the man who walked towards it was Ruddick, a colleague of Cameron, and the medical photographer at the

London Medical School. While Ruddick shone pictures of the baby's clothing on the screen, Cameron stood in the half light outlining the important patterns of bloodstain with a glinting wand and its concurring shadow. His voice was fluent and continuous. Sturgess was letting him run.

A slide came up showing two views of the jump-suit, side by side. The fabric glowed, the stains were black. An identification tag below said: 'Ultra-violet fluorescence'. Cameron said, 'That is the front of the jump-suit, and that is the back.' The tip of his wand circled smudges on the back, close to the left armpit. 'There are marks on the back of the cloth, here, consistent with fingerprints. Four fingerprints of a young adult. A young adult right hand on the underneath, or over, the left shoulder blade.'

'You said a young adult?' Sturgess said.

'I'm differentiating that from a child.'

'A child of four, or six?'

'It's far too big a print.'

When the lights came up, Cameron moved on to a print of the same shot, life size. He slid across it a transparency showing the outline of a young female's hand. Rice looked worried and perplexed. As it seemed to him, so confused was the array of smudges here that any attempt to select a form was a disturbing exercise in sophistry.

Cameron handed it up to Galvin. 'Act the superimposition yourself,' he said.

Galvin moved the transparency this way and that. 'I'm sorry, I can't see it at all, now.'

'Work principally, I would suggest, on the middle finger.'

But the coroner was not doing so well.

'It is not an exact fit,' Cameron said with some exasperation, 'because it is of another handprint.'

He held the jump-suit up and read from his report.

'As to the possible causes of death, in the absence of a body, one must assume an unascertainable cause of death. Having said that, however, in the presence of the bleeding on the jump-suit, and from its amount, and various other findings at that moment in time, it would be reasonable to assume that she met her death by unnatural causes, and that the mode of death had been caused by a cutting instrument, possibly encircling the neck, certainly cutting the vital blood vessels.'

*   *   *

After that, the newsreporters were anxious to get out of the court and on the phones. This was the story they had waited for, a cut throat, although it fell a little short of the vivid decapitation they'd been led to expect. But they had to stay where they were, for the moment, in line with an earlier order given by Galvin which prohibited movement while a witness was in the stand. With disinterest, they watched while Rice attempted a cross-examination. He did not delay them long. Without research he was without thrust.

Still, he was determined to illustrate, through Cameron, just how unfair and unusual the procedures at this inquest were.

'Professor Cameron, you were instructed to retain absolute confidentiality, in all respects, so far as your examination of the material submitted to you was concerned?'

Cameron conceded this was so.

'And you have maintained that, of course, without question?'

'Indeed,'

'You knew that you would be cross-examined on matters relating to your examination of the material?'

'I was led to believe that, yes.'

'I just want to put this in the right setting, if I may.' Rice stole a quick look at Galvin. 'You have been cross-examined time and time again, I suppose?'

'Indeed, yes.'

'Is it true to say that before you had been cross-examined, someone else has had an opportunity of examining the material as well as yourself? So that opposing counsel is at least acquainted with what has been examined by you?'

'That has been the normal practice.'

'And,' Rice said, 'you can understand the fact that in my position here I have not, for whatever reason, had that opportunity?'

'I sympathize,' Cameron said, and raised a laugh from the gallery.

11

IT DIDN'T DRAW A LAUGH from Malcolm Brown, who leaned forward in the second row to see how Lindy Chamberlain was taking this. Throughout the evidence he had watched her making notes, but now the pad lay on her knee. She was biting a lip. Her face wasn't in such good shape anymore. The cheeky college-girl had gone, and the usurper was a tired little woman, used to hard times.

Something of Brown's own was also taking a beating. It was his pride. Professionalism was a thing he strove for, and admired in others. Now he feared he had become too sympathetic to the Chamberlains. Since the time first rumours were abroad of foetal blood in the car, most newsreporters convicted them then and there. And he had done that himself, God knows. The trouble was, every time he met the Chamberlains face to face, he didn't see in them the shadows of cruelty and guile. The most affecting instance happened when he arrived in town for the hearing. It was late afternoon, and he had just booked in to the Oasis, a motel near the riverbank. The driveway filled suddenly with bounding photographers, intent on an approaching car. The lawyers Dean and Tipple were in the front seats. The rear doors opened, and Michael and Lindy got out. They were unsmiling and pale. Flashbulbs gave them expressions of shock. Lindy's unsteady hand waved away the microphones. Brown, from the steps, caught Michael's eye. It was Brown who turned away. He had found in Michael's gaze a bewildering amount of trust.

He was a man who made his decisions step by step, often by talking to himself, and sometimes very loudly. The task, and he saw it clearly enough, was to write his stories straight whatever the state of his sympathies. His pieces in the *Sydney Morning Herald* had around three quarters of a million readers, and he owed them accuracy. When he compared his pieces on the inquest with those of competing newspapers, it seemed he was somehow isolating the *Herald* from the mainstream. All this seemed to add up to a need for caution. But he had been reporting around the courts for many years now, and this one made him angry.

Andrew Kirkham was no longer at the bar-table. He had flown back to Melbourne for treatment of some ailment or other, as Brown had heard, and Rice was carrying the load alone, meantime. Brown watched Rice deal with Cameron's coeval Sims, a chubby odontologist who found no marks of teeth on the baby's clothes, and with a Sydney professor of textile sciences, Chaikin, who, in the voice of an excitable New Yorker, testified that the collar and shoulder of the jump-suit were cut rather than torn, and showed how loops and tufts were shed this way. Chaikin was voluble and difficult to pin down, but Brown thought Rice did better against Sims who conceded that his experience with dingoes was limited to the recent examination of one dried skull.

During recess Brown wandered out into the foyer. He was beckoned by a tall gentle woman who was standing with her displeased husband by the door. They were Adventists, friends of the Chamberlains, and had given him tidbits of information in the past. The woman's tone was low and breathy. 'What do you think of your Mr Rice now?' she asked.

Brown didn't bother with the attribution. He said, 'He's doing as well as anyone could, considering.'

'Oh no, we don't think so,' she said. 'I think you'll find none of us are happy with him at all.' Brown supposed she was referring to Adventists at large. He excused himself and headed back. He guessed that there was something deep in the nature of Adventist belief that led these folk to hope for some sort of courtroom messiah.

Sturgess put two women from Western Dry Cleaners through the witness-stand, in quick time, to prove the patterns of blood on Lindy Chamberlain's tracksuit, a child's parka and bedding. Lindy's friend Jennifer Richards, whose name had become Ransome by a second marriage, took a terrified few minutes to identify the tracksuit and quit the court without a backward glance.

There was now a day and a half left in this part of the hearing, before the Christmas break. The way Brown calculated it, Sturgess would try to finish the testimony in the current session, letting the legal argument and summations carry over into the next. If he was right, there were no surprise witnesses to come now. It left only Charlwood.

12

IT WAS STARTLING just how closely Charlwood's evidence of the Chamberlain interrogations accorded with the Chamberlain's own testimony about them. Any differences were of form rather than substance. This did not make great copy for the newswriters, who then had to beat it up, as they say, into something exciting. But it spoke well for the Chamberlains' truthfulness, or for Charlwood's truthfulness, or for both.

So unusual an occurrence is this degree of agreement, in the experience of lawyers, that Rice was suspicious. He wanted to be sure Charlwood was holding nothing back. First he called for the detective's notes, then, arms belligerently akimbo, got down to it.

'Mr Charlwood, did you—on any occasion at all—ever record any conversation you had, with either of my clients, by means of any instrument or device?'

'Yes,' he said. This caused immediate interest in the press benches. It was the first anyone had yet heard of a recording. Then Charlwood shook his head. 'When I say I recorded the conversation, a tape-recorder was in use during some of the conversation I had with them. Unfortunately, the quality of that tape was such that it was unable to be transcribed.'

'Which converstaions do you refer to as an "attempt" at tape-recording?'

'Yes, I refer now specifically to conversations that took place during the house-search on 19 September 1981. The conversations that I had with Mrs Chamberlain in the motor vehicle on the way to Toronto police station, and at that police station with her and Mr Chamberlain, wasn't recorded.'

'Are you saying that the only conversation that was recorded, or attempted to be recorded, was that at the house?'

'Some of the conversation at the house. Yes.'

Rice was really pushing this. He said, 'Just so that we have absolute clarity about it, no attempt was made to record any other conversation with them? Or was there an attempt made which was aborted for some reason or other?'

Charlwood raised his eyebrows. 'You are referring now to?'

'Any conversation you had with them.'

'I had a tape-recorder in the motor vehicle, but it just wasn't started. The tape never commenced.'

'Did you have it in mind to record that conversation?'

'Yes. I did at the time. Yes.'

'Was there electrical interference, or some such thing, which rendered the operation of the tape-recorder useless?'

'No, the tape just never operated.'

'So,' Rice said slowly, 'you attempted to record it. But that was the reason why you could not record that conversation, was it?'

'It just never operated. That's correct, yes.'

'Did you, at any time, tell either Mr or Mrs Chamberlain of your intention to record any conversation you had with them?'

'No, I never.'

Rice stood silent for a moment. There was something dissatisfying about the way these answers had come out, but the reason, whatever it was, was too elusive. 'Thank you,' he said, and sat down.

13

THIS WAS CHRISTMASTIME, the season of warm windless evenings and long dinner-parties. In restaurants, big tables were popular. The lawyers from about town took one, and sat around after the meal, talking. The inquest made an appearance in conversation only late in the night, perhaps because Gerry Galvin was sitting there.

Not everybody at the table thought there was enough hard evidence to show that the baby was killed by one of the parents.

'Do you know this,' Galvin said, 'the police discovered a baby's coffin at the Chamberlains' house?'

A lawyer, of sceptical bent, said, 'Why hasn't someone given evidence about that, if it's true?'

'It's in the police report, right enough,' Galvin said, which brought the argument to a close.

14

THE SUMMER RECESS provided the legal teams with five weeks in which to assemble their concluding arguments, and submit them in writing. Written submission was Sturgess's idea. A week before the inquest was due to begin, Malcolm Brown interviewed Rice, in Adelaide, for the *Sydney Morning Herald*. Rice was annoyed because he had still not received a copy of Sturgess's arguments, and time was running out. The law department was still playing it hard. Rice asked Brown not to quote him, but Brown wrote about it anyway.

When the court opened on 1 February, with the easterners astonished at the heat outside, Brown got there early, sought Rice out, and apologized. Rice was abrupt but seemed to have got over the worst of it. He was now angrier about the way other reporters had treated the Chamberlains when they arrived, chasing them all over town with carloads of photographers. Brown saw that Andrew Kirkham was back in the team, waiting at the bar-table. Behind him sat Lindy, in defiant red, and Michael in a pinstripe shirt and tie. Neither of them looked up as the gallery filled.

Sturgess called the biologist Joy Kuhl back to the stand.
'After you had concluded your evidence you were given a black vinyl camera-case, is that so?'

This was the camera-bag Michael Chamberlain had given to Charlwood.

She held it up. 'The camera-bag was turned inside out, compartment by compartment, and the screening test for blood was performed over all surfaces.'

'How long did these examinations occupy you?'

'Four days,' she said. 'In the front zippered compartment, most vinyl surfaces gave me positive reactions for the presence of blood. Strong reactions were observed along the base of the bag.'

'You are dealing with what you describe as the front compartment?'

'The front zippered compartment. The zipper was extensively tested, tooth by tooth.' She described blood on the teeth and on the clasp. 'Consistently positive reactions were found on that groove and from around this side of the zipper clasp,' to which she pointed, 'and precipitin tests made from an extract of those areas identified the presence of foetal blood.'

'The middle zippered compartment also gave me strong positive reactions.' She pointed to the bottom, to the flap, the right-hand corner, and then to the groove of the clasp. 'An extract prepared from that reacted as human haemoglobin.'

'The outside of the bag was subjected to examination, and the buckle on the outside gave me very, very strongly positive reactions for blood around the outer groove, around the top part of the buckle.'

'This is where the buckle attaches to the vinyl?'

'That is correct.' The rust on it she discounted. 'An extract prepared from around that outer groove also identified the presence of human foetal blood.'

The cross-examination was Kirkham's task now. He took her to the screening-test for blood, the orthotolydene.

'Would you agree, first of all, that the reaction can be obtained by substances other than blood?'

'Not the same reaction.' She went through the alternatives. 'Plant peroxidases tend to give a much greener colouration than blood does. It is a slower reaction. Chemical compounds which give false positives generally give a positive first-stage reaction, which blood never does. The colour development from a blood-type reaction is very, very distinctive, particularly in the hands of an experienced operator. And I consider myself an experienced operator.'

Kirkham asked, 'May you get a positive reaction from milk?'

'Yes. Occasionally.'

'Child's vomit?'

'Yes. But vomit would always contain traces of blood.'

'And therefore what? Give blood reactions?'

'Yes.'

'Did you do any tests to exclude the presence of child vomit in the orthotolydene tests that you did on the bag?'

'I'm sorry, there was not enough matter present to do any sort of test like that.'

'So, in the circumstances, you are prepared to assume that it must have been blood?'

'I have not assumed.'

'Despite the fact that you could not exclude, by way of testing, that it was the other agents. Is that correct?'

'I have not assumed. I have not assumed that it is blood. I have reported that a blood reaction was obtained. However, attempts to prove the presence of blood, and determine the species, were unsuccessful. I have written that in my report.'

'I have not seen your report yet, and I am going to, in due course, have a look at that,' Kirkham said, with a glance at Sturgess. 'Are you conceding, then, that what was on the bag,' and here Kirkham was talking about what was on the surfaces of the bag, 'may not have been blood?'

'I have stated that. Yes.'

This left Kirkham with the samples she had identified as human, and human foetal blood. These came from the car, the towel, the chamois container, the scissors, and the camera-bag clasps. The task called for detailed questioning about every test, and every step of every test. Kirkham asked Mrs Kuhl for her work-sheets, and began to take her through each notation, item by item. He began this at around eleven a.m. and was still going when court adjourned for the day. He began again in the morning. The spectator gallery was noticeably less crowded. The newspeople were bored and irritable. Questioning like this was unreportable. There was just no copy.

Kirkham questioned her until midday. It was an exercise in research rather than in advocacy. To Malcolm Brown it meant this: Kirkham was now preparing for a trial.

15

ARMS PERCHED ON THE LECTERN, Sturgess began his summation. Half-moon spectacles sat low on his nose. He cleared his throat often and sipped from the water-tumbler.

'Clearly the child, Azaria Chamberlain, came to her death at the camping area, or near the camping area, or at Ayers Rock, on 17 August 1980. The cause of her death is revealed by the condition of her clothing, discovered a week after her death. She must have suffered an extensive, and a fatal, wound or wounds to her neck or her head.

'Your Worship has to consider the manner of death. Here there are only two possibilities: that she was killed by a dingo that also took her away, or that it was a case of homicide. I have submitted to you that, reviewing all the evidence, Your Worship will conclude that this was a case of homicide. The dingo theory cannot be supported by the evidence produced in this inquiry.

'I have submitted to Your Worship, in my written submissions, that in view of all the evidence that has been called here, Your Worship will place Mrs Chamberlain on trial on a charge of murder, and that Your Worship will place Mr Chamberlain on trial on a charge of being an accessory after the fact to that murder.'

Galvin caught early what was happening in the gallery. Newsreporters were beginning to stand, as if the show was suddenly over. Some were still scribbling as they rose. Galvin raised a hand and said, 'Ladies and gentlemen of the press.' No one heard him. 'It is going to be hopeless for me to give the proper concentration on this if we are going to have people in and out. I know you have deadlines, but I also have a much more important job to do.' By this time the benches were half empty.

'It will just have to stop.'

Malcolm Brown stayed where he was. He had plenty of time

before deadline. In any case he was more interested in the silent drama in front of him. He was sitting directly behind the Chamberlains. While Sturgess spoke, they faced steadfastly ahead. Every time Sturgess uttered the word murder, tremors ran down Lindy's hair.

The written arguments which Sturgess had given to Galvin were kept from the press. Reporters had to glean what they could as he spoke, linking one orphaned point with another. The story came gradually clearer. Sturgess had abandoned the early police theory that the baby was slaughtered somewhere on the slopes of the Rock. She was killed in the car or somewhere close to the car. Lindy Chamberlain had cut her daughter's throat and told her husband about it later. The body was hidden in the camera-bag and then buried. The clothing was exhumed and laid out near Maggie Springs, damaged to simulate an attack.

The evidence of the Lowes and the Wests and the Whittackers seemed far away. It brought to Brown's mind a conversation he'd had with someone when the hearing began. He was talking to Frank Moorhouse who was writing a piece for a weekly but also had in mind a film, and was keen to isolate the themes. 'The first inquest was about dingoes,' he had said. 'This one is about blood.'

Rice did not take long to make the same point. Reciting from the pages of his own written submission, he read to Galvin, 'There is no attempt to discount the dingo hypothesis by any dingo expert.' He laid the paper aside. 'After all, Dr Newsome gave evidence in the first inquest. And whether Dr Newsome was studiously avoided by the Crown or not, I do not know. Nonetheless, Your Worship has the benefit of his observations, and the absence of any further attempt to discount the dingo theory was not resorted to by the Crown.' Rice was now well used to speaking of Sturgess's case as if it were the Crown case in a prosecution. 'And, so far as Newsome is concerned, I will be referring to his evidence as we proceed.'

'But the whole fortnight of the inquest,' Galvin said, meaning the Barritt inquest, 'was about that, I would have thought.'

'Pardon?'

'The whole fortnight of the inquest was about it.'

'Yes, of course.'

'But you are saying? On that specific aspect?'

'No attempt has been made to discount the hypothesis by a

dingo expert. That is what I am saying. It has been attempted by other means, but no one has been heard, as a witness, before Your Worship.'

During a recess, Rice and Kirkham pushed through the foyer towards the conference room. Lindy Chamberlain, impatient, tugged at Rice's arm. She was speaking loudly enough that reporters were encouraged to edge closer. Plainly she was giving Rice some vehement instruction, but no one caught more than the words 'the boys'.

The journalists stood around and talked it over. A rumour, then currently popular, attributed the slaying of the baby to one or other of the Chamberlain boys and concealment to the parents. Someone now flipped through a notebook and turned up an item from Dr Andrew Scott's testimony. Of blood on a boy's parka, Scott had said: 'Alternatively, the pattern is consistent with the wearer of the parka carrying a bleeding child.'

The intriguing point was that the Chamberlains didn't have to prove anything. To avoid trial they needed only to suggest other plausible culprits. Here was an exciting possibility. The reporters filed back inside. They might be about to witness a neat evasive trick.

Rice paused and rearranged his papers. Gestures like these were harbingers of an important topic. He picked up a copy of Sturgess's submissions. He said, 'I quote: "So far as Reagan, Mr Chamberlain, and Aidan are concerned, not only is there no evidence that either, or any, was responsible, there is positive evidence that each was not responsible." '

He held the papers high. 'So there is a clear and unequivocal assertion as to any participation at all. So all the rumour and speculation—which are rife—about some child having something to do with this is put at rest by the assertion of Mr Sturgess himself. Who better to make a comment such as that?'

The reporters were looking at Lindy Chamberlain. So this was what she had instructed Rice to do, scotch the rumour. Someone passed a note along the front bench to Malcolm Brown. It read: It's all over. He scribbled and passed it back. He'd written: Long Ago.

16

GALVIN took a little less than two hours to decide. He came back into court carrying a single sheet of paper. Rice and Kirkham knew what was coming. He had sent them a message.

'The evidence is, to a large degree, circumstantial. It is my view, having considered all that evidence, that a jury properly instructed could arrive at a verdict. I therefore consider that it is a proper matter for a jury to consider, on the two matters that are argued for by the Crown. And I propose to proceed on those two suggested charges.'

He turned to Rice. 'It will be in order for your clients to remain seated while we do it.'

Galvin held the sheet steady and prepared to read the arraignment. Sturgess slipped his folded spectacles into a pocket. Excitement was gone from the faces in the spectators' gallery. It was extinguished by a curious and perverse dread, although this was the event they had come here to see.

17

GRASSHOPPERS EXPLODED against the pavement. Television crewmen sat on the steps, out of the sun, watching a monitor. The picture had nothing to do with whatever the daydreaming cameras were gazing at. Here they were watching Australia and the West Indies at cricket. The first newswriter through the door came at a run. 'Get ready,' he said. 'He's done it.'

They plugged in the cameras and switched the monitors over. Everyone wanted to finish it off and go home.

It made banner headlines in every city daily. The *Daily Mirror* in Sydney, which was representative enough of the first coverages, ran:

CHAMBERLAINS
A 'Not Guilty' Plea at Trial

Lindy and Michael Chamberlain will plead not guilty in the Alice Springs Supreme Court on 19 April. Mrs Chamberlain was committed for trial charged with the murder of her 10-week-old daughter Azaria in August 1980. Coroner Mr Gerry Galvin also charged her husband Michael as an accessory after the fact, in trying to shield his wife.

Sons Not Involved Says QC

Azaria Chamberlain's two brothers were not involved in her death, Mr Phil Rice Q.C. told Alice Springs Coroners Court. Mr Rice said he agreed with a submission by Mr Des Sturgess, counsel assisting the coroner, that the boys Aidan and Reagan were not responsible.

The radio talks department of the ABC had a Sydney law school academic quickly to air. There, Professor Ralston was already worried about prejudicial pretrial publicity. He called for a prohibition against reporting of preliminary hearings and of coronial inquests. 'It is now very difficult to obtain a fair trial for the Chamberlains. The loss of freedom of the press is counter-balanced by the preservation of justice.'

One east-coast radio station saw the issues quite differently. Its reporter rounded off his bulletin with this sentence: 'When the trial goes to court, the world might find out just why Lindy Chamberlain cut the throat of her tiny daughter.'

18

MALCOLM BROWN checked his luggage in at the airport desk. The terminal was hot and crowded, but he was not yet persuaded he should take off his suit-coat. He made for the shopping counters. He had called his wife from the motel, and she reminded him to pick up something for the children. He bought a plastic crocodile and a fluffy buffalo. He chose them because they would fit in his pockets.

He picked through the crowd looking for his *Herald* photographer. The reason he was doing this was something of a sore issue. His office had phoned through. He must get an interview with Lindy Chamberlain. Another time, he would have been flattered that they thought he might pull it off, but he really didn't want to try. He had thought about it and called back, but his boss told him to do as he was bidden and rang off.

He found the photographer at the ticket-counter. It was a sure bet that the Chamberlains were around here somewhere, because the two Sydney flights left within a half hour of each other. Everyone seemed to have the same idea. A reporter had climbed on a chair to get a better view, and cameramen stood at the tarmac gate.

Brown beckoned his photographer outside. They walked through the baggage-depot and into the bleaching heat. A goods gate led to the tarmac. Brown had guessed well. There was a sedan parked in the lot here. The driver was no one he recognized. The couple in the back were the Chamberlains.

Brown was good at forcing surprise interviews this way. He had a reputation for it, and a break like this usually made him feel quite high. But the Chamberlains were, somehow, not a quarry to feel proud of now. All he could think was, Guilty or not, the worst thing that could happen to anyone had happened to them.

He drew the photographer away. 'I don't see them around here,' he said and headed inside to the bar.

NECROMANCY, SO TO TRIAL

ALWAYS RUNNING FROM
SOMETHING

1

SPREAD OVER A SMALL TABLE which took up much of the side wall of a room in the Medway Wing, a building in Kent, was a copy of the London *Daily Mail*. The man reading it was pale, a habitual pallor now, accustomed to nervousness, and over the last four years had developed a squint. The news report in which he was interested was headed 'U.K. Pathologist in Dingo Baby Case'. He was preparing to write a letter about it on ready-ruled grey paper, using a ball-pen from which the sharp clip had been removed. If, at this moment, you were to ask him his name, he would come to attention and recite 'B-22204 Godfried'. This room was his cell in the Maidstone jail. He was in for rape.

He addressed the letter: To the Lawyers for Pastor and Mrs Chamberlain, Alice Springs, Australia. It was the best he could think of.

Dear Sir,
I have just read in the morning paper today a report on the inquest into the death of the little girl Azaria Chamberlain. I feel I must write to you, as I noticed that Professor James Cameron is giving evidence at the inquest.

Sir, I speak from experience of having had this man give evidence against me at my trial and at this moment in time a police inquiry of my allegations against him is in process.

It is not sour grapes saying this about Cameron. I can back my allegations up. I have said this before to other people and he knows of what I said. Sir, to prove that he is (and there followed here an opinion about Cameron which was unmistakably Prisoner Godfried's very own) I have made inquiries on my personal behalf. And have to date found cases in which he has been involved, which, to put it mildly, made his evidence stink. The first is where he gave evidence (forensic) in a trial in which after his evidence three boys were found guilty of murder and manslaughter. However, after serving over three years in prison, these boys—whom I do NOT know—were proved innocent and eventually awarded over 60,000 pounds between them. The second case was a man who was robbing a supermarket and on coming out of the supermarket was shot dead by the police. The police said that the robber pointed a gun first, and was shot dead in self-defence. A pathologist confirmed this, by saying the robber (Michael Calvey) had been shot once from a handgun in the stomach, from which wound he died. That pathologist was again Professor James Cameron. Calvey's wife called for an independent autopsy, by another pathologist, whose findings were that Calvey had been shot not from the front but from the back. These two cases can be proved. Mine I am still working on, but will be proved sometime.

I want you to look at Cameron's evidence carefully, and you will see it does not add up. And to save others unnecessary suffering,
Yours sincerely

James Godfried

Both items of which Prisoner Godfried wrote were now celebrated causes in Britain: the Confait case and the Calvey. He was astonished that Australian lawyers had not heard of them, at least the newsreports indicated nothing of the sort. 'What amazes me,' he wrote to someone else, 'is why the pathologists in Australia did not come up with any evidence in the Dingo case, but on coming to England, out of all our pathologists in Britain, who but our Professor James Cameron! This man has caused so much heartache.'

He enclosed in the Chamberlain letter a photocopied extract from Lord Fisher's judicial inquiry into the Confait case. The passages criticizing Cameron were heavily underlined. To the envelope he attached the postage he though sufficient for surface mail. It ought to take around a month to get there. He closed the flap, and it was ready for the mailbag. This was the event of his week. Prisoner Godfried expected to be in this room, and in rooms like it, for the next eleven years.

2

IT IS NOT a usual course of action for barristers to do their own legwork but, for a brief of these dimensions, Andrew Kirkham thought it reasonable enough. So on 18 July, which was a Sunday, he filled a satchel with his papers, his wife Jenny packed his bag, and he caught a plane from Melbourne for Brisbane. He was making the trip in good vein, although he was at the same time losing money over it because advocates earn most in court. His humour was more a response to the need for a team effort in this case, than it was to any simpler professional duty.

Just how much ground they had to cover had come clearer in the closing days of the inquest. Michael Chamberlain had put it well. He gave one short press interview. To a reporter he said, 'We have a lot to do,' and walked away. What heartened Kirkham most about that utterance was not its accuracy but its brevity. Someone had at last convinced the Chamberlains that they should stop talking.

The defence's task was already far too complex. Most murder charges resolved their problems, sooner or later, to a single paramount issue: an act of self-defence, say, or accident, or mistaken identity. The Chamberlains' was exceptional. Here, it was like mending cracks in a piece of glass. You could go after them this way and that, only to find it was none of these which eventually shattered the pane. What they needed was a broad and co-ordinated effort. The choice of team they had now settled on was largely Kirkham's. After the Chamberlains decided against engaging Philip Rice for the trial—a process which Kirkham kept a firm, professional distance from—they asked Kirkham to recommend someone else. He took a week or so mulling the problem, setting the criteria. Rice was born in the Northern Territory, and there'd been some advantage having a home-town player, but most of the advocates Kirkham knew best lived in Sydney or Melbourne. He wanted a leader who was not, as he thought of it then, a three-ring circus-master. They needed, to use the phrase of the times, someone cool. So the team leader was now John Phillips. Kirkham had not, in his years at the bar, appeared with Phillips, or against him, but knew many who had. Now that the news was out, press profiles of Phillips dwelt most on his list of murder trials, which numbered around a hundred and fifty. For more human interest they described him as an opera buff and a passable amateur baritone. Kirkham thought of him in entirely different terms: as a very elegant street-fighter, swift and deceptive.

If anyone else was a runaway surprise in the team it was the Gosford solicitor Stuart Tipple. Kirkham's early impression, from their first meeting in Alice Springs, had not been encouraging. Tipple was introduced as the church's solicitor. It seemed an adequate assessment. He was a quiet young man with a moustache which had very little character beyond neatness, and the tidiness about him spoke more of proprieties than toughness or pragmatism. Kirkham clearly remembered the thought: What could a guy like this know about life? It was the surly face of life of which Kirkham was thinking, and he couldn't imagine that Tipple had caught sight of it too often. The surprise was not so much that Kirkham had somehow got it wrong, but that Tipple was now showing a capacity for the technical, the scientific. The way haematoligists and pathologists spoke, the jargon and formulae which for everyone else called for rote-learning made deep sense to him. It seemed that his neatness was an asset.

So the division of intellectual labour they decided on made Tipple responsible for the scientific evidence. Already he had gathered an arresting assemblage of pathologists and surgeons with whom to confront Cameron's adventurous opinions, an odontologist ready to rebut the doctors Brown and Sims, textile analysts who were examining automobile carpet and baby-clothing, and working in laboratories at Newcastle University, the professor of biological sciences who was simulating the tests on which the prosecution relied to show foetal haemoglobin in the Chamberlain car.

But Kirkham saw tactical dangers in all this. They might be drawn too far to the scientific front to be able to fight on the practical. Every case was a combination of the logical and the emotional, or as Rice had been fond of putting it, the scientific and the human. This was why Kirkham was heading for Brisbane.

He found the Seventh-day Adventist headquarters in Eagle Terrace, and a plump woman at the desk fetched Pastor Kennaway. Kennaway was the communications director, a lean man in his forties, his eyes lined at the corners by whatever responsibilities he bore here, but with a yet undefeated grin. They sought out an empty room. The pastor knew what Kirkham wanted to talk about. Michael Chamberlain's camera-bag was once Mervyn Kennaway's. He told Kirkham now, 'I carried it everywhere, rock-climbing and bushwalking, for five years, and I gave it to Michael somewhere about March 1980.'

'Five or six months before Azaria disappeared?'

'Around then.'

He couldn't think of any way it might have been stained with blood before, but fibres were a different matter. 'I carried T-shirts in it, that sort of thing, when I took it to the beach, a towel maybe, plenty of cleaning clothes, tissues, and so on.'

'You know Michael Chamberlain was a keen photographer?'

'We both were.' This recollection brought with it some amusement. 'It was a sort of well-known joke. We took our cameras and gear everywhere.'

'Did you ever see him drive with a camera-bag under his legs?'

'I can't say that I have,' Kennaway said slowly, 'but I can well imagine it.' He looked up at Kirkham. 'You're not a photographer yourself, I suppose? No.' Evidently, then, an explanation wouldn't be much use.

When Michael Chamberlain was posted to pastoral duties in Bowen, Innisfail, and Mt Isa, Kennaway called in often, and stayed as a house guest. He had, just six weeks before Azaria died, offered the infant's prayer for her at Sabbath Service. 'We don't have baptism at that age,' he said. 'It's a small service. I held her. She was a pretty baby. The tinyiness. She was two weeks old. Lindy lavished attention on her. The boys called her "our bubby". They were all so delighted.'

The next service he held there was the memorial. Kirkham asked, 'How did the parents take it?'

'Heartbroken.' Pastor Kennaway had lost his own child, who was then fifteen, a few years before. 'No outbursts, you understand, but heartbroken.'

On the flight out he held Kirkham by the sleeve. 'There is nothing wrong with the Chamberlains, you know.' Kirkham took him to be making, not one statement now, but two: there was nothing in Adventist belief that would condone the slaying of a child, and there was no aberration in the Chamberlains. We are the same as you in this, his plea said.

To see Ronald Bellingham, who lived in Warwick, Kirkham chartered a light plane two hundred kilometres west to Towoomba and drove a rented car from there on. Bellingham owned a roadside garage. While he talked, he kept wiping his practical hands with a rag. The family was touring Ayers Rock at the time the Chamberlain baby was taken. The day before, the Saturday, they were walking the road near Maggie Springs. A dingo followed them awhile, and they were pleased to see such a shy animal so closely, until it padded up behind and bit at Bellingham's heels. It bit through the sock. Since it would not go away, Bellingham took a snap while the family stood shoulder to shoulder behind. The dingo circled about, intent on some ploy which only became clear when it lunged for young Michelle and tugged at the pullover she had tied at the waist. They beat it off, flagged an opportune tourist-bus, and got out of there.

Kirkham liked the uncomplicated way Bellingham told it. He liked the rueful mixture of astonishment and afright. He decided Bellingham ought to be called as a witness.

On the flight into Mt Isa, three hours north-west from Brisbane, he had the smoke-stacks in view all through the approach. He took a cab to the hospital and spent a few minutes with Dr Weller. Weller had examined Azaria after her fall from a shopping-trolley at the supermarket and pronounced her unharmed. He thought Lindy Chamberlain an affectionate mother. But he didn't have the vividness Kirkham was looking for in a witness. Dr Irene Milne was altogether different. She was grey-haired and vigorous. In her voice, authority was not incompatible with grace. She was Lindy's obstetrician but was a little late at the birth, she smiled. When she got there, Azaria was already well into the world and doing fine.

Kirkham asked, 'So it was a normal birth?'

'Certainly.'

'You saw them how often, the mother and the child?'

'Every day, for the five or six days they were here. Then about every four days.'

'And normal growth-rate?'

She thumbed through the medical records. 'Yes. When I saw her last, 7 August, the baby had got up to nine pounds two and a quarter ounces.'

'And Lindy Chamberlain. How do you remember her attitude to the baby? Was she loving? Caring? Off-hand?'

'Not at all off-hand. It was her third, you know, her only girl.'

'I want to be careful about this,' Kirkham said. 'The prosecution is faced with an absence of motive, so far as we know. They might try post-natal depression.'

'Mr Kirkham, I am familiar with the dangers of depression. If a mother shows any sign of the baby-blues we don't let her out of hospital.'

A circumstantial case is one in which an essential element of the crime, and sometimes more than a single element, is proved by inference instead of by direct evidence. So circumstantial was the case against the Chamberlains that it seemed to establish a new category, as if it had speciated, as plant or animal biologists describe a changeling which begins a new class in the established order of things. Here, not only was the prosecution without eye-witnesses to identify a slayer, there was no body to display the fact of death, no weapon to illustrate the manner of it, and no motive to betray deliberation or intent.

Of all the deductions, of all the inferences to be drawn, Kirkham thought motive the most curious. It was not an essential ingredient in the definition of murder; it was made important by the other omissions. The way the case was shaping, there was no reason for this mother to kill her child. All the evidence was the other way. Sacrifice in the wilderness, the dispatch of a retarded child, post-partum depression, all were untenable now. The defence could disprove each of them at will. It occurred to Kirkham that the prosecution may choose to ignore motive altogether. The old rumours might then steal in and out of the trial just as they had in the press, beyond testimony, the beguiling creatures of bigotry.

He booked into a Mt Isa motel and rang Western Dry Cleaners from there. He wanted to talk to the pressers Beaman and Hansell, who had cleaned bloodspots from the Chamberlains' clothes and bedding. The call was put through, but each of the women refused now to meet him. This was a surprise. When he'd telephoned from Melbourne they were happy enough. They gave a reason for the change of plan. The police had told them to be silent.

Kirkham's last interview was the most important and the most far-away. He took the evening flight to Cairns, on the north-eastern seaboard. Cairns is closer to New Guinea than it is to the southern states. When Kirkham got there, the air was dank and warm, a condition difficult for a southerner to associate with a mid winter's night.

In Cairns lived the man whom the defence team now privately referred to as the Bleeding Hitchhiker. The name he was more generally known by was Keyth Lenehan. The Chamberlains had found him by the side of the Cook Highway in the dry season, as winter is called here, of 1979, the year before their holiday at Ayers Rock. Lenehan's car had overturned, he was injured, and they took him to the Cairns Base Hospital.

Lenehan walked into the foyer of the hotel in which Kirkham was staying, at noon and on time. Kirkham led the way into a lounge, although Lenehan made mention of thirst, because it was Kirkham's practice to work first and drink later. Lenehan was not dressed for the lounge, but he didn't appear to notice. He wore shorts and a work-singlet. His arms were long, and his chest was moist. His feet seemed held to the floor by the weight of his boots. He was not as tanned as Kirkham expected of north-Queenslanders. This was explained when he said he had come into town from a factory where he made pool-tables.

His style of speech was sparse and laconic. When Kirkham asked him to describe his automobile accident he said, 'I wrecked it,' and about the injury to his head, 'I was a mess.'

After a few minutes persistent work, the story Kirkham got was this: Lenehan crawled away from his buckled car through the settling dust and made it as far as the roadside. All he could do was sit. He couldn't see too well. He held his head, and when his hands came away they were sticky with blood. It matted his hair, ran the length of his face, and was soaking his singlet. The sight he made evidently did not excite sympathy in anyone driving past, until a yellow hatchback pulled off the road. The driver and his wife were first-aiders, so they said, and they loaded him into the car headfirst through the tailgate. He lay stretched out there, head between the two front seats. The hospital was three-quarters of an hour away. Lindy Chamberlain, he knew who she was now, was sorry she couldn't staunch his blood.

'Which front seat was your wound closest to?'

'The passenger's. See, I was on my back; the blood was coming from here.' He tapped the right side of his head. 'There was plenty.'

This was all Kirkham needed for the present. They moved

into the bar. Kirkham bought the beer, in a brace of pots, and then another. They went through six rounds before Lenehan's pace showed signs of slowing. He seemed to inhale beer rather than swallow it. He declined a ninth, on the ground that he was already late for work, and walked out with an unperturbed gait. Kirkham went up to his room for a nap.

The Bleeding Hitchhiker's haemoglobin patterns were already known. He had provided a sample, when Michael Chamberlain asked him last month, to a local pathologist. Analysis then showed around one or two per cent foetal haemoglobin, the proportion expected in a normal adult. This brought it nowhere near Mrs Kuhl's assessment of the blood in the Chamberlain car, which stood at fifty per cent foetal. But information already coming out of the work at Newcastle University now threw doubt on her tests. Foetal haemoglobin in the blood of a baby ten weeks old should amount to no more than twenty-five per cent. Moreover, Andrew Scott in Adelaide had found this was the level present in Azaria's blood. So something was wrong. The prosecution had found what it needed to find. This time perhaps it had found too much.

And Kirkham's diary note, written on the southbound flight to mark the end of the journey, read: All those interviewed to date believe the Chamberlains innocent.

3

SHE ALWAYS SEEMED to be running from something. This time it was from the Sydney *Sun*. Through the curtains in the front room she could see the car, and recognized the men in it. It was the second time this week. Now they were parked three houses down Avondale Drive and, in a ludicrous attempt at disguise, had changed cars. Somehow they had got onto her schedule. Class began in fifteen minutes.

She let the curtain fall and walked back to pick up the telephone. It was already off the hook and she said, 'That's them, for sure.'

'Shall we do it again?' asked the woman on the other end.

'Thanks,' Lindy said. 'I'm sorry.'

'No trouble at all.'

She waited until she heard the sound of a motor, threw on a

coat, and ran out the back door. She bobbed through the side fence and climbed into her friend's car in the driveway of a neighbouring house. At the bend in Avondale Drive, they were doing eighty, and the press car pulled in behind, tailgating all the way to the campus. Lindy put on sunglasses and turned up the collar of her coat. She had a hand on the door-handle as they swung into the parking-bay outside the administration buildings.

A light drizzle was falling on the roadway, and the cars slid to a halt as though they were interconnected. She let the door swing open and jumped. She could hear the shutter and the camera-drive from somewhere behind, ran the path under the trees, past white-faced students, and clipped up the steps. She knew the photographers would stay with the car. They were devilish people, and their business was devilish, in the plain sense of the word, the way people meant it around here.

At the top she was breathless and dizzy, unused to her matronly weight now. She pushed through the glass doors. The foyer was undergoing some sort of motion. She steadied a wall with a hand and caught her breath. With alarmed fingers she kneaded a sudden tightness in her belly.

4

IT WAS THE MOST PUBLICIZED PREGNANCY of the year. Columnists tried to guess the date of birth and the zodiac sign which would thereafter guide the development of the baby's character. A television crew caught the family at the Avondale fun run and got in everybody's way while it filmed her in side shots, so far as was possible with the crowd, the better to show her expanding outline. News reporters followed up every Adventist contact they had, but no one was talking. The timing was such that the pregnancy should be round and indisputable by the time the trial opened in Darwin on 13 September. The way reporters calculated it, this was some manner of gauche ploy, a plea for jury sympathy. Kirkham knew the fact was otherwise. The birth was due on 8 November. It would have been a simple matter, as Kirkham considered, to announce that date now, let everyone count back the days, and conclude that the date of conception was sometime shortly after the end of the second inquest. At that time, the trial was listed for April. She could have hidden a twelve-week pregnancy.

Lindy shrugged it off now. She said it was a family matter

and no one else's business. People could think what they liked. She wouldn't give them the satisfaction. Anyhow, if she wasn't meant to have a baby, then God would not have allowed the conception. It was as simple as that.

5

PEOPLE KEPT SENDING in information about dingo attacks. They had a long list already. Now Peter Dean had a letter telling of one around Tennant Creek in the sixties when a small Aboriginal child was killed and carried off. Dean yet hoped to track the story down. Stuart Tipple was sent a news-cutting which described the death of a lost two-year-old white boy, of the family Ford, taken by a dingo thirty-five miles to feed its young. The cutting was from the *Sydney Morning Herald*, dated 1902.

A current story, from the London *Observer*, although it dealt with Los Angeles, read:

Californians Declare War on the Coyote

One morning last summer, three-year-old Kelly Keen wandered away from the house. Her father came outside minutes later to find only her sandal. Up the road he saw a coyote, about four feet in length, dragging the baby along, its jaws clamped on her neck. 'It was like it was killing a sheep,' said Robert Keen. He chased the animal thirty yards into the brush before it dropped its prey. His daughter died of a broken neck.

Coyote control has triggered bitter argument. On one hand is a broad public demand for more trapping. On the other is the anger of environmentalists who claim the danger is being grossly over-rated. 'We have to re-instal a fear of man in the coyote,' said Lila Brooks, head of California Wildlife Defenders. 'We must drive them back to where they belong, not kill them.'

This report was of no direct evidentiary value but, all the same, Kirkham thought, it was a pity it hadn't made any of the newspapers here. It carried a reverberation, peculiar and trou-bling. There were enough similarities between the Chamberlain story and the Keen story that it seemed as if the seeds of the one event had blown into alternative and diverging streams of time.

6

A PRESS-RELEASE from the law department in Darwin arrived at the *Sydney Morning Herald* and was passed on to Malcolm Brown. It identified the barristers briefed to prosecute at the trial. There were three. Des Sturgess was no surprise, although if the government had wanted to maintain appearances, particularly the appearance of impartiality at the second inquest, he might have been excluded. Evidently no one cared about that now. Brown didn't know Tom Pauling at all, but cuttings from the file-room described him as a Darwin barrister who had once served time as a magistrate. The other was Ian Barker. Barker was now at the Sydney Bar, a small jaunty man much prized by press-reporters for his asides, which were witty and often reportable. Throughout the sixties he lived in Alice Springs. The following decade he lived in Darwin. He was then the Northern Territory's inaugural solicitor general. The law department had chosen, for its prosecution leader, a home-ground player.

7

THE LUGGAGE WAITED by the door. The car stood in the driveway. Aidan stopped sniffling long enough to tell his mother that she looked pretty in her big bright frock. Both the boys were tearful because they knew where their parents were going; they understood the nature of the moment. Lindy said she wouldn't tell them a lie; they must be brave about this. 'We might not be allowed to come back,' she said.

Cliff Murchison was a preacher even more than he was a father, and had made his daughter a scriptural gift. Lindy had the idea that, whatever the scientific evidence, she would be judged on the way she gave her testimony in the witness-box. She was terrified it might all go wrong. So, preparing for the family service, her father searched through his trembling notes for an apposite verse. He considered Psalm 82, 'How long will ye judge unjustly, and accept the testimony of the wicked,' and Psalm 35, 'False witness did rise up; they laid to my charge things I knew not,' but passed them over in favour of something more positive and lifting. He found Matthew 10, verses 18 to 20:

'And ye shall be brought before governors and kings for my sake, for a testimony against them and the ungodly.

'But when they deliver you up, take no thought how or what ye shall speak: for it shall be given you, in that same hour, what ye shall speak.

'For it is not ye who speak, but the Spirit of your Father which speaketh in you.'

'The Spirit,' said Avis, 'Amen.'

A WHOLE DIFFERENT TOWN HERE

1

THE ROAD FROM DARWIN AIRPORT into town doubles as the northern tip of the Stuart Highway. It carries here an extraordinary jumble of traffic, too much to expect near a city of, after all, not much more than forty thousand people. Territorians call it the Track. The Track runs the continent all the way to the south. Along the northern half, the thirteen hundred kilometres from Alice Springs to the outskirts of Darwin, there are only nine intersections of a status serious enough to be marked on the map. Not one of them is a cross-road, and the closest to Darwin, the Arnhem highway, ends somewhere between the Alligator rivers. So a good proportion of the city's traffic is driving along the top end of the Track at any time: sports cars, family sedans, four-wheel drives, pick-ups, road-trains. It is the only road connecting Darwin with anywhere else.

North of the airport, the Track is multi-laned, like a straightened ring-road. Traffic going in is separated from traffic going out by long road-centre plots. The plots have been grassed over. By September the grass is dry, and the road-trains raise a haze of fine dust. Malcolm Brown sat in a taxi-cab, inbound. It was hot. The driver was obese, so fat indeed that he kept his thighs akimbo to make room for the steering-wheel, and he fanned himself with a magazine although the cab was air-conditioned. This part of the highway runs through the sort of city approach you would find anywhere, past auto-shops, factories with saw-tooth rooflines, beer hoardings, and not until it becomes a coast-road does it enter the Darwin southerners think of, the lush, garlanded and fragrant hillsides, the streaky currents below in the harbour, the soft breeze that blows here from the Timor Sea.

The driver was inquisitive. When he found out why Brown was in town he said, 'The reporters are mostly staying at the Darwin.' By this he meant the Hotel Darwin. Brown didn't bother to tell him that was precisely why they were headed for the Motor Inn. The mention of the Chamberlain trial seemed to make the driver suddenly troubled and thoughtful, but it wasn't until they pulled up outside the reception office that he put any of it into words.

'She's strange, that one,' he said and left it at that.

'If it happens, I report it,' is something like the motto Brown would choose for his coat-of-arms, should he have one. He began reporting this trial before it began, in the press-room on Sunday afternoon, at the media briefing.

For the duration of the trial the second floor of the building next to the court-house had become the press-room. Fifty or sixty news-gatherers, the number depending on how the support crews were defined, were here from the press, radio and television networks all over the country. The long room would seat perhaps forty, which was fine since most of the photographers would be working outside. It had been proclaimed a court precinct, pro tem. They had here writing-tables and chairs, notice-boards and a coffee-bar. They had a Telex terminal and, along the length of a wall, telephones stood in enfilade, the charges for which would be billed directly to their employers. Proceedings in the court next door were covered by closed-circuit television cameras, one to show the action at the barristers' table, another the witness-stand and the bench. The receivers were set up here in the press-room. A pair of screens was mounted at each end wall. Although they could report the trial adequately without leaving the room, there were, in the court gallery, seats set aside for journalists, but it was not considered they would be in much demand. The windows on this floor looked over the bright court-house plaza, and down there white ropes and stanchions made a corridor along which the Chamberlains would walk to court unhindered by public curiosity, and in full view of the reporters and the photographers in the press-room.

The official whose duty it was to look after the press suggested that any dissatisfaction with these facilities should be directed to him. This invitation he delivered with an admirably straight face. An aide from the chief minister's department said he didn't want to read it suggested anywhere that the government was putting on a show, but when Brown wrote it up later as an opener for his coverage he found it hard to keep a tone of distrust out of the piece. He used the line: 'There is official recognition of the fact that the trial is going to be a centre of publicity.' It seemed, in the circumstances, a fair compromise.

But he decided to have nothing to do with the press-room and whatever it stood for. Anything he wrote from there would come out like a review of a stagey television drama.

Echoes knocked around in his mind awhile. The cab-driver's 'She's strange' was one. It was a cipher for distrust, perhaps for hate. People like that used to wait outside trials at the Old Bailey, at the gates of the Fleet Prison, or gather early in a town square before muffled carpenters had completed the gallows. There were crowds then. Now, the curious stayed at home. They were spectators at home. The government aides were wrong. Brown didn't expect full houses at this trial. A few, passing in and out on the hour as though it were a newsreel theatre. For the rest, it was left to the presses and the broadcasters.

There was a curious duality of roles here. Onlookers are important to an event, and every one of the journalists at this trial represented a crowd. Each stood for numbers ranging from a few thousand to a million apiece. Each was to provide an audience with the spectacle, and, somehow just as importantly, provide the spectacle with a crowd.

The cab-driver's opinion of Lindy Chamberlain echoed, in Brown's experience, the thoughts of most people all over the nation. It recalled another happening, this time in Sydney. A lunch-time party of reporters took a cab to a restaurant. They were talking about the Chamberlains. The driver straightened the argument out, simply but with great deliberation. 'They ought to burn the bitch,' he said quietly.

2

HE SET OFF for the court-house at nine the next morning. The pavement was already hot underfoot but he guessed this was the only part of the day cool enough for walking comfortably anywhere. By the time he got there he wished he owned a hat.

The centres of administration in Darwin are set, as they are in most capital cities, among parks and gardens. It is as though the symmetries of governance should take a place among the other blessings of nature. Because the blessings of nature are tropical here, the park between the police department and the chief minister's offices is also a garden of green fronds and soft clouds of insects. Red poinsiana petals litter the footpath. The grounds around the court-house opposite are grassy, and most of the trees are palms, spaced well apart like a new plantation on old ground. The view beyond is to the harbour, chalk-blue now, an indication that the tide is ebbing and strong. None of the buildings around here has the elegance of age, a result of the merciless cyclone of 1974 which, on Christmas day, blew much of the city as flat as a junkyard.

The new court-house is handsome. It is only two storeys high, hard-edged and modern, but tall fluted columns and dark glazing convey well enough that the rooms inside are chambers of judgement. On the flagpoles by the steps hang the ensigns of the nation and the Territory, waiting on breeze. This time of year they will wait until afternoon.

The session was an hour away, and television crews were unloading gear from rented automobiles and laying cables. A Channel Seven van took up part of the grass. On the forecourt steps, alone, sat a telephone. It was a smart salmon pink and would have been at home in the most flippant movie producer's suite. Impossibly, it rang. The man who ran to it was blond-haired and bouncy. It was Gary Tait. He picked up the hand-piece and said, 'Darwin footpath.' The call was from Brisbane, Tait had set up office on the pavement.

Just inside the sliding doors, the corridor was thick with journalists. The common idea seemed to be to catch the arrival of the Chamberlains, then watch the session next door on the video. Meantime they were renewing friendships. Most had covered the inquests: press, television, and voice-reporters, photographers and technicians, among them a stringer from the London *Daily Mail* who was at the same time writing a book, an American who was ordinarily the cricket writer for the London *Times*, a lonely and impenetrable German, and the Pacific correspondent for *Newsweek*. Here was the flavour of a reunion of an elite, an assumption that the networks had sent their best. And there was an attractive reasoning in that, for during the inquests most city newspresses had sold around forty thousand copies more every day than they were otherwise accustomed to, and this quantified boon was taken as a cue by everyone else.

3

UNDER THE RULES of court procedure in this country, people summoned as jurors are not examined about bias. The responsibility for fair-mindedness lies with the jurors. They are reminded of this by the judge—in this case the Acting Chief Justice James Muirhead, who sits now on the bench in crimson robes and grey wig—and thereafter it would take a provable incident of misconduct or prejudice to raise the matter again. The defence is permitted to challenge, without explanation, twelve of those called as jurors at a murder trial. This throws something of a burden on a lawyer's capacity for judging character quickly. A challenge must be made after the juror's name is called and before the juror takes a seat in the jury-box. It allows appraisal for about forty seconds. The system is eased along to some extent by a list of juror's names, addresses and occupations, given to the lawyers before the case begins, and the one Kirkham and Phillips now have in front of them lists those of a hundred and forty-two people. Cavanagh, their legal-aid contact here, has written brusque comments against thirteen names he knows, and he considers that twelve of them would harbour dislike for the Chamberlains. Kirkham wonders if this is some sort of omen.

So crowded is the courtroom that there is no space for spectators or reporters. Phillips and Kirkham expect the selection process will take most of the morning. The judge grants exemptions to two women who have insufficient English, to another whose father is ill, to two men in businesses too small to run without them, and to the wife of a police prosecutor. A nervous government clerk who fears she wouldn't make unprejudiced judgements is told to stay, but her name might not come up again in the ballot, and Kirkham makes a note to challenge her if it does.

A jury-list of this size is supposed to reflect the social complexion of the region it serves, but it never does, and no one is really surprised. The people who now pack the court represent, at best, a median in the spectrum. Various selection processes account for this, some of them informal. Doctors, lawyers and felons are exempt. Workers on short contracts and itinerant job-seekers have no place here, although they might make up fifteen per cent of the Darwin population at times. Judging by the faces in court, the Chinese, whose traditions in Darwin go back to the labour-gangs of the 1870s, do not register in the numbers they might. There ought to be more than three here. The two Portuguese will be hurried arrivals from Timor, very likely, and some of the Dutch names, a surprising dozen or so, could belong to families who migrated here after Indonesian independence.

The bulk of this panel anyone would call Territorians. Curiously, the majority of Territorians is less well established in Darwin than are the minorities. This, too, is a result of the cyclone in 1974,when three-quarters of the city's population fled south or east, and many stayed there. Most folk who live in Darwin now have lived here less than a decade. It shows. The urge that brings them here is the will to prosper, itself a fierce spell, and not unlike the need for conquest. They are peppy and ungentle, not at all a people of the tropics. They cut frangipani for their vases, but do not wear it in their hair.

Among the one hundred and twenty-three jurors in this panel there are no blacks. Most Aboriginals are thought, by registration clerks, too elusive to be worth the effort, but not all the fault lies here. There are plenty of indications that blacks hereabouts hold the society of Europeans in no high regard. A bold message of that nature is written in a public toilet which is no longer much frequented by whites. It is printed at face height above a urinal. The walls are otherwise free of graffitti. An improperly rendered plural accents the derisive tone, and it seems the verb is meant in its widest sense. It reads: 'All White Mans Fuck Each Other.'

The selection is done now, and the jury-box is full. The defence used eleven challenges to pare the panel down to these; the prosecution used seven. Kirkham feels a familiar brief shadow. Are these the faces of the open-minded, the fair, the prudent? Nine are men, three women. The women have chosen to sit together. As he looks them over, a barrel-bodied man with bristly hair who sits at the end of the front row gives a grin.

Phillips leans closer to Kirkham. 'I think we've done well,' he says. 'I like them.'

4

WHEN THE COURT was cleared of unchosen jurors, the spectators waiting in the corridor were allowed inside. Those reporters who didn't want to begin their coverage of the event from the video-room came in with them. Malcolm Brown took a seat in the front pew. He soon gave away the idea of describing the jury for his readers. His decision had nothing to do with contempt of court. This jury would become the most publicized in the country's history, but each face seemed to him as unremarkable as he might find on any peak-hour suburban bus. He made the note: None under thirty, none over fifty.

The courtroom was muggy. This was consonant with the rising tension, but was caused by overloading of the air-conditioner. The Chamberlains, sitting on benches in the elevated dock against the wall, seemed short of space. They were flanked by prison officers. Michael wore a dark tie, but no jacket. He was damp at the armpits. Lindy was wearing her hair short. Her cheeks were heavy, which set her eyes more deeply, and gave her a look of distrustfulness and exasperation. She held her shoulders squarely but this conveyed an attempt at comfort rather than resolve. Below, she was squat and burdened. Now and then she lifted her gauzy skirt and billowed air around her legs. Michael was as still as a snapshot.

5

BARKER GOT TO HIS FEET. This was the moment. He hitched his gown at the shoulder. The gown was frayed just there from years of that gesture. Brown made a quick note: Curly grey hair under the grey curls of his wig. When Barker spoke he sounded like a narrator opening an intricate play in which the audience must be given the plot before the drama begins.

'A baby was killed at Ayers Rock on 17 August 1980, during the evening, between eight and nine o'clock. It was a Sunday. The child was then just under ten weeks old, having been born on 11 June. She was called Azaria Chamberlain, and was the

daughter of the accused Michael Leigh Chamberlain and Alice
Lynne Chamberlain. The body of the child was never found but,
having heard the evidence concerning the baby's disappearance,
you will have no difficulty determining that she is dead, and that
she died on the night she disappeared. As to the manner and the
cause of death, one cannot be precise because the body was
never found. However, what will be proved, largely upon' scientific evidence of the baby's clothes, is that the child lost a great
deal of blood, in all probability from injury to the major vessels
of her neck. She died very quickly because somebody had cut
her throat.'

'The Crown does not venture to suggest any reason or
motive for the killing. It is not part of our case that Mrs
Chamberlain had previously shown any ill will towards the
child, nor do we assert that the child was other than a normal
healthy baby. The Crown does not, therefore, attempt to prove
motive, nor does it invite speculation as to motive. We simply
say to you that the evidence to be put before you will prove
beyond reasonable doubt that, for whatever reason, the baby was
murdered by her mother.'

This was already a better opening than the newsreporters
could have hoped for. Everyone was worried, in the reporting of
this case, that the evidence was now so well known that no
amount of skill could make it sound fresh. It occurred to
Malcolm Brown that Barker might have considered he had the
same problem with the jury that reporters had with their audi-
ences. So Barker was making it fresh. The trick for Brown now
was in his choice of lead. He wanted to begin his piece with a
quotation which would show, at the one time, the vigour of the
opening and the pith of the case against the Chamberlains. Then
Barker said: 'Shortly after the event the mother asserted, and
thereafter continued to assert, that the dead child had been taken
from the tent by a dingo. The Crown says that the dingo story
was a fanciful lie; calculated to conceal the truth, which is that
the child Azaria died by her mother's hand.'

Brown knew he would lead with: 'A Calculated, Fanciful Lie'.

6

BARKER'S OPENING ran all day, and the defence team took the transcript back to the Travelodge Motel in the evening and worked it over. The job they had in front of them was not unlike the task of a football coach. The Crown had now laid out the pattern of expected play and nominated the stars in the line-up.

Phillips ran his finger down the list of prosecution witnesses. There were two newcomers: the doctors Baxter and Culliford. Barker had himself already identified Baxter as Joy Kuhl's supervisor at the Sydney laboratories. Culliford was a London police biologist, a specialist in blood identification. 'A big name,' Tipple said.

'A big name, but he cannot have seen the tests carried out in Sydney.' Phillips guessed Culliford was to be called to block any criticism of the way Joy Kuhl worked the electrophoretic experiments. This would also account for Baxter's presence. Well, the defence would produce some big names too, when it came time to take to the field.

They picked over the transcript looking for weaknesses in the way Barker had chosen to present his case. A prosecutor is not compelled to disclose all the evidence available, but it was the best guide the defence had so far. Phillips quoted: '"The accused was absent from the barbecue area for some minutes. It is a bit hard to be more precise than that, but it was long enough, the Crown says, for the child to be murdered."'

'The Lowes put it five to ten minutes,' Kirkham said. 'I don't think we can get it down from that.' Striking, he thought, how the case against the Chamberlains had altered since the inquest. Then, they were defending accusations that the baby was long selected for death, was dispatched to Jesus from the slopes of Ayers Rock with sacrificial rites, that the parents had somehow mocked up, perhaps with a doll, an impostor with which to hoodwink bystanders until night-time, and their barbecue at the tentside was the finale in a pitiless play. So much had the police case modified, to accommodate the emergencies of incompliant evidence, that the defence was having a hard time arraying its armaments to face the changing angles of attack.

'"As the accused went back to the barbecue area, the dead child was in all probability in the car, and it is possible her body was in the camera-bag."'

'If that's so, where was the camera-gear?' Tipple said. 'No one remembers seeing it anywhere else.'

Phillips rang down to the bar for a bottle of Calvados. When it arrived, everyone but Tipple took a glass. Phillips read on: ' ''Michael Chamberlain apparently heard a noise which might have been a cry coming from the direction of the tent. The accused Alice Lynne Chamberlain then straight away commenced to walk back to the tent. There will be evidence that Mrs Lowe also heard a noise, but at this stage of course, on the Crown case, it was impossible that it was the baby.'' '

Phillips knew how high a hurdle this was for the prosecution. He had, in May, flown to Hobart to talk with the Lowes. If the jury saw in Sally Lowe the qualities Phillips found, honesty and homely sincerity in just about equal parts, the prosecution case ought to end right there. 'She won't back down,' he said. 'It was a cry, and it was a baby's cry.'

He read: ' ''It was now just after midnight. For a substantial period both accused had been left on their own near the car while the searchers progressed far out into the sandhills. So there was ample opportunity for them to have cleaned at least some of the blood from the front of the car.'' '

Tipple generally left matters of advocacy to the advocates, but now he leaned forward in his armchair. 'That is a very weak part of the case, I've always thought,' he said. 'They were away from the women at the tent once, maybe twice, and nowhere near the car.'

'Barker is puffing it up a bit much,' Kirkham said. 'We'll have to pare it down to size.' But it was his guess that the prosecution would treat the point by ignoring it.

Following what seemed to be a line of connected disquiet, Kirkham turned to this passage: ' ''You are going to be invited to find that it was not mere coincidence that the baby's clothes were found near the part of the Rock where the photograph of the lichen was taken.'' ' Something was wrong here with the sequence of the prosecution case. He worried at it until the answer came.

'The Crown case is now that the killing was not premeditated, more a spontaneous act,' he said. 'That photograph was taken long before the baby died, but they are still using it as if it betrays a plan.' And there was a connection here with motive, if he could find it. He recovered the words: ' ''The Crown does not attempt to prove motive, nor does it provide speculation as to motive." ' He knew this was double-talk. Barker was going to leave the jury open to any enticing fancy.

'We will raise motive,' Phillips said slowly, 'so that we can demolish it.' There were tactical problems in this, which he seemed to be solving somewhere in the pale cage he was making with his hands. 'If we call Dr Milne on some pretext or other, say, on the weight of the baby, we can then use her to exclude the only feasible motive there is now. Post-natal depression.'

Phillips drummed his fingers and said, 'But we've a long way to go before we reach that point.' He poured another round of Calvados. He was overweight, in the way a thin man gets big, all below the shoulders. He was no pacer about the room, but he was edgy. Kirkham knew they were all edgy. They wanted the evidence, and therefore the contest, to begin.

7

THE EASY MORNING was the gift of a fading sea-breeze. Malcolm Brown crossed to the park where, under the palms, a picket-line of photographers and a television crew were taking shots of two leggy girls in shorts and T-shirts. When he got to the forecourt, he found it empty, so he knew that the Chamberlains had arrived early. This accounted for the photographers' interest in the girls in the park. He headed inside.

Had Brown been more interested in things like this he would have found that these girls were not posing for glamour shots. They were modelling T-shirts printed, across the hummocky bust, with slogans of home-town support. The words said: 'The Dingo is Innocent.' The girls were happy to pose in any manner that best drew the eye to the message and, between bouts of interest the photographers showed in them, leaned against the palms and chatted with passers-by. They spent time yesterday afternoon this way. They preferred the city side of the park where there were plenty of onlookers. This was also the route the jury took to the court-house.

Brown found out about it from a Melbourne *Age* reporter, who predicted that the southern dailies would lead with the story unless better copy came up. When the session opened, Phillips got to his feet and made his complaint to the judge. He spoke as if he were an outsider who might be ignorant of local customs, but could not find neutral words to describe them.

'It is difficult for any rational person,' he said in a mystified but polite voice, 'to understand the mentality or motives of these people. And I do not suggest that this stupidity would in fact influence a juror, but it is clearly enough calculated to do so, Your Honour.'

Justice Muirhead ordered the demonstrators to desist and, in their fortunate absence, threatened them with jail if they did not. It was just the sort of action Brown would have anticipated on the information he had of this judge—a genial and diligent lawyer from whom everyone expected a fair and mannerly trial—and his order halted the offence without causing an irrevocable fuss. Brown's problem now was the reporting of the event. He couldn't ignore it since it would be all over the competing dailies. So he did what he thought ought to be done with shameful and contaminating human actions. He wrote it as an occurrence of little account and prepared to bury it, deep under something else.

8

SALLY LOWE looked as if she hadn't slept. Justice Muirhead told her she could sit while she gave her testimony, and she seemed grateful. She'd had her hair styled into cascades of fossy curls, and her smile was nervously bright. She was handed a map of the Ayers Rock camping-ground and took time to find on it the position of her tent and the barbecue.

Pauling, whose witness she was, said, 'I want to take you to Mrs Chamberlain going back from the barbecue to the tent, with the baby and Aidan.'

'Yes, that point in time,' she said, finding the groove in her memory. 'Right. Mrs Chamberlain had the baby in her arms, and Aidan was close behind her. I recall them walking along the footpath area towards their tent. I don't recall anything much after that. I have forgotten most of it. And I was involved in conversation.' She shook her head. 'The next I recall is them coming back, along the same path. About halfway along that path, I suppose, I recall seeing them again. And they walked back to the barbecue. Mrs Chamberlain had a tin of something in her hand, and I saw a can-opener, or perhaps something else, in her other hand. Aidan was behind her. And the next I recall, he was beside me, between myself and the second barbecue, which Mr Chamberlain had been using, and Lindy was just inside the railing, near the barbecue.'

'Are you able to tell us how long Mrs Chamberlain was away from the barbecue area?'

'Well, it's a fairly short period of time. But I've stated before, six to ten minutes would be roughly correct. Five to ten minutes away.'

Pauling asked her to keep going. She said, 'Well, she was just standing there. I heard the baby cry. Quite a serious cry, but not being my child, I didn't sort of say anything. Aidan said, "I think that's Bubby crying," or something similar. Mike said to Lindy, "Yes, that was the baby, you better go and check." Lindy went immediately to check. I saw her walk along the same footpath that they'd been on.'

'What happened next?'

'She was in the area on that footpath closest to where the car and the tent were, only inside the railings, and she yelled out the cry, "That dog's got my baby."'

'Yes?'

' "That dog's got my baby." We froze for a minute. Mike, and my husband Greg ran in the direction she was looking to the south side of their car, out in that general area. Then, as they went off searching, one of them shouted about a torch, and Greg said to get the torch from the car, which I did. I had my daughter on my hip.'

'After the police arrived,' Pauling said, 'a major search got underway?'

'That's right. People came from all directions.'

Pauling asked her if she had then entered the tent.

'Yes. Aidan was close by me after the men had started searching, and he was very upset, and said that the dog had got his baby in its tummy. And I cannot recall why, now, but I took him to the tent, and I had some thought in my mind of getting him to sleep. He showed me where he slept, his sleeping-bag, inside the tent. I had my daughter. I was holding her with me at the time. I knelt at the front of the tent and leaned in a little way. I think Aidan got in when he showed me where he slept. I saw a few spots of blood around the area at that time. After he showed me where he slept, I think my eyes caught sight of the bigger pool of blood in the tent.'

'Where was it?'

'I was leaning in from the middle of the tent, so it would have been a little off to the right, and it shocked me a bit, because it looked as if it had soaked into something padded, but was still wet on the surface. So, although the area itself wasn't large, I took it to be quite a lot of blood.'

'Can you describe it?'

'About six by four'—here she was talking in inches—'a squashed circle, I suppose. I recall it as a dark, red, wet pool of blood.'

Phillips took the cross-examination himself. The Crown had spent less than twenty minutes with Sally Lowe and, in an act of further relegation, presented her to the jury through the most junior prosecutor on the team. They were treating her testimony as though it was insubstantial, as if it led nowhere of any persuasive interest. For Phillips, she was the most important of all the campsite witnesses.

'I suppose it is clear enough from your evidence,' he said, 'but the fact is that prior to meeting the Chamberlains in the way you did, you had no contact with them, directly or indirectly?'

'No, no.'

'And no connection whatsoever, for example, with their church?'

'No.'

He was determined to show that no bias lurked in Sally Lowe. He pushed further. 'And, in the three-quarters of an hour, where had the acquaintanceship got to? First names, was it?'

'Yes, first names.'

He retrieved from the bar-table a copy of Barker's address and asked her to listen to the passage he was about to read: ' ''At this stage the Crown says the baby was dead. Her husband Michael Chamberlain apparently heard a noise which might have been a cry coming from the direction of the tent. The accused, Alice Lynne Chamberlain, then straightaway commenced to walk back to the tent. There will be evidence that Mrs Lowe also heard a noise, but at this stage, of course, on the Crown case, it was impossible that it was the baby, because the Crown says that the baby was then dead.'' '

He asked, addressing the jury more than the witness, 'Do you understand the importance of the evidence you can give to this court?'

Clearly she did, and seemed about to complain that it was the prosecution case she didn't really understand, so Phillips said,

'The Crown is saying that it is impossible you heard the baby when Mrs Chamberlain returned to the barbecue.'

She shrugged. 'I disagree with that.'

'Not only do you disagree with it, but you are absolutely certain that is the time you heard the baby? Are you?'

She nodded. Evidently the dispute was inexplicable, beyond the reach of words.

'Would you say, "Yes," please,' said Phillips, who didn't want any ambiguity about this.

'Yes,' she complied. 'All the Chamberlains, Aidan and Mrs Chamberlain and Mr Chamberlain were present. My husband, myself and child. And we heard the cry.'

'The cry came from the direction of the tent?'

'It definitely came from the tent.'

'Beyond any doubt?'

'I'm positive.'

'You knew well, from your own child, the sound of a baby crying?'

'Well,' she agreed. 'I come from a big family and am used to babies. I can tell the difference between a baby and an older child.'

'Apart from your own baby and rearing it through the same stages as Azaria Chamberlain, what other babies of that age had you had direct contact with, prior to August 1980?'

'I come from a family of nine, and they always seem to be having children. I'm just familiar with babies and children.'

'You are quite satisfied that the sound you heard was a baby crying out?'

'Yes. Positive.'

'I think it has been suggested to you in the past that it might have been the little boy Reagan, who I think was then four, crying out in his sleep? Do you reject that suggestion completely?'

'Definitely. It was a small baby.'

'What about this suggestion that Mrs Chamberlain stood up with the baby, took it over to the car and sat in the front seat, and cut its throat? In the three-quarters of an hour you were with her was there anything, anything, that indicated to you that such a thing was likely to happen?'

Sally Lowe smiled. 'No. In fact the opposite. She sort of had a new-mum glow about her. It's hard to describe.'

'A new-mum glow. Did she appear a loving mother to you?'

'Yes. Definitely yes.'

'Was she in a sullen, truculent, surly mood?'

'No. She was a little tired, but she still managed to be quite cheerful and happy.'

'Was there anything in her appearance and her demeanour, on her return, that indicated anything abnormal had happened?'

'No. She seemed to be solely concerned with feeding Aidan some more food.'

'Was she covered in blood?'

'No.'

'Did she have any blood on her at all, that you saw?'

'Well, I didn't look all over her. But just looking directly at her, I didn't see any blood, no.'

'She has told the police that the reason why she returned with Aidan to the barbecue was that he wanted something extra to eat, and she selected a can of baked beans and returned to the barbecue to heat it up. You can at least confirm, can you not, that she returned with a can in one hand?'

'Yes.'

'And a can-opener in the other?'

'Yes. I'm not sure, but I believe it was a can-opener, y-s.'

'Mrs Lowe, I would like to read you some more passages from the prosecutor's opening address. Mr Barker told the court that, as to blood in the tent, there were ''just insignificant traces''.' Phillips flipped through the transcript. 'And he again referred to ''tiny traces of blood in the tent''. Can I ask you this: the floor of the tent was covered, was it not, effectively, with articles of bedding, clothing?'

'Yes. You couldn't see any part of the—' She waved a hand.

'Of the fabric of the tent itself?'

'That's right.'

'Was this area of blood, that you have described, a tiny trace?'

'No. I woudn't have said that. That was what convinced me that the baby was dead. From the amount of blood I saw.'

'Did you also see some spots of blood?'

'Yes, that's correct.'

'Spots on a sleeping-bag?'

'Yes. There were spots on Reagan's sleeping-bag, to the right in the tent.'

'If forensic scientists later found eleven spots on a sleeping-bag, that would be consistent with what you saw?'

'It wouldn't surprise me.'

* * *

Sally Lowe could remember clearly, she said, the number of times the Chamberlains had walked away from the vicinity of the tent while she was there, which was until ten o'clock. They had left her once.

'Several ladies comforted Mrs Chamberlain during the time you were there?'

'Yes.'

'You can only recall one occasion Mrs Chamberlain was with her husband?'

She agreed it was only one.

'On that occasion they were in a lighted area?'

'Yes.'

'You could see them?'

'Yes.'

'They were never out of your sight?'

'They were quite visible, because you could see them crying.'

Everyone in the defence team had liked the idea, when they talked it through, of reading Barker's address back to the witnesses. It did more than merely clarify the realities of the evidence. It put prosecution witnesses directly at odds with the prosecutor, right from the beginning, and in plain view. Phillips kept it up. He quoted: ' "For a substantial period, both accused had been left on their own, near the car, while the searchers progressed far out into the sandhills, so there was ample opportunity for them to have cleaned at least some of the blood from the front of the car." Do you follow that?'

'Yes.'

'Limiting yourself to the time you can speak about, did you ever see anything remotely like that, either Mr or Mrs Chamberlain cleaning the inside of that car.'

'No,' she said, aggravated enough to add, 'and the car was here.' She placed the car, with a gesture of proximity, alongside the witness-box. 'You could see inside the car too, from the light.'

'Page fifty-five,' Phillips said, so that Barker could follow his own words, ' "Sometime during the night of 17 August, the body of the child, still dressed in its clothes, was buried in a very shallow grave on, or near to, a dune not far from the campsite. It is the case for the prosecution that there was ample opportunity for this to be done when the search moved away from the area close to the camp.'' Follow that?'

'Yes.'

'Was there anything done by the Chamberlains, during the time you were there, to suggest they were burying a body?'

'No, no.'

'Did you ever see them take any object out of the car and disappear into the scrub?'

'No, no.'

'You can be quite categorical, can you not, that nothing of the sort occurred during the time you saw them away from the car?'

'Yes,' she said, grim and sorrowful.

Justice Muirhead picked up the point. 'From the time you heard the baby cry,' he asked, 'until you went back to the motel that night, did you at any stage see anybody open the car doors?'

'No.'

'You yourself did not open them?'

'No.'

'At any stage, did you see the headlights, or any lights attached to the car, inside or out, illuminated?'

'No. The only light was from the barbecue area, and then later from the police vehicle.'

'Am I right in saying you never saw, after you heard the baby, anyone in the car?'

'No one,' she said, shaking her head. 'No.'

Neither Phillips nor Kirkham had expected the judge to intervene so early. It seemed, on balance, a happy sign.

'I do not think the prosecution suggests otherwise,' Phillips said, with a glance at Barker, 'but there is no doubt the baby was alive during the time the mother was nursing it at the barbecue, is there?'

'Yes, the baby was definitely alive.'

'Because you saw it kicking, did you not?'

'Yes,' she said. Sally Lowe knew this issue had a long and malevolent history. The Northern Territory police, who had interviewed her in Hobart, seemed to be interested in nothing else. That memory prompted her to volunteer now, 'Also the expression it made on its face.'

'Mrs Chamberlain has spoken, in conversations with the police, about a dingo which was present when you were all at the barbecue.'

'That's correct.'

'According to what she has said, the dingo at one point came very close, and pounced on some little mouse that was hopping about. Was there a dingo close to you at the barbecue?'

'Yes. One followed me back from the rubbish bins at one stage, just sort of fairly close behind, but keeping in the background. Then, I believe, the same dog appeared again, and it did make a dive for something under the bush, and someone made a comment about a mouse, but I didn't see the mouse.'

'As to the duration of the baby's cry,' Phillips said. 'That cry, as you listened to it, appeared to be cut off?'

'That's right,' she said. 'Going from experience with other babies. Yes.'

'It seemed to you to stop suddenly?'

'Yes.'

'And that was something you noted?'

'Right,' she said as if, at long last, someone had got the point of all this.

9

FROM THE WAY Greg Lowe kept rubbing the side of his gingery beard it was clear he was more than usually uncomfortable in court. Around the newsroom, the story ran that the prosecution could disable his testimony at any time it chose. At the barbecue with the Chamberlains he'd been drinking. The story was amusing because everyone remembered it was Lindy Chamberlain who berated him over his can of beer, and so made the incident memorable. It was a neat irony.

Lowe's discomforture had nothing to do with beer. He had a problem no one here knew about. Pauling got close to it when he asked, 'How long was Mrs Chamberlain at the tent?'

'For a maximum of ten minutes. I'd say about eight to ten minutes.'

'What did Mrs Chamberlain do then?' Lowe hesitated. This

was right where the problem lay. He had spent many sleepless nights revisiting these eight to ten minutes. It now seemed he could stand by the fireside at will. He was talking to Mike. Sally held Chantelle on a skewed hip. The tips of his ears were cold. The night would freeze, later. He watched Lindy carry Azaria to the tent, bend, shuffle inside. He hadn't taken much notice from there on. But the next scene in his memory showed this: Lindy in frock and parka, bare-legged, pushing out through the tent-flap, standing. The police case, since the time of the second inquest, had her murderously carrying the baby to the car. But when he saw her there now, her arms were indisputably vacant. The baby was still inside the tent.

He knew well the difficulty he faced. In Hobart, he had taken the problem to a local lawyer. The lawyer had, in the event, posed more problems than he solved. The lawyer advised Greg Lowe to give his testimony exactly as he had at the first inquest. He would be justified in including his present recollection only if someone asked him about it, in precise and inescapable terms.

'What did Mrs Chamberlain do then?'

Was Pauling referring to the beginning or the end of the scene? Greg Lowe kept his gaze on the floor.

'She returned to the barbecue with her son,' he said quietly.

'Did something then happen?' Pauling asked.

'Well, we were heavily involved in conversation, and Mr Chamberlain made some comment to his wife like, "Was that the baby?" She went to check on the baby. She got about five yards away, from my recollection about five yards away from the barbecue-site toward the tent, and she came out with an outburst: "That dog's got my baby."'

'Did you hear anything like a baby crying?'

'No, I didn't myself, no.'

'Mrs Chamberlain said, "That dog's got my baby." What happened next?'

'She chased in a direction where she was pointing, where she said a dog had gone, and then she veered back towards the tent, and checked the tent to find out whether the child was still in the tent or not, but by this time, of course, the outburst had raised a hue and cry, and Mike and I raced from the barbecue across to the tent and asked which direction the dog had gone, and we proceeded to search immediately.'

Kirkham cross-examined him about the statement he had made to the interviewing police. 'As to what she called out, you remembered two things, did you not, when you were talking to the police? One was, ''The dog's got my baby?'' '

' ''That dog's got my baby.'' Yes.'

'And you also indicated to the police that she said something to this effect: ''Somebody please stop that dog.'' '

'Yes.'

'It has been suggested,' Kirkham said, 'that Mr Chamberlain's behaviour, during the time of the hue and the cry, lacked urgency. The prosecution is claiming that, you understand?'

Greg Lowe nodded, grudging and brief, as if more definite assent might align him more closely with the prosecution than he wanted.

'Tell me this, is this how you described some of his conduct to the police?' Kirkham paused here, to emphasize that the police had long known about the behaviour he was about to comment on. He read, ' ''Mike and I must have searched for about half an hour, going at full pelt through the scrub.'' '

'That's right.'

' ''We kept covering different areas, and then coming to the tent to see if there was any news.'' '

'Yes, that's right.'

'What do you say? You were there. What do you say about this suggestion that Michael Chamberlain lacked urgency in his conduct?'

'Well, when the hue and cry first was given, Mike and I just froze for a few seconds. And then it was a full pace to get a torch, and to find out which direction the dog had presumably gone, and then we raced as far as we could up the sandhill to check it out. And then we broadened our scope of search.'

'Did he in any way, to your observation, lack endeavour in seeking his child?'

'No. I must point out, though, that Mike did go back to console Lindy on several occasions.'

Kirkham knew that Greg Lowe thought this was a helpful offering. 'Thank you,' Kirkham said.

'It is suggested by the prosecution that there were opportunities for the Chamberlains, or one of them, to clean blood from the front of the car during the search. Did you see either of the Chamberlains engaged in any such operation?'

'No, I didn't. There were quite a lot of people around at that time at the tent-site, and I'm sure if anything like that had happened it would've been noted.'

Kirkham turned to the jury-box. 'I hope the jurors can hear your evidence,' he said.

Greg Lowe walked from the courtroom, shambling, splayfooted, resigned to a helpless suspicion that nobody seemed to put much store by ordinary folk anymore.

10

EACH WITNESS SO FAR seemed to have a different grasp of timing and sequence. It was as if Lindy Chamberlain's cry from her tent had so unsettled time and shuffled events that the usual methods of judging these things were no longer apt. No one was having more difficulty with this than Judy West. A handsomely greying woman now in her fifties, she was thought calm by those who knew her well, even serene. The calmness, to which work on the farm and the strict application of meditation both contributed, was not of long standing. Judy West used to suffer dark bouts of disabling nervousness. It was a pit she climbed out of painfully. Now she seemed to be standing again at the edge.

Trouble had begun when she arrived in Darwin. The constable who met the Wests at the airport took them to a room in the police depot for a pretrial conference. Barker was there, and the legal officer, O'Loughlin, but Pauling did all the talking. Evidently the Wests were Pauling's responsibility. He began by saying, 'The Crown is impartial, you understand, but we've got a good case here, and we are out to prove it.' Some contradiction lay deep in there, but she had let it pass.

His pen hovered over a pad. 'You say you heard a dingo outside your tent on the Sunday night.'

'I did hear a dingo. I heard it growl,' she said. The regret that she had done nothing about it at the time had long pursued her now.

'And you later heard Mrs Chamberlain call out.'

She said she had. She knew Sally Lowe thought the cry began, 'Michael, Michael,' but the words that rang in her own ears were, 'My God, My God, the dingo's got my baby.'

'How long was that after the dingo growled?'

'I don't know, five to ten minutes, perhaps.'

Then, she recalled, Bill and young Catherine, went to see what had happened. Once they'd located everybody, Michael Chamberlain had asked for a torch.

Pauling asked, 'How long after you heard the cry did Michael ask for a torch?'

She ran through succeeding pictures: Bill and Catherine pulling on their shoes, the path from there outside to the barbecue, finding the shivering Aidan who said that a dingo had taken their Bubby, crouching to hug him close, the sudden appearance of Sally Lowe, and Lindy, white-faced, and then Michael, who had lost his car-keys and was calling for a flash-light. Talking in 'actual happening-time', as she thought of it, was implausible. Everything took an age.

'About fifteen minutes,' she said, which seemed to please Pauling more than it ought.

'Did you stay long with Mrs Chamberlain while the search went on?'

'Until the bush-nurse took them off to a motel.'

'You saw Mr and Mrs Chamberlain walk away, together, while you were there.'

'Which time do you mean,' she said.

Barker and Pauling exchanged glances. 'That happened more than once?' Pauling asked.

'Twice, for about ten minutes each time,' she said. 'No more.'

He had asked her to recall what they did when they came back to her. 'The first time,' she said, 'Michael asked us all to pray together. He put his hands on Lindy's head and said a prayer. The second time, I told Lindy Reagan cried and I'd shushed him to sleep.'

'So you had been inside the tent. What did it look like in there?'

'Everything was lying about. There was a trail of blankets strewn from the cot at the back to the flap at the front. I remember some blood. I was kneeling on a little blanket, a baby-rug, and there was a fine spray of blood on that.'

'When Mr and Mrs Chamberlain walked away from the tent, at either time, were they carrying something? A spade, a bag, anything?'

'No.' The scene in her mind was nothing like that. She was watching two bereft people who loved each other walk arm in arm, back and forth through the low scrub. She did not lose sight of them for more than a minute. They needed to be alone. They were not far away but beyond consolation. 'No,' she said 'they had nothing.'

They told her she could go. She heard Pauling and Barker talking as she reached the door. 'That's when they buried the body, right enough,' Pauling was saying.

She went through it all again in the attentive courtroom. For the first time she began to suspect just how much was amiss.

Pauling asked her to demonstrate for the jury the gestures Michael Chamberlain made looking for his car-keys. 'He was patting his pockets,' she said. 'He seemed very distressed.' She stood and tapped her own hips and vest. 'He seemed to have a coat on.'

'What was it he was saying?'

'I think he wanted a torch, and it was in the car, and he couldn't find the keys, but it was most unusual for him, because he was a very organized person. I knew we had a torch in the tent. So Bill offered it to Michael, and he said, yes, he'd like it, so Bill went over to the tent and brought the torch back for him.'

'Can you give us any idea how long after you had heard Mrs Chamberlain cry out that you had this conversation with Michael Chamberlain about the torch?'

'Ten to fifteen minutes,' Judy West said. She heard an indrawn breath from somewhere behind her. The dock was behind her. The breath was from Michael Chamberlain. It was then she realized that ten to fifteen minutes might represent an error of more that usual importance.

It fell to Kirkham to retrieve some ground.

'Could you tell the jury what time you arrived at Ayers Rock.'

'The Friday, in the afternoon, about five o'clock.'

'On the Saturday, did you see a dingo in close proximity to your tent?'

'It would be about sundown,' Judy West said. 'Catherine and I had climbed the Rock. She'd had a shower and was sitting outside the tent.'

'Did your daughter call out to you in a loud voice.'

Judy remembered that Catherine, who was then twelve, had screamed, rather than called. 'Yes,' she said.

'Did you see a dingo in the immediate vicinity of where your daughter was seated?'

'Yes.'

'What did you do?'

'I chased it away. It wouldn't go. It just stood there, and I was quite frightened. It moved, in the end, but it was just like shooing off a dog.'

'How long did you have to exert yourself to shoo the dingo away?'

'Not long,' she said with a smile, 'because I did not want it there.' She was familiar enough with the ways of courts to know that she mustn't give the reason for this, since it relied on hearsay from Catherine. The dingo had grabbed Catherine by the arm and pulled.

'In which direction did it proceed?'

'It went around behind our tent. East.'

'Towards what has been described as the sand-dune to the east of the camp?'

That was indeed where it had gone.

A story doing the rounds about town, which Tipple had lighted upon, spoke of these witnesses as if they were all friends of the Chamberlains. So Kirkham asked Judy West, 'Did you ever meet Mrs Chamberlain prior to arriving at Ayers Rock?'

'No.'

'Did you have a conversation with Mrs Chamberlain at the barbecue?'

'Yes.'

'Can you recall the details?'

'When we went over to have a look at the baby, she told me she'd called her Azaria because it meant Blessed of God.'

'It meant?'

'Blessed of God. And that she'd had trouble originally when they'd rung her parents about the baby, because the parents thought it was a boy called Azariah, so she had to explain she'd had a girl called Azaria.'

'Was there any conversation about the desire of the Chamberlains to have a girl?'

'They said they'd always wanted a girl, and she was very much the baby they wanted. Mrs Chamberlain was wearing a parka that was covered with travel badges, and she told me she had done the same thing: she'd sewed travel badges on a parka of Michael's, and for the two little boys. Wherever they went, she bought badges and sewed them on, and she'd started a parka for the baby that already had two badges on it.'

Justice Muirhead said, 'Mr Kirkham.' The judge had caught something everyone else had missed: Lindy Chamberlain, on her bench in the dock, was hiding her tears with her hands. 'We will take our afternoon break now.' He rose from the bench, but they still hadn't got it. 'I think Mrs Chamberlain is not well,' he said.

Kirkham pressed the topic. 'Were you able to make any observation of the manner in which she was caring for her child, Azaria?'

'The baby was wrapped, in the cot, and she offered to pick it up for me to have a look. I said, no, not if she's asleep, but she said it was time for the baby to be picked up. She had a great care for the baby.'

'Did you see that attitude change in any way?'

'No, I never did.'

'The next occasion I think you saw Mrs Chamberlain was again at the barbecue, in the evening of the Sunday. Was the child awake?'

'Yes. She was sitting. Mrs Chamberlain was dandling her on her knee.'

'Did Mrs Chamberlain appear in any way grouchy or unhappy?'

'No. She was a bit tired, I thought, but she wasn't grouchy or unhappy.'

'Were you in the concluding processes of washing-up when you heard the growl you have told us about?'

'No, I had given coffee to Catherine, and I had sat outside, myself, drinking coffee. Then I moved into the tent and was just sitting inside the door when I heard the dog growl.'

'I do not want to put words in your mouth,' Kirkham said, 'and if I am wrong please tell me immediately, but did the sound appear to come from the general area to the rear of the Chamberlains' tent?'

'About half way.'

'Half way what?'

'Between our tent and the Chamberlains'.'

'Would you be able to describe the growl?'

'It was a low, deep growl. It was the sort of growl our dogs give when Bill is killing on the farm and he gives them—'

Kirkham stopped her there. He wanted to sharpen the jury's attention for this. 'You may have a little difficulty making the jury hear you. It is a growl like your dogs give on the farm, when Bill is killing, you say.'

'Yes. Bill will give them a bit of offal while he is killing, and one dog will be sort of scared that another dog will get a bit more, so it growls to keep it off.'

The judge said, 'A type of threatening growl, is that it?'

'Yes,' she said.

'You told the coroner at the first inquest,' Kirkham said, 'that Mrs Chamberlain's cry seemed to come fairly quickly after the growl of the dog, although you could not estimate the precise time. Was that true?'

'Yes.'

This was the growl which had convinced Dr Newsome at Wildlife Research, and Les Harris at the Dingo Foundation, that two dingoes were at the tents. Phillips and Kirkham planned to call Harris to testify about that. The growl was important for another reason. It gave a presence, vivid and menacing, to the dingo which left its prints in the dust at the Chamberlain tent.

'You were, apart from occasions I will ask you about in a moment, in Mrs Chamberlain's company from the time the alarm was raised until the time she and her husband departed for the Uluru Motel?'

She agreed she was. 'There were times when I went away,' she said. 'I went to the barbecue at one stage, to make some Milo.' She recalled that occasion clearly, for Lindy had refused the Milo, saying if she drank it she would throw up. 'And I went to our tent a couple of times for blankets. It was very cold.'

'They were visits of short duration? Minutes?'

'Yes.'

'Are you able to say whether either Mr or Mrs Chamberlain removed anything from the car in your presence?'

'No,' she said, thinking back. 'Not to my knowledge.'

'Indeed, you were standing at times against the car. Leaning against the car, I suggest to you. And so were other people.'

'Yes.'

'And the light was sufficient so the people leaning on the car from the outside could see the interior.'

'Yes,' she said.

'When you first saw Mrs Chamberlain, after the alarm had been raised, can you recall what she was wearing?'

'She was wearing the same clothes she was wearing when she was at the barbecue in the morning.'

'Which was?'

'Sneakers, and socks, with a short dress or a skirt.'

'I would just like you to describe the light, for the members of the jury, if you would not mind.'

'It was a gas light on a long stainless steel pole.'

'Was Mrs Chamberlain standing in that light?'

'Yes.'

'Did you see anything on her clothes or her face, or her person, which would suggest to you that she had a child's blood on her?'

'No.' She shook her head. This was all the vehemence of which Judy West was capable. She wished she could express it more truly. But the choice for her was between calm and calamity, and she held to calm.

Justice Muirhead brought her back to Michael Chamberlain's loss of his car-keys. 'Your assumption from that, I suppose,' he asked, 'was that the car was locked?'

'Yes.'

'Did you see it unlocked that evening?'

'Not until they'd packed up.'

'And set off for the hotel?'

'They were setting off for the motel.'

'To the best of your knowledge, it remained shut during the entire period?'

'Yes,' she said.

Kirkham asked, 'Did any of the police, or the rangers, say anything in your presence to Mr or Mrs Chamberlain that night to indicate that there was little hope of the child remaining alive?'

'No.' Then she remembered something. 'The bush-nurse, when she arrived, asked Mrs Chamberlain if she was feeding the baby. And when Mrs Chamberlain said that she was, she indicated that she'd give her some tablets to dry up the milk.'

'Did you urge the Chamberlains to leave the area and go to a motel?'

'Yes.'

'And did other people?'

'I know Mrs Whittacker urged her to go. And the bush-nurse.'

Judy West well knew the importance of all these questions. Neither of the Chamberlains had the chance or the time to slay their baby or to bury it secretly. No one who saw them when Azaria vanished thought they lacked urgency, or grief. Those suggestions arrived with the press. The one advantage she could attribute to her own experiences of sorrow and anxiety was that she knew grief when she saw it.

It seemed they had done with her now. The judge was saying she was free to go. The first five paces of her route home took her by the dock. She looked up and risked a hesitant smile. It occurred to her then that the expression in Lindy Chamberlain's eyes had not changed at all since the desperate moment of loss.

11

THE LAW DEPARTMENT had booked part of the Telford Territory Motel for prosecution witnesses. Stuart Tipple went over there to interview the family of Whittackers. He came back nervous, told Phillips and Kirkham there were problems. Max Whittacker, for all the practicality to be expected from a high-school engineering teacher, was open-hearted but hesitant, changed the direction of his recollections mid stride, and delivered what was left of them in brutally dislocated sentences. The daughter Rosalie was graceful but shy. Amy Whittacker's capacity for recall was prodigious, but excessively exact. She was a short, determined, and tough-minded woman, a much qualified nurse who had turned to professional social work. Tipple thought her a gifted observer of emotional detail, but he worried that she might be fussy and overcautious in the witness-box. There was another thing. She had looked at him as if he were some sort of mountebank. Although she was clearly a religious woman, he suspected she might not like Adventists. She seemed to him detached, distrustful.

As it turned out, Amy Whittacker was, in her stern and precise way, quite spectacular.

Of the manner in which Michael Chamberlain burst into their tent, she told Pauling, 'A man appeared in the doorway: Michael Chamberlain. He said, ''You have a Christian record

aying. What does that mean?'' After a few seconds I said,
We are Christian people.'' Michael said, ''If you are Christian
eople, can you be praying? A dingo has taken our baby, and she
 probably dead by now.'' My husband addressed a remark to
im which I didn't hear, in response to which Michael turned
nd indicated outside the tent. My husband and daughter imme-
iately grabbed torches, clothing, and ran out. Because Max and
osalie had already gone, he raised his voice to follow them out,
nd I heard him saying, ''I am a minister of the gospel.'' He
urned to me and again made some request for prayer. I assured
im I would pray, and he left the tent.'

'Did you remain in the tent for some minutes?'

'Five or six minutes,' Amy Whittacker had kept her promise
 pray. She then walked the row of tents looking for the
hamberlains'.

'Did you then approach some women in that area?'

'Yes, I saw a group of women, standing. Three, as I recall.'
he had no trouble choosing the afflicted mother. 'I simply put
y arms around her and I said, ''God is good.'' '

'Did Mrs Chamberlain say anything?'

'She said, ''Whatever happens, it is God's will.'' And then
he pulled her body back from me, and looked at me directly,
nd said, ''It says, doesn't it, that at the Second Coming, babes
ill be restored to their mothers' arms?'' '

'I took her by the arm, and I led her over to the low fence. I
at her down and sat beside her, and there was another woman
ho sat on the other side, the right side of Lindy, Judith West.'

'During the balance of the evening, you spent some time
ith Mrs Chamberlain?'

'A considerable amount.'

'Did she indicate anything about the area in which she
elieved the search should take place?'

'There was one period in the night when she was quite
gitated because she believed the searchers were not looking in
he right place. She said, ''They're not looking in the right
lace.'' These are phrases I recall, but they may not be in the
ight sequence: ''The baby is just out there, it must be out there,
nder the bushes somewhere, and they're not searching, and they
hould be looking in that area.''

'I recall something else she said: ''I will have to live with
his the rest of my life, and I don't want to think that the baby
ould've been out there and simply because we didn't look in the
ight place it would die.'' '

'Did you make a suggestion to Mr Chamberlain, followin
on the conversation?'

'I said to him, "Look, take Lindy out there and let her se
for herself that the baby is not there." '

'How long were they away?'

'Fifteen to twenty minutes.'

'What was the lighting like where they went?'

'I think there were a few car headlights, but the area int
which they went would've been pitch black. It was out in th
bush.'

This incident was of arresting interest for Phillips and Kirkhan
On the prosecution case, the Chamberlains walked into the scru
to bury their baby. Now it seemed that, at least on the first c
two occasions, they went out there at the suggestion of Am
Whittacker, who watched them set off.

Pauling asked, 'When you were comforting Mrs Chamber
lain, did she say anything to you about the dingo?'

'I recall her telling me that as she was coming across fror
the barbecue towards the tent, she saw a dingo outside th
tent-flap. I think she said she then entered the tent, looked for th
baby, and it wasn't in the bassinet. The big clothing wa
disheveled, and she thought first of all maybe the baby had falle
out, and she searched around but couldn't find it.'

'After Mr and Mrs Chamberlain had been away for the fiftee
to twenty minutes you describe, did Mrs Chamberlain sa
anything more to her husband, in your hearing, about how th
baby could have disappeared?'

'She did look up at him hopefully at one stage, and she said
"Is it possible someone could have entered the tent and taken th
baby away?" He looked down at her and said, in a gentle tone c
voice, "But what about the blood?" '

'You suggested they go to a motel for the night?'

'I had several times asked what their plans for the nigh
were, and perhaps suggested they go, but they said no. It wa
after the nursing-sister came, and she renewed attempts, tha
they agreed to go.'

'Did you assist packing up things in the tent?'

'I didn't enter the tent, but Lindy was giving me articles t
take to Michael, to pack in the car. This would be something lik
twelve-thirty to one o'clock, packing the car. I ferried article
across.'

Pauling asked if, while they were emptying the tent, she had seen the baby's bottles.

'They were in a white plastic ice-cream container,' she said, and added that she recalled another with teats.

'Was there any liquid in it?'

Yes, she remembered liquid being emptied from the bottles.

It was not easy to guess what the prosecution was up to, with this point. Barker had not, in his opening, anointed the teats or the bottles with any significance. Nevertheless, Kirkham made a note.

'Did anyone switch on the lights of the car?'

'The interior of the car was lighted.'

'How?'

'Well, I assume because the door was open.'

'The first time you noticed the door open was when you were packing up, is that so?'

'Yes. I don't recall seeing the door open at any other time.'

So well had Amy Whittacker's testimony suited the defence that there wasn't much Kirkham had to do. 'Firstly,' he said, 'did you observe a dingo in the vicinity of your tent shortly before Mr Chamberlain arrived there?'

'Yes. I was washing up with my daughter, facing towards the sand-dunes, and I saw the dingo enter under the fence, directly across from me, and it passed to my left in the outer periphery of the light.'

'In relation to the Chamberlain tent and car, can you tell us in which direction it was travelling? Was it towards them?'

'It was travelling towards them in the time it was in the circle of light, but once it went beyond the light I don't know where it went.'

'When Mr Chamberlain arrived at your tent, what was his demeanour?'

'You want my impression?' Kirkham nodded. 'My immediate impression was that he looked strange,' she said. 'He appeared to be a man rigidly controlling some emotion that he thought may have been in danger of overcoming him.'

'When you went down to speak with Mrs Chamberlain, it was with the intention of giving her what support and comfort you could?'

'I guess I was wondering if there was anything, in a professional way, that I could give.'

Because Amy Whittacker held a university degree in social work, double certificates in nursing and midwifery, and had taught nursing, Kirkham asked her, 'Are you able to recognize signs of shock in a person?'

Her answer was untainted by doubt. 'I am certainly well qualified to do that.'

'When you saw Mrs Chamberlain, did she, to your mind, exhibit signs of shock?'

'Well, she was certainly numb. And she certainly appeared to be rigid, motionless, and oblivious, to some extent, of her surroundings. Those signs would be consistent with a person in shock.'

'When you spoke with Mrs Chamberlain in the course of the evening, did she describe to you the clothing the child was wearing?'

'Yes, yes. Because she was concerned about the exposure, and saying that the baby only had on a singlet and cotton jump-suit, and an old cardigan.'

'An old cardigan?'

'An old cardigan. I recall the cardigan, because it offered to me some comfort that at least the baby had one warm garment on.'

'People did come along, on and off, most of the night whilst you were there?'

'Yes. Every time they came, there was always the hope that, maybe, this time there would be something, something certain.'

'Mr Chamberlain, on a number of occasions, approached vehicles coming up, and asked for news, is that so?'

'I saw Michael several times go towards a car. As it came down the road and stopped, he would go off to the car.'

She delivered to them with that scene the Michael she knew: dutiful, uncertain, alone. Kirkham couldn't have hoped for a better line to finish on.

12

WITNESSES WERE EXCLUDED from the courtroom, on Justice Muirhead's order, until the time came to testify.

Orders like this are issued in the hope that the witness will then give evidence without knowing anything of the testimony already offered, but when Murray Haby was called by the constable at the door, he walked in with a rounded complement of knowledge. He had kept up with the newspaper reports, and the television bulletins were full of it. This didn't matter much in Haby's circumstances because his story did not compete for veracity with anyone else's, but it made him wonder just how efficacious these lawyers thought their orders were.

The Haby family had arrived in the camping-ground at Ayers Rock about an hour before the Chamberlain baby vanished. Before setting up camp, they had eaten an evening meal in the van, lounging about the main cabin, and it was to this time that Pauling directed Haby's evidence first.

'Were you sitting with your family in the Combivan, with the door open,' he asked, 'at about eight o'clock, after you had finished your dinner?'

'We were still in the middle of the meal. While we were having the meal, a dingo came up to the van. We had the sliding door open. It came up, and I took a couple of photographs of it.' It was the opportunity of more than one which had astonished him at the time. The Habys had been on the road three months, mostly spent in the outback, and he'd expected the dingoes here to be as shy as they were everywhere else. This one had stuck around while he'd set up the camera and fired off two shots. 'It was dark,' he said, 'so I used a flash.'

'At around eight-twenty p.m. did a woman approach your Combivan?'

So far as Haby could guess, it was in this conversation that the prosecution was most interested. 'Yes. It was Mrs Chamberlain.'

'Tell the jury, please, how she approached the van.'

'She was walking fast. She said, "A dingo"—or "a dog"— "has taken my baby, have you got a torch?" She repeated something similar again because I sort of looked at her in disbelief, I suppose.' Haby remembered that disbelief vividly, and, verbatim, his thought at the time. It was: Pull the other leg, it rings out a tune. He was appalled, now, to think how close he had come to uttering it. He had suddenly seen that she was serious. 'I asked how did she know. She replied that she saw a dog, or a dingo, coming out of the tent when she was walking to the tent, and she looked in and found the baby was missing. I then said, "Did you see the dingo, the dog, carry the baby out?"'

'Did Mrs Chamberlain reply?'

'She replied, "No, it wasn't carrying anything." I asked, "Which way did the dingo go?" The one she saw.' Haby had clear recall for this, too, for he had begun to suspect by then that the dingo with the baby might not be the one the mother saw. This would make the tracking difficult. 'I'm not sure of the exact words, but she said, "Up there," or "In that direction," and she pointed up the sand-dune.'

Murray Haby had not given evidence before. He was not called at either inquest, and suspected that for some reason the evidence he could give was not popular. Beyond that, he had not thought a lot about it. But now he didn't much trust the prosecution. His wariness had come about at an interview, before evidence began, with the prosecutors. Pauling had asked him then to recount his part in the search for the baby. He described leaving Lindy Chamberlain standing on the roadway. He had headed for the dune, happening on tracks here and there, too many tracks. He guessed a fugitive animal might make for high ground, and that was the way it worked out. He found a track on the slope which looked to him fresh, and he followed. It led to a depression in the sand where something had rested. A bundle, maybe. When he plied his torch there, he caught a pattern, in clear relief. Whatever the bundle held, the material covering it was either woven or knitted. He followed the trail on, but it faded away. When he backtracked, it took him all the way to the roadside scrub near the Chamberlain tent.

In conference Pauling's response to this story was not as Murray Haby expected. Haby, a schoolteacher, had some grasp of legal ways. He knew about the adversary system in criminal courts, the just fight between antagonists, but wasn't too sure it represented a methodology he was happy with, close up.

Pauling asked him, now, to show the jury where his Combivan was parked, and Haby marked the map with a careful oblong and his initials.

'Now, Mr Haby,' Pauling said, 'you had been asked for a torch, and pointed in the direction of the sand-hill. What did you do?'

'I went back to my vehicle and got a torch, and then proceeded up the sand-dune. There were two other torch-lights flashing around on the dunes. I looked around on the lower part, and we called to each other a couple of times—had we found anything?—and the answers were no. Then I thought, Well, if there was a dog carrying something, it would have to cross the ridge of the sand-dune, so I'll go up the dune. And I went to the top of the sand-dune and walked along it until I came across some tracks.'

Here was the point beyond which he couldn't go without first deciding how much he should say. It had irked him, since the time he'd read the newspaper accounts from the inquests, that no one had bothered to report to the awaiting parents the discoveries made on the dune. And now the Chamberlains were criticized for seeming too quickly dispirited. He couldn't see that this was at all justified, and it worked on him like a fortifying anger. He decided to tell it as it happened.

'There were a lot of tracks down lower,' he said, 'but this track stood out because it was a little bigger than the others, and quite easy to follow, and came along to an area where obviously it had put something down, this dog or this dingo, and had left an imprint in the sand which, to me, looked like a knitted jumper, or a woven fabric. And then, it obviously picked it up, because it dragged a bit of sand away from the front, and kept moving. And I followed it around past the Anzac memorial, to where a car-park comes off that road to the south of the sand-dune, and lost it in the car-park.'

Murray Haby thought himself a man of moderate courage, but when Pauling told him to pause there, he wondered if he was in trouble. Instead, Pauling asked about the size of the impression in the sand.

'To use the imperial, about seven inches by five or six,' Haby guessed.

'The shape?'

'A rough oval shape, It had defined edges. There wasn't a mark as if somebody had put down this, and left a straight edge.' He held out a finger stiffly. 'It was sort of a depression like that,' he said, showing a concave palm.

'Was there the impression of anything attached to it, or not?'

'No, it was just the one oval shape. And there was a drop of something there. Something moist. Like saliva had spilt there beside it.'

*　　*　　*

The judge was interested in the location of the trail. Haby said, 'I didn't follow it back as far as I could've. I only went a little way north,' which was in the direction of the camp, 'to where it would have been directly opposite the tent.'

'Did you go and tell somebody?' Pauling asked.

'Yes. I spoke to a ranger and a policeman, and told them what I'd found, and I took them back up to the crest.'

All he could truthfully say was now said, and he felt the better for having breathed on the scales of justice a little, himself.

PART OF THE FACT, ANYWAY

THERE MUST BE AN ARGUMENT in complicated cases for sometimes presenting commutative testimony, as it might be called, allowing witnesses to speak of an event until the evidence of it is exhausted, then recalling them when it is time to speak about other happenings. The way we do it now, leading the witnesses to the stand seriatim, in a picket-line queue, puts more store by convenience than comprehension. They pass through like actors who deliver all their words during uninterrupted, lonely appearances, leaving it to the audience to reshuffle the lines into appropriate scenes. Constable Frank Morris's narrative, for example, spanned a period beginning an hour after the baby vanished and ending the day after Wally Goodwin's discovery of Azaria's clothes. This represented nine days, and it overlapped, somewhere or other, with the testimony of fifteen other witnesses.

Barker seemed anxious to bring the big, agreeable Morris quickly to the first conversation the constable had with Lindy Chamberlain. Phillips and Kirkham understood the reason well enough. The Crown said she was then in the process of fabricating a story and had not yet got it straight.

Morris said, 'Mrs Chamberlain said that, originally, she was at the barbecue site, and she'd seen a dingo near the tent. It had what appeared to be something in its mouth. She hadn't taken a great deal of notice of it because she'd seen dogs and dingoes earlier in the day, around the campsite, around the rubbish bins and tourists feeding them to get photographs, etcetera, and didn't take undue notice until she returned to the tent site a short while later, and then suddenly realized that the dingo or dog must have taken her baby. She then called out for assistance, and called out that she needed lights and torches, etcetera, so as to illuminate the area to try and locate the dingo and the baby.' Doing his best to describe the mother's demeanour, he said, 'She appeared to be weeping, upset, and one thing Mr Chamberlain did make mention of, at the time, was that he thought he should stay with his wife, under the circumstances.'

The memory the chief ranger, Derek Roff, had of a similar conversation at the Chamberlain tent was this: 'Mr Chamberlain stood behind Mrs Chamberlain with his hands on her shoulders. The pastor had said, "Our baby girl has been taken by a dingo, and we are fully reconciled to the fact that we will never see her alive again." He then asked me, "The dingo would've killed the child immediately, would it not?"' Roff asked Lindy Chamberlain what had happened, and he recalled she'd said that she had seen a dingo come out of the tent and she had been worried and gone inside, to find that the baby had disappeared. He had asked her then, 'Did you see anything in its mouth?' She had answered, 'No, the dingo wasn't carrying anything.'

Morris had returned to the tent, between searches, to check his facts. 'On this occasion,' he told the jury, 'she said that the dingo had nothing in its mouth. I said back to her, "But you made the statement earlier that the dingo had something in its mouth," believing that the woman could have been upset and could easily have made a mistake. She stated she did not recall making that statement earlier.'

Morris later came close to conceding the mistake might have been his. In cross-examination, Kirkham asked, 'You told the coroner in the first inquest that your conversation initially with Mrs Chamberlain was very brief because you were more interested in getting on with searching?'

'That's correct.'

'You also told the coroner that you could not recall exactly the conversations that occurred between you and Mrs Chamberlain?'

'Not word-perfect, no.'

But the real point was this: 'In fact, you did not make any record of these conversations until, I suggest to you, 26 August.'

'That is also correct,' Morris said.

2

DURING THE NIGHT-TIME SEARCH, Morris had been shown dingo-tracks and the marks of something dragging. 'Very shallow, as though something had barely touched the ground—the Aboriginals pointed it out—if they hadn't, I wouldn't have possibly been able to detect it with my own eyes.' Asked by Phillips if he observed any indentation in the sand 'with a weaved pattern', Morris replied simply, 'I don't recall.' Ranger Roff's memory was better. He remembered it well.

'You likened the impression you saw in the sand,' Phillips said, 'to a crepe bandage?'

'Yes, Sir.'

'Is a knitted garment equally valid, Mr Roff?'

'I think it could very well be. Yes.'

'Whatever the object was, it had some weight to it?'

'Yes, Sir.'

'The dog or dingo pad-marks associated with this drag-mark, did they run on either side of it?'

'Yes, I ascertained that the following day, really, more than that night.'

'Mr Roff, the clear inference you drew was that the object causing the drag-mark was being carried by the animal in its mouth?'

'That was the clear inference, yes. But of course, you know, it could have been an object carried by anything.'

'Did you find more than one area where the object had apparently been put down?'

The answer was a surprise. 'Yes, Sir, three areas.'

So unremitting was Barker's pursuit of the detail of the searches—and he kept Morris at it for two hours—that Phillips knew it had more to do with the requirements of drama than of logic. Then he got it. The dune had been covered 'a multitude of times' in Morris's phrase. For three days they scoured the wider landscape. The inference was this: if there was anything to see out there, they'd have seen it. So Phillips asked, in cross-examination of Derek Roff:

'Because you knew that dingoes bury their prey, you took pains, did you not, to indicate to the searchers that they should look for signs of anything having been buried?'

'Right, Sir.'

'Nothing of the sort was found in the searches you were involved in?'

'No. It was very difficult because the country, you know, was obviously torn up from tourist activities, before and during.'

'But the fact is?'

The white-bearded ranger shrugged. 'We found nothing.' The shrug meant: it's a big country.

The constable had seen tracks in the dust around the side of the tent, the right-hand side as he faced the entrance, by torch-light. The next day, while he was there with the hurriedly arrived Inspector Gilroy, he watched the inspector lift the sagging wall to uncover other prints. They were at the corner where the bassinet was. Morris described them, in answer to Kirkham, as, 'right at the very base of the tent, what appeared to be dog-tracks or dingo-tracks.'

Roff had seen one paw-print there, 'a dog-track, a dingo-track', outside the tent, he said, at 'the same corner where the baby's basket had been'. Gilroy remembered two at the entrance to the tent, and others at the rear corner, a size 'similar to, or perhaps a little smaller than one would expect from a labrador or a German shepherd'. He had them photographed, but when the negatives were developed the shots were blank. But Gilroy had caught sight of something on the tent-wall which everyone else had passed by. There was, mid-way along the right-hand panel, a stain.

Phillips asked if it was blood.

'I saw a dark spray,' he said. 'It could have been blood.'

'Where was it?'

'From memory, perhaps fifteen or sixteen inches from the ground, in the middle of the tent.'

This was, very likely, the blood which Dr Andrew Scott could not analyse for species or group. But it was, Phillips thought, useful nevertheless. It added to the defence's list of significant coincidence.

3

'MR AND MRS CHAMBERLAIN were in the office,' Morris said, speaking of the Uluru Motel office early in the morning, 'and Mr Chamberlain was making telephone calls. I heard him say something along the lines of it was God's will the baby has gone, and not to worry, they were bearing up to the situation. After he hung up I told him that we didn't have any success with the search during the night, that we had been up at first light, and that we would keep them informed of any developments. I believe he was, once again, pleased with the work the rangers and everybody was doing.' Not long afterwards, Morris had Michael Chamberlain complete the form 'Information as to Death'.

Lytle Dickenson, the licensee at the Uluru who was later to drive the Chamberlains to the camp so that Michael could take a photograph of the tent for the Adelaide *News*, was right there in the office. He remembered Michael Chamberlain was then 'calm and cool', speaking 'very clearly and precisely on the phone'. The manager, Allan Barber, knew the telephone call was to Michael's mother. Barber was there for the beginning of it. 'He said, ''Our daughter Azaria was killed by a dingo last night, and we don't ever expect to find the body.'' ' Then other calls came in, and Michael Chamberlain took one from the Melbourne *Herald*. 'Mr Chamberlain made mention of the fact that he had not taken much notice of the signs erected at Ayers Rock telling people not to feed the dingoes, and he hoped that this tragedy would make people more aware of signs, not only at Ayers Rock but elsewhere.'

Phillips and Kirkham suspected that Michael Chamberlain was more unsettled by his feeding of the dingo at the barbecue than he cared to admit. It explained his preoccupation later with warning signs and with photographs. After all, his pastoral calling was in public health and safety education, which was another piteous irony.

4

'HE SAID, ''I would like to take a photograph of the dingoes that were shot, a close-up, especially of the head and jaws, so that people could understand exactly how this could have happened.'' ' The testimony was Gilroy's. The conversation he recalled was between Michael Chamberlain and the police at the Aboriginal compound, the morning of Tuesday, 19 August. Morris and Roff were there. Morris's version was very similar. Roff creased his tanned brow, which produced only 'a vague remembrance' of the incident. Michael Chamberlain had wanted to know, as they each recalled, if it might be possible to arrange a memorial to Azaria, like the plaques which mark the deaths of others at the Rock, but no one could give him an answer. The Chamberlains were, just then, on their way home with Aidan and

Reagan. Gilroy thought their departure a perfectly reasonable decision. Morris, troubled, wasn't so sure.

5

MORRIS was not prepared to concede that, after Wally Goodwin led him through the bush to Azaria's dishevelled clothes, he had at once picked them up. 'The clothing had been tampered with by myself,' his quaint phrasing ran, 'after receiving an instruction to do so,' which came by radio-telephone from police at Alice Springs. Four studs at the top of the jump-suit were already unclasped, and he then opened the others. He arranged the jump-suit and the scattered nappy to simulate the way they were when he saw them first, and immobilized it all in photographs.

Wally Goodwin would have none of this. Two years of misinformation was, he thought, more than enough. His face got ruddy and derisive. He was having trouble holding his temper. Of Constable Morris's first sighting of the clothes Goodwin said, 'He stood and glanced at them for a few seconds, then he bent down and picked them up.' When he was asked if Morris had first made a telephone call, he answered, 'He couldn't have, because he was with me all the time.' Of the studs on the jump-suit, he clearly recollected that the entire front was open, 'and I thought part of the leg as well'. And as for the police photographs, 'They were nothing like the way the clothing was found.' In Wally Goodwin's deep belief there was nothing about the appearance of the clothes which suggested an animal had not left them there, but he guessed he wasn't permitted to say anything so relevant.

6

STUART TIPPLE was keeping a list, begun some time ago now, of the demonstrable errors in the development of the police investigation. His interest was more partisan than jurisprudential. More and more he was astonished at the way the prosecution had been able to recover from its own mistakes. By any standards, the list of errors and refuted assumptions was remarkable. How wrong the investigators were, believing the baby was dead long before nightfall, was attested by families of

Lowes, and Wests. Everyone now agreed that the parents were distraught, even disabled by grief, at the campsite. James McCombe, called by the Crown to prove that the dingo Lindy Chamberlain had seen at Maggie Springs was not like the one she described at the tent, proved equally well that the dingo was there, although this was disbelieved earlier by detectives who thought it an obvious deception. The bush-nurse, Bobbie Elston, called to prove that Michael Chamberlain drove to the motel with his camera-bag under his legs, allowed that they were driving to the motel at her insistence, although the parents had wanted to stay near the search.

The phenomenon did not end with the lay witnesses. Forensic biologists in Adelaide had been given clothes and bedding to examine for hairs, without being told that animal hairs had been taken off in Darwin and were there still. Dr Scott ran his test on the jump-suit, looking for traces of saliva, not knowing that Goodwin and Roff remembered rain falling the night before it was found, or that the baby might have worn an outer garment, a jacket. Damage to the baby's rug, assumed to be inflicted by a knife or scissors, was later found to be the work of wool-moths. No one considered that a dingo might extract a baby from a jump-suit without first opening the garment wide, until a dingo managed the feat with the carcass of a goat at the Adelaide zoo. So long was the Chamberlains' tent held at the Darwin police depot that blood sprayed along the wall could no longer be identified. Michael Chamberlain was suspected of withholding a child's parka from the investigation until it turned up in an Alice Springs police room where it had been all the time. Photographs of paw-prints at the Chamberlains' tent came out of the developing vats unhelpfully vacant and were not mentioned at the inquests. The imprint of a knitted fabric found by Murray Haby on the dune was neither photographed nor guarded, and disappeared under the tramping of feet, forgotten. And Morris's photographs were no longer of the way the clothing was on discovery, as everyone had assumed, but snapshots of the way his memory worked.

It seemed now that the Crown could not call a witness to support its present case who did not also illustrate in some way how enthusiastically wrong the prosecution had been in the past. It added up, in Tipple's view, to culpable mismanagement and an action for damages, certainly writs for defamation against press and broadcasters, once this trial was all over. Given the publicity,

it could be the biggest libel action ever. He thought it would
serve the bastards right.

7

DEREK ROFF walked out of the court-house, thoughtful. The paving was hot and glossy, the glare humbled the eyes.
His safari jacket hung open. He was pleased to be out of the
courtroom, to have finished with it all, but he was walking
slowly, as if he were not certain any longer of the right direction.

The disquiet he felt now had begun before the trial, at a
conference with Ian Barker. He liked Barker, thought him skilful
and pragmatic, a straight thinker. They were talking about the
gully in which the baby's clothing was found. Barker wanted to
know whether it was a place frequented by dingoes.

'Dingoes were there, right enough,' Roff said. 'Tracks all
over the place.' He knew of the botanist Kuchel finding *Parietaria*
fragments through the clothes. Roff wasn't much impressed by
that evidence, and decided to straighten it out before it went too
far. 'The vegetation there was crushed, where the animal had
scrubbed the garment around, just fooling about, skylarking.'

Barker shook his head. 'There wasn't any vegetation then.'

'Of course there was. Morris's snapshots will show it.'

Barker laid the photographs out on the desk. 'There,' Roff
said. The bottom corner of one print had caught a patch of green,
a dark runner, an annual of some sort. Roff tapped it with a sure
finger. 'My memory is not that bad,' he had said, smiling.

Now he was walking away from court without having uttered
a word about it. He stood at the kerbside wondering if he should
alert the defence in some way, young Tipple perhaps. Then he
wiped his mouth with the back of a hand, picked a gap in the
traffic, and crossed the road. He much preferred the candid
desert.

ENOUGH MAGNIFICATIONS TO SEE BY

1

FOR THE SUNDAY edition on 11 September Malcolm Brown had written a colour piece so that weekend readers in the south might get to know something of Darwin and the manner in which trials are administered here. For 19 September he wrote another. He latched the door, turned the air-conditioning to maximum, switched off the Musak, and wrote at the vanity table under a lighted mirror, or weighing down the edge of the bed. He was writing to inform his readers; he was writing because not every reporter could get published this way and he liked to show he could do it; he was writing for some reason unconnected with any other, some reason inaccessible to him right now, and he hoped it might come clearer as he went along.

It could Happen only at the Top End

When photographs of an Ayers Rock dingo were tendered in evidence this week, and were described as 'the dingo blown up', the jury rocked with laughter.

Selected on Monday, the nine men and three women were well presented, apparently conscientious and objective. But for a jury to break into all-out mirth? To southerners arriving in Darwin for what has been described as the Trial of the Century, it is just one instance of the jarring oddities the frontier-north has to offer.

It does seem odd that a barrister could walk into a Supreme Court with unpolished [Brown had written 'filthy' but soon discarded it] shoes, or a Crown Law officer could sport a tattoo on his biceps, or a female Court Orderly, who may be efficient and professional, could wear a dress split most of the way up her thighs. The presiding judicial figure is quiet, droll Supreme Court Judge James Henry Muirhead, who ensures punctual adjournments so he can have a hallowed cup of tea.

As Azaria's pathetic clothing was produced, Lindy Chamberlain sat expressionless, her dark eyes occasionally darting across to the bar-table, and Michael Chamberlain, quite ashen, sometimes turned away and winced. Only one friend, Mrs Irene Herron of Queensland, has come here to be with them, although their Gosford solicitor Mr Stuart Tipple is as much a friend as a lawyer. Michael Chamberlain's brother Peter, who accompanied the Chamberlains at the second inquest, is not here. At the end of that inquest he returned to New Zealand, broke down, and cried for three days.

If the couple could have taken any heart, last week, it was from the impressive performance of their barrister John Phillips QC, who vindicated his reputation as one of the best criminal lawyers in Australia.

The reference to Phillips was prompted by an incident three months before at Avondale College, while Brown was at dinner there with the Chamberlains. They were exploring the terms on which Brown might ghost a book for them, after acquittal. Phillips had just been engaged to lead the defence. It seemed that Michael Chamberlain was only then finding out how high Phillips's reputation was, and the discovery was somehow cause for dismay. 'When we are acquitted,' Michael complained, 'people will say it's because we had a smart lawyer.' Brown remembered saying, with surprising gentleness considering his astonishment, 'Just get acquitted.'

The dingo skull, used for demonstrating the dingoes' biting action, click-clacked throughout the court and looked more ghastly than ever. The humour of Ian Barker QC, leading the prosecution, who said that 'well-mannered humans don't eat that way', scarcely relieved the atmosphere.

When Brown finished, he poured a whisky from the store of miniatures in the refrigerator and read the piece through again. He was no closer to the source of his disquiet, but he knew enough about his own writing to see that his obsession lay more now with those who populated the environs of the case than it did with either of the accused.

2

THE WITNESS on the stand was Charlwood. When he gave his rank, Brown noticed a promotion. Charlwood was now a detective sergeant, first class. The 'first class' was new, but it didn't help him to look any the more comfortable. He fiddled with his fingers and smoothed his slim moustache. The jury was excluded, because Phillips was objecting to the detective's use of his notes, and this was a preliminary issue. The notes were taken from tape-recordings Charlwood had made during his conversations with Lindy Chamberlain at Mt Isa, in person and by telephone. Phillips's task was to show that Charlwood had recorded her unfairly, unlawfully, and the conversations were not relevant enough to qualify. In this country, the mere unlawfulness of recording is, alone, not enough to disqualify its use.

'You had not the slightest difficulty getting her,' Phillips asked, speaking of Lindy Chamberlain, 'to agree to come to the police station that afternoon?'

'No,' Charlwood said.

'And you entertained every belief that she would come down and talk to you?'

'Yes, my purpose in returning was to pick her up.'

'Tell me this: on that day, did you suspect she may have killed her child?'

Charlwood paused. 'No,' he said.

'That is a truthful answer, is it?'

'To your question, yes.'

'It never entered you head that she may have killed her child?' Phillips was now looking at the judge more than at the witness. Clearly Phillips thought that the secretiveness of Charlwood's recording was incompatible with the answers the detective was giving.

'I felt she may have known more about the death than she had told,' Charlwood said carefully.

'Did you feel she might be involved in a homicide in some way?'

'In some way.'

'Tell us about this tape-recorder you used at the home. Where did you have it?'

'In my pocket.'

'There was no problem at all about putting the tape recorder on the table and saying, ''Mrs Chamberlain, I want to tape this conversation so that we have a record of it.'' '

Charlwood seemed to have no immediate answer.

'No problem at all about that, was there, Mr Charlwood?'

'I never entertained the idea. Nor did I put it forward. I don't know whether there would've been a problem or not.'

'The tape-recorder remained in your pocket without any decision on your part that it should remain there, is that what you are saying? It just happened to be in your pocket?'

'No, it never ''happened to be there''. I placed it there, and I activated it, and stopped it.'

'And you activated it in a way which she would not pick up, did you not?'

'It wouldn't have particularly worried me had she.'

'Kindly answer the question you were asked. You activated it in a way that you hoped she would not pick up? Yes or no, please.'

Charlwood looked a little more defiant now. 'No,' he said.

'How long was the tape that you had in your pocket? How long would it run?'

'One side runs an hour.'

'Did you change it?'

'Yes. It was changed at some stage.'

'At the house?'

'No.'

'At the police-station?'

'Yes, the tape there was changed.'

'Where was it at the police-station?'

'From memory either on the desk, or in a drawer in the desk.'

'Are you suggesting you took it out in front of Mrs Chamberlain and changed it?'

'Whether she was there or not I do not know.'

'You tape-recorded two telephone conversations with Mrs Chamberlain, did you not?'

Charlwood agreed he had.

'Did you regard your action in taping those phone calls as being above-board?;'

'Yes. I did not have any pangs of conscience.'

'Were you in complete ignorance, do you swear to His

Honour, of any legislation relating to the taping of telephone conversations at that time?'

'At that time I was not aware of legislation.'

'You know of no act of parliament, either of the Territory or of federal parliament, which related to the taping of such conversations?' Phillips asked with some incredulity. 'Do you swear that?'

'At that time, yes.'

'You gave evidence at the first inquest?'

'Yes.'

'Did you tell the coroner in the first inquest about these secretly taped telephone conversations?' After a derisive pause, Phillips added, 'Which you regard as being completely above-board?'

'No, I don't think the subject ever came up.'

'You gave evidence at the second coronial inquiry?'

Charlwood nodded.

'Did you tell the coroner at the inquest about these secretly taped telephone conversations that you regard as being completely above-board?'

'No, not that I recall.'

'When did you first tell a lawyer connected with this case about them?'

'I haven't told a lawyer at all.' Because Phillips conveyed, by silence, that more was expected in answer to the question, Charlwood went on, 'I passed information through my superior and I believe that he passed it on.'

'You told your superior that—'

'That the record of the conversation I'd had with Mrs Chamberlain existed, yes.'

'When?'

'About a fortnight ago.'

'Did you tell the coroner at the first inquest that you had secretly taped the conversation at the home?'

'Not that I recall.'

'Now, kindly turn your mind to the second inquest,' Phillips said, finding a page in the volume of transcript. 'Were you asked this question by Mr Rice: ''Mr Charlwood, did you on any occasion at all, ever record any conversation you had with either of my clients by means of any instrument or device?'' '

Charlwood conceded he might have been asked that question.

'Did you reply: "Yes, when I say I recorded the conversation, a tape-recording was in use during some of the conversation I had with them. Unfortunately the quality of that tape was such that it was unable to be transcribed."?'

'Yes.' Charlwood was still conceding, but he wasn't conceding much. 'From memory now, we were talking about, specifically, conversations I'd had with them at Cooranbong in 1981, and that was the situation.'

'I will just reread the question to you. "Mr Charlwood, did you, on any occasion at all, ever record any conversation you had with either of my clients, by means of any instrument or device?" That is the question you were asked, is it not?'

'Yes.'

A good display though it was by Phillips, it was not enough to convince the judge that Charlwood was evasive, or had enticed Lindy Chamberlain unfairly to answers she might have considered unreflective, if she'd known they were important enough to be recorded, and the judge decided the point against the defence. As the law allowed, Charlwood could have his tape-recordings. But the glimpse this exchange had given of secrecy from the early days of the investigation, of stealth only now coming to light, illuminated for Malcolm Brown what it was that made him so unquiet writing about it. It was displacement he felt, a chill sense of foreignness. Brown had worked as a police-roundsman around Sydney a good while, but up here it was taking him a long time to work out what the local game was. The Chamberlains might simply never know what they were up against.

3

A FREELANCE REPORTER from TwoDAY-FM carried another jugful of beer back into the garden and filled the glass on the table in front of Sergeant Cocks. The other drinkers were left to pour their own. It was twilight. The garden was cool, and the mosquitoes were not yet enough to drive everybody inside to the bar. The portly Cocks looked pleased with the esteem in which he was held here. His diligent experiments, with scissors and jump-suit, had suffered in importance as soon as the prosecution engaged a textile scientist from Sydney, but Cocks was still an insider, and reporters looked on him as a possible 'source'. The relationship between press and police is often described, on both sides, as symbiotic. In media circles, symbiosis is thought of as a biological interdependence stimulated by alcohol. No one wanted to leave while there was a chance it might pay off.

Someone asked Cocks why it was the Crown, rather than the defence, which called Keyth Lenehan to the witness-stand. Lenehan, who had given evidence that day, was the Bleeding Hitchhiker. It seemed to the journalists at the table that the Crown had provided a plausible source of blood in the Chamberlains' car without getting anything in return.

'No one can say we're not fair-minded,' Cocks said. He might have believed this was the reason, but it did not represent the whole truth. It was important that the prosecution prove Lenehan's blood type, and essential that it prove he was not a sufferer of thalassaemia, an anaemia characterized by high and continuing levels of foetal haemoglobin in the bloodstream of an adult.

'So far,' the radio man said, 'all you've done is convince everybody that Lindy is innocent.' His use of her Christian name implied nothing like compassion for her, as they all understood. No one now referred to her any other way, even in newspaper headlines. 'Lindy' was a name now more familiar to the nation than the first names of footballers and tennis stars.

Talk turned to the judge. 'He was right on to that towel,' a TV reporter said.

Cocks nodded. While Lenehan was describing the fashion in which he had lain in the back of the Chamberlain car, his damaged head between the two front seats, Justice Muirhead interrupted to ask if he had been given a towel. This was the towel which later showed the presence of human blood. The Bleeding Hitchhiker had said no, no towel, but the question seemed to show that the judge was interested in following up leads like that.

Cocks said, 'Early days yet. He's a judge, he'll get there.' He wiped the beer-froth from his lip. 'All the witnesses so far might just as well have been called for the defence. But,' he said portentously, 'the tide is about to turn,' and he laid a contented hand on his belly.

4

BUT THE TIDE was still ebbing for the Crown while Myra Fogarty was on the stand. She had left the police-force soon after Denis Barritt's criticism of her in the first inquest and moved to Miami, Queensland. She had come into a modest inheritance and was now soft-haired and light-hearted. Pauling, whose witness she was, had her identify the tent, the baby's two purple blankets, and Michael Chamberlain's sleeping bag, which were the items she had examined in Darwin for blood and hairs two years before. She remembered, she said, locating blood-stains on the tent-floor, on the larger baby-blanket, and three on the sleeping bag. When she cut the stains from the sleeping bag, so she could send them to Dr Andrew Scott in Adelaide, 'feathers went everywhere,' she said, and giggled at the memory.

She had vacuumed the bag and the two blankets and sent the debris she collected that way 'down south', by which she meant the laboratories in Adelaide. The tent she shook over a paper sheet to see what fell off. In the shakings were fibres she thought were hair. She mounted them on slides and dispatched them to the Adelaide biologist Harry Harding. These fibres, as Dr Harding was scheduled to testify in three days time, proved to be five human hairs and three strands of wool.

Kirkham went gently with her in cross-examination. He thought she'd had a rough enough passage through the inquest. At the time she was ordered on to the Chamberlain case, Myra Fogarty's experience in forensic investigation was barely three months.

'I am not being critical when I ask you this, because I do not think I was a very good barrister at three months,' he said, 'but is it true that you had no training in the examination of clothing, from the forensic point of view, during those three months, apart from on-the-job inspections?'

'That is correct,' she said, and agreed she'd had no formal training in the detection of blood or the identification of hair, either.

'You were not told what sort of hair to look for?'

'No.'

'You were not looking for short, white, animal hairs?' Kirkham was making a point of this description because Dr Harding had found hairs just like that on the baby's bloodied clothing.

'No,' she said, by way of agreement.

He asked her in what manner of packaging the tent and bedding was sent to her from Alice Springs. 'In a large box, is that so?'

'That is correct.'

'You took out · the blankets and the sleeping-bag, and subsequently took out the tent?'

'Yes. Possibly a day or two later.'

Kirkham was concerned to show that there might have been any number of animal hairs overlooked in so cursory an examination. 'Miss Fogarty, there was debris from the various items left in the bottom of the box, was there not?'

'Yes.'

'Did you vacuum that up?'

She twirled a tress of her hair with a finger while she thought. 'No,' she said.

'Do you know what happened to that?'

She supposed it might be somewhere around the police-depot, still.

Looking at the jury, Kirkham said, 'A very trusting presumption.'

Evidently Myra Fogarty thought so too. 'I left the section shortly after,' she said.

'How thorough was your inspection of the tent, Miss Fogarty? Did you spend a long time looking for signs of blood on it?'

'I spent a fair amount of time looking for blood, because that was what I was told, mainly, should've been on there, but I couldn't really do as much as I wanted.'

'Do you think some spots of blood could have escaped your notice then?'

'For sure. Yes.' She shrugged. 'Like you said, I'm not trained really to look for them.'

Hoping perhaps to make up some lost ground, Pauling asked her, 'You told us you found four hairs. What did they look like?'

'Gee, they looked like human hair,' she said. 'I really couldn't tell. They looked like hair. Well, what I thought hair should look like.'

'You had no special training in distinguishing dog, cat's fur, human hair?'

'No.' She laughed. 'The only thing I did was pull a few hairs out of my own head,' which she mimicked now with tweezered fingers, 'so I knew what human hair looked like under a microscope.'

Malcolm Brown, watching this from the press-pews, thought Myra Fogarty seemed so pleased to be out of the police-force that she was never far from laughter. And he noticed that she had handled her sunglasses, throughout, as if they were some sort of sunny aide memoire, to remind her that her dutiful appearance in this court was fleeting, transitory.

5

PETER DEAN, whose responsibility it was to co-ordinate evidence about the behaviour of dingoes, had not been able to locate the family of holidaymakers at Ayers Rock from whose car a dingo had dragged their three-year-old daughter. The incident was important for two reasons: it had happened only a few weeks before Azaria Chamberlain vanished, and the dingo had gripped the child by her neck. Ranger Ian Cawood was the investigating officer but until recently was out of the country. When he got back, he told Peter Dean that there was no record of the family's name or address.

So Phillips made application to the judge for permission to advertise, in the newspapers, a plea that the family contact the law department. It took Justice Muirhead only a few minutes to dismiss the application, but while he was talking it through he said, 'There is an abundance of evidence as to dingoes, their capacity to get very friendly, and to get very vicious. To go into rooms, and to go into tents, and upset rubbish bins and behave like pests. It seems that the jury will have to approach this case knowing that.' Of the capacity of a dingo to carry off a baby he said, 'It is not like saying it could not happen, or it does not happen. The evidence is entirely the reverse in this case.' Phillips did not press it further. The way he heard it, he was being told that, when the time came for the judge to direct the jury, this was a point the defence wouldn't need to worry about.

6

BARKER WAS ABOUT TO TENDER, as evidence against the Chamberlains, their testimony at the Galvin inquest. In the normal course of things, the transcript would be handed up to the bench and that way become part of the Crown case. Phillips and Kirkham wanted to block it. They both recalled Barker's opening address to the jury, in which he'd said, 'It would not be fair to closely and critically analyse everything said by somebody obviously under stress,' but neither of them believed he meant this stone-literally. Barker was too tough to pass up an opportunity to score, and the more the Chamberlains had talked, the more scoring-points there were. The defence would have had an easy time of it, Kirkham thought, if the Chamberlains were criminals, tight-lipped and case-hardened.

It was a difficult application for Phillips to make without sounding too critical of the coroner, Gerry Galvin. But the point he must make was that Galvin had allowed the Crown to summon the Chamberlains for public interrogation while taking steps to make sure that they did not find out, in the meantime, what the case against them was. There were not too many ways to beautify that procedure.

'Could not your clients,' Justice Muirhead asked Phillips, 'have said, ''Well, under those circumstances we are not going to wander in a maze, and we decline to give any further evidence on the ground that it might tend to incriminate us?'' There was that opportunity.'

'I say there wasn't, Your Honour. Because one just has to reflect back on the utterly unique way this proceeding was carried out with the publicity.'

'Do you say that the matters which would properly concern counsel in that situation would perhaps be almost peculiar to this particular case?'

'Yes,' Phillips said.

'In view of the prejudice, the conclusions that may be drawn by refusal to give evidence?'

'The potential consequences to their clients, of taking such a public course, may have been irreparable.'

Barker, over two and a quarter vigorous hours, argued that Galvin had acted lawfully and, because the Chamberlains could have taken early refuge in silence, their testimony was now admissible. In the event, Justice Muirhead did not disagree with that, but judges, in criminal trials, have a discretion to exclude admissible, but unfair, evidence. Of the Galvin inquest he said, 'As matters turned out, the general rules of evidence were substantially adhered to, save perhaps that counsel assisting the coroner, in examining the accused, did so forcibly and at times inquisitorially. But it was done according to law. At this time, the accused were the focus of national interest and national curiosity. Counsel involved in the inquest must well have known the extent of that interest. In looking to the future, the possibility of prejudice to their clients by a refusal to answer further questions, about a largely unknown subject matter, was a very real, albeit almost a novel, consideration: What were the prospects of their clients receiving a fair trial, by an unprejudiced jury in the Northern Territory, according to law?'

That about sums it up, Kirkham thought. When the judge ruled the testimony out, Kirkham whispered to Phillips, 'Well done.' It was not only the triumph which made him feel good, it was something closer to retribution. He hadn't been able to think about the way that inquest was conducted without it causing him a fresh reddening of anger.

7

IN THE MEDIA-ROOM next door, newswriters were unhappy with the amount of available copy. The legal argument was unreportable, not only because it was inexplicable in the column-space or the air-time these journalists had to work with, but because Justice Muirhead had prohibited publication in case the jury came to hear about it that way, off duty. So the journalists could report only the evidence, and the way Prosecutor Barker had ordered the witness-list was making the reporting task difficult. As Dudley Doust, the American-born correspondent for the London *Sunday Times*, put it, the prosecution had reached 'the middle-order batsmen', who were there to 'dig in and consolidate'. Doust liked sporting terms because he was normally a cricket-writer. He was referring now to those witnesses who might not do the prosecution much harm if they failed to score. Doust's metaphor was troublesome, as Malcolm Brown saw things, because it implied tailenders to follow. This, on any view, was not the case. Brown, who had once hoped to pummel his way to a career in prize-fighting until a horrified promoter eased him out of it early, preferred the language of the ring. They were watching, Brown said, 'the preliminary bouts'. He meant it didn't matter a great deal who won them.

The defence was clearly not so troubled now by Dr Harding's evidence that hairs found on the baby's bedding were cat more probably than dingo, since he was even-handed enough to allow both possibilities and, anyway, Myra Fogarty had shown just how little care was taken to preserve anything passing through her untutored and vigorous hands. The gingery dentist, Kenneth

Brown, whose nervousness in the witness-box was betrayed by repetitious clenching of the eyes, conceded that some of the damage to Azaria's singlet might have been caused by the teeth of a dingo. In any event it was he who had attributed, to some manner of blade, marks in the baby's blanket which were caused by moths, and the press, at least, found it hard to take the rest of his evidence to heart anymore. The soil analyst, Torlach, who, in his slow campfire voice, likened the sand in the baby's clothes to sand he dug near the campsite, on the sand-dune, and near the ranger's dwelling, didn't enhance the logic of the investigation. All those areas were searched so often for signs of digging that it seemed impossible the body had been interred there, either by a dingo or by a grave-digging Chamberlain, without discovery. Dr Andrew Scott's identification of blood on bedding and garments suited the defence as much as it did the prosecution. The absence, during testing, of saliva on the damaged jump-suit was nowhere near so forceful if the child had been wearing another outer garment, or the clothing had been rained upon.

As the evidence was coming through, some favouring the prosecution case and some the defence, it made for tricky reporting. Not uncommonly, a journalist will sit through thirty thousand words during a day in court and must trim that down to four hundred. A precis exercise of that heroic magnitude requires the reporter to decide which way the story ought to be slanted. Many choose to weight it in favour of the party calling the witness, prosecution or defence. Hard decisions of this nature cause competing journalists to criticize each other roundly. One argument like this was settled in the media-room with the words: 'We're supposed to be reporting the prosecution case, right?'

8

FRIDAY NIGHT. Brown had more than enough copy.

Michael Chamberlain Ill after Bloodstain Evidence
Michael Chamberlain was suddenly taken ill in the Northern Territory Supreme Court yesterday as a forensic expert gave evidence about bloodstains on the jump-suit of his daughter Azaria.

Near the close of yesterday's hearing, Dr Andrew Scott, a forensic biologist from Adelaide, was describing patterns of blood.

Dr Scott said he believed the blood flowed heavily from the neck downwards, and had soaked through the singlet.

Mr Ian Barker, QC, for the Crown, then asked what blood related to a hole in the left sleeve of the jump-suit, and Dr Scott indicated a stain. Suddenly Mr John Phillips, QC, for the Chamberlains, rose and said, 'Mr Chamberlain is not feeling well.'

Mr Chamberlain, who had sat for two weeks revealing little emotion, slumped forward in his seat, bending over his knees. Justice Muirhead adjourned the hearing until Monday. Mrs Chamberlain rose from her seat and stood by her husband as two correctional services officers approached. They then left with the officers through a side door of the court.

Earlier, Detective-Sergeant Barry Cocks gave evidence of tests he had conducted with scissors on a baby's jump-suit. Sergeant Cocks said that if he cut the jump-suit in a particular way, using curved scissors similar to the pair found in the Chamberlain car, he could obtain the same incisions as appeared on Azaria's jump-suit. He had tried to reproduce the incisions using a scalpel and a razor blade, but had been unable to obtain the same result. Sergeant Cocks said he considered scissors the most probable implement to have made the incisions. He also found that, cutting a jump-suit, he could produce tufts and loops of material similar to those found in the Chamberlain car and in Michael Chamberlain's camera-case.

Brown phoned it through to Sydney, leaning back then on his bed holding a tumbler of whisky. Fashioning the piece had taken him three laborious hours. It was not the writing, for he was a fast writer, but the choice of material which took the time. The space to which he was restricted had never seemed so tight. There was plenty of rich incident in Phillips's cross-examination of Cocks, for example, which, if the piece were longer, produced an entirely different result for the reader.

Phillips first question was, 'Sergeant Cocks, do you consider yourself an accurate person in your duties, including the giving of evidence?'

'Yes,' Cocks said, adding by way of credentials, 'I would have to be, to perform the type of work that I perform.'

'Do you consider you have a proper, scientific approach to your duties?'

Cocks agreed without hesitation.

It was the sergeant's opinion that fibres through the collar and sleeve of the baby's jump-suit were severed by cuts, rather than by tearing. 'These were all consistent with having been cut,' he said confidently, and it was to the word 'all' that Phillips now directed him.

'Is the sentence you included in your statement for the first inquest correct: 'I examined the fibres under a microscope and observed that the majority were cut, not frayed or torn''?'

'Yes,' Cocks said. Explaining the shortfall between majority and totality, he offered, 'The cut in the collar, the fibres that I could examine, had straight-cut edges. That was my opinion back in 1980, and again today.'

'Are you saying, now, you could not examine all the fibres in the collar?'

'Some of the fibres have withdrawn back in,' Cocks said, meaning back into the weave. 'The fibres that I could examine were distinctly cut.'

'Are you saying, now, you could not examine all the fibres in the collar?' Phillips repeated, pursuing the point because withdrawal of fibre into the weave is also a characteristic of tearing. 'Yes or no.'

'That is correct.'

'Do you not think you should have made that clear to the jury?'

Cocks thought about it. 'Possibly yes, on reflection,' he said.

'With people on trial for murder,' Phillips said, not requiring an answer, his voice tight, angry.

'Is there anything you would like to tell us, in the interests of fairness, about these loops you found in the camera-bag, Mr Cocks?' Phillips was talking about tufts of cut cotton which, in the sergeant's view, came from a baby's jump-suit. 'Anything you would like to add to your evidence?'

'No,' Cocks shrugged.

'Nothing that strikes you as important?'

Cocks couldn't think of anything.

'Did they have any indication of blood on them?' Phillips said, helping him out.

'No.'

'What about the loops that came from the car? Would you like to add anything to your evidence about those?'

The line of questioning did nothing, evidently, to give Cocks the clue he needed. 'No.'

'Any indication of blood on them?'

'No.'

'Did you test them?'

'No.'

Surprised by this answer, Phillips reached for a volume of transcript. 'You were asked about the loops from the vacuuming, at the second inquest, were you not?'

This jogged the sergeant's memory enough to have him recall examining all the loops from the camera-bag and the car for 'any vestige of blood' and finding none. He remembered testifying at the inquest that he'd found nothing which gave the 'reaction to blood'.

It was this phrase 'reaction to blood' which interested Phillips. All attempts to prove the presence of blood inside the camera-case had failed, but the prosecution still insisted it had once held the dead infant or its cerements. The loops which were found in there were important, particularly if they were unstained, bloodless. So he asked again, 'Did you test them for blood?'

'No, I'm not an expert in testing for blood.'

'How were you able to give that evidence?' Phillips was referring to the evocative term 'reaction' again now.

'Under a microscope you can see the appearance of blood, and I did not see any trace of any blood. Therefore I gave the reply, ''I could not see any blood on any of the loops and fibres, or threads or tufts, that I'd removed from the car or the bag.'' '

Phillips brought his hand down hard on the table. 'That is not what you swore at the inquest at all, Mr Cocks. What you swore was,' and he opened the volume again, ' ''Nothing that gave the reaction to blood.'' And, ''They didn't give a reaction, that is the point.'' That is what you swore.'

The sergeant played with his necktie, as he had done throughout, while he was thinking. He tucked the fall behind his belt buckle. 'Then what I said at the inquest, if that is how it was recorded, is inaccurate,' he said.

'It is not the first time you have given inaccurate evidence in your career, is it, Mr Cocks?' Phillips said softly.

'I don't consider that I've ever given what I'd call inaccurate.'

'Do you remember a case of Van Beelen?'

Sergeant Cocks remembered that case, as did several of the reporters in the gallery. Van Beelen was tried in Adelaide for the seaside murder of a schoolgirl in 1971. Cocks was on the scientific investigation team. He was then specializing in the identification of hair. Strands identified by Sergeant Cocks as

characteristic of Van Beelen's hair connected Van Beelen with
the slaying. Cocks had committed enough mistakes in the course
of his scientific labours that the state's chief justice, sitting on
appeal, bothered only to list a few and then referred to them as
'these and other errors'. The case was sent back for retrial.

Now Phillips wanted the jury to know about it, in detail.
'You gave sworn evidence, didn't you, of the thickness of some
hairs?'

Cocks conceded he had.

'And you gave three times the correct thickness, in your
sworn evidence.'

'I gave evidence three times of an incorrect measurement.'
While this was an admirable deflection of the attack, it wasn't
the truth. 'You didn't give evidence three times,' Phillips said
with increasing volume. 'I suggest you gave evidence of three
times the correct measurement. Triple what it should have been.'

The sergeant confessed it was so.

'In that case, did you produce slides and photographs?'

'Yes.'

'Your evidence was wrong, was it not?'

'There was evidence that some of the photographs had been
mixed up, and were in the wrong place, yes.'

Phillips repeated the question slowly, as if instructing a child.
'Was your evidence wrong?'

'Yes.'

'Did you also swear in that case that a sample of hair came
from a red and black jumper, when in fact it came from the
accused's head?'

Cocks could not remember that one.

'In the same case, did you swear that a particular exhibit
contained a number of slides of dog hair?'

'Yes.'

'In fact, it contained a combination of dog hair and human
hair.'

Cocks scratched at his head, but the association did nothing
for his memory. He could not recall confusing the hair of a dog
with human hair. Phillips let the topic go. He'd done enough
damage.

'I want to ask you about this vegetation material you
said you saw,' Phillips said, referring fragments of leaf which

Cocks and the botanist, Kuchel, had picked from the baby's clothing. 'You swore it was of a broad-leafed plant?'

'Yes.'

'Embedded in the fibre?'

'Yes.'

'You talked about "a lot of other material",' Phillips said, lingering on the phrase, emphasizing quantity. 'Green, broad-leafed material.' He turned to Barker. 'I call for that material to be produced.'

'It is produced,' Barker said, as a clerk laid three vials on the table. This was the first time the prosecution had produced them.

Phillips held them aloft. Here was the debris which had convinced Cocks and Kuchel that someone had 'deliberately and forcefully' rubbed the clothing in *Paretaria debilis*, to counterfeit dragging and rough usage.

'This is how much was involved?'

'Yes,' said Cocks.

The quantity in any of the vials wouldn't have covered a fingernail.

Barker took the point fast. 'Your Honour, I would like to say of these exhibits that my attention was drawn to them, and I intended to produce them. I showed them to Mr Phillips.'

'I accept that Mr Barker had not seen them when this witness was giving evidence,' Phillips said pleasantly, and went on passing the vials up to the jury.

Brown could fit none of these exchanges into his copy. He knew that not one of the other dailies would run them either. The readers of newspapers had nothing on which to judge the reliability of the testimony they were reading about. They could only assume that evidence like Cocks's went through unscathed. This raised questions of newspaper philosophy which Brown didn't enjoy mulling over. And here was another curious thing. Outside the adjourned courtroom, he could find no other journalist who thought Phillips had diminished Cocks in any way. Brown had shaken his head and walked away.

The telephone rang, and he rolled over on the bed to reach it. The call was from his wife Inga, in Sydney. 'How is it going?' she asked.

'I don't know,' he said. 'I can't judge things like that anymore.'

9

CHAIKIN, THE PROFESSOR, was a great performer. He walked to a table near the witness-stand on busy and resolute feet, so not to lose anyone's attention for a moment. It was time for him to demonstrate to the jury what happens when fabric is cut with scissors. An orderly handed him a square of black cloth. He already held a spare jump-suit in hand. Scissors were somewhere in his pocket. He wanted to show, now, that a Bond's jump-suit cut by these scissors would dislodge tiny loops of towelling, like those found in the Chamberlain car and in the camera-case.

He smoothed the cloth over a board on the table. It was a satin square, a profound blackness, like the boards conjurors use to show off their glittering tricks to best advantage. He shot back the cuffs of his shirt as if to show nothing was hidden there. He held up the garment, turning it this way and that. It was entire. He produced the scissors. Professor Chaikin had been away from the United States a long time, but his voice still belonged to New York, and now it seemed that he might be just as happy busking a routine like this on a sidewalk somewhere off Broadway, alert to any sign of the cop on the beat. 'If you take this fabric and cut it,' he said, and the scissors flashed, 'some fall off and that is—' He shook the garment once, twice, 'there.'

Tufts feel like stardust.

The laughter which followed was confined to the media room, where the journalists were watching the show on video. Chaikin flourished a hand, triumphant, and the audience here broke into applause. They were as delighted as he was. 'The Great Chaikin', said someone. Sergeant Cocks, who was following the evidence from a seat here rather than in the courtroom, thumped his thigh was a fist. 'There's no one like him,' he said, grinning. 'Just no one.'

10

THE PROFESSOR held the chair of textile technology at the University of New South Wales. He was a small talkative man with troublesome wavy hair and such enthusiasm for work that, as was often said around the textile school, anyone else would tire of a problem long before he did.

In October 1981 two policemen called to see him. They were Sergeant Cocks and Constable Metcalf. They brought with them Azaria Chamberlain's clothing, damaged and bloodied, a stained towel, and a small blanket. The visit was no surprise. Chaikin was often consulted by police investigators in celebrated cases. Cocks spread the infant's jump-suit and the singlet over a bench. 'The central question is,' Cocks said, 'whether these holes are cuts or tears, and how they were produced.'

Two ancilliary issues, how the slim incisions in the blanket were caused and what sort of action had stained the towel, were quickly resolved. The eye of a microscope found, in the fibre of the blanket, the same larval casings which Dr Andrew Scott had discovered some time ago. 'These are not cuts,' the professor said. 'Insects caused that.' On the towel, most of the bloodstain capped only the elevations of the pile, and very little ran deeper in the weave. Something had been wiped on the cloth, but the professor could not determine what it was. Sergeant Cocks was interested, for some reason, to know if it might have been the blade of a knife. 'Sure,' the professor said, 'I don't see anything inconsistent with that, anyway.'

He ordered a supply of Bond's jump-suits and singlets and, when they arrived, got down to the business of identifying the characteristics of damage. He was familiar with the weave from which the jump-suit was fashioned. Shopkeepers called it towelling. Nylon yarn formed the base and cotton the loops. It was the cotton loop, fed loosely into the loom during manufacture, which made up the pile.

Cotton is not as elastic a thread as is nylon, and here was the first problem. The commonest distinction between a cut and a tear is this: a cut severs the threads leaving the ends in position, a tear pulls the ends out of alignment. But here, the nylon was both elastic and under tension, while the cotton was inert and loose. The nylon might withdraw, however precisely the cloth was cut. So the professor took to the weave with scissors and, under a microscope, watched the nylon thread migrate through the weave.

He took the problem to the next level of magnification. Since the disparity between threads caused a reaction all its own, it seemed to follow that he should choose a plane at which he could compare nylon with nylon, or cotton with cotton. A single thread is made up of fibres, much the way a rope is. If he magnified a nylon thread, say, enough that he could see each component fibre, he should be able to judge the precision of alignment and distinguish a cut from a tear that way.

The magnifications of which he was thinking were in the order of a thousand or so, beyond the range of optical microscopes and well into the realm of the electron. He teased, from the damaged shoulder of the Chamberlain jump-suit, the fibres he wished to examine and mounted them on a stub. His laboratories were well furnished with imported transmission microscopes, which shower the examined substance with electrons and display the picture on television screens, but they have trouble seeing materials which absorb moisture, unless the materials are plated with gold and held in a vacuum. Coating these fibres would deform the ends he needed to look at. So he chose for this job an instrument developed here in his department, a scanning microscope, which used a back-scatter of electrons to get around the moisture problem.

The picture Chaikin had on his screen looked like a jungle. He searched through the turmoil of fibres horizontally, vertically. Altering the focus gave the pleasing illusion of strolling forward. Some of these fibres were aligned, some not. There was nothing conclusive here. It was not until he replaced the fibres from the shoulder with a stub taken from the collar that he found what he was looking for. The fibres were, as he recorded in his notes, 'pretty much in a plane.' More important, here was a single fibre on which the end was clean, abrupt. To his mind this was 'a classic nylon cut'. And his bet was scissors.

He photographed the picture on the screen before he touched the controls. Such was the confusion in this minute territory that he might never find the locality again.

The cotton singlet gave him trouble. The weave was ribbed, good for stretching around a fattening infant, but difficult to pierce with an implement, however sharp. The weave gave, unless the cloth was under quite considerable tension. A dingo's tooth, which he mounted on a mechanical arm, pecked away like a weary ibis but had no success at all. He filled the singlet with the carcass of a freshly skinned rabbit. The skin ruptured under the tooth, but he could find no damage to the singlet. He stretched the fabric more tightly over the flesh, and only then did the tooth penetrate the pliant and hardy weave.

Later in October the detectives delivered another problem, together with several bottles containing cotton tufts, to the professor's laboratory. Twenty-five tufts were, as his instructions ran, found in the Chamberlain car. Three others were taken from Michael Chamberlain's camera-case. He was asked if he could match any to the baby's jump-suit.

Under the optical microscope, they looked like fragments of cotton yarn. He snipped through a section of jump-suit cloth and was rewarded with enough cotton tufts to convince him that he was on the right track.

The tufts the detectives had sent him seemed, at thirty magnifications, to approximate the right size and shape, but he needed a tighter grid of comparison. He decided on three tests: fibre diameter, number of fibres in each thread, and evidence of twist. Three tufts from the camera-case plainly qualified. Of those from the car, he was satisfied that five could have come from the Chamberlain garment. Among the twenty rejects, some were partly synthetic, a possibility he had not thought likely earlier. These must have come from another material altogether.

Following the line of reasoning through, it occurred to the professor that he might find severed tufts at the sites of damage on the baby's suit, imprisoned by the weave. He picked over the threads with a pair of tweezers. They were here, all right.

His work had shown another complication. New garments shed tufts of cotton, mostly from the seams, in the ordinary course of handling. It was a normal product of manufacture. How sinister, then, was their appearance throughout the car? Or in a camera-case? The arrival of a further twenty-five tufts, from the Darwin police department, seemed to highlight the point. He could classify only one of these as the sort of fragment he might expect from a Bond's jump-suit. There was certainly a lot of tufts around. An uneasy excess of fortune.

On 5 January the biologist Joy Kuhl had arrived at the laboratory. She brought with her Michael Chamberlain's camera-case. The professor led the way to a bench and set down the bag under an adjustable lamp. He laid back the lid. The interior was divided into compartments. He pushed back the walls, letting the light fall in. There was no debris here, but this was no surprise because the bag was vacuumed elsewhere, perhaps more than once.

The professor was looking for hair. He could see fibres, which clung to the surfaces of each compartment, and lifted off with forceps as many as he could find. More came away when he patted the sides with strips of stationers' adhesive-tape. He discarded those strands which were, even to the unassisted eye, vegetable. The remainder he took to the scanning microscope.

The picture on the screen panned over crimped wool, more vegetable fibres, and hair. Hair viewed this way looked curiously metallic, like poles armoured with plate. There was a good deal of hair from the bag, but he couldn't see what helpful inference could be drawn from this. Judging by length and diameter, half the hairs were adult.

He found six he thought infantile. Three he had taken from the middle compartment in the bag, the others from smaller pockets in there. They were smooth-scaled and slim, around a centimetre long, and the taper showed they had never been cut. And there was another reliable distinction: the hair from an infant is cellular all the way through. It lacks the medullar, the hollowness, of adult hair.

Two others showed signs of much washing. He pointed them out to Joy Kuhl, jabbing a finger at the screen, where the edges of the scales, 'here and here', were jagged and agape, characteristics which set them apart from their fellows. He discarded them. Mrs Kuhl suspected the bag was washed inside and out, but this seemed to him unlikely. The other fibres there showed no mark of it at all.

The final assessment, colour, was back in the demesne of the optical. Four strands he described as 'a light straw-yellow', one 'light yellow-brown', another 'mid to dark brown'. The real question was: had he detected enough similarities to link all six with the same infant?

Sturgess, leading the professor through his evidence now, put the question this way: 'Do you get variations in colour when looking at hair from the one individual?'

'That can happen. But in respect to that question,' Chaikin

said, frowning, 'I would not be able to say that all this hair came from the same head.'

11

'ALL ROADS lead to Chaikin,' Tipple had said, explaining his failure to find anyone else so well qualified. So Phillips knew that whatever the defence needed to fortify its case he must get from this witness, now.

'Professor, if I could ask you about your examination of the camera-bag first please.'

'Certainly.'

'We propose to call evidence that the bag was not a new bag in the hands of the Chamberlains. It had been previously owned by another family. When the Chamberlains had it, it was not used exclusively as a camera-bag but was used for family excursions, and so forth, putting clothing and that sort of thing in it. In those circumstances, do you find it at all surprising that you found baby hair in the bag?'

'Well, I'd rather not comment on that. All I know is that there was baby hair in the bag. I wouldn't know how it got there.'

'Could you indicate just how many hairs a baby might lose in a day?'

The professor consulted his notes. 'On the average baby there are fifty or sixty thousand. Babies start shedding at different times, so one cannot come to any definite conclusions. But when they start falling out, they fall out in large numbers. It can be measured in hundreds of fibres a day.'

'Even at one hundred a day, according to my indifferent mathematics, this baby would have had the potential to lose seven thousand in its short life? In nine and a half weeks?'

'On the average, it could be calculated that way.'

'Professor, reference has been made to the apparently washed appearance of some of the fibres. Does that relate, in any way, to the possible washing of the bag?'

Chaikin shook his head. 'I wouldn't have thought so.'

'Can I now ask you to turn your mind to the napkin? You said this: "As far as the nappy is concerned, there were several indents and one tear when I saw it, and the material is a soft plastic, and I simply came to the conclusion that any method which involved the pushing of a slightly pointed object into the plastic would have caused those, and that's all I could conclude." Is that right, Professor?'

'That is correct.'

'You are certainly not prepared to exclude that damage as being possibly caused by a dingo's tooth or claws, are you?'

'I could not. No.'

The judge took the point. 'You could not exclude that?'

'I could not,' the professor repeated. 'No.'

'We are told that Professor Cameron, from England, will be giving evidence, and he will offer the view that, if a dingo were to have taken hold of this child by the neck, with the jump-suit collar up—so that the fabric of the collar is between the child's flesh and the dingo's tooth—that would involve the infliction of damage onto the collar.' Phillips paused, allowing Chaikin time to assemble the image in his mind. 'Do you follow that proposition, Professor?'

Testily, the professor said, 'I follow it.'

'Your experiments would very strongly run against that proposition, wouldn't they?' Phillips had in mind Chaikin's work with dingo teeth, rabbit flesh, and cloth.

'My experiments would tend to indicate that the proposition would not necessarily follow.'

Phillips said, 'In fact, your experiments show that, not only could a tooth press against a child's flesh, but penetrate it for some distance, and still not cause damage to the jump-suit or the singlet.'

'Obviously when it was being held, there would be an indentation, but subsequently that fabric would recover.'

'Exactly.'

'Mr Sturgess made the point, with your electron-microscopy, that you did not examine every fibre end. You agreed with that?'

The professor agreed again now.

'On the other hand, what you did, Professor, was to zero in on any end which looked like a cut, did you not?'

'We scanned the cut, and wherever it looked as if we could take a reasonable picture of either a bunch of fibres coming

together, or of an individual fibre that looked like it had a sharp
end, we looked at those, yes.'

'You picked the best of the crop.'

'I wouldn't put it that way. I mean, I picked those where we
could get a photograph which I believed exhibited the state of the
yarns and the fibres along the edge.'

'You ended up with one,' Phillips said slowly, 'which had a
classic appearance of being cut.'

'That is correct,' Chaikin said, bluntly, disdaining evasion.

'Professor, you voiced a conclusion that for the holes
you observed in the singlet to have been made, there would have
to have been some tension in the garment, is that right?'

'Yes. If the garment was held, and there was a continuous
pushing into the fabric, this would then create the tension.
Alternatively, you could hold it apart, and then there would be
less extension required for you to get to the breaking-point.'

'Or an animal could create the tension by holding part of the
garment with its paw or paws, for example, and the other part
with its teeth?'

'I wouldn't exclude that.'

'If a child wore a new suit without it being washed, the
potential is there for tufts to fall from it, is it not?'

'Correct.'

'How many loops would be produced from a new suit,
Professor? Quite a few?'

'In manufacturing a new jump-suit, some loops would fall
off, some would be loosely held, and some would be tightly
held. On the average, for every inch of cut, about fifteen loops
would fall off, ten or fifteen.'

'Is it fair comment to say that a new suit would probably
have quite a few cut loops? As distinct from one or two?'

'Oh, yes.'

As Phillips judged things, there now remained only one
item on which the professor's evidence was inarguably damaging
to the defence: the single 'classic nylon cut' of a fibre at the
collar of the baby's jump-suit.

'In stating the opinion that you have—that it was not a
dingo's tooth that produced the damage—you do that without
ever seeing a live dingo bite anything, don't you?'

'That's correct.'

'Without ever having examined the clothing of a person who has been bitten by a dingo?'

'I have, as I said, carried out experiments with dingo teeth on this particular fabric.'

'Will you please answer my question. You state that opinion without ever having examined the clothing of a person who has been bitten by a dingo?'

'That's correct.'

'We propose to call evidence that a dingo is capable of biting through metal, like a chain.'

'I certainly wouldn't dispute that,' the professor said, 'because I have never experimented with dingoes biting through metal. But may I say this, that has absolutely no relevance to whether a dingo could bite through these nylon fibres.'

Phillips didn't press the argument. At best it was 'a jury-point,' as lawyers say. The hope is that juries prefer the practical to the theoretical, when the time for decision comes. Phillips sat down. He'd done better, overall, than he'd thought he might. He couldn't expect his luck to hold forever.

12

EVERY NEWSWRITER is afflicted with the need for brevity, and the trick for a radio-reporter is writing something not much longer than a telegram, retouching it on air with the colours of the voice. 'Exaggerate the inflections more,' Murray Nicoll said. 'So much that you'd be ashamed to hear yourself talk like that anywhere else.' He was instructing Tracy Bowden, his partner. Bowden was suffering an unusual lapse of confidence. She was a good voice-reporter, a fact everyone knew, it seemed, but herself. Her delivery was at the one time serious and melodious, which precisely reflected the sort of woman she was. 'Just keep going over the top,' Nicoll said.

They worked for the Macquarie network, Bowden for Sydney, Nicoll for Adelaide. The normal run of bulletins called for reports and up-dates during the day, each around thirty seconds' broadcast time. These they covered separately, using the telephone link between the media-room and their home-state studios.

The evening bulletins allowed time for much longer reviews. Bowden and Nicoll made them together, alternating voices. They called them duets. The performance required lower background noise than the busy media room allowed, so Nicoll converted one side of his bedroom at the Darwin Hotel into a studio. By six o'clock any evening, the array on the vanity bench comprised a tray of electrical cables, switches and relays, a stack of shorthand notebooks, a typewriter, a completed script of about three hundred and fifty words, a partly consumed six-pack of beer, two microphones, a tape-recorder, and an amplifier. A cable from the amplifer was taped with adhesive strip along the wall, left the room through the gills of the air-conditioner, leapt to the crown of a palm tree, skirted the swimming-pool by way of a tall lattice, and made the footpath outside where it disappeared into a plug. From here the signal journeyed more legitimately to capital cities on the eastern and southern seaboards under an arrangement between the Telecom authority and the Macquarie network, which Nicoll didn't have to worry about.

Into a microphone Nicoll said, 'Murray Nicoll here. Anyone alive out there?'

The first voice through the speaker said, 'Sydney here.'

'And Melbourne, Murray.'

After a pause Nicoll said, '4BH is tied up with the Games, huh?' The City of Brisbane was then hosting the Commonwealth Games carnival. There was no answer.

'Adelaide?' he asked. 'Bugger it, Adelaide?' 5DN Adelaide was Nicoll's home-station.

'We're here,' Adelaide said. 'Don't get your beard in a knot.' This cheap shot was accurate enough. Nicoll's slatey beard had a hard time of it whenever he was agitated.

'Brisbane here. We need thirty seconds.'

'Give you thirty,' Nicoll agreed.

Brisbane didn't need that long. 'BH is rolling now.' Other studios said they were rolling too, meaning that from here on Nicoll and Bowden were on tape there.

'Roger, stations. Here is your intro.' This was to be the introduction used by the studio newsbroadcaster as a lead-in. 'In the Darwin Supreme Court today, Sydney textile and forensic scientist Professor Malcolm Chaikin gave evidence in the Chamberlain murder trial.'

He allowed a few seconds blank space. 'Okay, here we go. Five, four, three, two, one: ''The professor, head of the textile sciences department at the University of New South Wales, said he had examined the clothing worn by the abducted baby under a high-powered electronmicroscope. In his opinion, damage to the material could not have been caused by a dingo. The professor believed the fabric was cut with an instrument, most probably by sharp scissors." '

Tracy Bowden came in on cue. 'The court-house—sorry, sorry, coming again. Take two, from "scissors". Three, two, one: The courtroom was in near darkness during what was virtually a lecture illustrated with projected slides, showing the cotton and nylon weave from which the clothing was made. He showed the jury a photograph of the one fibre which he described as a classic nylon cut.'

This time the performance ran the full script. By the end, Nicoll's stopwatch showed two minutes fifty.

'This is Murray Nicoll,'

'And Tracy Bowden,'

'For Macquarie National News, Darwin. Okay playmates, that's it'.

'4BH. Got it.'

Melbourne said, 'Thanks,' and Sydney said, 'Goodnight.'

5DN Adelaide stayed on. 'Murray, it seems from this far away that the prosecution is pushing it uphill. One cut fibre, you know? Can they hang her on that?'

Nicoll thought for a moment. 'They might,' he said. 'We've got the blood to come.'

The plain fact was that nobody wanted a fizzer.

13

THE LUNCH-ROOM in the Darwin Hotel was rigged out in the style of the South Seas: bamboo tables, green foliage. Lazy punkahs stirred the air. The reporters had joined two tables together to make room for Charlwood, Metcalf, and Professor Chaikin. The professor was still excited enough to recount anecdotes from his day in court. 'Phillips said dingoes could bite through chain. I pointed out that you could break a chain with a hammer but not necessarily damage a singlet.' Someone yawned. Chaikin was old news already.

Charlwood evidently caught the drift. 'We still have aces up the sleeve' he said.

The prosecution played a new card that day in the form of Rohan Tew, whose name did not appear on the witness list. Rohan Tew's job was the fitting of audio equipment to

automobiles. On 7 November 1980, while he was working at
Floyd Hart's Highway Sound Centre at Mt Isa, Pastor Chamberlain delivered a car there, a yellow hatchback. Tew did not see
the pastor, but he saw the docket, which called for the fitting of
a stereo-deck. Everyone knew who the Chamberlains were. The
proprietor, Mr Hart himself, carried out much of the installation,
then told Tew to finish it. The job took three hours. Tew began
cleaning up. It was then he noticed dark stains on the centre
console. It looked like blood.

Now, Rohan Tew had a peculiarity. There was very little
feeling in his right arm since an occasion on which he had cut it.
He was then going through a plate-glass window. Thereafter, he
could injure himself quite badly without noticing. Looking around
the pastor's car now, he saw another stain, on the driver's door,
near the new speaker. His first thought was that he had cut
himself, working. He checked his arm over, but it was not he
who had bled.

His story gave the reporters something new to write about,
but no one in the press-room could find much point in it. The
real question in this trial was not whether there was blood in the
car, but whose it was. Malcolm Brown could only guess that the
prosecution had thrown Tew in for the same reason a boxer feints
with a left, just to keep the other fellow a little off balance.

14

THEN PHILLIPS FOUND OUT that someone had
broken into the Chamberlain car, before the trial, while it was in
the police-compound.

Metcalf was the witness. He testified to his discovery of the
bloodstain on the ceiling of the passenger footwell. This stain
was, by now, famous enough that everyone called it the Arterial
Spray, and on it hung the suggestion that the baby was held down
there and slaughtered. When he found it, Metcalf said, it was
still 'sticky to the touch', a recollection which tested the credulity of the defence team because the blood was then more than a
year old. But there was some sort of pattern under there, right
enough. Metcalf produced the steel plate, which had been
excised from the car, and passed it up to the jury. This was the
one stain which, if it was blood, could not be accounted for by
either the Bleeding Hitchiker or the transfer of blood from
bedding in the tent the night the baby disappeared.

Phillips was not prepared to concede that the stain was blood, but he was determined to show that there might be more than one way it could have got there. In cross-examination, he reminded Metcalf of an extraordinary event.

Four months back, the law department officer Mick O'Loughlin went to the Alice Springs police-compound to take some material from the car. With him were a solicitor from the defence, the pathologist Tony Jones, and three police including Metcalf. Inside the car they discovered part of a plastic syringe. It was of a size used by veterinarians. The instrument was lying on the floor. Metcalf said it was not there when the car was last inspected. Since the time of his last vist, the cage around the car was locked and only O'Loughlin had the keys.

Because Phillips was so clearly keen to show that the Arterial Spray might be accounted for by a syringe or something like it, the prosecution put O'Loughlin in the witness-box to explain what had happened. Then the story came out. The mystified O'Loughlin had returned to the police-depot next day to look around for signs of entry. He saw ragged cobwebs hanging from the roof. Someone had climbed in, over the top of the cage. Under the car the dust was scuffed. Someone had crawled underneath, heading for a gap in the cabin floor where the gearbox once was. That gap would admit the passage of an arm, up to the shoulder.

No one could explain the happening further. Phillips decided against pushing the issue any harder. But it remained a disquieting phantom, eerie and inexplicable, like a shadowy face at a window-pane.

15

THE SEVENTH-DAY ADVENTIST pastor for the Darwin congregation was an ex-cop. Malcolm Brown sometimes saw him walking home after court. He was Graeme Olson, a burly but still athletic man in his middle forties, a long-strider. Pastor Olson lived in the manse beside the church, and the Chamberlains were billeted in quarters behind. Brown's motel was at the same end of town. Meeting the pastor, en route, was easy.

It was Olson's job to shield the Chamberlains from the sightseers who often loitered on the footpath outside the house, and from the press. When the telephone rang, it was Olson who took the call; if the door chimed, he answered it first. But the more he talked to Brown, the clearer it was that he didn't much like the Chamberlains. It seemed to come down to the way they spoke. They thought Sergeant Cocks a fool, and said so, and they spoke of the police-force as if it were some agency of devilment. Olson had known Barry Cocks a long time and had once worked with Police commissioner McAulay. He didn't like to hear the police spoken of that way.

Brown wondered how long it might be before Olson gave him some useful information. In the event, it took about a week. Olson told him the date on which Lindy Chamberlain expected the birth of the coming baby. If the pregnancy ran full course, delivery was just five weeks off.

The information gave Brown a clear break. As gossip currently ran, there was any number of willing contacts at the Darwin hospital ready to call some reporter or other, the minute Lindy Chamberlain entered the maternity ward. Brown wasn't worried. The arrangement he now had with Olson was more reliable, and closer to the action, than anyone else could hope for. The code 'the bird has flown' would mean that Lindy was on her way. The message Brown most hoped for was 'the bird is fluttering'.

Brown broke the news of the expected date in a story which the *Sydney Morning Herald* headed: 'November 11 is the day for Lindy's baby'. There was no point to a heading like that unless everyone already knew they were reading about the most infamous mother in national history. It was the sort of story which confronts the reporter with the cruelties of the trade. Next day, before the session began, Brown watched Lindy walk into court. She was carrying a pillow. She caught his gaze, and shook her head sorrowfully. Then she smiled. Brown took this exchange to mean that she understood a fellow had to make a living somehow.

THE MOLECULAR STRUCTURE
OF TRUTH

1

THE COURTROOM FLOOR was now cluttered with the merchandise of testimony. When Joy Kuhl was called into court, as the thirty-fifth witness, she picked her path between stacks of photographs, maps, plastic containers, automobile parts, floral mattresses, blankets, hats, baby-wear, camping-equipment, and clothing. Everything was labelled, like the possessions of a family about to be sold up for enough to cover a judgement debt.

Constable Metcalf set up a silver screen against the wall. A projector already lay on the table. Kuhl sat, not in the witness-box, but alongside the screen, wand in hand. She smiled at Metcalf, smiled at the jury. She smoothed her skirt. She was ready to delivery, with Sturgess as prompter, a home-course in the identification of blood.

Sitting behind Phillips and Kirkham now was a man whom Phillips had identified to the judge as Barry Boettcher, a professor of biology. Boettcher was tall and stiff-limbed. His baldness was of the sort which seems to have been caused by an expansion of the temples, rather than by loss of hair. While Kuhl gave the jury a glossary of the terms they should get used to, Professor Boettcher found a notebook and set a briefcase over his lap to use as a writing-bench.

In the next recess, Metcalf joined the pressmen chatting in the corridor. None of them knew Boettcher, and someone asked, 'Who is the guy?'

'An egg-head,' Metcalf shrugged. 'No one we're worried about.'

2

BOETTCHER was the head of biological sciences at Newcastle University. Indeed, he had been the chairman there since the biology school opened ten years ago. His doctorate was in genetics, and his special interest was blood. He spent much of his time researching the relationships between the components of blood and genes, and pursuing problems of one sort or another in immunology. A good deal of his work had to do with the mechanisms by which immune reactions are inherited, the way those reactions work, and with the structures and identification of blood.

He wrote papers in genetics and immunology at a great rate. He edited, or helped to edit, journals of biology in Australia, South Africa, and the US. He sat on two international committees which were concerned with immunology in reproduction. Because immunological reactions are important to researchers who want to distinguish proteins in blood, he produced anti-sera to specific proteins, enough of them that, if asked how many, his most accurate estimate lay somewhere between twenty and fifty. He taught the practices of immunological testing and the principles which justified them. He taught scientific method, the principles which justify any conclusion. He supervised graduate students. He administered his department. If there was any time left over he made for the campus pool. He often swam so many laps then, that students wondered if the professor had simply forgotten to stop.

He was not especially pleased when someone passed another chore his way, but it sometimes happened, and it happened again on an afternoon in March 1982 when a young man came to the laboratory and asked to see him privately. The young man was quiet and apologetic. He had graduated in science here three years before, as the professor recalled, and was a Seventh-day Adventist from the community at Cooranbong, which was not far south. When mention was made of the Chamberlains, the professor knew he was about to be asked to review the biological evidence.

The documents arrived at the end of the month, and he took them home. There were about twenty pages of foolscap entitled 'General Worksheet', reports of the forensic biologist, Joy Kuhl, on which she brought her conclusions together, and a transcript of the scientific testimony at the second inquest. The work-sheets displayed sketches of some of the items she tested for blood: a small knife on which she had found no blood, scissors, a ten-cent coin, parts of automobile seats and doors, and a camera-case. On some pages she had sketched the immunological tests she carried out, showing the position of the wells holding the testing solutions, and anti-sera, and marking the bands of reaction against the blood she was testing.

It was all plain enough. The tests she used were appropriate and well known. The blood she was testing reacted in some instances as foetal blood, in others simply as human blood, but it was all old blood, denatured, some of it cooked in an automobile by thirteen months of Australian heat. It was bound to cause problems. The unsettling thing was that the problems it seemed to cause were not those he would have expected.

He came back to the puzzle a week later. He had in mind, now, to turn the problem about. It had occurred to him that more was known about the dead child than that it was simply an infant. They knew which infant it was.

He picked through the work-sheets and the transcript again, making notes as he went. Azaria Chamberlain was nine and a half weeks old when she died. The blood of a normal infant that age should contain haemoglobin of around thirty per cent foetal and seventy per cent adult. Indeed, as he read in the inquest testimony, Dr Andrew Scott had judged just those percentages in the blood on Azaria Chamberlain's own clothing. Here was, at the least, a reliable starting-point.

He went first to two tests which were not immunological, that is, they didn't rely on the blood sample's immune reaction to anything. They were molecular sieves, plates made from polyacrylamide gel, through which the haemoglobin is moved by an electric current. When the current is switched off, the haemoglobins have swum as far as they can, separated because the molecules of the adult component are different in size from the foetal, and the gel is graded so that just this happens. It is not a test designed to identify how much of each there is, but the strength of the bands gives a good indication. If the blood sample was Azaria Chamberlain's, Boettcher would expect the foetal band to be much less marked than the adult, about half strength. But here, Kuhl had found them equal.

He turned to the immunological tests. Here, Kuhl had tested the blood samples of reactions against several anti-sera. She had used anti-HbF which is the anti-foetal component, and antiHbA the anti-adult. She had included an anti-species, for example anti-pig or anti-sheep, for use as controls to show that the test was working properly, for if there is a reaction against anti-pig or anti-sheep the whole thing has somehow gone wrong, and the test is scrapped. Importantly, she had often added a known sample of cord blood, blood drawn from the umbilical cord of a new-born and comprising around eighty per cent foetal haemoglobin, twenty per cent adult.

He checked the results of tests which included a cord blood control. Cord blood contained nearly three times more foetal haemoglobin than did Azaria Chamberlain's blood. He would expect the reaction between the testing solution and cord blood to be around three times as strong as the reaction between the testing solution and any sample attributed to Azaria Chamberlain. But it was not. In nine results, out of seventeen, the strengths were the reverse. In eight they were, just as inexplicably, equal. In no case were they the way he might have expected.

There were other ways he could check it out. He looked at the manner in which the blood attributed to Azaria Chamberlain reacted against an anti-foetal testing solution, and the way it reacted against a wide anti-haemoglobin solution. Only thirty per cent of Azaria Chamberlain's haemoglobin was foetal, so only thirty per cent of it would react against the anti-foetal solution, whereas all of it must react against the wider anti-haemoglobin. But there were incidents here, in the work-notes, in which the vehemence of the reactions worked precisely the other way around.

No, something was very wrong.

Why had these results not alerted Mrs Kuhl? He scanned again the transcript of her testimony. He found her saying this: 'I was getting very strong reactions against the foetal haemoglobin, and much weaker ones against the adult haemoglobin, which is very consistent with gradual changing of the blood from the foetal to the adult condition.' So there it was. It seemed she anticipated, in the blood of a nine weeks old baby, more foetal haemoglobin than adult.

She got the reactions she expected.

Some results seemed, even on the evidence of her own tests, to show the presence of adult blood, not foetal. One of the samples taken from the floorwell of the motor car reacted only against anti-adult anti-serum. So did the zip-clasp on one of the inner compartments of the camera-case. Was there blood of more than one origin in the car and the bag? Or was none of it foetal?

Since he had no sample of Azaria Chamberlain's blood to work with, he took adult blood, cord blood, and a mixture of both, and proceeded to run similar tests. He chose the mixture of cord and adult to simulate the blood of a baby of nine weeks. He chose testing solutions of the brands Kuhl had used. He used the same dilutions for his samples. And things went wrong.

First, he found that the dilutions Kuhl had used weren't appropriate. They were often too strong. There were just too many antibodies in there, warring. The fallen were everywhere. Often they hid the real regions of battle, of hard resistance, and the lines of precipitation weren't clear where they ought to be clear. He rediluted and tried again. The manner of test he was running called for a thin plate of gel into which he punched small wells to hold the testing solution and the blood samples apart until it was time to oppose them, each advancing towards the other, emboldened by an electric current. Now he found that reactions between the testing solution and the sample sometimes gave two bands of precipitation instead of one. And elsewhere the lines formed between testing solution and the wells holding each of the samples had joined into one band involving all blood specimens.

The testing solution which seemed to be giving him trouble was an anti-foetal anti-serum. It was made in Germany. Its validity as a testing solution depended on the claim that it would cause a reaction with foetal haemoglobin and with nothing else. The term which describes this reliable narrow-mindedness is specificity. The testing solution, if it was specific, ought to cause a reaction with the foetal component in infants' blood and not with the adult. The reaction should occur, in the sort of test he was running, in one battle-line of precipitation. It was showing two. The testing solution was, for some reason, reacting with the foetal component and with something she hadn't identified.

He wrote to the German manufacturers asking if they knew that this could happen. They replied with a tight letter, directing him to the Australian agents, but added this: 'The observed (precipitation line) of the unknown component is most likely due to denaturation.'

They had misunderstood him somewhat. He had not yet experimented with denatured blood. But the blood which Kuhl examined was denatured by age and heat, whether it came from Azaria Chamberlain or from Lenehan, the Bleeding Hitchhiker.

He experimented with denatured blood. The older blood was, the less was it sensitive to the testing solution, but the foetal and the adult haemoglobins lost sensitivity at much the same rate. So denaturation alone could not be blamed for any change in the ratio of foetal to adult haemoglobin in old stains. The ratios Kuhl had found were wrong for Azaria Chamberlain, and they were as wrong for her denatured blood as they were for the fresh.

It remained now to show that the testing solutions Kuhl used at the Sydney laboratories were identical with those he had faulted at Newcastle. By this he meant not only the same manufacturer, but the same batch, and he needed to know the code. He thought an inquiry of this nature ought to come from a solicitor, so Stuart Tipple wrote to Mrs Kuhl, asking the batch numbers for the testing solutions she had used in each test.

The refusal came back in polite terms.

They would have to make do without it. On the work so far, Boettcher thought the ample irregularities in Kuhl's results invalidated them all entirely. Whatever batch of testing solution she used to identify foetal haemoglobin, there was sufficient detail in her own work-sheets to show that the solution was not specific. It was enough.

And there was another advantage yet to come. Kuhl had so far displayed only diagrams of the way her test plates reacted. No one in the defence team had seen the original plates. They ought to be somewhere around, colour-stained and preserved. Phillips was determined to insist that she produce them, at trial.

3

'NOW, MRS KUHL,' Phillips said, pointing to a gel-plate she had brought to court, 'that is a demonstration electrophoretic plate?'

'Yes,' she said. She had produced it as a teaching-aid. It had nothing to do with the tests she had run for this case.

He had Kirkham hold up two photographs. She had used them, as examples of testing technique, in her testimony. Phillips asked, 'That is a demonstration photograph of a gradient gel?' And of the other, 'a demonstration photograph of an Ouchterlony plate?'

She agreed to both.

'What about the real thing?' He went first to the plates. 'What about the actual electrophoretic plates that you ended up with at the end of your tests? Do you produce those?'

She shook her head. 'No.'

'What about the actual Ouchterlony plates that you ended up with at the end of your tests? Do you produce those?'

'No.'

'What about the actual gradient gel that you used in your tests? Do you produce that?'

'No.'

'What about the plate that you used for attempt at a haptoglobin grouping? Do you produce that?'

'No.'

'They are in Sydney, are they?'

'No,' she said. They were not in Sydney. They were not in Darwin.

'Where are they?'

'They have been destroyed.'

'The plates are destroyed?'

'Yes.'

'All of them?'

All of them.

'Whose decision was that? Who is to take responsibility for this?'

'I don't see it as anyone's responsibility,' she said. 'It is standard procedure in our laboratory.'

'Did you take any photographs of them? Or did you direct that any photographs be taken of this evidence, before you destroyed it?'

'No. We have not the facilities for that,' she said abruptly, as if that ought to dispose of the matter. Her gaze followed the slow passage of Phillips's hand, which was now reaching across the bar-table. He picked up one of the items she had produced already. He let it dangle, aloft, from his fingers. There was hardly the need for a question. It was a photograph.

'To produce my visual aids,' she said. 'Yes.'

'Now, at the inquest, did you swear this? ''Human foetal haemoglobin is different from adult haemoglobin. While a baby, or a foetus, is in utero it does not have any adult haemoglobin.'' '

'Yes, I did.'

'That was demonstrably false.'

'I used that statement for the—for purposes of making things clear and simple. It was not a false statement.'

'I say false in the sense of incorrect?'

'It was incorrect, scientifically,' she said. 'It was used as an indication of the relative amounts.'

'You are perfectly entitled to give any explanation which you have,' Phillips said, tugging irritably at his robe, 'but the fact is, scientifically that statement is utterly incorrect.'

'Scientifically,' she said, 'it is not correct. Yes.'

She considered that the bloodstains found in the Chamberlain car were old enough to be from the dead baby but not old enough to be from Lenehan, who had bled in the car fourteen months earlier. She conceded her experience with old stains was little. She conceded she had never worked with stains which had survived a summer. She conceded that the age of blood could not be determined accurately. But she stuck with her opinion, nonetheless. Phillips knew he must find a way to shift her.

'Are you suggesting that we should, as it were, shut the door as at September 1979?'

'That would have been consistent with my opinion, yes.'

'These stains could not date from August 1979? Do you swear that?'

'It is an opinion. Based purely on experience. I can't swear that.'

'Do you swear they cannot date from July 1979?'

'Once again, no, I can't swear that.'

'Do you swear they cannot date from June 1979?'

'No,' she said curtly. They had come to the end of it now. The Hitchhiker had bled on 17 June 1979.

Because the testing plates were no more, Phillips had only Mrs Kuhl's demonstration plates, photographs, and diagrams to work on. He had Tipple set up an overhead projector, and it threw the pictures up on the screen. An orderly darkened the court. Phillips stood by, pointing to this well and to that, wherever the bands of reaction were unexpected.

He wanted to show there were often two bands where there should have been one. 'Here are two bands, Mrs Kuhl?' he said, pointing.

'A band and a smudge.'

The slide made way for another.

'There is a band, and a faint impression of a second band?'

'No,' she said. 'I can see only one band.'

He sought out more.

'That is a band, is it not?'

'It is not a band. It is an artifact in the staining procedure.'

Professor Boettcher muttered and scribbled in his notebook. There were demonstration plates, and they were demonstrating something wonderfully important. The plain fact was: Kuhl's batch of anti-foetal testing solution had gone wrong here, too.

She was a remarkable witness by any standards, Malcolm Brown thought. She was resilient and spirited. She let go no point that she could possibly retrieve. When she was pleased with an answer, she beamed at Metcalf who stood in court throughout. In the hottest exchanges with Phillips, she made disparaging faces, and no one was in any doubt how silly she thought his questions were. For the most part, her eyes ignored him, and she answered directly and confederately to the jury.

The press was having trouble turning the secrets of the bloodstream into anything like readable copy. The reporter sitting next to Brown whispered, 'God knows how much of this the jury can understand.'

'It doesn't matter,' Brown said. 'It's not the point.'

Professor Boettcher closed his notebook. He felt a flush of self-consciousness, of foolishness. He had been naive. He recognized now that he had been waiting for the point at which Kuhl would recognize her errors. He had expected her to recant. The pencil in his distracted fingers had somehow snapped, and he slipped the pieces into a pocket. He had awaited the messianic triumph of science.

She had a parting shot for Phillips.

Barker had returned the topic to the camera-bag. 'Did you form a view whether anything else had been done to it at some stage?'

'Well, to me it looked like it had been through a washing-machine, but I guess that's—' She trailed away a moment. 'The vinyl was cracked, very flakey. It was in very poor condition.'

Angry at the mention of 'washing-machine', Phillips was about to object, but Justice Muirhead got there first. 'I think we have got far enough on the camera-bag,' the judge said. Phillips insisted the jury be told to disregard Kuhl's remark. Justice Muirhead agreed. There was no opposition from Barker. 'I must say the washing-machine was not something I had heard of before,' he said, and sat down.

4

JOY KUHL looked tired but happy. She wore sunglasses and sipped her drink. They were sitting in the garden-bar, under the wide umbrellas, a half dozen reporters and two detectives.

It seemed some current of nostalgia was rising in her. 'I said it was an artifact of the staining process and, in a way, it was true. But it was all Baxter's fault.' Baxter was in charge at her laboratory. 'Baxter had overcooked the plate. He left it in the dryer for an hour and a half, he forgot about it altogether, and it collapsed. She grinned. 'But I wasn't going to tell them that.'

She turned her recollection to the jury's excursion to view the Chamberlain car. The court had convened in the police-yard, where the car lay dismantled, while she pointed to the location of bloodstains.

'And all the time, She,' here meaning Lindy Chamberlain, 'was there behind me, staring. She just stares. She is, you know, a witch. I could feel her eyes burning holes through my back.'

Murray Nicoll took this reference to be a joke, but the turn of conversation was unsettling. He raised his glass to her. 'And Happy Birthday for yesterday,' he said. 'I didn't know.'

'And the jury,' she said, 'no, someone on the jury had a birthday too. And they wanted to sing Happy Birthday to Joy.' She waved the glass. 'When they found out it was mine.'

5

PROFESSOR BOETTCHER sat in court throughout Joy Kuhl's evidence. He sat through the testimony of the Sydney biologist, Baxter and the Englishman, Culliford. Baxter, Kuhl's supervisor, had inspected the test plates at the laboratory. He remembered agreeing with her opinions at the time, although he could now clearly recall no more than one of them. He was too self-confident a young man to let this worry him. When he was asked, 'Is the experienced biologist likely to confuse a reaction from household bleach or heavy metals with a blood reaction?' he replied, 'Not while I'm around,' and his knuckles whitened as he gripped the rail.

Culliford had not seen the test plates before they were destroyed and, so far as Boettcher could tell, Culliford seemed to be here at all only because he had developed one of the tests Kuhl had used, the cross-over electrophoresis. Boettcher wondered why a law department would bring a man halfway around the world to say that.

The notes Boettcher were making included:

With regard to the specificity of the anti-haemoglobin F antiserum that the FB [his cipher for Kuhl, Forensic Biologist] had used in the tests, it was agreed that, if the anti-serum would react with something other than haemoglobin F, the conclusions reached by the FB from results of tests involving the anti-serum would not be valid. This was agreed to by the FB, and by the OE [Culliford, Overseas Expert.]

Really, this appeared to be the nub of the problem in accepting the interpretation that the reactions between test samples and anti-haemoglobin F anti-serum could be accepted as being due to anti-gammaglobin chain antibodies rather than to the contaminant I had found, anti-alpha globin chain antibodies.

He considered this plain language, clear to the most casual reader. It meant: Everyone agrees now that, unless the test solution was specific to foetal haemoglobin, the tests were worthless.

In the media-room next door, journalists abandoned the video-screens. Their task, making all this catchy and explicable, was hopeless. They needed another diversion, until things got better. Geoff DeLuca had hit on an idea. he was running a sweep.

Everyone crowded to one end of the room, waving banknotes. Tickets were a dollar a time. DeLuca drew up a chart. Each line was marked with a date, like a calendar for October/November.

The stake would go to the person who drew the day on which Lindy Chamberlain's baby was born. Winner take all.

6

EVENING was the only feasible time for running in this climate. Brown saw Kirkham running the grass reserve between the high-rise hotels and the foreshore, so Brown ran there too. He fell in beside Kirkham. They ran a length, which was around a kilometre, and started back. Kirkham asked how Brown thought the defence was doing.

'You're holding your own,' Brown said between breaths. 'But the blood evidence is not easy to follow, just now.'

There was a breeze, north-west, off the Timor Sea. Seed pods high in the trees, slim and papery, whirred like locusts' wings. There were blacks below the cliff somewhere, singing.

'Well, you aint seen nothing yet,' Kirkham said. His singlet hung heavy with sweat. 'If we can show the anti-foetal serum will react with other things, we destroy the basis of the Crown case.'

He glanced sidelong at Brown. 'And Malcolm,' he said, 'we can.' Then he sprinted away, enlivened.

7

AT A CORNER TABLE, Dr Tony Jones was dining with a visiting lawyer. They were talking about the trial. Jones was the government's pathologist in Darwin, a heavy man with a gruff beard and serious eyes. He was the first pathologist to examine the Chamberlain infant's clothing, and was now the next scheduled witness.

The lawyer asked Jones what he knew about the pathologist James Cameron.

'Well,' Jones said, as if he did not much enjoy the question, 'you've got to understand that these chaps belong to a certain school of forensic science. The Spilsbury school. They're keen on what they call court-craft. For them, the court-craft is as important as the science.'

The lawyer said, 'You don't like that?'

'Let's just say that I think tactics are for lawyers, science is for scientists,' Jones said.

The evidence Jones was to give sometime tomorrow was not nearly so far-reaching as everyone expected of Cameron. As Jones judged the bloodstains, they might have come from a crushing injury to the baby's head, or damage to the neck, and he could not exclude, with any certainty, the jaws of a dingo. He did not see a convincing handprint on the clothing, as Cameron did. The Arterial Spray was Jones's own term for the stain over the footwell in the Chamberlain car, but he could not see that he could fairly push judgements like this into the realm of certainty, either.

'The scientist shouldn't become too adventurous,' he said, 'too competitive.'

His gaze was on a long table near the centre of the room, where Charlwood and Metcalf were eating with the press people.

'The trouble is, we're all so human.' He shrugged, his eyes dark and uneasy. 'I've never seen a case more governed by human frailties.'

8

HE THOUGHT KIRKHAM had finished with him. Then Kirkham asked, 'Doctor, would you be kind enough to look at this?'

An orderly carried to the witness-stand an oblong metal plate. Jones took it. This was very like the plate Metcalf had cut from the footwell of the hatchback Torana. At least from the same sort of car. He turned it over. Here were droplets, dark and blebby, like those he had called the Arterial Spray. He nicked at one with his finger. It was dry and hard.

'Can you observe an apparent spray pattern?' Kirkham asked.

Jones did not bother to hide his surprise. 'Yes,' he said. 'I can.'

'Does that spray pattern appear to you similar to the spray pattern you have described?'

'It is a fine spray of similar character,' he said carefully. He expected someone would tell him more about it now, but Kirkham sat down. Jones stood there, turning the stain one way and another, wondering what the hell it was.

9

NO ONE in the defence team had any idea what it was either. Michael Chamberlain had, in March, checked around the locality looking for a Torana, model LX SL, with a spray over the passenger footwell. It seemed a foolish and unlikely chase, but nobody had the heart to dissuade him. Then he found one. It was in Maitland, owned by a clergyman by name of Roberts. The spray pattern was unmistakable.

The supplier couldn't say what had caused it, although the best guess was some circumstance of manufacture. Chemical analysis was no use, since no one could say what the stain might look like afterwards. So Phillips and Kirkham decided it should go to the jury unexplained but entire.

10

MALCOLM BROWN'S SHORTHAND description of the London odontologist Bernard Sims was, 'The proportions heavyweight wrestler, long retired.'

Sims, answering Barker's inquiry about how many dog attacks he had investigated, said, 'Perhaps about twenty-four altogether. A number have been written up. One of them in which ultra-violet photography was used to elucidate dog marks on a man's arm six months after they occurred. And a case a couple of years ago, in which a boy of ten was savaged and killed by four alsatians.'

'And I think you had the unpleasant task,' Barker said, 'of examining the bodies of people who have died naturally but have subsequently been attacked by dogs.'

'The family pets,' Sims said. 'If the person has died of a heart attack in the front room, and no one knows they are there, the family pet has to survive, so it usually eats the owner.'

Brown added to his memorandum about Sims the words, 'Has lost all repugnance for the horrible.'

Sims passed a photograph, by way of an orderly, to the jury. It showed a punctured human arm. The wounds were clean and oval. 'That is typical of a dog bite, an alsatian dog.'

'Under what circumstances,' Barker asked, 'would you expect a dog merely to close, without tearing or twisting?'

'It wouldn't be usual if the dog was going after its prey,

going after food, because it would tear and twist. Probably only trained dogs would go in and grip.'

Barker handed up Azaria Chamberlain's garments. 'Is there anything about the damage to that jump-suit consistent with a dog attack?'

'In my opinion, no. There are none of the typical hole and tearmarks I would expect to find in the relationship of the four canine teeth.' He held up the left sleeve. 'To the arm, that is not the sort of shape one would expect to have from a dog bite. One would have at least two canines, or four canines, going in and causing a dragging. And it wouldn't be as regular an outline as that.'

'What about the collar?'

'Again, that seems to be too linear. The family of the dogs wouldn't have sharp enough teeth to do that.'

He dismissed any possibility that a dingo might have taken the child by the neck. 'The difficulty would be of a dingo being able to get into the neck alone, without leaving any damage to the clothing.'

'What sort of bleeding would you expect if the dingo had savaged the child's face?'

'Copious,' Sims said. 'And there would be spurting. The facial artery comes out onto the side.' He put a finger to his dampling cheek. 'Here.'

'Can you imagine a situation where the dingo was able to fasten its teeth on the child's face, and carry it off?'

'It wouldn't be able to. The facial tissues would be ripped away.'

Frowning, Justice Muirhead asked why this was so.

'The facial tissues aren't as tough as ours,' Sims said. 'The musculature of the child's face wouldn't be able to support the weight of the child. The features would come away.'

He held up the dingo skull. The jaws fell open. He took up a doll, which was dressed as a baby, and which he said was the size of a three-month infant. 'The dog I examined, which was larger than this, was only able to open its teeth nine centimetres, between the points of the upper canine teeth and the lower.'

Plainly, the head of the doll would not fit into the jaws of the skull he now held.

Kirkham took over. 'Do you suggest a dingo is not capable of seizing the head of a child,' he said, pointing to the doll, 'that size, in its mouth?'

'The entire head?' Sims asked, incredulous.

'The entire head.'

'I don't believe it is capable of it. The opening of the mouth wouldn't allow it to get that sort of purchase.'

'If, for example, the head of a child with a circumference of forty centimetres was placed in the jaws of a dingo, there would be a disarticulation of the jaws?'

'Yes. The dingo articulation, the dog articulation, is a simple hinge joint.'

'Using lay terms,' Kirkham persisted, 'if a dingo seized the head of a child with a forty centimetre circumference, the jaws would be dislocated?'

'Yes.'

Kirkham handed him a photograph. It showed the Dingo Foundation president, Les Harris, holding a russet dingo by the collar. In the animal's mouth was the head of a doll, like the one Sims was holding. It was a sleeping-doll. One eye was lazily closing. So much of the head, crown first, was accommodated by the jaws that the canine teeth reached very nearly to the doll's ears.

'Do you concede, having seen that photograph, that a dog could perfectly easily encompass the head of a child, Azaria Chamberlain's size, with its jaws?'

'If that—' Sims paused, staring at the photograph. 'If that doll's head has not been forced into the dog's jaws,' he said, hunching a shoulder, 'I would accept that.'

Kirkham sat down, grinning. It would do no harm if the jury saw just how pleased he was. He risked a glance their way. A bristle-headed young man at the end of the front row, who generally sat forward with his heavy arms on his knees, caught Kirkham's eye and winked.

11

THE JOURNALISTS WERE BORED with eating at the hotels night after night. Murray Nicoll gathered a group together, and they set off down town. With him was the writer

Frank Moorhouse, and Lindsay Murdoch, who looked like a football coach but wrote for the Melbourne *Age*. Most of the others were photographers. They found Christo's, a crowded Greek place in a lane off the Mall, which served spicy seafood and resined wine. They had agreed to embargo, in conversation, any mention of the trial. The pact lasted through the first two bottles of retsina, but did not survive the third.

The day's testimony had included Mrs Elston, who was once the Ayers Rock nurse Bobbie Downs. The prosecution called her to prove that Michael Chamberlain had driven from the campsite to the Uluru Motel, insisting that his camera-case ride on the floor under his knees. She said the case seemed tightly stuffed with something. She then demonstrated by jamming it with wadding.

'What I don't understand,' said McNeil, a press photographer, 'is where was all the camera-gear? If the bag was full of bleeding baby, someone would have seen the lenses and the other gear somewhere in the car.'

Murdoch chose the moment to voice doubts of his own. 'The real point is, she doesn't get blood on her clothes,' he said. 'She gets out of the car clean.'

Nicoll was troubled for altogether different reasons. He thought this sort of argument did not reflect the hidden indices of guilt or innocence. They inhabited the shadowlands of a police investigation. You had to be very close to the sleuthing to get anywhere near the real story. 'The fact is,' he said, 'the police found, at the Chamberlain's house, a baby's coffin, and the clothes Lindy used to dress the kid with. The dresses were black. No mother in the country would keep black clothes for her child.' He waited for this to sink home. 'That's a devil's child.'

'Who told you that?' Murdoch asked, sceptical. 'A cop?'

'Not a cop. A scientist,' Nicoll said. He tapped his temple, signifying serious consideration. 'A forensic scientist.'

No one pressed him further. If Nicoll wanted to protect his sources, that was his affair.

Moorhouse, the story-writer, was taken with a quite separate aspect. 'A scientist, peddling black-magic stories,' he said, refilling glasses. 'it has nice congruence.'

When this conversation was later recounted to Malcolm Brown, he said he'd heard 'something about a black dress, but the coffin was a new one'. Brown had no reason to disbelieve rumours of this nature, beyond the fact that they made him uneasy. He knew Charlwood still believed the child may have been slain hours before anyone saw her at the campfire, despite all contrary evidence. So ineradicable a belief seemed like an early touchstone of the investigation, an orthodoxy, a superstition.

12

'BE IN COURT for Cameron,' Kirkham had told a friend, and the friend told Malcolm Brown. They guessed it meant the defence had surprises in store. The public gallery had filled, which had not happened for some time. Cameron was a celebrity.

He looked confident and sturdy. His face and head had ruddied more since the second inquest. Brown had heard tell the professor was currently one of the consulting physicians with the British team at the Commonwealth Games in Brisbane, in whose performance he held a passionate interest, and wouldn't be staying long in Darwin once his testimony finished.

While Cameron was sworn, Kirkham took, from a stack of files on the floor, a thick folder. It was an astonishingly bright shade of green. It lay on the table, closed, an item of some presence, as if it drew the eye not because of the vavacity of the colour but because it held matter of exceptional gravity.

Cameron's curriculum vitae was the record of an impressively vigorous man. Barker read it out, pausing for the professor's assent less and less frequently, as though there was a danger the list might never finish. Cameron presently held two professorial posts at schools of medicine and an appointment in forensic medicine at a school of law. He consulted to the Royal Navy and to the Army, and lectured at the London University, the University College, the Royal Free Hospital, and to classes at four police academies. He had practised at hospitals in Scotland and England, edited journals, and contributed a plethora of articles on pathology, criminology, child abuse, infanticide, cot deaths, forensic dentistry, 'and as a digression', Barker asked him, amused, 'you have written about the Turin Shroud?'

The professor conceded he had somehow found time to do that, too.

By Brown's wristwatch, it had taken Barker six and a half minutes recitation to get this far.

'Have you carried out many autopsy examinations?'

'In excess of fifty thousand,' Cameron said. 'Cases reported to the coroner, requiring a medico-legal autopsy.'

Brown made a quick calculation. Cameron could get through fifty thousand at the rate of five and a half cadavers a day, on average, assuming he had not taken so much as a day's rest in twenty-five years. Most coronial autopsies took upwards of an hour to perform, sometimes a good deal longer. It seemed he must mean by 'carried out' something much more like supervision.

Cameron turned the rumpled jump-suit over in his hands. 'I saw no evidence on any of these garments to suggest that any member of the canine family was involved. I cannot say anything about dingoes. I speak about the canine family in general.'

'In your opinion,' Barker asked, 'is there evidence suggesting to you that the child was not killed by a member of the canine family?'

'There is evidence to suggest it was killed in another method. It suggests there was an incised wound around the neck. In other words, a cut throat.'

'Caused by?'

'A cutting instrument across the neck, or around the neck.'

'Held by?'

'Held by a human element.'

'What do you say about the possibility of a dog or a dingo having savaged the child in the head?'

'I do not think there is enough evidence on the jump-suit, alone, to support that theory.'

'What happens if a dog bites a child's head?'

'A lot depends on where, on the head, it bites. It would be very difficult for me to imagine a dog grasping the head from above. That would be the only way in which I think a dog could possibly grasp a child without damaging the collar. But, in so doing, I would have expected extensive bleeding, but not around the collar of the jump-suit.'

'Why?'

'Because when you get a head injury, you get rivulets of

blood draining down, and missing the collar. It goes down the front and down the back. Depending on which way the head is bending, certainly, you'll get bleeding around the back of the collar, depending on how the child lay afterwards, where there's pooling of blood.'

He traced the blood pattern with a finger. 'I would have anticipated that it could only be described by a cut-throat type of injury.'

'Had the child been lifted and moved by a dog, what do you say about saliva?'

'I would have anticipated saliva from any member of the canine family lifting a garment.'

13

Station TwoDAY Newsbreak

At the Chamberlain trial in Darwin today, the court was told that baby's clothing found after Azaria's disappearance bore the marks of bloodstained human hands.

James Cameron, London professor of forensic medicine, showed projected colour-slides of the infant's jump-suit and singlet made from photographs taken in his laboratories using ultra-violet light.

He pointed out to the jury smudges on the stained clothing which indicated to him the pattern of bloodied fingers, and another he thought may be a thumb.

Lindy Chamberlain, charged with her baby's murder, watched as the professor took up a life-size doll and held it to demonstrate the grip that could produce the marks he found.

He said the stain gave him the impression of a hand belonging to a small adult.

14

WHEN PHILLIPS got to his feet. Cameron paid no attention. He sat facing the judge. He recrossed his legs. He shot a cuff. He presented impeccable relaxation. Phillips reached for the green folder. He thought the professor knew what was coming.

*   *   *

'Professor Cameron, I would like to ask you some questions about a famous English case, called the Confait case, in which you were involved.'

'Yes?'

'Because I want to suggest to you it illustrates some of the difficulties in giving forensic opinions in court.' Phillips took up a document. He didn't need to read it. It was a convincing prop. 'Professor, let us go through the history of the Confait case, so the jury will follow it, please. In April 1972 the body of a man called Maxwell Confait was found at a house that had been set on fire, and he had apparently been murdered.'

'That is so.'

'You attended, in the early hours of the morning and examined his body.'

'Correct.'

'Three young men were charged with his murder.'

'Yes,' the professor said, but it seemed he could wait it out no longer. 'If you could go back. On that occasion, I refrained from taking a rectal temperature.'

'I will come back to that later. I will give you an opportunity to say what you want to, about what you did,' Phillips said, almost pleasantly. 'Three young men were charged with Confait's murder?'

'Yes.'

'Tried at the Old Bailey in November 1972?'

'That is correct.'

'You gave evidence for the prosecution?'

'Yes.'

'One of them was convicted of murder, another of manslaughter, the third of arson?'

'Yes.'

'They were all sent to jail.'

'All.'

'The case of these three lads was referred to the Court of Appeal?'

'Yes.'

'A Professor Teare gave evidence on behalf of the boys?'

'Among others.'

'The report of a Professor Simpson was produced?'

'That is correct, yes.'

'You, indeed, gave evidence yourself.'

The professor agreed he had.

'At the end of the evidence, the Court of Appeal,' Phillips began, but that was as far as he got before Barker interrupted.

'I object to that,' Barker said. 'What the Court of Appeal did has nothing to do with this witness.'

'I am just going to say what the result of the appeal was,' said Phillips.

'That is what I object to.'

'Very well, I note the objection,' the judge said. 'But I will allow the question.'

15

WHATEVER THE FACILITIES at the Maidstone jail, they were generous enough that Prisoner Godfried could lay his hands on back issues of the London newspapers and of the local press, the *Kentish Times*. His selection of cuttings about Professor Cameron's roles in the Calvey and the Confait cases reached Phillips and Kirkham a few weeks before trial. The Calvey, in which an escaping hold-up man was shot through the back by an apprehending policeman, did not impress Phillips as material of promise. But Confait was, on any reading, rich with disquieting incidents of scientific misjudgement.

Maxwell Confait had lived in the upstairs room of a house in Catford. He was dark and lithe, a Seychellian, and a practitioner of the martial arts. He was taut-muscled and swift, but many frequenters of London night-spots knew him as Michelle and would have been surprised to see him dressed in anything but sequinned gowns or slinky cocktail-frocks. He was saving for a surgical change of gender, and worked nights, mostly out of rooms rented by the hour.

Catford was then having its share of fires. Early one Saturday morning, not long after one o'clock, firemen were called to a blaze in a house in Doggett Road. They got there in time to put it out. This was the house in which Maxwell Confait had his room. He was found on the floor. He was dead, his face bloated, strangled by some manner of cord. The fireman who lifted the body found it was already stiff. A Dr Bain, called to the scene, diagnosed rigor mortis as complete.

Detectives picked up three boys for questioning. They were each teenagers, and intellectually retarded. They very much liked setting fire to things, and two of them had lit several of the fires that afflicted Catford. At around the time the firemen put out the blaze at Doggett Road, the three were caught burgling a shoe-shop not far away.

Interrogation by the police was very successful. The boys confessed to the killing and the arson. Although they couldn't seem to keep the details straight for any great length of time, they kept them straight for long enough to sign confessions at the police-station in front of their anguished parents. The confessions were repudiated the moment they set foot on the pavement outside.

The oldest boy, Colin Lattimore, then remembered where he was earlier that night. It was a belated memory, but his parents considered it a good effort in the circumstances because the last time psychologists tested him he was able to score only sixty-six points in an I.Q. test. He recalled he was at a youth club. The police checked it out. It amounted to an unshakeable alibi. The people who ran the club were Salvation Army workers and they remembered him well. He had left at eleven-thirty. On the medical evidence, Confait most probably died somewhere between eight and ten p.m.

At trial, the Crown was at pains to delay the possible moment of the murder until midnight, giving the boys time to commit it. The pathologist who examined Confait's body at the mortuary early the same morning was called by the Crown. The pathologist was Professor Cameron.

Cameron testified that 'rigor was commencing' at the time of his examination at the mortuary. Confait's death, he said, might have occurred as late as midnight.

The confessions stood. The boys were convicted, one of murder, another of manslaughter, the third of simple arson. An appeal was lost. An inquiry, by Lord Fisher, called Cameron back to the stand. He was asked if he had known, when he testified at the trial, that Dr Bain found rigor mortis complete at the scene of the fire. He said he had not. He was asked if he had known a fireman found the body stiff to the touch. He said he had not. He conceded he had not taken a rectal temperature of the body, against his own usual practice and his teaching. He explained that by 'rigor was commencing', the words he used at the trial, he meant rigor was fully present.

Lord Fisher did not find that enough had gone wrong with the trial to warrant releasing the convicted boys. By this time they had been in jail three years. Then Maxwell Confait's housemate, Winston Goode, killed himself with a handful of cyanide. Goode was himself once a suspect, discarded by the police when the boys confessed. It was now found that Goode was Confait's lover and was in the house the night Confait was slain.

Parliament authorized another inquiry, this time before three Lords of Appeal. At this hearing, Cameron was in court while Professor Teare, an eminent pathologist, put the most probable time of Confait's death at around eight p.m., five hours before the fire. Professor Cameron gave evidence again. 'I would have thought the time of death less likely to be near the midnight mark,' he said then.

The parliamentarian and commentator Christopher Price appraised the scientific errors this way: 'It was mostly Cameron's fault. The law trusts forensic medicine to produce accurate, clear, unambiguous evidence in serious cases of this kind; Professor Cameron's evidence was inaccurate, vague, and equivocal. Perhaps this says something about the psychology of expert witnesses in the courtroom. Once allied to a particular side, a feeling of team loyalty tends to overshadow their ''expertise''.'

The boys were pardoned, sent home.

16

'YOUR HONOUR, I do object to this,' Barker said.

'Yes, I know you do, Mr Barker,' the judge said kindly, 'but I will allow it.'

'I suggest,' Phillips said, pressing Cameron, 'the attorney general announced in parliament that he was satisfied the boys were innocent, did he not?'

'Yes,' Cameron said, 'that is correct.'

'And the boys were awarded some sixty thousand pounds compensation, because of their imprisonment?'

'That's right.'

'The problem illustrated by the Confait case is that, when you gave evidence at the trial, you did not have a completely correct understanding of all the attendant circumstances, did you?'

'I think that would be an unfair criticism,' Cameron said, 'of the police.'

It was a good parry, and made Phillips smile. But he was determined to resist distractions. 'But that is the fact: you did not?'

'The whole substance of the Confait case was that I did not

take a temperature at the scene, and was therefore only able to give as accurate a time of death as I would normally give, if there was such a thing as an accurate time of death. There have been so many variables in the case. And I saw them. Because of the type of case it was; I did not feel there was any justification in doing a temperature.'

'Your difficulty was, when you gave evidence at the trial, you did not know what the police surgeon Dr Bain had found.'

'That is correct.'

'And you did not know what the fireman had found?'

'No, that's correct.'

'Consequently,' Phillips said, 'when you gave evidence at the trial, you were not armed with the correct knowledge of all the attendant circumstances.'

'I agree entirely.'

'Now, I want to suggest to you, Professor Cameron, that you have done the same thing in this case.'

Phillips leaned across the bar-table as though to get closer to an antagonist. 'You formed the view that you have expressed here, that a dog or a dingo did not have anything to do with the disappearance of this child. Really, you first formed that view at the time you wrote your report, did you not?'

'That is correct.'

'And your report was introduced into evidence at the inquest?'

'Yes.'

'And indeed it largely, but not entirely, forms the basis of your evidence today, does it not?'

The professor agreed it did.

'You believed, at the inquest, that the proposition that a dog or a dingo could take a child out of a jump-suit like that, leaving only two press-studs open, was quite incredible, did you not?'

'That is correct, yes.'

'And you voiced that at the inquest?'

'I did, indeed.'

'You believed that when the clothing was found only the top two studs were undone, Professor?'

'That is so, yes.'

Phillips read him passages from the inquest. Constable Morris testified there that the jump-suit was open except for studs at the crutch, and Goodwin testified the garment was entirely open.

'Will you now agree you were acting, even up to the second inquest, under a completely false impression as to the state of the studs that were undone, on that clothing, when it was found?'

'Putting it that way,' the professor said, 'yes.'

'The fact that you believed only two studs were undone was an important factor in causing you to conclude a dingo or a dog had nothing to do with it—because you regard it as incredible that a dog or a dingo could get a child out of a jump-suit, and undo only two buttons.'

The professor conceded it was true.

'Have you given evidence under any other false impressions of this case, Professor Cameron.'

The professor answered, 'Not that I know of,' but his voice was no longer sure.

'You were not aware that you were wrong until this morning, were you?'

'Well—' he began, but was interrupted.

It was the judge. 'His understanding was wrong,' he said.

'My understanding was wrong,' Cameron said, 'depending on the variability of the other statements,' referring to Constable Morris and Wally Goodwin.

But Phillips would have none of it. 'You can vary them as much as you like, but neither of them ever said only the two top buttons were undone.'

'I accept that,' the professor said quickly. 'I accept that.'

'I would like to show Professor Cameron photograph 10 B,' Phillips said, and passed it up. This was the coloured photo of the clothing, arranged by Constable Morris to represent the way it was found. 'Do you seriously suggest that this shows the clothing in a ''neat bundle''?'

'I was told the clothing was found in a neat bundle.'

'I know you were. But do you seriously suggest that photo shows the clothing in a neat bundle?'

Barker objected. The clothing was found by Goodwin, he said, not Morris.

Phillips amended the question. 'But you were told the clothing was found in a neat bundle?'

'Correct,' Cameron said, 'yes.' He was told by the odontologist, Brown, and by the police.

'You said, in your report: "Suffice to say I have never known a member of the canine family leaving clothes in a neat bundle." '

'That is correct.'

'Did you put this in your report: "On reading all the evidence, it would suggest the last time the child was seen, by an independent observer, was 1530 hours on the day of the alleged disappearance of the child, although there is evidence given that the child moved, or was seen to be held by the mother. Nobody actually saw the child, apart from an alleged kicking motion seen at the barbecue site." Did you put that in your report?'

'I put that in my report.'

'Your beliefs expressed there were part of the process of forming your opinions, where they not?'

'Yes.'

'And 1530 hours, if I can remember back to my army days, is three-thirty in the afternoon?'

'True.'

'Did you read the deposition of Mrs West properly?'

'I'm afraid I don't attach names to a thing.'

'It is clear, from Mrs West's depositions, that an independent person saw the child as the sun was setting.' Judy West had said she saw Azaria, who was then unwrapped and dressed in a little pink dress, at sunset.

'Yes, it would appear. But no exact time was given.'

Phillips almost laughed. 'The sun would not be setting at half past three, would it.'

'No.' The professor shrugged. 'I don't know when it was.'

'Do you agree that your conclusion, having regard to Mrs West's deposition, is a false assumption?'

'It is a false assumption if, if one negates, as I have apparently negated, Mrs West's evidence.'

'Have you made any other false assumptions, before you gave evidence, Professor Cameron?'

'Again, not to my knowledge.'

'Not to your knowledge,' Phillips mused. 'Did you swear this at the inquest: "I rely entirely on Dr Scott's negative evidence, in that there was no saliva present."?' Phillips was referring now to the child's clothing. 'Correct.'

'Did you read Dr Scott's deposition properly?'

'Yes.'

Phillips read a passage from Scott's testimony, which ended with the words, 'Of course, there is no guarantee that there is no saliva elsewhere.'

'That,' Phillips said, 'is a completely different thing from swearing that there was no saliva present, is it not?'

'There was no saliva present on the samples taken.'

'That is what he said: "Of course, there is no guarantee that there was no saliva elsewhere." '

'I would accept that.'

'A nappy was one of the articles found by Mr Goodwin?'

'Yes.'

'I suggest a Constable Noble referred to "bits of scattered nappy"?'

'I remember that.'

'He referred to "larger pieces of torn nappy". Do you remember that?'

'Yes.'

'Mr Goodwin, the finder of the clothes, referred to "a nappy lying next to it", that is the suit, "with a few tear-marks in it, and the plastic liner, with the inside exposed"?'

'Yes.'

'Constable Morris, looking at one of the photographs, said, "Of the bits of nappy on the ground, I think they would be pretty much where they were found." Did you read all that?'

'Yes.'

'Did you say this, in your report, and I will just read the material part now: "Suffice to say I have never known a member of the canine family pulling off a nappy intact." That is what you reported, was it not?'

'That is correct, yes.'

'You reported that without seeing the photographs?'

'Yes.'

'What? On the basis of what Dr Brown told you?'

'No,' the professor said. 'The appearance of the nappy when I examined it.'

The answer nonplussed Phillips. All he could assume was that the nappy had somehow reconstituted itself by the time it got to London.

*   *   *

Phillips took the topic to the stains on the jump-suit.

'You indicated an area, which was on an ultra-violet photograph of the back of the suit, and pointed to "a possible, more diffuse area there which gives the impression to me of the heel of the hand, with extended fingers". Right?'

'Yes,' the professor said. 'I corrected it, and said it wasn't the heel. It was that part of the hand.' He tapped the side of his palm.

'And referring to other marks you suggest "they could be the fingers of the right hand", but you couldn't be dogmatic about it.'

'Correct.'

'So we are talking of impressions of impressions, and suggestions based thereon, are we not, Professor? Or, to be more to the point, that is what you are talking about?'

'That is a play on words.'

'Well, they are your words.'

'And they are my impressions.'

'Arising out of the Confait case,' Phillips said, 'you would be one of the first to agree that blood, from an injury, can take up apparent patterns of objects, quite by accident?'

The professor tugged at his chin. 'I don't see the connection with the Confait case.'

'Perhaps I will explain,' Phillips said.

An English barrister, Louis Blom-Cooper, who was then pursuing new facts in the Confait case, came across photographs not shown at the boys' trial. They were photographs of Confait's neck, showing the wounds of strangulation. It seemed to him that something was written there in blood. He couldn't quite make out the word. The photo was too fuzzy. Then he found that Confait's neck was not destroyed. It was chemically preserved. Professor Cameron had it in his laboratory.

New photographs were taken. The prints were enlarged by three hundred magnifications and showed a pattern on the skin. Professor Cameron said he could make nothing of them, they were random. Blom-Cooper was convinced otherwise. He saw the word: 'WANK'.

*   *   *

'You looked at the photo, did you not,' Phillips asked Cameron.

'It was blown up three hundred times, and there was an apparent W. But if that can be inferred as a letter—' He shook his head.

'Next to the apparent W, was there a letter A?'

'According to the eyes of this particular attorney that you're referring to all the time, yes.'

'Whether he was right or wrong, it did have the appearance of an A? Did it not?'

'It was good courtmanship.'

'I'm sorry,' the judge said, leaning forward. 'I did not hear you, Professor.'

'It was good courtmanship,' Cameron said, louder.

'Whether he was right or wrong, there was a general appearance of those letters on the throat, was there not,' Phillips persisted.

'That is correct, yes. On the photographs that were blown up.'

'Three hundred times,' interjected Barker, who seemed as irritated as was the professor.

'The veins in the parchment skin had dried, and had given an artifact,' Cameron said. 'Which Mr Blom-Cooper agreed with.'

'By sheer accident?' Phillips asked. 'By sheer accident, producing that apparent word?'

'For his satisfaction, yes.'

Then Phillips got down to the connection. 'I want to put it to you again: Would you not agree that blood from an injury, purely by accident, can take up apparent shapes of objects?'

'They must have a contact point. By or against an object.'

'It can occur purely by accident, an apparent pattern of an object?'

'A pattern of an object can occur, certainly, yes.'

'By accident?'

'By whatever means, accident or not.'

Phillips was happy that it was so.

And when the defence team got back to the motel room that night, they toasted, in Calvados, Prisoner Godfried.

17

THE KNEW the prosecution had, with Cameron, expended its last witness. Tomorrow Barker would close the Crown case. So heady were they over the state of things now that they sat around late in Phillips's room talking about the chances of a 'no-case' ruling.

There is a saying that the high point in the conduct of a defence occurs the instant the prosecution case ends. The cruel and humorous implication is that, most often, a defence goes downhill from the moment it begins. Such fears make an application like this beguiling, but it is a tricky enterprise. The evidence must be so insufficient that it could not, on any arguable view, justify a conviction. Phillips said slowly, 'But that is not what we have here.'

They knew he was right. This case was somehow both too complicated and too simple to be dismissed now. Phillips made interlocking circles on the table with a moist glass. 'I think we will just have to win this one the hard way.'

18

FOR KIRKHAM, this was a familiar dream: he was running a footrace, a four-lap mile, a distance to which he was not suited unless the early pace was favourable and he could surge home, fresh. He made it through the last lap and into the straight, feeling good. As he sprinted for the tape it vanished. The groundsman tolled a bell. The final lap had only just begun.

2 TIMOTHY, 4:7

1

THE DEFENCE OPENED its case to the jury on the morning of 13 October. It was a hot Wednesday. The public gallery was packed tight. The defence is not obliged to nominate its list of witnesses, and the team had kept the secret close. Most journalists privately predicted that neither Chamberlain would be allowed, by their barristers, anywhere near the witness-stand. Malcolm Brown thought this assumption took little account of Lindy's own headstrong opinions.

Phillips, standing, turned his chair about so it gave him something to lean on. 'Mr Foreman, ladies and gentlemen of the jury, I want to begin by mentioning some legal matters of fundamental importance to this trial. Very shortly you are going to see and hear witnesses for the defence, and it is of critical importance that, when you are listening to and looking at witnesses for the defence, you never once allow yourself to slip into an attitude of mind where you say, in effect, to the witness for the defence; "Come on, you convince me that the Chamberlains are innocent." You see, as His Honour will tell you later on, persons accused of crimes like these under our law never ever have to prove their innocence. That is the law. His Honour will tell you more than that, I have no doubt. His Honour will tell you that an accused person does not have to prove a single, solitary thing in a criminal trial like this.'

He was spending time on the responsibilities of proof for an unsettling reason. He had discussed it with Kirkham. They were both uneasy. They agreed that in this case, more than any other, the accused might have to prove innocence.

Brown's gaze drifted to the Chamberlains. Lindy was not sitting on the pillow, it rested on her lap. She kneaded an embroidered kerchief. She kept trying to clear a persistent discomfort in her throat, as though ready to say something. This morning she wore a sunfrock, white and blue, frilly and meticulously pressed. Brown nudged Moorhouse. 'Lindy is going to testify,' he said.

Within a minute, Phillips confirmed it. Both Chamberlains would testify, he told the jury, as would 'a considerable number of other witnesses'. He did not name them. He nominated, instead, the prosecution witnesses whose testimony they would confront.

'Issue number one involves the opinions of Mrs Kuhl, supported to the extent they are by the opinions of Dr Baxter and Mr Culliford, to the effect that there was foetal blood in the Chamberlain car and on the camera-bag.

'We dispute those opinions, and we will be calling expert evidence to the effect that those opinions are not valid.

'The second issue relates to the opinion of Professor Cameron that the bloodstaining around the neck of the jump-suit means that the child's throat was cut by some sharp instrument, suggesting a human agency. Allied to that is the impression suggesting the imprint of bloodstains on the jump-suit.

'We dispute that opinion, and that impression, and we will call expert evidence that Professor Cameron's opinions are not valid.

'The third main issues revolves about the opinion of Professor Cameron, Mr Sims, and Dr Brown, suggesting no canine involvement in the disappearance of the baby.

'We dispute those opinions, and we will, again, call evidence to the effect that those opinions are not valid.

'And finally, as I see the main issues at any rate, there is the area of the opinion of Professor Chaikin and Sergeant Cocks, suggesting that the damage to the clothing is occasioned by a bladed instrument.

'Ladies and gentlemen, we dispute those opinions, and we

will call expert evidence to the effect that those opinions are not valid.

'You will also hear evidence, from lay people, as to dingo attacks and behaviour at Ayers Rock, mostly involving children. Fortunately, it would appear in each case, considerably older than Azaria Chamberlain. Not helpless children, but children that were able to do something, and I think in practically every case it was in daylight, and a parent of the child concerned was nearby and able to intervene, but you shall hear evidence as to the conduct of the animals in that connection.'

Every one of the jurors was with him: the three women sitting together in the front row, the garrison of serious men, the foreman with lined and reliable eyes. So attentive were they all that it seemed their gazes were not in the least individual, but served one concise and cohesive system of reasoning. Phillips felt a sudden surge of confidence, and recognized in it the signs of danger.

'You do not want me to spend a couple of hours telling you what the evidence is going to be, do you? You would like to hear the evidence, so let us go ahead and do that now.' The deep fall of his gown swept out as he pointed to the witness stand. 'I call Mrs Chamberlain.'

She lifted the Bible and took the oath. To Malcolm Brown, sitting on the press-bench, her voice seemed small and shaky. She settled on a chair in the stand, slipped the pillow behind her. She didn't look sturdy anymore. Her eyesockets were bleak and blotchy, in pitiful contrast with the effort she had made with her spotless frock. It was as if, so close now to the end of tribulation, she might be in peril of losing her grip.

Brown wondered how Phillips would handle the problem. He wasn't left guessing long. Phillips drew her through a few questions accounting for bloodstains in the car: the boys' injuries, bandaged Pathfinders, the baby's vomit, the Bleeding Hitchhiker. He allowed her to explain, briefly, where in the tent her tracksuit pants lay, then changed the subject. Her description of the baby's disappearance he restricted to a precis. Brown saw what was happening now. Phillips was rushing her through.

An obedient orderly handed her the jump-suit. In her hands, the limp thing was melancholy, dismally vacant, a cerement which represented a death so old now that as she laid it open the rusty neck gave off a wisp of coppery dust. Her mouth was ashen.

The judge asked if she felt all right.

'Yes, thank you, Your Honour.'

'Perhaps I can approach it a different way,' Phillips said. 'Without opening any of those articles, do you confirm they were the clothes your child was wearing, apart from a matter I will ask you about in a minute.'

'Yes.'

'Right,' said the judge, quickly. 'Put the clothing back.'

'Please state what other article Azaria was wearing.'

'She had a white knitted Marquis jacket.' She closed her eyes too late, and the tears stumbled down. 'With a pale lemon edging.'

A movement in the jury-box caught Brown's attention. A woman had lowered her face to her hands. The woman next to her, and a man behind, were also in tears.

The judge called a recess. The orderly, holding a tumbler of water, helped Lindy Chamberlain from the stand. The jury filed out. The women dabbed their averted eyes with kerchiefs. A jury weeping was an event with which Brown had no experience, but he was too sceptical a reporter to jump to ready conclusuions. Which tragedy were they really mourning?

After recess Phillips called for the life-sized photograph of the jump-suit. It was one of Professor Cameron's exhibits, showing the smudges of blood. He stood Lindy Chamberlain in front of the jury-box. He asked her to align her own index finger with the mark which had impressed Cameron. He turned it towards Barker, and then to the jury. Her finger was longer by half an inch.

'I object to that,' Barker said. 'The hand is flat.'

'I was going to make sure that was put on the notes, Mr Barker,' the judge said. 'Is there a mark definable, Mr Phillips?'

'You can see the finger extending beyond the mark, Your Honour.'

'Because the hand is flat,' said Barker.

'How many black smudges, or splotches, do you say you see in that light,' Phillips asked Lindy Chamberlain.

She counted them off from the photograph. There were four.

'Now just hold your finger up.' Phillips had come to the real point of all this. The mark which Cameron had identified, as the length of an index, seemed to have been made by someone whose stubby finger was blessed with four phalanges. The rest of the world has three.

Phillips abandoned her to Barker.

The accused's cross-examination is said to be the 'loneliest time' for defence counsel. Disabled by fears that objections will seem like confessions of weakness, they sit on the sidelines guessing the patterns of opposing play like footballers ordered from the field.

Barker took off his grey wig and reset it, straightened. A spur of hair at each temple gave him an impish look. All suggestion of good humour had gone.

'Mrs Chamberlain, should we take it from what you said about Mrs Ransome that you accept you told her to see that stains were cleaned from the pants?' Mrs Ransome was once Jennifer Richards, the friend who had taken Lindy's tracksuit pants to be dry-cleaned in Mt Isa.

'I accept there must have been some conversation, about something with the trousers. I don't recall any of it.'

'I understand you do not recall it. But do you accept what she said about having stains cleaned from the pants?'

'Yes. I just said: if she says that's what I said, I accept it.'

'Do you accept there was blood on the pants?'

'No.'

'You do not?'

'No.'

'Do you deny there was blood on the pants?'

'I have never seen blood on the pants at all.'

He asked her to recall the testimony of Mrs Hansell, the dry-cleaner. 'Do you remember she indicated with her hand a sort of splashing motion?'

'Yes.'

'She said they ranged in size from about her fingernail.' He read from the transcript. ' "Sort of tapering off with little drips, sort of, and went down to very small points, very small blobs, just splattery. Between one to three dozen, all told, and they were tapering off, and running down towards the bottom." Do you remember her saying that?'

'Yes.'

'Do you accept that is what she saw?'

'Yes.'

'Do you deny it was blood?'

'I have never seen any blood on them myself. There could have been blood on them because they were in the front of the tent.'

'Is that the way you would account for it, if it were blood?'

'Well, that's the only explanation I have.'

'Is that how you account for the blood on the tracksuit pants, if that be the case?'

'Yes.'

'Notwithstanding that it was seen to be only below the knees, and only on one side?'

'I don't know how they were folded or placed in the tent. It's the only explanation I have.'

'You would discount the possibility that it came from you?'

She took a breath and said grimly, 'That is not my blood, Mr Barker.'

At the bar-table, Kirkham lowered his head. It had not taken Lindy long to make the transition from nervousness to anger.

'Did you have any blood on your shoes at any stage?'

'My own opinion is that there was blood on my shoes. It hasn't been confirmed by any tests, though.'

'When did you become aware of the blood on your shoes?'

'It was the first time I went to wear them after I got home. It would have been a week later.'

'When was that? That you became aware of blood on your shoes?'

'I said: about a week later.'

'How do you say the blood got on your shoes?'

'I think it would be from crawling over things that were in the doorway, and things in the tent.'

'I take it from what you said about the possible application of blood on the tracksuit pants, and the other blood you saw, that you accept that the baby was bleeding in the tent?'

'Yes,' she said. 'Yes.'

'And according to you, there is no other way of accounting for the presence of blood in the tent?'

She could not think of any.

Kirkham's train of thought was running in the opposite direction. He wondered how Barker was going to account for the spray of blood Judy West saw, and the pool recalled by Sally Lowe.

   The topic reached the dingo she saw emerge from the tent. Barker asked, 'Do you recall this animal going around the car? That is, on the southern side of the car?'

   'No. As I said, I only watched it with my eyes for a couple of feet or so, and after that it was guesswork as to where it went.'

   'Did it just disappear?'

   'I didn't watch where it went at that stage. I went into the tent.'

   'Do we take it that it had progressed at least to some part of the car?'

   'Well, it had gone somewhere,' she said with sarcasm. 'I don't know where it had gone, Mr Barker.'

   'Did you see it again at all?'

   'I saw a dingo standing by the car on the southern side. The trackers told me it was a different animal.' She shrugged. 'It was the one I chased, though.'

   Then Barker said with some surprise, 'There were two dingoes there, were there?'

   'According to the trackers, there were two,' she said.

   Although a second dingo seemed now to have made an unscheduled appearance in her testimony, Brown remembered he had heard the suggestion somewhere before. He located it in his memory of the first inquest. Dr Newsome, the zoologist from Wildlife Research, said he thought two dingoes likely, on his reading of the events. But the evidence was new to this trial, and the additional animal stood there, shadily, like a convenient and evasive figment.

   'When it was shaking its head,' Barker said, referring to the dingo she saw leaving the tent, 'was it somewhere on top of the two parkas, is that right?'

   'Somewhere in that area.'

   'Apparently, if it be blood, shaking blood onto your slacks?'

   'Yes.'

   'Onto Aidan's parka? Do you know?'

   'In my opinion,' she said carefully, 'Aidan's parka had blood on the inside of it, but I don't think there have been any scientific results on that.'

'You know that none has been detected, do you not.'

'I said scientifically. I don't think they've picked it up.'

'You account for the blood on Reagan's parka from the shaking?'

She conceded that without argument.

'You know, do you not, that Dr Scott closely examined the tent for blood?'

'Yes. I believe it was Dr Scott.'

'You know he found a small spray, on the southern side of the tent.'

'No,' she corrected him, 'I understand there was a couple of small sprays.' She waved her hand to indicate the right side. 'Along the southern side of the tent.'

'But then you know he said it is most unlikely that it was human blood?'

'I know he said he couldn't detect what it was, apart from the fact it was blood.'

'If this dog, carrying the baby, ran to the south of the car, the spray or sprays on the side of the tent could have very little to do with this case.'

'If it had gone around the car,' she agreed. 'But if it had gone in between, that would be a different matter.'

'You suggest that as a possiblity?'

'Yes,' she said, 'I think it's a possiblity. Yes.'

'That it went between the tent and the car?'

She nodded.

'When did you first consider it as a possibility?'

'When I heard about the sprays on the side of the tent.' After a moment's pause she added, 'During the first inquest.'

'Before that, your view was that it had gone around the car?'

'I had thought that's where it had probably gone, yes.'

'Because you saw it there,' Barker said slowly, emphasizing it for the jury.

'I saw a dingo there,' she said laying an emphasis of her own on the comparative singular.

The day ran out before Barker finished with her. Phillips and Kirkham went back to the motel room. They had an aperitif or two. They talked the day over. Phillips thought Lindy was 'going fine', considering the circumstances. The circumstances he had in mind included the making of three full statements to the police, God knew how many press and television interviews, and the delivery of testimony at two inquests. Despite the number of times she had described the event, Barker was finding it difficult to pick up many contradictions. 'In the legal history of this country,' Phillips said, 'there can't be another accused who has talked so much.' So true did this line seem to be as he uttered it, that he made a note to say something of the sort in his closing address.

There was a knock at the door. It was Lindy Chamberlain and Stuart Tipple. The legal team was not permitted, by ethical rules, to talk with her about the evidence, but it was permissible to discuss the way she gave it. Her demeanour in the witness-stand worried Kirkham. When she was annoyed with Barker she sounded like a fish-wife.

'I know it's difficult for you,' Kirkham said, 'but you must hold your temper. You sound too harsh, too angry.'

'I am angry,' she said. 'What do you expect?'

'It's not going to go over well with the jury. Try to be more,' he cast around, 'demure.'

She was angry all over again. 'I am the way I am,' she said. 'The jury will have to get used to it.'

Plainly she was not prepared to take notice of him. He glared at her. Kirkham's eyes are generally described as 'piercing blue'. Whatever goes on in there in the midst of fury, it is not the abode of warmth. 'Understand this,' he said, in a glacial voice, 'When this case is over, I am going to climb on a plane and get the hell out of the place. You could be staying here for a fucking long time.'

Her hand flew to her mouth as if the words were her own. She began to cry. It occurred to Kirkham that she was the sort of woman who might never have been sworn at before.

And before court next morning, an astonished Michael took Kirkham aside. 'What did you do to my wife?' he said.

She was still upset when she got into the witness-stand. She shakily held a kerchief. As Barker took her through every item she could recall in the tent, she was pale and reflective. Kirkham thought the quality of reflectiveness, however involuntary it was, could work well. It might keep her temper in check.

Evidently Barker was in the mood for lists. Having exhausted the contents of the tent, he began on the stains in the Torana. 'You have heard quite a lot of evidence, have you not, about the presence of blood in the car?'

She nodded.

'You have heard quite a lot of evidence about the orthotolidine test?'

'Yes.'

'And you heard Mrs Kuhl say that she received positive reactions for blood from the carpet from the driver's side?'

'Yes.'

'And the driver's seat?'

'Yes.'

'If it were the case, do you know why there would be blood on the driver's side carpet?'

'No. It could have come from a number of places, I suppose. I don't know.'

'What places would you suggest?'

'Children crawling around the car,' she said, 'or people moving.' She put a helpful hand to her temple. 'Or from people Michael had fixed up, with injuries. I don't know.'

'Who did he fix up with injuries?'

'Oh, we often used to stop for road-accident victims.'

'Often,' Barker said, managing to convey disbelief.

'Yes,' she said.

Phillips made a note: Ambulance certificates. This was to remind him to make clear, in re-examination of her, that she and Michael were practising holders of St John's Ambulance certificates for first-aid.

'How many road-accident victims has he carried in that car,' Barker asked, 'beside Mr Lenehan?'

'I don't mean he carried them in the car. I mean he stopped to assist at the accident site, and then he—'

'Yes? Well?'

'He had to get back in the car to drive.'

'And you think he might have carried the blood with him.'

'He could easily have done that. It is quite possible to have some on your hands when you get in.'

This line of questioning was beginning to trouble Phillips. Barker was treating, one by one, the locations at which orthotolidine had reacted with something. Orthotolidine gives a positive reaction to many things other than blood, like milk, vomit, and rust, for example. A positive reaction merely indicated that the stain was worth testing further. This critical distinction seemed to be getting lost, somehow.

Barker said, 'And you heard about the positive reaction to the cross-bar under the passenger-seat?'

'I can remember a cross-bar. I'm not sure which seat it came from.'

'You heard about the reaction to the stain on the ten-cent

'Yes,' she said. She recalled the coin was found under the seat.

'And the floor? And the bracket? And the hinge?'

She remembered all these.

'What do you say about that?'

'I don't know that I've got any opinion on it, particularly.'

Phillips relaxed a little when Justice Muirhead interrupted. 'You are not being asked, Mrs Chamberlain, whether you accept the validity of the findings.' Phillips thought, He's onto it. 'It is merely that,' the judge said, 'if there were positive reactions, what have you to say about it?'

'Well,' she said, 'I don't know that I've really formed any opinion, Your Honour.'

Barker kept on with it. 'Can you account for the presence of blood on that side of the car?'

'I know Mr Lenehan's blood was on that side of the car,' she said. 'And a number of other incidents I have related here in court, but other than that,' she shrugged, 'I don't know anything about it.'

'The blood around the console? Can you account for that, if indeed it was blood?'

'It could have got there when Reagan hit the dashboard. I don't know.'

'When was that?'

'A couple of months after we bought the car, in 1979. Reagan was about twenty months old.'

'What about the window handle?'

'Well, that could've easily got there when I got back into the car after attending to Mr Lenehan.'

'The chamois?'

'That's been used on a number of occasions to clean up the car.'

Barker took his time delivering the next one. 'What about the spray under the dash.'

'I'm not convinced in my mind how that got there.'

'Can you offer us any suggestions?'

Phillips wondered how she was going to handle this, the Arterial Spray. Her gaze drifted to the exhibits sprawled about the courtroom floor. Somewhere there lay the plate Michael had found with a similar spray, from another Torana. It was inconceivable that both were blood, and possible that neither was.

She seemed to be choosing her words carefully. 'It would only be pure speculation,' she said.

'You prefer not to speculate,' Barker said. 'You just have no idea how it got there.'

She was firm. 'I'm not going to speculate on how it got there,' she said.

'You would not suggest it came from Mr Lenehan, would you?'

'No.'

'A nose bleed?'

She dismissed that too. 'Not under there.'

'What about the towel in the wheel-well at the back?'

'That had been used to clean up the car, and wipe down the car, on various occasions. One of the car towels had been on my knee when I was nursing Mr Lenehan.'

'The scissors?'

'I don't really know whether there's any blood on the scissors or not,' she said, adding that if it was blood she didn't know how it got there.

'The camera-bag?'

'There could've, quite possibly, been some blood on Michael's hands that night, from collecting the gear out of the tent,' she said. 'Zip up his camera-bag, it could easily get on the zip.'

'What gear did he put in it that night? Do you know?'

'In the car? All the stuff out of the tent.'

'In the camera-bag,' Barker meant.

'He wouldn't have put any gear in the camera-bag, but he may have zipped it up before he travelled.'

'There were large areas in both the front two compartments which reacted to the positive screening tests for blood, the orthotolidine tests. Now, if indeed that reaction was for blood, can you account for it?' Here Phillips thought it time to enter the argument. 'Your Honour, I do not want to intervene, but did not Mrs Kuhl specifically say that after four days she could not prove the presence of blood in the bag?'

'I think Mr Barker may be restricting it to the orthotolidine test,' Justice Muirhead said.

'That last little piece that slipped in,' Phillips said, 'got it into the area of actual blood.'

The judge turned to Barker. 'Could you restrict it?'

'I said "if it were blood", Your Honour.'

'If it were blood, and if the orthotolidine test did give a positive reaction,' the judge said, by way of spelling out the ground-rules. 'Put the question again.'

'She said screening-tests of the vinyl surfaces gave consistently positive results in both the front compartment and centre compartment. You cannot account for that?'

'If it was nasal secretion, or something like that, I could understand it.'

'Nasal secretion?'

'Well, it had held used handkerchiefs, and I carried used children's clothes in it, and things like that.'

'On the night of 17 August?'

'I wouldn't expect so, on the night of 17 August, but it had been used for some four months, by us, before that, and it was about five years old when we got it.'

'You see,' Barker said, 'you heard it put that other substances can cause a positive reaction, did you not?'

She had.

'And that one of those substances could be vomit, provided the vomit contained blood?'

'Yes.'

'The baby had vomited in the car on about five occasions, is that right?'

'Yes.'

'Did it ever vomit blood?'

'To your knowledge,' the judge added.

'She had projectile vomiting. I've never analysed it to see what's in it but it's—rather painful.'

'On each occasion you were holding her?'

'No,' she recalled, 'on at least one occasion Reagan was. Reagan was burping her.'

'Do you suggest that the vomit could account for the presence of blood?' Barker corrected himself. 'For the positive reaction in the camera-case?'

'Well, this is—' She waved her hand as if to clear away some misunderstanding. 'There are things that had been at different times in the camera-bag.'

'You say vomit?'

'The face washers,' she said, 'were used to wipe up vomit at some stage. But whether they had blood in them, I don't know.' She made a face and lowered her eyes. All the messy complications of motherhood were beyond explanation.

'I'm just saying it's possible,' she said.

*   *   *

'You know there was no blood on the flyscreen,' Barker said, meaning the flyscreen on the tent.

'I presume there wasn't, because it hasn't been mentioned.'

'Do you say this dog had its head halfway through the flyscreen, shaking a bleeding baby?'

'I said it was emerging through the flyscreen.'

'Shaking its head vigorously?'

'I couldn't tell you, now, whether it was shaking its head as it was going through, or before it was through. Its obvious movement was shaking the flyscreen at some stage. It was all in a matter of a few seconds, from the time I first saw it to the time I was in the back of the tent, very very fast and moving.'

'Your evidence is that you saw it shaking its head vigorously, and it was moving the flyscreen in the process.'

'I don't know whether its head was shaking the flyscreen, or whether what it had in its mouth was hitting against the flyscreen.'

'And what it had in its mouth,' Barker said with increasing volume, 'we know now, according to you, was a bleeding baby.'

Her reedy voice broke halfway through the answer. 'That's my opinion.'

'Pardon?'

'That is my opinion,' she said, taking care.

'Well, is there any doubt about it?'

'Not in my mind.'

'Is it merely your "opinion" or is it something you know as a fact?'

'It is something my heart tells me is a fact.' She was screwing the kerchief tight. 'Other people don't think so.'

'Does it surprise you there was no blood on the flyscreen?'

'No. There was blood on the pole. It doesn't really surprise me there was none there. It would depend which angle the animal was,' She took a breath. 'Or which angle the wounds were.'

'Mrs Chamberlain, you say this child was in the mouth of a dingo which was vigorously shaking its head at the entrance to the tent. That is what you firmly believe, is that right?'

'That's right.'

'The dog having taken Azaria from the bassinet?'

Her reply was a thin and dismal sound. The words wouldn't come.

Justice Muirhead said, 'Take it steady, Mrs Chamberlain.'

'You saw blood on the parka?' Barker said.

'Yes,' she said through her fingers.

The judge asked, 'Would you like a spell, Mrs Chamberlain?'

'No,' she said, 'I'd rather get it over with, Your Honour.'

'I do not want you to have to answer questions when you are feeling distressed,' the judge said. He suggested a ten-minute break.

'No, I'd prefer to go on,' she said. 'This has been going on for two years. I want to get it over with.'

Barker, who did not seem to be taking any pleasure in this now, obliged her. 'You say the blood on the parka must have come from the baby?'

'Yes.'

'When it was in the dog's mouth?'

'Somewhere around that time.'

'What other time could it have come from the baby?'

'Look, Mr Barker,' she said, 'I wasn't there. I can only go on the evidence of my own eyes.' She was close to wailing now, in need of some amnesty, but not prepared to accept it. 'We are talking about my baby daughter,' she pleaded. 'Not some object.'

'We will adjourn for ten minutes,' the judge said, firmly.

'I would like to remind you of some evidence given by Constable Morris,' Barker said. 'He told us this: "Mrs Chamberlain said that originally she was at the barbecue-site and she'd seen a dingo near the tent. It had what seemed to be something in its mouth. She hadn't taken a great deal of notice of it, because she'd seen dogs and dingoes earlier in the day around the campsite, around the rubbish bins, and tourists feeding them to try to get photographs etcetera, and didn't take undue notice until she returned to the tent-site a short while later, and then suddenly realized that the dingo or dog must have taken her baby." ' Barker lowered the transcript. 'Did you hear him say that?'

'I—I don't recall his evidence greatly. That is not, to my knowledge, what I told him. It may have been the impression he got.'

'Did you tell him you had seen a dingo near the tent, and it had what appeared to be something in its mouth?'

'I told—I told him I had seen a dingo in the tent with—appearing to have something in its mouth, yes,' she said, wary.

'Is this the case: when you first saw the dingo you did not take much notice because you had seen them around the camp earlier in the day?'

'Yes, that's probably it. For the first half second, or something like that, I thought it had a shoe. I didn't really take much notice. That's why I just yelled at it to get out of the tent.'

'When you say "much notice", you mean that you did not feel alarm?' the judge asked.

'Yes.'

Barker said, 'Did you tell him that you did not take undue notice until you "returned to the tent site a short while later", and then "suddenly realized a dingo or dog must have taken the baby"?'

'Not to my knowledge.'

'Do you deny telling him that.'

'I said I don't remember telling him that.'

'Do you deny telling him,' Barker insisted.

'I just don't remember telling him anything about it. I don't know whether I did or I didn't.'

'You might have told him?'

'It's possible,' she conceded. 'But I don't see why I would have, because it doesn't connect with any of my memories of what happened.'

'Which is totally inconsistent with your evidence, is it not?'

'Yes,' she said simply.

'You know Constable Morrris, do you not?'

'I do now, very well.'

'I suggest to you that he came back to try to find out what the baby was wearing.'

'I can remember him running across, at one stage, and saying, "What was the baby dressed in?" and me saying, "White" and him tearing off again. There just wasn't an opportunity to give him a full description. He had to let the searchers know basically what they were looking for.'

'Did you tell him, again, that you saw the dingo near the entrance to the tent?'

'I could have, quite possibly.'

'Did you tell him the dingo had "nothing in its mouth"?'

This was a discrepancy to which Barker had returned more than once. 'I think we've been over this a number of times before,' she said. 'I told him I saw nothing in its mouth.'

'Did you correct him?'

'To—to my remembrance I, yes, I know we had several discussions on his impression, and my impresison.'

'You do now remember the conversation, do you?'

'I know that when he came to see us just before we left he was still confused.'

'He was confused,' Barker repeated, doubtful. 'By the way, did you tell him the baby was wearing a matinee-jacket?'

'I did mention it. But I don't know if he was close enough to have heard. He was on the move.'

'You heard him say here that you did not say anything about a matinee-jacket at the time.'

'It was quite possible he was too far away to hear.'

Phillips thought it high time he straightened this out. 'Your Honour,' he said, 'I object to selected passages being put. My recollection is, when he was cross-examined, the constable clearly said that he may be mistaken.'

'He said that it was not verbatim,' Justice Muirhead said. 'He made no notes.'

Unwilling to let the point go, Phillips said, 'More than that, with respect Your Honour. He said he may be mistaken about that.'

'I was not trying to argue with you, Mr Phillips,' the judge said, amused. 'I was kind of basically agreeing.'

'I would like to remind you of what you told Inspector Gilroy the day after all this happened,' Barker said. He held up a transcript of Gilroy's tape-recording. 'Now, what you say there, do you not, is that you found the baby was missing when you entered the tent, not when you were running towards it?'

'I think it's just a matter of how it's put.'

'Is it? What you say there is, do you not, you called to your husband that the dingo had the baby when you emerged from the tent? Not before you went into it?'

'Well,' she said, 'I did both.'

'You did both. You dived into the tent, did you not, and saw that she was gone? Is this what you told Gilroy?'

'Mr Barker,' she said, 'that interview was a short interview, to give them some facts to work on. He told me they were coming back to take a statement with all the details in it. I don't pretend that everything in there is exactly one after the other as it happened. I was totally confused, and still in shock, when that was taken.'

'Is it the case that what you say here,' he waved the document, 'cannot be relied upon?'

'I am saying that it may not specifically be lined up, one thing after the other. It may be jumbled. I'm not saying it's incorrect. I'm saying it may be in the wrong order.'

'I suggest to you that it is not merely a matter of jumbling. It is simply incapable of being reconciled with what you say here. Do you understand that?'

'It isn't,' she said, 'in my mind, Mr Barker.' Kirkham and Tipple exchanged glances. Her voice was, once again, brittle, ungenerous, and combative.

'Did you see, as you approached the tent, that the baby had gone?'

'Yes.'

'Why did you not tell that to Gilroy?'

'Well,' she said, 'I thought I had.'

'Why did you say to him: "I dived straight in the tent first to see if there was anything I could do. I never thought of him taking her"?'

'To know that something's true, and to accept it, are two different things.' This glimpse of turmoil suddenly seemed to hold as much immediacy now as it had then, and she covered her face with her hands. The judge told her to rest awhile. Then he said, 'Mr Barker, she did say, when she was discussing with Gilroy the next day, that it may be jumbled up. I don't know whether—' He waved a bothered hand. 'I do not want to limit your cross-examination, of course. It is not as if we were dealing with—' He did not finish the sentence. Unease had no form in law.

'Go on,' he said.

Barker went on another hour. Phillips and Kirkham knew they were close to the end of it when Barker asked, 'Mrs Chamberlain, may I respectfully suggest to you that the whole story is mere fantasy.'

'You have suggested that before,' she said.

'Mrs Chamberlain, is it not the case that your husband declined to search actively on that Sunday night because he knew that the baby was dead, and he knew that you had killed her?'

'No, definitely not.'

'And is it not the case that this is why you declined to
actively search?'

'No.'

'I suggest to you that the reason that you and your husband
stayed near the car whilst people were searching was that, for
some portion of that night at least, the child's body was in the car.'

'Definitely not.'

'You invented the story of the dingo removing the child from
the tent.'

'I definitely did not invent that story,' she said. 'It's the
truth, Mr Barker.'

Her face had dried streaky. The pillow had slipped from
behind her, but she did not trouble with it. When Barker sat
down, he took off his wig, and his pate glistened. She sat
straighter. She had somewhere found reserves enough to outlast
him. I have fought a good fight, I have finished my course, I
have kept the faith: 2 Timothy, 4:7.

2

THE DEFENCE TEAM went back to the motel that
night for the most part happy with her testimony. Phillips was
surprised at the amount of time Barker had spent examining
Lindy about the stains on her tracksuit pants. Phillips thought it
merely served to illuminate the weakness in the Crown case,
since the campside witnesses testified that she wasn't wearing
the trousers until late in the night. 'Barker must be the only man
in the world who puts her in them when the baby vanished,' he said.

Kirkham was still perturbed about motive. 'Not once did
Barker put to her any reason why she would kill her own child.'
It seemed it was simply to be assumed she might. Plainly the
defence would have to call Dr Milne sometime, to show she
was suffering no psychological malady, post-partum. 'Otherwise,'
Kirkham said, 'it's a latent issue, a sleeper.' He didn't like it at
all. Then the mood in the room took hold of him. He poured a
drink. There was no reason to be this jumpy.

Malcolm Brown knew enough about Lindy Chamber-
lain to guess she would ascribe credit to some form of heavenly
sustenance. He also knew enough about the ways of the world to
doubt that she had made as good a witness as she might think. In

medieval times, when the adjudication was by water, those who sank were the innocent. They were acceptable to the elements. They spluttered and were acquitted. It was a social mechanism designed to exact public sympathy. There wasn't much around for Lindy Chamberlain. She might have done better to sink.

He walked to the Mall next morning and bought the *Herald* at a news-stall. He found his piece was entitled: 'Lindy Denies Coverup.' He thought it a harsh heading. It did not reflect the tenor of the copy. But the error underscored something he had been thinking about the case for some time now. No one seemed capable of understanding anyone else.

The Mall was busy. He was used to the odd glances his awkward gait drew. Brown seemed to have been constructed from parts which were overtightened in the process of assembly. He folded the paper, forced it into his suit pocket, and lumbered doggedly on.

3

LIKE FESTIVITY ORGANIZERS everywhere, social club committees in Darwin had a hard time devising themes for the annual ball, and the club which held its fancy-dress extravaganza over the next weekend asked that guests exemplify as best they could, in their costumery, Bad Taste. It turned out a lively affair, festooned and frolicky, the last gala before the Wet set in. There were the usual impersonations of spiky punks, here and there an ambiguous hippie made a dreamy appearance, and those who came as raucous drunks did not seem at all out of place, but it was clear, early, that the judges of costume faced a problem. Around a third of the merry-makers were dressed as Pastor and Lindy Chamberlain, the wives bellied with padding, the clergy swinging camera-bags they draped with swaddling clothes. The ball ran until the early hours of the morning. Couples wandered home, happy, replete, trailing streamers. A still dawn, lighting the court-house in Mitchell Street on Monday morning, uncovered a basket someone had delivered to the terrace steps. To the duty-constable it must have looked like a foundling. It was a white bassinet. A doll lay inside, headless, gory. He whisked it away before the press got onto it.

4

RATHER THAN DISSENSION, Stuart Tipple would have called it something like constructive argument, but the fact was that the team was not entirely agreed on the final shape of the defence case. Tipple, thin-faced and anxious, favoured leaving open to the jury a suggestion that 'a human agency' might account for the disposal of the infant, or its clothing. After all, this was the finding at the first inquest, and he thought Coroner Barritt had come closer to the elusive truth than anyone else so far. Kirkham was keen to reshape the case by bringing the discussion back to dingoes. 'When the arguments were about dingoes, we won,' he said. He wasn't too happy about 'human intervention'. Phillips, beetle-browed, ruled it out altogether. 'Look,' he said, 'the baby was taken by a dingo, and our clients think it was disposed of by a dingo. Anything else is just too complicated.'

Otherwise they were, as Phillips said, ad idem. Their witness-list stood at twenty-six, the Chamberlains aside, easily arranged into four categories. Testifiers to the Chamberlains' good character, or to their evident sorrow, comprised Lindy's Mt Isa friend Natalie Goss, Pastor Colin Lees from Avondale College, Pastor Mervyn Kennaway who was also the one-time owner of Michael's camera-case, a perplexed teacher David Haslem who thought the Chamberlains 'decent, kind people of the community', and the Ayers Rock tourists Gren and Jack Eccles and grey-haired Flo Wilkin who remembered Lindy Chamberlain as 'a perfect little mother'. Kirkham proposed to bring in the tiny obstetrician Dr Irene Milne somewhere under this heading, although her real usefulness lay in that part of her testimony which militated against post-natal depression.

Justice Muirhead had ruled already that testimony about the behaviour of dingoes must be restricted geographically and temporally, so the witnesses John Cormack, Erica Letsch, Ron Bellingham, Elizabeth Fisher and Lorraine Hunter, all of them vividly harrassed and still indignant, were testifiers only to attacks around Ayers Rock within the few weeks before Azaria Chamberlain's disappearance. This group should begin with the dingo expert Les Harris, Phillips said, 'so the jury might know what sort of predatory animal we are dealing with', before the more anecdotal evidence of the others.

Their answer to the Arterial Spray—the spattered plate Michael Chamberlain had found in a Torana in Maitland—was to be

proved through its clergyman owner, Weber Roberts, and by Mrs
Jennifer Jones, the Justice of the Peace who supervised its
removal for evidence.

This, then, left the scientists, of whom there were eight.
Phillips thought the order in which they were to be presented
would determine the thrust of the defence. They should lead off
with Barry Boettcher and splinter some bulwarks with a first
brute salvo. Findlay Cornell, a biochemist working in immunology, ought to be able to damage the prosecution a great deal
further by testifying that Mrs Kuhl's phosphoglucomutase estimate was, in the result, 'dubious' because the blood was so old.
Arnold Russell, a chemist who for ten years had worked with the
Melbourne Coroner's Court, had tested samples of carpet from
the Chamberlain car and, where Mrs Kuhl found 'a soap reaction', he could find no soap at all, and could detect only as much
detergent as you would find in drinking water. The Royal
Melbourne Hospital pathologist, Dr Rose, would prove the
astonishing pliability of an infant's head, 'like a pingpong ball',
he said in interview, which a dingo could crumple without
swamping the tent with blood, and the neurosurgeon Professor
Keith Bradley would show that the pattern of bleeding on the
baby's jump-suit was of the sort to be expected 'quite definitely'
from puncture wounds to the neck, and did not at all suggest a
cut throat. Hector Orams, an oral pathologist, was in quiet
admiration of the 'scissorlike action' of a dingo's carnassials and
of the keen, slender canine teeth. He could not distinguish the
damage to Azaria Chamberlain's clothing from damage which
could result from a masticating dingo. Of the two remaining
pathologists, Professor Nairn considered Mrs Kuhl's blood tests
inexpertly carried out and insufficiently controlled, and Dr Vern
Pleuckhahn, the director of pathology at the Geelong Hospital,
could find little anywhere in James Cameron's testimony with
which a responsible pathologist could agree. Pleuckhahn and
Cameron were once colleagues in the production of a forensic
medicine text-book. Tipple especially liked that conjunction. A
sweet, insolent touch.

5

THE PROSECUTION BROUGHT Simon Baxter back
into court to listen to Boettcher. Tipple saw that it was Dr
Baxter, rather than Barker, who was making the copious notes.

Phillips said, 'Professor, had you received prior to this trial a copy of Mrs Kuhl's work-notes?'

The professor said he had.

'Had you been supplied, too, with a copy of her deposition, her sworn evidence, made at the second inquest?'

'Yes,' he nodded. 'Yes.'

'During the course of this trial, I think everyone is aware, you were present during Mrs Kuhl's evidence?'

'Yes,' he said, adding that he was also in court during the testimony of Dr Baxter and Mr Culliford.

'Professor Boettcher, in your opinion, should it be concluded, on the results of any of the tests performed by Mrs Kuhl, that foetal haemoglobin was present in any of the samples tested by her?'

Barker was on his feet in a second, objecting. Justice Muirhead didn't seem pleased with the interruption. 'What is the basis of the objection?' he asked, as if nothing had suggested itself to him so far.

'Is my friend putting it to the witness as a conclusion which ultimately has to be drawn by the jury? Or is he putting it to the witness as a conclusion which he would draw as a scientist? Because, whatever the witness may think, the jury are entitled to draw what inferences they like on the evidence.'

Phillips thought this more an early reminder to the jury of its sovereignty, than a form of objection, but he held his peace.

'Mr Barker,' the judge said, 'I assumed it was put to him as a scientist, by way of opinion after hearing her evidence and looking at her work-sheets, as to whether, as an omnibus question, the conclusions as to foetal blood can be scientifically sustained.' It all seemed perfectly plain. 'I think that is all he is asked.'

'I think it should be clear, that's all,' Barker said, and sat down.

This was the most important and comprehensive question the witness would be called on to answer, so Phillips wasn't too displeased at the opportunity to repeat it. 'In your opinion, should it be concluded, on the results of any of the tests performed by Mrs Kuhl, that foetal haemoglobin was present in any of the samples tested by her?'

'No,' the professor said. 'It is my opinion that such a conclusion should not be reached from the results presented by Mrs Kuhl.'

*   *   *

'The anti-serum known as anti-haemoglobin has in it antibodies that react with both the alpha and the beta molecular chains which are found in haemoglobins. The alpha chains are found in all haemoglobins, adult and foetal. The beta globin chain is found only in adult haemoglobin. Foetal haemoglobin contains both alpha and gamma haemoglobin chains, and if one is testing a blood sample that has some foetal and some adult material in it, one expects that, if you obtain a reaction with anti-foetal haemoblogin anti-serum, that should be directed only at the gamma chain, which is found only in foetal haemoglobin. If you perform a test on the same sample with an anti-haemoglobin serum which is specific for the alpha chain which is found in both adult haemoglobin and foetal haemoglobin, you would also expect to get a positive reaction.'

Something about Boettcher was unsettling Stuart Tipple. The professor's concern with the molecular precision of things was making him sound pedantic and prolix. He had no gift for easy sentences. Although he addressed his careful words to the jury, he was clearly unable to produce a smile at the same time. The muscles in his neck squeezed out beads of moisture. He was carrying a heavy load. It was as though the professor has assumed the task of restoring to its proper level the entire reputation of science.

During recess the Melbourne *Age* reporter Lindsay Murdoch took Malcolm Brown aside in the corridor. 'This is impossible,' Murdoch said. 'What is the guy saying?' No one in the media-room could translate it into copy. Brown filled him in as best he could. Brown's grasp of immunology and molecular structure wasn't all that wonderful either, but he knew from Kirkham that Boettcher was demonstrating the failure of Kuhl's testing solution. Brown had understood the real point. 'It's not so much a series of unrelated errors, but a repetition of the same mistake.'

'Pity the jury,' Murdoch said as he wandered off.

Station TwoDAY Newsbreak:
Proceedings in the Azaria murder trial were dominated this morning by a courtroom battle between the defence witness Professor Barry Boettcher and the prosecutor Ian Barker.

Professor Boettcher testified that serum used in the Chamberlain case by prosecution analysts was defective. This serum is widely used in government laboratories and is manufactured in West Germany.

Under persistent cross-examination the professor conceded he was an academic biologist and not a specialist in criminal investigations.

But he also told the prosecutor that Mrs Joy Kuhl, called in the case against Lindy Chamberlain, seemed not to understand fully the principles behind the tests she used to identify foetal blood in the Chamberlain family car.

'Professor,' Barker said, with a sudden distaste for the title, 'you heard Mrs Kuhl give evidence.'

'Yes.'

'You heard her say that in her experience she has examined a wide variety of forensic exhibits?'

'Yes.'

'That she regularly gives evidence in courts in New South Wales?'

'I believe so.'

'That she works in a laboratory that handles some six hundred criminal cases a year?'

'Yes.'

'There is no doubt, is there, that Mrs Kuhl has vastly more experience than you in forensic biology?'

'I will agree that Mrs Kuhl has vastly more experience than I have in dealing with forensic samples.'

Phillips and Kirkham knew what to expect from this line of questioning. Barker was about to imprison the professor in an Ivory Tower.

'You heard evidence, did you not from Dr Baxter?'

'I heard Dr Baxter's evidence.'

'Do you suggest Dr Baxter does not know what he is talking about?'

'No. I think that Dr Baxter has had wide experience. I think he came here and spoke correctly of his observations.'

'You wouldn't doubt his competence?'

'His competence as a technician?' the professor asked.

'As a forensic biologist.'

'I have no reason to doubt his competence as a forensic biologist.'

'He told us that the anti-sera at that laboratory is routinely tested, did he not?'

'He told us that in one respect,' the professor conceded, 'but he also gave us information in another. He, I think, told us that the anti-sera are tested against the material that they are supposed to react with. But I think he also informed us that, if the anti-sera contained unwanted antibodies, they would not be detected in the tests they do.'

'You heard evidence from Mr Culliford, did you not?'

'Yes.'

'You heard him tell us that he's been actively engaged in the identification and grouping of blood?'

'Yes.'

'Probably the world's leading forensic biologist?'

'I don't believe I would argue with that. He's certainly very well known.'

'He invented the cross-over electrophoresis test?'

'Yes.'

Barker read, from the transcript, passages in which Culliford had said he found nothing in his reading of Mrs Kuhl's methods or conclusions to cause him to doubt them, either in the finding of haemoglobin, or of the phosphoglucomutase grouping which she judged inconsistent with Lenehan's. 'That,' Barker said, 'was Mr Culliford's opinion of her work, was it not?'

'Yes.'

'An opinion with which you, I take it, disagree?'

The professor did not get as far as an answer. Justice Muirhead said, 'You say you did find fault with her methodology, do you not?'

'With the conclusions derived from her results, Your Honour.'

'You are critical of her interpretation of what she saw?'

'Yes.'

'And her scientific examination? Am I right in saying you believe she was misled by believing that the anti-sera was specific, where you say it was non-specific?'

The professor nodded. This was the crux.

'You don't know whether it was specific or non-specific, do you,' Barker said. 'Apart from what she can tell you, and what Dr Baxter can tell you.'

'Unless one of the two batches I used was the same batch that Mrs Kuhl used.'

'You've given a great deal of evidence arising from your use of a particular batch of anti-serum.'

'Two batches of anti-serum.'

'Which is not the same as the anti-sera used by her in this case.'

'I don't know that,' the professor said.

'You didn't inquire, did you?'

'No, I haven't inquired.'

'You made no attempt to get, from her, a sample of the anti-serum she's spoken of in this court, did you?'

'No,' the professor said, 'I did not contact Mrs Kuhl.'

It was not the professor but Tipple who, before trial, had asked Mrs Kuhl for the batch number of her testing solution, and Tipple was refused. Although Boettcher believed that Kuhl's own demonstration plates showed the anti-sera plainly misbehaving, the defence would have been on stronger ground if it knew which batch to experiment with. Phillips considered that, if anyone should be blamed for this, it should be Mrs Kuhl. 'Your Honour, I'm sorry to intrude, but our instructions are that Mr Tipple was in touch with Mrs Kuhl about this matter.'

'You can re-examine,' the judge said, directing Phillips to bring it up again with the professor when Barker finished.

'I don't think this witness knows anything about it,' Phillips said. 'That's the difficulty.'

'I'm not going to stop the cross-examination,' the judge said.

'If the anti-serum she was using was specific to foetal haemoglobin, that's the end of the matter, isn't it?' Barker said.

'I wouldn't like to say if it was the end of the matter. It's the end of the matter with regard to specificity, yes.'

'It rather destroys the thesis upon which your evidence rests.'

'There are two theses upon which my evidence rests.'

'You say you got an unexpected result? That is, the two bands.'

'Yes.'

'You tried to relate this to her work, to suggest that her anti-serum was also defective, because of the two bands? Is that what you are saying?'

'Partly, yes. When I saw Mrs Kuhl's demonstration slide here, it indicated to me that, on that slide, there was the same sort of phenomenon I had observed previously.'

'You heard her evidence in that regard? That the two bands were of no significance?'

'Yes.'

'You heard Dr Baxter's evidence in that regard? That the two bands were of no significance?'

'Yes.'

'What Mr Culliford said was: "If it has been shown that the anti-serum is specific to foetal haemoglobin, then, it has no necessary bearing on the issue, it is a positive result." Do you agree with that?'

'Yes, and I would take particular note of the last comment there: "If it has been shown that the anti-serum is specific to foetal haemoglobin." '

'That is what was shown to Mrs Kuhl's satisfaction by her own testing, was it not, and to Dr Baxter's satisfaction?'

'I believe Mrs Kuhl understood that the testing had been done by a laboratory technician, and she was assuming the anti-serum was specific.'

'But she then tested it herself, didn't she, two hundred times?'

The professor remembered that she had said something like that, but the number of times was of no moment. 'She was testing the suitability of the reagent to work under those circumstances, which are different from the circumstances under which she worked on the test samples that she was studying in this case.'

That was a roundabout way of saying she was testing with fresh blood from a reaction to old. 'Well,' Barker said with a deprecating smile 'that's your view, is it?'

'That is my view,' the professor said. By size alone he was ill-fitted to a witness stand. The rail hardly reached to his hips. He seemed remote, precarious, the odd man out, made the odder by an awkward and inflexible conviction that he was right.

6

THE BARMAID was new to the hotel. She wore her hair in an erect pony-tail and was, very probably, working her way around the country mixing drinks. A reporter asked her to mix him a highball. He wanted lemon juice served in a flute, with a double shot of vodka and a few drops of red grenadine over the top. This drink he had devised in the media-room watching Professor Boettcher in the witness-stand, on video. The barmaid added the grenadine to the brimming glass, drop by drop, using a drinking-straw like a pipette. She asked what the drink was called. 'A Tube Precipitin', he said, watching the colours form. The grenadine spread into a ring, crimson and glowing. It hung halfway down. 'There's the reaction,' he said. She walked to the other end of the bar. She thought he was drunk.

At a table in the garden reporters were drinking with Dr Baxter, Mick O'Loughlin and two detectives. Everyone was in shirt-sleeves. Baxter seemed to be carrying the conversation which was, until then, about the Commonwealth Games. A copy of *The Bulletin* magazine lay on the table. Someone picked it up. This was an issue in which the reporters were reported on. A piece about scientific testimony at the Chamberlain trial described, in comical terms, puzzlement and confusion in the press-rooms. The reporter flipped the pages through but couldn't find it. Baxter needed hardly a second's reflection. 'Page sixty-seven,' he said.

Sean Flannery, who had put in as perplexed a day as anyone else, was keen to know what the prosecution thought of the evidence so far. Flannery was a voice-reporter with radio 2UE Sydney, a short feisty man with a professional reputation for tenacity and a personal reputation for trouble. He asked Baxter how he thought Boettcher performed in the witness-stand.

Baxter inspected his fingers a moment, then looked up, rueful and amused. 'Extremely well,' he said.

Not everyone thought so. At the Travelodge Kirkham and Tipple were at the swimming-pool. Phillips was preparing for a run on the foreshore, a new habit encouraged by Kirkham. None of them was happy with the day's work. As far as they could guess, the jury missed as much of it as had the press. Overkill, Kirkham thought. The most disappointed was Stuart Tipple, who was commonly believed to understand the blood evidence better than any other lawyer on either side. Tipple had said of the professor, 'He'll hit them for six.' It simply hadn't worked out that way.

Tipple sat at the end of the pool, legs awash. The sun sank behind the trees, but the air was still hot. Jennifer Kirkham, who had flown from Melbourne with the children for a few days, splashed with them at the far end. Cherie Tipple, an Adventist girl who might have the longest legs in Christendom, sat in a deckchair nibbling soap powder out of a packet, a foible she attributed, laughing, to her pregnancy. The professor was swimming endless laps in pursuit, somehow, of relaxation. He had not yet sought anyone's opinion of his testimony. Tipple knew it would come. It came when the professor's swim ended. He hauled out of the water, seal-sleek and contented. 'How do you think I was today?' he asked.

Tipple slapped the professor on the shoulder. The fact was, a courtroom was a theatre of combat so foreign to the man that he couldn't distinguish success from failure. 'Great, Barry,' Tipple said. 'You were just great.'

7

EARLY THURSDAY MORNING, 14 October, Les Harris opened the cage at the back of the house and tethered the dingoes to exercise chains in the yard. They ran the periphery, snouts high, sniffing. Harris replenished the water-bowl. He brushed two tidy rolls of scat into a pan, and inspected them for health. When he went inside, the dingoes trotted to the mesh gate at the driveway, where they generally watched him leave for work. Harris left the house by the front door, carrying his suitcase. He passed the mesh and Kua, a big rufous male, let out a howl of disappointment. The animal either understood the significance of luggage or it was picking up clues from its owner's demeanour.

By the time Harris's flight landed in Darwin, it was late in the afternoon. He checked into a motel and met Kirkham at the legal-aid office in town. Harris had brought with him copies of everything he had sent to the coroners, to the solicitors, to the barristers. It represented years of learning, and observations of dingoes captive and wild. Kirkham laid it all aside. He had seen it all before. 'Most of these points are duplicated already,' he said. He was referring to the testimony of the ranger Derek Roff. The defence needed to prove now the expanse of a dingo's bite, how it hunted and fed, the manner in which it carried its prey.

The way Harris normally dealt with differences of opinion was to press on with his own. He said, 'The most important point is this: food is the absolute imperative for a dingo, and the circumstances at Ayers Rock were so perfect that if a dingo did not carry that baby off it would be atypical, even incomprehensible. The probability is nearly one hundred per cent.'

'The judge won't allow testimony like that,' Kirkham said. 'Probability is for the jury.'

The ways of the law never failed to make Harris irritable. He wrote that night in his diary:

Briefing with Andrew Kirkham. He is looking for confirmation of jaw openings, nothing else. Andrew maintains they have 'already won' everything else (motivation of predation, the recorded killing of children by canis pallipes and latrans, natural canid c.f. dog, possibility, etc. etc. etc.) and 'won't risk losing any points'. No one has made any attempt to investigate the ONE claim made by Lindy Chamberlain. And now she's being tried for murder. And still no one is paying any attention to the basic claim. Why?

He spent the next day walking around town. When he left Melbourne yesterday, the weather was crisp. Here the air was like steam. He wiped his gingery beard, and his palm came away wet. The newspaper reports added to his chagrin. Professors Boettcher and Bradley, Dr W. McI. Rose, specialists in this and that from universities here and there. It looked as though the case wouldn't get back to dingoes for another three days yet. He wrote:

There are now more Ph.Ds in Darwin than in the halls of a university. The case, which began two years ago with a single claim that a dingo took the baby, is now only 0.01 per cent dingo. It is now a battle of the professors over everything but dingoes.

That evening Harris was taken to dinner by Annie Warberton, a quiet ally to the Chamberlain defence, a solicitor with the legal-aid office. They ate at the Darwin Sailing Club, not an elaborate place as yacht clubs go, but it had a serene view over the waters of Fannie Bay. They sat at a table with other lawyers. This was a happy arrangement until the conversation turned to the trial. A local lawyer, who did not believe a dingo would carry a baby off, and had never heard of an Aboriginal child dying that way in the bush, made the mistake of saying so. The several accounts of what next happened vary a good deal, but Harris recorded in his diary:

* * *

I tried to explain to him that the comparison was not valid. Unfortunately, it was the end of a long, hot and tense day, and I was less than patient. His response was to shout at me, calling me a pseudo-expert, using some less than polite terms, scoop up his wife from the table and storm out. This unnerved me quite a lot. Here was a man whose professional livelihood depended absolutely on being very analytical and not missing a detail. If this was his response, what chance do the Chamberlains have?

He was called into the courtroom mid morning Tuesday, after, he noted, an applied chemist and a biochemist. Kirkham opened with his qualifications: Dingo Foundation president, field observer, guest lecturer to the Wildlife Department, the Forest Commission, National Parks, and the Conservation Ministry. Harris was permitted to offer some anecdotal material about a dingo's surprising capacity for the destruction of inanimate things, for example, shearing in two a steel cable using the sharp carnassials, and of livelier objects, like a twenty pound swamp wallaby which Harris had seen a dingo kill and then carry away without discernible effort. He was an engaging story-teller, and Kirkham had him entertain the jury with accounts of dexterity and cunning, while Kirkham watched Barker for signs of objection.

Then Kirkham got down to it. 'I am more concerned,' he said, 'to explore the situation in relation to stationary, or slow-moving, prey.'

'Stationary or slow-moving prey is usually taken head-on, because that is the way the dingo has constructed the situation and, if we are talking about small mammals, it will take the entire head. It will seize the entire head in its jaws, and in one motion it simple closes its jaws, and it will crush that skull. Usually they will accompany this with a sharp shake, which is calculated to break the neck of the animal at the same time.'

He was given a photograph of a doll wrapped in blankets lying in a bassinet, 'in the position in which Azaria Chamberlain was said to have been', Kirkham said. Only the top of the head was visible. 'With your knowledge of dingo behaviour and capacity, are you able to offer an opinion as to whether a dingo would be capable of grasping and carrying the child?'

'Yes, it would,' Harris said, without hesitation. 'There is enough showing that the dingo would make the assessment that it was a mammal, and therefore viable prey. I would envisage that a dingo would, immediately after the instant of identification, make seizure, which would be of the entire head, and it would close its jaws sufficiently to render that mammal immobile. As a continuous operation, it would then continue by making off with the acquired prey. It would have made the seizure by head, and it would be unlikely that it would change its grip in any way. That would have been enough to immobilize the prey.'

Kirkham asked if the dingo was likely to have spent much time in the tent.

'No, particularly not in those circumstances.' The beast was not likely to 'hang around' while it had food in its mouth. 'A dingo, a pair of dingoes, will have a territory, and they take their life-time's food supply from that territory. What makes the Ayers Rock area unique is that there has been an artificial food supply provided by tourists, and a number of dingoes forage in one area, and that is very rare. To our knowledge it doesn't happen normally in dingo society.' Danger of competition should, he said, cause the dingo to make off with its prey, quickly.

'With your knowledge of dingo attacks, would you expect to see a large amount of blood?' Kirkham was referring to the floor of the tent.

Barker said, 'I object to that,' and the judge asked him why. 'Your Honour,' he said, 'the man is not a pathologist dealing with the body of a baby.' Then he added something which annoyed Phillips, since it was said in front of the jury: 'We have already been told that the dingo grabs the head, crushes, and shakes.'

Phillips asked that the jury and the witness retire, then complained that, if Kirkham's question was ruled out, 'an exceedingly unfair situation will obtain for our clients'. It concerned him that Professor Cameron, whose 'knowledge of dingoes is minimal' suggested there would be blood in the bassinet if a dingo had taken the baby. Of Les Harris, he said, 'This man, in our submission, is clearly qualified to speak about dingoes.'

'There's no doubt about that,' Justice Muirhead said, but ruled that Kirkham should restrict questions about blood to observations of animals in the wild. 'The ultimate question of blood must be a question for the jury.'

When the jury and the witness came back into court, Kirkham asked Harris if he'd observed the letting of much blood from a kill in the field.

'No, there's been very little, and it's characteristic of a kill in the field that little bleeding takes place.' He put it down to the fact of death, the failure of the heart.

'We've heard evidence that a dingo in the Chamberlain tent was seen to shake its head, in the vicinity of the entrance,' Kirkham said, and asked if that was inconsistent with behaviour Harris would expect.

'No, that's quite consistent, because they are observed to also shake it after they have made the seizure, and the shake is obviously intended to,' here he shot a glance at the Chamberlains, who were staring at the floor, 'to break the neck.'

In cross-examination Barker was happy enough to encourage Harris in his praise of a dingo's strength. This was a clever twist, the implication being that the beast would not need to hang its burdened head as Lindy Chamberlain saw it, or cause the drag-marks Murray Haby found. Nevertheless, Kirkham thought, Harris is doing very well. He seemed to have two missions: to show how likely it was that a dingo took this infant and, at the same time, to re-educate the nation in line with the teaching of the foundation. It was a task of some magnitude, a little like opening the window of an air-conditioned room hoping to cool the world.

Harris flew back to Melbourne, and to the foundation committee, uneasy that he had not been able 'to convey even a fraction of what we knew to be relevant'. Kirkham thought they had got away with a wonderful amount.

8

IN PHILLIPS'S ROOM at the Travelodge, the defence team had a last conference with Professor Richard Nairn before he was scheduled to testify. Nairn was a neat man, in his early sixties, the professor of pathology and immunology at Monash University.

He was drawn into the Chamberlain case by Phillips. To his office at Monash, Phillips had sent copies of Kuhl's testimony and work-notes, with a request that he comment. The comments came back in around a fortnight. In Nairn's view, the work Kuhl conducted with Tube Precipitins, with electrophoresis, and Ouchterlony tests, all of them immunological techniques, did not establish the presence of foetal blood at all. The reasons he gave supported Boettcher. The testing solution was not specific.

The peculiar significance of Nairn's opinion was this: he had worked in laboratories in the production of anti-sera and knew what could be expected from them. It was always of critical importance, he said, to retest the anti-serum daily and, ideally, a part of the test run on the sample to be identified. Not only had Nairn worked in laboratories where anti-sera like this was manufactured, he had worked in the very laboratories in Germany which produced the anti-serum Kuhl had used in this case.

When the conference was done, and the professor had gone, Tipple confessed to Phillips that Nairn made him nervous. There was an air of the generous witness which Tipple didn't like. He seemed in some way intellectually eager, a fine trait in a scientist, a weakness in a tough courtroom. Barker would break him in minutes.

'Don't be fooled,' Phillips said. He had begun to laugh. A private joke, evidently. 'Richy Nairn is a gutter-fighter.'

Sitting easy in the witness-box, a trim, well-shaven, dapper man with precisely combed hair, he didn't much look like a fighter of any sort. If he had given his occupation simply as gentleman, no one would have been surprised. His only concession to nervousness was the need sometimes to ask Phillips for the question again in case he'd not got it fastidiously right. He explained methodology to the jury in concordant tones, and as if they were carrying out the exercise together, in the way Kuhl ought to have done it.

'For example, a sample could have been taken from the *baby's clothes*. Such a model would have made a perfect control, to see whether your serum is working. And then you would want to know, "What kind of concentrations am I working at?" demonstrating the sensitivity of the serum. With what small quantity will it react? When you have demonstrated that, you then have to ask yourself, "What is the *specificity* of the serum?" A sacred word. How will it react? Will it react only with *one* thing, and with no other? And you have to test that out with a model. The third thing you must do is to say, "The system of testing that I am going to use is such-and-such a system," and you *test*. You put in the model samples you have made, and you put your serum in, which you have shown to be sensitive enough, and you *demonstrate* that they are specific, and you demonstrate their specificity by those reactions, the reactions of identity or non-identity, and then, when you are satisfied that your system is working perfectly—you have the perfect sera, you have the perfect models—then you put in the samples. In this case, so as not to make it too hypothetical, the samples from the

Chamberlain car you put into your test system. Only *then* do you put your samples from the car into your test system. That avoids wasting them if the thing doesn't work, and it makes absolutely sure that you have got the chance of doing things like recognizing the *absolute* identity of one thing with another: foetal haemoglobin with your control foetal haemoglobin, adult haemoglobin with your control adult haemoglobin.'

The process seemed orderly, authentic, harmonious, even charming.

Having in mind, perhaps, the same Ivory Tower for Nairn to which he had already consigned Professor Boettcher, Barker asked: 'May we take it, Professor, that you are not a forensic pathologist?'

'In one sense I'm not,' Narin said, amiably. 'In another sense, I am responsible for the forensic pathology teaching in my medical school, and have been for the last twenty years.'

Of forensic biology Barker said, 'A great deal of it is to do with identification of blood from trace samples and old stains, isn't it?'

Nairn's agreement with this was not unqualified. 'Most of their work, of course, is on fresh stains.'

'All your work is on fresh stains, isn't it?'

'By no means. All my work is on all sorts of tissues. Some of it is very old. I've actually made a study of the ageing of animal tissues—'

He got no further. 'I was talking about blood,' Barker said.

'Including blood, as an example of an antigen.'

'Have you ever done it to assist in a criminal case?'

'I've never actually been asked to identify blood, in a criminal case,' the professor said carefully, 'other than by just looking at it, but it doesn't differ in any way from the identification of any other human or animal tissue. Blood is a tissue. It doesn't differ. It just happens to be red. People can see it. And it comes out easily. But the principles are precisely the same.' His smile was a beam of pure reason.

'You have never ever before been involved as a witness in a case of suspected homicide, is that right?'

'No, it is not right,' the professor said. 'I've been an expert witness in four cases of suspected homicide during the last six years.'

'In Victoria,' Barker was now referring to Nairn's home state, 'is there a forensic science laboratory?'

'Yes.'

'Does that employ biologists?'

It employed biologists, though Nairn confessed he didn't know exactly how many.

'Does it concern itself with mayhem? Or wounding? Suspected cases where blood requires to be examined for forensic purposes?'

'Yes.'

'By forensic purposes, we mean for the gathering of evidence for presentation to a court?'

Nairn agreed with the definition.

'This is the speciality of the forensic biologist, is it not?' The implication was clearer now. Barker meant to distance Nairn from any involvement with the practical.

'Yes. As a matter of fact, the forensic pathologist to that group attended a course I gave sixteen years ago,' the professor said, thinking back. 'To learn how to do it.'

Richard Nairn had taken his first degree in 1942. This was at the medical school at Liverpool University, U.K., and he graduated with honours intending to go on to higher degrees. But that was the third year of the war, the Royal Navy lost HMS *Eagle* and then *Manchester*, both sunk on convoy to Malta, and a convoy to Russia repulsed. off Norway, the heaviest German air attack anyone afloat had set eyes on until then. This seemed reason enough to choose the navy in which to see service, and Nairn spent much of the rest of it as sea-going surgeon lieutenant to a flotilla of minesweepers which cleared passages for fleets in convoy between Europe and the Far East. For peacetime his choice was pathology. His higher doctorate came in two years and a Ph.D in another five. By 1963 he was a specialist in immunology, a fellow to two Royal Colleges of Pathologists and took up his chair at Monash. He added another Royal College, this time of physicians in Australia, and the Royal Society of Edinburgh. He lectured and researched now in London, Toronto, Cleveland Ohio, and the University of Texas.

'How much of your day is spent teaching?'

'Regretfully little, teaching undergraduates. I would suppose two hours a week.'

'How much on administration?'

'Two days a week.'

'How much in research?'

'My research happens to be immunological, and my professional work and immunological work would make up all of the rest.' He added, in case it seemed rather a lot, 'My week, of course, being a seven-day week.'

'I'm happy to inform you that you are not the only person who so suffers,' Barker said. 'How much of your time is devoted to the identification of blood?'

This was becoming a familiar theme. 'As I said, very little. Rather more, in the last few weeks, since I wanted to make myself competent in being able to give opinions in this court.'

It seemed like an opening. Barker said, 'When did you commence to make yourself competent?'

'I began to make myself competent twenty-five years ago,' the professor said.

'When did you commence to make yourself competent to give evidence in this court?'

'When I was first asked to give an opinion about certain aspects of this case. About mid July. I have repeated all of these things in my own laboratory.'

'And before that, was very little of your time devoted to the identification of blood?'

Nairn wagged an amused finger. 'I don't accept that blood is any different from any other tissue. A great deal of my time has been devoted to the identification of human and animal tissues. Some of it forensically, in the identification of remains. I am considered to be, possibly, the final consultant in this, in many cases.'

'May we confine our discussion to blood?' Barker said.

Justice Muirhead seemed to think the dispute was not getting very far. 'I think what he was trying to point out is, you can't really confine your discussion on immunology only to blood, when you are looking at questions of experience and endeavour.'

'He seems to have managed it so far, Your Honour,' Barker said in a gritty voice.

Barker turned to matters of specificity and the testing solution. 'If you tested your anti-foetal haemoglobin anti-serum against over two hundred samples of adult blood, and if you did not receive a positive reaction to any of them, that would be a good practical method of determining that it was not specific to any component of adult blood?'

The professor shook his head. 'Not necessarily. It would depend entirely upon what test you were using, what concentration of adult blood you were using.'

'But two hundred tests, by a competent biologist, in which no positive reaction was obtained?' Barker was referring to Kuhl.

'I have already referred to the inferiority of quantity over quality. Two hundred *bad* tests are poorer than one *good* test.'

'I know your opinion of forensic biology as a science, Professor,' Barker said.

But Nairn would have none of it. 'Anti-sera can *alter* on storage. They are kept frozen, and then they are taken out again for another time, and this is why all testing has to be done at the *time* when you make the test. It can't be based on what happened last week. Even yesterday.'

'Professor, if they are done properly, by someone who knows what they are doing, that would be rather an adequate series of tests? Wouldn't it, for the purpose?'

Were they done on the same day?' Nairn insisted. 'Or is this a series of tests done in the course of a month?' He smiled, waiting.

There was no answer from Barker. He sat down, as Tipple noticed, heavily, looking weary, ragged. He let out a sigh that might have been in him a long time. It seemed exasperation was all he had left.

9

IN A BURST of confidence, long since out of date, a detective had told journalists, 'The moment a defence witness steps off a plane in Darwin, we'll know about it.' Evidently the intelligence system was not working well. The prosecutors Barker and Pauling were now openly complaining that the defence was taking them by surprise with each additional scientist.

During a recess, a southern journalist took Phillips aside at the door to the conference room, 'John,' he said, 'I need to know when we are likely to finish. Family reasons, you see.' He then asked Phillips the number of witnesses yet to called by the defence. The correct answer was three, but something in the man's eyes suggested caution, and Phillips doubled the figure. The grateful journalist headed off, a progress Phillips watched through a space in the partly closed door. The man changed direction, once he was alone, and made for the police-room. 'Spies on our tails,' Phillips said, grinning, to Kirkham.

10

IF THE POLICE intelligence system was going to recognize anyone, it ought to have been Vern Pleuckhahn. He was not, by nature, commonplace. A stalky, greying man of striking energy, he was well used to interstate and international assignments and, if he was not first off an aeroplane, he was not far behind, an impatient gatherer of luggage, an imperious hailer of taxi-cabs. Any policeman watching for a myopic boffin was way off.

He was well known to the medical and scientific communities, at least those of the southern and eastern states, as a forensic pathologist, physician, and biochemist. He was director of pathology at the Geelong Hospital, a consultant to others, and senior examiner in forensic medicine at Melbourne University. He belonged to the societies of his profession in Britain and the United States, and Americans who read their forensic medicine journal carefully would find his name familiar because he was on its board of directors.

When he climbed into the witness-stand, Phillips began to read the curriculum vitae. Pleuckhahn had provided a summary for the purpose, which they were able to get through in twelve minutes. Then Phillips said, 'Dr Pleuckhahn, I'd like now to refer you to some evidence given by Professor Cameron.'

Pleuckhahn did not present himself as a tolerant man. It was as if he wouldn't bother with that manner of deception. His voice was abrasive. Many of Cameron's opinions, when Phillips read them out verbatim, seemed to stimulate in the doctor something between disappointment and anger. Phillips and Kirkham hoped he would be able to keep any excess of it in check.

Quoting Cameron's examination of the baby's clothing, Phillips read, ' "The only way in which one can reproduce this pattern of bleeding is by a cut-wound across the neck." '

'From my experience and my study of this clothing,' Pleuckhahn said, 'I would say that Professor Cameron's statements are completely unfounded.'

'Have you seen circular patterns of bleeding, on clothing like this, from head injuries?'

Cut-throats and head injuries were wounds familiar to Pleuckhahn. He was a pathologist to coroners and to busy hospitals. He had seen patterns of blood from head injuries there which 'were not dissimilar' to those on Azaria's clothes.

He looked relieved to be able to agree with Cameron over something. The jump-suit was, most likely, fastened up to the neck while the child bled, and the collar upright. But their comity did not last long. He showed photographs of a dead child Azaria's age, its head over the gaping jaws of a dingo's skull, to dispose of Cameron's belief that no canine could take a child that way. When Phillips read out another, '"The child would have had to have been alive for the bleeding to have occurred,"' Pleuckhahn showed that the dead bleed too, holding up a photo of a man two days dead, in a gloomy mortuary, whose blood had then seeped away to the floor overnight. Asked if he would expect, as Cameron did, more blood in the Chamberlain tent if a dingo had taken the child, Pleuckhahn said, 'I wouldn't necessarily expect, if it was taken by an animal with a firm grip, that blood would immediately come out.' He threw open his hands to show the airy and abundant possibilities. 'Depending on the vessels punctured at the time, if it is a vein punctured, a tooth could well form a plug. It depends on how tight he gripped.'

'Does extensive bleeding necessarily follow from severe crushing injuries to the skull of an infant?'

'I have seen extensive crushing injuries of a child's skull, also adult for that matter, without any real, obvious external injuries.' He was talking of children run down on highways, of a child dropped twenty feet on its head, and of three others, he said, striking his palm with a fist, killed by the blows of a carpenter's hammer.

In the video-room next door, the air was grey and bitter. The air-conditioning could not cope with the cigarette smoke. No one could open the windows. Monitors at both ends of the room showed a duplicated Pleuckhahn inspecting Cameron's photographs of Azaria Chamberlain's clothing. He looked, on the screens up here, like a contestant in a television quiz show. 'You have ten seconds, starting—now,' Lindsay Murdoch said, wiping sweat from his chin.

Pleuckhahn said, 'I've looked at this very carefully and, with due respect to Professor Cameron's opinion'—respect did not seem about to overwhelm him—'to me I can find no evidence, whatsoever, that would convey to me, even on this highly contrasted ultraviolet fluorescent photograph, the imprint of a hand.' He shook his head, marvelling. 'I've attempted to, but I can't.'

From the top of another screen, the judge asked, 'You express the opinion, do you, that the blood further down the jump-suit in the area of the chest, of the tummy, is direct-flow blood?'

'Yes. It could all be direct-flow blood.' Pleuckhahn shrugged. 'I can't see anything to convey to me that it is any different from the top, other than it's less concentrated.' When Phillips sat down, Murdoch said, 'He's finished.' Pleuckhahn's testimony had taken less than an hour.

Barker rose, his back to the screen, but not to cross-examine. 'I seek leave,' he was saying, 'to have the cross-examination of this witness deferred until tomorrow.' In tones of complaint he added, 'Your Honour, I have three times asked Mr Phillips to give me some indication when he was calling a professional or technical witness, and some indication of the general area of the evidence.'

'We can go on to someone else,' Phillips suggested, without rising.

Justice Muirhead asked if Phillips objected to the doctor's deferral.

'Not at all,' Phillips said, and Pleuckhahn stood down.

The court took the morning's recess. Radio journalists telephoned voice-reports through on the interstate lines, and the rest took a coffee-break. The monitors caught the lawyers again at the bar-table and the return of the judge to the bench. The witness-stand was empty, and it suddenly occurred to Murdoch that there was here an opportunity for the defence to keep Barker under pressure.

'Phillips might throw Michael Chamberlain at him, right now,' he said, 'just to give him a hard time.'

'Chamberlain will go last,' someone still at the coffee-bar said. 'There are three more scientists yet, I happen to know.'

The monitor quietened. Then Phillips called Michael Chamberlain.

11

THREE PRESS ARTISTS sat in the gallery sketching Michael Chamberlain while he testified. The one next to Malcolm Brown was a slim young woman with short dark hair. She was a freelance, and Brown had bought some of her drawings for the *Sydney Morning Herald*. He thought she was excellent. Of her name he only knew the syllable Jo. She also sold flowers and seldom wore shoes. She came from Perth, circumnavigating the continent in some fashion which did not always involve proceeding forward. Today she was in jeans and a T-shirt, and sketched, with a felt pen, on umber paper she took from a folder. She made four drawings of Michael Chamberlain, and discarded each of them. When Barker got up to cross-examine, something in her subject's face must have changed, and she worked more quickly, but she rejected another two before she passed one to Brown.

The scene she had created was truthful, although it did not, in fact, exist. Brought from other places in the courtroom to do duty here were the grave escutcheon of government, and an ominous shadow of the jury-box. The witness-stand imprisoned him to the chest. Whatever sudden understanding had informed her pen, it had got him right, this time: exerted brow, a hesitant underlip, and a gaze resigned to all manner of expected wrongs.

Barker said, 'What did your wife tell you had happened to the child?'

'That a dingo had taken her.'

'When did she tell you in detail, Mr Chamberlain, precisely what she had seen?'

'We talked about it, on and off, during the evening.'

'What did she tell you?'

'I don't recall exactly the conversations we had.'

'There is no doubt, is there, that your wife was the last person to see the child alive?'

'No doubt,' Michael said.

'And do you tell us that you are unable to say just what she told you about the child's disappearance?'

'In no detail can I tell you.' He lowered his eyes. 'We prayed,' he said.

*   *   *

'Did you think then that the child had died?'

'I knew she was in great danger.'

'From what?'

'Dying.'

'Of what?'

'Dying.' He was unsure of anything else.

'What did you think was going to cause her death?'

'Either exposure or bleeding.'

'You didn't know from where she was bleeding?'

'No.'

'You didn't inquire whether your wife could help you find out?'

'No.'

'Why?'

'It didn't occur to me. The fact was she was bleeding, and she was in danger of death.'

'Could it be because you knew that the dingo did not take her, and that she was dead at the hands of your wife?'

This time he met Barker's gaze. 'No,' he said softly.

Sister White had said: 'The Evil One is the accuser of the brethren, and it is his spirit which inspires men to watch for the errors of the Lord's people, and hold them up to notice.'

'Did you say to Constable Morris something like this, on the occasion he came back to make some inquiries: "It was the will of God; there was nothing that you or I or anybody else could do about it"?'

'I don't recall saying it.'

'Do you deny it?'

'I'm not going to deny it.'

'It's something you believe?'

'I believe in God's will.'

'Did you believe it was the will of God when you told Morris?'

'God's will is over all.'

'I suggest you couldn't see then, and you can't see now, why your wife would not have seen a baby dressed in white being carried in the mouth of a dingo out of the tent, and past the front of it.'

'I believe my wife's account, Mr Barker.'

'I suggest the whole story is nonsense, and you know it.'

'No, Mr Barker.'

'How do you account for the damage to the collar of the jumpsuit?'

'I can't account for it.'

'Did your wife cut the sleeve?'

'I don't think she did.'

'Did she cut the collar?'

'I don't think so.'

'Did you bury the jump-suit with the child in it?'

'No?'

'Did your wife?'

'I don't think she did,' Michael said, lips pursed, candid, and close to missing the point of his own words.

There was no spirit to his answers, only form. Brown now recognized in this a phenomenon from his days in the fighting ring. There sometimes comes a moment when an opponent, out-matched and damaged, concludes that nothing worse can happen to him than has already. He simply discards the seriousness of his plight. Brown had seen it in the eyes, in the tardy and incautious face, in the shockingly undefended mouth. Brown had to force himself to hit it.

Next morning Brown walked to the court-house with Pastor Olson. Olson said the Chamberlains were planning to move, on the last day of the case, to a 'secret destination' from which they could slip away, quietly, from the press after acquittal. From the way Olson spoke, it seemed he now thought acquittal a possible course of events. Brown wondered if this also reflected the thinking of Olson's friends in the police-force.

When Brown got to the courtroom, it was unattended. From waiting journalists came rumours of a suicide overnight. A court orderly, estranged from his wife, had shot himself through the head with a revolver. Although the incident had nothing to do with the case, Brown couldn't shake off the feeling that no sorrowing human being ought to work in a place like this. Everyone sat around, hushed and gloomy, until court resumed.

*   *   *

'Mr Chamberlain,' Barker said, 'your wife, I suggest, told you that the story of the dingo was false, very soon after the child was killed.'

'No,' he said. His voice was limp. It seemed he might not have slept much overnight.

'Did she not?'

'She did not.'

'She told you she was going to suggest that the dingo at the tent was the same as the dingo she saw at the Rock' Barker said, meaning the dingo Lindy and the McCombes had seen near the Cave of Fertility.

'Could you repeat that please?'

'She told you that she was going to suggest that the dingo at the tent was the same as the dingo she saw at the Rock.'

'I don't remember that,' Michael said, wearily.

He seemed now to understand little: not the questions, not the answers, not the dangers to come, not the manner of enemy he faced, not the ways of the world around him. He had none of the equippage of combat. So bereft was he that Brown now saw the prosecution's sudden paradox. It was in danger of showing that Michael had neither the wit nor tenacity to carry out the long and complicated deception with which he was charged.

Had Phillips and Kirkham forseen this all along? If sacrifice had anything at all to do with this case, Brown thought, the offering was Michael Chamberlain.

Barker asked how it came about that, the day after the baby vanished, Lindy Chamberlain had suggested they take the troublesome boys on a drive to Mt Olga. 'Did she say, ''Why don't we go to the Olgas so the boys will stop playing up?'' Or something like that?'

'No. No, that wasn't said.'

'What did she say about the boys ''playing up''?'

This was a conclusion Michael had come to, alone, 'because our children had to go on with life—normal, as much as possible, and it was just something—just to keep life as normal as possible'.

'Look,' Barker said, 'didn't it occur to you that there might have been a remote possibility, however remote, that the child was still alive on Monday morning?'

'Miraculous,' Michael said, by way of concession.

Barker recognized the tone. 'You believe in miracles, don't you. There are plenty of precedents for them, aren't there.'

It was a neat dilemma, and took some moments' thought, but all the pastor could come up with then was, 'I'm also a realist.'

Nothing seemed further from the truth.

When Michael Chamberlain stood down, Brown watched him walk slowly to sit beside his wife, and watched them hold hands in the quiet space between the chairs. In his face was fatigue, relief, even a little ludicrous pride, but not a line of bitterness or rancour, and Brown recalled a time he had asked the pastor about emotions like those. It was at Cooranbong. They'd had lunch, and Brown was leaving. He stood with Michael in the driveway. The day was overcast, autumnal although the season was spring, and brittle leaves blew across the grass. The trial was not long off. Brown asked Michael why there was no bitterness in him now, no outrage. 'I must not commit the sin of bitterness,' Michael said, 'if I am ever to see my daughter again.'

He was thinking of Paradise

12

Station TwoDAY, Newsbreak:

Pastor Michael Chamberlain finished giving evidence to the Darwin Supreme Court this afternoon, after six and a half hours in the witness-box.

The defence then recalled the forensic pathologist Dr Vernon Pleuckhahn, who had previously given evidence opposed to the prosecution's expert from London, Professor Cameron.

In cross-examination by prosecutor Ian Barker, which at times became a shouting-match, Dr. Pleuckhahn said the patterns of blood on baby Azaria's clothing could not support Cameron's opinion that the baby's throat had been cut.

Dr Pleuckhahn also said he had found microscopic traces of congealed blood in the damaged fibres of the jump-suit collar. This showed that the clothing was damaged while the baby's blood was still fluid, and not, as the prosecution believed, long after she was dead.

Then, at the end of this twenty-seventh day of the trial, John

Phillips announced that the evidence in defence of Lindy and Michael Chamberlain had closed.

13

NEWS BULLETINS foreshortened the proceedings somewhat. After Barker finished with Pleuckhahn, having made the most of the doctor's short temper and unrelenting resistance to compromise, one brief witness remained. This was Lorraine Hunter, a nurse whose young son was bitten by a dingo at the Ayers Rock camping-ground the day before the Chamberlain baby disappeared. Phillips closed the defence evidence at 4.20. It was a Friday, so Justice Muirhead released the jury for the weekend.

Phillips then handed up to the judge a series of submissions. One asked for a 'no-case' ruling, others that he should direct the jury it would be dangerous to convict as the evidence stood. Justice Muirhead said he would consider them later, but he looked doubtful. 'You should act firmly on the assumption that the matter will proceed to its ordinary conclusion,' he said. Phillips seemed disappointed for only a moment. He hadn't expected it would come off, anyway. It was more an expression of their risen spirits.

He was hopeful about the fourth submission. This asked the judge to strike manslaughter from the list of possible verdicts. The defence was ahead. He wanted no half measures in the jury-room.

14

CAMERAMEN backed down the courthouse steps, shooting, crouching like supplicants in front of the descending Chamberlains. Brown watched them go. They had three hours left now before their last Sabbath of the trial. It was hard to tell how pleased they might feel. They were not giving much away, anymore. Brown had heard it said that Lindy was ready to sue everybody in the police and in the media, just everybody, once the trial was over. Tipple ushered them into a little red sedan, and they pulled out into the traffic. Lindy had turned her face from the flashbulbs.

Barker came through the doors and reporters caught him on

the top step. Today was his birthday, as they all knew, and someone asked how old he was. 'Forty-seven,' he said, 'going on a hundred.' When Barker broke from the journalists, he offered Brown a lift to the motel. Barker chatted as he drove. Brown rather liked him, liked the attractive mixture of jauntiness and gravity.

Brown asked how the prosecution team thought the trial stood now. 'Don't quote me,' Barker said, 'but we've got to be realistic.' He thought the prosecution couldn't hope to nail home convictions any longer. 'We might have a chance for a disagreement,' he said. He laughed. 'For another trial, the Crown can get someone else.'

'I don't know if the Chamberlains could take another trial,' Brown said. 'The will of God notwithstanding.'

'If I had to take what Michael Chamberlain had to take,' Barker said quietly, 'I'd be an atheist.'

Brown walked the remaining block to his motel. Because it was Friday some of the light trucks and four-wheel drives passing by were loaded with camping-gear. Weekends here are of some moment, treated as if they are longer vacations, the very reason many people choose to live in this part of the country. In a few weeks now the Wet will come in, the air will be damp to the touch, the creeks broken, the tracks bloated, foliage become the freehold of leech and mosquito, and no one will want to go anywhere.

While Darwin gamblers waited on the completion of a new casino at Mindil Beach, they rode money on roulette wheels, blackjack, and two-up in the plush rooms of the Don Hotel. The restaurant there was crowded most evenings, and impatient diners could play the numbers while they ate. A party of pressmen and lawyers had taken a table. Bill Hitchings, a Melbourne reporter with a wide grin and a nose broken long ago, was there, alongside the prosecutor Pauling. They had been aware for some time now of a rowdy party at another table and were trying to take no notice. Evidently some of the jurors had decided on a celebration to toast the close of evidence. They toasted it many times. An incident which caught Hitchings's eye was the quick departure, towards the powder-room, of a woman over whose gown her partner had thrown up. Pauling must have glimpsed it too, so intent was he on looking the other way.

Then the event Pauling seemed most to dread happened. One of the jurors was heading over. He was unsteady. Cigarette ash streaked his shirt-front. Not many hours ago he had sat in court while the judge warned jurors against discussing the trial with anyone, but there was no doubt what he was about to do. His was the compatriot smile of inspired drunks everywhere. When his gaze adjusted from the general to the particular, he said to Pauling, 'I want to talk to you about this case,' and looked seriously about for somewhere to sit.

With as much good humour as Pauling could muster in the time available, he got to his feet, spun the man around, and set him on his way, a change in alignment that the juror acknowledged with a wave of his reluctant hand, which turned then into a finger beating time to some infectious dance-step as he contemplated the amusements of the path ahead, gay dog. Pauling flopped back into his seat. 'Jesus Christ,' he said.

Saturday morning Sabbath school took most of the hour from ten o'clock and, since Bible study was not only for children, it was often the same congregation which stayed on then for Divine Service at eleven. The church stood on a neat and unfenced block with a grassy border. The apex of the roofline was high, the fall steep. Altogether it made much the same shape as a pair of hands lightly pressed in prayer. They seemed to be somehow Northern American hands, more than any other, perhaps because of the association between slender, modern gables like these and the snows of New England, but the affinity is just as strong inside, where the appointments are pinewood.

The congregation, on 23 October, half filled the church. Stuart Tipple, who would cut Sabbath short when he got back to work this afternoon, sat near the gentle Irene Herron, Lindy's friend. Michael Chamberlain sat with a space at his side for his wife. No one was certain if she would attempt the journey from the bungalow behind, considering the heavy and uncomfortable condition in which she was. This was the usual time now, while folk waited for the beginning of the service, for the church proclamations. Pastor Olson read from a list of imminent events. He stood with his feet planted wide. A bunch of keys hung from a clasp at his belt. Tipple thought about the indelible nature of a policeman's training.

'Right,' Olson said. 'There's one more thing. The trial that has caused so much fuss in this town is nearly over. Those prosecuted under the due process of the law will be acquitted, and as they rightly should be. We have all prayed, and everybody will be pleased when it's over. Now, every one of us has suffered the jibes of people who thought they were guilty, but I don't want to hear about any paying back of old debts. No mocking, no unpleasantness, no unchristianly behaviour. And the first test is right there, just outside that door.'

This brought an appreciative giggle because, outside, newshounds and press photographers had the building staked out.

A carload of photographers returned Sunday night, fresh from Lim's. Lim's is sometimes called The Cage because the concreted beer-garden is surrounded by wire mesh to keep drinkers under control, either inside or out. The current attractions at Lim's were bouts of mud-wrestling between slippery and very nearly naked girls, but the show was over. It advertised spaghetti-wrestling for next month. The journey from Lim's to the Seventh-day Adventist church had lasted long enough that someone in the back seat had rolled a joint, a surprise because it was considered perilous to carry dope interstate by aeroplane, and nobody did. The burning leaf smelled green and sweet. He passed it around. Asked where he got it, he said, 'On a junket.' He meant one of the trips on which the government here was sending pressmen at weekends: sailing, fishing, or shooting, anyway outback. One of these excursions was led by a local detective and a guide.

'I didn't have any of my own,' the photographer said. 'I thought it would be a straight trip, just a drunk, you know? And then the cop,' and here he named a detective they all knew, 'said to the guide, "Have you got any?" And the guide had nothing. And the cop said, "Have you smoked all the good stuff I got you last week?" Well, I could have fallen over, you know? So I scored later.' He tapped his forehead wisely. 'It's a whole different town, here.'

When they pulled up outside the church, it was dark. They got out and looked around. The church was still. The door was locked. They heard music, fluted cascades and a fervent bass, but it came from the manse. So far as they could tell, it was not a recording. Someone was playing the organ. They considered ringing the doorbell and shooting film as it opened, a speculative expenditure of effort, but something in the music sapped resolve, and someone who was still thinking straight suggested they drive to Dick's Disco instead, in case it was raging there, and it seemed the best suggestion of the night.

Phillips was working in his motel room. He had, on Monday, to address the jury before Barker did so. Because the defence had called evidence beyond the accused, it forfeited the right of last reply, of the final word to the jury. He worked sitting at a coffee-table, with the window-drapes closed halfway against the glare until early evening when he flung them apart for the dusky sun asquat on the Timor Sea.

They'd been working like this for two days, and it was almost done. Kirkham and Tipple flipped through the transcript for passages of testimony he might read to the jury, indexing those he had already decided on. The transcript made six volumes now, at a guess three-quarters of a million words.

He'd made a list, selecting quotations from Barker's opening address he wanted to use. The prosecution might yet shift its ground, assume some other form, unanswerable, as soon as he turned his back and sat down. It had tried to do that from the day the investigation began. He wanted to nail the accusations to the wall, answer them line by line.

He wrote: 'This is the case we were called on to meet; this is the case we met.'

The themes divided with ease into five: support for the Chamberlain testimony by the campsite witnesses, corroborative trails and drag-marks on the dune, dingo behaviour at Ayers Rock, the Chamberlains' response to the tragedy, and the destruction of the prosecution's scientific case. There were seventy-three witnesses he must cover in some way, many in detail. God, it would take two days' talking.

Two items deserved treatment separately from the main architecture of the speech. The Arterial Spray which Metcalf found over the passenger footwell stood out because it was upon this the Crown based the suggestion that here the baby's throat was cut. Well, Michael had found an answer of some sort with the duplicate from the Torana from Maitland. And Metcalf found it 'sticky to the touch', so whatever it was, it didn't originate from Azaria Chamberlain a year earlier.

He should spend the early time restoring Sally Lowe to the narrative. Any jury must have loved her: gentle, observant, manifestly honest. If she heard the baby cry from the tent when the Crown said it lay already slaughtered in the car, the case was over, right there. Barker couldn't avoid meeting that.

Phillips wrote: 'Sally Lowe is an absolute bar to conviction.'

Tipple turned up the passage in which Barker said, 'There will be evidence that a Mrs Lowe also heard a noise at this stage. Of course, on the Crown case, it was impossible that it was the baby, because the Crown says the baby was dead.' So Barker will say she heard it in her imagination. If she did, she imagined it at just the right time, the time Aidan heard it. And then Michael, who the Crown said was not yet in on the secret, hears it. She imagines it at a time when a dingo has freshly dragged something up the dune in the darkness, something which leaves furrows for Roff to discover and when it is laid down leaves the pattern of a knitted garment for Haby.

Phillips wrote: 'What are the odds against two independent witnesses, searching the area Lindy Chamberlain indicated, making that find fortuitously? Astronomical.

They were quite right, the way Phillips thought about it, to worry so much about motive. In any other circumstantial case it would have been treated as an essential, a crucial step in the inferential path.

His task was to make it so again. The problem had as much to do with the nature of human understanding as with the equations of logic. He didn't yet know how he would handle it, but he wasn't worried. He knew it would come.

15

'ONE OF THE MOST fundamental facts in nature is the love of a mother for her child. A mother will make all manner of sacrifices for her baby. A mother will die for her baby. We all know that, it happens again and again. We know, too, from the evidence at this trial that some mothers may harm or kill their babies. But we know, from the evidence, that's not contrary to nature when it happens because we know the natural love of those mothers for their babies has been distorted, and warped, and removed by the effects of a severe, depressive illness. So the killing by mothers of babies in that connection can be said to be "motiveless killings". Killings without reason.

'Now just listen to what Dr Milne, Mrs Chamberlain's doctor, had to say about it.

'Question: "On the occasions you saw Mrs Chamberlain" —and I interpolate, we know they were many, daily in hospital and routine check-ups thereafter—"On the occasions you saw Mrs Chamberlain, did she show any symptoms, even of the mild form, of post-natal depression?"

'Answer: "No."

'So the result is this, isn't it, that the defence—which doesn't have to prove anything—has proved beyond any doubt that Mrs Chamberlain does not come within the category of mothers who might commit a "motiveless killing". We know that's confined to mothers who suffer from this severe form of post-natal depression, and she didn't have a scrap of symptom. Even of a milder form. So the question of a "motiveless killing" caused by illness is, in this case, gone for ever.

'Now, what are the alternatives? There is only one alternative, and that's a killing with motive. A killing with reason.'

Here was an opportunity to wedge the Crown into a corner. 'The prosecution has had two years and three months to think of a reason. They can't. They can't supply you with a reason why she should do it. And we have excluded a "motiveless murder" on Dr Milnes's evidence. In this area of the case, the supply of a reason why this mother would kill her baby, the prosecution is bereft. Bankrupt. But the defence isn't bankrupt. We have been able to obtain, from witness after witness after witness, ninety per cent of them independent of the Chamberlains, proof after proof after proof, of this mother's love for her baby.

'Ladies and gentlemen, if anything, we are suffering an abundance of riches.

'Listen to Mrs Lowe: "She sort of had a new-mum glow about her."

'Listen to Mrs West: "They said they'd always wanted a girl, and she was very much the baby they wanted." And later, "She had a great care for the baby."

'Mr Eccles, the afternoon before the baby disappeared: "She treated the baby like a true mother."

'Mrs Eccles: "A very caring mother, an affectionate mother."

'Mrs Wilkins, who saw her near the climb: "She was a perfect little mother."

'Mrs Goss: "She was very warm, an affectionate mother."

'Pastor Kennaway, who performed the ceremony which is apparently similar to a christening: "I am convinced they loved the baby."

'Now, what have we got? Ten people there, from north, south, east, and west of our country, every one of them telling you the same thing. And we have traced it from the time of the pregnancy, through the birth, through the nine and a half weeks, and,' here Phillips pounded the table with the flat of his hand, 'up until minutes of that child's disappearance.

'All these people tell you·the same thing. This mother was not the sort of mother that Dr Milne explains might commit a "motiveless killing", a mother who had rejected the child. This lady,' he pointed behind him where Lindy sat now with her heavy legs supported by a chair, 'was a caring mother, a mother who loved the child, a mother who wanted her, who welcomed her, and who looked after her.

'And notice—it's a feature of this case—that people like that, all the civilian people there, in terms of this woman's relationship with her baby, all support her up to the hilt. That is a feature of this case: every one of them. So much for the question of a "motiveless killing".'

Sydney Morning Herald
Crown's Azaria Arguments Laughable—Q.C.

The words and actions of Pastor Michael and Lindy Chamberlain at the time of their daughter's disappearance in 1980 and in the events following were inconsistent with guilty knowledge, a QC submitted in the Northern Territory Supreme Court, yesterday. Mr John Phillips, representing the Chamberlains, said that in too many instances the couple's actions would have been illogical if they had wanted to cover up their baby's murder. He submitted, in his closing address to the jury, that there were too many people around in the three and a half hours the Chamberlains had spent at the campsite, after the baby disappeared, for them to have done anything secretly. Discussing the prosecution case, relating to Michael Chamberlain's camera-bag, Mr Phillips said that the scenario painted for the Chamberlains would have been, if not so serious, laughable. The defence had met, and answered, the Crown case. Mr Phillips said the Crown's assertion that the Chamberlains would have had 'ample opportunity' for secret burial of the body had not been borne out by the evidence.

*   *   *

Brown caught Phillips outside court on the second day, after the address finished. Phillips asked how it seemed to go over, and Brown said, 'Excellent,' which caused Phillips some embarrassment, as though he might be thought fishing for compliments.

'It was a team effort,' Phillips said. 'We've answered the Crown, scientist for scientist. I had never seen a defence case better put together.'

Brown couldn't remember a more thorough one, certainly. But the phrase 'scientist for scientist' seemed to miss some deeper and more elusive issue. He wondered if this were a scientific case at all. It had more to do with simpler beliefs. The astonishing notion of unfathomable evil had been around so long that Lindy Chamberlain wasn't judged by the same assizes as everybody else. She inhabited some closet of immortal experience, ancient and unnatural.

16

'I SAID in my opening address, the Crown does not venture to suggest motive, nor does it invite speculation about motive,' Barker said. 'That was my position then, and it is my position now. We haven't shifted. We don't know why this happened. All the Crown says is that you should find it did happen. The only question here, so far as Mrs Chamberlain is concerned, is whether or not you are satisfied that she is guilty of murder. I told you quite openly at the start, we can't prove a motive, and I haven't come here to prove a motive, I've come here to prove a murder. And that, I respectfully submit, is what has been proved.

'Now let's examine the dingo story. I have said, and I said it seven weeks ago, it's preposterous. It's been seized upon by the accused to explain what otherwise was incapable of explanation. Having told the lie, she was stuck with it. I suggest to you it has continued as a lie with various twists and embellishments since 17 August 1980. It was conceived as a lie, it was a lie told to Inspector Gilroy, it was a lie told to Sergeant Charlwood, it was a lie told to the coroners, and it was a lie told to you.

'What is the dingo supposed to have done? It managed, if he
story is true, to kill the child in the bassinet, drag her from the
basket, divest her of two blankets and a rug, shake her body
vigorously at the entrance of the tent, then carry her off into the
night in such a way that it left virtually no clues in the tent by
way of blood or hairs or anything else. It left no blood o
drag-marks by the outside of the tent. It was able to pass by the
child's mother in full view without disclosing that it was carrying
a baby. It managed to kill the child while all the buttons on the
jump-suit were done up, and managed to carry the baby a long
way. At the shortest, it walked some four or five kilometres, i
the story is true, to the base of Ayers Rock and, if during part o
that distance it walked through the bush, it managed to do so
without tearing or pulling the fabric of the jump-suit, collecting
almost nothing in the nature of seeds or sticks, or other vegetation along the way. So, all in all, ladies and gentlemen, it was
not only a dexterous dingo, it was a very tidy dingo.

'It managed to cut the collar and the sleeve with a pair of
scissors. An unlikely circumstance, you may think, even if we're
dealing with the most intelligent and perceptive of animals. And
be clear, with respect, about this evidence. It remains unanswered
The overwhelming evidence is that the jump-suit was cut by
scissors.

'Supposing the dingo was on trial here. How could you
possibly convict it on this evidence? Where is the evidence?
Where is there one substantial clue, apart from the account given
by the child's mother, pointing to a killing of this child by a
dingo? There isn't one. The case against the dingo would be
laughed out of court.'

This put Malcolm Brown in mind of a bumper-sticker
seen around town. It read: 'Save the Dingo'. He watched Tipple
whispering, at the bar-table, to Kirkham. Tipple scribbled something on a notepad, tore it off, and headed for the door. He
looked pale and angry.

Tipple carried the note outside, past the cameramen lounging
in the shade, then stuffed it into a pocket and made for the
car-park. The errand involved a trip to the hotel to fetch a
volume for Kirkham. It was a welcome respite. Barker's gift
for deadly humour seemed designed to appeal to some affinity

or derision deep in the national character. He kept thinking, We
aven't come this far with the case to be treated like a joke.

When Barker finished, Phillips asked that the jury retire
moment while he addressed the bench. He had objections to
nake. First, Barker had told the jury that criticisms of Mrs Kuhl
nd Dr Baxter in this trial cast doubt on convictions in cases in
vhich they testified elsewhere. Phillips said, 'In our submission
here is a danger, once that is said, that the jury may feel that an
cquittal would in some way operate professionally as a reflec-
ion on Mrs Kuhl and Dr Baxter. Of course, it wouldn't do any
uch thing.'

Justice Muirhead found a note of his own of the comment.
Have no worries about that,' he said. Evidently he had decided
lready to say something about it in his charge to the jury.

'The second matter is this. It was said consistently, Your
Ionour, that the only basis for the dingo story—as it has been
haracterized—is Mrs Chamberlain's evidence. It was said there
s no support for her assertion that a dingo was involved, at all.
n a detailed final address, not a single reason was given why
Mrs Lowe's evidence of hearing the baby cry should be discounted,
o reason whatsoever advanced as to why she should not be
elieved.'

'I will be dealing with that,' the judge said.

But Phillips thought he had not yet made the full point. 'It's
ust not correct to say that it all rests on Mrs Chamberlain,
ecause if Mrs Lowe is right—'

'That is what you would call ''the absolute bar to conviction''.'

'Yes, Your Honour.'

The judge found Phillips's agitation amusing.

'Don't worry,' he said.

17

AT MIDDAY on Thursday, 28 October, Justice Muirhead
djusted his chair so he could face the jury-box and said, 'Mr
Foreman, ladies and gentlemen of the jury, it is common ground
hat Azaria Chamberlain, then only nine weeks of age, died at
Ayers Rock on or about 17 August 1980. In this court, her
nother stands her trial on a charge of murdering her baby, and
he father of being an accessory after the fact. Inquests have

come and gone. The tide of opinion and innuendo has ebbed and flowed—'

The public gallery was full. Others waited in the corridor. Lindy Chamberlain leaned on her pillow. Her nervous fingers were never very far from her mouth. Michael stared at the floor. The judge turned the pages of his notes and spoke quickly, and those reporters who had shorthand judged the rate at a hundred and fifty words a minute. The charge was expected to take two days and by late afternoon radio and television reporters were describing it as 'even-handed' and 'straight down the middle'. With no bias to reflect, newspaper editors had problems choosing captions.

The *Sydney Sun* asked:

> Do You Believe that Azaria could be taken
> by the Head without Leaving Bleeding?

The Melbourne *Age* chose:

> Dingo can not be Ruled Out, Jury Told

Running the foreshore reserve in shorts and sneakers, Malcolm Brown saw Phillips on the path ahead and caught him up. The air was sticky and slow. Brown asked how he felt about Muirhead's charge.

'Okay. So far.' Phillips seemed to be fitting the syllables to his laborious breath. 'How are the vibes now?'

Brown gathered he was being asked how everyone saw the likely outcome. 'Fine,' he said.

'I think so too,' Phillips said, turning for his motel.

The way Brown cleared, with Lindy Chamberlain, the information he was given by her talkative friends, was through Irene Herron. Brown now wanted to write something about 'the eve of the verdict' and asked Mrs Herron to carry the message. He didn't want to jeopardize any chance of an exclusive interview with Lindy later, so he had waited in the corridor after court for the answer. Mrs Herron walked by without turning her head. 'That's all right,' she said.

Chamberlain Family Making Plans

Pastor Michael and Lindy Chamberlain are preparing to return to their home in Avondale College, Cooranbong, N.S.W., immediately after their trial in Darwin if they are acquitted.

Mrs Chamberlain is due to give birth in less than three weeks, but the couple will try to obtain a medical certificate saying birth is not imminent and Mrs Chamberlain is fit to travel. Alternatively, they will ask a doctor to travel with them.

A source close to the Chamberlains said they preferred the idea of having their baby in N.S.W. and would want to leave Darwin without delay.

The couple are anxious to be reunited with their children Aidan and Reagan, who are staying with Mrs Chamberlain's parents, Pastor and Mrs Cliff Murchison. The boys have been following reports of the trial closely.

The chef at the Hotel Darwin set up a charcoal grill in the garden-bar. He turned purple buffalo steaks and pale fillets of barramundi with tongs, and a waitress sold tickets at a counter. It was a birthday party for a press photographer everyone called Spider, who seemed to be shouting all the drinks. The television crews had been here some time now, since the major bulletins went to air in the eastern states between six and seven. Journalists from morning newspapers with evening deadlines phoned copy through from the media-room and got here late.

Gary Tait, the head technician for Channel Seven, was telling the crew of a rival station that he had asked Justice Muirhead for leave to televize the judge's charge. It was Tait who had televized Coroner Barritt at the first inquest. 'Muirhead said he'd think about it, but then he knocked me back,' Tait said. The rebuff hadn't made him at all glum. He considered he had the best transmission arrangements of any crew here. He had a high-frequency dish set atop the nearby Hooker Building, for which permission had been denied all networks. Tait hadn't bothered to apply for permission. He had carried the equipment up there himself, disguised as a maintenance man.

At a table by the pool, Sean Flannery from 2UE and Murray Nicoll from the Macquarie network sat with Barker, Pauling, and some court staff. Flannery had taken time off between courses to dive in the pool and, misjudging the depth, came up with a gored nose and an affronted expression. He sat around wet and dazed. When the conversation got to the trial, someone asked Margaret Rischbieth how long she thought her judge would go. Margaret was the judge's associate, a young blonde-haired woman who, while the judge read through his charge, handed him volumes of transcript and successive pages of notes. 'He's got a hundred and twenty pages altogether,' she said, 'and we're through seventy now.'

Nicoll did the sum. 'He might finish at lunch-time,' he said.

Concerned with the newsbreaks too, Flannery said, 'They could be out a long time.' He asked Barker what the odds on conviction were now.

'Pauling is still hopeful,' Barker said, grinning. 'He thinks we could get a hung jury.'

'Ten against two,' Pauling said, but he wouldn't tell them which way he thought the ten and the two would vote.

The party ran late. Someone played guitar and sang Country and Western. Those who furtively ascended the poolside stairs to the rooms above descended more serenely later, smelling of musky smoke. They made a conga line, chanting, until the tailenders fell into the pool, helpless and splay-legged. They trod water in billowing shorts and floated half-filled goblets, of champagne now, from one to the other. The festivity had changed its substance. It was a celebration. Soon they could all go home.

In Kirkham's room at the Travelodge, Tipple stood up from his chair, but he didn't look anxious to leave. He wasn't feeling so good, he said.

'I know,' Kirkham said, 'I get tight in the guts too.' He told Tipple they had done everything now that could be done. 'It'll be all right,' he said. 'You're too close to it to be able to see that.'

Tipple walked down the corridor to the elevators. He was too close to it, right enough, he thought. He came from the same New Zealand town, Christchurch, as did Michael Chamberlain years back. He remembered Michael's inaugural address as a young preacher. He even remembered the topic of the sermon. It was: 'Should Adventists Suffer Nervous Breakdowns?'

Malcolm Brown couldn't sleep. He turned the air-conditioner off, but within a half hour he was sticky so he turned it on again. It occurred to him that a clattering fan had become the true sound of the tropics. He reached into the liquor cabinet and poured a heavy shot into a tumbler. He socked it down and lay back. When he drifted to sleep, whatever part of his mind that was still in touch with things now knew it was a mistake. He was entering a dream he'd had before. The first time was the night after the Galvin inquest, and then he'd had it three nights in a row. It always began the same way. He was somewhere so remote there was no periphery to the world. It was dark. He could see a pale bundle on the ground. What drew him closer was an appealing gurgle of childish delight. He could not help but look. It was a baby with a doll's face and glassy eyes, and it was gagging on its life's blood. He lay there until the sound of it was loud enough to wake him.

18

REPORTERS got to the video-room early, around eight-thirty, because the court was due to sit again at nine. Brown went there to telephone the *Herald* so his editor would know the judge's charge would last the rest of the morning session, and they might get a verdict anytime between two p.m. and midnight. He wanted plenty of space, front page.

While they stood around drinking coffee, Mike Lester was taking bets. Lester was a television journalist. Tanned and pinched, he looked more like a strapper than a bookmaker. He was offering five to four on for acquittal and two to one against for a hung jury. Anyone wanting to ride money on conviction could begin the haggling at tens.

Brown had caught Lester's telecast at the motel last night and didn't like it. He told Lester, 'You're favouring the defence case too much.' It wasn't any of his business, but he was glad to have said it anyway. He wanted to see dignified, Queensbury Rules professionalism everywhere. 'Where's your objectivity?' he said. He thought the judge's charge impartial and punctilious, and ought to be reported that way.

Lester's riposte sent Brown angrily for the stairs. 'You're not listening between the lines,' Lester said.

Brown crossed the courtyard, where television crews were laying out cable. Inside, the corridor was crowded. He shouldered through, short tempered. The sketch artist, Jo, was selling her courtroom drawings. Those of the Chamberlains were sold out already. She discounted the others at six for a hundred dollars and was doing good trade.

Nothing was going to convince Brown that he was not listening as intently between the lines as anyone else, but by mid morning Lester seemed about to be vindicated by subsequent events.

The judge said, 'With the question of the experts, pay such heed as you are convinced the opinions of experts require. Where they differ, I direct you to tread warily, especially where the circumstances with which they are dealing are in doubt, or in a state of confusion. That is to say, where the evidence is beset by many possibilities, or contingencies, be cautious. You will not convict on circumstantial evidence unless it is sufficiently strong to be. inconsistent with any—with any—reasonable hypothesis other than the guilt of the accused.' He gave some examples and went on, 'It is perhaps fair to say it is a case of novel and unique circumstance. Opinions are opinions. Impressions are impressions. Bear those things in mind. We are not treading on the ground of unequivocal, unchallenged scientific opinion. To the contrary, the scientists' opinion on vital issues is divided. Don't forget that.'

Brown thought, Without the scientists, the Crown is nowhere; we are back to the campsite. Some similar understanding evidently led the judge's reasoning. He said: 'I spoke to you earlier of the presence of foraging dingoes in the area, and the further evidence called by the defence has highlighted that evidence, and of the fact they could be menacing and dangerous. You may think, to put it simply, If ever there was a time when dingoes were becoming a problem, it was in August 1980. Is it but coincidence, fortuitous from Mrs Chamberlain's point of view, that she put forward—as the Crown asserts—this false explanation for a murder just at that time, in August 1980?'

'I turn for a moment to the evidence of character. It is common ground, ladies and gentlemen, that neither Mr nor Mrs Chamberlain have ever been in trouble with the law before. You have heard this. You have heard of their capacity to help people such as Mr Lenehan.' The judge read passages from the testimony of those in praise of the Chamberlains. 'It is trite to say that people do commit crimes for the first time, of course they do. But when you are considering whether you are prepared to draw the inference, in this case, that Mrs Chamberlain deliberately cut Azaria's throat in the car, you must, in considering that, bear in mind the character evidence as a factor which may help you in considering the likelihood of her committing this appalling crime, and of her husband being an accessory after the fact of that crime.

'So you will consider all these things as a background to the allegations that this mother carried out a sudden homicidal attack on her baby. You will consider the evidence of those people who were there on that night—quite independent people—who saw them both, and comforted them both, after Azaria disappeared. It may be, as I have said earlier, that Michael Chamberlain and Alice Chamberlain were strong, but you may think, ladies and gentlemen, that the evidence justifies no conclusions other than that their subsequent sadness was at times manifest to others.

'You will bear in mind the preservation of that camera-bag, the preservation of that car, the exposure of that car so early afterward to the opportunity of an inspection. I ask you that you'll bear this in mind, if your wife had murdered your child in that car, what would you have done over the ensuing months? Would you have still had the car? Would it have been thoroughly scrubbed? Would the scissors be still left in the car?'

He reserved to Sally Lowe the last word. 'Well, you saw and heard her,' he said, 'and it is for you alone to determine what reliance you place on her memory and on her evidence. But I know you'll bear this in mind: if Mrs Lowe heard that cry, and if it came from the tent, you may think that the only inference you can draw is that it was Azaria's last cry. And if it was, you may think that the only further inference you can draw is that Azaria was still living. She was not, and could not, if Mrs Lowe is correct, have been, as the Crown asserts, then lying dead in the car.'

As the jurors filed through the jury-room door Phillips leaned toward Kirkham and let out a breath. 'You couldn't complain about that,' he said.

Brown wrote, 'So the case ends as it began, with a cry in the dark.'

THE LORD SHOULD HAVE BEEN
HERE BY NOW

1

JOURNALISTS STOOD AROUND in the video-room talking, smoking. The screens were empty. Radio reporters, who would be live to air all along the eastern seaboard the moment the verdict came through, jotted in their notebooks, trying out newscasters' phrases, useful alternatives whatever happened.

A reporter came in with a message from Kirkham. 'He wants an undertaking from us,' the messenger said, 'that Lindy and Michael can walk out of the court-house without being mobbed for quotes. He thinks we owe them a dignified departure if they're acquitted.' He laughed. 'I said we'd consider it.'

It provoked more anger than consideration. 'Tell them nothing doing,' someone said. A reporter from a Sydney tabloid suggested making the promise, 'and then we hit them anyway.' Lindsay Murdoch didn't think that was on. 'Let them go,' he said. 'We can turn up at the church later.' Sean Flannery turned away and pushed through for the door. 'Don't count me in on any deal,' he said, 'I'm paid to get interviews.'

This summed it up. In the pause that followed, everyone seemed to be thinking the same thing: the Chamberlains will want to talk sometime, and nobody wanted to blow the chance with some petty and fruitless deception.

2

PAUL WHITE, the newscaster for Channel Seven, Sydney, was designing a 'wrap-up'. The idea called for his narrative, a retrospective he would first establish from a 'stand-up' in the witness-box, over a cut to library film of the Chamberlains, cut back to pan along the vacated jury-box while he quoted from the judge's charge, cut to the interior of the jury-room. This last shot he needed to film now. The jurors were at lunch in a private hotel room, so the deputy sheriff, whose domain the court was, let the crew in for ten minutes. When they had enough footage, White ran the tape back on the monitor in the truck outside. The shot in which White was interested took in the long room, the narrow table crazy-paved with notepaper and documents, the skewed and discarded chairs, and executed a pull-back slow enough to give the impression of respectful withdrawal. Having in mind transmission a few hours from now, White wanted a sense of completion, to establish the occasion, ahead of time, as history.

The retreating lens caught, lying on the near end of the table, a photograph. He stopped the frame where the photograph was clearest. This was a print of the last snap Michael Chamberlain had taken of Lindy, dandling Azaria on the slopes of the Rock, the world aslant underfoot, the child mystified, the mother happy. White told the technician to end the scene on that shot. 'It says something,' he said.

3

NOTHING WAS GOING ON in other courts in the building. Orderlies closed the doors along the empty and resonant corridors. They left open only a side door, since the Chamberlains were in custody now, waiting it out in the defence conference room rather than the basement cells. The journalists had made for the Darwin Hotel, leaving behind a sentinel with a pack of beer, a promise of relief after a half hour, and a hand-held CB. The arrangement called for another radio in the pool-garden at the hotel, where the waiting reporters lounged, and traffic on that frequency betrayed a third, placed somewhere on the noisy counter of a cocktail bar, through which they were ordering drinks.

At around five-thirty, Margaret Rischbieth, at a shady table with Nicoll and three other radio journalists, checked her wristwatch. The jury had been out a little over three hours. 'They were told to take a quick vote first,' she said, 'so they must be talking about something.' Nicoll was in a more cynical frame of mind. 'They live here,' he said. 'They can't be seen to knock it over too quickly.'

The garden-bar was getting crowded and the waitresses busy. Murdoch sat with the photographer McNeil and Shears, the correspondent with the London *Daily Mail*. Murdoch said, 'The verdict may come out on their Sabbath.' The sun had gone off the garden. The frangipani smelled moist and fragrant, which seems here the soft nature of evening-time. 'The Chamberlains drove to Ayers Rock on their Sabbath,' he said.

A table in the main lounge was taken by two young lawyers and a counsellor from the legal-aid office. They had arranged to meet here the travelling entertainers Jan Wositsky and Debbie Sonenberg, who were busking in Darwin for enough to get by. Earlier they had worked the Mall, Jan playing harmonica and clacking spoons while Debbie, whose body is articulated wherever she chooses, folded herself double into a costume and became, for all the purposes of ilusion, a duo of high-stepping ballroom midgets with embroidered smiles. The last place they stayed for any length of time was Ayers Rock. Jan was saying, 'The Pitjantjatjara think this trial is a waste of money. Of course the dingo did it. The dingo is a spirit of death.'

Margaret Rischbieth, called away to a sudden telephone call, walked back to her table. She had a message from the deputy sheriff. 'The jurors will stay out at least until seven-thirty,' she said. The waitress who arrived with their drinks had just come off shift at the Travelodge. She told them Phillips had ordered a six of champagne. 'Not for now,' she explained. 'Just on hold.'

4

LONG BEFORE he got there, Brown could see spotlights on the courthouse.

It looked now like a military Shrine for the Fallen. The crowd he could see only in silhouette, but it obliterated the forecourt and spilled on the footpath. His fear as he crossed Mitchell Street was that he was unaccountably too late, but by shading his eyes he made out folk sitting in the gardens, quiet and asprawl. The glare came from luminaires, floodlamps mounted on grids, six of them, set to face the fastened doors. A high telecamera raked faces in the throng and lingered a moment on three women sitting on deckchairs playing cards, while another held on a performing newscaster who was connected to a

kerbside TV truck by a thin microphone wire, which ran down
the inside of his left trouser leg and crossed the pavement like a
discreet surgical prosthesis. Brown supposed all this was on air
right now, at home.

He found Frank Moorhouse standing on the roadside plantation. Moorhouse, who loved commotions of any sort and thought
he might write something of this one into his film script, had
wandered around, eavesdropping. 'They're talking about everything except what they're here for,' he said, as though this were
far more interesting than the converse might have been. He now
had a half bottle of bourbon stashed in a healthy shrub nearby.
After a glance around for meandering policemen, they each took
a slug. A boy hurried past carrying a can of Coke and a freshly
minted pizza. Brown craned over to look along the kerb and saw
a kitchen-van, which he had taken earlier for a television truck.
It was puffing smoke and doing brisk business.

Sean Flannery, leading Nicoll and Murdoch, pushed past
heading for the video-room, and they were in a hurry. Murdoch
turned long enough to shout 'Verdict' in Brown's direction and
kept going. Everyone now knew something was afoot and packed
around the doors, and Brown guessed that those with
pocket-radios had heard the message on a newsflash. Over the
heads Brown could make out a picket-line of policemen inside.
The doors remained inexplicably closed, and he sprinted instead
for an entrance at the far end of the forecourt. When he got
there, he saw that the police were directing everyone that way.
Some calming measure of crowd control, evidently. Inside, a cop
motioned that he should not run in the corridor. The guard at the
door of the court had been doubled. He pulled out his press pass.
His mouth was dry.

5

JURORS WHO AVERT their eyes from the dock when
they walk into court will convict, because, as Brown knew the
given wisdom, they cannot bear to look upon the faces of the
damned, so he watched their slow procession all the way, men
and women with evasive faces, every one, and the erect foreman, on the verdict of them all, adjudged guilty the first
accused, guilty the second, in a quiet and unhesitant voice beside
two women who covered their mouths with porcelain fingers and
wept, and Lindy's bloated and stupefied face drained away all

the colours of life when the judge committed her to prison for as long as she live and departed the bench leaving everyone to break the moment as best they might, Michael by rubbing his shining cheeks with a cuff, the jury by turning to follow a resolute orderly towards the door, while Brown knew he was shouting something after them, the word 'bastards' sounding in his suddenly flaming ears, and someone had him by the sleeve and was sitting him down.

6

IN THE VIDEO-ROOM, the two reporters who were of such standing that they were assured of immediate clearance to air, on demand, were Flannery and Nicoll. Nicoll's direct line to Macquarie was in the next room. He ran, the moment sentence was passed on Lindy Chamberlain, a journey of a dozen lanky paces or so, composing copy as he went. Others broke for the booths by the wall. They found Flannery there, his palm pressed over one ear, on air already. He had opened his line to 2UE in Sydney as the judge came on screen, and Flannery then divided his concentration to cover both the proceedings of court and the radio programme he could hear through the ear-piece. The studio announcer selected a music track and waited on Flannery's cue. When the jury filed into court Flannery said, 'Come to me—now,' and heard the announcer say, '—to Sean Flannery in Darwin.' Assuming the harsh and streetwise tone he liked for crime rounds, Flannery began, 'And the jury, lined up, standing quietly now—' The transmission lasted four and a quarter minutes, and he calculated that his listeners were never more than two seconds behind the precise course of events. He signed off, slammed the phone down, and walked to the deserted centre of the room, cocky, preening his shirt-front. Everyone else was still talking, and some hadn't got to air yet. A tabloid journalist who had missed the announcement that Michael Chamberlain's future was not to be considered until tomorrow, roamed about asking, 'What did he say?' but was shrugged off.

Someone shouted from a booth, 'What's "Life" in this town?'

'A real long time, pal,' Flannery said.

7

THE STAIRWELL to the basement cells was spiral and shadowy. Kirkham followed Phillips down. Their iron footfalls sounded like the slow strokes of a clock. Kirkham expected Michael would want to know how things could go so wrong, and he couldn't think of an answer. Lindy, judging by the way she looked in the dock, wouldn't see so much as a light passed in front of her eyes. He could hear her sobbing now, somewhere in the hollow shafts below, lost and piteous. The air down here was hotter, step by step, as if they were measurably closer to the netherworld.

8

AS BROWN RAN UP the stairs to the video-room, everyone was coming down, anxious to catch the departure of the prison van. Brown phoned the duty editor at the *Sydney Morning Herald* and promised him copy on time. Then he looked the empty and strewn room over. He could hear a cleaner's broom tapping the stairwell. A notice-board on the wall announced briefings, excursions, parties, long past. An inclined Darwin Casino postcard, hanging by a surviving thumb-tack, showed a baize-green roulette table surrounded by a dozen posed and delighted gamblers. The bets were down. A smiling croupier was about to spin the wheel. Written underneath, weeks ago now with a fading pen, was the caption: 'A Jury Considers its Verdict'. Brown tore it down and flipped it into a bin.

He walked out into the oily night, crossed the forecourt, descended the steps. Trampled wrappers and winded drink-cans littered the ground. There was no one about. A television van straddled the kerb, a door ajar. Gary Tait's footpath telephone sat on a step. A retreating foot had sometime dislodged the hand-piece, which lay disabled on the ledge beneath like an upturned bug. Brown decided against joining the mob he guessed was covering the vehicle exit behind the court-house. That was his photographer's job, he thought by way of excuse, but he didn't have to search far for the truth. It was his private fear that the custodians now, whoever was arranging the final event, would choose to send her off in a limousine, uncurtained, blatant, exposed to the flashbulbs and to the tumultuous gaze, just as jailers once drove the condemned through village streets in uncovered carts, and for much the same reason.

9

AN ORDERLY LED Phillips and Kirkham along a carpeted corridor to the judge's chambers and knocked. When he opened the door, they saw Justice Muirhead refreshing a tumbler from a whisky bottle he then set on the desk. He was in shirt-sleeves. 'Well,' he said, raising his glass by way of a greeting, 'I didn't think I exactly summed up in favour of a conviction, did you?' The orderly withdrew, closing the door on the rest of the converstation.

10

THERE SEEMED TO BE parties offering all over town, but Brown wasn't keen to go to any of them. After he phoned his copy through to Sydney, he had a few drinks in the lounge at the Darwin Hotel with one of the sheriff's staffers, who said the first jury-vote came out four for conviction, four against, and four undecided. He was then asked not to use the information, but told the man not to be a fool and walked off. He drank with Murdoch in the Regency Room, watching a table where the waiter refused to serve three journalists who were rolling joints on a dinner-plate in full view of a nearby party hosted by a uniformed superintendent of police. Brown knew those journalists were upset with the verdict, and plainly he was observing some calculated gesture of insolence, more than anything else. When he walked through to the garden-lounge, things were peaceful enough, until two radio reporters who were otherwise firm friends got up, grey-faced and shouting, from a poolside table and knocked each other into the water. He walked, from there, the slow length of the quietening town, kept walking, sat down on the foreshore awhile hugging his knees, watching the interminable tide grow milky with the ebb change, and the sun came up over his shoulder.

11

JUSTICE MUIRHEAD convened court at ten o'clock next morning, although it was Saturday, and called on Phillips to speak for Michael Chamberlain. Phillips read directly from notes. The argument he put, for some measure of leniency, concentrated for the most part on the prisoner's previously blemishless character, the needs of his now motherless boys, and his certain notoriety for evermore. Reporters thought Phillips seemed surprisingly unfamiliar with the document from which he was reading. Indeed, he had never set eyes on it before. He had told Kirkham that a sentencing plea was simply beyond the powers of concentration he had just now. So, although the voice was Phillips's the words were Kirkham's.

The public gallery held only a few spectators now. Most of those seated in the pews were journalists. They heard the judge sentence Michael Chamberlain to eighteen months hard labour, which seemed about what everyone expected given the gravity of the conviction, and someone whispered to Brown, 'Par for the course.' The the judge said, 'I have, in this Territory, the power to suspend the operation of sentences and, in this case, I consider it not only appropriate but in the interests of justice to do so.' He ordered that the prisoner he placed on a bond of good behaviour for three years, and fixed the amount of the bond at five hundred dollars.

12

THE FIRST TIME Brown tried to get into the women's compound at Berrimah jail he was arrested for loitering. The mistake he'd made was assuming he only had to ring the bell and wait, but when no one came to the gate, he decided to take a look around the grounds, and two turnkeys took him away, an arm each, into the men's division for questioning. Brown was of a size that he could have clapped their heads together, but he went quietly, unmanned by his gawky embarrassment rather than funk. He told them he was ghosting a book for Lindy Chamberlain, but they looked as if they'd heard everything now and sat him in the superintendent's office upstairs. The superintendent, a gingery man with fingers which tirelessly roved the edge of the desk, stared at Brown a long time, then told him to get out. When he stood on the hot pavement outside, and the clatter of the closing latch had died away, Brown took a breath and looked for a telephone. He found a coin-phone in the visitors' room and called a cab. Next time he came here, he'd make sure he was armed with more authority than a press pass. He had decided already to stay around Darwin until he'd got his interview.

The Berrimah penitentiary stands on the side of a ridge, a

caricature of entombment, stony-faced, a terminal of the spirit. There is in the air, always here, the moorish smell of rotting bodies and ignoble deaths, which, although known to panic newcomers, has nothing to do with the prison. Much of the paddocky land around is owned by a livestock company, whose slaughter-yards are here, and decaying offal is thrown into sodden pits between which a few wormy horses graze. Long-term prisoners say they get used to the stench in a few months. As if to underscore the richness of allusion, this is the end of the road, of Tivendale Road, which loops this part of the hillside enough to service the penitentiary gate and doubles back to the highway. Guards high on the prison walls have a clear view the entire length of the roadway, of the mown grassy field it encloses, of the single-storey women's block in the centre of it, and of the few women on exercise schedule in the compound. If all the women went to exercise together there would, on any normal day, still only be eight. There is a garden with well-disciplined flowers and a small games-court. This tidy complex might resemble, more than anything else, a sports pavilion of steamy showers and locker rooms, surrounded by a mesh fence whose only purpose is to restrain an absconding basket-ball, if it were not for the strands of razor-wire glinting in the sun like gossamer caught high on the posts, and the way every green thing growing outside is close-cropped so not to impede the fire-power of sentries sighting from the penitentiary walls.

Not long after Brown's cab took him back to town, most likely a half hour afterwards, a bright red sedan drove up to the main gates and reversed into a parking slot. Stuart Tipple and Michael Chamberlain climbed out and walked to the visitors' room. A warder there, behind an armour-glass pane like a bank teller's, told them which way to go and reached for an intercom. They crossed to the women's compound, walked to the gate by way of the concrete path, carefully avoiding the grass, eyes straight ahead and held level. They were exhibiting, Tipple noticed, the excessively predictable behaviour of those who knew they were under unwavering surveillance from above. He wondered if it was any different for people who didn't believe in God.

He'd heard all manner of stories about the sort of women who worked in these places and was happy that the blonde warder leading them from the gate to the accommodation block was homely. He guessed there were more than a few prisoners who knew precisely how many paces there were to the path he was treading. The corridor they entered seemed to run the whole length of the building. The wall paint, which would grow dew once the wet season came in, was now cool and glossy. A gecko clung to the ceiling with sticky fingers spread, waiting slyly for mosquitoes. Visiting room was first right. Lindy was already there, waiting. Her arms flew around Michael's shoulders while Tipple and the warder stood back. The warder said, 'Well,' in not too reproving a tone and told them to sit down. They sat at a spindly table and the warder withdrew to the corridor.

'They'll take me to the Casuarina Hospital to have the baby,' Lindy said, 'if I'm not out on bail for the appeal.'

Tipple nodded. He had promised to begin work on an appeal, Monday. Lindy had, herself, all sorts of suggestions for grounds of appeal, but Tipple was guarded. 'It's a highly technical area, appeal.' Of bail he said, 'You just have to take things day by day now.'

She seemed to have thought about this already. 'I'll act as if everything is going to happen today and plan as if I'm going to live for ever,' she said, which was familiar enough to be a quotation from somewhere, but Tipple couldn't place it. It wasn't the scriptures.

She was anxious to talk to Michael about arrangements for the boys when he was away from the house. 'Jenny Miller will help out,' she said. Jenny Miller was an Avondale College girlfriend who had helped out before. Lindy didn't want to forget anything. She was alert and efficient, far more than her husband, who kept asking her to repeat things. She had instructions about clothes, meals, school. They had dressed her here in a light blue smock which did nothing to hide the size of her belly. Tipple supposed she was not allowed notepaper, since she kept glancing at a pale wrist on which she had jotted single words with a leaky ball-point. Prison-wise already, Tipple thought, a marvel.

It seemed as if Michael was not responding to all this with the enthusiasm of which she thought him capable. His lips were pinched, his eyes clouded. She took his hand. Tipple knew her quick eyes were searching for something cheering. 'Michael,' she said, as if speaking to someone half her age, 'I think you can buy yourself a new camera.'

It was a purchase on which they all knew his heart was set for months, and this was the sort of gesture Tipple thought quite typical of so astounding a woman, but the event which drove him now to leave the table for the window, for the view of a grim exercise yard and a forbidden world beyond, was the change in Michael's face. He was visibly happier.

For the flight home, Tipple rebooked on an earlier aircraft, and registered Michael as Pastor Olson, a subterfuge designed to beat a press stake-out at Darwin airport. It paid off by seating them within a few rows of Ian Barker and a half dozen ogling journalists. As the crusty and deserted Birdsville Track passed underneath—the deadliest roadway in the history of the automobile, as an easily amused captain announced over the PA—Michael reached for his camera to shoot through the porthole. He took it, as the journalists reported almost without exception, 'from a black camera-bag he kept beneath his legs'. He put it back afterwards without the lens cap, a slipshod lapse, but it was his 'old' camera now, although the new had not been bought.

13

TIPPLE liked to walk to work in the mornings, around eight-twenty, from his villa on the residential hill overlooking Gosford, and it felt good to be doing it again. He strode through the town centre and turned into Baker Street. The easterly had in it the fresh tang of the cool Pacific. Gulls rode the breeze from the rooftops. The law office occupied the ground floor of a crisp building built in the seventies. He was the only Adventist lawyer here, and a partner for almost a year, although his name was not yet on the shopfront. He walked the length of the typing-pool, and the chatty young women seemed pleased to see him back. He collected his mail and carried it into his office. The room was low ceilinged, around four metres long by five across, little larger than Lindy's now, he caught himself thinking. He opened the *Sydney Morning Herald* and saw that Malcolm Brown had somehow got into the jail to interview Lindy and was astonished by her high spirits. Brown ought to know her better than that by now, Tipple thought. He opened mail and sorted it between the out-trays, annotated in his neat hand for action. There was an envelope postmarked New Lambton, near Newcastle. It was from Barry Boettcher.

'Although the jury has not yet had to consider its verdict, I am confident of the outcome. There is only one verdict appropriate. I am confident that the Chamberlains will not only be found not guilty, but there will be a wealth of commentary—' Tipple checked the date of postage, 25 October. Phillips began his final address that day. 'Andrew Kirkham and John Phillips are excellent in court and other members of your profession will give them the acclaim their abilities deserve. However the credit for assembling the material with which they could work goes to you. I applaud you for the tireless effort—'

He held his head in his hands. He couldn't have believed he would cry like this. He was okay right up until now. A secretary looked in, and pulled the door quietly closed. '—you will always carry with you a feeling of personal satisfaction—' It was so joyous a voice.

A QUIET PLACE ON REDEMPTION STREET

1

THE BIRTH was celebrated everywhere.

Melbourne *Herald*
IT'S A GIRL

Sydney *Sun*
GIRL FOR LINDY

The *Australian*
LINDY HAS 'BIG STRONG HEALTHY GIRL'

New York Times
Australian Killer Gives Birth

Darwin, Australia, Nov 17—Lindy Chamberlain, who was jailed for life last month for killing her baby daughter, gave birth to a second girl today, but the baby was taken away from her four hours later, prison officials said. Australia's Northern Territory Government, acting on medical advice, said she could not keep the baby with her in prison.

She called the baby Kahlia. 'Let them try to make something out of that,' she said.

2

KIRKHAM WAS SITTING in his law chambers in Melbourne drafting documents for an appeal. He had a tough job finding appellable errors in the judge's charge. The transcript only served to remind him how well they'd thought the defence had done. The afternoon mail brought a letter headed Maidstone Prison, Kent. It was from Prisoner Godfried.

'I am enclosing a copy taken from papers of last Saturday, 6th November. I do hope these will be of some assistance in the appeal of Mr and Mrs Chamberlain. Please, if it is possible, could you give them my condolences.'

The cutting, from the London *Daily Mail*, was entitled: 'Judge Attacks Dingo Trial Doctor.' Kirkham had already seen a version in the Melbourne *Age*, the report of a neglected-baby trial in which Professor Cameron had given evidence of a post-mortem examination, recording the dead baby's weight 'on a piece of blotting paper' rather than in a more durable manner and estimating, wrongly, the weight the baby ought to have been if properly cared for. Kirkham laid the cutting aside with a smile. Evidently Prisoner Godfried hoped it might somehow constitute a separate ground of appeal.

The appeal, to the Federal Court sitting in Sydney, was scheduled for February 1983. Phillips and Kirkham asked Tipple to consider briefing a specialist in appeals at the Sydney bar, and Tipple chose the Queen's Counsel Michael McHugh and the junior Miller. With spectacular early success they had Lindy Chamberlain released on three hundred dollars bail, and she went home to Cooranbong where reporters and television crews, who were barred at the boom-gate entrance to College Drive, skirmished with fit and implacable students. The appeal ran from 7 February to 3 March, and coincided with lunatic tempests and bushfires all over this end of the continent. In Victoria an early death-toll had reached fifty, and in South Australia no one yet had time to count. In Sydney, foyer windows darkened outside the Appeal Court on the twenty-first floor, which seemed to be at storm altitude, and liftwells sighed. A journalist brought a radio into the press-room, and everyone crowded around listening to Murray Nicoll who was covering, live to air, wildfires in the Adelaide hills. He was weeping. The blazing house he was then describing was his own, collapsing room by room.

When legal argument finished and the appeal adjourned, journalists held a renunion in the upstairs bar of the Surrey Hotel. Even reporters who were no longer covering the case

made it. So did Joy Kuhl, in a canary yellow frock, chatty but
not staying long, and Brian Martin, the Northern Territory
solicitor general, in Sydney on business unconnected with the
Chamberlain case. 'But forgive me a passing interest,' he said,
loosening his tie. His pate was ruddy, and he drank with his
feet spread wide. He was used to having the floor when
reporters were around. Another journalist joined the circle. 'Is
he one of us or one of them,' Martin said, so the man could
hear. The newcomer, perplexed, said he was just a reporter,
which caused Martin to laugh. For Territorians there is no
such thing.

On the morning of 30 April, the day of the Federal Court's
judgement, Malcolm Brown met Tipple going up in the lift.
Tipple thought the judges were split, 2-1, win or lose. Brown
knew this was wrong, but he couldn't say so. He knew a girl
who worked in the judges' typing pool. Lost, 3-0.

3

THE THING that got to Barry Boettcher was, when he
thought about it, that having started he couldn't pull back out
now. He still needed to know that the anti-serum Joy Kuhl used
was the same, and from the same batch, as the anti-serum he had
demonstrated was not specific to foetal haemoglobin in his own
laboratories. He and Tipple climbed aboard a flight to Germany
and visited the manufacturers. Boettcher was interested in the
batch numbers of anti-serum exported to this country between
April 1975 and September 1982, which covered the period
amply. He found that throughout this time all supplies were from
the one batch prepared in 1973. The Germans were still a little
sceptical, so he suggested he run his tests again then and there.
To make sure no one was in any doubt that the testing solution
was reacting with the blood of an adult, he bared his arm and
donated blood of his own. They dried it out. He used the
concentrations Kuhl had used. The anti-serum reacted, and
the manufacturers gave him a certificate to attest this was
so.

'Non-specific immune reactions can be observed under certain conditions due to denaturation of haemoglobin A in adult
blood and due to alteration of the relative concentration of
antigen and antibody. The anti-serum against haemoglobin F
(foetal) of this company, therefore, is not suitable on its own for

the identification of foetal or infant blood and adult blood.'

It was wonderful news but, very likely, too late.

4

ENOUGH LETTERS sympathetic to the Chamberlains were published in correspondence columns of the city dailies that two law-school academics called for an embargo, a Sydney barrister wrote to the *Herald* complaining of disrespect for the legal system, and Lindy Chamberlain Support Groups grew up all over the country. Facilities at the Berrimah jail could not handle the increased volume of mail and neither could its famous prisoner. She began a monthly bulletin with a readership list numbering in the hundreds. 'God and I are doing okay,' she said. A 'Plea for Justice' committee in Melbourne began collecting signatures for a petition, and was soon joined by the National Freedom Council. An Adventist businessman, whose enterprises included newsletters about health and the investment of monies, sent a squad of investigators to Ayers Rock in search of new evidence, and announced his intention to stand against Chief Minister Everingham at the next elections. An analyst commissioned by the Sydney *Sun* now pronounced Lindy Chamberlain a person without 'aggression or dishonesty', a conclusion lately reached on the shape of Lindy's signature and a discipline called graphology, which was the analyst's profession. Just after midnight on 18 August, at the Inland Motel at Ayers Rock, a road-train driver by the name of Crabbe, who was still sore from being thrown out of the bar, walked to his truck, backed up until he had the bar dead ahead, gunned, and rode her through. It was a Mack Superliner. The bullbar picked up the shopfront, and the truck made it through the bar-room easily enough, carrying much of the wall like a runaway fork-lift, but the momentum was not sufficient to take the load out again the other side. The truck stalled halfway, smoking. Crabbe climbed out of the cabin while the debris and the dust were settling and, according to one of those still alive, smiled and walked out the way he had come in. The date, newsreports noted, was the third anniversary of Azaria Chamberlain's death, and the blacktracker who trailed meandering Crabbe across the sand-dunes was old Winmatti.

5

DEEP IN FRENCH'S FOREST—a misdirection that will make Sydneysiders smile, because this part of the forest is as built-up as a Hollywood hillside—is a belt of private bushland which Michael Thornhill Productions was renting as a movie-lot. The attraction for Judy Rymer, the director, was the nature of the scrub, which was arid and sparse, and where it was too healthy they stunted it with chainsaws. Trucks spilled red sand everywhere, and they trampled it down, counterfeited a solid barbeque, built knee-high railing, and brought in Toyota Landcruisers repainted with Northern Territory insignia. Along the track, far enough that the lights wouldn't bother the filming, were mobile offices, caravans, kitchens.

Moorhouse's script called for two versions of drama, separately: the Chamberlains' account and the Crown's. The shooting schedule specified crisp dark nights. Under the lamps, the lead actress Elaine Hudson ran to the tent and scrambled inside—while the camera and a boom microphone pressed in through an abbreviated panel—checked the empty bassinet, pummelled the strewn bedding with anxious and incredulous hands, and flew out again, shouting.

'Print it,' Rymer said, after the fourth.

The nights they filmed the prosecution scenario, Moorhouse stood about behind the crew wrapped in a broad anorak and trailing a scarf. When Rymer called for action, Elaine Hudson carried the baby from the tent to a seat in the yellow hatchback. She slaughtered the infant with icy scissors while the camera looked up at her towering face from below, and cleaned the car and herself afterwards, all the while in thrall of demonic obligation. It was a tall order, and they tried it again and again. The scene had no persuasion in it. 'Cut,' Rymer said.

The actress threw up her hands. 'I'm sorry,' she said into the glare. 'It's not the writing. It's the idea.' She shaded her eyes, looking for Moorhouse. 'It just won't hang together.'

Moorhouse rubbed a cheek with a palm. The scene was faithful to the prosecution case. 'It's the way it is,' he said.

'Take nine,' Rymer said. They had three hours before the moon came up.

6

AN APPEAL to the High Court of Australia was lost, three judges to two, on 22 February 1984. The next letter Lindy Chamberlain wrote from Block J Berrimah Prison said:

The total effect of the last four years on the lives of myself and my family are permanent and far reaching. No one who has been touched by our tragedy, and the subsequent events, can claim to have been unaffected. I don't cry myself to sleep much anymore. I just grit my teeth determinedly. Although I've felt broken at times, with God's help I've risen, armed for the fight. Others haven't been so lucky, and will show the scars for life.

Others with 'scars for life' seemed a mysterious reference until this item appeared in city newspapers:

Chamberlain Resigns as Minister

Sydney—Pastor Michael Chamberlain has resigned his position as an ordained minister with the Seventh-day Adventist Church. Church spokesman Pastor Russell Kranz confirmed the resignation today. 'For some time Michael has been seriously thinking about his future, and realizes he cannot continue effectively as an ordained minister,' he said.

There were rumours about awhile now that Michael Chamberlain was suffering a crisis of faith. Lindy wrote: 'May God forgive those involved in doing this to me and mine.'

7

IT SEEMED TO TIPPLE now that everyone was speaking out. He was keeping a running-list. The Chamberlain Support Groups were drawing good publicity. In Tipple's private assessment, the newspapers were in the pursuit of sales rather than justice, but either way the publicity resulted in a press statement from Joy Kuhl, which he thought was indicative of something. Kuhl announced her resignation from the New South Wales Health Department to join the Northern Territory Police Forensic Science Unit, as its director, and moved house to Darwin. She had retested her anti-serum, the statement said, and her opinions remained the same. The importance of this diminished unexpectedly when a carefully anonymous juror broke silence long enough to explain that scientific evidence played no great part in the conviction. 'It really came down to whether you believed it was a dingo or not,' he said, at a secret press interview condoned by the law department, and then he disappeared again. The family Cranwell, who the defence team was unable to trace, came forward and described the way an Ayers Rock dingo dragged their child from a car eight weeks before Azaria Chamberlain's death. On 23 March this letter appeared in the *National Times*:

A Plea from Ayers Rock

Now that Mr Max Cranwell has told of his daughter being attacked by a dingo at Ayers Rock in June 1980, it may be that certain experts will give the Chamberlain case more detailed consideration.

Legally the case is finished, all appeal rights having been exhausted. It is a pity Mr Cranwell did not give evidence at the trial because I believe his story would have suggested that it was unsafe to convict Mr and Mrs Chamberlain.

Since the incident of Azaria's disappearance I have heard 'dingo experts' stating that a dingo would not enter tents or attack humans whether adult or juvenile.

Having lived at Ayers Rock for 16 years, I know that the dingoes of this area are conditioned by and to the people. Consequently their behaviour is not that of a true wild animal and not fully understood by anyone.

I have no doubt that a dingo is capable of attacking children and the possibility of a dingo carrying away a baby is therefore quite feasible.

The doubt that is now being cast by scientific people on the forensic evidence given at the trial, together with my experience of dingo behaviour, leads me to hope that despite legal channels having been exhausted, humane considerations will result in some form of inquiry into the evidence given at the Chamberlain trial. I do not think any of us should feel comfortable with the present situation.

The signatory was the chief ranger, Derek Roff.

Ten days later, thirty-one scientists, twenty-five of them members of the Australian Society for Immunology, signed an open letter protesting against the conclusions drawn from Joy Kuhl's tests and directed the original to Chief Minister Everingham. On 16 August, Dr Frederick Smith, a Northern Territory Health Department psychologist who examined Lindy Chamberlain at

Berrimah prison, gave a television interview at which he made his report public: 'Psychologically I am unable to account for any criminal behaviour on her part. On the contrary, all of the indications available to me suggest that Mrs Chamberlain is clearly among those persons in society who would be least likely to engage in crime, whether in an habitual or isolated fashion.' In a letter to the governor general, he went further. 'Having interacted closely with hundreds of prison inmates as a psychologist,' he wrote, 'I believe Mrs Chamberlain to be the only one whom I have known who is totally innocent.'

The Plea for Justice Committee and the National Freedom Council had one hundred thousand signatures on a petition to the governor general, and organizers still hoped for another twenty thousand. An embarrassment of riches, Tipple thought, then recalled Phillips saying something like that at the trial.

A heavy envelope arrived on Tipple's desk postmarked London. It held a copy of the medico-legal society's quarterly journal, sent by a British friend who thought he might be interested in an account of the society's quarterly gathering. The meeting was held on 12 April, in the evening, at the Royal Society of Medicine. The report didn't note the number of members present but otherwise seemed to give the proceedings in full. Tipple imagined a modest function-room, the remnants of dinner cleared away, decanters of agate port, throaty cigar-smoke. The chairman, a judge, rose to introduce the speaker, Professor Cameron. The record noted applause. Cameron then delivered a paper, which must have taken a full hour to read, committing throughout so many errors of fact that Tipple, with some measure of dark pleasure, couldn't readily keep count.

The recorder, Tipple supposed it was the secretary, gave the rest verbatim.

The chairman: The word 'fascinating' is the right one. Professor Cameron has been good enough to say he will answer questions and hear comments from anybody.

Mr Leonard Caplan: What was it that led to the prosecution naming the wife as the supposed murderer, rather than the husband?

Professor Cameron: This was a problem which we, as prosecution witnesses did not need to worry about, but I do know that a number of legal views were expressed, or cast doubt as you do, on the veracity of differentiating the charges.

A member: The two boys were never questioned?

Professor Cameron: The two boys were questioned, and from what I am led to believe, when interviewed they gave identical statements, and, when re-interviewed and breaking off the interview halfway and starting again, they went and had a playback, and carried straight through. They never changed in any way whatsoever, but naturally they could not be interviewed too often. In fact, no blood samples were taken from the children at all because it was considered totally unnecessary, in view of there being no challenge to the clothing being that of baby Azaria.

The chairman: Are there any accounts of dingoes attacking human beings? Particularly babies?

Professor Cameron: There are a number of cases in Australia, particularly in the Aboriginal legends, of the dingoes attacking livestock, and alleged children, but there is no factual proof whatsoever of dingoes attacking such objects, unless they already be dead. They go mainly for insects and small mammals.

The chairman: And do they eat carrion?

Professor Cameron: Not often. I have no definite proof. There were a number of dingo experts called, both for the prosecution and for the defence, and there seemed to be considerable diversion of views, as to whether they were four-legged animals or eight-legged octopi, and their views changed from day to day.

The secretary: Professor, I thought you were saying that it looked as if the body had been buried in the baby-grow, and then the baby-grow had been dug up again.

Professor Cameron: No. When one examined the baby-grow, there were no bloodstains whatever on the baby-grow, or on the carry-cot. There was very little blood on any of the six blankets in which the child was wrapped like a cocoon. There were a couple of drops of blood on a couple of parkas that were found inside the tent, and also on Mrs Chamberlain's trousers, which were only detected after they had come back from the cleaners. As to the clothing of the jump-suit, it was my view that this had been buried in sand, or in the red sandstone adjacent to Ayers Rock whilst something was inside it, because there were no crease-marks in the clothing, and it was uniformly stained with sand as if it had been buried in sand and not as if the clothing had been buried empty.

Mr Evans: What was the defence's explanation for the bloodstains on the mother's trousers, and the bloodstains in the car?

Professor Cameron: As far as we were led to believe, the Chamberlains' view was that the blood in the car was not that of Azaria. They did offer the explanation initially that, being Seventh-day Adventists, they were very good Samaritans, and if they knocked down an animal and they picked him up and threw him in the back of the car, this would cause the blood contamination. That was one story.

The second was that, as was pointed out, it was a child's blood; it was then suggested that their two boys frequently fought in the car, and this was coming from them. Then when it was pointed out, or suggested by Mr Barker, on Mrs Kuhl's evidence, that this was a child under six months, no explanation was given. There is, and there always will be, considerable disquiet by many forensic biologists as to the presence or absence of foetal haemoglobin in the bloodstain of that age, and as categorically as stated in this case.

Mr Eric Newham (Oxford): I had the privilege to attend a conference in Australia where this subject was discussed. This was, in our view, a wonderful determination by pathologists to show, without question, that the defence put up would not stand up. I think that because of the weird background some of us might think that there might be something in the defence. I am quite certain, in talking not only to the forensic scientists on the spot, but also to lawyers there, that there is no question whatever that the right decision has been made. I think there is a danger—do you not, sir?—that because something is peculiar and weird, therefore we do not believe the obvious scientific evidence; but the scientific evidence here, as I understand it, is absolutely clear.

The report ran for pages yet but Tipple was too angry to read any further. He slammed it shut.

8

A WELL-WISHER sent her a poem.

A little bird I am
shut in from fields and air,

and in my cage I sit and sing
to Him who placed me there,
well pleased a prisoner so to be
because, my God, it pleaseth thee.

Within a fortnight she had news that Reagan was caught in the
face by shrapnel from a bottle which exploded at a children's
party and he was lying in hospital, blind in one eye.

9

AN ADVENTIST CHURCH in Melbourne was daubed
with red paint. Two nights later, the same insistent brush drew
outsized paw prints on the pavement leading to the church door.
In Sydney, a housewife chased Adventist teenagers from the
street outside her home. At the top of her voice she identified
them, by way of explanation to passers-by, as child-killers. At
the Erina church near Gosford, families who arrived early for
Sabbath School found a sign scrawled by the doorway. The
message read: 'Dingo Pups for Sale, Apply Within'. So popular
now were jokes about dingoes and the inexplicable disappearance of Adventist babies that a publisher released an anthology.
The Anti-discrimination Board of New South Wales reported:
'The church once had a rather benign image which it will now
take years to regain unless it involves itself in an active campaign.' The *Adventist News*, a lay journal, predicted in an
editorial that the problems the community now faced would take
up the greater part of debate at the next meeting of church
governance.

The executive committee convened in a boardroom in
Wharoonga, on Sydney's north shore. The administrative complex here is headquarters for that part of the christianly world
called the Seventh-day Adventist Australasian Conference. These
precise titles are important. The church is of a hundred and forty
years standing, age enough to see change and meet rivalries.
There are, now, congregations which no longer hold so fast to
the prophetic guidance of Ellen White, and a reform movement,
estranged over objections to military service, has not been part of
the mainstream since the first world war.

The Wharoonga centre is on Highway One. The church on

the east side, lofty and solid, has a bell tower which speaks, in architectural terms, of constant vigil for the first shining sign of Advent and of expectations undiminished by disappointment. The office building on the opposite side of the motorway resembles a comfortable, late Edwardian mansion. Sedans in the carpark behind are modest and clean, and the most common fender-sticker carries the neat outline of a fish.

Fifty-two delegates to the executive assembled in the boardroom, all men, all pastors. They represented around a thousand congregations. They were hushed and solemn. Each one of them had felt the swift unpopularity of their church at first hand. The rate of recruitment to Adventism, which was once a proud and reliable eight per cent a year, was now halted. Their annual appeal for public donations to the health and mission programme was a vivid failure. House-to-house collectors returned with quiet tallies. They had found distrust and evasion. They were met at times with curses and often with slammed doors. Everywhere the story was similar. They were expected to dispel adversity with what they called 'lives of patient example', but the times were exceptionally ill. Everyone knew of pastors who had answered the telephone late at night to abusive callers. On a popular radio programme, a public-affairs commentator had associated Adventism, by some feat of reasoning, with the Jonestown massacres. Not long afterwards, a religious studies researcher was asked, by a serious reporter, to supply the texts which detailed the ceremonies appropriate to the ritual sacrifice of Adventist babies.

Those delegates who anticipated, as did the *Adventist News*, a discussion of the current plight were surprised by the agenda. It was a heavy list, routine and familiar. It opened for debate the usual labours of their lives in Christ. They spent time speaking and voting on measures to do with public health, education, regional administration, outreach, everything but the acute problem of the day. General business brought an expectant pause, a cough or two, the white reflection of a tentative hand, but nothing came of it. By then it was clear what had happened. The guiding elders had determined, in discreet concert, to leave redemption to the proper intercession of the Lord, should He so choose. Neither the conviction of the Chamberlains nor the bitter predicament of the church would be raised at this session, or at any other. They closed the meeting with prayer.

10

Sun
Lindy Guilty of Murder, Say Most
Most people believe Lindy Chamberlain murdered her baby Azaria, according to the Gallup Poll. Of those sampled, 53 per cent believe she is guilty, and 52 per cent say she should not be pardoned.

11

IT IS THE DEFORMITY of prison-time and prison-space which so credibly tampers with the mind. She was finding now that a cell is not confined by the walls. The fault lies with the ungenerous corners. Time makes progress here to the ringing of bells but idles in the muted intervals between. It takes less than a year for the bell to do duty as a biological metronome, persuasive enough to control sleepiness and wakefulness, tolling all the obedient rhythms of the body. The next bell will command darkness, but meantime the high globe burns brightly, and she sits on a chair at a table she uses for writing and holds a pencil as if she were judging its length against the pad. Her fingers are bony. She is so light now that she could scarcely creak a wicker chair. In her own judgement she has lost twenty-five kilograms and knows her photograph would alarm her friends. She is dressed in a flat blue smock, and her abruptly cropped hair does nothing anymore to hide the inquisitive shape of her ears. An abandoned shoe lies under the table.

It is early August. The afternoon temperature made thirty-one degrees, and the night air is little cooler now, but these are conditions she has come to think of as soft and pleasant. By day, the window gives her a view over a scrubby plain, dry and ruddy, to a horizon she long ago decided was south. An inlet, some shiny part of the harbour, dribbles in from the west. This is now as familiar to her as a landscape hung on the wall, and at night is repaced by an abstract of cross-hatching where chain-wire from the stockade shadows the window-pane.

The most unsurprising change—the replacement of daytime by night, to choose an example near at hand—is evidence valuable to her of the fleeting nature of things. A notice she has taped to the wall reads: 'Tough Times Don't Last'. To friends she writes of God's waiting-room, as if she were at a siding, momentarily between trains. The tasks she has set herself, during prison classes in the useful crafts, include leatherwork, weaving, and apparel, and there would be nothing remarkable in this were it not for the unison of purpose in the items she has chosen to make. The fashioned and embossed hide belts for the boys to wear to school. She made small suits, soft and snug, for Kahlia to wear outdoors in winter, then added a muff and sent them off to Cooranbong. She crocheted a jacket for her mother and mailed it to Nowra. In a locker, and ready for despatch, lay a pair of shoes for Kahlia, which matched a pair she planned for herself, and a partly completed tapestry—a caravelle in full sail—bound for the long wall in Aidan's room. These are all, one way or another, expressions of motility, as any quick analyst would see, but her own interpretation is far less mystical. She now has a presence in the midst of her family, wherever they are.

The surprise, in so disciplined a place as prison, is the truancy of the mind. She finds repetitive tasks easy, but a book cannot hold her for longer than a slow page. she discovers grammatical errors of the simplest kind in her own letters, re-read. In conversation she sometimes refers to Azaria instead of Kahlia, and transposes the names of the boys. She often wonders if there is some significance to this she should better understand. Right now she is struggling with the words of a poem. She has slipped off the other shoe and perches her toes on the rung. In less than a week is the anniversary of Azaria's death, and she has in mind an item for the 'In Memoriam' columns of the *Sydney Morning Herald*. This sort of composition had given her no trouble as a pastor's wife when, for some defeated family, she helped out with an apt and sweet rhyme, but now the words come slowly. She has folded the discarded pages under the pad in the belief that a fresh sheet invites thought. The verse she wants will show the permanence of love, compared with temporary death, and will carry the gentle tones of prayer-time. She hopes to do better when her mind sharpens but, so far, she is confident only that it will close this way:

Not a day has ended
With the fading of the light
That I have not remembered you,
Azaria, goodnight.

12

BENCHES IN THE HALL began to fill, beginning with the second and third rows, since no one ever seemed keen to sit in the very front seats. The rally was due to begin in ten minutes, at eight p.m. The speakers stood around backstage. Judy West, although pleased that everyone thought her habitually serene, wasn't sure she felt any better than the trembling Sally Lowe. Greg Lowe has gone off somewhere searching for water with which to wash down his sedatives, but Judy's guess was that he was also looking for a dark corner for a quick cigarette. They had played town-halls in most city capitals now, afforded top billing, if that wasn't too theatrical a term, because they—Judy herself, the Lowes, and sometimes Wally Goodwin and Murray Haby—were onetime witnesses for the prosecution, dismayed and disaffected.

Someone switched on the footlights. They crossed the resonant stage and sat in an enfilade representing the order of speakers tonight: Guy Boyd, the founder of the Plea for Justice Committee, clutching notes, then the Crown witnesses, a space to the lean and peppery Les Harris, this time without a dingo to parade about the stage, and Barry Boettcher, stiff-legged and impenetrably silent. The hall was around a third full, allowing for the vacant seats between. A good many couples of middle age and older, muffled against the cold, some of them rank-and-file Adventists, Judy guessed, a dozen or so young people, from Christian youth groups perhaps, a junior reporter alone in the front row on the most dismal assignment of the editor's night-sheet but hoping for enough to lift her to the prominence of a by-line, and otherwise maybe fifty others, singly or in quiet company who had seen the newspaper advertisements.

No hecklers this time, so far as Judy could tell. She had recognized in herself a new wilyness for such things now. This was a travelling show, and they were evangelists of a sort, offering the message with what they hoped was persuasive clarity and confidence, while watching, as if at the periphery of vision, for the first signs of disbelief and ridicule.

Volunteers were closing the doors. The hall fell silent. Boyd walked to the lectern. To applause, he held his hands aloft, a handsome pilgrim, white-haired and sad. He fiddled with the microphone. Judy had a vision, which she got from a second-hand story, of Boyd standing outside the opening doors of the High Court after the appeal was lost, lone and bewildered, handing to outrushing journalists the press-release he had prepared for victory.

They had, she rather thought, each joined the troupe for different reasons: Les Harris out of fierce anger, Barry Boettcher because plain facts had been mislaid, the Lowes because, as they often said, the tragedy could have been theirs. Judy's reasons were harder to come by. She simply knew she must. She was not here because she was a Christian, indeed of the speakers tonight probably only Boyd was, in any real way. Judy sustained her own system of human understanding and love with a belief in a more general God, with pragmatism and patience, and with a calming discipline of meditation, on demand. But she was not beyond the charming philosophies of the testaments. The one she now carried around in her mind was from Isaiah 26. 'Hide thyself as it were for a moment, until the indignation be overpast; for behold, the Lord cometh out of his place to punish the inhabitants of the earth for their iniquity.'

This seemed to meet the deep and simple needs of the moment. It made the world explicable.

AFTERWORD

WERE IT FICTION, no new and risky character would appear so late, but the ways of unruly fact drew in David Brett, leading him here from a quiet English village. Brett was a young man with a belief in the occult and a liking for the rituals which bring good fortune. He had in mind to see as much of the material world as he could while his own fortunes stayed good enough. From Harley, in Kent, he journeyed to the Australian east coast and lived there for around four years. His close friends were mystics, in whose judgement David Brett could expect some peak of destiny only with his death, by suicide, which they were encouraging. He was not as convinced of this as they were, and he left them for his mother, and home.

While Brett was back in Kent, people whose beliefs lay more in the direction of the hard sciences were still investigating how Azaria Chamberlain may have died. In a laboratory in Germany, Doctors Baudner and Storiko were fast coming to the conclusion that blood found in the Chamberlains' yellow hatchback should not be identified as foetal, but may well be as adult as the Chamberlains said it was. They were much persuaded by Professor Barry Boettcher, who not long before had walked into the laboratory and pumped a sample from his own bared vein for its routine identification, which then classed the professor as a newly born baby.

At Kansas State University in the U.S., Randall R. Bresee, an associate professor in textile sciences, was comparing, under many magnifications, damage to the fibres of babies' jump-suits and singlets sent to him from Sydney. The clothes had been chewed by a dog and by a dingo, the threads neatly sliced by the teeth, in no way different from damage the professor had seen before on textiles bitten by coyotes. They were also identical with the cuts on the Chamberlain garments.

Inside the High Court building in Canberra, where the baby's own garments lay in custody, three inquisitive laboratory analysts who were picking over the tousled and sordid fibres for any other indications of chewing, happened on specks of flesh, glistening as the magnifications were turned higher, suddenly and shockingly meaty. So far as anyone could tell, these were the remnants of Azaria Chamberlain. Around that time, at the Turnbull Research Institute in Melbourne, Hans Brunner, who had now developed a method of classifying species of mammalian hair, turned to the identification of hairs taken five years ago from the jump-suit and the singlet. There were nine of them, and throughout the trial they were thought to be cat. Brunner found two were human. Another he couldn't place at all. The other six he was sure about. They were canine.

And away at Cooranbong, Leslie N. Smith was tracking down the source of the blood pattern in the footwell of the Chamberlain car. This was known to everyone by now as the Arterial Spray, the baby's very last heartbeats, the vivid and indelible place of slaughter. Smith worked with the Sanitarium food factory. He was responsible for automated equipment there, and this made him fussy about patterns which seemed to betray some sort of repetitive structure. He took photographs of the car-panel, close-up, and enlarged them further. He could see, over the peaks and ridges of these dark stains, a haze of colour that reminded him of overspray from paintwork. From the spray to the bottom of the footwell he drew lines in the air with taut strings, a cat's cradle which pointed slyly at a grommet in the sedan floor. Then he made for the car-assembly plant. This was not the blood of a murdered child. It wasn't blood at all. The Arterial Spray was a sound-deadening emulsion which General Motors called Dufix HN1081.

Not much of this was known to anyone beyond the inquiring scientists and the people to whom they reported their findings, and certainly none of it was known to David Brett in Kent. Brett had discovered in himself certain familiar longings. He was taking telephone calls from his friends in Australia. His mother didn't like it. More worrying, he was making plans to go back.

When certificated copies of those scientists' reports landed on the desks of the Law Department in Darwin, they came with a petition for a judicial inquiry and for Lindy Chamberlain's release. She had so far served two years of her term, long enough to outlast the term in office of Chief Minister Everingham, who had moved to political life on the other side of the continent. His replacement was Ian Tuxworth, a politician of blustery mode, but there was no one now with legal qualifications on the high benches of government, and Tuxworth chose, as his attorney-general, Marshall Perron, who had the clean and regular features of a graduate from law school, though he was nothing of the sort. Perron passed the new Chamberlain plea back to the Law Department. The petition was denied.

To clear the air, Tuxworth handed around a press release, and brought to the debate a perspective all his own: "This campaign has as its intended effect the building up of antagonism toward the Northern Territory Government, which it seeks to portray as hard, cruel, and lacking in compassion. At stake is law and order, and faith in the due processes of a legal system recognised as the fairest in the world."

Newspapers which carried this statement also ran reports, attributed to ministerial sources, that Lindy Chamberlain should expect to serve twenty years. Avis Murchison, her tiny and vigorous mother, didn't believe it for a moment. From the Adventist manse in Nowra she wrote to a friend, "We know that, in God's good time and in His way, this terrible injustice will be resolved. May victory come, and bring glory to His Name."

The friend to whom she was writing was not religious. So Avis penned, by way of a defiant letterhead, "Our God Is Able."

When David Brett got to Ayers Rock summer was at its worst. Six months living on the east coast again had taken off the pallor of Kent; he was robust enough now, but here the sky was mercilessly clear day after day, the sun blazed, the desert oaks sighed, and the heat seemed to come equally from the zenith and the sand underfoot. There weren't many tourists around. If Brett had been a follower of the Chamberlain case he would have seen that the settlement here was much changed. The faded motels had gone. New camping sites, and hotels with outdoor bars and veiled swimming-pools, lay in a discreet hollow.

Brett had come here to climb the Rock. He was camping alone, so he had no one's capacities to consider beyond his own. He was fit, but so hot was it that a day climb was out of the question. He chose evening, and set out just before sundown, carrying a small knapsack of light clothing in case the air up there got chilly. He took the ascent route on the western side, with the post-and-chain as a guide, as far as a ledge below the peak. No one had told him that a dawn climb was preferable to dusk because the arcose of which the rock is made holds the heat a long time on the west ridge. He rested a while there. Then he swung the knapsack over a shoulder and started up again.

The sun had well gone, but there was still light to see by, enough that a group of departing tourists watched him climb, a small figure, high above the southwest face. He kept climbing east. The air was cool, but not crisp enough yet for need of a sweater. There was something happening, now, of which he would have to be careful. It was as if the altitude and the stillness of the night were together pressing from the air a faint but tricky dew. He came to a bluff, which must have located him then somewhere above the great smudge of lichen the Pitjantjatjara call the camp fire of the Sleepy Lizard.

It seems he had chosen a nighttime climb because of the radiant wonders of the heavens, and here they were, within happy reach of the mind—the stars, the planets, the luminous ways, the whirling galaxies, the emblems that begat the zodiac, all the forces of the universe, in glittering and dizzy display.

David Brett's body was found below the bluff, eight days after his fall, in the scrubby gully with which newsreporters were already familiar. It was here that Wally Goodwin had found Azaria Chamberlain's clothes, five years back. The local police sergeant, Mike Van Heythuysen, roped the ground off for a hundred paces each way. He didn't want anybody watching this. The dingo lairs around here were many, and now the corpse was not entire. By radio he called in rangers and maintenance staff, and directed a search. It was not that he thought they might find any trace of the smaller parts, but the right arm was gone and there might be a chance of finding bone that size.

They walked abreast, kicking aside shrubs and dusty grasses. The dingoes had evidently pillaged the fallen knapsack, and they located a T-shirt, shorts, a kerchief. Further along, a ranger next in line to Van Heythuysen gave a grunt and stooped to inspect the sand by his feet. He tugged at a knot of something buried there, the gritty crust broke away, and he pulled it free. Whatever it was, it had once been white. The sergeant took it and turned it over. A baby's jacket, knitted, with stiff, tiny sleeves. A button at the neck hung by a thread.

"Stay right here and don't move," the sergeant said, and headed for the radio in his truck. He wanted some very clear instructions about what he should do now.

Police Commissioner McAulay was heading for the chief minister's office. McAulay was a stocky man, precise in his ways, who was happiest when things ran according to police manuals and statute books. He'd had the feeling, for some time now, that the Chamberlain case was guided by rules with which he wasn't familiar. When the Chamberlain's petition had come up with solid scientific support, he had expected an inquiry as a matter of legal course. A lawful conviction was one thing, but it seemed to him that scientific opinion had unbalanced the sort of scales of justice he had trained with, and the time had come for someone in judicial authority to rule on it. When he said so, he was told it was a legal matter for Cabinet. Since there were no lawyers in Cabinet, it seemed he was being told it was a matter for politicians.

He expected the matinee-jacket should turn the manner of debate around, even in the judgement of politicians. It was always part of the prosecution's case that there was no matinee-jacket, and that Lindy Chamberlain had lied when she said there was. It was thought a convenient phantom, to explain why no saliva was found on the underlying clothes, and an effort to link the after-image of a knitted fabric, which Murray Haby found in the sand, with the dingo tracks alongside. More importantly for McAulay, the jacket now altered certain slight balances of authority. It was recovered during a search under his jurisdiction. He had already decided to have it sent to independent laboratories in Melbourne for examination rather than to the Darwin Forensic Science Unit. The jacket gave him some standing in the argument, right where he wanted to be.

A secretary led him into the chief minister's office. Tuxworth, too big for his chair, Perron, easing his neat slacks, and the sweaty Crown Solicitor Martin lounged around the desk, jackets off. They stopped talking when McAulay entered. This was the wet season, the air-conditioner at full blast, the vapours damp and smelly.

They let him stand. Perron took the easy question. 'So it is the jacket?'

''Without doubt.'' McAulay said. Since no one seemed ready to offer anything more, McAulay said, 'You have to hold an inquiry now. There's no alternative.'

Martin ran a hand over his sparse hair. Tuxworth sat back in his chair. Perron shook his head, irritated, as if they'd spent too much time talking this through already. 'No,' he said, 'that's not the way to go.'

McAulay turned for the door, red-faced. He had decided to put his recommendations in writing from here on and let them deal with it that way. And he was coming closer to a conclusion of a different nature. He had seen, in a government bulletin, an advertised post with the federal police force. More and more it seemed an attractive way out of here.

Maybe the falling out of allies should play no part at all in the administration of justice, at least no executive role, but that is the way it was, and no one in government seemed to understand the rate at which it was happening. At the offices of the *News*, Darwin's daily, a short stroll up Mitchell Street from the chief minister's suite, one of the government's long-standing alliances was in poor shape. Anyone who could remember the last time the *News* and the government fell out had a long memory, but a scoop was a scoop, and right now the *News* had one it wasn't going to let slide.

Journalists at the *News* had discovered that someone had been feeding them misinformation. The acting editor then was Jack Ellis. When the attorney-general denied the Chamberlains' petition for an inquiry, the department's reasons satisfied Ellis, until he found that they didn't at all satisfy two of the prosecution's own scientists, Andrew Scott and Tony Jones, who were now calling for a new investigation. Not long after, the leader of the political opposition in this town, Bob Collins, took up the issue in the House, but word got around to the presses that Collins was a Seventh-day Adventist. People at the *News* thought this explained a great deal, until they found that Collins was an Adventist for a time brief enough to fit between his fifteenth and sixteenth birthdays and had been a church-going Catholic ever since.

Ellis doesn't like to be made a fool of, and at times like these anger makes him unusually single-minded. He assigned staffers to the Chamberlain case, full time. Because he judged that the finding of foetal blood was the crux of conviction, he instructed his reporters to head in that direction. They came up with a copy of Andrew Scott's report, and another from Professor Orjan Ouchterlony, who had written, from Sweden, protesting the way the prosecution had used the procedures which bore his famous name.

But it was the Germans who gave them the lead story. The *News*'s staffers telephoned Behringwerke, makers of the testing solution. Dr. Baudner came on the line. He spoke a convenient amount of English. Certainly, he said, he had advised the Law Department in Darwin that the testing solution should not have been used as it was in the Chamberlain prosecution. So dismayed was he over the denial of the Chamberlains' petition, that he had written again to the crown solicitor, asking for reconsideration. The date on the letter was two weeks old. The astonishing fact was this: since that time, the Law Department had kept Baudner's judgement to itself.

Ellis decided to run everything he had. It was a Friday morning. A nine o'clock radio bulletin reported that 'Government ministers are confident there will be no new inquiry into the conviction of Lindy Chamberlain.' The layout Ellis chose ran the Behringwerke story, page one, with the Scott and the Ouchterlony letters in support. It was more space than the *News* had ever before used on the Chamberlain case. There were small-town niceties to be observed here, so Ellis despatched a messenger-boy to the attorney-general's press secretary, with a copy of the lead story and a courteous note.

The *News* generally hits Darwin streets at three in the afternoon. Ellis sent the stories off to the setting tables at around midmorning. A reporter fresh back from the government offices said something was going on there, an emergency meeting of Cabinet was scheduled in a few minutes' time, and the police commissioner was in the attorney-general's office. Ellis drank coffee and waited at his desk. The presses would roll in an hour. The way things were done in the Territory, he could expect a visit from a ministerial aide anytime now.

The call came at midday. It was the chief minister himself. He addressed Ellis as 'Jack,' and his voice was loud and amiable. 'I know what's on the presses, but I've got a better story for you,' he said. 'We're letting her out.'

Perron called a news conference. Every reporter and newsphotographer in town was there. He handed around copies of a prepared statement which announced an inquiry, and the immediate remission of Lindy Chamberlain's sentence. He read it aloud. By the time he finished, no one doubted how deeply he wished the problem over. 'Although Mrs. Chamberlain's remission is subject to the usual condition of good behaviour,' he said, 'it is not my intention that she should be taken back into custody, regardless of the outcome of the inquiry.'

Then he turned, leaving the cameras agape, and walked out.

Melbourne Age:

CHAMBERLAIN IS SET FREE
Rejoicing as new evidence leads to inquiry.

The Australian:

LINDY FREE   TOP-LEVEL INQUIRY
The story that intrigued the world.

The Telegraph:

LINDY SET FREE
NT promises: She will never go back to jail.

Adventists at the Avondale College painted 'Welcome Home Lindy' on a cotton banner and carried it, skipping, to hoist above the gates. On the way back, they tied every tree for the length of College Drive with a yellow ribbon. The pastors responsible for Sabbath prayer were in merry conference, fashioning a service of thanksgiving around the verse 'I waited patiently for the Lord, and he inclined unto me, and heard my cry' (Psalms 40:1). A juror from the trial, Yvonne Cain, told journalists of a recent prescience, a dream in which Azaria had spoken to her from the dead, and was joyful.

At his desk on the editorial floor of the *Sydney Morning Herald*, Malcolm Brown had been taking calls, all afternoon, from reporters with news like this. Every stringer in Darwin had print-fever. A freelance newshound outside the gates of Berrimah Prison had watched Lindy Chamberlain, frail, in pink frock and sunglasses, climb into the rear seat of a darkened limousine while a tearful woman in slippers and a housecoat tried to get close enough to give her a clutch of flowers. Reporters in hire-cars and taxi-cabs dawdled the inbound traffic lanes but were warned off by motorcycle police. Photographers were staked out around a bungalow in town where Lindy Chamberlain was thought to be now, but frangipani and bougainvillea blocked any sidewalk view of the windows.

By the time Brown had used enough incidents of this nature to fill a newspage headed 'The Final Chapters,' it was late. He sent the sheets away with a copy-boy. Brown preferred a typewriter to a terminal, and since he was now the paper's chief reporter he could work any way he chose. He still liked, for example, to stand his typewriter upright on its heel at the end of a day. It implied a natural conclusion, and was at the same time his salute to tradition. He slipped into his jacket and snapped out the light. No one else was around. All the activity in this building was closer to the presses now. He rode the lift down and stepped out onto the pavement. It was a warm evening, soft and indigo. The bright footpaths of Broadway were busy with summer-night crowds. A sudden need to be with them made him pass up a cruising cab. He strode seriously along, huge and splay-footed. Brown would have described his gait as jaunty, but the hint of anything so personal rarely makes it as far as his shoe-leather.

These happy crowds and garish lights seemed to him emblematic enough of a carefree and splendid world, but a candid source for his own humour was not so easy to come by. Brown knew there was a deep sense in which Lindy Chamberlain's freedom had somehow released us all, but he was thinking, now, more of the other casualties, those along the way, the Lowes, Wests, Whittackers, Murray Haby, and Wally Goodwin, all of them united in a chill understanding that they had not so much taken part in a courtroom trial as in some theatre of illusion. And all of them imagine a measure of personal blame, because they did not see early enough what the prosecutors were making of them, because they did not think quickly enough in the witness-box, because they did not give their testimony well enough.

Justice was not done, as they reckon it, by their default. They are quite wrong about that. We know, when their voices are gone, when the stories close, our lives don't work that way, at all.

ABOUT THE AUTHOR

John Bryson studied law at the University of Melbourne and later joined the Victorian Bar and specialized in jury trials.

His fiction is published in literary magazines and in periodicals, his feature articles in leading Australian newspapers. He was a member of the Literature Board of the Australia Council and later its deputy chairman. His collection of short fiction, *Whoring Around,* was published in Australia in 1981.

Evil Angels has occupied him day and night for the past four years. It was published by Viking, Australia, in 1985 and has also been published in England. Bryson was awarded the Allen Lane Award for the book in 1986.